Larkhall Gre

Narrative and illustrations
for the HAT Archive

Dr Robert Woodward

Over 50 years of a family business
manufacturing and marketing
health, beauty and food supplements
advertising, PR, writing, regulations,
creating employment, brands, formulas,
staff, factories, takeovers, home and export sales
from sweeping floors to Managing Director and out

ISBN-13: 978-1537488547   ISBN-10:1537488546

LARKHALL GREEN FARM

Chapters

INTRODUCTION

Our family business began in 1946 when my father started on his own with one tableting machine making saccharin tablets. For the next twenty-five years it was a largely pharmaceutical based contract compressed tablet producer. In the early 1970s after reading Ivan Ilich's "Medical Nemesis" I had a damascene moment and rebelled against the chemicalisation of health. Over the following 30 years, as the Managing Director with professional qualifications, this inevitably led to the company's primary interest becoming Alternative Health Care.

Keeping independence to ensure that we could research our ideas was vital. Luckily, we had acquired a leading cosmetic product and a medical appliance that generated resources to enable my ambition to change direction successfully without detriment to family and staff. The cosmetic put us into leading retailers and the appliance into direct mail supply to consumers.

The asset of skilled tablet production, the basis of my father's original company, made transition from pharmaceutical drugs to food supplements relatively easy. Retaining ability in the medicinal area was important because the ever increasing regulatory environment made distinction between medicines and foods a legal minefield. Technically, we were unique in the health food field.

By the mid 1980s our products covered not only food supplements but also herbals, marital aids, biochemics and special diet foods. Our successes in research and publicity raised hackles. Skirmishes with government authorities were challenges but suddenly in the 1980s we became a prime target for powerful interests particularly the sugar based junk food industry and their academic supporters when we blew the whistle on the poor diet of schoolchildren. We made really powerful enemies who, for several years, tried to put us out of business.

Whilst our courage and victories ensured survival they also enabled our competitors to continue too. In the late 1990s, I realised that the future as an independent business was unlikely. Whilst I enjoyed commercial battles my family preferred a quiet life. So, a takeover was accepted when the opportunity arose and in ditching our principles our successors fared poorly.

The world of Alternative Health Care continues to flourish in 2016 but under sufferance from regulators and mainstream (orthodox) medicine. Acceptance that diet plays a vital part in general health and chronic diseases is still far from mainstream established truth. The excessive levels of sugar and salt consumed daily together with too little vegetable fibre largely continue unabated. As a Nobel Prize Winning maverick remarked to me "Like so much in science time alone will bring acceptance but those who fought for change will be conveniently forgotten as their critics reap the accolades".

Dr Robert Woodward BPharm.,PhD., FRSC., C.Chem., MRPharmS (Retired)
January 2017

CONTENTS

GLOSSARY

ABPI   Association of the British Pharmaceutical Industry
BGP   British Glandular Products
AHB   Professor Arnold Beckett
AHF   Associated Health Foods
AMA   American Medical Association
ASA   Advertising Standards Authority
AWH   Arthur Humphreys
BEP   British Ethical Proprietries
BGP   British Glandular Products
BOT   Board of Trade
BHMA   British Herbal Medicine Association
BHFTA British Health Food Trade Association
CA   Consumers Association
CAP   Committee of Advertising Practice
CHC   Consumers for Health's Choice
COMA   Committee on Medical Aspects of Food Policy
CRM   Committee for Review of Medicines
DHHS   Department of Health and Social Security
DOH   Department of Health
DR   Doctor
DRF   Dietary Research Foundation
EPO   Evening Primrose Oil
EHPM   European Health Product Manufacturers
GLA   Gamma Linolenic Acid
GLC   Greater London Council
GNC   General Nutrition Corporation
GOW   George Orange Woodward
GP   General Practitioner
HCSG   Hyperactive Childrens' Support Group
HDRA   Henry Doubleday Research Association
HFMA   Health Food Manufacturers Association
HRL   Huntingdon Research Laboratories
IHFR   Institute of Health Retailing
MCA   Medicines Control Agency
MD   Managing Director
MS   Multiple Sclerosis
NACNE National Advisory Committee on Nutrition Education
NGA   National Graphical Association (Trade Union)
NNFA   National Nutritional Foods Association
OTC   Over The Counter
PAGB   Proprietary Association of Great Britain
PATA   Proprietary Articles Trade Association
PhD   Doctor of Philosophy
PR   Public Relations
PPR   Pharmacy Products Review
QC   Quality Control
RAMC   Royal Army Medical Corps
RG   Rita Greer

RJW	Robert John Woodward
RPM	Retail Price Maintenance
RPS	Royal Pharmaceutical Society
SNCMA	Snack, Nut & Crisp Manufacturers Association
SPNT	Society for the Promotion of Nutritional Therapy
FDA	Food and Drug Administration (USA)
USM	Unlisted Securities Market
WLU	Wright, Layman & Umney
WOC	Walter O'Connell
WHEN	World Health and Ecology News
WHO	World Health Organisation

Beginnings

The family background and beginnings - World War II - Staff - Expansion - Lemons - New Premises - Takeovers - Mother Seigel's Syrup – Advertising - Founders sons join their father

Background and beginnings I never knew either of my grandfathers as they both died before I was born. On my mother's side, my grandfather was a dentist in Newbury, Berkshire, with a passion for horse racing and football. He died before the age of 50. Robert James Woodward, my paternal grandfather was a Parliamentary Agent who married late in life and had retired at the age of 40. He died aged 77. His wife, a tiny person called 'Doll', worked as the cashier at her family's butchers shop in Clapham. In 1911 their only child had been born (my father), a son to whom they gave an unusual middle name of Orange. My grandparents were hardworking, thrifty and shrewd, buying properties in Clapham which they rented out. Doll saw to the cash in the butchers shop, collected the rents and kept an eye on the properties. She also took care of her blind sister. Doll worked looking after her properties until the day she died at the age of 79 in 1949.

My father   My father, George Orange Woodward (GOW), was not academically inclined, although he was a talented church organist who began playing for church weddings at the age of fourteen. He defied his father by refusing to take up a career in banking and instead sought employment at sixteen, as an organ-builder. Failure resulted in him taking up a quite different a job with Menley & James, manufacturing chemists in Brixton. His father had died suddenly and as his mother was carer to her blind sister, George Orange, still only sixteen, found himself the head of the family. He had to grow up quickly. He worked hard and learnt well, rising to managing the Tableting Department with an office. He had learned his tablet making art (*Secundum Artem*) under the guidance of men who had been trained at Burroughs Wellcome, the originators of the modern Compressed Tablet (Tabloids). He was keen and ready to start his own company but this progress had to be delayed, due to WWII and the fact that he had married Mary Stillman from Newbury. She had trained as a Norland nanny and her job had been looking after babies for the well-off, including the young Tony Benn. Now George Orange had new responsibilities, both at work and at home.

The Second World War During the war Menley & James worked on secret Ministry of Defence contracts for the forces, such as anti-malarial tablets. Like George Orange, most of their employees were not called up to serve in the forces because of their specialist knowledge. They were in what was called 'reserved occupations'. Brixton had its fair share of sirens, bombs, doodlebugs, rockets, electric cuts, shortages, food rationing, the blackout, fear, stress, worry, lack of sleep, overwork and all the other miseries and inconveniences of being at war. Thieving was a problem and so was the constant threat of a telegram arriving to say a relative had been killed or reported missing, presumed dead. The Home Guard and fire watching were major duties for the staff, with the Managing Director as the Commanding Officer. Mainly these were carried out at night and weekends, adding to their workload.
  I had been born in 1937, just before war broke out and was christened Robert John. My brother, Charles Edward, was born six years later in 1943, two years before it ended. Thankfully, neither of us were stuck with the second name 'Orange'. My mother insisted that we were not. Once she had married, she did not go out to work again. My father would not allow it, deciding her life was to be a wife, housewife and mother.

LARKHALL GREEN FARM

The war years were very difficult times and in the spring 1944 my mother, baby brother and myself went to Newbury to live to escape the London bombings, leaving my father in Clapham on his own. An incendiary bomb burnt out the top of my grandmother's house which was also in Clapham. She moved into the basement with her blind sister and made the best of it. In the autumn we moved back to Clapham from Newbury and were all together as a family again. We had hardly seen my father throughout the war as he worked long shifts as a manager in the daytime and did Home Guard duties at night.

A new family business One of the things that inspired my father to to start his own company was his family background of small business. It was a world he understood and enjoyed. In 1946, a year after the war had ended, he was able at last to fulfill his dream and start up his own company -- 'G O Woodward and Company Ltd Manufacturing Chemists'. At the age of 35 he left his secure manager's job at Menley and James and began to work on his own, making saccharin tablets with a single rotary tablet machine. The work premises were in one of his mother's small shops at 146 Larkhall Lane in Clapham. He was the managing director and his mother was the other director, making it a family firm, 'Woodwards' as it came to be known locally.

The first customer was a Mr Goodall who owned chemist shops in Ealing. Goodall remained a friend and customer for many years and was revered by George Orange as he had been his very first customer. The major customer was Edward Hack, an entrepreneur who had an office and store in Guildford. He had excellent connections in those difficult times of rationing and quotas, and ensured that G O Woodward & Co Ltd continued to grow - albeit very slowly. Saccharin tableting was the mainstay of the business and George Orange had to work hard to ensure he had a quota of this costly material, to satisfy demand, sugar being on ration. I remember my father bringing home 100,000 Saccharin tablets and the family sitting round the kitchen table packing them into envelopes of 100 tablets.

There were many controls regarding raw materials after the war and the company joined the Wholesale Drug Trade Association, which later became the Association of The British Pharmaceutical Industry (ABPI), to help qualify for and negotiate its quotas.

Staff In order to grow the company, staff were needed. The first one was the man who lived as a tenant on the first floor of 146 Larkhall Lane, where my father had installed the tablet machine. My father himself trained him in compression, to look after the rotary tablet machine while he himself was out visiting customers. My father made a drying oven in the garage at his home to enable the wet granulation, an important part of the tableting process, to be done.

Several staff came from either family or past colleagues from Menley & James. A cousin, who had spent several years in Kenya, was taken on as a p/a to GOW. He didn't stay long as he had no knowledge of tablets or pharmacy and fancied himself as the managing director rather than a cousin of GOW. He was replaced by Eric Hill, a colleague who had worked with GOW at Menley and James. He and his wife moved into one of Doll Woodward's rented out flats in Larkhall Rise and Eric took over all the administration work, including invoicing, wages and buying. He was destined stay with the firm for another 23 years, as company secretary, until 1970.

John Rugless was another employee who stayed until his retirement. He was taken on as technical assistant and buyer. He had previously worked in the London factory of Stafford Allen Ltd. who were galenical (traditional drugs) manufacturers and herb growers with farms in Suffolk. Inevitably, changes in personnel were the norm at Woodwards but by 1947 it had settled down and some 10 employees, mostly women, were established.

2

They included some packing ladies in another shop at 130 Larkhall Lane. Here, hand filling and the labeling of bottles and tins of tablets were carried out. It was all contract work and George Orange had to be salesman, formulator and driver for the business.

Customers   Competitive prices, quality tablets and excellent personal service soon enticed top pharmaceutical companies to become customers, including Rexall (of Loughborough) and Bayers (of East Molesley). Woodward's contract customers now included Paines and Byrne (of Greenford), Halewood Chemicals (of Paddington) and one or two herbal companies including Pierce Arnold and Co of Beddington, near Croydon. The products made under contract for large pharmaceutical companies before 1950 included Barbiturates, synthetic hormones, glandulars and early vitamin tablets such as Ascorbic Acid (Vitamin C) Aneurin (Vitamin B1) and Multivitamin compounds.

Sugar Coating   The sugar coating department was developed and soon many millions of tablets were being sugar coated every year.

Expansion and contracts   By 1950 expansion was underway with takeovers of similar small manufacturing businesses such as CF Abel (of Peckham) and Crickmay, Matthias & Pepper (of Vauxhall). The attraction of Abels was its modern tableting factory in Nunhead, coupled with some contract customers including the PDSA who had Homoeopathics, whilst Crickmays was a general chemist supplies producer of a range of ointments, creams and liquids, with a London base of customers. By now George Orange had a broader product range to offer. Abels had the contract to make Cantassium Discs and G O Woodward & Co. were soon making them for the Twickenham based company that also embraced Associated Preparations. Latterly, these products were to form an important base for the move of G O Woodward & Co from contractor to brand owner. Abel's had contracts making products for herbal medicine companies which added to the company's expertise in that area.

Lemons!   The company could now undertake larger contracts and the first was one for Edward Hack who had recalled the success enjoyed with Saccharin tablets back in the late 1940s. Hack had the bright idea of presenting pure lemon juice in plastic lemons and asked Woodwards to pack them. The product 'Hax Lemon' was a huge success and produced a boom for Woodwards at just the right time. The factory went on overtime but later Hack felt he could not refuse a good offer for his lemon juice business. The purchaser renamed it the 'Jif Lemon', still on sale today (2015).

Hack had already conceived a range of fruit flavoured juices used to make milk shakes. They were marketed in handy-sized plastic fruit-shaped containers. Calling it 'FLIP', all went well until fermentation caused the packs to burst or explode! The product had to be abandoned and the dream ended, probably due to Hack's lack of credibility and practical vision. Hack went on to invent other products but none equalled the plastic lemon.

New premises   In 1955 George Orange purchased 45 Morrish Road, London SW2 from Stewart Plastics Ltd and so the mid-fifties saw rapid development of the Woodward business. The 10,000 sq ft factory and office building would house all aspects of manufacturing and administration. It was on two floors and its main office jutted out over the road to provide a car park beside the goods entrance. The cost was about £25,000 freehold (about £2 million today). In order to obtain a loan from Barclays Bank all stocks and shares were sold and our family home at Valleyfield Road SW16 had to be used as collateral.

3

Whilst contract tableting and packing remained the core of the business, George Orange was always open to other ideas. His friend Denniss Hubble was a wealthy fruit farmer in Kent and a new company Woodward & Hubble supplied his farms with fertilizers and pest control items. It worked out well.

Hubble had a magnificent Bentley Continental and used to visit the Morrish Road factory with fresh apples from his farm for my father. He would sit in the back of the Bentley, smoking a large cigar whilst the chauffeur delivered the apples. He was a keen organist and both he and my father were great friends of Osborne Peasgood, the sub-organist at Westminster Abbey whose wife became Secretary of Woodward Hubble. My father, who still played the organ, would often turn the pages for Ossie while he was playing. Business friendships did not necessarily mean just business.

Takeovers In 1957 the business took a bold step, expanding with the purchase of generic tablet manufacturer Matthews & Wilson (founded in 1894) from Eucryl Ltd, an over-the-counter (OTC) chemist product maker. M&W had expertise in export and were competitors of many of Woodward's contract customers. Based in Cole Street, off the Borough High Street, M&W were not far away from the Woodward base in Brixton. Several staff from M&W joined the company. Despite losing many of their contract customers Woodwards successfully expanded as planned.

I join the company After Westminster School I had studied at College and graduated from The Chelsea School of Pharmacy (1959). I then worked on my PhD. By 1961 I had joined the family firm as Assistant Managing Director. My father had made sure I had started at the bottom, sweeping up and cleaning plant from the age of 13. At 14 I was working in the holidays at the factory. I had also gained experience outside the company in my regular student holidays job with Public Analyst Noel Allport in Kennington, who was working on analysing samples of water from the river Thames and general chemist product samples from local authorities. These were collected by officials on their inspection visits to chemists and food retailers under the Food and Drugs Act.

Getting a good education was one thing but the experience of working in manufacture was quite another. My father had wanted me to gain knowledge in the same way he had done -- the hard way. Later on, again in the school holidays, I was the Van Boy, working with a driver, delivering orders to all the London customers who were chemists, druggists or sundriesmen. All this was useful experience and a long way from studying at Public School and College. It kept my feet firmly on the ground and I learned about the practical side of factory life and business and how to get on with staff and customers at all levels. I also gained an understanding about the world of work that suited me no end.

Mother Seigels Syrup and Advertising The purchase of Mother Seigels Syrup from A J White Ltd (later part of Glaxo Smith Kline) took the company into the OTC speciality pharmacy market. Seigels was a popular product in South Africa and the distributor subsequently acquired the UK rights from M&W in 1961. Lessons learned from the marketing of Seigels encouraged me to pursue development of a range of my own pharmaceutical specialities. However, my father undoubtedly feared costly brand advertising which he felt resulted in too much commercial uncertainty. That made him uncomfortable. To him, taking risks with property and machinery was all right but advertising was far too uncertain and expensive. He was way out of his comfort zone.

Networking and The Troc   My father had always believed that networking and entertainment were vital to business success. He had joined trade associations, attended meetings regularly and made important contacts. These were nurtured at conferences and at some special places such as the famous Trocadero Restaurant near Picaddilly Circus in London. This was a luncheon haunt much supported by sales people and buyers with Pharmaceutical (Drug Trade) connections. Personal commercial relationships could be built by regular lunching there. I was lucky to be taken there often and came to know many important trade personalities. The skills learned at the Troc were probably the most valuable ones I ever experienced. In those days entertaining was a tax deductible expense as it should be today. Oiling the wheels of commerce is vital.

I qualified and my brother also joined the firm   Soon after I joined the company, I gained my PhD in Pharmaceutical Chemistry and also brought to the company professional qualifications as a Pharmacist (Member of the Pharmaceutical Society) and later Chemist (Associate of the Royal Institute of Chemistry). My father, very proudly, assembled the staff, announced the good news and told them that in future I should not be addressed as 'Mr. Robert' but instead, 'Dr. Woodward.' As my father had no professional qualifications he was keen to have people around him who did. My research in Pharmaceutical Chemistry inspired ambition to finance my research ideas, using company profits. Sadly, this became a forlorn hope because research within companies could soon be rubbished by academics. Whilst those same people often control University research facilities funded from commercial sources, they can happily tow the line of their sponsors, unbeknown to the public and the media. As journalist Simon Heffer wrote in 2009, "There is an age old problem with academics being envious of people from outside who trespass on their field".

In 1962 my appetite for risk led the company in a new direction. This alarmed my father considerably as he was a strong minded man and was determined to stick to the old ways that he understood from experience. If he was the old dog then I was the young puppy. We had a lot of arguments.

There was also the problem of my younger brother Charles who was five years my junior. As expected, he had not done well at school and had begun to study music at the Royal College of Music. He still lived at home and when my parents moved to Charlbury, near Oxford, he moved with them, abandoning his music studies for a job helping my father in the new factory. He saw this as a great opportunity and a much better idea than studying to be a musician. Sadly, his lack of any qualifications and basic knowledge of science would always cloud our relationship in the business. He had never shown any interest in pharmacy or business, never had a job or trained for anything. He had enjoyed a completely different childhood from mine and for several years had been educated away at boarding school. However, he was family and was brought into the company. Like many owner managing director fathers at that time, George Orange was determined his sons would work in the family business, whether they liked it or not. He had a fixed idea he was founding a dynasty and that was that.

From Brixton to Putney (London) and Charlbury (Oxford)

Second Premises near Oxford - Alternative Health Care - Pet care - Pharmaceuticals - Direct Mail - Health Foods - Bribery - Biostrath and Advertising claims - Corruption - Unfair competition - Export development - New Staff expand company expertise - The Royal Institute of Chemistry - Sainsbury Committee - Middle East visits - Family tensions - Putney move

Two factories instead of one and changes By 1963 it was clear the company was doing so well it needed larger premises. George Orange found premises in the Cotswolds where it would be possible to do the strip packing. He had always had a dream of living in a country house to get away from life in London and this was his chance to do so. He found a small factory owned by a pharmaceutical company called 'International Laboratories'. It was situated near the station in the Wool Town of Charlbury, near Oxford and surrounded by fields. The main shareholder was Mr Harry Pickup who had invented a popular household cleaner and called it 'Harpic'. As part of the deal, George Orange was offered Pickup's country house. This was Wychwood House, a Victorian, six bedroom house with 4 acres of land. He bought both the factory and the house, seeing it as an opportunity too good to miss.

My brother Charles, then nineteen and still living at home, moved with my parents to their country house and began work at the factory as second in-command to George Orange. Three or four local staff were taken on and one experienced worker from the London factory moved to work with them and become the caretaker, living in a small house at the entrance to the site. George Orange traveled up to London one day a month to keep his eye on things and telephoned me every evening for a daily report. I personally was in charge of the London factory and head office with 50 staff, concentrating on tablet making, packaging, general sales and administration for both Brixton and Charlbury. I was just twenty-five years old and thrown in at the deep end. It was time to make my mark. As this was the year I had left home, married and moved into a house of my own in Banstead, Surrey, I certainly had a lot on my plate. My wife had wanted to continue working as a secretary in a West End estate agents but my father would not hear of it. He made it quite clear his daughter-in-law was to be my wife, a housewife and later on a mother, just like my mother was. He was the Managing Director and his two sons worked for the family firm under his guidance. He was the patriarch and determined on starting a business dynasty.

New avenues My training as a pharmacist had failed to provide awareness of herbal medicines apart from the few mentioned in official Pharmacopoeias such as senna, digitalis, nux vomica and belladonna. Homoeopathy had been totally ignored. Meanwhile, the family company was making many herbal formulations in large quantities and a few homoeopathic products too. The synthetic drug industry was growing fast and most new products were being developed using high purity, fine chemicals. I saw these as the way forward for the company. To me, at that time, compared with the new synthetic drugs, herbals and homoeopathics seemed to have had had their day. Twenty years later I thought very differently.

Pet products and direct selling In April 1963 Deryk Manton Cotterill contacted me. He had recently returned to England from South Africa and now lived with his mother in Acton, London. He had successfully marketed a Dog Worming and Conditioner tablet in South Africa, called AD-VA-TABS, and it was attractively packed in a carton with the logo of a dog on a lead.

6

LARKHALL GREEN FARM

The formula was a Charcoal and Sulphur plus blend – hazardous and very dirty to make into good compressed tablets. Cotterill was insistent that he wanted to use the trade mark AD-VA-TABS in England. I gave him the name of our Trade Mark Agents (Wildbore & Gibbons) and Mr Cotterill then spent many months in correspondence with them but failed to find a Trade Mark that he could use.

I was well aware of this kind of problem, and although we had several marks registered, I was doubtful of their value for small turnover products. Common Law rights to Trade Marks were often enforceable if a product had been openly marketed. In the end I suggested Cotterill should use Abels as a Trade Mark, with our permission. In November Abel's Brand of Dog tablets mail order developed and sales were made from Charlbury but I did the marketing myself. I saw a great future in Direct Selling and experimented with marketing approaches intending to have measured responses reported by GOW in Charlbury. Unfortunately he failed (and didn't want) to understand Mail Order principles as they didn't interest him and so no results were reported to me that were even remotely accurate. As I was designing and writing all the advertisements in conjunction with a London Agency, inevitably results were disappointing. My father simply would not co-operate.

Pharmaceutical Specialities By February 1964, the pharmaceutical specialities in the Matthews & Wilson portfolio were Peroidin (Potassium Perchlorate 200mg), ReponeK (a sustained release Potassium formulation) and Ferronate (an Iron Gluconate tablet). All were typical Pharmaceutical products, well researched of high analytical purity. ReponeK competed directly with Slow K produced by a Swiss pharmaceutical giant and competed on quality and price. Peroidin stood alone in the market as it was perceived as dangerous to make owing to the explosive chemical nature of its active ingredient, Potassium Perchlorate. I determined there was no risk provided purity was high. Research in Scotland had found Potassium Perchlorate a very safe and effective medicine for hyperthyroidism (over-active thyroid). I designed an advertising campaign to GPs quoting the new research and Peroidin began to succeed against more costly synthetic chemical drugs.

Added businesses Commercially, 1960s growth was driven by Export success and involvement in Alternative Healthcare in Britain. Harry Smith, a pharmacist MPS, joined M&W from Gale Baiss of Peckham. Smith had in depth experience of the medicines market in many countries. Good contact with the Crown Agents in London, who acted as buyers for many Commonwealth (Empire) Countries, enabled us to ship products to many countries where our name became established. In the mid sixties, we also took over the small general overseas distributor business attached to Sanitas of Clapham. This proved successful and we became involved in supplying Mission Hospitals, Charities and Oil Company medical facilities as well as small independent pharmaceutical traders throughout the Middle East. The Sanitas company were manufacturers of Woodward's Gripe Water, one of the largest brands in the baby medicine market. There had been confusion between the two completely different Woodward companies in Clapham for several years.

Alternative Healthcare Meanwhile, the Alternative Healthcare Movement was developing away from the strict vegetarian towards nutrition and dietary supplementation. The company picked up some contract work in this area because of its experience in the contract manufacture of Vitamin C and multivitamin tablets for pharmaceutical companies from the late 1940s. The need for vegetarian ethics in the growing 'Health Food Trade' led to supplements made using gelatin (non vegetarian) capsules not being desirable.

7

Tablets could easily be made to meet vegetarian standards but up until then no-one appeared to have thought about this.

Pills for Nigeria   There were several companies in London who specialised in selling to Nigeria, a country with an insatiable appetite for proprietary medicines. Silver coated Blaud's Pills were very popular as was a compound herbal Iron formula known as Female Disorder Pills -- probably recommended by 'fringe local medicine men' for women whose monthly periods failed to start at the correct time each month. Many more formulas, in simple packing for many disorders, were shipped in millions to Lagos and Port Harcourt. Methylene blue pills were used by the native Nigerian medicine men as antibacterials because they coloured the urine that indicated successful treatment to patients. (I understand that Gentian Violet pills were available in the markets too!)

Dexamphetamine   The amphetamines were invented before the second world war. By the 1950s they were widely used by students to prevent fatigue and by slimmers to suppress appetite. Several formulas combined them with thyroid gland extract that boosted metabolism. Many Harley Street private doctors were using such combinations in high strengths within their practices. In the 1960s we were approached to make a specially coloured and shaped 5mg Dexamphetamine tablet to be packed in lever-lidded, gold coloured tins of 1000. The labels had either a picture of two cockerels or two bulls and were for export to Nigeria. Demand came through two well known companies, Kingsgate and D J Gilbrook. We regularly supplied them with 'specialities' for export to West Africa.

During the mid 1960s we supplied many millions of these Dexamphetamine Tablets but price competition was fierce. As time went by the price fell from 3/6d (17p) per tin of 1000 tablets to 2/3d (11p). I often wondered about the significance of the pictures on the labels and many stories were related about their meaning. Some said that the Nigerian Farmers gave them to their livestock so that they could get them many miles to the markets without stopping on the way to forage. Others that they were used to boost food production from the livestock with less feeding required. Looking back I think that they were probably used as a recreational sex drive medicine and were sold singly by native herbalists/witch doctors!

At this time the amphetamines, although restricted to doctor's prescription, were not controlled as dangerous drugs in the UK but were the most popular illicit recreational drug among Britain's youth. Each of those 5mg tablets, which were commercially shipped to Nigeria for less than today's equivalent 0.01pence, could be sold in South London Pubs for around 50p. Unsurprisingly, after some three years of doing this business we experienced break-ins at night, burglaries and petty theft of these tablets as news spread that our factory was making millions of them a week. One day, at lunchtime, a policeman came to see me in my office and showed me a handful of our dexamphetamine tablets that had been in the possession of a newly recruited member of our tableting staff an hour before. Sure enough, this man had clocked in at 8 am and clocked out at midday – we never saw him again. That was enough for me. I decided this was something the company should not be making and gave up bulk dexamphetamine manufacture immediately.

Bribery   The newly independent African Countries who had previously ordered western medicines from the Crown Agents, soon imported from non UK sources and prices were seldom viable for British producers. Bribery was rife. I recall a moment in the company of the Managing Director of one of the new suppliers. We had just walked past a new Rolls Royce Corniche and I remarked, "that's a nice car", to which the director reacted with the comment "If you had been one of those ----- I would have bought it for you".

Abels, Crufts and direct selling   Abels took a stand at Crufts Dog Show for the first time in February selling its pet products direct to the public. I went on the stand myself. This was successful but Pet Trade retailers were very reluctant to stock Abel's 'Anti-worm all in one conditioner'. I visited several stores as did Cotterill but thought the discounts and initial free stock demanded made the required investment unviable. Using pilot stocking in a few stores soon showed that the market leaders 'Bob Martins' and 'Benbows' presented real problems to newcomers with conditioner tablets, without highly risky initial launch advertising costs. Cotterill and George Orange were unwilling to invest. I felt that retailers were fickle friends and did not earn the margins most demanded. Multiple Chemists willing to stock OTC Pet Products such as Boots and Timothy Whites drove very hard deals. So, the mail order direct selling route was chosen and this was to be the method used for the next 35 years for the company when launching new products. Its attraction was the receipt of money up front and the full profit margin available. Consumers didn't seem to mind paying for postage and packing on top as their orders were delivered to their homes, by post.

Once a product established itself using direct selling methods then many retailers, including Boots, would order small quantities direct at our standard trade price. Several years later we took over companies who were already selling large quantities of some of their products eg Lipcote (1971), Ruthmol (1972) to multiple chemists and this gave us a way-in with additional products. These were invariably disappointing for many reasons, not least because of our involvement in direct selling, a fact used by our competitors to denigrate us and offer copycat items. I was often pressured by sales staff to abandon mail order business but was adamant that there was no better route to the market for a small company than direct mail. It enabled us to test consumer acceptance but instantly my brother said it was too much like hard work. He even demanded that I should predict all new product sales accurately before introduction. I doubted any human being could make such predictions and if they could they would be very rich for sure.

International Generics   This was a company owned and managed by Leon Tamman, a Sephardic Jew from The Sudan whose father was in banking in Geneva. The opportunity Tamman subsequently presented, led to much export business over the ensuing years. This was nurtured by my empathy and technical expertise, enabling rapid expansion into new London premises. Tamman frequently made generous overtures to take over the Woodward Companies but however tempting these were, they were rejected by me because I cherished my independence most of all.

Polish Aspirin   From time to time supplier companies would approach hoping to supply us with their bulk ingredients. They had cottoned on to our rise in the market and would flatter. A Polish firm commented 'knowing of your very high standard'. Their product, Aspirin, did not meet the quality we expected and was not found to be of pharmaceutical quality in our tests. We did not buy from them whilst many of our competitors did.

Alfonal and the Health Food trade   AAHF group owned the magazine 'Here's Health', the wholesaler 'Brewhurst', the retailer 'Holland & Barrett', 'Heath & Heather' and the 'Healthcrafts' brand. I was first introduced to this group by Frank Lewington, who, when working for Albion Laboratories, a manufacturing chemists, had known my father. Frank introduced George Orange, my brother and me to Jimmy Lee-Richardson, the owner of the group and much business resulted for us.

Healthcrafts The Healthcrafts Brand had been developed by Jimmy and his company was selling millions of soft gelatine capsules (which were not vegetarian) to vegetarians. Frank said that it would be more appropriate to sell tablets that needed no animal derived ingredients such as gelatin in their formulations. I also emphasised that the gelatin capsule shells, both hard and soft, contained synthetic technological ingredients that were not declared on labels. Jimmy wanted wholesome natural products to sell under his 'Healthcrafts' brand and I was confident that I could satisfy this demand. So began the company's involvement in the Healthfood Industry. This was helped by the fact that we had been making vitamin C tablets since 1948 and multivitamins since 1955. At that time, we had an unequalled manufacturing skill to offer Healthcrafts. Unfortunately, when Jimmy sold his company and then left Bookers (his successors) in 1971, all the ethics of 'Natural' manufacturing were ignored and synthetics soon became the norm for the brands. Bookers were close to sugar producers and grocery trades people. Like most Supplement manufacturers they did not seem to appreciate the difference between a 'naturally formulated' product and a junk food made with 'pure processed and synthesised' ingredients.

BIOSTRATH and Advertising Claims In the late 60s Jimmy Lee Richardson's wholesale and distributor business had several agency lines in the Healthfood Area. The first major one was Biostrath Elixir, a Swiss herbal tonic made from flowers collected from unpolluted alpine slopes. These herbs were naturally fermented and processed naturally into an elixir with an appreciable alcohol content and great health giving properties – feel younger, full of energy, sexy, slim, athletic etc etc. The sole importer was a small company Straten Imports. Jimmy, being a generous man, put Straten in touch with the romantic novelist Barbara Cartland who was a brilliant publicist for natural remedies. She had real credibility with those she described as "My people". Barbara was sent samples of Biostrath to try and she loved it – perhaps it was the alcohol. She was soon giving samples to leading health journalists on national newspapers and to TV personalities. Michael Van Straten, whose family owned the importers, became a guru and before long Biostrath was coming over to the UK by the 'plane load. Switzerland had difficulty keeping the market supplied. Biostrath was undoubtedly the most successful natural elixir since the war. It soon became heavily criticised by nutrition academics and experts who, twenty years later, were to found 'Quackbusters'.

The Advertising Standards Authority (ASA) were soon involved and advertising claims were curtailed. Many products of this kind in succeeding years would encounter similar problems but Biostrath was the first and set the pattern for many more wonder health givers such as ginseng, royal jelly, pollen, propolis, glucosamine etc. Michael Van Straten still held sway in alternative healthcare and by 2008 competed with 'Dr' Gillian McKeith and many others for the media's attention.

Mission Hospitals During 1965 Wright Layman & Umney, a division of Sanitas Ltd, owners of 'Woodward's Gripe Water' (no relation to us), wished to dispose of their extensive business with Mission Hospitals in the Middle East. We were already supplying several Oil Company Health Clinics and Charities overseas with tablets and various other Pharmaceuticals. The WLU business would take us to new levels and enable us to expand our list of products as wholesalers and manufacturers. Bob Aylmer Hall was the MD of WLU and I well remember meeting him in his office in the Sanitas Building in Clapham Road and debating an appropriate offer over a glass of sherry. We paid £5000 plus stock at valuation and agreed to take over all outstanding orders.

This proved to be a difficult addition for the company at the time because it took us into wholesaling of medicines including many covered by the Dangerous Drug Regulations (Morphine, Cocaine etc). However after some six months things settled down and the wholesale export business gained us many new export customers for our own tablet products. Some of the WLU customers were lost but the core ultimately gave us a business that expanded rapidly over the next ten years and was key to enabling us to continue in business when our manufacturing licences were lost in the early 1970s. Indeed it was probably because the bureaucrats were unaware of this side of the business that made them select us for special treatment as an example to others. I was always convinced that the company was singled out for closing down, long before an Inspector called.

Corruption   In February there was trouble in the London factory at Morrish Road. Sidney Mitchell had been employed for several years, initially as a builder to construct internal services and partitions. He then became packaging floor manager but I knew he was a bully. A very useful member of his staff resigned because of Mitchell's behaviour and we soon discovered that he was receiving 'backhanders' from the supplier of our export packing cases. George Orange personally dismissed him because he had been responsible for Mitchell's original employment and promotion to manager.

ABPI   In April I was elected to the Council of Division A (Standard Formulary Medicines Committee) of the ABPI (The Association of the British Pharmaceutical Industry). This indicated the company's standing as a generic pharmaceutical manufacturer.

Unfair competition   In June a letter arrived from Mr Ray Simons of Inter-alia Pharmaceutical Services Ltd enclosing a cheque for payment of a longstanding debt. I had seen him on a stand at a trade fair the week before and prevailed on him to pay up. He was obviously not a man to be trusted and his company soon went bust when the Medicines Inspectorate started work in the 1970s. The factory was in Thetford, Norfolk where government grants aided new businesses. Inter-Alia were competing against us with lower prices taking plenty of credit from suppliers and grants from the Government. This was hardly fair competition. No wonder I longed to get out of the generic industry and into branded proprietaries.

Patents and MPs   In July a controversial Parliamentary Question from a Dr Wyndham Davies criticised one of the company's customers, Biorex Laboratories, together with DDSA and Inter-Continental Pharmaceuticals. I had known Biorex for many years and had extensive dealings with them through Dr Gottfried, the Romanian owner. Gottfried retained two Labour MPs as directors (Sir B. Stross and Mr Harold Davies). It was legitimate for Biorex to supply patented Drugs to the NHS, since the NHS could purchase supplies by invoking new laws that permitted the Government to obtain products from companies other than the patent holder. Enoch Powell, when he was Minister of Health had promulgated the patent-breaking law that was opposed by the ABPI's branded medicines companies.

Trade Mark   In July we received notification of the successful registration of the Trade Mark 'Stabevit'. This was a product containing Tin and Tin Oxide for the relief of acne - not a success. However, the company continued to try and register Trade Marks over the years but I became disillusioned as to the real value of such registrations because legal enforcement was always difficult and costly. Common Law protection was usually enough. Selecting product names was difficult and had to be done carefully so that risk of an infringement would be unlikely.

11

Extra premises and new staff In 1966 I enlarged the manufacturing area at Morrish Road by renting a small 2500 sq ft warehouse and office in Sulina Road, about 400 yards away. This was used to store all raw materials, to assemble them for batch tablet manufacturing and as the goods in and out facility. We were desperate for more space because expansion was going well.

I learned that John Bell Hills & Lucas Ltd of Lower Sydenham were closing their factory and some staff were looking for employment as tablet making operators. The factory was for sale (£325,000) and was over 40,000 sq ft, fairly modern (1934) with good offices and services. I went to see it and whilst it was a possible base for the company, the whole responsibility would have been mine and it was unlikely to prove viable for us unless the whole family management returned to London. This was impossible as neither my father nor brother would contemplate giving up their agreeable life in the country. However, I took on two new people, W. Lilley as Stores Manager and Baldeo Ramsarran a Tablet Maker. Bal, who was born in British Guiana (now Belize), stayed with the company until 1999 and became a key member of staff. He would lead the manufacturing team in Putney for the next thirty years. He was a very skilled tablet maker and had an ability to make good compressed tablets from herbs, vitamins and minerals in every conceivable combination without recourse to synthetic additives. I would devise a blend of ingredients and Bal would produce a satisfactory tablet within hours. He had an instinctive feel for materials that was uncanny. He had had no scientific training and was a puzzle to those soon to be all powerful Medicines Inspectors, who always looked down on such people, ignoring his talent and positive genius for such work.

In 1967 George Orange hired a new manager at Charlbury -- Dennis Hooker. A motor bike accident had left him with leg injuries which caused him trouble throughout the rest of his life. He had previously been a sales executive for Mr Lovatt, an engineer who made strip-packing machines. Dennis Hooker brought with him a good working knowledge of packing machinery and enabled the company to invest confidently in modern machinery. The contract work was growing at the Charlbury factory at this time. Dennis Hooker was a knowledgeable, loyal and hardworking employee who stayed with the company as manager at the Charlbury factory until he retired in 1999 -- after over thirty years service.

Royal Institute of Chemistry I was elected as an Associate of the Royal Institute of Chemistry. (A Fellowship would come a few years later). The letter notifying me of my election to this prestigious organisation was signed by Frank Hartley, the President. Hartley had examined me for my PhD degree in 1962 and later was most unhelpful when acting as chairman of the tribunal regarding Medicines Act Licensing in 1974. He was a typical example of an establishment appointee who would see that the Bureaucrats came out unscathed by critics. Eventually, he was knighted.

Lord Sainsbury's Committee George Orange received a letter from Lord Sainsbury, the Chairman of the Labour government's Committee of Enquiry into the Pharmaceutical Industry's relationship to the NHS, the aim being to see, if by company nationalisation, medicines could be provided at less cost. Our company replied that whilst willing to take part we thought we were too small to have any meaningful data for his committee. This was accepted in the reply received on 3rd June. Nevertheless, the selection of our company to take part in the enquiry indicated that G O Woodward & Co was now perceived as a much larger company than it really was. This misconception persisted for many years. I think this was because we generated publicity and participated in pharmaceutical affairs to a greater extent than competitors of similar size. My qualifications gave me some clout with authorities that I never hesitated to use.

12

Export developments   In May, Eric Hopkins joined the company from Thomas Morson Ltd (A Chemical supplier recently taken over by multinational Merck Sharp & Dome). He was well known to George Orange and me through the ABPI. Eric Hopkins worked in the export department that had relocated to Sulina Road in Brixton. It had recently expanded through the purchase of the Mission Hospital Supplies Service from Wright, Layman & Umney. M&W were now supplying overseas Clinics and Hospitals under the control of Christian Missions and Oil Companies such as Shell, Iraq Petroleum and Anglo Iranian Oil. This business was wholesaling general medical goods and whilst the margins were modest, the sales were worthwhile. We did supply some generic tablets to these customers but it was only a small percentage of the total sales to them. This business meant that we were no longer dependent on just manufacturing.

These new customers provided us with connections in the Middle East and visits to these facilities as well as small retail importers was undertaken by OS Burton (Jim), an old friend of George Orange, who enjoyed travel to the Middle East. Correspondence between myself and Jim on his travels make interesting reading. The contrast between those countries in the 1960s and in 2016 is incredible.

In December 1967, Jim Burton undertook his first trip to visit our Middle East customers, combining this with a sightseeing holiday. In Beirut he drew a blank but his report indicated the likely difficulties in doing worthwhile business. In Cyprus he had some complaints to report. Jordan was much the same with a complaint about Codeine Compound Tablets - a notorious formulation in warmer climes and expensive to keep replacing -- better not to offer it. Jim then went on to Tehran but had no luck there. By January he was in Doha seeing our agent Al-Baker. In Abu Dhabi there were few hotels and Jim had to sleep in any room available including the lavatories.

At the end of his trip Jim wrote to George Orange saying how much he enjoyed the experience. I believed we now knew more about these countries but whether there was really long term business with them I was unsure.

Crown Agents   In January, I took H D Smith to lunch with Mr Bew and his colleagues from the Crown Agents to help cement our ongoing relationship with this important buyer.

Administration led to family tensions   In February Jim Burton came to the London factory in Morrish Road to help me with the growing mound of administration work. His customers in the Middle East had been complaining about our service and Jim believed he could help. He did, attending the office regularly until his next trip planned for August/September. HD Smith, although a very good salesman, was not an organiser and Eric Hill (Company Secretary), John Rugless (Buyer with a background in Pharmacy) Gladys Lewis (Book Keeper) and Ellen Haynes (Office Manager) were not leaders. Jim helped me greatly whilst the key family members George Orange and my brother Charles remained at the smaller site in Charlbury, the packing factory in the Cotswolds. I was concerned that a disproportionate amount of the management work was shared unequally and I was working very long hours. Arguments about this matter within the family proved hopeless because both my father and brother had found themselves a very pleasant country lifestyle. No way would they ever give it up. My wife was continually complaining about the unfairness of it all.

Finance   In May my brother left home and married a musician from Abingdon, near Oxford. The toast to the bride and groom included a bold reference to the bride's good fortune to be 'marrying money'.

This was far from the truth and I was baffled at how such a wrong idea had arisen. George Orange didn't mind the reference as he was always keen to give the impression that he had done well in business and prospered. It wasn't quite like that and the debt to the bank was a worry. Those two words were to have severe and lasting consequences for my relationship with my brother and his new family. Thinking back, it is often that an ill considered public comment can do lasting harm. The indebtedness of the Company was high and working for fringe companies such as Biorex Laboratories and International Generics, both, in reality, fringe operators was hardly a formula for security. The company was at risk every day and the Medicines Act 1968 heralded huge problems for the coming years. The finances of the company were a constant worry to me, especially as it was now responsible for a large number of staff at two sites eighty miles apart.

More work on Exports August found Jim Burton in Cyprus visiting several customers including the Government Hospital who were supplied with our products either through a local agent or The Crown Agents. By September he was in Jordan where we had problems with the major Hospital including 'Black Listing' for poor service. Jim was a good diplomat but was suspicious of the people (Army Officers) with whom he had to deal. He said a monetary direct contribution (incentive) was probably needed. I would never agree to this. Jim noted the tension between Arabs and Israelis. Fortunately, we had orders from the 'Save the Children' charity who seem satisfied. Jim then went on to Doha Qatar to experience prayers in the office of our agent Al-Baker. He was our best private customer in the Gulf States. Jim then went to Bahrain to see the American Mission Hospital. Other visits indicated that it was expected that suppliers 'look after buying staff'. At the end of September Jim was in Dubai, having been in Abu Dhabi and Sharjah, before his return to UK.

Moving to larger premises in Putney I knew we had to move the London factory to larger premises. We were bursting at the seams to keep up with production with just a total 10,000 square feet at Morrish Road and Sulina Road. I had been looking for two years and eventually found the empty branch of the Scottish Cathkin Laundry at 225, Putney Bridge Road in Putney, London, SW15. It was 30,000 square feet area and no longer required. The idea of people sending their laundry out to be washed and ironed every week was becoming a thing of the past. There were laundrettes everywhere and a washing machine in many homes. The Cathkin Laundry in Putney had become a white elephant after many years of service and was shabby and run down.

My father agreed we should buy it in 1968 for £115,000. A bank loan secured on the property and personal guarantees from the directors made it possible. (I was convinced that within the next 25 years it would become a valuable property.) It fronted on to Putney Bridge Road and included a small shop with caretaker's flat over it, a large area which could be made into the warehouse and packing department, plenty of room for manufacturing, a small yard at the rear and offices at the front of the building on 2 floors. The side of the building opened on to Bective Place for goods inwards. There were 2 enormous oil-fired Lancashire boilers in place and a lot of drains. It was on a main bus route, near Putney Bridge tube station and Putney main line trains too. It had possibilities, but needed a great deal doing to it before we could move in and make pharmaceuticals.

V B Tuhill was appointed my assistant to oversee the building works and the move from Brixton to Putney. He had worked in the pharmaceutical industry and it was hoped he might become a key manager after the move. Unfortunately, this did not occur owing to serious disagreement about the way ahead. We were on different wavelengths.

We had no option but to keep Morrish Road and Sulina Road going until enough of the Putney building had been made fit for Pharmaceutical Manufacturing. We were then in a position to transfer to Putney. Of course, we still had the smaller 4000 sq.ft unit at Charlbury.

Changing Interests driven by Takeovers

Putney premises - New Takeovers - Safeseal - New Staff - Asbestos - Medicines Act - Hong Kong - Advertising - International Generics - Cantassium and Blakoe - Family - Jimmy Lee Richardson - Tissue Salts - Boom for Blakoe - Threat - More Takeovers - Clinical Trial for Blakoe - Lipcote - Bribe sought - Range 200 products - Decimilisation

The Putney Factory The old laundry we had bought was originally the 17th century, three-storey Miller's House (Mouliniere House) which fronted on to Putney Bridge Road. It had a large cellar at the front with a bricked up smugglers' tunnel to the Thames, which was only 200 yards away. There was a very large wooden front door with a canopy, which was listed. The rest of it was a hotch-potch of brick buildings, corrugated iron sheds, a huge area of warehouse with a wood block floor, a flat roof that could be walked on, a yard at the rear with big factory gates and a side entrance in Bective Place. At the front of the building was a small shop with a flat over it for the caretaker/boilerman, whom we kept on. At the rear of the building was a 60ft brick factory chimney -- a local landmark.

There was a great deal to do before we could move in. Basically, it was a clapped out laundry and it needed to be gutted. Part of the roof leaked. Some of the building had to be pulled down and rebuilt. The oil-fired Lancashire boilers eventually had to be taken out and replaced with two large gas-fired Windsors. Partitioning to make the various production areas, lowering the ceilings, new flooring and general modernizing had to be done before the move. Enough work was finished by September to make the factory functional and the remainder had to be done piecemeal as we could afford it. (It went on until the end of the century. It was like the Forth Bridge.)

As 'The Cathkin Laundry' sign had been carved out of the concrete at the front of the building, I ordered a painted signboard to cover it. It read 'Larkhall Laboratories'. Larkhall came from the first factory my father had started in Larkhall Lane and 'Laboratories' had a pharmaceutical ring to it. It became the name of the building. A small signboard by the front door listed the names of our companies based inside the building.

After 6 months, we were able to sell Morrish Road and Sulina Road in Brixton. We moved into 225 Putney Bridge Road as the new premises were now up and running. At the end of the year, in spite of all our efforts and expense, the Factory Inspector found 'deficiencies'. Well he would, wouldn't he?

Changes We began work at the new premises by concentrating on manufacture for export and home trade, contract tableting and generic medicines. As the regulatory environment was about to change dramatically, due to the implementation of the Medicines Act 1968, I realised we had to change or go under. We looked for profitable areas outside the Act where we could use our skills, equipment and premises. Gradually, we would have to give up generics and medicinal contract work, find new products and get into our own brands. There was no alternative if we were to retain our independence as a company.

New takeovers were **Cantassium, Blakoe, British Glandular Products, BGP Cosmetics (including Lipcote) and British Ethical Proprietaries (including Ruthmol).** They all had some products threatened by the Medicines Act but their key sales generators were outside the Medicines Act. The threats to small companies were huge and those who couldn't or wouldn't change would go out of business. Being broadly based was a help but we had to build new business as the old one wound down, keep the staff working and the production running. It was not possible to suddenly stop the old business and begin with a new one -- it had to be done gradually. Export was useful and I hoped Alternative Healthcare and Mail Order would be the way forward.

LARKHALL GREEN FARM

ABPI I was elected to serve a further term on the Division A Council (Standard Formulary Medicines) of the ABPI. Serving on the Council was a front row seat regarding the regulatiory threats and how others were coping. Other than ourselves very few of the companies in Division A of the ABPI survived as Independents more than ten years. Later I was elected again as Chairman of the Division. Talk was invariably about the Medicines Act including Fees, Product Licences of Right and Inspector demands. Constructive, but I could see obtaining an understanding with the DHSS would be difficult.

   After some ABPI meetings there were informal lunches at Browns Hotel, Dover Street. These were a great source of gossip and information and I learned far more from them than I ever did at the minuted Management meetings.

Safeseal and new staff   In 1969 I had designed a method of strip packing to make tablets and capsules **childproof**. Having spent time and money on developing it I was loath to abandon because it would save lives. So far 'Safeseal' and had got us nowhere in spite of appointing an advertising agency to help.

   Arthur Humphreys (AWH), who had agreed to join the company in the autumn as Home Sales Director wrote a business plan that laid the foundations for formation of 'The House of Woodward', to work alongside Matthews & Wilson which was under the management of HD Smith in Export and Walter O'Connell in UK Retail. O'Connell was a large, ebullient, enthusiastic drinking Irishman who perpetually kissed the blarney stone. He believed he was the greatest salesman on earth. It was envisaged that he would work with AWH and H D Smith would continue export sales separately with Eric Hopkins as his assistant.

   AWH was well known to George Orange and me through the ABPI (Association of the British Pharmaceutical Industry). Before joining us he was Sales Manager for Thomas Kerfoot Ltd, a leading contract and generic pharmaceutical manufacturer. He had very good contacts in the wholesale, retail and contract manufacturing pharmaceutical trade and it was hoped he would develop our business in those directions. When I explained the 'Safeseal' idea to him he saw an exciting way forward with Doctors and Pharmacists.

   Safeseal gave AWH something to talk about when visiting retailers, wholesalers and hospitals and helped give essential credibility to 'House of Woodward'. Substantial progress was made in finding contract tablet making and strip-packing business but retail was slow. AWH certainly helped build our connection with wholesalers. I looked after Unichem myself, Walter O'Connell did Sangers and some London based retailers, whilst AWH worked throughout the country. We hoped to appoint more sales persons in the future.

   Substantial money was spent on trade advertising of Safeseal and communication with editorial departments of the trade and professional journals. Encouraged by comments such as "I must say, I think your client Matthews & Wilson Ltd are on to a winner", FC Littlewood Advertising Manager of The Pharmaceutical Journal, "I am hoping that departmentally official encouragement can be given", Dr Roy Goulding (Department of Health & Social Security). Goulding was very involved in the drive to protect children from accidental poisoning.

   In January 1970, AWH, was on the road following-up on customer enquiries or cold calling on some of his old contacts. He was trying to establish 'Safeseal' special orders from Hospitals and obtain wholesale orders for our specialities Matthodorm and Reponek, that were copies of popular prescription products -- lower prices proved appealing to dispensing doctors. I hoped new 'Safeseal' products under such a banner would prove successful using this route.

Company Secretary and Finance Eric Hill the company secretary for nearly 25 years retired, aged 58. He was diabetic and had found the move from Brixton to the larger factory a strain. He decided that he did not want to continue his employment with us. So he left and was replaced by a young accountant, who stayed a couple of years.

The company was expanding with sales up to £750,000 from £600,000 in 1968/69 and profits were holding up well, despite the substantial costs incurred in moving from Brixton to Putney. By now over 100 staff were employed by the company with a small workforce and manager at the Charlbury strip packing factory and the remainder in Putney. By then much of the packing was still done by hand, by women workers. About 40 staff worked in manufacturing at Putney with some 15 to 20 office staff.

Fire Escape problems with the GLC In moving to Putney we experienced a major problem because the building came within Section 20 of the London Building Act. If a building was over 20,000 sq ft ,which it was, it had to be fitted with a sprinkler system and have a Fire Certificate. When we partitioned the building to make it suitable for Pharmaceutical Manufacture we inadvertently transgressed the Building Laws. This led to many problems over the coming years but initially we had got off on the wrong foot because we moved in before obtaining full clearance from the GLC. That would have taken months. I had been assured that the architect had looked after the matter but alas, he had not. No fire had broken out. There was no danger to staff as all exits were clearly signed etc. and only some 20 persons, apart from contractors' staff, were actually working in the building at that time. They were all within thirty feet of an exit. We ended up in court, paid fines and undertook to complete the work within an agreed period. In fact the work had already been done before the case was heard. Nevertheless we were still fined and so had a black mark against us.

Asbestos We were against using asbestos for the partitioning but, by law, it had to be used. There was no way round it. If we hadn't used it we'd have been back in Court again and there would have been more fines to pay. Some years later this had to be removed by a costly process.

The new Medicines Inspectorate In April 1971 I received a letter from the newly formed Medicines Inspectorate. It requested an informal visit to form an impression of the range and variety of medicinal products being made by us. Messrs Baker and Jones duly visited Putney on 5th June They were very pleasant and went away apparently satisfied, but I was not fooled and did not plan the future based on the inspectors' words. We were expected to apply for a **Manufacturer's Licence of Right.** This would be granted and a legal inspection would take place later. I knew that this would very likely cause problems owing to the great variety of generic medicinal tablets we manufactured. My policy for survival was still to concentrate future activity in the non-medicinal area. The grey area between Medicines and Non-Medicines was a legal minefield but G O Woodward & Co had to get involved there to survive.

Far East Opportunity In May 1970, H D.Smith our Export Director, was approached by a representative of a company in Hong Kong called 'China Engineers'. The multimillionaire owner of the company, Mr YH Kwong, had recently taken a small pharmaceutical manufacturer into his group and was looking for a partner in the UK to invest in the company and develop its sales. In May I visited Hong Kong at Mr Kwong's invitation to view the facility, with a room at The Mandarin Hotel that was then the top hotel in that city. In the event, the quality of the products being made was very poor and I declined the opportunity. The factory was well equipped but the technical expertise of the staff was low.

Quality control barely existed and the cleanliness standards of the factory were appalling. In fact they were shocking.

This visit was far from a waste of time, as whilst in Hong Kong I unexpectedly bumped into Dr Colin Roberts, an old College friend who was also staying at The Mandarin Hotel. I had dinner with him and his colleagues from the Huntingdon Research Laboratories including its founder Dr Alastair Worden. HRL was then in its infancy but later became the leading contract research Company in the Pharmaceutical field. Soon our company was to use them for some contract research work.

On the return flight the Boeing 707 aircraft developed engine problems and was forced to land in Delhi. An opportunity for a day sightseeing presented itself and I was left with the indelible impression of a hot, smelly, dirty and poverty-stricken city, in contrast to Hong Kong which was hot, sticky and smelly but vibrant with a very rich strata of society.

Exports   Jim Burton was prepared to visit our Middle East customers again. We were experiencing payment difficulties with Mission Hospitals who we supplied with bulk tablets and special items on a regular basis. A customer in West Africa had given us an order for £6000 worth of stock. It came to nothing. Various excuses were offered by the customer but it boiled down to his inability to obtain a letter of credit. This was a major blow to the company as raw materials had been purchased and the goods made. This happened frequently.

Factory Inspectorate   Around this time we were being questioned by the Factory Inspectorate as regards handling of what they considered harmful chemicals including Steroids, Oestrogens, Antibiotics and Mercurials. I explained that we were upgrading our facilities and would soon be under the Medicines Inspectorate. Their requirements were likely to be similar to the Factory Inspectorate and I said would keep them informed. I could see they would always be a problem as they had little knowledge of tablet manufacture.

Advertising - Caples and Ogilvie   "There are only five good ads" was the headline of an article in the marketing press by Michael Pulman, a creative director of a new agency, French Gold Pulman. I found this helpful in judging ads submitted by agencies dedicated to blinding their clients with 'science' and those dreamed up in-house. Much of advertising is common sense but a grounding with books such as John Caples **Principles of Advertising**, a USA publication from 1950s, and **Ogilvie on Advertising** were very useful to me as I had to start from scratch and teach myself about creating effective advertisements.

International Generics   The new facility at Putney impressed Leon Tamman, the managing director and owner of International Generics Ltd a company with whom we had been trading as contractors since 1964. They had a cosmetic/perfumery manufacturing unit (Berkley Perfumery in Lancing) and Mr Tamman wanted a Pharmaceutical facility. I persuaded him that he could have just such a factory by co-operating closely with G.O Woodward & Co. Their name would feature on the company list outside the front door of the building and our staff would say they worked for IG if questioned by visitors. Tamman's real need was for a facility that would convince his government customers in Africa that his company was a 'manufacturer of pharmaceuticals'. I agreed to become a director of IG for £150 a year and Tamman agreed to assist financially with fitting out the offices and flooring at the factory. A large office was furnished by IG and this was used to entertain IG guests when they visited.

Substantial regular business from IG resulted from these arrangements.

In March Leon Tamman admitted he wanted a share in Matthews and Wilson Ltd. I visited IG in Brighton/Hove to meet officials from N.Ireland where Tamman hoped to base his new factory. Tamman was very keen but I was not in favour because of the political situation and difficulty in finding good pharmaceutical manufacturing managers prepared to move to Belfast.

The Cantassium Company and Blakoe In late 1970, I was approached by Mr Nelson Roberts of the Cantassium Company trading over the Post Office at Kings Cross (London), to purchase the stock and goodwill of his business. Our company had made one product for Mr Roberts, called 'Cantassium Discs', under contract. Roberts had previously owned a small Pharmaceutical business, Castle Huskisson Ltd, which he had recently closed down. He now wanted to retire completely. Sales of the discs were mainly by Mail Order and turnover was less than £2000 per year.

When I went to see Roberts at his office in March 1971, I proposed not only to buy the Cantassium Company but also all effects and stocks. On looking round the effects I came across an upright wooden chest with a folding cover over the drawers. I asked Roberts what the strange piece of furniture contained and to my surprise the reply was, "Oh that's the Blakoe Ring stock". Puzzled, I asked what the Blakoe Ring was? "It's a patented device for male impotence and incontinence and comes in 21 sizes," was his reply. Roberts was going to close the business down and dispose of the stock to a single customer in the West Indies. I said I could be interested and asked for more details. Recent correspondence from Dr Robert Chartham indicated that this well-known sexologist was very interested in the ring and was proposing to test it on his clients, after finding great benefit himself. I immediately said I was very interested in buying both the product and the Cantassium Company. Roberts said I could have it and the stock at cost (£200).

The following weekend I arranged to clear the effects and all stock of these two mail order companies to Putney. **Cantassium Discs** (a bio-chemic remedy) and **Blakoe** (a sexual and incontinence aid for men) together with certain supplement tablets and creams including Blavig, Male Glandular and Male Hormone Cream. I believed that the way forward for a small independent family company following enactment of the Medicines Act 1968, would be in Alternative Health Care with brands. Cantassium and Blakoe were seen by me as fitting in well with the company's food supplement and herbal interests. However, our ownership of the Cantassium brand made relations with some contract customers more difficult. There was antipathy to any company in the mail order vitamin business because manufacturers were very retail-shop orientated.

Our association with Blakoe was used against us in the shops by competitors' representatives, always referring to Cantassium as 'The Sex people'. In fact Cantassium Discs were formulated in 1921 and mentioned in the book 'Victory over Cancer' by Cyril Scott. The word Cantassium was derived from combining 'Cancer' and 'Potassium'. A free booklet entitled 'The Cantassium Dietary System' was widely advertised and brought in many customers. The system was a dietary programme high in Potassium and vegetarian (no red meat). It was also high in Fibre and low in Sodium (Salt). In fact, it was not far off what many health professionals recommend as a healthy diet in 2015. The Discs were packed in 280s and nine were taken daily. Many users reported darkening of their grey hair and this news found us many elderly customers. Cantassium Discs were very much a remedy of the twenties and a forerunner of todays food supplements. These had arrived in the UK early in the 1950s as synthetic vitamins became available from many fine chemical manufacturers. (Fine chemicals are those made pharmaceutically pure with modern processing).

The Blakoe and Cantassium mail order businesses (Associated Preparations Ltd, renamed Blakoe Ltd) developed well. Testimonials containing wonderful personal stories of success were received regularly and extracts from these were used in advertising and promotion.

19

Fresh stories were always guaranteed to improve customer responses. Wheat Germ Oil with its Vitamin E content was an ideal add-on for the Blakoe range. There was much publicity about Vitamin E's benefits to potency and fertility. Sales were increasing well but advertising costs were high.

N.Ireland   Leon Tamman and General Sir Alexander Drummond visited me in Putney to discuss the future of business with International Generics. They planned to open a new factory in Northern Ireland to gain tax advantages. I was very sceptical because the IRA were sabotaging companies working with the Northern Ireland Government. IG had just been at an exhibition in Ghana and maintained very good business there, no doubt with plenty of 'incentive' on offer to the locals.

In July I went to Brighton again to see Tamman and General Drummond. Apparently the Northern Ireland venture was not definite despite the recent positive publicity.

Later in the year, Tamman and General Drummond brought Mr Dunbo, Ghana's Minister of Health, to Putney to show him 'their' factory. The next day they all returned for a photographic session.

Rolls Royce   In the middle of January I had the usual early evening 'phone call from my father who said he wanted a Rolls Royce car -- his other long standing ambition to go with the Country House. (In those days a car could be run and purchased by a company with full tax allowances.) Soon after, George Orange said he had seen a second hand Rolls Royce he liked. I said, "No, we can't afford it." He took no notice as he was determined to have one so he bought it -- a Silver Shadow. He was in a foul mood when I saw him that evening with my brother, -- no doubt aggravated by my attitude to the purchase of such a car. Later in the year George Orange put a £500 deposit on his second Rolls Royce Silver Shadow car, this time a brand new one. He had always been a man who liked his own way and I really had no influence on him.

Postal Strike   20th January saw the start of the threatened postal strike. It meant all Mail Order businesses would be badly hit. It didn't end until 8th March -- nearly 7 weeks later.

Anne Summers   I met Mrs Nixon, an executive of the new sex shop, Anne Summers. They would have liked to sell the Blakoe Ring but required far too much discount. I believed the item was better commercially kept mainly to mail order and surgical stores who had expert staff to advise and measure customers. The energising ring was really a medical aid designed by a Doctor of Anatomy and offering it for sale in a chain of sex shops would have tarnished its image.

Customer complaint   A customer buying Barker's Liquid of Life tablets complained again. He expected every bottle we packed to contain exactly 40 tablets. It was normal for machines counting tablets electronically to err on the plus side for legal reasons. This meant that customers' packs of tablets might last longer than expected and therefore postpone purchase of a new bottle. This loses their company money -- so they said. Apparently, their MD actually re-counted each bottle himself. The bottles were not pilfer proof in those days.

Staff matters   Kay, my secretary resigned. Trained as an actress, she was much too unreliable but very good on advertising copy. She would be better suited to a creative job. Happily, she went into magazine journalism and did well.

HD Smith, the export sales director of Matthews & Wilson 'retired' after George Orange had a row with him. He had made several expensive mistakes. We found out later that Smith had really left to go and work for one of our competitors, All Countries Export, a London export agency. So much for his retirement.

Family matters   At a family Sunday lunch in March at Wychwood House (George Orange's country house at Charlbury in the Cotswolds), he was in a foul mood again. There was a report in The People, the Sunday newspaper, on Blakoe, which was not favourable, but fortunately my father didn't know about it or he would have been incandescent.

I told General Drummond that I was worried about my father's health. Drummond promised to arrange for a consultation with a top specialist through his contacts at the RAMC. (Drummond had been head of the RAMC sometime in the 1950s.) Tests showed that George Orange had Type 2 diabetes.

In April my parents visited us in Cheam, in father's new Rolls Royce for which he had paid £7900. I had a drive in it very nice! George Orange now had five grandchildren -- four girls and one boy. (There were to be no more as it turned out.) He singled out my brother Charles's son Ben and said a policy was needed for him. Even at that stage my father had ambitions for his grandson to lead the family companies, whether or not the boy would want to or have the right ability. I was already determined that my daughters would never come into the company as I did not want history to repeat itself. Without family pressure and my father's bullying I would have been able to choose a quite different career.

Sales   Mail order Sales of Blakoe reached £1000 in a week for the first time. Forum Magazine passed some enquiries about the Blakoe Ring over to me at a meeting. These had been generated by an article in the magazine by sexologist Robert Chartham. Jimmy Lee Richardson left Alfonal (AHF group) after a serious dispute over policy and what he considered unfair treatment of the small independent Health Food retailers.

In May 1971, at last, George Orange came to realise that Blakoe was a real winner and asset for the first time.

Opportunity missed   Jimmy Lee Richardson wrote telling me of his resignation as Chairman and Chief Executive of Associated Health Foods, a subsidiary of Booker McConnell, a large Public Company. Bookers had owned AHF for some eighteen months but knew little about the Health Food Trade. Jimmy had established himself as pre-eminent in the trade through sheer hard work and dynamism. He was a firm believer in the Health Food Movement and a friend of the small retailers. It was the arrogant attitude of Bookers to the small trader, when merging the Heath & Heather chain of shops with Holland & Barrett that led to Jimmy's resignation. Jimmy leaving AHF was to lead to a substantial loss of business from them as new buyers joined the company over the coming years. Sadly, I always found the big company ethos somewhat alien to my ideals and could not agree to some of their demands.

I replied to Jimmy's letter after a meeting with him when he strongly advised me to buy the company New Era, the 'Tissue Salt' Biochemic/Homoeopathic brand. Jimmy subsequently introduced me to the owner Leonard Stocks but unfortunately we were unable to progress business in this area. I thought Tissue Salts had no basis in science and could not understand why the overt claims for their effectiveness were permitted. Latterly these claims have been reduced but by that time Tissue Salts were owned by the giant company Seven Seas. They still have a following as Biochemic Remedies. George Orange was not in favour of the takeover, the amount wanted (£400,000) was not within our capabilities. The risk of losing the product health claims were great, particularly if the authorities realised that the Woodward's owned the New Era brand. In hindsight this was a bad decision because the claims were permitted for many more years and we could have merged it seamlessly with the Cantassium supplements (Cantassium Discs was a Biochemic preparation).

Business matters   I visited Butler's of Leicester (Pharmaceutical Wholesalers) who had bought generic tablets from GOW & Co for many years. I looked after this account, not AWH or W.O'Connell because I had built the contact over several years, before either of those staff joined the company, and, the customer would only deal with me.

Hugh Butler and his father, who were the family owners, had known me for many years through the ABPI and The Wholesale Drug Trade Association.

In early July a customer Mark Morris of Richmond Order Co brought in an order for Ex Lax tablets. He seemed to me to be a man with a lot of good contacts.

I told Jim Burton that I was becoming very concerned about the company's future because of the ramifications of the Medicines Act 1968. I felt that neither GOW nor CEW really understood what was likely to happen because of this Act. Their negative attitude to the New Era deal demonstrated this family problem but was understandable. Perhaps, we should have immediately abandoned Orthodox Medicine manufacturing and gone into 'Biochemics and Homoeopathics' plus the alternative health care products. Hindsight is wonderful but would the bank have backed me? Probably not.

The success of Blakoe and perhaps with effort Lipcote, (agency to be acquired in 1972) and the wholesale export side now under Eric Hopkins began to look as if they would all be crucial to survival.

The development of the Putney facility was going well but I worried whether we would we be able to convince a zealous Inspectorate, in the first flushes of power, that we were worth saving. They were bound to need a firm to close, to show others what they could do to them. We were ideal – an English family company in London (not far from the Inspectorate's office). Already we had black marks from 'Safeseal' that contravened the professional division between doctors and pharmacists. **Doctors could prescribe any products but not their packaging.** We had also had tussles with authority (GLC Fire Brigade).

In July, I was out at lunch, at the Playboy Club (home of the bunny girls) with Gordon Grimley who was working with Penthouse and Forum Magazines. Blakoe was advertising with them. Their subsidiary 'Evelyn Rainbird' sold by mail order sex aids including the Blakoe ring. The real boom for Blakoe was after the Chartham article appeared in Forum, before Evelyn Rainbird was started. Grimley had worked previously for Robert Maxwell the press tycoon who had been criticised by the Board of Trade Inspectors as unfit to run a public company. Grimley was unequivocal that Maxwell was a crook and the BOT inspectors were right. I bore this in mind and steered well clear of Maxwell and his companies. The demise of Maxwell was a great scandal in 1991 with thousands of pensioners impoverished and creditors swindled.

In August, The Division of the family Companies was agreed and new share certificates were issued. We purchased a ¾ acre plot of land adjacent to our Charlbury Factory to be used for future expansion.

Inspector future   Ministry of Health supplies division Pharmacist, Haydock, came to Putney. In his opinion our in-production quality control was inadequate. He told me he was soon to be transferred to the new Medicines Licensing Division so would probably take his opinion with him. This did not auger well.

Blakoe threat   Mr Crouch, the top craftsman model-maker who made the Blakoe rings, reported that he had been approached by men from London (in an expensive car) to make energising rings for them in red, blue and yellow plastic. He refused, but I wondered who these men were and who told them that an obscure little one-man firm in Haverhill in Suffolk would make these rings? I suspected the sales rep O'Connell was the informant and that the men were from Pellen Personal Products (Paul Rimmer). He certainly had some dodgy business friends. Whoever leaked the information put me on my guard. Whom could I trust? Surprise, surprise! O'Connell soon did a special price deal on the ring with Pellen -- so it had been them.

Changes A shop called 'Birds and Bees Phyllis Wright' opened in Croydon and had installed a Blakoe product display. A chemist, Richard Dreyfuss, showed interest in the ring and we offered him special terms. AWH and and Walter O'Connell were both at the opening and afterwards I decided I would have to drop 'Safeseal' as it seemed to be going nowhere and concentrate on the Blakoe and Vitamin business instead. It was then that AWH told me that he thought Walter O'Connell a really outstanding representative for the company that I found reassuring.

AWH had had an inconclusive meeting at the ABPI regarding the legality of Safeseal in Psychiatric Hospitals. By now it was obvious there was no future in this project and no more effort should be spent on it.

Purchase of British Glandular Products, BGP Cosmetics (including agency product Lipcote)

I learned that **British Glandular Products** were in Liquidation after the effects of the postal strike. I was contacted by Mrs Arnold whose son Giles had been a friend at school. She worked at BGP and was the sister of the owner Mr Jeffree. On Friday 27th August the liquidator (Bernard Phillips) accepted my offer of £2500 for the BGP mail order business assets, to include **Lipcote** UK rights, pending agreement with its New Zealand owner.

Lipcote had once been manufactured under contract by George Orange in the late 50s so we were confident that making it would not be a problem. British Glandular products had a range that fitted well with Blakoe. These were Trade Marked products including Vitatrop, SPHP, SPHP Forte, Virules, Overones, Testrones, Prostalin and Phrodisine that were glandular and vitamin tablet formulae for adults. There was an excellent wrinkle preventative called 1934 Female Hormone Cream in the range. At the time there were many similar ranges on the market sold by mail order through advertisements in fringe magazines like Health & Efficiency and Psychic News. Hygienic Stores in The Charing Cross Road sold Damaroids 'The Great Rejuvenator', as proclaimed by a large banner above the shop entrance, seen by every upper deck bus passenger when the buses stopped outside their shop.

I met Mrs Arnold and Mr Jeffree at 67 St Mary Abbots Court. They were very helpful with the detail on BGP. I was confident the takeover would be smooth.

Business matters In November Walter O'Connell went to Dublin to set up a Blakoe Distributorship. He was full of bluster and confidence that he would succeed. He failed miserably.

I went To Huntingdon Research Company to see Dr Alan Cooper and discuss a Blakoe Ring Clinical Trial. Dr Colin Roberts, the old college friend who I'd met in Hong Kong joined the meeting. Soon after this meeting both had left HRC. Cooper would continue with the trial on his own.

In December I recorded in my diary that I was writing a new booklet covering Blakoe and British Glandular tonic and vitamin products. This was the first time that the company had produced such marketing material and laid the foundation for many of the catalogues and brochures that were developed in the 1972-1998 period. Many of these were in-house written, photographed and designed by me and later on with Rita Greer. There were many staff changes throughout that period and although substantial inputs from these people took place – the themes were mine and hers. We had the unique advantage of knowing the products thoroughly which was something advertising agencies generally lacked.

Lipcote   The BGP agency product, Lipcote had been sold in Boots and chemists with some success using advertising in the national press in both magazines and newspapers. It was a cosmetic product used to apply over lipstick to keep it on the lips. George Orange was a believer in this product and it was decided to plough all its profit back into advertising. Unfortunately, we did not own the rights to its trade mark or formula and spent well above the amounts expected by the principal. I discussed the advertising of Lipcote and Blakoe with Hugh Winthrop, the managing Director of Edward Walters Advertising in Richmond, Surrey. George Orange met Winthrop and approved the new photography and copy in connection with the advertising.

Ruthmol takeover   I saw an advertisement in the Chemist & Druggist concerning a business for sale in Taunton, Somerset. This was British Ethical Proprietaries Ltd who manufactured a salt replacer **'Ruthmol'**, based on Potassium Chloride. They also marketed a small range of barbiturate tablets with a built-in emetic (Emetine). This range appealed to me as I saw the emetic barbiturates as a natural successor to Safeseal whilst Ruthmol complemented Cantassium Discs the Biochemic Remedy based on Potassium Bicarbonate. There were some good utensils and machinery available and the advertising materials were good. After discussion with George Orange, I arranged to visit Mr Gray the owner and a deal was done at £5000 plus £300 for plant. Stock was purchased at cost. The whole deal was put together and the items received in Putney within a week of my having made contact with Mr Gray.

   BEP soon proved its worth and Ruthmol the Salt Free Salt ultimately became number one in the salt replacer market. It was not permitted on prescription but was widely recommended by Doctors to their Blood Pressure patients. There was evidence that its use in place of salt in cooking and as a table condiment could help prevent strokes and heart attacks. It was superior to competitor salt replacers because it did not 'cake' in its shakers and was virtually salt free (Sodium has a ubiquitous presence in fine chemicals as an impurity and can never be totally absent). It also had a taste close to sodium chloride. Reduction of salt in the diet was still a long way from being accepted as a good healthy diet choice. By 2009 things had changed but Ruthmol was no longer available. Products are now labeled 'Low Salt' and sold as salt substitutes but they all contained more than traces of Sodium and their benefits to health were unproven. The same could be said of Sea Salts. Potassium Chloride is a costly material in comparison with Sodium Chloride and the Low Salt salt replacers have taken Ruthmol's place in the market on a false prospectus. The public was misled but the authorities did not care. Barbemets, the emetic preparations, prevented suicides by barbiturates (Phenobarbitone, Butobarbitone, Amylobarbitone, cyclobarbitone). They were prescribed by doctors to patients who they suspected might attempt suicide and to those with a previous record of attempting suicide. I saw these products as appropriate to my thoughts on 'safer prescribing' and hoped to increase the range soon. Again, my hopes were dashed by authorities who frowned on combination formulae in general and on combining in a formulation ingredients with no cumulative therapeutic benefit. Saving lives was not accepted as a benefit by officialdom. As usual the bureaucrats acted by the book but not rationally. Emetine was an emetic not a narcotic and was later seen as basically 'unsafe'. It was thus never combined with other popular suicide drugs such as paracetamol, methaqualone etc. Indeed a safe formula of paracetamol was marketed a few years later but received similar rejection by the authorities. However, Paracetamol frequently features in accidental/suicide deaths.

Problems in Cyprus I wrote a letter to our Cyprus distributor about a dispute over tablet quality with the authorities in Cyprus. The Chief Pharmacist of the Cyprus Ministry of Health had visited the factory in Putney and had taken a dislike to Matthews & Wilson. He was openly critical of our staff and systems. I thought that there was probably a hidden agenda because at the time we employed a PhD from Hong Kong as our head of Quality Control. Dr Lee was a competent analyst but obviously the official from Cyprus, a Greek Cypriot, did not gel with him. I had often recruited from outside the UK and had become aware of as many tensions between Indians and Pakistanis as between English and Poles. Prejudice was unconfined. The Cyprus ministry opened its own Laboratory and took delight in rejecting our products, in every case, without justification. In the end we refused to ship products to Cyprus without clearance of a sample before shipment. We would not pay the expected 'incentive' so the business ceased.

Product range and Decimalisation By the end of the 1971, the range of products stocked amounted to over 200 items. Most were pharmaceutical generics under The House of Woodward together with specialities by Matthews & Wilson, Blakoe & British Glandular Products. Lipcote came in two sizes small (7ml) 25p retail and large (14ml) 35p indicating that decimalization had occurred.

Year end notes 1971 The company Blakoe Ltd sold by Mail Order but 33% of sales was spent on advertising and promotion. Thus mail order advertising cost much more than to the trade and George Orange became very concerned about this. He could not really get his mind round advertising being an investment. He was used to his network of business contacts, drinks in pubs and friendships with customers. This was a problem for me and was to continue for many years. My father could see buildings and machinery as an investment but not sales promotion. In reality machinery is far from an investment as much of it dates and deteriorates rapidly – value being lost, often far in excess of 'depreciation' allowances.

'House of Woodward' to Amygdalin

Child Safety - Inspections - Medicines Licensing - Alternative Healthcare - Mechanotherapy - ASA - Cantamac - Manufacturer's Licence - A Black February Day - Homoeopathics - Aquamaid - Three day week - Appeals Tribunal - Saccharine Disease - Environment and Health - Calcium Pantothenate - Medicinal Product definition - Omniped - Amygdalin (B17)

Child Safety In 1972 Child safety packaging was still a live subject with questions in Parliament, but it was obvious that the method of providing this was likely to be through use of childproof closures on bottles of dispensed medicines. Safety through strip-packing was too bulky to be a practical answer.

In May the BMA published a special report on the transmission of Pharmaceutical preparations from manufacturer to patient. In the area of packaging there was implicit recommendation of unit packing for dispensed medicines and for clear labeling 'Keep out of the reach of Children'. The use of unit packaging (when medicines were packed into the unit prescribed by doctors, eg 28 capsules for four weeks at one-a-day) for dispensed medicines was still not universal in 2009. In 1969 there were **3,023 fatalities** from poisoning by Pharmaceutical preparations of which **28 accidentally occurred in children** under 15. Of course, there were many more non-fatal events but these were not recorded. Whilst Woodward's 'Safeseal' (branded under House of Woodward) had contributed to the debate it was time to move on as already decided in 1971.

By February 1972 'Safeseal' had been discontinued and AWH was still trying to obtain retail chemist business in generics. He was also endeavouring to find contract tableting. However, I was becoming increasingly concerned at the on-going profitability and growth available in this area. We had AWH and Walter O'Connell on the road, and, whilst there was pressure to increase sales representatives, I was doubtful of their likely success in a very crowded market. The fact that some retailers realized we were selling non-medicines direct to consumers through mail order did not endear us to them or to firms that had contracts to give for similar products to those we were direct selling. Mail order, with Blakoe and Cantassium, was proving profitable. Payment with order was an enormous boost to the company's cash flow. Many chemists and health food retailers took a very long time to settle even the smallest debt yet insisted on big discounts. Contractors were very ready to find slight faults with the colour of sugar coated tablets especially if a competitor had come round recently offering a penny less per thousand for the same tablets.

Sales policy Mail order required good office based customer relations and no quibble return of goods but this was manageable on the margins earned by the company selling direct and cutting out middlemen. Good store relations had to be generated by travelling sales staff. The overhead associated with mobility was considerable. To obtain one order worth £25 gross out of three to five visits to stores a day was hardly exciting, especially if customers took four months to pay. The decision was taken to concentrate efforts towards Mail Order, Export (mostly through London based buyers), UK based Wholesalers and the large multiple retailers such as Boots and Timothy Whites. The company continued with some larger established contract customers, making and packaging tablets, including strip packing. Both our factories had enough work for their staff.

LARKHALL GREEN FARM

RIP House of Woodward' (AWH's idea) was abandoned and Blakoe Mail Order, Export under Matthews & Wilson, wholesaling and contract work under G O Woodward & Co Ltd, became the core activities.

Inspectors   Inspections at the factory seemed to be never ending -- the building, offices, environment, fire exits and alarms, health and safety, electrical appliances etc, etc. The Factory Inspectors inspected machinery and tools, guards, noise, dust, hygiene, toilets, canteen facilities, offices and safety of the workforce.

When the Medicines Inspectors started to come to the factories they inspected the goods inwards, warehouse, checking and storage of raw materials, the staff, quality control, the laboratories, the departments for granulation and mixing, compression, coating and packaging; hygiene standards and facilities. However, they did not concern themselves with the sales office and general office, the telephone switchboard and reception, accounts department or the reps' transport.

Medicines Licensing   June 1972 brought the first real effects of the Medicines Act 1968 into focus – Product Licensing and Manufacturing and Assembly Licensing.

On 30th June all applications for the so called **'Product Licences of Right'** had to be received by the Department of Health and Social Security Medicines Division. We submitted **several thousand applications** on agreed abbreviated terms. This was a huge task and had taken our technical staff many months. We heard little more about these applications for a long time after submission of the data but could continue to sell all the products. There was much confusion as to what made a product a 'Medicinal' and we actually registered many preparations that we found were exempted in later years. The crucial property of Medicinal products was their effectiveness on physiological processes. The labeling became of vital importance. The lack of a medicinal claim and a formula not containing established active (evidence based) medicinal substances, would take the product outside the licensing system. The grey areas were soon exploited to the full and throughout future decades caused authorities and industry real problems.

In February we had applied for **Manufacturer's Licences** in Putney and in Charlbury. A Medicines Inspector called by appointment in February at both locations. He said very little on his visits and would not be drawn into an open discussion of the situation he observed. In June, some three months later, we received a very critical assessment of both facilities. To add insult to injury the Inspector had not even bothered to sign his letter -- so much for his attention to detail on the simplest of matters whereas he expected us to be 100% on detail in very many functions. He had 30 critical matters to mention about Putney and added just 4 more about Charlbury, which was the smaller facility, making very few medicines but strip-packing and bottling many. (The latter procedures were classed as 'assembly'.)

The vast majority of the criticisms were nit-picking but that was to be expected -- Inspectors have to justify their existence. They had bees in their bonnets and could change their minds between visits. They were often impossible to deal with rationally.

My father was disgusted with the Inspector whom he thought inexperienced, with very little idea of practical tablet making. He and I decided to close the small tableting function in Charlbury and in future this would only deal with packing. Putney ultimately concentrated on manufacturing and was Head Office for the group. This meant a large lorry went from Putney to Charlbury once a week with bulk tablets and returned to Putney with packed stock for the warehouse. If we hadn't been in two places this expense would have been saved. It would continue until 1999 but there were positive aspects too.

I replied to the Inspector's letter on **13th June** and had a reply from his superior that seemed to imply that a Manufacturers Licence would be granted. Therefore we did not apply for a Manufacturers Licence of Right by **30th June**, which was the deadline. If we had, then we might have been in a stronger position later. I believed that the timing of their inspections and letters amounted to a deliberate ploy by the Department of Health, to ensure we did not obtain a Licence of Right and so obtain more protection for our business. They had no idea that we were already changing the commercial structure of the business to ensure that we became independent of 'Medicinals' as defined in the Medicines Act 1968.

At this time all our commercial effort was moving towards expanding in the **Alternative Health Care** area. The hope was that in a few years time, we would have a Manufacturer's Licence but be making Alternative Health Products, within a facility of Medicinal Standard. It was likely that in about five years the inspectors would become less zealous as they found themselves a permanent niche in the burgeoning, well-pensioned Department of Health bureaucracy.

Gaining a Manufacturing Licence was some years away but as we had an application for Manufacturers Licences at both facilities we were able to continue operating. This meant we faced the possibility of an unannounced inspection at any time, and, Putney was not far from the Inspectorates' HQ. I expected an attack and in 1973 I actually dreamt of an unannounced inspection that forced closure of Putney. It was constantly on my mind. Nevertheless, we increased our loan facility from the bank by £40,000 to enable faster development of the Putney laboratories.

It was obvious from that first visit by the Inspectors, that problems would arise in the future if we did not cut down on our involvement in Medicines and expand in the alternative healthcare area. The recent purchase of British Ethical Proprietaries would be our last in the medicine field but its product Ruthmol would lead us into dietary healthcare where we would become a leader.

Mechanotherapy   Blakoe developed too, thanks to the advice of Dr Brian Richards, a visionary GP who had a special interest in the growing area of 'Sexual Medicine'. With his help we published 'The Manual of Mechanotherapy'. This outlined the case for appliances to aid sexual dysfunction. Doctors were mailed, we employed a brand manager, three sales representatives (visiting Doctors and Pharmacies) and took advertisements in the medical press. Articles appeared in the lay and medical press to promote the ideas, but in the event it became clear that whilst Doctors were users of the aids themselves, they did not prescribe them for patients. Many Blakoe Energising rings were sold to Doctors following our publicity but business did not grow sufficiently to warrant greater sales effort to the Health Professionals.

Commercial progress 1972   For M&W and G O Woodward Group sales amounted to under a million pounds with virtually no profit. Staff had reduced to barely a hundred. The reductions were attributable to the Medicines Act effects and the costs associated with complying with the demands of the bureaucracy. Gross margin was maintained and we still had a small reserve.

Blakoe was trading separately with most sales direct to consumers and increased sales of 150% meaning that total sales of all the companies might exceed one million pounds in 1973. However, in the event they did not. The gross margin on the Blakoe Ranges were good and enabled investment in the brand to reach nearly 50% of sales including consumer advertising, mailings and Medical Consultants' fees. These margins were totally alien to George Orange who needed persuasion to let so much cash go into the ether. It was the old problem "I can see machinery and real estate but not advertising and sales promotion". Nevertheless, it managed to carry forward a revenue reserve and paid to the company group over £21,000 as management charges. I was determined to continue my policy that was showing good results so soon.

Within its trading, G O Woodward & Co Ltd included the Pharmacy only products bought from British Ethical Proprietaries and Lipcote, the BGP Cosmetic product. Advertising for these products was beginning to increase and so gain wider distribution for them in Boots Stores and Retail Chemists. All Pharmaceutical Wholesalers were stocking Ruthmol but Lipcote was only stocked by one or two. Both these products were presented in more than one pack. Ruthmol (shakers of 50g and 200g, and a bulk 400g), Lipcote small 6ml and large 11 ml.

The **Blakoe** range was already extensive and embraced Tablets, Capsules, Creams, Liquids, Powders and Mechanical Sex aids -- in all, a range of about 100 items. There were some wonderful names! Blavig, Virules, Testrones, Vigmasc, Phrodisine, Carry on Cream, Bliss Cream, Rise Cream, Dr Blakoe's energy formula, Blakoe's Natural Pile remedy, Improved Compound No.1, Salfree (Ruthmol for direct sale) etc. Sex aids included the Dr Blakoe Energiser, Vacuum Developer, Virilex (Hydrotherapy for Men) together with Prosthetics, Stimulators and Vibrators.

Associated Preparations was the mail order section of the company embracing the Blakoe, Cantassium and British Glandular ranges. The diverse product range covered alternative health care and was growing rapidly. Testimonials were received daily from happy customers and extracts from these letters were used in our promotions and when the advertising rules permitted in our national press advertisements. The testimonial was undoubtedly the most powerful of all mail order sales tools. However many companies were already taking liberties and using them to promote miracle weight loss, hair restoration and wrinkle prevention, 'cures' for arthritis and rheumatism, colds and 'flu and sometimes even cancer.

ASA and bogus claims   The Advertising Standards Authority had been formed in the 1960s to enforce voluntary codes of sales promotion and the Trades Description Act 1968 had been passed. Together, these affected all companies and many ads were stopped and court cases brought. However, despite this, there continued to be many ways of circumventing the rules and the authorities could not keep up with many transgressors. Even in 2009 there were many hugely successful promotions for very dubious products. The campaigning charity 'Healthwatch', that was formed in the late 1980s to expose bogus claims for healthcare products and services, was still kept very busy despite the large bureaucracies that should have been acting swiftly to eliminate the cowboys. The inefficiency of Government regulators often amazes me. In 2010 there were still many products promoted from off-shore addresses and on the internet, that seem to make monkeys out of the enforcement systems and indirectly force losses on law abiding UK based companies.

Unfortunately, my decision to take the Alternative Health Care route in 1972 led to many run-ins with the ASA and the Medicines regulatory bodies, but that made business a real challenge. Importantly, these problems often gained us publicity and sympathy and so helped sales development. I was also writing letters to the professional and lay press extolling the virtues of the **alternative way** – my argument being that if the NHS and orthodox medicine did the job properly then alternative care people would not exist. After all, the NHS was free at the point of use but alternative healthcare was a pay-as-you-go system. This was a powerful message and much feared by the establishment bureaucrats and healthcare professionals because they had no answer except bluster.

Cantamac In mid 1972 a Professor Roger MacDougall (A Professor in Theatre Studies UCLA) and MS sufferer came to our office at the suggestion of Dr. Jean Munro, who had been treating him. MacDougall was a playwright who had written one really successful play, 'The Man in the White Suit'. He said he had **cured** his MS (Multiple Sclerosis) by adopting a Gluten Free Diet and taking several Food Supplements. I looked at the quantities of vitamins and minerals he was taking daily (a combination prescribed by Dr. Jean Munro, and said I would formulate two supplements to replace the ten he was using, making the dosage closer to what MacDougall deemed ideal for his MS. It had to be two tablets because there was some confusion about using Vitamin B12 as a non-medicinal product. We held a Product Licence of Right for 50mcg Vitamin B12 tablets so had a legal product, should the authorities question our marketing it as Cemac B12, to compete with Glaxo's 'Cytacon'.

The name we used for the new supplement was 'Cantamac'. In collaboration with me, MacDougall wrote some information and the product was soon being widely prescribed on the NHS for MS patients. I was interested in keeping Cantamac ethical (only for prescription) but such was its popularity that many orders were being received direct from patients with MS, who had heard about the MacDougall diet. 'Cantamac' was accepted for prescribing on EC10 NHS prescriptions by Doctors. This was a real breakthrough and led to regular sales.

Since Cantamac was a vitamin product many local drug authorities would not permit it for free prescription on the NHS. The rules in that area were unclear but the government was anxious to prevent costs of prescriptions increasing. Patient groups fought to obtain Cantamac prescribed free and won in several areas of the country. Cantamac sales helped sustain the company for two or three years and was still being prescribed into the late 1980s. Unfortunately, several years later Cantamac was included in the Black List of non-prescribable items on the NHS that became law. However, Cantamac still sold steadily until the late 80s on private prescription. It was discontinued in 1995.

Macdougall enjoyed a substantial commission on sales of Cantamac but after a year he became greedy, decided to take my formula and found one of our competitors to make it. He called the product 'Regenic', for which he made the many dubious claims that I had told him should not be used. He put forward the idea that all degenerative diseases could be cured with his pills and hoped his title of 'Professor' would make people think he was a doctor and enable him to make a fortune. We ceased to pay him and soon lost touch. No MS patient was ever cured by his methods.

Rationalisation At the end of 1972 The G O Woodward Group of companies was widely respected but was becoming involved in too many areas. The companies needed to rationalise their ranges and structure as soon as possible. Could they do it in time and so survive? There were rumours that many small pharmaceutical manufacturers were already being closed by the Medicines Inspectorate, not directly but indirectly because they could not afford the new overheads caused by inspector demands -- safety must be 100% regardless of reality -- don't walk on the pavement anywhere!

Big Changes Prior to this time our company had been predominantly an ethical and generic medicine manufacturer - a member of the ABPI.

Our company had been through very difficult times with sales not reaching expectations and overheads increasing. The 1968 Medicines Act was having devastating effects throughout the Pharmaceutical Industry. As had been predicted by the Chairman of the Standard Formulary Medicines Committee of the ABPI in 1968 – 'Life would never be the same again'. Many companies were closed and products banned. Fear ran throughout the smaller companies but the bureaucracy's policy of divide and rule paid off.

The officials achieved their aim of less work for them with fewer facilities to inspect and less products to worry about. They would be left with the bigger companies and monopoly products, all in the cause of 'Consumer Safety' and rising salaries and pensions for themselves.

Very few companies had the resources or the courage for a fight – many feared for their profits and director lifestyles, so were fodder for the officials who displayed duplicity beyond belief. Many found their first inspections torrid experiences with verbal complaints about dust, cross contamination, oil traces on machinery and written records then extended in letters after their visit, to forty or fifty detailed shortcomings. No one ever reported a note of encouragement – it was all denigration by people with personal grudges and scores to settle, few of whom had real experience of manufacturing or running a small company.

George Orange was alarmed by the Inspector at Charlbury whom he thought ignorant of real life in factories. It was very much the communist approach that 'I am the master now'. The fact that an owner had given work to hundreds over time and used their own resources of savings and work to build something was immaterial to most of these inspectors. There were some exceptions, but they seldom lasted as inspectors for long.

The Medicines Act 1968 was the forerunner of later so called 'Enabling Acts' but it was not until the methods of Medicines Inspectors became stock in trade to Trading Standards, Food Hygiene, Environmental enforcers, Health and Safety Inspectors etc. that many companies throughout manufacturing came under the cosh, and the UK lost so much of its manufacturing base. We will never know how much was lost in exporting as the little firms closed down.

I predicted that manufacturing would move away to countries where Inspectors were less zealous and general overhead costs were less. Most of the new countries were granted reciprocity rights with the UK, eg India, Bangaladesh, Nigeria etc. There, UK authorities trusted local inspections. Even the Pharmaceutical giants moved their manufacturing to these countries to save costs.

Many of these overseas facilities were far below the average standards (don't ask about hygiene!) operating in Britain whilst bribery of officials was endemic in those countries, but the UK government turned a blind eye. By the 21st century, counterfeiting of medicines became a number one problem for the NHS – thanks to the shortsighted government actions twenty-five years before. Whilst on the subject of bribery – I often had a feeling that some Inspectors were suspect in that regard but I never positively reacted to their 'hints'.

A Manufacturer's Licence granted but soon suspended In January 1973 we received a letter from the Department of Health (DOH) informing us that a 'Maufacturer's Licence would be granted to us, but restricting our range to active ingredient strengths above 5mg and disallowing Hormones, Steroids and Antibiotics. I replied that I did not accept such restriction and asked for a meeting with officials. My brother and our new Quality Controller attended the meeting with me on Friday 2nd February, with about twelve officials, including Inspectors and Lawyers led by a long service bureaucrat. He insulted us and implied that the factory was a slum and that we had had plenty of time since 1968 to get our act together. I protested that since we had no idea as to what demands were likely to be made by the DOH until about a year ago, that he was being unreasonable. The new Orange Guide to Good Manufacturing Practice had been published in late 1971 and the DOH had stated that it had no statutory force and was not to be regarded as an interpretation of Medicines Act requirements. In typical bureaucrat language, they referred to the Guide, 'Observance or non-observance of any of its recommendations does not amount to compliance or non-compliance with particular requirements of the regulations'.

At the end of the meeting I felt crushed but even more determined to fight what I considered outrageous behaviour by a senior civil servant and his cohorts. It began to look as if we had been singled out by the DOH as an example to others, of DOH power. Our facilities were not perfect but I could have taken him to many more which were really bad and still operating as medicine manufacturers. I had never hidden my contempt for the bureaucracy in letters to the press and to journalists – I was a marked man in their book. Good.

After that meeting we were promised an inspection by appointment within a couple of weeks. Instead, we received an unannounced inspection by two inspectors on 6th & 7th February. That was one working day after the last DOH meeting. This visit was a disaster. One of the Inspectors had been at Chelsea School of Pharmacy around the same time as me and was heard to say, sotto voce, "He was born with a silver spoon in his mouth, I want to get him".

One minor error effectively finished us as generic tablet makers but was the beginning of a commercial recovery that lasted until 1999. During this time most of our then competitors fell by the wayside. The Inspectors took samples of various tablets and dust at random. These samples showed traces of penicillin as a contaminant. I could not understand this because we had not made penicillin tablets for many years and cleaning was always rigorous.

I accepted total responsibility for the problems and asked for a meeting at the HQ of the Inspectorate with Mr Whiffen our Quality Controller. Unsurprisingly, this was not a success. There were some fourteen officials, including Inspectors, ranged against two people from the Company. We were told that if we appealed their decision to revoke our licence they would cease informal discussions. It was to be my last experience of this kind. Our Licence was suspended. That was our **Black February day** but actually as I have said previously, a springboard for recovery.

Paperwork and more inspections   At the meeting the officials said that if we cleaned up the premises to their unknown standard and notified the Inspectors, an inspector would be down in hours. In the event, we had the factory industrially cleaned and notified the Inspectors in early April, but the inspector refused to attend unless the paperwork documentation was in order. Mr Whiffen, a registered pharmacist and our quality control manager, resigned -- a broken man. I took over the paperwork myself, and helped by Mr SGE Stevens, an analytical and quality control consultant who had worked for a major pharmaceutical company, submitted paperwork for six products with some 50 pages of paper for each. Hundreds of pages were submitted by the end of April. On 11th May some derogatory comments on the paperwork were received. Much of the comment was trivial criticism on points that pharmacists could always disagree about. Consumer safety was not compromised by these so called 'errors'. Mr Stevens pulled out of the project as they had rejected his paperwork and I was left on my own once more.

On 16th May we had another inspection and the premises passed with compliments from the two Inspectors on the cleanliness and organization. However the problems with the paperwork persisted and it seemed obvious that the DOH were expecting me to give up soon. I did not oblige.

In July we were offered a very limited licence (just 3 products Hexamine, Dapsone and Vitamin B12) but our paperwork was not 'internally consistent and mathematically accurate' -- a cliché used all the time by the bureaucrats. It meant there were a few typographical errors. This sort of thing is always discovered when the documents go into practical use and are corrected in situ. Aspirin was added to the licence and there were subclauses in it that apparently permitted export manufacture of any product. Since most of our business was export I accepted.

If, as it became clear later, Export Production was not permitted, how did the officials think we could survive on a four product licences? It proved that they had no commercial considerations and their claim not to want to put any manufacturer out of business was nonsense if not downright evil.

New QC Manager A new Quality Control Manager was appointed in August 1973. He prepared more documents but the problems were repeated – the Inspector was too busy to deal with them promptly and again found petty points to raise. The restricted Manufacturers Licence was received on 6th December but expired on 31st – just 25 days later. Incredible! I suppose we were expected to work over Christmas and then apply for another Licence. We did apply but it was rejected. The DOH seemed to be playing games with the company, just hoping for that all important factory closure and publicity to make an example of us and to warn others. The Medicines Act 1968 was enacted to prevent a recurrence of Thalidomide but the officials had a different agenda – to drive out the small companies, by burdening the makers of simple medicines like Aspirin and herbals, with criteria close to those applied to powerful new drugs like Antibiotics and Antidepressants. I was convinced that the fact that our family was middle class, white and English did not play in our favour.

Homoeopathic Veterinary Product and the Medicine's Act In July 1973 we received a rather aggressive letter from a top official, at the Medicines Division of the DHSS. It concerned a homoeopathic veterinary product that contained a trace of Nux Vomica (a natural source of strychnine). As a Homoeopathic, the actual content of strychnine in the product was virtually undetectable and totally harmless to animals and humans. Incredibly, this official was devoting his time to writing to us about the product and had obviously not checked with the relevant office at his department to find that this was a product licensed to us. I thought it crazy that a bureaucrat should be concerning himself about animals being administered Homoeopathics when his Licensing organization had been voted into being to prevent the recurrence of the side effects of powerful prescription drugs like Thalidomide. He seemed to be out of his depth. Even by 1973 it could be seen that his outfit was not achieving those aims but was certainly using draconian policies to wipe out tens of thousands of useful health products, close good companies and drive manufacture overseas.

The multinational drug industry, as I well knew, could have been complicit in all this because it always wanted 101% of the market. The DHSS appeared to be their ally in ridding itself of their competition. As for the vested professional interests in healthcare, they knew that the power lay with the drugs industry and it was not in their interest to interfere with the deeds of the Regulators.

This true story of bureaucrat behaviour is a microcosm of what always happens in regulatory bodies worldwide. They are brought into being for unexceptional reasons, but once installed they lose sight of their real objectives and grow logarithmically, involving themselves in peripheral matters in order to appear 'efficient'. People seldom question these organizations because consumer or public 'safety' is paramount. No wonder the highly regulated UK was £178 Billion in deficit in 2009.

Sunflower oil price increase As an example of the way the bureaucrats worked, in October 1974 we had a letter from the PRICE Commission asking for a reason for the increase in price of our Sunflower Oil (Cemoil) from 60p to £1.90 per litre -- a 200% increase. I replied that the raw Sunflower Oil on the world market had gone up 400% from £160 to £800 per ton, which seemed to have escaped them. I told them we only sold 500kg a year and our price had to be competitive. I received no reply from them. What a waste of space these government bodies are.

A Possible Sale of the business 1973   In late 1973 the directors had an approach from Barclay Pharmaceuticals to purchase the Tablet and wholesale businesses and the Putney Factory. Had the sale gone through we would have moved the Blakoe Ltd business to Charlbury and, at a stroke, reduced our involvement with generic pharmaceutical tablets. The sales and development office would possibly have moved to Surrey. Although much documentation was produced no acceptable offer was received. It was an interesting exercise and I was never really in favour because I could not envisage Charlbury becoming the company HQ with all the Woodwards together. It just would not have worked. I did not get on with my brother and had a tense relationship with my father. He was more in favour but possibly had similar reservations to me. In the event, 1973 was a low point, but no one could have foreseen the success of the Blakoe/Cantassium/Lipcote businesses.

Blakoe and Cantassium progress 1973   The range of products grew substantially and the Mail order Price List of October 1973 demonstrated this. It included Blakoe and BGP (23) Special Formulas, Pile Remedy with syringe, Energising Ring standard and de Luxe, Wire Wool. Marital Aids (32), Hydrotherapy Breast Conditioner (Aquamaid), Foods (3) including Vitamin E powder and Salfree Baking Powder, Health Courses (7) comprising several products eg Contour Course for Ladies (Galegae Tablets, Vitamin E cream and an Aquamaid Hydrotherapy device). Blakoe Products on a new colour leaflet (21) including Creams, Tablets, Capsules and a liquid Blakogerm. Cantassium Supplements (19), Herbals (1) Galegae Tablets. Biochemics (1) Silica 6X (a homoeopathic). Approximately 110 Products.

This range was unique in the alternative healthcare field and established our Company as a credible entity. The range was to undergo many changes and refinement up to 1998 but the basic range conceived by me in 1973, was its foundation. Mail order gave the company a market entry at minimum advertising cost. It enabled us to test a new product's or range's likely demand, at an affordable launch cost. It meant that products sold into trade outlets had an established basis of demand which gave most retailers confidence to stock them.

Many retailers were apprehensive of our mail order sales division but we gave them margins to ensure they could compete with these. Retailers do not accept that many consumers prefer mail order as their route for supply, whilst there are others who much prefer to see and be advised by a person in store.

The large range also gave the company great credibility in trade and consumer minds. We had a qualified staff of scientists and pharmacists unknown in other companies in the Health Food area. We knew our products from basics because most were made in our factory and we had quality control far ahead of our competitors in alternative healthcare. Product knowledge built from those early days of tablet manufacture stood us in great stead and made us the envy of our rivals. Unfortunately, there were few opportunities for patent protection and many of our successes were soon copied, but that kept us on our mettle to develop new ideas. Research into new products and nutrition trials continued throughout the period 1970-1998.

Our mail order price list was used as a promotional tool as were package inserts. Some extracts from the wording on the mail order price list well illustrate our approach:-

*   Associated Preparations Limited ... Your Key to Good Health

*   When you buy from AP you have the guarantee resulting from 35 years experience in the Health Product field.

*   The purest, finest, Natural ingredients are used. We keep ahead of the times too and cater for the daily stresses, the figure conscious age and the "Getting the Most out of the era in which we live".

* If you are overweight we will help you....if you want to put weight on – our Protein sweets will help give you the extra pounds that you need.
* If you are tired (and who isn't at times these days) our Energy-giving Wheat Germ and Vitamin E preparations will help you to carry the strain.
* Our proteolysed liver tablets are perfect for convalescents and Athletes needing extra nourishment.
* For men with virility problems, we cater for them with the wonderful Blakoe Energiser "to help your love last a lifetime". We also strongly recommend our Gland Tablets. Testrones, SPHP and Overones – as their names imply we make them for both sexes. They are excellent tonics and help to restore that sense of wellbeing once more. Our Cantassium discs are an established name.... we get letters of gratitude from Gout and Rheumatism sufferers everywhere.
* Our new range of Marital Aids are top quality and guarantee satisfaction.
* By pin-pointing the everyday ills that beset us all we are endeavouring to maintain a well balanced and healthy mind and body....our key and yours to perfect health.
* We now have Special Dietary Foods available. Send for details.
* The famous Blakoe Galvanic Wristlets, Anklets and Body Belts are now available. Send for details.

All copy and design was generated within the company. No agencies were involved in that work in 1973.

Aquamaid Hydrotherapy device for Breast enhancement This intriguing device fitted well with our company's mission of non-drug therapy and was purchased by me towards end of 1973, from Leslie Green of Ilford, Essex. Green, a naturist, had patented his design using a special sprayer. The spray operated as a small rotating shower within a plastic cup that fitted over the breast. A similar device was made in France but was poorly designed with a fixed metal spray held within a plastic breast shaped cup.

Les's wife Cathy, also a naturist, had used the 'Aquamaid' with great success and through his press connections -- he drew all the maps for a national newspaper -- Les had achieved a persuasive two page story in a tabloid Sunday newspaper. The before and after photos of Cathy must have been the clincher for the publicity. Les was inundated with orders but after two years had been unable to repeat the story and paid advertising was difficult in national press and magazines, owing to advertising restrictions surrounding 'Breast Improvement' claims. Sales of the device were declining, despite persuasive advertisements in the fringe press especially 'Health & Efficiency' the Naturist Magazine.

Within our product range I thought Aquamaid had a future. Breast feeding was an area of increasing Medical Nursing interest and I thought that stimulation from an Aquamaid might well make this easier for some mothers. The discomfort of the cold water spraying on the breast was a minor point but still a drawback. But, like the Blakoe Ring, we could have a dual purpose device – impotence/incontinence for the ring – breast enhancement/breast feeding for the Aquamaid. A subsequent clinical trial by Dr Saha, of St Mary's Hospital, Newport, IOW in 1974, proved the breast feeding benefit. Attempts to publicise this trial proved nearly impossible despite the widespread medical view that 'breast is best'.

We also had great difficulty with press advertising but using our growing Mail Order customer base we managed steady sales for many years until sourcing the sprays became impossible in the small quantities needed. Nevertheless, Aquamaid became the brand name of our growing range of naturally based beauty products and continued in use beyond 1999.

35

Inspector Hell and the three day week   1974 heralded further harassment from Inspectors. A telephone call was received in January from someone in the Licensing Authority who expressed surprise at finding we were "still open and taking calls". Soon after, we received a short visit from two Inspectors who said little but took samples of tablets away with them. We were operating under the **three-day week** restrictions as a result of a miners' strike. Another short inspection by three Inspectors took place soon after. The surprise nature of these visits meant that my brother had to come up from Charlbury in order to deal with them. I was engaged in trying to keep business in non-medicines expanding and not available to be sidetracked by talking to or deferring to the Inspectors whenever they felt like it.

Alas, the limited Manufacturers Licence in Putney London was lost within weeks of these visits. Having two premises really was a good idea. The assembly-only licence in Charlbury was not affected because the technical demands on products was not so dependent on highly qualified personnel and advanced quality standards.

The Medicines Inspectors were still causing havoc among many UK medicine manufacturers but there was no coherent opposition because each company was fighting for itself hoping to survive whilst competitors went out of business. This enabled Inspectors to make different demands on each company and many ceased to make medicinal products for commercial reasons. There seemed no way to satisfy the power-crazed bureaucrats within predictable budgets, so few bothered. This meant that soon there were far fewer manufacturing sites left in the UK and ultimately most manufacturing of modern medicines was transferred to overseas facilities with so called 'reciprocal' licence recognition by the UK authorities. As a consequence in the UK, many people lost their jobs.

Air conditioning   Once we had been asked by one Inspector to change the filtering method and the direction on an outside air conditioning intake. Cost was £12,000. Within a year another Inspector visited us and demanded we reverse the air intake reverting to the previous filter method. Despite protest we had to obey and the reversal cost another £15,000. Madness – yes, but a real problem with these Inspectors.

Independence   Over the years my determination to pursue independence at all costs was rewarded with the growing strength of the Blakoe, Aquamaid, Omniped and non-medicinal Cantassium products. We also maintained an excellent export wholesale business in pharmaceuticals to Oil Companies, Mission Hospitals and Charities eg Caritas Congo. Holding on to the Assembly Licence in Charlbury was very helpful too.

An appeal tribunal   The alternative health care activities were going well enough for us to be building funds to fight these unreasonable, power crazed officials. First was a planned appeal under Section 22 (2) of the Act. We had been warned that if we did appeal then co-operation by the Inspectors would cease. If their behaviour for the last 12 months was their idea of 'co-operative' – I didn't think their non co-operation was worth worrying about. Airing our case with an appeal would at least mean our plight would be known to the wider world. Whether the hearing would be fair was another matter. I did not expect it to be, in view of the way they had behaved so far.

The Appeal Tribunal took place in the week beginning 1st July 1974 at The Insurance Institute, 20 Aldermanbury, London EC2. The Tribunal Chairman was Dr Frank Hartley CBE.,DSc who had been my examiner when I gained my PhD in 1962. Hartley had since moved from Academia and become an Establishment figure – soon to be knighted. Our Company was represented by Sir Peter Rawlinson QC (a former Attorney General) and Mr Norman Cox of Kenwright & Cox Solicitors. At this time there was no case law in the area and no specialist lawyers were available. Our representatives did a very fine job. We had as experts Professor Arnold Beckett OBE.,DSc a Past President of the Pharmaceutical Society and Mr Arthur Chamings FPS who had been a Director of a major Pharmaceutical Manufacturer and was an expert in Herbal Medicine. Our own staff and directors were also present. Two inspectors attended but were not called to give evidence as they had only come as observers and therefore could not be cross-examined. This was their policy and it made a mockery of the whole process. It was a Kangaroo Court and the outcome was a foregone conclusion. Hartley refused to visit the Putney factory and gave the impression in his final address that he had not really comprehended our arguments.

After two days of strong representations and open criticism of the Inspectorate we had to wait more than three weeks until the end of July for a result. This was entirely as expected -- a whitewash for the Inspectors. However, we had made our mark and were still in business but not making 'Medicinal Products' as defined by the Medicines Act.

At the end of August we received a letter from the licensing authority totally rejecting our previous December 1973 submission for a Manufacturing Licence. It was not unexpected because we were 'at war' with a powerful bureaucracy. They would have to be defeated and thanks to their arrogance this was to happen. I had the resources and courage to do it for the sake of freedom. The DHSS had made a fatal error as they thought I could be bullied into submission. They totally underestimated me, as they would later find out.

I still thought that the aggressive visits of the two inspectors in February 1974 could lead to a prosecution in a Magistrates Court. I hoped it would, because after the toothless tribunal hearing I thought that a real court case could be useful in the longer term. I believed that these Inspectors were exceeding their remit and so long as the wider world remained ignorant of their behaviour, medicine producing companies would continue to suffer hardship and injustice. Sure enough, summonses were received by us towards the end of the year and 28th February 1975 was set for the hearing at Wells Street Magistrate's Court, London. The Licensing Authority had expected well under a day would be enough, thinking we would capitulate easily. As usual they underestimated my determination and the case lasted two full days. (See Chapter 5)

Larkhall not alone I began to learn of the problems at other wholesalers and manufacturers. Many of these were not as courageous as Larkhall and tried to placate the Medicines Bureaucrats by going along with their crazy demands in the name of 'safety'. One company, on losing its licence, went for supplies to a licensed company but on checking the products supplied by this company found serious quality deficiencies. These included mixed identity tablets in the same bulk container, pink dye contamination of white tablets, a piece of wire in a tablet, discoloured and spotted white tablets, soft tablets, 'sticking' of tablets during compression so that more than 30% of the tablet weight was lost, bulk tablets supplied in old barrels with filthy labels etc, etc. No doubt the paperwork was in order at that factory but the skill of the operators was low. Such are the effects of bureaucracy everywhere -- perfect paper records to please the man with the power in his ivory tower.

The Saccharine Disease and the Wholesome Diet, TL Cleave, GD Campbell and D Burkitt In 1966, three doctors -- Thomas Cleave, GD Campbell and Dennis Burkitt -- caused great controversy when their books claimed that refined carbohydrates, especially refined wheat, was a major causal factor in many health problems. These included major degenerative illnesses -- Diabetes, Colon Cancer and Coronary Heart Disease. Burkitt had discovered that primitive Africans who consumed a high fibre diet did not suffer these diseases. The outcome was that the Health Food movement, dating back to the great Dr Allinson in the late 19th century, realised that the natural style of diet with the wholewheat brown bread that they had been advocating for decades, was confirmed by Burkitt's research.

The food industry did not warm to these claims. Industrial scale production of breads, biscuits, cakes, cereals etc. needed raw materials with consistency of specification. It also required long shelf life for its products. Refining flours is essential, not only for economic production, but for long storage time too. Many unrefined flours soon deteriorate and taste and smell stale. This is because of the fat content associated with the fibre (Bran) that oxidises and the food becomes rancid and malodorous.

Processing flour to remove the fibre takes away the natural vitamins and minerals too. Millers add exact quantities of synthetic vitamins and minerals to correct that nutritional deficiency and provide consistency. They believe this makes a product that is better than the whole grain they started with. This is nonsense. There are many minerals and vitamins in whole grain cereals and just putting a few back after refining, as required by governments, is wrong. Breads are staples and if they lack micronutrients and fibre have a potential to cause malnutrition. Industrial bakers are permitted to use many synthetic chemical additives to achieve the economics of scale and long shelf life. The side effects of those combined additives are, as yet, unknown. Additives are usually safety tested individually, not in meaningful combinations.

Whilst fibre food products are often available as individual items they are not in widespread dietary use like breads, cakes and biscuits. Several proprietary brans contain plenty of sugar and salt to make them palatable. Oats is an honourable exception and one of the best sources of fibre to include in the diet.

Cleave and his colleagues have had a significant influence on the concepts of what constitutes a wholesome healthy diet. The F-plan diet of the late 70s owed its success to them. The Food Industry is very powerful and there has been much controversy about the research. Some believe that it has been the food industry behind research papers that contradict Cleave and Burkitt. They used those results, many emanating from their own funded researchers, as they attempted to persuade consumers that their refined carbohydrate with additives products were best.

Soon after taking over Cantassium in 1971, I realized that the Cantassium Dietary System following the ideas of Cyril Scott (author of 'Victory over Cancer') and Forbes Ross was a vegetarian based, high-fibre diet. I met Dr Cleave by appointment one lunchtime, on a bench at Waterloo Station, (without lunch), and was impressed by his character and belief in the correctness of his ideas. These ideas already formed the basis of our company's philosophy of the healthy diet. I believe that Cleave and Burkitt did not look to the Health Food Movement for support because, as Doctors, their faith was still in the medical establishment. In 1974 I thought that wrong but my later experiences with that movement was to disillusion me. By 1990 it was, for me, a plague on both their houses.

Chemical Environmental Factors and Health   I saw an opportunity for good publicity for the company. I wrote articles and letters and gave talks concerning the importance of dietary factors in degenerative diseases. I was advocating cutting out drug treatments and looking to Health Food Movement methods. The harm from chemicals both as drugs and as additives in junk food was a root cause of so much disease. Oliver Gillie of The Sunday Times and Richard Mackarness of 'A little bit of what you fancy' fame received letters from me on environmental factors affecting health, as did the BBC programmes Today and The World this Weekend.

Medical News entered the fray with an article by Joan Morgan in June about adulteration of breads by industry and the superiority of wholemeal bread made without additives to industrially made breads. The industry was quick to respond to Dr Joan Morgan but offered only platitudes and did not take up her challenge and prove their product superior to wholemeal bread. This argument continues to this day and the industry has fought its corner well. Alas, the consumer still gets a nutritionally poor product range from the mainstream food industry with too much use of refined basic ingredients, and, far too many synthetic chemical additives about which little is known of their combined safety profile. Individually, these agents may be 'safe', but what about the many combinations? No one knows. Add in the chemical prescription and over-the-counter medicines and people can ingest more than a witch's brew.

Calcium Pantothenate 1974   Dr Eustace Barton-Wright contacted me about his theory that Arthritis was a degenerative disease caused by deficiency of Vitamin B5 (Pantothenic Acid). He had trialled Injections but since the trial managers injected Barton-Wright's preparation directly into the affected joint, it did not work. I thought that perhaps high doses of 500mg Calcium Pantothenate in tablets, three times a day, might be worth a trial. Such a trial was carried out under Larkhall auspices and produced positive, but not scientifically significant results. Nevertheless, Cantopal 500mg and 50mg tablets were marketed with some success. Cantothen Injections (Barton-Wright's preparation), a licensed medicine, also sold well. Many competitors jumped on the bandwagon and claimed ownership of the research. This experience was enough to make me contemptuous of the Health Trade and its leaders like the Trade Body's President.

What is a Medicinal Product?   The aggressive stance of the Medicines Regulators began to be tested in mid 1974. The Chairman of a Health Food company, visited our Putney offices in May. His company had encouraged Roger MacDougall to leave us and they made my formula (as Cantamac) into Regenics tablets. This company was already selling Ginseng for more than food supplement purposes and was taking the Health Food movement in a distinctly Medicinal direction. A classic example was when I warned MacDougall of the danger of allowing his Regenic tablet to become a 'medicine' by law, but he took no notice. Some years later Regenics had gone and the company had many problems with their wild claims.

The public did not really appreciate the difference between a medicine and a food whilst the regulators feared losing a test case in Court because the definition of a 'Medicinal Product' was imprecise enough for clever lawyers to use to a Health Food company's advantage. Power Health of Pocklington in Yorkshire had a victory over the DHSS concerning Ginseng in the mid 70s and this landmark case provided succour to the supplement industry for many years. The borderline area was a fruitful source of revenue and avoidance of the licensing system enabled many small companies to survive commercially. However, the forces of the drugs industry and mainstream health care professionals were alert to these problems and made every effort to oppose the development of the alternatives in Healthcare. These matters became very relevant to the Woodward Companies as time went by as will be seen later in this narrative.

OMNIPED and International Foot Appliances. Continuing our quest for mail order products in the healthcare field that were not likely to be subject to the Medicines Act, I was offered a company involved in foot care. International Foot Appliances owned the Omniped Foot Cushion that was an arch support, invented and patented in 1936 by Dr E Allschoff, a German foot specialist practitioner. It was unique in its field, being very soft yet providing excellent support to the arches of the feet. It was mainly needed by elderly people but many athletes also found them useful. Regular users would probably need about three pairs a year so the market was attractive from the longterm user aspect. Its problem was that it came in two sizes for ladies and two for men. Stock needed was substantial. It was being advertised in the National Press and the response rate was very good.

George Magnus was the owner and he drove a hard bargain. His father, who had started the business in England, had retired some three years previously and the lease on their City Road property was about to expire. I thought the product would fit well in the range and went ahead with the purchase, despite a contrary view from AWH. Magnus had good contacts with suppliers of the components through his experience in the footwear trade. Special sandals were included in the range but these were fashion driven and quickly axed. A foot cream was more successful but never approached the Foot Cushion in sales volume. Unfortunately, suppliers of the really soft cushions required to make an Omniped became scarce and when in the late 80s we had to use a firmer cushion component, sales reduced.

The Omniped Foot Cushion proved an enduring product for mail order sales over many years. It was one of the few products that was easy to advertise and sold well off the page. It was always among our best sellers but product returns and sizing were always problems. Obtaining components of consistent quality was a constant headache too. Omniped drew people to our service and users often bought other products.

The Product Range growing with special diet foods added (the original 'Free From' range) Owing to consumer and retailer confusion because of the diversity of the Blakoe, Cantassium and Prescribable Ethical Preparations, efforts were made to distinguish these ranges using different price lists and order forms. The importance of Gluten Free, Salt Free, Refined Sugar (sucrose) Free and Saturated Fat Free was beginning to be important. We had our first Gluten Free Flour (Maize Starch), Fructose and Sorbitol (Sucrose Free) Salfree baking Powder (Salt and Gluten Free) Ruthmol (Salt Free condiment) and Sunflower and Safflower oils as substitutes for saturated and hydrogenated fats. Skimmed Milk was on our lists as a low saturated fat item. All Cantassium Diet Supplements were labeled on that platform too. Whilst we introduced Cantabran, which was from wheat, we also had Cantocel (a granular Methylcellulose) as a gluten free fibre item; some 10 special diet foods in all. I think that this was probably the first such range in the world and years ahead of its time.

The most successful products included the Blakoe Ring, Lipcote, Omniped, Cantamac Cantopal and Ruthmol. We were not a one product company by a long way. Thus our independence was assured despite all the problems with the Medicine Men from the Ministry. In all over 120 products were in the ranges.

AMYGDALIN or Vitamin B17 Vitamin B 17 was one of the most controversial substances with which I ever became involved. Chemically, it was known as Amygdalin or Laetrile. It contained an organically bound cyanide molecule. It was found in apricot kernels and bitter almonds. The originator of B17 and B15 was an American, Dr ET Krebs (no relation to Krebs of the famous Krebs Cycle in carbohydrate metabolism). ET Krebs postulated that the reason for the longevity and freedom from cancer of the Hunza Tribe in the Himalayas was their diet rich in apricots including their kernels. Krebs patented his substances in 1958 (UK) and 1961 (USA).

The vital constituents of the apricot kernel were B17, postulated as a cancer cure and B15 for energy and youth. There were very few manufacturers of either and promotion was impossible. However, several private doctors were looking for supplies of both substances in powder and injectable form. Several journalists became aware of the substances and many articles appeared in the press and radio and TV. Demand for apricots became great and powdered kernels (Canta B17) sold well without any claims. One doctor asked us to source him injections of Amygdalin B17 and these were sold to many patients against prescriptions. Later tablets containing 250mg were made and these sold on prescription for many years before being banned by the Medicines regulators.

Was anyone harmed by Amygdalin? This is an interesting yet unanswerable question. The fact was that only patients in terminal decline were ever prescribed B17. Many were given days to live yet survived for months and years after being put on Amygdalin, combined with special cleansing diets. No successful clinical trials were documented but there was much anecdotal evidence for effectiveness and many believed that Laetrile was opposed by vested pharmaceutical interests which invested heavily to ensure it was discredited. The substance did contain a cyanide radical and this was a prime reason for the successful legal ban. This cyanide radical was found in foods such as bitter almonds and peach stones but they were never banned.

Could Amygdalin ever be legally licensed? No, because the costs of technical and clinical data to satisfy regulators could never be afforded for a substance that was not fully patent protected. It was not a medicine under the Medicines Act so fell within our sphere of interest.

Year end   At the end of 1974 we had a successful Alternative Heathcare business and eagerly looked forward to our days in Court with the Medicines Men in February 1975.

Company with a Mission

Diet and Health - National Sick Service - Court Case vs the DHSS and Judgement -
Helfex 1975 - WHEN - Bookers all powerful - Product Licences of Right review -
Demise of Herbals - Medicines Men make me Sick - Sinister forces - Company mission
- Closer to nature with Non-Drug Therapy - Ellis Kopel - Lipcote PR - Blakoe Middle
East - Exporting is Fun? - Multiple Sclerosis - Zsa Zsa Gabor - Leslie Kenton - Mother
Brown destroyed by the Medicines Act - Products 1974/5

Some Dietary approaches to Disease Management
To commemorate 50 years of involvement in Dietary Means to Healthcare, The
Cantassium Company published a booklet for health professionals entitled 'Some Dietary
Approaches to Disease Management'. Copies were distributed free to many Doctors,
Nurses and Pharmacists. Written by a Medical Doctor, it served as a basis for the next 30
years. Some journalists were informed of our work under the heading 'A Company with a
Mission'. We set ourselves standards far ahead of our competitors and gained many
followers, pioneering a road that many were to follow some twenty years later.

National Sick Service   The Cantassium booklet was the first of many to be published by
the company throughout the next 25 years. Although the professionals were the toughest
target audience for us to tackle, I was sure that it was ultimately only that group who could
lead us out of the prescription drug dependent health culture into which, as a nation, we had
fallen. That was our mission, but progress was impeded, at every step, by that very group
and its allies in the junk food industry. It was our success with direct appeal to lay people
that gave us the resources to continue our dialogue with the professionals. Many laymen
quickly saw the sheer commonsense in our argument that more chemicals were not the right
way to the 'Health of the Nation'. Some even said that the National Health Service was
wrongly named and should be called the 'National Sick Service'.
   I wrote many letters to journalists and opinion formers about our non-drug approaches to
healthcare. BBC TV and Radio were included. Whenever an article or programme was seen
that covered diet or side effects of drugs I wrote to the media offering our solutions. Many
friendly replies were received. I even wrote to the Chairman of British Leyland, regarding a
report that he had a serious eye problem. I suggested he could be helped by Dr Stanley
Evans, a nutritional eye therapist's Ocutrien Vitamin/Mineral Powder, the Chairman, of
course, replied graciously. This sort of in-house Public Relations resulted in much
favourable publicity.

The Court Case, February 1975, Woodwards versus the Medicines Inspectorate   As
expected, the first ever Medicines Act 1968 case was brought against our company on
February 28th 1975, at Wells Street Magistrates Court, London. There were 14 offences all
logged from a visit by Inspector Sharp and two of his henchmen in March 1974. The counts
covered making products without a licence, assembling (packing into bottles) unlicensed
products and storing certain medicinal substances in an unlocked store. Our company
pleaded not guilty on all charges.
   Unfortunately, Sir Peter Rawlinson QC, who had acted in the Tribunal hearing in July
1974, was not able to lead our side but a very able colleague, Christopher Sumner, proved
an excellent deputy. The Crown called the Chief Inspector and Inspector Sharp whilst we
had Arthur Chamings an experienced industrial and academic pharmacist, Professor Arnold
Beckett DSc., and Dr Brian Richards. The case lasted two days over a month apart (reported
in Chemist & Druggist March 8th and April 12 1975).

LARKHALL GREEN FARM

Much of the evidence for our defence involved the inordinate delays and inefficiencies experienced by us from the Inspectorate. Our counsel made clear that we were victims of an over zealous bureaucracy and very unjustly treated by disproportionate enforcement.

The magistrate, Mr Christopher Besley, found us guilty on 11 counts but not guilty on 3. However, most importantly, he fined us a mere £20 on each (the minimum by law) and refused to award the Crown its costs. The Inspectors were absolutely devastated by this judgement.

Full judgement: "It seems very surprising to me that no full licences have been granted and it seems stranger still in view of all the correspondence in August 1973. In that sense I have a great deal of sympathy for the Defendant Company. It seems to me that the Department were not being at all helpful in August. It seems extraordinary that there was no further correspondence after 21st August. One would have expected the Department to have done its duty to the public and helped this company and get them producing. It seems astonishing to me that if there were apparently few things to clear up, these things were not cleared up by the Department.

I am left with a feeling of sympathy for the Defendants. At the same time I am satisfied that they went into the matter knowing the Licence had not been granted and even when the Licence came, I don't think they took notice. Possibly they had got exasperated with the Department – with possible good reason"

The Inspectors were basically told by the Magistrate to give us cooperation in future and change their attitude. So far as I am aware, no further cases of this sort were brought and the Inspectors adopted a more conciliatory approach to all companies. It was made clear that the Act was not intended to put companies out of business and make examples of them. I was convinced that much of the problem had been caused by jealousy and prejudice against me by Inspectors. I was a marked man, perhaps from student days. "Born with a silver spoon - we can get him now", as one Inspector was overheard saying.

There were many reports on the case in Pharmacy publications and some National Newspapers. The Times carried about eight column inches under the headline

"Ministry criticized over delay on drug licence"

I received many letters and 'phone calls after the case. All were supportive and some grateful that we had had the courage to take the overweening Inspectorate on and morally win.

A few days after the case I was contacted by Mr Arthur Fishburn the Chief Inspector and recommended Mr Adamson as a consultant to help us. We had a friendly meeting and this proved invaluable in going forward. I dropped my threat to go to the Parliamentary Ombudsman. Changes in the Inspectorate personnel soon occurred and better relations were established. It had been a hard few years and undoubtedly took its toll on my father who was very upset by his family name receiving notoriety. I was soon to drop the Woodward name from all trading companies. Instead, we would use **Larkhall Laboratories** trading title derived from the company having been founded in Larkhall Lane, Clapham, London.

After his experience of the workings of the Medicines Act, Norman Cox, our solicitor wrote a letter to The Times questioning these matters and calling for the act to be amended. There was no reaction apart from the Chemist & Druggist that carried a small piece about the proposal. The Act is an enabling act and as such it makes the bureaucrats very powerful unless they are challenged in the Courts when commonsense often prevails, as it did in the 'Woodward Case' of 1975. In 2010 many traditional forms of healthcare such as Ayurveda and Traditional Chinese Medicine were threatened with extinction by the Medicines Act.

I helped to fight the Department's policy towards these and many other threatened therapies to ensure their continuance.

This is not a question of enforcing the safety and efficacy criteria of western healthcare on these ancient practices but of Human Rights for ethnic people to have the benefit of their traditional Healthcare unhindered by ignorant European bureaucracies.

Helfex 1975   In April, at the International Health Food Fair, Helfex, Cantassium Company exhibited and promoted their new philosophy of Natural Food Products including Supplements. Their 'Company with a Mission' statement was amplified and was to remain the bedrock of all product development. Non Drug Therapy was a difficult message to get across regarding the importance of hypo-allergenic food and avoidance of synthetic ingredients in natural supplements. The introduction in the late 1970s of a symbol system by Rita Greer helped greatly and consumers became better informed. Later amplification of the mission 'Closer to nature with non drug therapy' was sometimes used.

Many competitor companies were trying to jump on the bandwagon of purity yet displayed pathetic ignorance of the concepts. Several even labeled their products 'Gluten Free' yet included and stated, as present, wheat derived items in their formulas. (Wheat contains the highest gluten content found in nature.) Food labelling regulations did not require technological trace ingredients to be listed on labels and few consumers realised that all those elegant gelatin capsules contained such chemicals to aid elegance and preserve the products. Tablets could be made without these substances and Cantassium warned that elegance and pure appearance, like pharmaceutical medicines, was attained at hidden cost to real product purity. Indeed, any company which quoted 'pharmaceutical standards' as their ideal immediately displayed their ignorance of 'natural' food supplement or 'herbal medicine'.

Among the products exhibited at Helfex by Larkhall/Cantassium were Cantabran, Cantapollen, Cantamac and Cantavite.

WHEN - World Health and Ecology News -- new UK version   In July 1975 I met Charles Royal, the owner of an American publication 'World Health and Ecology News'. Royal was a typical American with a ready patter but was serious about naturally based healthcare and the environment. I was supportive of his ideas and agreed to take advertisements in his new UK version of the magazine.

Bookers   At this time the largest company in the Health Food Trade was Associated Health Foods, owned by Bookers, the multinational Sugar, Engineering and Supermarket Group. This company was vertically integrated within the industry. It owned Heath and Heather a chain of Health/Herbal Stores (soon to be combined with Holland & Barrett), Brewhurst/Realfare (a wholesale Health Food supplier), Healthcrafts (a major Vitamin and Mineral brand), Allinsons (Flour Millers) and most importantly Newman Turner Publications which published Here's Health Magazine. Ninety percent of health food manufacturers needed Brewhurst/Realfare to ensure distribution of their products to retailers. Most producers wanted to advertise in Here's Health and to receive the favour of good editorial publicity in its pages. Naturally, they all wanted their products on the shelves of the largest retail chain, Holland & Barrett.

How could Bookers fail with such a vertically integrated group? Their market dominance was soon questioned by authorities. The group was broken up with sale of its divisions and by 1992 they had gone from the Health Industry. In 1975, I and others coveted their position and by taking an interest in WHEN I hoped to build a more focused business with a greater charisma than Booker.

Bookers were closely associated with the makers of that pure white and deadly substance (white sugar) and competitors made much of that fact to the detriment of their 'Health Food Group'. Refined sugar is not an acceptable product for Health Food Movement followers. We kept the emphasis of our company on 'Natural wholesome' products and services. Our mission was to be closer to nature through non drug therapy.

In the last forty years (1975 to 2015), has the acceptance of the too many drugs idea progressed with professionals? Sadly no, but the improvement in diet through more fruit and vegetables, less saturated fat, salt and sugar has taken place – with a small thanks to Cantassium perhaps.

New Compression Department opened During the year the extensive rebuilding begun in 1970 had enabled a new Compression department to be opened at a cost of £100,000. This was the subject of a small piece with picture in the Chemist & Druggist 6th September. The article announced that we now had a full Manufacturing Licence and had overcome our problems with the Inspectorate. The compression area was on the ground level and there was a storage cellar underneath and a Quality Control Laboratory above.

1975 CD Indicator The agency for this device that helped women calculate the time of ovulation in the menstrual cycle was passed to us from Wassen, through the kindness of Ray Matthews. The Wassen company was growing rapidly in the Health Food Supplement field and did not need the distraction of the CD Indicator. Pollen B was their first major Pollen product sold in the UK. Later, I helped Ray develop Selenium ACE, a very successful Food Supplement product. Wassen clinically tested many of their products but the results were never accepted by the medical establishment, without patent protection more research was impossible. The Health Supplement Industry did very little research and usually copyists did better and sold at lower prices than originators.

March 1975 Review of Product Licences of Right, the demise of Herbals starts
We had registered thousands of products and gained Licences of Right in 1973. It was now proposed by the DHSS that these be reviewed and very searching questions asked of producers. I was horrified and wrote a letter to the Pharmaceutical Journal saying that there was no justification for this 'review' which was very costly for industry and also for a Government Department -- especially relevant when the country was in economic crisis. This letter was picked up by the international SCRIP publication (a weekly newsletter read by opinion formers in the medical field). This must have riled the Department. It made the very valid point that most of these products were in small demand and would die through commercial pressure within a few years without the review. In the event the review process paper work and technical specifications demanded by the Inspectorate would not be economically justifiable and so most products would be lost. The vast majority of these preparations were harmless natural herbals. So began the demise of many UK herbal companies.

A few of the relatively rich herbal companies saw an opportunity for profit by letting the Inspectorate drive out their rivals. Their duplicity was unforgivable and I was a vociferous opponent of these companies despite having our own product licences

Maker tells CRM (Committee for Review of Medicines): You make me sick
Medical News, a newspaper for General Practitioners, reported on another dispute I was having with the Medicines Department of the DHSS. This concerned the product licence review of the 'Barbemet' range. These were the formulations we had taken over from British Ethical Proprietaries in 1973. Anyone overdosing on these products would be very sick (vomit) and so eject the overdose of barbiturate. The CRM was declining to permit these products to be sold, the reason being that they said emetine had cardiotoxicity problems.

45

However, these were mainly associated with high doses by injection. The real reason was that they disliked polypharmacy (multi ingredient products) and the presence of ingredients in sleeping tablets that had no connection with sleep. They totally ignored the prevention of suicide aspect of these formulas at the time when Barbiturates were one of the major causes of deliberate/accidental suicide. This was well documented and accepted fact. Medical News described me as never less than outspoken and quoted a letter I had written to the Lancet criticizing the CRM decision. If the Medicines Department is legally bound to promote safety of patients how can it possibly reject a 'safer' barbiturate. Proof that the bureaucratic mind is illogical and obtuse. Barbemets continued under threat but were still available in 1975 but their demise was coming.

A sinister force   Ironically, in October Dr Eric Trimmer, prompted by a letter from me, was praising the Barbemets and saying how they are much better for insomniacs than fashionable diazepam and other benzodiazepines, promoted with vast marketing resources of the drug industry. Sadly, Dr Trimmer's slightly maverick approach cut no ice with the regulators. So it was not just herbals that were being forced out of the market but many small demand, useful ethical medications too.

Since 1975 several attempts have been made to market drugs used by suicidal patients in 'safer' formulations but all have failed to achieve licences.   In later years it was the benzodiazepines that were found to be addictive and whether patients would be better served if the old barbiturates had never been so maligned is something we can only ponder. What is certain is that the demise of all barbiturates, including the Barbemets, was not just caused by the regulator but by the Drug Industry's costly public relations efforts. Barbiturates were addictive for some people but so were their successors including the benzodiazepines. The industry drew the attention of doctors and consumers to the addictive side effect of barbiturates and then at the same time offered, in quite separate stories, a new series of synthetic drugs to replace them. These were all patented and vastly more costly to the NHS than barbiturates. These were hugely profitable and because they have not been available long, there was no addiction problem -- as was to be expected that followed some years later.

After a few years the barbiturates were forgotten but the new drugs which were then out of patent were found to have addiction problems too. The story then repeats with a new series of compounds for the same medicinal purpose with no addiction and high price and profit. This happens all the time in all drug classes for the commonest ailments and yet few see through the scam. What if we had never progressed from herbs and found the right diets instead?

The products and Medical Profession credibility   I continued to take opportunities to promote the company to the medical profession. The Blakoe Mechanotherapy approach created interest but patients continued to want tablets, capsules and injections for their sexual dysfunctions. Attempts were made to emphasise the Energising Ring as a helpful item for diabetic men with potency problems.

The Pantothenic Acid research carried out by Dr E.C. Barton Wright and Dr Elliott had produced two prescription products Cantopal Compound capsules and Cantothen Injections. These were marketed by The Cantassium Company but actually licenced to Koch Light Laboratories. They were launched as ethical prescription products but were seldom prescribed on the NHS. Private doctors prescribed them and sales grew slowly. Professional data sheets were produced and many arthritis patients were helped by these very safe preparations.

Ellis Kopel Public Relations   In late 1974, on Barton-Wright's recommendation, I appointed a medium sized public relations consultancy, 'Ellis Kopel', to work on promoting the Cantassium Company and its mission of 'Non Drug therapy', using Pantothenic Acid preparations as credible examples of what the company was doing.

The theory of Barton-Wright regarding the connection of Pantothenic Acid and Arthritis led to his writing booklets for lay and professional people. One entitled 'Arthritis, Its Cause and Control' and the other 'Arthritis, a Vitamin Deficiency Disease'. These directed people to adjust their diets to increase Pantothenic Acid naturally as a preventative measure. The effectiveness of special supplements by sufferers was also noted. Sadly, Dr Barton-Wright, a biochemist, died in August 1975 before his booklets were published. These were subsequently published by our new publishing arm Roberts Publications. I was interviewed on Radio London that helped greatly with our efforts.

At this time, specialist public relations agencies were in their infancy. Public relations was a way to promote a company and its products in editorial to complement normal commercial advertising. The advantages were that you could have more written about the products and editorial had more credibility than advertisements. However, you have no guarantee that your press releases will be used and little prospect of repeats in the same publication. Kopel's worked successfully on many of our products in the late 70s but concentrated on those in the dietary area. They eschewed mechanotherapy despite my contention that the mission was 'Non Drug therapy' not just 'diets for health'. This dichotomy was to bug our company for many years.

This is well illustrated by press cuttings from 1975. There was the diet and disease connection covered in June by Doctor Magazine, that went to all GPs free. The Scottish Daily News brought Gluten Free diets to the fore, castigating Doctors for failing to diagnose Coeliac Disease that was maybe affecting 200,000 people in the UK. Cantassium was marketing naturally Gluten Free Flours and criticizing the authorities for permitting use of 'Reduced Gluten' Flours on NHS prescription but not allowing 'Naturally Gluten Free' Flours for free prescription. The fact that traces of gluten can adversely affect patients was conveniently ignored by the bureaucrats.

Lipcote and Public Relations   Lipcote did not interest Ellis Kopel so we decided to employ another public relations agency to complement our advertising agency SF Advertising. Mr S Fiorentini, the owner of Stephens, recommended Jean Sainsbury who operated as an independent PR consultant. Mrs Sainsbury organized a very successful press campaign that further enhanced Lipcote's profile. Over the years, Jean also worked on the Aquamaid Bust improver, the Dietary Supplements, Omniped and Books. So we had two PR firms working with us.

(In October 1985, long after we ceased our connection with Jean, I read a report in the Times that she had received a large legacy from her estranged father (not a Sainsbury) and made a donation to Covent Garden Opera House which would enable £80,000 to be spent on a Ballet or Opera every two years into the future.)

Blakoe Middle East Ltd – as Harold Wilson our Prime Minister famously said, "Exporting is fun" Exporting was not fun for us in 1975 but rather a series of headaches and expense, as this sorry tale illustrates.

In late 1974, Walter O'Connell, our Sales Manager, received a letter from his brother Tony who was working in the Lebanon for the United Nations. Tony had made contact with a Mustafa el Jundi, a Lebanese entrepreneur. Jundi was interested in importing health and beauty products into Lebanon and distributing them throughout the Middle East. Jundi claimed to know many influential politicians and civil servants in all these countries. I knew that registration of these products was a complex undertaking aimed at making importing difficult. However, Jundi and Tony O'Connell maintained they could circumvent the problems with their 'connections'. Tony O'Connell accused me of not being enterprising - a typical English backwoodsman.

47

Jundi came to the UK and managed to persuade me to consider the business possibilities more carefully. Walter O'Connell was totally enthused with the possibilities and I thought that perhaps this venture could make up for the loss of sales caused by the Medicines Act problems.

In January 1975 Jundi and his legal associate Maitre Chaouki Boustany, together with the O'Connell brothers, visited me at home in order to discuss the possibility of Jundi representing the Blakoe company throughout the Middle East. I was persuaded to forget my reservations and it was arranged that Walter O'Connell would visit Beirut to set up the Office there. On 15th February a provisional agreement was signed by both parties in Beirut. This agreement was brief but the countries to be covered exclusively were:-

Lebanon, Syria, Egypt, Jordanian Kingdom, Saudi Arabia, Iraq, All the Trucial States (now the Emirates), all North Africa. In all these countries Jundi claimed to have excellent business contacts.

W. O'Connell made recommendations on the product range and back in London extensive work was carried out to produce Free Sales Certificates and other registration documents required by the Lebanese authorities. I was concerned about the threatened civil war in Lebanon but was assured by Tony O'Connell, a senior UN staff officer, that this sort of thing was nothing new and business conditions would be unaffected. After spending some weeks in Beirut, Walter O'Connell returned to London and arranged shipment of the stocking order, value £15,000, to the new storage warehouse and office that he had helped set-up in Beirut.

In order to launch the business I agreed to go to Beirut on 17th June where a large lunch party would be held at the Holiday Inn Hotel, and where politicians, opinion formers and journalists were to attend. To show the strength of Blakoe, my brother joined the Blakoe Group from the UK.

All went well apart from the engine of M Boustany's BMW falling out as he drove us to dinner at his home and me enquiring about a hole in the living room window where we were dining! 'Oh, that was a stray bullet from last Saturday', said Boustany.

On 18th June, over 20 journalists were joined by the Lebanese Minister of Foreign Affairs Mr Lucien Dahdah (who was assassinated some years later) at a very professionally arranged PR lunch. The coverage in newspapers and magazines was extensive in the following days. One headline read "A Sexy Luncheon at Rooftop Restaurant". The whole business appeared to be off to an excellent start as far as publicity and advertising were concerned. As one would expect, the enthusiasm of the locals for the venture led both my brother and I to think that good business would soon follow. However, I was concerned that the store/warehouse was yet to be fitted out and there was no sign of the stocking order goods that had been shipped from the UK several weeks before. 'Held up at the airport but will be delivered in a few days', I was told. At Jundi's request, Walter O'Connell remained in Beirut to sort out these matters.

On return to London I awaited developments and regular reports from O'Connell. Unfortunately, no encouraging news was received, no payment as stock was sold nor any new orders that would have had to be paid in advance, as they would be replacing the Blakoe Stock held on consignment in Beirut.

O'Connell returned to UK in July and informed me that all was going well but that registrations were delayed. Meanwhile he said many orders from retailers in Lebanon were being fulfilled satisfactorily. Following the event at the Holiday Inn, enquiries had been received from Kuwait and Saudi Arabia which he and Jundi wished to follow up as soon as possible because these were larger markets than the Lebanon. He asked for more registration documents for these two countries to be drawn up as soon as possible and he would take them with him when he went later in the year. He also said Jundi would be paying all his travel expenses for the visits to these countries.

48

I somewhat reluctantly agreed to send him with the registration documents because the further expense for Blakoe would be minimal and would be a true test of the real potential for Blakoe in the Middle East.

O'Connell left for this trip in early 1976 and after two months of silence returned to Putney with a very large order from Kuwait. I agreed to ship the order as soon as the promised letter of credit materialized. O'Connell also intimated that an even larger order was expected from the distributor in Jeddah -- Saudi Arabia. When I asked about initial stocking orders for these new distributors I was told these had been satisfied from Lebanese stocks in Beirut. Of course, we waited in vain for the Letters of Credit and news from new distributors.

The war in Lebanon was now getting worse but after receiving a letter from me, threatening him with loss of the agency in July 1977, Jundi contacted me by 'phone and sent a letter saying the war was over and that he was ready to start business once more. I did not object but laid down strict terms for Jundi, including stocking of pharmacies before any advertising began. Jundi requested another visit from O'Connell to train new staff but I refused because I thought that enough training on the Blakoe products had been given and I was looking for evidence of a positive commercial contribution from Jundi and his associates. Advertising and PR had not proved of commercial benefit. I also suspected that Jundi would soon be looking for a large contribution from Blakoe in London towards the costs of setting up the Blakoe Middle East venture, including travel and subsistence for O'Connell and the PR and Advertising back in 1975.

By February 1978 there had been no positive news from Beirut and the war was continuing. Tony O'Connell visited me in Putney and was told about the situation. He expressed surprise at the lack of progress but promised to visit Jundi soon. On contacting Jundi he sent a fairly positive letter to me at the end of February. Jundi was serious about the business and was expanding distribution to Tripoli the second city of Lebanon. He would return the Saudi Arabia registration documents, would pay the outstanding amounts due, less a credit to take account of W. O'Connell's travel and subsistence and an unspecified percentage of the promotional costs. Some items would be shipped back to London at our expense for credit but these were not listed or itemized. Tony advised against Walter visiting Lebanon despite Jundi's request because the war situation was still serious. On 24th April I wrote to Tony O'Connell and told him nothing had been heard from Jundi.

Eventually, in 1981 I wrote off the venture as hopeless, after hearing finally from Jundi in February that he had decided to abandon Blakoe Middle East, blaming the war and his own involvement in other businesses. He wanted me to compensate him for many of the losses. I replied that until the stocks and registration documents were returned and full account of items sold and allegedly destroyed were rendered that no compensation would be considered. I heard no more from Jundi.

Years later, Walter O'Connell arranged to meet Jundi at the Ritz Hotel in London but when he arrived at the Hotel there was no sign of him. However, there was a box of cigars left for O'Connell's collection. Impressed by this gift he opened the box and found it was empty.....

Multiple Sclerosis The increasing professional credibility of the Cantamac supplement together with polyunsaturated fatty acid oils (sunflower and safflower oils) was bringing us into contact with Multiple Sclerosis patients and their various groups. Dr Michael Crawford, who was head of the Nuffield Institute of Comparative Medicine, had found that all MS patients he tested had a deficiency of polyunsaturated fatty acids in their blood. He postulated that this deficiency was a causal factor in MS. These fatty acids were essential for the proper development of brain and nervous tissue. The quantities of polyunsaturates needed in the diet were more than could be included in a few capsules. Ounces not grammes were required.

Crawford recommended a diet very similar to that of Roger MacDougall but not Gluten Free. MS patients were experimenting with their diets with the help of their relations and some MS charity groups.

However, the largest and very well funded MS Charity 'The MS Society' did not support any of these diets and was close to the medical establishment whom they funded with research grants. I thought that their domination of MS research, which was very similar to the Coeliac Society's influence on medical research in their area, was regrettable. Mavericks like MacDougall, and later Rita Greer, with many others were easily discredited by these powerful interests. Perhaps this was not really in the best interest of the patients suffering these two chronic illnesses that had not been successfully 'cured' by modern medicine.

Rita's husband Alan was a severe (chronic relapsing) MS sufferer. He had been given two years at most to live by a panel of ten doctors when diagnosed in 1970 and was bedridden or in a wheelchair. He had been told categorically by the ten doctors that he would never walk again. There had been no help for him from the NHS and in those days MS sufferers of the type of MS he had were just expected to become bedridden and die. Rita realised a complete change of lifestyle was all they could do now. Alan was already taking the Naudicelle (EPO) capsules as well as Cantamac and Vitamin B12. He also followed a diet which was Wheat Free, Milk Free, Egg Free, Sugar Free, Cholesterol-free and Vegetarian. He was able to exercise well and had his MS well under control. The Greers never claimed a cure had taken place in spite of a great deal of pressure to do so. They were hounded by the press to say Alan was cured but did not -- ever. (100% proof of MS could only be obtained by post mortem, so a diagnosis was always just medical opinion.) They also took pains to tell MS sufferers that what had worked so well for Alan Greer might not work for anyone else and did not use the situation to make money as Roger McDougall had done. They gave information away free to MS sufferers on request and to doctors.

MS is particularly difficult to research because some patients can go into long, spontaneous remissions at any time. So any 'cures' can readily be rubbished as owing to natural remission or misdiagnosis. This is probably why it remains such a puzzle despite millions of pounds expended on medical research. In 2015 no progress had been made in discovering the cause of MS and in the UK there are over 100,000 sufferers. Positive thinking is best and giving hope not to be derided. Despite the efforts of the MS Society to prevent other patient groups succeeding, several still exist today and do excellent work.

In 1975 the Crawford dietary approach coincided with the discovery of a concentrated natural source of the important polyunsaturated fatty acid, gamma linolenic acid. It had greater protective power than ordinary linoleic and linolenic acids found in sunflower and safflower oils. This new dietary item was 'Evening Primrose Oil'. It was claimed that EPO was at least ten times stronger than sunflower oil. Patients who were taking 30ml doses of sunflower oil could gain the same dietary benefit with 3ml of EPO (six 500mg capsules). The cost of EPO was much more than sunflower oil but dosage meant its convenience for patients was exceptional. It only remained to obtain approval of the capsules for free prescription for MS patients (see 1977 Chapter 6 onwards).

Health and Beauty unsolicited promotional positives Sometimes journalists tell stories with unsuspected effects. The Aquamaid device had apparently enhanced the breasts of Zsa Zsa Gabor as reported in a National newspaper. The Contraceptive Pill was causing vitamin imbalances that could be corrected with supplement pills like Cantamac reported the October issue of Here's Health Magazine. Meanwhile, in June the News of the World did an exposé of 'Sex Pills' that involved some of our products sold by a mail order company, using copy that was theirs, not ours. This frequently happened because most people in the Health Food Industry wanted to make exaggerated claims for effectiveness. Through ignorance they treated supplements as if they were medicinal drugs.

This was a problem that had plagued the industry for years and the message that dietary correction can help with all sorts of illnesses was lost, because consumers believed it was the pills (although labeled as supplements) that were the effective miracle agents.

Leslie Kenton The daughter of the famous jazz musician, Stan Kenton, was one of the first Health Food guru journalists. She was Health Editor of Harpers & Queen – one of the most influential women's fashion and living monthly magazines. Every month she would write interesting articles on Natural Health and soon built up a large group of followers. She wrote to me after she had seen a letter from me on Food Additives in Medical News Magazine. She expressed great interest in natural ways to health and was concerned at the levels of synthetic chemical additives and pesticides in food. I wrote back with as much detail about the company mission as possible and Leslie subsequently used the information in her articles. She was on my wavelength and proved a great ambassador for the natural health movement over many years.

Product Range developing 1974-5 Our flexible manufacturing units put us in a unique position in our market. I determined to stay independent and build for the next twenty years. We could develop new unlicensed non-medicinal tablet products within a few weeks. We could test their demand through our growing list of health food and alternative healthcare consumers. Our technical knowledge base was second to none in this field and we had scientific expertise within the company to hold a Medicines Manufacturing Licence. Answering all customers questions was simple for us and our advice was greatly valued. In direct selling this was very important. We had enormous credibility both in the UK and in overseas markets where laws surrounding this product area were very different from the UK. I made myself au fait with many of these differences and was able help the company use them to its advantage.

Product range By the end of 1975 the product range spanned over 130 products with several being available in different pack sizes. Many generic supplements such as Brewers Yeast and Bone Meal Tablets were sold in packs of 7000 direct to consumers at £1 per 1000. Over 50 diet supplements and herbals were stocked. We made all the tablets in the Putney factory (Larkhall Laboratories) whilst the Charlbury factory concentrated on packaging the supplements and manufacturing Lipcote, the Lipstick sealer, which was developing sales quite well in Boots, Chemists and Drug Stores. There were two sizes 7ml and 15ml that sold at 30 and 45 pence respectively.

The Blakoe range of mechanotherapy aids embraced over 40 items with several available in different sizes – the standard Energizing Ring came in 21 sizes whilst the De Luxe model had only two sizes. A special fine grade of wire wool was needed to maintain the Energiser's potency and this sold well, as did the unique 'Stand-Fast' wipes and creams to aid sexual performance and satisfaction. The CD Indicator for calculating peak female fertility was a most successful addition to the range. The rhythm method of conception control was permitted by the Roman Catholic and Orthodox Churches and this was responsible for successful sales. Many couples were looking to increase their chances of having male babies. Accurately calculating the time of ovulation was thought to pinpoint the best moment for intercourse — hours after ovulation for a male because sperms carrying the male gene were slower travellers than those carrying the female gene.

The Aquamaid Bust enhancing hydrotherapy device was our leading direct mail order beauty item and had sister products in two creams of Vitamin E and Female Hormone, a galegae herbal tablet enhanced the Aquamaid's benefit.

Limb Support with Mother Brown   Omniped Foot Cushions were a major item but came in 4 sizes – we even stocked Omniped sandals in 3 different ladies designs. The 'Mother Brown' range dovetailed well with Omniped.

It consisted of specially impregnated knee, ankle, wrist and back supports claiming to fight aches and pains externally. The formula of the impregnating solution was a secret and was made by the managing director of the Mother Brown Company, Mark Morris. Mark had recently moved his operation to a shop adjacent to our Putney Laboratory and we provided him with an outbuilding to do his impregnation and packing. Mark had been a long time friend of the Woodward family and had spent over fifty years in the pharmaceutical industry. I was delighted when he came to Putney. His knowledge of generic and contract manufacturing was useful. Mark and I were to work closely both on manufacturing and business development until Mark's death in December 1978. I miss him to this day. Mother Brown soon enhanced our range and replaced the less comfortable Blakoton electrically energized limb and back supports.

In 1978 the impregnating solution was reformulated to comply with the Medicines Regulations. However, the technical requirements of the Inspectorate were such that there was no hope of the products surviving and despite great efforts being made to meet the quality and efficacy criteria. The bureaucrats unreasonably banned their sale as medicinal by 1985. No customer complaints regarding efficacy or side effects had ever been received. The Inspectors just referred to reference books, looked at ingredient properties and found an obscure report of mild skin irritation being associated with one of the ingredients (concentration not even known or specified). This was enough for them to refuse the licence renewal. Once a renewal was refused, that effectively opened vast technical areas for examination, not limited to the ingredient they had highlighted.

To fight that decision would have used up all Mother Brown's commercial profit for centuries with no certainty of success. They were judging these products as if they were powerful new drugs and well knew that no commercial company would oppose their decision. They saved themselves work and the interests of the company and its customers were ignored. As usual, their policies worked for them (less work more pay) but what possible justification there was for the banning of Mother Brown's Knee Supports on grounds made possible by an Act of Parliament designed to protect people from a recurrence of the thalidomide problem –- a drug which caused multiple, serious foetal deformities. Only the Almighty knows.

Business progress   The years from 1972 had seen us gradually lose sales of the Barbemets and many other medicinal products, yet overall sales grew and in 1975, after nearly three years of commercial hell, we managed to pass the £1,000,000 sales for the first time. Profitability was well down because of the huge investments in the manufacturing facilities and sales promotion expenditure required by the relatively new 'Brand' business. Inflation was beginning to take hold in the UK economy and this was inevitably a contributor to our sales expansion. Nevertheless, at the age of 38 I looked forward to exciting times ahead and was confident that we still had an independent business to grow and make a contribution to 'The Health of the Nation'. A pompous but not a mean aspiration.

Contract work still played a major part in the business but its promotion was restricted to personal calls on major customers and advertising in the Chemist & Druggist Annual Directory, which was still a main source of information in the Pharmacy Trade. The Two companies advertised Matthews & Wilson Ltd for strip packing and G.O.Woodward & Co Ltd for general tableting.

Interests and Threats

Gluten-free books - Lawrence Hills and Comfrey - Alternative Medicine Books - Rita Greer - Contract to Brand - Evening Primrose Oil the real history - Maurice Hanssen - Medicinal status - Dr David Horrobin - New Competitor Start Up - Magic bullets versus Holistic Health - Opportunity missed with wrong turning after Thalidomide - Food Allergy - Slimswift Homespa another cautionary tale

1976 Plan At the beginning of 1976 I was trying to plan the year ahead. (The financial year then ran from 1st April to 31st March, so year end for 1976 was March 1977.) The export business was predicted to grow by 20% but the out-turn was some 10%. In order to fund this growing business an increased overdraft was required. Capital expenditure on plant and machinery was expected to be substantial whilst improvements to the Putney facility would absorb considerable funds to be provided through an additional bank loan with full director personal guarantees.

I was worried about holding on to the manufacturing licences and keeping tax to a minimum. A Labour Government was in power and one needed one's wits to use their excessively bureaucratic policies to advantage. Export and stock valuations were important aspects of our commercial approach to the balance sheet. We needed to keep share valuation low and to dissipate any profit in advertising and factory renovations.

The brand values were increasing because of good advertising but as these had no capital value for accounting purposes there was no profit for taxing. I noted that in the future these brands would be easier to sell as a business than machinery and a list of contract customers. However, I was also adamant that the plant be kept up to date and in first class repair. No wonder the bank demanded such an onerous guarantee from the directors.

Inflation continued to be a problem and whilst sales value increased the number of units increased at a lesser rate.

Bank entertained In October I was invited to join our local Bank Manager at the Barclays Bank London Branch Managers' Club dinner, on November 24th in the Great Room at the Grosvenor House Hotel in Park Lane. William Rees Mogg, the Editor of the Times, proposed the health of the Bank and a Bank deputy Chairman replied. There were some thousand people there and I remember seeing Henry Cooper the boxer enjoying himself. Looking back, it seemed unimaginable that a bank would be so generous to a thousand important customers. Those were the days when you felt appreciated by the Bank.

Gluten Free Food Books by Cherry Hills The company was becoming more involved with Food Allergy and Cantassium Supplements were made using as few excipients as possible and always without gluten. The gluten free food ingredients were becoming more popular and I became interested in producing a cookery book with recipes using our ingredients. I contacted Hilda Cherry Hills, a writer living with her Coeliac husband Lawrence, in Bocking near Braintree in Essex. Lawrence was the founder of a Charity called 'The Henry Doubleday Research Association' (HDRA). This charity had a great interest in agriculture and preserving plant lines for posterity and fighting against new regulations from Brussels. It is thanks to him we still have King Edward potatoes. It had a membership of thousands and a small-holding in Bocking where the elderly couple Lawrence and Cherry lived their vegetarian life. He grew many varieties of vegetable and was particularly keen on **Comfrey** a large plant that contained protein and Vitamin B12. For vegetarians this plant was an excellent food source. Lawrence wrote about Comfrey in National newspapers and had published booklets on its merits, especially as a health food.

LARKHALL GREEN FARM

Some years later Comfrey was found to contain certain natural ingredients (pyrrolizidine alkaloids) that were said to be poisonous to humans and ingestion of the foodstuff by humans was banned. Poor Lawrence never really recovered after that bombshell but did not have the resources to prove that the authorities were wrong. Comfrey was still used in ointments and as animal feed – it also made excellent composted fertilizer. Jenny Pitman used it for making poultices for the racehorses at her Lambourn stables.

I visited the Hills and asked Cherry if she would be interested in helping us by writing a gluten free recipe book. In fact she had just written such a book 'Good Food, Gluten Free' which was sold by HDRA. She had also written another book 'Living Dangerously' which promoted all aspects of living without using synthetic chemical pesticides, food additives and synthetic chemical fertilizers. Many Doctors with an interest in treating allergies, especially food allergy, were recommending Cherry's books. I subsequently helped her with 'Good Food, Grain Free and Milk Free' as well as 'Good Food to Fight Migraine'. Cherry had a distributor of her books in the USA (Keats Publishers in Canaan, Connecticut). The US was already ahead of the UK in Food Allergy treatments. Rachael Carson's book 'Silent Spring' had come from there in 1960s and caused an international outcry. The Organic Movement was well underway by 1976. Our company's interest in selling books was now a natural progression for us in Alternative Medicine.

Rita Greer   In June 1976 I wrote to Rita Greer, having been shown an article in Woman's Own on her treatment of her husband's Alan Greer's MS with a healthy but restricted diet, as he had several allergies including wheat, gluten and meat etc. (The magazine had had to cope with over 17,000 requests for the diet etc.) John Williams of Bio Oils was supplying Rita with Evening Primrose Oil Capsules and these were being used in Alan's daily regime instead of several tablespoons of sunflower oil. He was not taking any synthetic drugs and found Cantamac of great benefit. I was already in correspondence with Rita regarding the way she was coping so successfully with her husband's MS. There was great interest in his success from all over the world.

Rita was helping John Williams by collecting samples of Evening Primrose seeds from the wild and growing plants for him in her garden. He was looking for a strain that would produce the most oil with the highest levels of gamma linolenic acid. When he did find the one he wanted, Rita made the botanical drawings of it for the Agronomist as there did not seem to be any.

I wrote to ask Rita if she would like to co-operate with me and Cherry Hills in a new cookery book with illustrations of the special diet foods, showing how appetizing they were. Rita soon came on the 'phone and told me she had already produced one herself, after four years in the kitchen, with her own new recipes and illustrations. She sent me a copy and I saw it was actually written in her own hand -- 'Rita Greer's Extraordinary Kitchen Notebook'. Rita, a former Royal College of Art scholar, was an artist and designer. She had to continue with this work alongside her special diet cookery as she had to be the breadwinner. Her lectureship at a college had had to be abandoned as she now had to care for her husband and knew she would never be able to hold down a full time job away from home again. Her fate was sealed as one of the self-employed for the rest of her working life. Because her husband had made such a wonderful recovery and had his MS under control he was not allowed state benefits even though he would be unemployable for the rest of his life. Rita had to provide for them both.

As regards her book, ability to do her own artwork ready for a printer had kept costs to a minimum. She had had the courage to publish it herself, in spite of the NGA (The National Graphical Association - a printer's Trade Union), and was one of only eight so-called 'backyard ' publishers in the UK who dared to take on the big publishing houses and the print trades unions.

This was at the time of RPM (Resale Price Maintenence). She had generated huge publicity by her own effort (no PR agency) and was inundated with orders at home that she mailed out. She had produced promotional flyers and informative publicity herself. I added Rita's book to the company's book list as it was ideal for allergy sufferers and it began to sell immediately. Rita seemed to be a magnet for journalists and womens' magazines. Her free publicity was amazing and she also made broadcasts on TV and radio. In this era the media were keen on happy stories as opposed to murder, violence, fraud, theft, warfare and other bad news. The Greers even made it into the News of the World and the Sun which paid for Alan to be re-diagnosed to make sure his recovery and control of MS was not a hoax. The press were keen to say it was a miracle but it actually was the result of hard work, new thinking, commonsense and dedication.

Contract to Brand Changing from a contract base to a brand one was a turning point for our family business. The Greers were just two of the new kind of people I would meet in contrast to business people in the pharmaceutical trade. John Williams was another, a biochemist who had worked in industry.

By August, owing to demand, Rita had her book reprinted, changing from a perfect bound to a spiral bound spine which was much easier for cooks to use. Bookshops hate spiral bound books but most of her books were sent out in the post and provided money up front (MUF). Bookshops usually had to be chased for payment and didn't pay. Soon she was doing the spiral binding herself – to save time and money. What a woman! I had corresponded with her for a year or so and spoken to her on the telephone but had never met her or her husband face to face.

Rita's enthusiasm, drive, all round creative skills and feel for business were something unique and I saw that with someone like her working closely with the company, business could develop and cut many of the crippling advertising and marketing costs that were slowing our progress. Rita was a lateral thinker who came up with ideas such as symbols on recipes for showing absence of Wheat, Milk , Salt (Sodium), Refined Sugar and Low Cholesterol, already being designed by her for use in her next book. All were years ahead of their time and were to prove useful later for our Cantassium Range in the 1980s.

Evening Primrose Oil (EPO) In June I was aware that this very potent source of polyunsaturated fatty acids was being made available to MS patients. It was Oil of Evening Primrose and was ten times the strength of sunflower oil in effective polyunsaturates that included GLA (Gamma Linolenic Acid). This was the polyunsaturate factor said to be really helping MS sufferers and was thought to play a part in rebuilding the myelin sheath of nerves. The nerve sheath was destroyed in MS, becoming scarred by each attack or gradually over time.

Larkhall was already selling bulk sunflower oil as a special diet food where the regular dose recommended was 30ml. The new Evening Primrose Oil (EPO) was available in 0.5ml capsules and just 6 of these capsules were needed each day by MS patients to replace the sunflower oil in their special diet. I thought that adding these capsules to our range would fit in well with Cantamac and Cemac B12 Tablets.

Rita Greer, whose MS husband was already taking Oil of Evening Primrose to good effect, suggested that I should meet John Williams, the owner of Bio Oil Research and the only person involved in trying to produce EPO on a commercial scale. I corresponded with him and he visited our Putney Office in June. His EPO product was 'Naudicelle'. He had been researching EPO and other polyunsaturated Fatty Acid Oils whilst working for Burroughs Wellcome at their Crewe Laboratories. Those labs were closed in the early 70s and the polyunsaturated fatty acid research was discontinued by them. GLA could be made synthetically in a laboratory but was prohibitively expensive and so not commercially viable.

The only alternative was from Evening Primrose grown as a crop, bred from wild plants. The Greers had been to stay with the Williams so that John could study Alan and had been shown the hundreds of bottles of different strains of Evening Primrose oil, kept stored in the roof of their bungalow.

In agreement with Burroughs Wellcome, John had retired and took over the patents relating to his research as part of his retirement package. This had enabled him to found his small company, Bio Oil Research, which he ran from his home. At that time MS patients had been found to benefit from large doses of Sunflower Oil (30ml at least per day). John Williams realised that in EPO he had a much stronger polyunsaturate source and much less would be required by the MS sufferers to achieve benefit. Sunflower Oil was not pleasant to take but EPO capsules were very acceptable and more 'Medicine' like. Through Bio Oils he offered the capsules to patients with the agreement of their doctors. Soon clinical trials were underway and news of the benefits of EPO capsules soon spread to many MS sufferers through press articles. Sadly, the MS Society (a Charity) was very much against its use and put MS sufferers off. They were also very much against the Greer's work and success. Although the clinical data on EPO appeared positive for MS the results did not yet satisfy the demands for efficacy applying to medicines, so could not be widely prescribed on the NHS.

Medicinal status for Evening Primrose Oil envisaged   John Williams was very keen to maintain his ethical medicinal route of supply to MS patients via doctors prescription, hoping to obtain approval for Naudicelle on a Free NHS prescription. He was convinced that the scientific evidence for EPO effectiveness for MS patients would soon be enough to satisfy the government that EPO should be prescribed on the NHS. From my experience with the DHSS I thought this was very unlikely. EPO was a dietary item not a drug.

In these early days John Williams had a surplus of capsules and agreed that I should supply the Health Food Trade and Mail Order customers with EPO capsules providing they did not bear any mark to equate them to Naudicelle, his own brand. Larkhall launched the products F-500 capsules and FF 100 tablets using EPO supplied by Bio Oils. Unfortunately, the quantity of oil available was limited and John had to give his professional research supply priority. Effectively, EPO was rationed for Larkhall and there was no other supplier. This meant that advertising and promotion had to be limited. Sales were significant and we eagerly awaited the next season's larger crop. The EP plant is biennial in northern countries, taking two years to come to harvest, so John had to look two years ahead for his unique supply. This was his downfall because his great expectation of NHS prescription never materialised. The seed grower pressed for payment that John could not meet and so the grower went out into the market, via one of its subsidiary companies. John would no longer control EPO supply.

Dr Horrobin anxious to research Evening Primrose Oil   Later in the year I was contacted by Dr David Horrobin who was researching EPO in Canada. I made an appointment to meet him one evening at The Royal Lancaster Hotel in Bayswater, London. He did not turn up but I understood from an earlier 'phone call that he was interested in researching our EPO tablets (FF100). Since EPO was in such short supply I was unable to consider supplying him free tablets or capsules for his research. I believed he had met John Williams before our proposed meeting and persuaded John to supply him with free capsules. Horrobin promised to use these in research that he would share with John to help him secure NHS prescription status. Actually, he sold them to MS patients in Canada so had obtained them under false pretences and misled John Williams. Within a year the EPO story had taken a very sinister turn.

New company founded to market Evening Primrose Oil   By 1978 a company called Efamol with a director who was a pharmaceutical marketeer as MD, assisted by a Dr David Horrobin, took the sales with aggressive advertising and PR. Dr. Horrobin had double-crossed and bullied John Williams, terrifying him and his wife, threatening to take their lives and forcibly stealing all his EPO research documents from their house. The police were unable to help.

Rita Greer was approached by Horrobin to say that her husband was **cured** of his MS by taking **Efamol's EPO** capsules, in spite of them never having been on the market or been taken by her husband and that he was not cured of MS and never would be. She refused. Horrobin who then suggested a cheque for £2,000 would get her to change her mind. Again she refused. Horrobin then turned nasty and pointed out she lived very near the Thames and a concrete overcoat would be easy. Still she refused and put the 'phone down. When the phone call had been made to her, in the background she recognised the voice of someone from the health food trade -- Maurice Hanssen. She also heard someone in the room call him by his name. Terrified, because her life had been threatened, she 'phoned the police. They said nothing could be done about it unless they had a body, floating in the Thames (hers). This was a frightening experience and her husband suffered a bad MS relapse over it. There was no way of knowing if Horrobin's threat would be carried out.

Efamol subsequently formed Scotia Pharmaceuticals, an ethical pharmaceutical company, that went on to obtain a Product Licence but then lost it. Nevertheless, Evening Primrose Oil had become big news, a major product and a big seller. For a while it became a fashionable 'cure-all' but then settled down to become yet another generic health food supplement.

Over the years from 1976, Evening Primrose Oil, sold in several different products, did well for our companies. From time to time rogue sellers of bulk 'Evening Primrose Oil' would turn up at the Putney factory. We would test their oil in our QC laboratory and sometimes it would turn out to be just sunflower oil. In business, wherever there is money to be made, you can be sure cowboys will appear. If something is being offered when it is scarce and at a price too good to be true, it is usually a con. I wonder how many firms fell for it and how many MS patients were cheated?

G O Woodward   In November, George Orange Woodward, my father and the founder of the company, had a bad fall down some stairs, after a dinner in London. He was taken to hospital. He never regained his full health and he had to retire from active participation in the business during 1977. Much of this was caused by the stress he had experienced from the Medicines Inspectors. As a tablet maker, who could trace his training from Wood, the originator of the compressed tablet, he found the incompetence of those Inspectors who had no real experience of tablet making, hard to bear. He definitely felt persecuted by these people, as I did, with an inevitable strain on his health. My mother always said her husband's health was destroyed by the Medicines Men and would always name them in conversation.

Magic-bullets versus holistic health ---- mid 1970s   I was still writing letters to the medical press and arguing generally for a change in direction in Healthcare with a move away from synthetic magic-bullet drugs towards a more holistic approach with healthy diet and lifestyle as the main considerations.

I believed that chemical synthetic food additives were a danger. Whilst the authorities approved these individually with basic safety tests – no attempt was made to look at the effects that cocktails of these additives might have. As a chemist I thought it was wrong to ignore the possibilities of complex reactions taking place in the human body between the many synthetic chemicals that people were ingesting daily in their food and through drug treatments. Why was ill health becoming so common?

The National Health Service had not achieved the aim of its founder Aneurin Bevan of making people healthier in the widest sense and so reducing in cost to the exchequer. The reverse was happening, despite efforts by the authorities to re-define illness so that many people who thought that they needed treatment were denied it. Enoch Powell had been right in the early 60s when he said that the NHS was 'a bottomless pit'. Yet still the population believed that doctors within the NHS had the magical powers to give their patients everlasting healthy lives. They didn't see how a doctor could possibly prescribe a patient a harmful substance.

Our company would strive to change people's expectations of what healthcare could achieve. The dangers of the magic-bullet beliefs had to be exposed and the benefits of following gentler natural approaches advocated. These ideas led the company, yet again into conflict with authorities, mainstream health professionals, the pharmaceutical industry and the giants of the food industry with their junk products rich in sugar, salt, saturated fats and chemical additives.

Opportunity missed An exchange of letters in the Pharmaceutical Journal in October highlighted my view that the thalidomide affair had offered an opportunity in 1962 for the Pharmaceutical Industry to be forced to change direction from synthetic drugs to researching alternative approaches to healthcare. It is a philosophical view that may stand the test of time. Instead, commercial and regulatory forces after 1962 have ensured the continuance of magic-bullet research. However, its enemies have not yet achieved the extinction of alternative healthcare in 2015. In 1976 our company was firmly set on that new direction.

Food Allergy was already one of our established interests. Rita Greer (RG) and I set out to expose the over-processed food ingredients where naturally occurring micronutrients had been extracted, replaced with a few token synthetic substitutes and then used to manufacture junk food. The sale of partially extracted wheat flour (wheat starch) as 'Gluten Free' to Coeliacs, when it was not 100% gluten free, with the connivance of the Coeliac Charity and the Government. It took years of work to try and stop it. These initiatives took up much time but the commonsense of our arguments carried our followers with us. Lay people never argued against us but the authorities, the vested interests and their cohorts in academia fought hard and tried to put us out of business many times. It was our open criticisms in letters and interviews that ensured the opposition never let up on us. We had to be fearless no matter what the consequences were.

The product ranges 1976 The ranges remained much as they were at the end of 1975 but we were seeking greater distribution in Health Stores and Pharmacies. Boots were stocking Ruthmol and Lipcote in their main warehouses whilst other products were ordered direct from us by individual stores. The pharmaceutical wholesalers were not listing many products but the Health Food wholesalers were becoming very supportive and this helped distribution in the Health Food stores that were, at that time, beginning to grow in number.

The mail order customer list was growing steadily but we kept a low profile so that we did not antagonize the retailers or our contract customers. In hindsight this may have been a mistake but mindful of the knife edge that the business was on, maybe it was an understandable position. There was considerable uncertainty about the future of the diet supplement industry thanks to our joining the Common Market a few years previously. Brussels was threatening directives in our product trading areas. Indeed there was seldom a year when new regulatory threats were not in evidence.

To keep our options open we were trading in the following product areas:-

1. Blakoe Mechanotherapy Sexual Aids including Energising Ring and Powermaster.
2. Special Diet Foods – main product Ruthmol Salt free salt substitute.
3. Single Vitamin Supplements including Vitamin F (Evening Primrose Oil)
4. Multivitamin & mineral supplements including Dolomite, Kelp and Cantamac.
5. Herbal Ginseng 250mg
6. Beauty products including Aquamaid Hydrotherapy appliance, Lipcote and FFCream (Evening Primrose Oil cream)
7. Slimming Aids including Aquabran, calorie counter and S-40 (Kelp,B6,Lecithin & Cider Vinegar formula)
8. Specialities for Men and Women including Testrones & Overones.
9. Arthritis treatments Cantothen Injections and Cantopal Compound by Barton Wright.
10. Omniped Foot Cushions.
11. Books on health matters and special diet cookery.

The major products were Lipcote, Ruthmol, Blakoe Energising Ring,Cantamac and Evening Primrose Oil preparations. All were exclusive Larkhall items. The S-40 was a tableted version of the best selling 3+6 Soft Gelatin Capsule formula. This diet supplement was the most successful slimming supplement sold in Health Stores during the mid 70s. Advertising was minimal but Public Relations in all media was sensational. The formula was devised to complement huge publicity for Cider Vinegar and Lecthin to be combined within a calorie controlled diet advocated in a recent diet book. The capsules were much more palatable than the neat Cider Vinegar recommended by the person who devised the diet. They soon sold in great quantities despite the fact that the amount of Cider Vinegar in the capsules was vastly less than the amount specified for daily consumption in the original diet.

It is not unusual, in the food supplement industry, to find foodstuffs with purported and widely publicised health benefits if consumed in 30ml/30g portions, three times a day. This can be converted to 0.5ml or 500mg capsules/tablets, with a recommended dose of 3-6 capsules/tablets daily. 30ml of a bitter tasting oil is seldom pleasant to take but a couple of capsules is easy for consumers and more commercially attractive for the retailers and manufacturers. Unfortunately, consumers would be taking perhaps up to 20 times less than their real requirement without realising this.

Slimswift -- a cautionary tale In early 1976 I was contacted by Len Coleman, one of the owners of the 'Slimswift' Brand. The company was known as Colrex Ltd and the other owner was Rex Green. Both lived on the south coast and the office was in Preston Road, Brighton. The product was a special multimineral Bath Salt with a dietary regime leaflet. The formula was such that when you added the salts to your bath it became a 'Spa' Treatment at home -- 'Homespa'.

We had made the Homespa Bath Salts for Colrex under contract for over twenty years and Coleman knew of our involvement in Health and Beauty products. He and Rex wished to retire and so offered the brand to us. The business appeared attractive -- a simple product, well known to a large list of satisfied users, marketed with an advertisement that apparently complied with ASA rules. There was a diet plan and report system where it was recommended that the customer send back a record of their progress for the company records. In cases of no positive benefit, then refunds were given.

This long established product was advertised in small ads in Theatre Programmes and in a few National publications such as Reveille. Larkhall bought it on condition that it complied with the ASA code but in the event, it did not, despite the fact that it had been advertised regularly up to the takeover, without any comment from the ASA.

Larkhall purchased the company with the proviso that ASA problems did not occur. As soon as we submitted the first advertisement to a National newspaper, unchanged apart from the sellers address, the balloon went up. ASA officials objected and said the advertisement had not been approved. I took the matter up with Colrex and it transpired that the advertising by them had been so low key that it had not been noticed by the ASA. They thought that Slimswift had been withdrawn from sale years ago. Endless correspondence with attempts at modifying the copy to please the ASA ensued and in the end it was evident that the Proprietary Designation 'Slimswift', with its logo and the words 'Homespa Treatment', were at the heart of the problem. Ultimately, Colrex agreed a reduction in the price and we went on to do mail order with the Brand over many years, including it in our catalogues and mail shots. Add-on products were introduced, including Calorie Counters and updated diet plans. We had occasional skirmishes with CAP but no real problems with the Slimswift brand because we kept the profile low. Slimming Treatments seldom last more than a few years and Slimswift had had a good run by the time it was withdrawn from sale in 1990.

Plate 1

George Orange and Mary Woodward, my parents 1951

146 Larkhall Lane, Clapham, London, SW4
The Company's first small premises 1946

Peckham Factory, Nunhead Green, London SE15
C.F Abel 1954

Brixton Factory,45 Morrish Road,
London SW2 1955

Starting a new business in London
after the war was more than difficult.
There were shortages of materials,
premises, delivery vans, petrol and
suitable staff as well as orders.
However it was managed somehow.

Hobart Mixer and operator John

Robert Woodward,
elder son, 1954

Plate 2

Mother Seigel's Advertisement 1920s

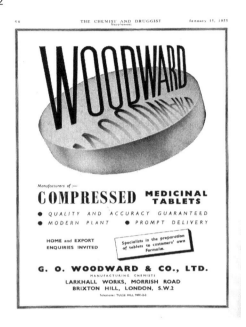

GO Woodward's contract advertisement 1955

Moving the factory from Peckham to Brixton 1954

Charles Edward Woodward younger son 1968

Plate 3

Tablet Compression Department at Brixton Premises 1960

Sugar Coating Department at Brixton premises 1960

Male Staff Office &
Production at
Brixton
premises1960

Standing from left

F.Moore,
S.Mitchell,John
Rugless,Roy
Crawford,Taffy
Davies,
L.Morris,N.Smart

Seated from left
W.Simper, E.Hill,
GOWoodward
W.Burke

Plate 4

Forest Works, Charlbury, Oxon 1962

1965 Forest Works, Charlbury extreme right
is the old retort house of the Gas Works
circa 1890

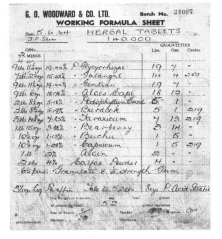

Working Formula Sheet for Herbal
tablets 1964 written by John Rugless

Wychwood House, Charlbury, Oxon.
G.O.Woodward's Country House 1965

Jim Burton 1965. Our Middle East
envoy

C.F Abel's Stand at Cruft's Dog Show at Olympia
in London, Deryk Cotterill and his mother 1965

Plate 5

House of Woodward
Trade Price List 1969

Caretaker's House at Forest Works,
Charlbury. New buildings on right 1970

Dr Robert Blakoe, Proprietor of
Blakoe Appliances and Doctor of
Anatomy 1930

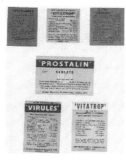

British Glandular Tonic
Product Labels 1971

GOW's Rolls Royce Silver Shadow 1971

Safeseal and Contract Strip
packaging service advert 1970

Removal of Machinery from Brixton to Putney 1969

Plate 6

Selected Examples of Architecture.

IN CONTINUATION OF
"THE PRACTICAL EXEMPLAR OF ARCHITECTURE"

Moulinière House, Putney Bridge Road, London.

MOULINIÈRE HOUSE, WANDSWORTH,
(Built circa 1700)

Rebuilding the Cathkin Laundry's old wash house showing the roof rusted away by the steam used by the washing machines. 1972

This is the original Moulinere House built circa 1700 on Putney Bridge Road, London. By the time that we moved into it in 1969 all that remained was the door and canopy. The grass had been replaced by road and pavement.

The bulk powder store and sugar coating departments in the Putney Bridge Road Laboratories. 1974

Symbolic and Defining Years

Founder's Health - Amygdalin (B17) an Alternative treatment from Mexico - Herbal struggle - Self medication saves GPs time - Special Diet Foods - Dr Hugh Sinclair - 100% Gluten Free standard -- Rita Greer and first 'Free From' range - 100% Gluten Free Bread Mix - Commercial Dispute and another battle ensued - Bureaucrat's view - Diet & Health reference point for 1977 - Diabetes and Guar gum - Chelation - Vitamin C Royal approval - What is a Health Food? An alternative medicine. - Healthmark - Natural and Synthetic - Official Approval for Evening Primrose Oil failing - Books for Allergics aimed at Professionals & laypeople - Symbol System - WHEN - Allergic's Charities - Clinical Ecology - Book reviews - Festival of Mind and Body - Junk Food criticised

Finance and George Orange's health. Bank correspondence indicated a borrowing facility of £152,500 was available but with personal guarantees of the Directors (myself and my brother) of £225,000 demanded. This included our own houses. I was invited to lunch with the local directors in Chelsea in March and subsequently I took one of the local directors, and our local bank manager, to lunch at a restaurant, after showing them round the Putney factory. I was building a new relationship with our Bank because of my father's illness. I knew we had to maintain good relations because we depended upon them for the continuation of our business.

Amygdalin/B17/Laetrile still in the news   on 1st January the BMJ published a leader on Laetrile: 'Quacks and Freedom'. A critical review of the 'false hope' argument applied to Cancer sufferers. It made the point that as long as patients felt failed by the medical establishment then products such as Laetrile (B17) would have brief success in the market. B17 was only really stopped in US and UK by extensive regulatory action. Most B17 came from Mexico where there were legal hospitals and suppliers specialising in B17 and other alternative treatments, just over the US/Mexico Border in Tijuana. It was inevitable that that was where patients went for treatment if it could be afforded. Bans on this sort of product might be counterproductive. Cases brought against US practitioners were costly to taxpayers and only made lawyers richer. It was better to ensure people were properly aware of the official view that the products were useless and let them decide for themselves.
   Since healthcare was free in the UK, there was little incentive to use expensive 'quack remedies'. Why not let the rich waste their money rather than taxpayers finance lawyers and regulatory officials? This was very much a 'Freedom' issue, like smoking.
   In October 1977 a clumsy piece of publicity was released by the US FDA. It stated, "Whether sold as a drug (Amygdalin) or as a 'vitamin' (B17) laetrile was worthless in the prevention, treatment or cure of cancer. The substance had no therapeutic or nutritional value. Furthermore patients were also warned that laetrile was dangerous because it contained cyanide and could cause poisoning and death when taken by mouth". It would have been better to have said unequivocally, "Laetrile (Amygdalin, 'vitamin'B17) was useless in the prevention, treatment and cure of cancer. It has no medicinal or nutritional value and its side effects included deadly cyanide poisoning."

LARKHALL GREEN FARM

The Herbal Medicine fight In January, the Daily Telegraph printed an article by Philip Barron entitled 'Not so healthy for the Herbalist' which referred to the proposed legislation for controlling Herbal Medicines. Times did not change and years later similar threats to herbals remained. Many have been lost since 1977 because that legislation was enough to drive out many small companies and thousands of products. However, many companies, especially from overseas, either ignored the laws or sidestepped the problems with clever marketing. The Regulators were constantly seeking to ban these fringe products but even in 2015 there were many hundreds of herbals sold as 'Food Supplements'.

Self medication saved GPs time. I wrote to the Daily Telegraph, protesting that it was unreasonable to try and disproportionately regulate herbals and other Alternative Health Care systems with the aim of driving them out altogether. It could only be justified if the public accepted that modern scientific evidence based medicine had provided them with ideal health. Surprise, surprise my letter was not published. Herbal remedies have a rich history of knowledge and experience going back centuries. Why waste it? However, it was pleasing to read Medical columnist 'Jotter' writing in Pulse (a GP weekly magazine) on the 'bogus remedies' which the DHSS wants to ban. These were the herbals and similar alternative care products. Jotter pointed out that if consumers find such remedies have cured him/her why should pharmacological pundits, for whom words mean what they want them to mean, consider them bogus and ban them?

Special Diet foods and Dr Hugh Sinclair By the end of 1976 Allergen free tablets and Cookery Books for special diets had become of great interest to the company. I wanted to explore the possibility of developing a Special Diet Food Range for Coeliacs and Food Allergy sufferers. This ambition became the subject of correspondence in late 1976 when my brother, through his contacts, was recommended Dr Hugh Sinclair as a dietary consultant. He was an Oxford scientist who had founded The International Institute of Human Nutrition based in Abingdon. I knew of Sinclair's organization through Jimmy Lee Richardson who had been behind its original founding after he saw Sinclair's research as a positive benefit to the Health Food Movement and Industry. My view was that consultants tended to be quite costly to employ and seemed to have little to add to our knowledge and were invariably unaware of the problems surrounding advertising of 'Health' products.

Sinclair had already made his name with Fish Oils through his research into the Eskimo people who avoided heart disease because of their oily-fish based diet. His work subsequently led to the marketing of many Fish Oil Supplement Capsules. Cod Liver Oil, one of the oldest health supplements, dating from the 1930s and widely used as an addition to children's diets in wartime as a source of Vitamins A and D, now became even more popular as a very low cost source of Fish Oil in the diet. Sinclair emphasized that people should consume more oily fish (Salmon, Herring etc) in their diets rather than use supplement capsules. However, consumers demanded the capsules of the protective polyunsaturated oils rather than eating fish. Not everyone could afford to eat fish. Capsules were good for supplement manufacturers and retailers but whether people benefited as much as they would have from eating more fish may never be known.

I met Sinclair at the Athenaeum Club in Pall Mall in February. We had a friendly meeting but the funding of the development of the products through him proved impossible for us and nothing followed. However, I was determined to proceed somehow.

I had been working with Hilda Cherry Hills of the Henry Doubleday Research Association who wrote 'Good Food Gluten Free' and other titles including 'Living Dangerously' and Dr Jean Monro of the Breakspear Hospital, who wrote 'Some Dietary approaches to Disease Management'.

Cantamac had been formulated on the low allergen concept in 1973 and this idea would form the basis of the entire Cantassium range of Supplements and Herbs from now on.

Rita Greer and the first 'Free From' Range After meeting Sinclair, I remembered my contact with Rita Greer who had needed Cantamac to help her husband Alan who was an MS patient. I was aware of her talent as a cook using natural wholesome ingredients and so wrote to her in February, to see if she would be interested in formulating a range of Special Diet Foods for Coeliacs and allergy sufferers who needed a 'Special Diet'. The range should enable users to easily cook good healthy, low allergen food.

By coincidence, she had already been approached, in the same week, by Marigold Foods and a newly retired businessman who had a chain of chemists in her area on the south coast. We all knew of her success with her allergy cookbooks and her talent for free PR. The three of us saw that she would be able to come up with formulas suitable for a range of special diet foods. Which one would she choose?

Of the three companies, she decided to team up with Larkhall for its Cantassium range because of our **manufacturing facilities,** which the two other companies did not have. I asked her to come to the Putney factory for discussions as we needed to get on with the work as soon as possible. She came up by train and we had a very good meeting. All dealings with her prior to this had been by letter or telephone so it was good to meet her in person at last. I found her bright, sparky, enthusiastic and highly intelligent. Additionally, she was a highly qualified artist and writer and seemed businesslike.

I had been alarmed to discover that the Gluten Free foods permitted on prescription for Coeliacs were made using Wheat Starch from which gluten had been chemically removed. I knew that it was impossible to remove 100% of any ingredient from a raw foodstuff. There would always be traces left and this could be harmful to patients. Equally, the cheap by-product from glue manufacturing known as 'wheat starch' used by manufacturers of gluten free breads and flours was stripped of its vital healthy ingredients such as B Complex vitamins and trace minerals as well as most of the coeliac's poison gluten. Wheat starch was an extreme junk food yet was actually being openly prescribed to sick Coeliac patients. One dietitian famously told me that this did not matter because "The bread from wheat starch was only used as a vehicle to carry nutritious foods like jam".

Rita agreed to undertake the development of the special diet range in her kitchen at home. There would be seven dry mixes made to her own formulas. They would all be 100% gluten free and wheat free. The company supplied her with most of the ingredients and often weighed them out accurately for her, the very small quantities needed in some of the early formulations as she only had kitchen scales. She worked with real speed, determination and passion to achieve results. No commercial laboratory could have done what she did in ten times the time and without many technicians. Even during the development stages she was doing her own publicity on the project including Radio and TV interviews. She used her connections developed from promoting her original 'Extraordinary Kitchen Notebook' and even those who knew her artistic work on Miniatures and Designer Jewellery. When the 1976 summer heatwave made working in her small kitchen too much to bear she worked in the very early hours to get the work done when it was a little cooler.

Cantassium Range of 'Free From' foods The range was unlike any other products on the market and needed to attract attention on the shelf. We immediately ran into trouble with our sales agency who couldn't find anyone to design the boxes specified. Rita stepped in and designed brightly coloured patchwork cartons. Then nobody could be found to match up the patchwork or do the artwork so she did it herself. The agency just had the typesetting done and a professional photographer took the photograph for the front of the packs. It was of Rita, cooking in her kitchen. The packs turned out really well, were completely original and fascinated people, looking colourful and inviting on the shelf. The agency was absolutely furious.

The Rita Greer/Cantassium range of Wheat and Gluten Free ready mixes were developed in 1976 - 77 as a pilot study and introduced to the market in September 1977. It comprised the following powder items:

Tomato Soup	Jubilee Bread Mix (grain free)
Fruit Cake (fruit to be added)	Crumble Topping
Sweet Biscuit Mix	Bedtime Drink (using carob)
Bolognese Sauce Mix	

The largest health food store chain refused to stock the new Cantassium Diet Food range as a matter of policy - why? Perhaps it broke the mould for this kind of product, they had nothing to even remotely match it. This action demonstrated the lack vision of that company.

100% Gluten Free Bread Mix The most interesting of these was undoubtedly the bread mix -- a world first. It was revolutionary, made up with yeast but did not require kneading or proving which cut down the preparation time to 5 minutes instead of hours. It could be put into the oven immediately it had been mixed and rose during baking. It had a crust and was an attractive golden colour. It looked, tasted and smelled like bread and nutritionally, had the same value as wheat bread. The standard of nutrition and taste, ease of use and appeal was far higher than anything produced for coeliacs before this time. The range was designed to see what market was out there.

Range not accepted for NHS prescription It was hoped that some of these mixes would be accepted for NHS prescription under the ACBS classification (The Advisory Committee on Borderline Substances). Unfortunately this was not possible because the products were all naturally 100% free from Gluten and the bureaucrats argued that if they were permitted then all naturally Gluten Free foods would be prescribable, eg eggs, steak, oranges etc. We argued that these were naturally gluten-free mixes that were direct substitutes for foods that were usually wheat based and could not be logically compared to steak, eggs etc. The authorities remained adamant and a long battle ensued.

Internal commercial dispute The authorities were not the only ones involved in the battle. My brother proposed that for commercial reasons we should make our products from **LOW** Gluten Wheat Flour like other manufacturers. He reasoned that by calling it LOW, that was the end of the problem. RG, backed by me, would not agree to compromise her quality standards for commercial expediency. Rita had spent years on research to formulate blends of naturally gluten free flours that would behave and taste like real wheat flour and be far superior to the run of the mill, very limited special diet foods for coeliacs on the market. She didn't see the point of producing inferior products that were not 100% gluten/wheat free. She had the experience of cooking for allergics, some of whom had appalling problems if they ingested something to which they were allergic. My brother's attitude made RG inclined to think she had just wasted years of research but I insisted we went on with it and managed to persuade her that her work was worth continuing.

The Bureaucrat's view on Gluten Free foods The Government stuck to their argument, supported by the Coeliac Society with its doctors and advisors, that if Rita's mixes were permitted on prescription then so would all naturally gluten free food. This view was specious and had nothing to do with 100% Gluten Free but all to do with the marketing of very highly profitable wheat starch based foods of poor nutritional quality. The profits made enabled the manufacturers to make large donations to the Coeliac Society that were used to fund their activities, pay their staff and fund medical research teams to discover how to grow 'Naturally Gluten Free Wheat'. A total waste of effort when perfectly good bread and cakes could be made from grains other than wheat. However, that can't be done in the UK because there is another law which ensured 'bread' must be exclusively made from wheat and her brand was wheat free as well as gluten free.

RG and Larkhall were besieged and because we told the truth, got no mercy from the vested interests. We just wanted the patients to be prescribed healthy foods and not potential poison. Luckily we had one or two people with us and ultimately succeeded in having our 100% Gluten Free flour mixes on prescription in 1979 after a struggle. I understand that some thirty years later most manufacturers have changed their formulas away from wheat starch, which is extremely limiting, and towards naturally gluten free blends, but it still persists in a few foods for coeliacs in 2016.

Diet & Health reference point for 1977   In June The News of the World published an article on Rita and Alan Greer that made a useful reference point for 1977 regarding how dietary control of health problems was not encouraged by the medical establishment. For them, there was no acceptable scientific evidence or proof of efficacy. In 2015 little had changed but the Free From shelves in Supermarkets show that special diets were still being followed by hundreds of thousands of consumers. Was RG the first to switch on this business with her publicity, cookery books and special food mixes with a symbol system guide?

My Weekly Magazine published an article by Michael Alcott on the Rita and Alan Greer story. He went to stay with them so he could write an in depth article. Years later Rita found out he had actually been diagnosed with MS himself.

The launch of the Free From range.   Health Food Trader carried an article 'First-ever special diet range launched by Rita Greer and Cantassium Company'. It gave details on the range, prices and symbol system. The Chemist and Druggist and the Pharmaceutical Journal announced the introduction of the Special Diet Food range and the publishing of Rita's 'The First Clinical Ecology Cook Book'. So did The Health Food Trader and 'The News' in Portsmouth carried a piece on RG with recommendation of her cook book. Southern TV featured RG with a 10 minute piece showing her special diet foods. All this important PR was free and no agency was involved.

New Inspector   In March a new Inspector, Mr Warburton from DHSS, visited and only had four comments for attention. He seemed to actually appreciate that we were making progress both with paperwork and construction of new production areas. How the situation had improved since the court case!

Jo Grimond   I attended a meeting of 'The Association of Independent Businesses' at which Jo Grimond, the former Liberal party leader, spoke of the real dangers that Trade Union Power was causing. I already had had trouble with them and so had RG with the NGA. There was to be more in the 1980s.

Guar and Diabetes   In October a paper was published in the Lancet regarding the benefits of 25g of Guar gum, a natural fibre, daily in Diabetic Diets. There was a 50% lowering of urinary glucose excretion. The researcher suggested that a specially formulated bread made with guar gum could be useful. At his invitation RG and I visited the lead researcher in Oxford, to discuss the possibilities of marketing food that contained Guar Gum. Palatability was a major problem and nothing resulted from these discussions. RG baked a crispbread using Guar Gum but it was brittle and tasted awful. Guar was a most unpleasant food ingredient with a taste that is impossible to mask. It not only had a very unappetizing texture but stuck to the teeth like superglue.

The research team had worked for a long time, trying to get enough Guar Gum into products and had failed. RG worked on it for a couple of days and solved the incorporation problem but did not recommend putting Guar Gum into any food. As far as I know, no commercially available foods were ever marketed. RG was not impressed with the Oxford boffins who were adamant that people in the UK did not eat fibre, especially beans. She queried the popular convenience food, Baked Beans. They had never heard of them and admitted they had never been into a supermarket. RG was unimpressed and me likewise.

Chelation   Chelation of minerals had become a buzzword in the Healthfood area following the introduction of 'Chelated Minerals' in the USA. Chelate formation was a complex chemical phenomenon and in biological systems the structures of the chelate complexes are infinite. The 'chelates' offered in tablets and capsules were usually organic salts of minerals such as aspartates, glycinates, or gluconates. The minerals in these were claimed to be better absorbed by the digestive system than those from simple inorganic acids such as carbonates, sulphates and chlorides. There was little convincing proof of this but undoubtedly the minerals combined in the organic acids were easier on the stomach because they were in lower concentrations in the tablet/capsule. The mineral combined with inorganic acids was likely to be more available for biological chelation too. The arguments continue to this day but can the average person hope to understand them?

Vitamin C - aristocratic approval   July/October 1977 I received two letters from Earl Mountbatten of Burma thanking me for sending him free 1000mg Vitamin C, which Barbara Cartland has told him will prevent colds – he said they worked.

What is a 'Health Food'?   Health Food Trader carried an article by me entitled "Health Foods - a changed meaning". In this article I argued that the term 'Health Food' was not restricted to the maintenance of health through wholesome diets but also embraced foods that can prevent poor health and even alleviate symptoms. In the minds of many consumers health foods were as effective as the doctor's medicines. The words Health Food could be taken over by pharmacies to the detriment of the real Health Food Stores. Health retailers were advised to become more knowledgeable in alternative medicine areas. There was a borderline between Health Foods and Medicines, but where it was would provide lawyers and bureaucrats employment for decades.

Trading Standards Officials charged with enforcement in this area would have liked to see the term 'Health Food' outlawed because they believed all food was healthy and thus when applied to a food or store 'Health Food' was a false trade description. If this were to happen it could lead to imprisonment for an unlimited time. Indeed, the words 'health food' were already banned in most European Countries and so UK authorities would have liked us to come into line. Happily, consumer led lobby groups have thwarted this ambition and are likely to succeed into the future because the borderline is so blurred.

I warned the Health Trade that chemist chains would compete with health stores but without knowledgeable advisers, were unlikely to succeed. The profits to pharmacists in dispensing drugs far exceed those offered by Health Foods. This reduced their genuine interest. They were in the enemy camp.

Healthmark   Around this time the 'Healthmark' scheme idea was introduced for discussion within the Health Food industry. This was to clearly distinguish **'Natural' from 'Synthetic'** products using an independently assessed standard. Sadly it failed to obtain support because of the extensive grey area between naturally and synthetically made products.

More difficulty for Evening Primrose A consultant who had connections with Bio Oils approached Cantassium regarding a monograph on Ruthmol.

I asked RG if she had heard of him and she told me that this man approached Bio-Oils in 1975 and became an investor. Correspondence relating to this revealed how John Williams was becoming concerned about the 'evidence' required to satisfy authorities for permitting prescription of Naudicelle. He ultimately failed to ever obtain approval.

In November 1977, 'Ministry ignoring new MS treatment' was the headline on an article from a local newspaper referring to the problems that Bio Oil Research were experiencing in obtaining approval for Evening Primrose Oil on NHS Prescription. This was a classic example of the problems faced by many nutritional supplements that attempted to gain real credibility.

A retired Oil Company Director, invested in the Bio Oil company. He was typical of many 'investors' in the Health Industry, fired up by publicised research which was appealing to lay people but cut little ice with regulators, advertising standards authorities and the mainstream medical lobby. Such people were soon out of their depth and go away disappointed or 'broke'. This gentleman opened a Health Food Store but soon sold it.

Books for Food Allergics aimed at Health Professionals and Laypeople By September RG was preparing to add 'Fruit and Vegetables in Particular' to her special diet cook book range. She was also working on the introduction to a Gluten Free Cook Book. This would give her account of the development of the food mixes from concept to store shelf of her products in their colourful packs.

'Fruit & Vegetables in Particular' was reviewed in Health Food Trader and stocked by Newman Turner, the mail order and publishing arm of Booker Health Foods. Such was the demand for her books.

Health Food Trader had a piece entitled "Food for mental health" which publicised Hilda Cherry Hills's new book 'Good Food: Grain free, Milk free' written to help special dieters. The author said 70% of people could improve their mental health by applying current knowledge of food allergy and exclusion dieting. Hills's books were aimed at medical professionals to recommend to their patients. Rita Greer's books were aimed at both laypeople and health professionals. A divide that was always difficult to close.

1978

Can diet cure disease? An article from Family Circle magazine in 1978 that referred to Rita Greer as "An energetic Portsmouth lady", gave many examples of the successful application of special dieting to fight disease and maintain health.

Symbol System problem The March Issue of Nutrition and Food Science published a two page article on the RG special diet foods and symbol system. This was a most comprehensive review of the products and showed the excellent rapport that Rita had built up with the Editor, Dilys Wells, of this prestigious publication with leading experts such as Dr Magnus Pyke on its editorial board. Rita wrote the article and did the artwork for the cover of the magazine and article herself.

This article stirred the establishment and undoubtedly increased awareness of Rita, Cantassium, Larkhall and myself. Leading academics wrote to the editor of the publication, angry about the concept in general but mostly concerning the symbol system. Was this a case of "not invented here?"

This system was way ahead of its time but her critics had no idea that Rita was not only the developer of the food formulas but an artist and writer too. The fact that she had produced the total concept and design package herself enabled her to fully answer those critics without receiving a reply. They were left speechless.

Symbol System Controversy The most controversial symbol was RG's Gluten Free one. There was already a 'Gluten Free' symbol that had been instigated by the Coeliac Society and called 'the crossed grain'. It was used by many manufacturers whose products were included in the society's official food lists for Coeliac patients. It was not available to just any company to use as they had to be vetted by the Coeliac Society and it cost the manufacturers money. The Coeliac Society was not a Government body but a charity set up to help patients with information and fund research into Coeliac Disease. It had many volunteer workers and raised substantial funds for medical research. The beneficiary researchers were naturally interested in protecting their benefactor and provided the lay-person run Charity with a professional front. The food manufacturers who used the 'Crossed Grain' symbol on their food packs were often major donors to the Charity. Thus there seemed to be a web of vested interests behind this Charity.

For sometime, I, RG and Cantassium's medical advisers had openly criticized the application of the Crossed Grain symbol to foods for Coeliacs made from wheat starch which was low gluten, and not truly gluten free. Gluten cannot ever be totally removed from wheat using chemical means (solvent extraction) – a first year chemistry student knew that. We were already considered *persona non-grata* by the Coeliac Society. We had no wish to use their tainted symbol on our food products so when Rita designed her symbols she used a new pictogram for Gluten Free. The symbol also meant Wheat Free, Barley free and Oats free. This stimulated an outcry from the dietitians who questioned the need for another symbol and Rita's right to design it. When Rita answered these people and they realized the importance of what she was saying, ie that their precious symbol was on foods that were merely low gluten – they suddenly went quiet. However, the stir caused was great because Cantassium and I became notorious for upsetting the apple cart for those manufacturers who were close to the Coeliac Society and great fans of wheat starch.

It is a fact that Coeliacs have an enhanced chance of contracting bowel cancer and one reason is likely that they were continuing to ingest gluten from the traces of gluten present in their prescribed foods. Dietitians, GPs and Consultants were only too ready to accuse patients of not complying with the diet but their support of wheat starch based foods probably meant that patients were not responsible for breaking those dietary rules.

The process of extracting gluten from wheat involved removal of many vital micronutrients such as B Vitamins and trace minerals that hardly helped its nutritional value for protection from cancers and other illnesses. Wheat starch was a by-product from glue manufacture, used for making paper white, starching laundry and for animal feed. RG and I believed it should not be used for human consumption. The international Codex Alimentarius organisation backed by their 'Experts' did not agree. They thought wheat starch was suitable for coeliacs and the Coeliac Society hid behind them. The Government hid behind the both the Codex Alimentarius and the Coeliac Society, as did the NHS, GPs dietitians and consultants. Bureaucracy overruled common sense but what about those 'experts'? Had they other interests supporting their livelihoods?

Whistle blowing was always a dangerous pastime. Exposure of the flawed policy of permitting Low Gluten Ingredients to be officially sanctioned for prescription to Coeliac Patients must have caused great consternation in official, medical and industry as well as Coeliac Charity circles. If our arguments were accepted by them then there was a great risk of law suits from patients. These could have proved very costly to all parties. Trading Standards Officials could have quickly grasped this nettle, but as Government servants were probably told to do nothing.

It was some 20 years before wheat starch was eliminated from most gluten free mixes/breads – yet even today (2015) you will find it in some prescription and 'free from' foods. The vested interests got away scot-free but of course Coeliac patients may have suffered premature deaths and from degenerative illnesses as a result of this negligence. No wonder Larkhall, me and Rita Greer were pilloried for so long by these people.

74

The other symbols criticized were the oil droplet for Low Saturated Fat and the split heart for Cholesterol Free. Rita held to the view that these were on pack as tiny pictograms to help the consumer and had no relevance to disease states. It is interesting to note that one of the most lengthy letters came not from just the National Dairy Council but The Eggs Authority and another, along exactly similar lines from an apparently non-aligned dietitian. They were all from a private address. Undoubtedly all three letters were from the same ultimate source – a vested interest group.

The Eggs Authority, although it sounds like a government body, was actually an egg-industry pressure group. Rita's egg free symbol had already appeared in her cookery books. They insisted this was wrong, complaining bitterly that only one in ten people were allergic to eggs in the UK -- that was about five million. We were delighted to have this information as we had no idea the percentage was so high. The Eggs Authority was later closed down.

Rita received a threatening letter from an animal cruelty organisation. They claimed she had copied their symbol of a rabbit for 'not tested on animals'. The said they would sue if it was not removed from the symbol system. The letter was aggressive and the telephone calls more so. On checking our records I found that Rita had used her rabbit symbol for over a year before the animal organisation had even had theirs designed. We appraised them of this fact and did not hear back from them. They didn't think to apologise.

Rita had problems from the Pepper Council, because in an article, and in her books, she told patients to be beware of gluten in white pepper when eating out. This was good advice for anyone allergic. There is actually no gluten in white pepper as such but, cafeterias and restaurants often 'stretch' their expensive white pepper with wheat flour. The Pepper Council denied all knowledge of quite a common practice in catering.

WHEN (World Health & Ecology News) Roberts Publications, the publishing arm of our business, had been publishing books and pamphlets on Alternative Medicine and Healthcare since 1975. Dr EC Barton-Wright's treatise on Arthritis – A Vitamin Deficiency Disease, was its first success but both the Cantassium Dietary System dating from 1921 and the Cantamac System of 1973 were brought into the fold in 1975. The Dr Blakoe story from 1928 soon became a best seller too.

In the mid seventies I had met Mr Charles Royal from the USA who claimed to be having huge success in the USA with an Alternative Health tabloid newspaper. He claimed selling millions of copies in the USA and wished to launch in the UK. He had even moved his family to Marlow in Buckinghamshire because he thought the lifestyle better over here. Meanwhile he would commute to the USA, having a well established office there. It was a good story, nevertheless I was suspicious yet I could see a UK edition of WHEN succeeding. There was nothing like it available in the UK. Royal already had advertisers and was ready to print and distribute in the UK.

I decided to advertise in the first issue but as Royal had no Audited Circulation figures I asked for a printer's declaration of copies printed. Speculating £1000, all went ahead. However, before long Royal was back with Issue Two with plans and demands. Another £1000 was speculated and we undertook to distribute some magazines to our retail stockists. By the end of 1977 Royal approached me with proposals for a takeover of the UK edition with a royalty payable. He was returning to the USA. His wife would control the UK end. Since we had already been heavily involved financially through being the main UK advertiser, I thought a further gamble worth taking and asked my friend Dr Dick Richards if he would Edit and Hugh Winthrop, then our advertising agent, would arrange production. Dick had contacts on the professional side and Hugh had access to other writers and so did I. (Rita Greer was also enthusiastic, calling it in jest 'Robert's Rag'.) She wrote healthy recipes and cookery and did black and white illustrations for it. By now we had enough product lines to support advertising without having many other supporters – for at least three more issues.

The new publication would be printed on paper similar to the best GP Medical Publication 'Pulse'. We hoped it would appeal to the important opinion forming groups of Health Professionals – GPs, Hospital Doctors, Nurses, Dentists and Pharmacists as well as to the Alternative Professionals such as Osteopaths, Homoeopaths, Herbalists, Chiropractors, Nutritionists and Health Store owners and their customers. An ambitious project, but we would invest enough to test viability. I feared that the ambition to soon have it on a paid-for subscription basis could fail.

The first Issue of the UK WHEN was published in March 1978 and was well received. A selective mailing resulted in 10% of Doctors, 20% of Nurses and over 25% of Pharmacists asking to be mailed WHEN regularly. This was an encouraging result – maybe the first issue headline about Natural Cancer Treatments helped. I decided to continue and made WHEN the main recipient of our health product advertising budget for the ensuing 12 months. Unfortunately, after that time our expectations had not materialized and it was obvious that no one would pay a viable subscription and our competitors would not advertise. They had no vision and could not appreciate that here was a unique publication that reached out to the established Medical Professionals whose ultimate support would be important for the long-term credibility of the Alternative Medicine industry and professions.

Even today 2015, they remain as blinkered as ever and still fight at the edge of what seems to be a losing battle with the medical establishment and regulators.

RIP WHEN   WHEN possibly generated huge benefits for the company as regards awareness but maybe we were many years too soon. I had to close it down in the 1980.

Dr. Richard Mackarness   In mid 1978 Mackarness met me at the National Liberal Club with RG. I thought Mackarness was a member and was surprised when he asked me to pay for the lunch by passing him cash under the table so that no one would see. Mackarness asked for Cantassium to sponsor Clinical Ecology meetings. We sponsored one in Basingstoke in July that Rita attended with her husband. We had a table with a display of our allergy aid products. As it was a Saturday there was no way I could go – (my wife insisted, no business at weekends). I was missed, especially as W O'Connell, our rep, didn't do any work but spent the day in the little bar. The barman was Irish and kept serving him. WO'C became very drunk. (If I had been there he would not have dared to do this.) In spite of this, which didn't go unnoticed, Mackarness seemed well pleased with the symposium. RG had spent two days cooking special diet food and preparing really healthy food which was given to the attendees for lunch. Mackarness was supposed to reimburse her for the ingredients but he never did. RG was rather disturbed when she sat at the back of the hall to hear the end of Mackarness's lecture. He claimed to have cured her husband of MS! RG told me I could count her out for anything more to do with Mackarness.

Action against Allergy   Richard Mackarness was establishment qualified but unfortunately found few followers who were. He retired to Australia in the early 1990s and was made Doctor of the Year by Action Against Allergy – a charity run by a most entertaining lady, Amelia Nathan Hill, who lived in Wimbledon and ran antique shop near South Wimbledon Station called 'Junkatique'. She percieved Mackarness to be something of an icon for patients with allergies. RG saw her at a lecture when she had her tortoise and a couple of other pets with her.

Sanity   The Charity 'Sanity' run by Mrs Marjorie Hall, arranged a symposium including Dr Theron Randolph, a Clinical Ecologist from the USA lecturing.

The organizer, Dr Ellen Grant assured me that there would be many attendees but in the event there were not more than 20 present including Mackarness. A costly venture and a waste of resources. it was the last to be sponsored by Cantassium at the Charing Cross Hospital, although Mackarness wanted bi-annual events.

Clinical Ecology? I had misgivings about the future for Clinical Ecology in the UK and did not intend to plan Medical meetings two years in advance. Pharma companies do this but their products are more profitable than special diet foods and books. The number of UK Doctors practising Clinical Ecology was few and most practitioners advocating it were really 'Alternative Health' people, many with qualifications from US mail order outfits. Many lay people cannot distinguish the establishment qualified Doctor from the alternative rivals. This was an enduring problem and was highlighted dramatically in 2009 by the exposure of a (Dr) Gillian McKeith, who had been accepted as a real Doctor by National Television and Media, but was really a US by-mail Doctor. I came across her in 1996 with her husband Howard Magaziner and had been taken in by their convincing double act. I am sure that many Clinical Ecologists are honest people but getting deeply involved with this area was commercially dangerous.

Wyndham Thomas This gentleman contacted Dick Richards in June about a boy he was treating naturopathically for eczema. This boy had been eating large quantities of sugary foods and no fruit. Thomas prescribed large reduction in the sugary foods and more fruit plus a vitamin C supplement. His condition cleared in 10 days. This boy had been attending Hospital for several years without ever being asked about his diet. Thomas indicated in his letter that many conditions had responded to simple diet change including Psoriasis.

ABPI I resigned from the Standard Formulary Medicines committee of the ABPI in March. Although the company retained its membership for a few more years, it was becoming clear that the company had lost any affinity with the organisation. We would resign our membership of it in a few years time.

Personal Efforts by R Greer and me -- we were courting trouble from the Establishment. RG and I were working on publicising the work of the company with Radio interviews and Magazine articles.

 The spring issue of Health Now (a publication distributed in Health Stores and some Pharmacies) published an article by me on the dangers from pollutants and allergens in common Foodstuffs. It dealt with problems that can be successfully addressed using special diet foods and RG's books. She was by now writing a book a year and they were all published, by different publishers. Some were translated into other languages and published abroad.

Good book reviews and free PR The April issue of Nutrition Abstracts and Reviews had given an excellent review of Rita's Extraordinary Kitchen Notebook. "In devising these recipes, the author has tried to produce dishes that were acceptable to the whole family and that were nutritious and inexpensive. In this she has achieved her aim. To those people having to produce a diet without gluten, cane sugar or cholesterol, and low in animal fat, the book would be invaluable." John Williams of Bio Oils had sent it in to them as he was so impressed with it.

Liverpool Daily Post printed an article on the amazing story of Rita and Alan Greer. A comprehensive article on her story and the development of the Diet Range in collaboration with me.

In April I went on the Ed Doolan Show to talk about Alternative Medicine -- 20 minutes. Independent London Radio followed by a ten minute 'phone-in. This was a first 'phone-in experience for me.

In August I was on ILR for Mike Matthews on Alternative Medicine -- 3 minutes but no 'phone in.

Festival of Mind and Body   Cantassium exhibited Diet Foods and Supplements and RG's Books at The Festival for Mind and Body at Olympia. 29th April – 7th May. Rita Greer and her husband attended the stand every day and stayed in a hotel.

More PR, May - October   We supplied the Bishop of Southwark with Apricot Kernel powder prompted by Barbara Cartland.
    Chelsea Post paper on Helfex exhibition at the Royal Lancaster Hotel Paddington with a photo of The Earl Mountbatten. He opened the exhibition. Barbara Cartland was also there. He said he was using Cantopal, the Calcium Pantothenate Supplement by Cantassium who were exhibitors. A very forthright article on Food Dangers by me was featured just below a photo of Lord Mountbatten. Perhaps this was the start of publicity of my attacks on junk foods that made me a marked man by the vested interests?
    Article from "Healthy Living" magazine outlining scheme by Cantassium for providing regular information to Doctors on nutritional research.
    Article from 'Family Circle', Can Diet Cure Disease? Discussed threats to health from additives including Hyperactivity in Children and MS. Cantassium and Rita Greer mentioned positively.
    In the Portsmouth News Rita had a large article entitled "The life-saving counterfeit cook". An excellent human interest story was always guaranteed to obtain publicity. Large photo of Rita and Alan looking through a display of the special diet foods with their patchwork packs.
    A Vogue Health columnist wrote about the benefit of Nucleic Acid rich foods to fight ageing. She recommended Cantassium Supplement Cantarna 450mg four daily, to assist those adopting this diet.
     London Evening News article on Jacqueline du Pre who has MS and had been helped by the Greer Diet.
    Lets Live Magazine (USA) carried an article on ALS with mention of Rita's books and dietary ideas. She was very concerned about it because her husband did not have ALS but the article said he did. She was inundated with calls from the USA, especially at night from ALS sufferers given false hope by the article.
    A nice piece in Alive Magazine (for Vegetarians) recommended Rita's kitchen notebooks with orders sent to her Portsmouth address.

Chemist and Druggist Interest   In July I was asked by the C&D to provide information on the Vitamin and Tonics market for their annual review of Alternative Healthcare Products available in pharmacies. I replied with a letter in August with my opinion that Alternative Health Care was in the ascendancy, proved by the response to WHEN magazine.
    In October I wrote to Ronald Salmon, the Editor of the Chemist & Druggist, regarding his support of Alternative Medicine. Under the heading "Healthy Future" the letter put the case for that support and expressed fear that the powerful interests of big Pharma and the DHSS (MCA) were seeking to squash small companies and non-establishment practitioners.

In November Chemist & Druggist published a letter from me on Alternative Medicine and the WHEN magazine popularity with Health Professionals, following a mailing of the magazine with reply for a free subscription. Nearly 30% of Pharmacists responded positively.

Possible Export to USA of Gluten Free Mixes. A letter arrived from the American Celiac Society of New Jersey. Anita Garrow from that society visited us later in the month and discussed the Gluten Free vs Low Gluten situation in US. No business developed as the cost of freight was too great. Our products would soon be copied anyway, even the packs but not the correct formulas since no amounts of each ingredient were divulged on the UK packs, and we would not be able to do a thing about it. Rita's books were selling well in the USA but as copyright did not apply in that country there were no royalties for her.

Larkhall vs Junk Food Industry An article in the Guardian on October 10th by Judy Graham reported on Rita's research and anger at the poor quality of so many Supermarket foods like Muesli ('Measly' according to Rita). In National Newspapers this sort of comment was sure to mark you as an enemy of the junk food industry. So I was making enemies together with RG and Cantassium. We were unaware of it at the time but it would lead to revenge in ten years time. The power of the vested interests should never be underestimated.

In November The British Medical Journal published a letter from me on Borderline Substances. Congratulations were received from Paddy O'Connor of Medical Digest. This letter had criticized the policy of the ACBS in only permitting chemically modified ingredients as prescribable on the NHS, thus forcing Coeliacs to consume their poison Gluten in these foods. The logic of not permitting mixes made from naturally gluten free ingredients was non-existent. The fact that the BMJ, a top world medical journal, published this letter no doubt increased awareness of the vested interests behind Cantassium products as well as mine and RG's views. At this time, unbeknown, we were using a PR agency with indirect connections to the Snack and Biscuit Alliance, a Junk Food Industry pressure group. It's possible that this link put us more at risk of attack – the agency was not used after 1979. A similar letter under the heading 'Gluten Free' Foods signed by Roger Baxter (our Pharmacist Registration Manager) and me to the Pharmaceutical Journal was published in October.

Inspections continue Visits and reports of Medicines Inspector B.A. Curran on Charlbury and Putney operations. It will be noted that regulatory life was an ever increasing burden. At this time John Gregory MPS was managing the works in London and Cyril Blau LRSC the quality control laboratory. In Charlbury, CEW managed the operation assisted by D.A. Hooker. I had already distanced myself from direct inspector contact except at reception and debriefing. This whole bureaucratic nonsense was achieving little except gradual elimination of the smaller independent pharmaceutical manufacturing companies. We were now 10 years into the Medicines Act 1968. Our companies continued to move away from Medicine production but the holding of the Manufacturing Licence ensured that we kept greater credibility with all our customers at home and abroad. Most of them didn't know the difference between a medicinal product and a health supplement.

Small Company destroyed by the Medicines Men In June George Mercer who used to make all our injectable products wrote to me sending a payment that had been outstanding for a long time. We had helped him try to overcome problems with the DHSS Inspectors but at his age he had decided to give up the struggle in Boxford in Essex. He was now in poor health – I sympathised with him and referred to the deterioration in my father's health having been caused by the Inspector-generated stress.

LAETRILE B17 April – October   The most controversial cancer cure had bad publicity in Medical News, a free GP Newspaper sponsored by advertising from the Pharma Industry. Cyanide poisoning in Dogs and some patients. "So what," said the proponents, "dogs Have different metabolic systems from humans and anyway the drugs promoted for curing cancer by Pharma have lots of side effects too."

In the same month, a more balanced article appeared by Miriam Polunin in Here's Health, the Health Food magazine. It covered the history of B17 and its development in the USA. No conclusion was reached, but people should be free to choose it and also apply the strict dietary regime. By October Medical News was reporting that an official trial might take place soon in the USA. In the event a trial was done but because other factors especially the strict dietary regime were not obligatory, the results indicated no beneficial effects. In clinical trials dietary control was almost impossible so the Laetrile trial was irrelevant and a waste of resources.

The Mail Order department (Associated Preparations of PO Box 53, Cheam, Surrey) of items required to supplement natural raw diets as recommended in Cancer dieting by the newly formed Bristol Cancer Centre in conjunction with German doctor Hans Nieper was often mentioned in these articles.

The range in 1978 constituted about 130 products. Most were diet supplements but special diet foods were growing.

Year of Destiny

Mark Morris - Wassen International - Family matters - BHMA - Annie's Room - Inspection problems - WHEN demise - B17 still under threat - Atheroma - Ireland - Nigeria - Alternative Healthcare - Eye Health - Cantabread - A disastrous promotion - Gluten Free double standards - Pharmacy and healthy eating - Trufree - Body Image Books - Foresight Preconception Charity - Death of GOW - Brands vs Generics - ABPI exit - Key staff problem

Mark Morris The new year had begun badly with the funeral of Mark Morris. He had gone away for Christmas with his wife, to stay at a hotel, and died suddenly aged 76. His death was critical for the business because his experience from over 50 years in the pharmaceutical industry had proved invaluable to me since 1972. Mark had worked with George Orange at Menley & James in the 1920s, (part of A J White Ltd later to become Smith Kline French and most recently Glaxo Smith Kline). He had later joined Thomas Marns Ltd in 1956 that was founded by Thomas Marns, a Past President of the Pharmaceutical Society and a founder member of the PATA (Proprietary Article Trade Association). This was a trade association for patent medicine companies that protected their interests including competition and maintaining prices (RPM). At one time Thomas Marns held the agency for **'Carter's Little Liver Pills'** which had been one of the world's best selling patent medicines in the 1930s. Later they sold **Juno Junipah**, a very successful ladies laxative containing Phenolphthalein. We made this product for Marns. Mark left Tomas Marns to help found Pharmacal Supplies Ltd that was a direct competitor of GO Woodward & Co and we lost the Juno contract. This upset George Orange but when Mark retired in 1968 he bought the Richmond Order Company maker and distributor of **Mother Brown's Kneecaps.** The office was in the middle of Richmond, not far from Putney. Mark also opened a consultancy and operated as a middleman for several overseas and UK marketing companies who trusted Mark's knowledge of where to buy products and were happy for him to take a commission. Mark came to see us to discuss co-operation with him. This approach appealed to us and soon good business was developed and we became one of Mark's major sources of products such as Cascara Extract tablets, Iron Sulphate 200mg tablets and Blaud's Pills (Silver Coated) etc – all for export to West Africa. Products were made in Putney and packed in Charlbury.

In the early 1970s Mark Morris was faced with a large increase in rent on his office in Richmond. We still had unused space in the Putney factory and he moved to the empty shop (previously a Cathkin Dry Cleaners) at the front of the building to use as his office. He also took space on the flat roof of the factory in a small brick shed which had previously been used as a ladies toilet for the Cathkin laundry and was redecorated for Mark's use. This was where he impregnated the kneecaps, anklets, wristlets and bodybelt pads with Mother Brown's (medicinally licensed of right) solution that contained traces of Thorium Nitrate (very slightly radioactive) and methyl salicylate. (This licence, since it applied to an externally applied product, was not reviewed nor banned until the mid 1980s). Mark and his assistant impregnated the pads by dipping them in a bucket of Mother Brown's solution and drying them in a domestic spin dryer, which recycled the Mother Brown solution back to the bucket.

LARKHALL GREEN FARM

Wassen and Pollen B Among Mark's customers had been Wassen International, recently founded by Ray Matthews, a gifted copywriter and advertising man. Being inquisitive, as usual, I asked Ray where the name Wassen came from? He told me that when he was seeking a name he put a map of the richest European country on the dining table at home, put on a blindfold and pushed a pin into the map. Thus Wassen the town in Switzerland became the company name. He said it was a 'disarming' name. Ray was an advertising genius.

We were soon making a major product for Wassen called Pollen B. Through advertising and Public Relations, Ray built Wassen into a multimillion pound product company selling its Food Supplements worldwide. Bee Pollen became a legendary health enhancer in consumers minds for all those everyday nebulous health factors -- feel young again, look youthful, boost your energy, overcome aches and pains, enhance sex life etc. There was anecdotal evidence in its favour but I thought it was that magical insect the bee flitting from pretty flower to flower, over unpolluted fields, that enhanced the story. Ultimately, it was perhaps the antioxidant polyphenols in Pollen that held its secrets.

The major problem with natural pollen in its raw form was its nutritional value to many insects, meaning that long term storage after collection could only be sustained by sterilization. Such processes were essential for making capsules and tablets. When consumers learned that their wonderful pollen product had been subjected to sterilsation by irradiation, the growth in sales halted. Opponents of alternative healthcare ensured the message about irradiation being harmful was not counteracted properly.

Pollen B's time in the top sellers list expired but Ray had many other products in his mind and Wassen became a leading brand of one-a-day Food Supplements under his guidance. Most were copied but never bettered. Despite all the efforts of authorities, doctors and academics to rubbish and prevent meaningful advertising of what they termed 'Snake Oil' products Wassen's success continues today (2016) -- because consumers are not fools. Food Supplements have positive health benefits but neither they nor the industry should consider them medicinal. There is too much misleading publicity that attributes medicinal benefits and cures to 'Food Supplements'.

Wassen contract lost Later, my brother managed to lose the Wassen contract for us by being unbelievably abusive to Ray Matthews at the Charlbury packing factory when he visited one day. Ray was so incensed he did not use us ever again, either for manufacture or packaging. This did not affect my friendship with him as this split only concerned business. However, the loss of the Wassen contract was a blow to the company. Ray never spoke to my brother again. My friendship with Ray kept up until he died at the age of 92 and we enjoyed many good lunches and discussions about business and clinical trials for supplements even after we had both sold out and retired.

New Architect When our company lost its manufacturing Licence, Mark Morris came to our aid by finding a new architect, George Messervy, and working with him and our own in-house builders to meet the requirements of both Fire and Medicines regulators. This was no easy matter when dealing with competing bureaucracies. His working knowledge going back to the 1920s baffled the poorly experienced inspectors who lacked practical awareness of many processes used in small companies. George Messervy also had the measure of them and baffled them with his eccentric charm. When dealing with builders and workmen he would let them solve the problem and when they had finished their work he would draw up the plan. He never argued and never fell out with anyone. A supreme diplomat.

Family matters -- a possible move? After Mark's death I came under family pressure to consider leaving London and basing our whole operation in Charlbury or elsewhere, thus avoiding the expense of running two factories. My wife refused point blank to move as did my brother's. It was a pity that the new generation of wives did not support a business that provided them with considerable lifestyle benefits. My mother, Mary Woodward, always put the needs of the company first. She saw that as her supportive role as the wife of a businessman. Sadly her daughters-in-law were basically anti-business despite of the rewards it brought them.

General Industry interests – The BHMA (The British Herbal Medicines Association) I had just retired from involvement with the ABPI standard medicines committee and although the company remained members of the ABPI I knew that that trade association would be of little use in the areas of Health Care in which it was now involved. One body that was still of some relevance was the British Herbal Medicines Association (BHMA). I had been to their meetings but was disappointed with their approaches to the regulators who were decimating the herbal preparations and producers using totally disproportionate enforcement procedures. Sadly, it seemed that BHMA policy was in the hands of a few powerful companies whose aim was not to help consumers but to achieve a monopoly for them in herbal products through close co-operation with Inspectors who only really believed in synthetic drug standards. I viewed them as cowards who put profit before all else and kow-towed to the bureaucrats, to ensure their survival and the demise of the small manufacturers, whom the officials despised and found a nuisance to regulate.

I advocated a new and proportionate system of regulation for herbals organized under the DHSS but with its own structure and herbally qualified officials. This is still unrealized in 2015.

Family attitudes   It was after one of these trade meetings that I returned home late, around 6pm, to a furious reception. Nothing new, but it had become clear that my wife could not accept that running a small company employing over 120 people, in the very specialized highly regulated health sector, actually involved more than the hours of nine-to-five, five days a week. To develop and survive I would need to work more, not less. I realised that if my wife's attitude did not change, running the business would eventually mean the end of our marriage. The family members depending on company resources had now grown from three to eleven and my father could no longer work owing to his poor health. It was all a huge stress for me.

I moved out of my home in April. After years of rows and unhappiness I had finally split up with my wife. By now we were totally incompatible and the marriage had broken down completely. She departed to her parents' house with the children. A divorce was inevitable. I could not give up the business as too many of the family depended on it, including my parents. She was adamant she didn't want to be the wife of a businessman. I sold the house and bought my estranged wife a brand new house, near her parents for her and the children. I gave her everything she wanted from my original house, a new estate car, paid school fees and new uniforms for the children plus an income. This left me with no home of my own and nothing much to put in one, but an end to the unbearable daily friction and blazing rows about my work for the family firm and how my brother and his wife had it so much easier and did better. At last I would be able to travel abroad to cope with increasing the export side of the business. I saw the children when allowed, took them skiing in the Easter holidays and battened down for a lengthy divorce.

The bank, key personnel and no lifestyle spending   The business was pivotal to more than one person's life. Whilst it had good liquid assets it was heavily dependent on bank borrowings and was far from a readily saleable entity in view of the very uncertain regulatory environment in which it operated. There was also the problem of key personnel able to run it in my absence. Many of our old competitors in the generic and contract drug industry had gone in the last five years and more would follow in the eighties – as Mark Morris had predicted after our loss of the Licences in 1974, "There will only be a handful of independent Generic and Contract Pharmaceutical Manufacturers by 1990". He was proved right. Profitable and rewarding sale of the business remained an aim for perhaps the year 2000 but work needed to be done to do that –- lifestyle spending was out of the question for me. I had to invest in the business, keep independent and achieve the structural change I envisaged.

Annie's Room   There was no way I could afford a house and a mortgage for myself was out of the question but there were spaces at the Putney factory which were unused and we had an on-going situation of renovation, having moved from 10,000 square feet to 30,000. I asked RG if she would help our new architect to sort something out on a tight budget for a kitchen and directors' dining room. We already had services on site and I wasn't fussed about spending a lot of money on it. They soon found something that would do -- 'Annie's Room'.

Many old factories have an 'Annie's Room', a store where junk is put and forgotten. Next to the tall factory chimney, at the rear of the big gas boiler shed and level with the flat roof, was a brick built old working area shed, where, in Victorian times the pressing of mens' heavily starched evening shirts had been done at the Cathkin Laundry. Underneath, was another store made out of the old stables that had been used for the big Shire horses that pulled the huge carts of grain when the building had been a mill, centuries ago. The way down to the yard at the back of the factory was an iron fire escape. It wasn't a space that could be used for staff to work in as there were no windows and only a skylight in the roof for light. Originally, it had been the hay loft over the stables. The bricks were of different sizes and there weren't any straight lines, cavity walls or damp course. The roof was slated, the floor was just concrete and the room was full of old junk that took two days and several skips to clear. There was no ceiling but the slate roof was covered by wooden boards. However, RG thought it had exciting possibilities in spite of the architect throwing up his hands in despair.

I had already decided that it would be more productive to entertain customers and other visitors on site rather than take them out to a restaurant. It had the huge advantages of being much less costly and gave privacy. It also meant I wouldn't have to be away from the factory during working hours. We also needed a kitchen for testing the new special diet flours as part of quality control and for research and development of these products. When my wife had had a new kitchen at home I had not thrown the old one away as there was little wrong with it. I had stored the old one in the cellar at the factory. It was perfectly good with formica surfaces and still had a lot of wear left in it. Now it could be used again.

The stainless steel sink was a really good one and I still had the original taps. Two cheap basic domestic type gas stoves were purchased and large fridge. A large extraction fan was fitted over the kitchen part and a plasterboard partition made a third of the brick shed into the kitchen with the remaining two thirds as a sitting/dining room. We had two maintenance men employed full time at the factory and an electrician. Between them they did the plumbing, decorating and electrics. Central heating was installed. The floor was tidied up and a white vinyl floor in the kitchen was laid with inexpensive, hardwearing carpet in the sitting/dining area. The walls could be just painted over with white emulsion to make the most of their texture rather than have them plastered.

RG said it was a really a Barn Conversion and all the rage. A little entrance hall with bookshelves, a new factory type front door to suit the fire regulations and Annie's Room was beginning to take shape, ready for its new function.

The maintenance men made some racks for a display of medicinal herb plates I had been given by a Swiss pharmaceutical company -- ideal. A large black table and set of black chairs with cane seats were bought in a sale for the dining area. Two enormous Japanese paper light shades lit the room. RG lent me a large oil painting and I had a rather shabby grandfather clock which my father had given me which had seen much better days in a Newbury pub. It had lost its clockwork innards but kept good time with electric works. RG's husband painted it for me -- matt black to match the table and chairs. Two large sofas my wife had left behind, fitted nicely into the sitting area with a black coffee table from Conran. Some decent Wedgewood bone china and cutlery was purchased, also wine glasses and basic pans etc. for the kitchen. The last things to be done were painting the fire escape black and signwriting 'Annie's Room' on the front door. Nobody could be found to do the sign-writing, so Rita did it herself, this being one of the skills she had learnt. She painted it in black on the pale grey door. (The maintenance men were astonished as they didn't know women could sign-write.) The whole project was amazing! A grotty old brick shed full of junk had been transformed into a state of the art directors' dining room and kitchen, on a shoestring. It had only taken two weeks. Whatever would the cost have been if an interior designer had been called in and how much longer would it have taken?

George Meservy, the architect, had made sure everything was in accordance with the fire regulations and pointed out it would always be unsuitable for staff to work in as it had no windows, only a skylight, and no cavity walls. However, the rules for customers and the MD didn't come into this remit and RG would be able to work in it as she was self-employed and therefore not classed as 'staff'. During working hours there was the low hum of the factory machines and the muffled noise of the big gas boilers so it was very much part of a manufacturing factory.

In the kitchen, Rita Greer was able to develop many of her diet foods, QC test her flours and importantly, entertain journalists to meals prepared for the special dieters. The publicity generated by these one-to-one meals – not always lunches – probably made Larkhall one of the best known companies in that field and more than doubled our market profile. Everybody wanted an invite. We entertained a wide variety of people in Annie's Room over the years. MPs, doctors, overseas clients, suppliers, the media, publishers, the bank, advertising agencies, my mother, my children... It also doubled as a boardroom when necessary and it could be used for confidential meetings. RG did the cooking. She would do breakfast for clients from overseas who came straight from the airport, elevenses for clients, lunches for clients, the media, Environmental Health Officers, bank directors and managers, the trade etc. Sometimes we held dinners in the evening too. Because of the privacy enjoyed, meetings in this environment with a nice meal and good wine paid dividends in terms of goodwill. It was beyond anything that could be achieved in a restaurant. In the evenings the factory was silent and had quite a different mood. For more details on Annies Room see appendix p.338.

A Boardroom for meetings With Annie's Room such a success, a proper boardroom was made at the front of the building behind the reception where there was a jumble of old stores. RG worked with the architect and the result was very useful for meetings. It had coffee and tea-making equipment with proper china, a sink and hot water, hidden in a cupboard. The reps were allowed to use it for dealing with customers instead of taking them up the pub. RG and I could also use it for doing live broadcasts on the telephone that saved us travelling to studios.

Brazilian Brothers of Africa   Mr S A Oduneye owned this company -- our most important customer in Nigeria. Until recently this company had been reliable and always paid its bills. However, by 1979 Nigeria was in a poor state and corruption was rife. I knew that Oduneye was doing his best to pay us but my brother decided unilaterally to add interest to the outstanding BBA account each month, without telling Oduneye. I was not surprised when Oduneye visited us and discovered what his debt had mounted up to, he was shocked. He was polite and left. I felt really bad about it, but not my brother. We had shipped Oduneye a Mercedes Car but he never paid us as promised. We lost most of our money and I believe Oduneye was killed in the tribal war. A card dated 5th April 1980 was the last I heard of him.

Complexity of Larkhall's Alternative Healthcare range   For 1979-80 I drew up a publicity programme that I hoped would simplify Larkhall's group product interests, by trying to tie in Blakoe and Omniped with Vitamins, Slimming and Special Diets and a Food Allergy Clinic. Although all these apparently disparate products and services had 'Alternative Healthcare' at their root, acceptance by the public was proving difficult. Looking back, I realize that this concept was not just difficult for consumers but for staff too. Customer Services efficiency and knowledge were vital and most staff were unable to grasp what the company was about – so what chance our customers?

PR   I was writing articles on health through diet and giving radio interviews – one on BBC World Service. RG and myself were becoming well known advocates of Alternative Healthcare – particularly dietary aspects. The willingness of Rita to discuss her regime for Alan was very important in obtaining PR articles with the 'human touch' example so sought after for stories by the newspapers. She spent a lot of time denying that her husband was cured of his MS and stressed that everyone ought to be on a healthy diet.

Both the Greers were aware that Alan's MS was progressive and that all they could do was try and control it -- a very novel idea for its time. In a good year Alan had two relapses. In a bad year he might suffer four. After each relapse he would have to recover and work hard to get back to health again. His story was compelling for the media who saw it as a love story and two people, a hero and heroine, fighting against all the odds and winning. In those days the media tended to concentrate on happy stories. When he had been diagnosed in 1970 Alan was so ill and disabled he had been given only a few months to live by a panel of 10 doctors but he had now lived on well for ten years. For someone who was told he'd never walk again to be able to play golf was exciting to journalists and the public lapped it up. MS had been around for many generations but there was still nothing the doctors could offer and still no definite idea of what caused it. In 2015 there are several kinds of medication but none is particularly effective and so expensive that very few MS patients are given them on the NHS. Still the cause of MS is unknown.

B-17 Laetrile fight   Throughout the year, the B17 Laetrile cancer dietary treatment was having to fight against the establishment on both sides of the Atlantic. In the USA the FDA was attempting a total ban but individual freedom even for terminally sick and elderly people was an important defence. In the UK the authorities were building their case against its use but the very restricted methods of distribution used by Larkhall continued legally. To buy the products containing B17 required a doctor's prescription and a full record of any sale had to be kept on file.

A letter was received from J.C. Wiggins regarding Dr Doug Thorogood who had promised to supply us with B15 and B17, this indicated that there were problems with his undertaking to manufacture them in the UK. Thorogood was moving to Wales. This gave Larkhall a serious supply problem.

Whilst the Laetrile (B17) debate continued there was Official and Medical Establishment opposition. Quality specifications for Injections from companies in Germany and Monte Carlo were unsatisfactory. I was trying to establish agreed quality standards for the injections. There were currently no problems in supplying the injections on a named patient basis. The terms B17 and B15 were permitted by Trading Standards. However, I had not been in favour of our magazine, WHEN, covering Laetrile again without independent scientific support.

WHEN Both Dr Richards and I had been aware of problems with independent articles and lack of outside advertisers which was leading to WHEN being seen as a promotional sales tool rather than an independent journal. He resigned as editor as WHEN was absorbing quite a lot of his time. At the beginning of the year I had been aiming for 6 issues but by mid year No.5 would be the last. Alternative health care had lost out.

Mark Morris Obituary In early January I received a letter from Jackie Jhaveri, an Indian chemist who had worked for several years in Production at Putney. He expressed his feelings of sadness on the death of Mark Morris, in December 1978. Mark had helped him with the Medicines Manufacturing problems in the mid 1970s. I wrote an obituary for Mark that was published in the Chemist and Druggist. I subsequently had a nice letter from our Medicines Inspector who respected Mark's knowledge of the Pharmaceutical Industry going back to the 1920s.

Dust and Inspectors There was a Medicines Inspection at the Charlbury facility and cross contamination issues were raised. Cross contamination had been a constant concern for Inspectors because 'dust' was always generated in the production and packaging of 'Dries' (a term for pharmaceutical products made directly using dry ingredients eg tablets). Dust extraction systems were used to control this but design and construction required expert engineers – most Inspectors had no in-depth knowledge of this technology. Sweeping statements were made by these people as soon as they saw traces of dust in the air in manufacturing departments. Analytical techniques for detecting traces of contaminants were becoming more sensitive so that minute traces could be found in the air in quite sophisticated constructions. Reporting such traces could be used by an Inspector to impress his superior official back at the MCA of his efficiency and perhaps help close down a factory. Larkhall did regular tests to overcome criticisms of this nature.

Atheroma An early February issue of the British Medical Journal carried letters arising from a previous article on 'Fats and atheroma'. I had seen this correspondence and thought of producing a food supplement tablet/capsule to help correct dietary inadequacies leading to arterial disease (atheromas). The result was that the FF-E range was developed around this time to conveniently provide the diet with Vitamin E and the powerful polyunsaturates from Evening Primrose.

Special Diet Foods for Ireland -- a promotion In February, Cantassium had launched Rita Greer Foods in Ireland with a 3-day trip to Dublin with Rita, her husband Alan, Walter O'Connell and me. We began with a meeting in the Montrose Hotel attended by Health Professionals, Coeliac Patients and their families. The place seemed to be in the middle of nowhere and ten minutes before the scheduled start the hall was still empty. Ten minutes later it was packed out. There were many pharmacists there, all wearing cardigans.

Rita did a baking demonstration, making a loaf of bread at the start of her hour and taking it out of the oven baked, at the end. It was well risen with a golden crust and it smelled gorgeous, just like wheat bread yet 100% gluten free. It was enthusiastically received with applause. One man (a coeliac) came up to the stage and asked for a slice of the bread. Rita cut him a slice and buttered it. He ate it and said, 'real bread at last'. The look of joy on his face was amazing. It brought the house down. Someone came up to Rita and asked if she would do an hour on the Gay Byrne radio show the following day. What a coup!

RG and I were under a misapprehension regarding the Irish Prescription Market for Gluten Free Foods. Our distributor and sales representative were sure that the launch would be a great success. However, they failed to tell us that there was virtually no free prescription of this class of product in Ireland and patients had to pay for their foods. The only product allowed for free prescription was bulk Wheat Starch labeled as Gluten Free Flour (of course not really Gluten Free but merely reduced Gluten). In addition the supplier of this Gluten Free Flour was contracted on a price agreed with the Irish Government each year and as a result there were no resources available for dissemination of informative advertising. Cantassium's Rita Greer Mixes, whilst wanted by the patients, could not be afforded by the vast majority. Had RG and I known about this state of affairs we would never have even bothered to do this PR trip.

Despite Rita going on the Gay Byrne popular radio programme live for an hour and getting a huge response to a 'phone in, unsurprisingly, this Irish venture was a complete disaster and I castigated both the sales representative and the distributor for lack of market knowledge. Rita took calls at the hotel one after the other for hours. Seven full sacks of mail were sent to her at the radio station but she didn't receive a single letter as an Irish postal strike had begun. All attempts to retrieve the sacks failed -- I wondered why? We flew back to UK in the opposite mood to which we had flown to Dublin. It was our most brilliant launch ever but nothing could be followed up. A disaster. WOC failed to obtain the sacks of mail or the tape recording of the Gaye Byrne show despite staying on a few more days in Dublin for that very purpose.

Gluten Free double standards   In March, I was in correspondence with a GP Dr B. Morgan-Williams regarding Gluten Free foods on prescription. I argued that whilst the Department of Health closes factories making medicines which have minute traces of contaminants present, the department openly permits Gluten Free ingredients containing Gluten as a contaminant to be used in foods prescribed to Coeliacs. Subsequently Dr Morgan-Williams wrote an article for the GP magazine 'Pulse' about the dilemmas and history surrounding prescription of Gluten Free flours/mixes. Useful but reaction from prescribers was unknown.

Pharmacy and Heathy Eating   I had an extensive interview with Chemist and Druggist outlining my plans for improving the Nation's Diet advocating that pharmacies promote Wholefood Healthy Eating. I emphasised that the term 'Balanced diet' was not specific enough nor was its content understood by consumers.

Inspections   At the end of May we had a Medicines Inspection. There were still plenty of queries. It was felt that on this visit that the inspector was asking for greater detail on Raw Material Certificates of Analysis received from our suppliers than was being asked of larger companies. I was convinced that the Inspectorate was playing games with companies, trying to drive up regulatory requirements unnecessarily.

Our Inspector was certainly one of the awkward squad. We would not accept all his requests and asked for justification. Cross contamination was the Inspectorate's current favourite topic. I believed the Inspectors were poorly qualified in the design of air filtering systems and would soon capitulate to scientific results measuring cross contamination and a letter from a real air movement expert. They did.

Success: Cantabread approved for prescription on the NHS   In May, there was a Parliamentary question on Gluten Free prescribing. There were congratulations for achieving Cantabread on the Prescription list. (It was 100% Gluten Free made to RG's formula.) In July Cantabread officially achieved its NHS prescription status -- the first 100% Gluten Free Bread Mix to do so. It was for Coeliacs but not MS Patients. This caused some distress to MS sufferers but there was no scientific evidence of a Gluten Free Diet benefiting that illness. On prescription it could not be advertised to the public and could not be displayed in pharmacies. It had become an under-the-counter product. We needed to ensure dietitians to spread the word as this was our only hope of promoting it. So we tried that route.

Another disastrous promotion   RG had done the artwork for a black and white pack for the Cantabread suitable for a prescription product. My brother had it printed on such poor quality card that was so weak it failed to hold the inner bag of flour without collapsing.

The promotion to dietitians, using a sample of sufficient Cantabread Flour Mix to make a loaf, was organised and took place in September. Unfortunately, the factory at Charlbury made a major error when preparing the flour mix and used **ten** times the correct amount of carob bean powder. They completely ignored the quality control required. The sample mix should have been sent to Rita for testing and she would have spotted the mistake immediately. It was not sent to her for testing but sent out to dietitians as the free sample. This error ruined the effectiveness of the mailing promotion because the bread mix baked to a solid brown, chocolate flavoured brick! What a disaster.

I was very angry when I found out. As a consequence, I stopped all future manufacturing of the flours at Charlbury and had the machinery sent to Putney, where proper skills and quality controls operated. This caused a major dispute with my brother but I felt he just could not be trusted with manufacturing. Sadly, he could turn on the charm for the Inspectors but any criticism of the Charlbury operation from Putney was always unacceptable to him. Not a recipe for family harmony. "We never make mistakes at Charlbury" was his claim - perfect people!

RG was furious about what had happened, particularly after she spoke to my brother about it. He shrugged his shoulders, laughed and said, "that's manufacturing". He couldn't have cared less about the error and its consequences. She decided she had no option other than to abandon her range of Rita Greer Foods after the 'chocolate bread' debacle and start another brand under a different name instead of her own. Cantabread would have to be abandoned.

From the sales of her mixes it had become obvious that the bread mix was by far the most popular and the first of them was now on prescription. She formulated special flours for different kinds of gluten/wheat free breads and plain and self-raising flour blends for home bakers. Rita Greer Foods had been a useful toe in the water but it was time to move on. It would require two brands -- one for prescription that could not be advertised to the public and one for shops and mail order that could, in one-colour packaging to save on printing costs.

Trufree and Jubilee brands RG decided on the name 'Trufree' which indicated the brand was entirely free of gluten/wheat. As the flours were produced by pharmaceutical methods she would be able to flag up 100% gluten free -- something our competitors would not be able to copy. She designed a logo style name where the 'f' curved back on itself and crossed an ear of wheat. The packs were to cost less and be larger, in one colour on white. Each type of flour would be in a different colour for identification and have a large number on the front. She immediately registered the Trufree name and logo as trademarks.

As the rules regarding advertising of prescription products were so severe as to be ridiculous, Rita also designed Jubilee packs that looked very similar. This was in case the rest of her special diet flours went on prescription so the Jubilee version would be for 'prescription only' packs and the Trufree flours, made to the same formulas could be advertised, sold over the counter and by mail order. Rita worked on the packaging designs for her upcoming range of Flour Mixes herself. By designing her own packaging she was avoiding the costs of an agency doing this work.

I thought it most unlikely we would achieve the flours on prescription but she was much more positive and determined about it than me and believed we would. Time proved her right.

Purchase of a Health Store Walter O'Connell indemnified me regarding purchase of Nature's Store in Streatham. Walter had become involved with this Health Store, supposedly to be managed by his wife who had previously worked in a bank. He said she had agreed to help him but there was a snag that I had pointed out -- there was a lease involved with the property and O'Connell was taking on a serious liability. He wouldn't listen and went on with it. Subsequently he tried to bring me in. I refused, and to ensure my position I insisted on an indemnity from him. In the end it all came to nothing, like so many of his schemes.

Body image books In August, Dr Richards and I had a meeting to discuss the future after closure of 'WHEN' magazine. The Body Image series of books would be written by him and he hoped for product spin-offs following widespread advertising of these books. I believed there would be no problems with the Advertising Standards Authority since other companies were promoting alternative healthcare books at that time. However, by the end of the year the ASA were clamping down on this sort of product promotion through books and the project was forced to become very low key and consequently without commercial success. Dr Richards had big ambitions but seemed to not fully appreciate the regulatory straitjacket surrounding manufacture and supply of Heath products in the UK. Titles in the series included' Live to be a Hundred', 'The Bust', 'Hair', 'Skin', 'Female Problems' etc. They were produced by a small printer and RG did the illustrations.

Dr Cicliteria a researcher into Gluten Free ingredients In September I received a letter from Dr Ciclitira, a gastroenterologist at Addenbrooke's Hospital in Cambridge, inviting RG to demonstrate her Gluten Free foods. A meeting in mid October was agreed. This was a good opportunity. Ciclitira was one of the people researching cultivation of a strain of wheat to be naturally gluten free. His, ultimately unsuccessful, project was partly funded by the Coeliac Society. As RG said, "What is the point of that research when people can make perfectly good bread with many naturally gluten free cereals?". As it turned out, the meeting was called off. The Coeliac Society had been informed of it and that was that. Sadly, in spite of all the trail blazing work she had done to improve the life of coeliacs, to the Coeliac society RG was somebody that had to be stopped.

Foresight, the first Charity for Preconceptual Care   In October I had my first contact with Mrs Nim Barnes, the founder of Foresight, The Association for Preconceptual care. This charity was founded in 1978 and Cantassium's emphasis on natural purity product standards appealed to Mrs Barnes. For the next 20 years we were to be their only supplier for dietary supplements that helped the organization to achieve remarkable success in preventing Birth Defects, Miscarriages and Enclampsia. It also helped many previously infertile couples achieve a healthy baby naturally.

Death of George Orange Woodward   My father's health had gradually deteriorated since his stroke, he also had dementia as well as diabetes. He died on 12th November 1979 at the age of 68, having been nursed at home by my mother. I sent an obituary to the Chemist and Druggist with a special reference to the role of the DHSS Medicines Inspectors in his death.

"Unfortunately, in his latter years the policy of the DHSS Medicines Inspectorate towards his company caused him great distress because he took it all as if he was criminally accused by these people. He was a small businessman who had built a company by hard work only to see it crushed by the might of a merciless bureaucracy who had no understanding of how a small family firm operated. His health suffered and undoubtedly these troubles led directly to his premature death". His obituary was published, but unsurprisingly without the last paragraph.

Bank relations   In November I attended Barclays Bank London Branch Managers Dinner once again at Grosvenor House, in the Great Room. In July, John Ball, a local director, had visited our Charlbury factory. Afterwards, the Bank was reluctant to approve money for the proposed extensions. He did not seem to have been impressed at all by my brother. Our established facilities had been approved in March but I was left in little doubt that without me directing the company these facilities would have been in jeopardy.

Gluten Free products still create interest   The Pharmaceutical Journal published a letter from me about the Gluten Free controversy and told of the failure of the Coeliac Society to come to terms with scientific fact that some so-called 'Gluten Free Foods' were not actually gluten free, although legally labeled as such.

I had a letter from an MS sufferer who was doing well on a gluten free diet but could not have the prescribable items because MS was not a permitted disease for coeliac foods. He hoped Cantabread would be permitted – alas, it was not.

Pharmacist David Hammond expressed interest in naturally gluten free products. At least one health professional was listening.

Generic vs Brand continued   In December the Generic vs Branded Drugs argument was highlighted in the Daily Telegraph. I wrote emphasizing that the large discounts given by some generic companies made their products suspect. In the last analysis, Brand is best but my views were based on the importance of quality and purity of the powerful drug industry chemicals – I did not support their excessive use and prescription. My letter entitled 'too many drugs' is still of interest. It advocated less prescription of medicines, more emphasis on wholefood based diets and less body abuse (smoking & drinking).

A letter in 2010 to the Daily Telegraph from a Doctor (29.11) was entitled 'Too many medicines' and demonstrated that the problem was worse 30 years later, but no reference was made to the role of wholefood based diets and body abuse. So the message was not yet clear but by 2014 press articles on the importance of lifestyle and diet and against wonder pills for every ill were becoming more frequent.

Smells I received a complaint from the local Environmental Health Department about 'smells' emanating from the factory in Putney. This was an on going problem and continued, despite our new air control system. These complaints varied so much that there was little we could do. Garton's sugar factory was not far away and we continually attracted the blame for their 'smells' which were really unpleasant. After they closed down the number of complaints fell markedly. However, an impecunious titled lady moved into the house next door to us, at the side of the yard. She lost no time in demanding that the factory be closed down and sending in complaints to the council who then had to send an officer round to take tests which proved negative. A man who had moved into the street opposite also wanted the factory shut down as he had allergies. A different man came and did the tests all over again with the same result. No wonder the business rates on the premises were so high.

Future In 1979 I experienced many changes in my life and attempted to plan for a future business based on the Brands. I had realized in the mid 70s that growing the business with contract work was unlikely. The decade had seen the demise of contractors unable to cope with regulations or who were bankrupted by the demands of regulators. Too many companies thought that by upgrading their facilities all would be OK – but there were too many chasing a static market with a greatly increased cost base. Larkhall upgraded their two factories but with the intention that regulated medicinal production would be allowed to decline gradually. Companies had to decide between large contract orders for marketers or serving consumers with their own brand. Marketer companies would be unlikely to purchase their products from a manufacturer competing with them with own brands of similar products.

Larkhall had now established their brands and plans for future promotion were sketched out with a broad natural Health and Beauty base.

Training videos RG and I made training videos for the mail order staff at no cost except our time. We made them in Annie's Room. The mail order staff would watch them in the boardroom and were kept up to date with new products. These videos proved immensely popular and educational with the office but the sales reps hated them as they left the mail order sales staff better informed. They had to be discontinued when my brother intimated they should be made by a professional film company - that would have cost a fortune I thought. Spending thousands of pounds to regularly make a training video for a handful of office staff was ridiculous. Sadly, my brother could never accept that our in-house efforts were ever right. He was always in favour of consultants and agencies.

Publishers and gluten free cooking Rita Greer's book 'Gluten Free Cooking' was published by Thorsons. They had approached her as they saw her success with her own published gluten free books and said the law was on their side -- they could copy her books and just change just 10%. They were correct. She had no choice but to agree to write one. It is still in print in 2015.

ABPI swansong In October, I attended the annual conference of the ABPI in Gleneagles Hotel, Perthshire with W. O'Connell. It was the last conference attended by G O Woodward & Co, who subsequently resigned. My father had joined this Trade association back in the early 1950s to gain contact with the more important Pharma Companies. He had networked hard to gain membership. This had been a good move, but by the 1980s the Company had distanced itself from Pharma. The subscription was totally out of line for what we could afford and there was little commonality of interest.

Key staff change   Towards the end of the year, I wrote to Medicines Inspector explaining the departure of a key qualified employee and subsequent diminishing of the qualified Pharmacist level at Larkhall. New arrangements were in hand and hopefully would be in place soon. We had to refer these matters to the Inspector because that was a demand of the Inspectorate. At this time a review of our Manufacturer's Licence was imminent.

All packaging of Medicinal Products was transferred to the Charlbury premises. Fortunately, Dennis Hooker had proved to be a dependable and hardworking manager.

Family Differences   When my father died this year, the old era ended. I thought my brother understood the changes that were needed but he did not. My mother then came into her own and defended the work I was doing as she had seen the contrast between life in 'Sleepy Hollow' Charlbury in the Cotswolds and the huge burden and continuous stress in Putney, London.

New Direction Established

Cantassium Prize and guiding principles - Legislative threats - The Crossed Grain - Members of the Lords and Commons - Health Food a criminal trade description - Food Allergy a fashionable illness - Pebble Mill at one - Coeliac Society upset - Bryce Smith and Zinc - The Mark Morris legacy - Belief and Evidence Based Treatments - Rt Hon David Mellor MP - Pharmacists not interested in non-drug treatments - HFMA conflict of interest - W5 Skin nutrition - Blister Packing - Purity of Life subliminal Advertising

Cantassium Prize. In May we exhibited at the Helfex Exhibition in Brighton. RG came to the rescue by engraving a glass decanter with a countryside scene and an inscription as I couldn't find anything suitable for the first prize. We presented it at the exhibition, the first Cantassium Prize, to the retailer that our judges had found to meet the criteria essential for a Health Food Store. Unfortunately, most stores were stocking products that were closer to Pharmaceutical Products than natural preparations. Most were packaged in ways that wasted nature's resources. They were conceived by advertising agencies rather than those who were grounded in the fundamental principles of the original wholefood stores which began around 1900. We felt that the Healthfood trade had to return to those ideals if it was to overcome its enemies who saw them as 'Snake Oil' salesmen. This vulnerability could soon mean that they would be put out of business by the Medicines legislation unless something changed.

The prize created some difficulties with the reps, one had promised the first prize to two of his retailers and when they did not impress the judges he was furious. Many of the entrants thought it was a fix as they didn't understand what it was about.

Legislative Threats and Poor Industry Standards Thanks to my knowledge of Pharmaceutical manufacturing, I could see the danger more clearly than the grocers who controlled most of the Health Food industry. Having come from the food industry these people were attracted by the much higher profits of drugs over foods. Make our 'Food Supplements' appear like pharmaceuticals and you can sell Seaweed at the profit levels of Librium. This was dangerous but with the growing popularity of items like Ginseng, Pollen, Royal Jelly, Vitamin E etc, investigative journalists could soon sink the industry if it was not vigilant.

Our company produced several pieces of publicity used to inform journalists, retailers, doctors and consumers about the fundamental difference between wholesome Diet Supplements and Pharmaceutical Drugs despite their apparent similarity. This perceived similarity was growing as High Street Chemists began to take an interest in 'Health Foods and Supplements'. They had always stocked items like 'Redoxon' Brand of Vitamin C by Roche and the Yeastvite, Phyllosan, Sanatogen and Seven Seas Cod Liver Oil but were now looking at Healthcrafts, Efamol, Red Kooga Ginseng and Pollen B.

The big pharmaceutical companies had no interest in 'Naturally Based' supplements and made their products using the same methods, chemical sources and additives as for their drugs like aspirin, penicillin, tranquillisers etc. Some Vitamin Supplement makers, in their ignorance, were also adopting the 'Pharmaceutical' construct for their products even openly describing their product ingredients as 'Pharmaceutically Pure'. In other words they were offering Food Supplements that were stripped of all the naturally occurring substances found with vitamins and minerals in the natural environment.

LARKHALL GREEN FARM

It was not surprising that before long Trading Standards Officials would be saying that the designation 'Health Food' was misleading and should be outlawed. Unfortunately, the leaders of the Health Food Trade failed to understand the truth and did not insist that Health Shops only stocked real health products. Attempts later by the health food industry (mid 1980s) to enforce a 'Health Mark' standard failed because of lack of support from the dominant companies who were happily misleading the public with poorly made synthetically based products. Even worse was the development of publicised standards, stated to meet the requirements of official sounding bodies such as 'The International Office of Food Standards' -- all with no independent assessors and financed entirely by manufacturers.

Earl Mindell leaflets and The Vitamin Bible Earl Mindell was an American Pharmacist who wrote a best selling book 'The Vitamin Bible'. On the basis of his brilliantly titled book he authored leaflets 'Deficiency Symptoms of Vitamins' and 'Deficiency Symptoms of Minerals' and many others. These leaflets all dated 1980 were widely distributed in the Health Food market in the USA and later in the UK. They tell you much about the Vitamin Industry. Mindell put most illnesses down as probable deficiency diseases. No wonder the Industry was facing legal opposition as the 'Snake Oil seller of the 1980s'. The caveat on all leaflets was 'The information in this article is not intended as Medical Advice but only as a guide in working with your doctor'.

Good Review The Staffordshire Sentinel published a review of Good Food to fight Migraine by Hilda Cherry Hills. This was the first of Cherry Hills's books published by 'Roberts Publications' and was well received both in UK and USA. We also distributed and reprinted her three other Books: Living Dangerously (1961), Good Food Gluten Free (1973) and Good Food Grain Free Milk Free (1978).

The Coeliac Society Much time was still being taken up by the Gluten Free disputes. The ideas of Genetic Modification were being explored to modify Gluten in wheat to render it safe for Coeliacs.

Our Advertising Agents were finding it impossible to obtain acceptance of our advertising by the Crossed Grain (Coeliac Society Magazine). The excuse of lack of space was credible as the magazine was very small. However, by the end of October a different agency was refused space on the grounds that it was from the Cantassium Company. The Coeliac Society itself would not permit that company to use its publication. (RG was told all their space in their magazine was fully booked up for years.) This was a restriction of trade and illegal. So, we had a fight on our hands because their magazine, key to the Gluten Free market, was used by our competitors. All the products advertised in the magazine were made from wheat starch that contained gluten. This was incredible and so wrong that something had to be done by us to protect the coeliac patients from their own charity.

At the end of December I wrote a letter to Coeliac Society complaining that our special diet foods were not listed in their official list and inferring that this was deliberate.

International Generics Through the good offices of General Drummond, I learned that International Generics were concerned about the status of their relationship with Larkhall. They wanted the front of a manufacturers licence but did not order product from us. I said that without orders then I could not co-operate on the Licence. Leon Tamman sent his son Danny to see me in April, followed by lunch with the General at the RAG (Army and Navy) Club in St James's.

95

There was no apparent progress regarding sales but I succeeded in obtaining for our company an annual fee without strings from IG. This enabled IG as a UK based export company to put 'Holder of a UK Medicines Manufacturing licence' on commercial documents to impress and reassure all their customers.

Lord Rank   In the spring, I had correspondence with Joseph Rank (later Lord Rank) the Chief of Rank Hovis McDougall, one of UK's largest Flour Millers. The correspondence did not attack our Gluten Free stance. He first heard of me after listening to an interview on LBC radio at 6.35 am one morning in April. His importance as an honorary Vice President of the British Nutrition Foundation and honorary Fellow of the Royal College of Physicians may be relevant to future awareness of me and Larkhall at the centre of Nutrition Establishment.

Too many drugs   Rt Hon Stanley Orme MP wrote thanking me for my support for the argument that **too many drugs were being prescribed**. Orme was trying to have his views aired in Parliament but he was not successful. No doubt the Medical Profession and the Pharmaceutical Industry lobbied against him.

Inspections   We had appointment-arranged visits from Medicine's Inspectors to Charlbury and London. Charlbury did well but was only an assembler of medicinal products not a manufacturer. London's more complex operation still had much to do although its medicines were mainly made for export. However, the month's delay in receiving the letter following the visit meant we had no critical problems. There were no major problems either. The reports were nit-picking but confirmed my view that the future for the family business, as currently capitalized, did not lie in Licensed Medicinal Product manufacture.

New Premises near Oxford?   In May my brother reported on a visit to an empty Tweed Mill near Witney that was for disposal, leasehold. I went to see it but thought it unsuitable for Larkhall except at a very advantageous price. Nevertheless, the advantages of putting the London and Charlbury functions together were worth exploring. Sadly, the differences in approach and vision between my brother and I were already becoming obvious. There was family tension and intransigence to be overcome before progress could be made. It was vital that compromises were made but there had to be give on both sides. We didn't go ahead with it.

'Health Food' a criminal trade misdescription   The June issue of Health Food Trader carried headlines about this legal threat from a Trading Standards Officer. I reacted with a long letter explaining the purpose of the 'Cantassium Prize' that was aimed at retailers who gave their stores a professional environment, in line with the products stocked. In response I sent about 1000 words on the way that the Health Food Industry was making big mistakes – praising products that are basically 'Pharmaceuticals' and pretending they are 'Natural'. If read in conjunction with the Trader letter mentioned above, a very good case was made for going in a different direction, as Larkhall did.

Health Food Personality   CTP Marketing carried an article by Kim Pearl on Health Foods. Many personalities in the Health Food Trade were quoted including Maurice Hanssen, Cyril Argent and me. I was given the last word. Not unconnected with the author's contact with me in June, I had, as usual, replied immediately on receiving a letter from Kim Pearl. These direct PR efforts with no agency involved were vital to the company at this time.

Cheated MS   August, article on Alan Greer, 'The Man who cheated MS', by Tom Tobin in the Limerick Weekly Echo. Tobin was an acquaintance of Walter O'Connell and staying at the Tara Hotel in Kensington where he had interviewed Alan and Rita. This was the title of the resulting article and there was also a Radio interview with Rita on the local station. We had still not given up hope in Ireland for the Special Diet Foods but this article, despite emphasizing the importance of 'Gluten Free' to Alan, made no impact whatsoever on sales or prospects.

Food Allergy - fashionable illness   Here's Health Magazine carried an article entitled 'ALLERGY -- Fashionable disease of the Eighties' by former editor of the magazine Simon Martin. Quite a perceptive and comprehensive article mentioning many of the people, lay and medical, taking Food Allergy seriously including Larkhall and Rita Greer. Simon was a friend and a frequent guest at lunches and dinners held at Larkhall, in Annie's Room, for journalists and medical professionals. All food was prepared by RG and tailored, if necessary, to cater for individuals suffering Food Allergies. Simon's article was followed by one by Vicky Rippere a medical professional at 'The Institute of Psychiatry' at the Maudsley Hospital attached to Kings College Hospital in Denmark Hill. Hans Eysenck was the Professor there and he was to help Larkhall in their fight against Shropshire Trading Standards in 1992. (Tandem IQ). Like me, Eysenk held many controversial views that clashed with the establishment line.

Lectures   In October, following a successful lecture in Sheffield, Rita and I went to Plymouth, invited by eminent pharmacist and homoeopath Mervyn Madge. We talked to the local branch of the Pharmaceutical Society on 'A prescription for Health Foods' including Special Diet Foods. These lectures were always well attended but were very time consuming for us. Sadly, there was no-one else on the staff we could rely upon to give these talks and correctly answer the questions arising. We came back from this one at 2.30 in the morning, all the way from Devon -- a long day.

Balanced Diet   I argued with journalist Arthur Smith of the Daily Mirror, regarding the myth of the 'Balanced Diet'. This diet only covers the single referenced and familiar Carbohydrates, Fats and Proteins. I told Smith that without further qualification this description was useless and would not help improve public health. The importance of including wholesome and combined sources like wholemeal flours and vegetable oils and excluding synthetic and purified items such as white sugar, white flour and hydrogenated fats, with a reduction in salt (sodium) must also be highlighted. Junk foods were not limited to fizzy drinks, sugary cakes and confectionery.

Recommendation for Blakoe   Marjorie Proops, a very much respected 'Agony Aunt' on the Daily Mirror was recommending Blakoe Ltd as a bona fide source of information on sex and health.

Naturtabs The concept of 'Real Food Supplements' was explained in a colour advertisement used in Health Magazines like Here's Health.

Healthmark   A leader in the magazine Food Manufacture was somewhat critical of the Health Food Trade and the new 'Healthmark Code'. This illustrated the academic debate going on at this time.

Steady Progress

Pebble Mill at One (BBC1 TV) Through a personal contact (no agency involved), in March, Rita and Alan Greer went on the BBC1 TV programme 'Pebble Mill at One'. Live in the Birmingham Studio, it went out nationally at lunchtime to over two million viewers. Rita and Alan were interviewed about MS and how a change in lifestyle and the special diet designed by Rita and exercise had helped Alan overcome his disabilities. Rita prepared a loaf of bread from the Trufree Cantabread Mix. At the end of the eight minute slot the address of Larkhall Laboratories, 225 Putney Bridge Road was shown on screen and read out by the presenter. (We couldn't believe it.) The resulting mail received at Larkhall via the TV studios was about 18,500 letters and took RG three months to open, read and answer. They put out a mention on the programme a week later to say the postbag had been overwhelming but everybody's letter would be answered. And they were.

Another fight The interest generated by this single programme had major repercussions for both Rita and the Company. It increased Larkhall's profile in the gluten free food area and greatly angered our competitors but more significantly the Coeliac Society. The Society used their unique position to try and undermine Larkhall's development and were aided by their food industry sponsors and supporters. Much vested interest was at stake -- the Society's staff, the medical researchers they supported, their medical advisers and the Wheat Starch Producers. The Society used its power in all these directions to undermine Larkhall and effectively banned them from advertising in the Crossed Grain Magazine and exhibiting and contacting Coeliac Area Leaders of Patient Groups.

This situation was outrageous but unexceptional. Throughout the 70s, 80s, and 90s Larkhall's views on the diets and lifestyles of the UK population constantly brought them into conflict with the vested interests of Government, Charities and Industry. The Coeliac (Gluten Free) dispute was the first major one but would be followed by the School Children Diet (Tandem IQ) at the end of the decade. Then it was not just wheat starch manufacturers but the entire Junk Food industry, with the assistance of their close allies in the Pharmaceutical business who opposed us with a ferocity calculated to finish us.

The Food Allergy Clinic, Laboratory and Books This clinic was opened at Larkhall in June under the direction of Dr Jean Monro. It operated on Thursdays using a small facility within the reception area. The patients were tested using a reaction to challenge on skin. Many also purchased foods and supplements that met their allergy purity demands.

This pilot was successful so that by September I made arrangements for the front half of the building facing Putney Bridge Road to be converted from a canteen to a laboratory, enabling blood tests to be carried out. This would mean we could analyse blood samples for hidden Food Allergies and discontinue use of the skin applied challenge tests that could cause anaphylactic shock in patients. (A new canteen was built in the corner of the warehouse.)

Food Allergy books were in demand and Rita Greer and I wrote 'Food Allergy, A Practical Easy Guide'. This book and others gained good publicity as Food Allergy became an almost fashionable illness for many, mostly female, sufferers. These books gained us many radio interviews through our PR agency.

The Sanity Charity The Charity 'Sanity', under the direction of Mrs Margery Hall in Pinner, Middlesex, was recommending Cantassium low allergy supplements and arranging Hair and Blood Tests for mentally affected patients. Most of these tests were being carried out in the USA although some UK firms were showing interest particularly in doing Hair Analysis. It was recommended that Peter Fennel be contacted and interviewed as a possible leader of the Allergy Services at Larkhall. He had been a captain in the army, working in a blood unit. Around this time Dr David Freed of University of Manchester Medical School was becoming well known in the Food Allergy world. I went to see him and his colleague Janet Ditchfield in Manchester to discuss new tests they were researching.

Professor Bryce Smith I began to hear much about the research work of Professor Bryce Smith of Reading University. He was making a name for himself through his research into lead pollution and its affect on mental efficiency. It was through his work that lead was removed from petrol. Bryce Smith was an excellent communicator whose researches were supported by several charities. He was a friend of Sanity and Margery Hall. Later he became involved in Zinc research in connection with the common cold but this time his ideas failed to obtain credibility and his proposed remedy for the common cold failed to obtain a Medicines Licence – unsurprising since there was the powerful OTC medication lobby who wanted no threat to their cold symptom remedies from food supplements.

Lipcote Whilst not a direct fit within Larkhall's health ranges, the lipstick sealer Lipcote had become our best selling brand. I was contacted by Nigel Halsby of Dendron Ltd in Rickmansworth offering to act as the Chemist Trade distributor of Lipcote. He had seen its growth in recent years through wider advertising. By August we had agreed to go ahead with Lipcote and Ruthmol our Salt Free Salt. Initially, we excluded Boots from the agreement but within 2 years Dendron were distributing the products to the entire UK Chemist Trade. Their sales force of some 12 people were fairly successful but I thought that Larkhall's products were inevitably in the second slot so far as the sales people were concerned. Only by developing our own sales force would we ensure optimum exposure and distribution. Dendron tried other Larkhall Products including the Cantamegas over the years but none got off the ground despite considerable investment.

This was a dilemma experienced by many smaller manufacturers. Sales forces were costly to operate and, at that time, difficult to control but could give valuable feedback from the retailer/consumer interface. I set out in the 1970s to do without a sales force and rely on direct sales drives using trade advertisements, loose leaflet inserts and direct store mailings. On several occasions I tried the sales force route with regrets. Ultimately, we used a sales agency with no products of its own but even these took on exclusive agencies from overseas that were always treated as 'number ones'.

Advertising In developing a Brand Business, advertising and promotion were the most costly items. So called Full Service Advertising Agencies operated in an unreal world surrounded by restrictive practices. I was finding this overhead too much and determined to breakaway.

So, In June the company bought a second hand IBM Typesetting Machine that Rita could use in her studio. It was portable enough so that she could work on it in London and at her home. The costs of advertising production using our agency had reached 75pence a word in small classifieds. Using Rita's skills this was reduced to under a pound per advertisement. She did artwork for a fraction of the agency charges too. The days of Larkhall using full service advertising agencies were nearly over. The only problem was the print union National Graphical Association (NGA) who operated something akin to a protection racket with printers, insisting that all print artwork be stamped by them or blacked for printing. Rita had to become a member of this union as she had already been reported, so we kept costs low.

We worked together on copy writing, design of both advertisements and new products. We could have a new product available for sale in weeks instead of the usual months without frittering away time on endless meetings. With the number of products we now had and the diverse nature of the range, I felt it was beyond any handling by an agency. The costs would have been enormous and crucifying.

I thought Larkhall still needed a prestige advertisement and took the outside back cover of Here's Health on a regular basis to ensure awareness of the Cantassium Brands was maintained. A scatter of small advertisements throughout that magazine ensured no one forgot the Larkhall ranges. All design and copy was produced in-house without any delay.

The Mark Morris legacy After Mark's death in December 1978, I helped Joan Morris to continue his Richmond Order Company business. Mark had intimated several times that he had left the business to me but on his death there was only one Will found and, quite rightly, that left it all to his wife. Strangely, I was not the only one led to expect to have control of Mark's company – Eric Mapley of Laleham Packers and John Rugless, our raw materials buyer were also expecting to inherit, as was Walter O'Connell our sales representative. I accepted the situation and actively cleared up the outstanding contracts with export firms, took direct control of the Wassen Pollen Contract and helped Joan with the Mother Brown Knee support business. There were several loose ends that were never really cleared because records were incomplete. This was inevitable with a one-man company. Joan was advised to liquidate by Mark's accountant of many years.

Joan did not know anything about the business, believed that the Mother Brown Kneecaps had a future and that the little company was worth millions. I told her that threats from the regulators would soon become great because of the radioactive Thorium used to impregnate the kneecaps and that the products were now old-fashioned. By the end of 1981 Joan had left the Putney Office and Mother Brown's came under Larkhall supervision as it rapidly declined. The financial area was cleared up but I always thought that Joan believed she had lost out. Her complete lack of knowledge about Mark's business made it impossible to talk to her rationally. When she tried to sell Mother Brown as a going concern she failed to find a buyer. Her letter to me dated 15th September 1981 said it all.

The start of the 'Belief Based' and 'Evidence based' argument and Ocutrien In November I wrote once more to the Pharmaceutical Journal, deploring the way that evidence based healthcare was depriving people of excellent treatments. Why not permit products with good anecdotal evidence to be recommended by Doctors and Pharmacists provided they were clearly labeled as such? The product used as an example was the Eye Nutritional Supplement 'Ocutrien' formulated by Dr Stanley Evans. My long time pharmaceutical friend Arthur Chamings introduced Evans to me and over the years Ocutrien became a good line in Larkhall's lists but it never received official recognition from either the Optical Profession or doctors. Yet Evans knew it saved many Africans their sight through his work as a young man in Nigeria, where the eye disease glaucoma was widespread.

These arguments have continued for many years and even in 2015 I am promoting the concept of Placebos/Health integrators being drawn together in a legal framework within 'Belief Based' healthcare and to be clearly separated in stores/catalogues/websites from 'Evidence Based' care. Perhaps one day the authorities will see the advantage to both regulators and consumers of these ideas.

The Coeliac Society and Frank Skingsley   In February, at last, the Coeliac Society wrote asking for our list of Gluten Free products for admission into their list of safe food for Coeliacs. This was a bible for those patients and we submitted the list. There seemed to be progress in our relations with the Society and we were hopeful but by June things were not so good. Our advertising was again refused for their Magazine. It was where all our competitors advertised. They used their regular Delegate Conferences to ensure we were not favoured as a manufacturer of GF foods. Frank Skingsley, our new sales representative, became active and tried to mend fences with the Society. His reports make interesting reading. We exhibited at a medical Exhibition in Glasgow in September. The hostility from other manufacturers of low Gluten foods was palpable. Our stance on the 100% Gluten Free issue was hurting them and baked up samples (by RG) such as rich fruit cake showed what a superior product Trufree was compared with the run of the mill GF products sold by other companies.

Bread Mix labelling problem madness   In April, Officials from Wandsworth Council visited Larkhall to report a complaint from Herefordshire Trading Standards concerning Jubilee Bread Mix. Since the mix did not contain wheat it could not lawfully use the term 'Bread Mix' in any way. We argued that this was nonsense so far as Jubilee Bread Mix was concerned. The regulations had been promulgated before the era of Free From Foods and were out of date. It was obvious that the officials were anxious not to be involved in a court case. It was eventually agreed that the product would be renamed "Jubilee Wheat Free Bread Mix" and this satisfied them. However this was not the last of this problem. For some time it has had to be called 'loaf mix' which was only allowed because there was a food product called meat loaf, also allowed.
In the pipeline, a few years ahead, was more trouble regarding bread/loaf versus cake. By then our relationship with our local Wandsworth officials had deteriorated, owing to a change in staff who seemed dedicated against our ideals.

'Cure for Arthritis'   I complained to the Royal Pharmaceutical Society about displays in the leading health food chain shop windows for 'A cure for Arthritis', a claim that had been unlawful for decades. This was never followed up but the displays were withdrawn.

David Mellor MP for Putney   In March, David Mellor MP for Putney visited Larkhall's factory. The visit was reported in local papers. I had recently joined the local Conservative business group, later led by my friend from Glaxo, Sir Austin Bide. At this time Austin had retired from executive management at Glaxo. Mellor came to dinner with his wife and father in August. Later in the year I asked for his assistance with the Coeliac Society and NHS prescribing. A meeting was arranged at the House of Commons but he failed to turn up. Many years later I was out at lunch with Leon Tamman of International Generics, sometime President of Sephardic Jewry, after Mellor had made a speech as a Foreign Office Minister, criticizing Israel. Leon said that as a result Mellor might be a marked man. That probably meant trouble. I got back to the office in Putney and put a call through to Mellor who was at that time Chief Secretary to the Treasury. My call was refused so I could not warn him. He did not return my call as I had asked. The next weekend the Antonia De Sancha scandal broke and finished Mellor's ministerial career.

Pharmacists were not interested in Preventative Care with Health Foods   In the April-May period we used a new loose insert in Chemist & Druggist headed 'How to profit from Naturally Ethical Health Foods'. This was an effort to find out whether Pharmacists might yet be persuaded to consider how real health food products could feature in their stores.

Although a few responses were received the interest was generally disappointing. I concluded that Pharmacists were doing nicely with their current OTC ranges and their dependence on the Pharmaceutical Industry and Medical Profession. Dispensing NHS prescriptions was their real interest and a concept of 'Preventative Health Care with Ethical Health Foods' made little professional or commercial sense to them.

Thirty days to better health   In August, a booklet 'Thirty Days to Better Health' was published by Bruce King, who was a friend of Walter O'Connell. This book was written to sell supplements in his shop. His book recommended a multi antioxidant formula based on the ideas of Dr Roger Williams the American discoverer of Pantothenic Acid. By chance the formula was close to that of Cantamega 2000, one of Larkhall's most successful products. I thought that helped Bruce promote his course.

The Health Food Manufacturers Association (Fighting Fund)   In June I was encouraged by Barry Taylor the MD of Healthilife Ltd (A Health Food marketing company) to join the HFMA Fighting Fund, a group consisting of the major companies in the Food Supplement Trade. This group soon became the 'Council for Responsible Nutrition'. After attending a couple of their meetings I declined membership because I feared the group would have little credibility with the media or Health Professions because of the way it was financed. Equally, the actual ethics of the group were grocery rather than science based. Maurice Hanssen was its Secretary who was a skilled lobbyist, but when the scientific chips were down, was depressingly short on real knowledge. Hanssen's independent consultancy that acted for overseas companies entering the UK market gave these competitors unfair advantages over indigenous companies. In my opinion Hanssen had a conflict of interest that precluded his employment by the HFMA and all its committees. Larkhall would be its own master for now but reluctantly joined the HFMA later in the 1980s.

Gluten Free in Parliament and Internationally   In the summer Jack Ashley MP had been asking Parliamentary questions about allergy producing additives in Pharmaceuticals. I took the opportunity to draw his attention to the outrageous situation in the 'Gluten Free' food market. Mr Ashley quickly made enquiries and managed to obtain a letter from the Minister. Whilst not very useful to Larkhall at the time, this little episode doubtless left its mark on the controversy and may well have stimulated behind the scenes activity. I was meanwhile pursuing the international food standards 'Codex Alimentarius' bureaucracy on the same subject with vigour but little response. These bodies moved slower than snails but I doubt their staff starved or were unpensioned.

W5 a youthful skin brand   In 1928 Dr J F Kapp invented the W5 serum in Leipzig. In 1930 the tablets were produced containing the serum under Dr Kapp's direction. In 1932 friends of Dr Kapp, the Gelty brothers, took over the marketing and were very successful in Germany and the UK. Dr Kapp regularly travelled to all countries where W5 was available to give advice to consumers. This gave the product an excellent profile. At the outbreak of war in 1939 the production facilities were lost and all advertising and promotion stopped. After the war Leipzig became part of the Russian Zone, W5 was no longer made and the royalty agreement with Geltys was sequestered. Subsequently the Geltys purchased the business, such as it was, but failed to agree a way forward following the death of one Gelty. In 1956 the UK W5 company and know-how was bought by Milesden Ltd who then sold the tablets by mail and exported them to some British Empire countries Rhodesia, South Africa and New Zealand. (A comprehensive history of the W5 Tablet during Milesden's ownership is in the HAT Archive)

In September 1981, I purchased the W5 business from Mr Nightingale, who then owned Milesden, for £3000. My brother refused to invest. I moved it from Goodge Street off Tottenham Court Road north of Oxford Street, London. We had made W5 tablets in the past 1970-1973 but in 1979 the product Licence of Right had been withdrawn by the DHSS. The justification for this decision was purely bureaucratic. There was no real safety issue but the chemical analytical quality criteria demanded by the authorities were impossible to meet. Complex vitamin and mineral mixtures can never meet the disproportionate standards established for single synthetic chemicals – nor should they be expected to. As for serums, like that of Dr Kapp, in the presence of such mixtures only fools would request such inappropriate standards. However, the cry of 'Safety' and memories of thalidomide meant reason was cast aside and lay people tended to agree with the bureaucrat. The producers were branded as 'Profiteers' and consumers lost their trusted products.

Nightingale was a successful antiquarian bookseller so his wife had looked after the W5 business. I changed the marketing platform to dietary and sales developed. There was never a 'Medicinal' basis to W5 – it was always a cosmaceutical but such classification was unknown in the 1930s. It should never have been classed as a medicine under the Medicines Act. The term serum was probably the reason for it falling foul of the 1968 Medicines Act. I called it Kapp's RNA/DNA extract, retained the brand W5 and emphasized its dietary supplement role. Many products in the diet supplement class have been very successful since the 1980s using the platform first used by Larkhall. Whilst the authorities have not approved they have failed to legislate to outlaw the products.

Importantly, Barbara Cartland was a great fan of W5 but the animal origin of the key ingredient was unacceptable to many health stores who were promoters of vegetarian and vegan products. There were many satisfied and regular users. A course lasting 3 months was recommended every year for the best effect.

In December there was an interesting enquiry from European Royalty asking for W5 Tablets (no offer to pay for a few packets). She was a friend of Barbara Cartland.

Blister packing   In June, I wrote to Esther Rantzen who presented a popular TV show 'That's Life' about her interest in Child Proof Packaging. My letter outlined the difficulties experienced in 1970s with 'Safeseal' -- all problems so similar to those experienced with Gluten Free 1981 and later Tandem IQ 1991. Vested interest controlled opposition.

Larkhall were actively working to produce packaging for their products that would enable the increasingly complex and extensive information legally required to be printed clearly on labels. There was demand for pilfer proofing too. Using and developing blister packaging design, we decided to pack more of our products in blisters and less in jars/bottles. Labelling these legibly was often a huge challenge when large amounts of detail was required by various regulatory bodies. Cartoning bottles was favoured by many of our competitors to overcome the problem but using two layers of packaging -- carton and bottle -- wasted nature's resources and should not be used for genuine Health Food Supplements. Blisters were the right answer. Whilst these are not really 'safeseal' they are not far from it and dangers to children from food supplements are not life threatening.

Ignorant journalists often criticise manufacturers for wasteful packaging not appreciating that the legible information that governments demand on food packaging cannot be accommodated on small packs. Ironically, it is often journalists that stimulate these rules in the first place.

Purity of Life - Subliminal Advertising   In September Bert Schwitters from S & A Survival, Larkhall's largest customer in Europe for vitamins and minerals brought an example of a promotional card and poster he had designed for Cantassium in Holland. It had the most wonderful photograph of the sea. He suggested we might like to use some in the UK and other countries. We purchased some and distributed them to customers, both mail order and trade. The headline was "Enjoy the purity of life, enjoy Cantassium vitamins, minerals and enzymes".

I was told this was our first venture into subliminal advertising.

1981 New Product Miscellany   Vitamin D 400iu. Most people keen on supplements obtained Vitamin D from Cod Liver Oil so Cantassium's tablets of Vitamin D were not popular but did complete our range. This was important for market credibility. If we had remained in business after 1999 a Vitamin D microvitamin product would have become a very good one. There has been so much positive publicity linking deficiency of Vitamin D to a variety of common illnesses from weak bones, cancer, MS, arthritis since 1999. Vitamin D supplementation is widely recommended by Doctors.

1981 Womanadds   This was a supplement made on a suggestion of a feminist group, Canadian lady Mary Ann Hushlak. We brought this out for Feminists but it failed to sell.

1981 The French carton for Trufree Bread Mix was made following an initial order from a French dietary company. Sadly, no second order ever materialised.

Are we Mavericks?

ABPI - Gluten Free Bake Book - Codex Alimentarius - Trufree Communion Wafers - Healthfoods and Pharmacy - Laetrile - Diet supplements are not Medicines - Dr Graham MacGregor - Blister Packing - Computerisation - Cytotoxic Blood Testing - Senta Runge and spiritualism - Lipchic - Maseur - Tryptophan - Serving two Masters - Trade Union - Natural form Vitamins - Foresight supplements - Cantamega 2000 - Dutch distributor Film

Balanced Diet and need for Vitamins The argument in this area is covered well by the sheet first published in the USA in 1982. If I eat a 'Balanced' diet do I have to take Vitamins? By Earl Mindell.
Dr Hugh Cox visited Larkhall and was a good friend in developing Larkhall's interest in Alternative Health Care. He was a qualified General Practitioner and thus had more credibility than the many 'mail order qualified nutritional doctors' who were proliferating in the UK. (An article about him from Here's Health is in this file at the HAT Archive.)

ABPI Larkhall (as G O Woodward & Co Ltd) was still a member and contributed to their long time Secretary's, Arthur Shaw's, retirement presentation. He had been a good friend of mine and soon after his retirement we left this Drug Industry body because we were too small a company and our interests were no longer allied to big Pharma. I attended the Annual Dinner at Grosvenor House for the last time in April. As usual, several politicians and top academics were present. After over 30 years of regular attendance most of the personalities I had known had retired and there were few people left who I knew well at the dinner.

Gluten Free Foods, dietitians and the Codex Alimentarius The argument continued with Coeliac Society and the Borderline Committee. Jack Ashley MP had joined in our fight and his letters probably helped achieve a result because the Trufree Flours became prescribable for Coeliacs but the Society still refused to accept Larkhall's Advertisements in its magazine that was distributed to all Coeliac sufferers (the best possible medium for Gluten Free Advertising). They said no space was available and would not be available for many years to come.
    In November Rita Greer and I went to Basildon Hospital to demonstrate Trufree Flours. As this was an Official Dietician Meeting it was good progress for our ideas on totally Gluten Free standards. When we arrived the dietitians were having their tea in the lecture hall. Out came carrier bags of junk food and they tucked in. Fortunately they didn't offer any of it to us!
    Half way through the talks the head dietitian walked out in a huff because of our views on Wheat Starch. The remaining dietitians ignored this.
    I was still in correspondence with the International Standard Codex Alimentarius as regards introducing a 100% Gluten Free standard for coeliac foods. There was little progress because of the opposition of powerful food industry interests.

TRUFREE and The gluten-free and Wheat-free Bumper Bake Book Rita Greer worked on this 156 page book for a year using Trufree flours for all the experiments. Once she had finished all her formulas for special diet flours it required a cookbook to show how they could be used.

LARKHALL GREEN FARM

She had always hoped during the years of research that she would be able to formulate flours that could be used with ordinary cookbooks. However, it did not appear to be possible and a Trufree cookbook was required with slightly different amounts for ingredients and shorter baking times, on slightly lower temperatures, for use with the new Trufree flours.

She designed it, did the typesetting and illustrated it with helpful diagrams. A professional photographer helped her with the photographs but she baked up all the food and arranged the sets herself for the colour plates. For a small company to produce such a marketing tool was unheard of. It would not have been possible if an agency had been employed and it would have required a whole team of experts. As it was, she was able to do it all herself as well as financing it. The result was excellent.

Trufree was remarkable. It would make everything and was a giant leap forward in gluten-free baking. It was in complete contrast to wheat starch baking which had a very narrow range of possibilities, was tasteless, difficult to use and not nutritious. For the first time, with Trufree, coeliacs could have shaped breads, crusty rolls and breadsticks, home made pasta, scones, crispbreads, crumpets, rich fruit cakes, over 40 kinds of cakes and over 60 kinds of biscuits. It was the kind of food that people who can eat wheat take for granted but up to now had not been possible for special dieters. It was easy to use and each flour was a blend of naturally gluten/wheat free flours with a binder such as pectin or methylcellulose. This completely new idea eventually became commonplace among other manufacturers but Trufree was the first of its kind and blazed a trail.

The first run of books cost RG thousands of pounds and she decided to sell it by mail order. She needed to find the funding for the next run. The reps were furious as they thought it ought to be free and given away as a promotion. (Generally speaking, when any good product came along the reps would find some great fault to explain why they weren't selling many. They never had any idea of how much products cost and seemed to believe that all money that came in was profit for the bosses.)

The Bumper Bake Book (BBB) immediately went into our lists and sold well. For the second edition RG went over to spiral bound plastic spines that meant that the cookbook could open out flat for use in the kitchen. She bought a hand operated machine and put the spines on herself to keep the costs down.

(By 1992 The Bumper Bake Book was in its 4th Edition and it can still be bought secondhand from Amazon in 2015 although the Trufree Flours no longer exist.)

Quality Control for Trufree   RG tested every quarter ton of the flour blends herself, either making a loaf of bread or buns. The latter were very popular with the production staff as she would take them down to the production unit or the lab, in her white lab coat and white trilby hat, and hand them round. It was very moreish QC and there were never any complaints. RG said it was good for the staff as they could see the point of what they were making by the ton and be enthusiastic about their work.

Baked up Trufree samples   If the reps wanted any Trufree food for a promotion RG used to have a bake-up in the Annie's Room kitchen and box them up for the stand. One of the real show-off cakes was rich fruit cake suitable for a birthday or Christmas cake. She would make large cakes to be cut up for the stand, as required. Dietitians were a problem as they were used to wheat starch and could not believe Trufree was 100% gluten-free. It meant that food baked with Trufree flour was truly acceptable for all the family to enjoy and not just the special dieter, which was a good selling point.

However, the reps didn't really bother their heads with it. Walter O'Connell was the worst as he would give all the samples RG had baked up to the first Irish person to come to the stand. It meant RG always had to go on the exhibition stands herself as she couldn't trust the reps to do a good job and anyway they didn't have the knowledge required to talk to the public. One rep in particular would eat the samples himself.

Mail and PR for Trufree Every day RG always had bundles of letters and enquiries. She answered them all herself and sent out replies including samples by the next post. Literature tied in with The Bumper Bake Book and 50g samples of Trufree self raising flour, enough to make 6 sponge buns, were sent out. She found a kitchen shop in Hampshire who would mail out the special size tins for the bread making when they became generally unobtainable owing to the forced decimalisation from the EU. Realising a poster would help people to sort out their gluten/wheat free diets, RG did new artwork herself. The posters were given away free and featured packs of Trufree flours. The switchboard put through any 'phone calls connected with Trufree for RG to deal with herself.

She was someone who knew the product inside out as she had invented it and she had the experience of cooking for her husband who was on a difficult special diet that excluded gluten and wheat.

Trufree Communion Wafers One of the things that could be made with Trufree flour was communion wafers. These were normally made with wheat flour as they represent bread but even such a small amount of gluten/wheat in the wafer thin discs can cause ill effects for a coeliac or a wheat free dieter, especially children. A baker in Kent began to produce Trufree communion wafers and it wasn't long before they were sent out by post all over Europe. He would ask for a bulk order of Trufree flour every so often to make them.

All went well until there was trouble from the Catholics. The Bible indicated they ought to be made from wheat to represent real bread and this is what Catholic coeliacs should have at communion, as decided by Rome, irrespective of the bad effect they might have on communicants. The baker ignored this and continued buying bulk Trufree for the wafers. He received stern letters from Rome but still continued. Not being a Catholic himself, he didn't accept he should be told what he should and shouldn't bake and sell. I had a nasty 'phone call from a nun about it and so did RG. She was vitriolic about our Trufree sin. Then the baker had a visit at his Kent bakery. A cardinal arrived all the way from Rome, via Liverpool in a big limo to argue his case. By now it had reached the Pope himself and the cardinal had been despatched to sort things out. The baker lost patience when the cardinal told him he had upset the Holy Father and consequently said some rude things about the Pope. The cardinal departed back to Liverpool in high dudgeon. The matter was only resolved when the bakery was sold out to another company and production of communion wafers ceased as they didn't want to be bothered with them.

The communion wafers were baked by nuns in a Catholic convent in the north of England. We supplied the same bulk Trufree and continued up until 1999.

RG had a letter from a priest who had the idea of everyone in his congregation taking communion with Trufree bread as many of them were coeliacs. He wanted them all to have the same, not two different sorts. His wife used to bake the Trufree loaves and the congregation would all be given a little. It was very popular as it tasted so nice and the coeliacs didn't feel left out. They were C of E, not Roman Catholics.

By 2014 many churches and cathedrals were using wheat communion wafers and gluten/wheat free communion wafers, round or square to differentiate them.

Laetrile (B17) The clinical trial failed and its demise was predicted. Larkhall continued to offer supplies but on an availability platform only. It subsequently was permitted for prescription only but not on the NHS.

The Health Food dilemma continues   I wrote to the Pharmaceutical Journal arguing that Pharmacists should take an interest in Health Foods because they have a responsibility for patient health in the broadest sense. This letter was published by the Irish Pharmaceutical Journal in May. Is dispensing a free prescription for a powerful synthetic chemical on the NHS really a 'healthy' action? As for a doctor prescribing such a substance in the first place.....

Legislate against Supplements   In December 1981 the Pharmaceutical Journal had reported that the Pharmaceutical Society was reminding government to legislate against unlicensed medicines. Most of these were 'Diet Supplements' and the one giving special cause for worry at this time was Tryptophan. Despite countless attempts to legislate for this 'problem' by governments in Europe, USA and many other places there had been little progress. Why? The Health Food Industry was popular with consumers who saw their products as 'safe' whilst those same consumers often saw the Pharma Industry and its friends as 'greedy blood suckers' who sell and promote dangerous synthetic chemicals. When legislators bring in new laws – Judicial Reviews are often demanded by manufacturers. In the event of a seller's prosecution 'offending' supplements or herbals the defence often mount a persuasive case and win. The legislators soon lose heart and their political masters would not sanction more taxpayer money and resources for continuing their fight. They knew that the Health Food Movement has thousands of taxpayer sympathisers.

The Diet Supplement Quandary   In April I wrote again to the Chemist & Druggist on the credibility of Evening Primrose Oil. This letter was the result of an article in that publication (27th March). I put the case for complete separation of 'Medicines' and 'Dietary Supplements' and point out the hypocrisy of the Health Food Industry when it promotes medicinal properties for its products without first specifying a healthy diet and lifestyle as essential to benefits from its products. I inferred that the healthy diet alone would be enough to be effective in most cases and supplements were probably unnecessary and just 'placebos'. This view did not endear me to the Health Food fraternity and since I had already alienated the drug/pharma interest I had few friends. Unsurprisingly in 2015 the situation remained the same – the vested interests remain and the consumers are probably still misled.

Journalist and expert medical activity   Pam Dotter from Family Circle magazine visited Larkhall for lunch and asked RG to be a consultant on Special Diets for the publication. We also had visits for lunch from Leslie Kenton (Health Editor for Harpers & Queen). Helene Hodge, Editor of Healthy Living, was helped with editorial appropriate to Health Foods. We gave her lunch in Annie's Room. There was a similar situation with Miriam Polunin (Editor) and her assistant Alan Lewis at Here's Health, at this time the number one Health Food magazine. The Dining Room directed by RG was very popular and Here's Health did a long article about her and Annie's Room with recipes. RG was always prepared to cater for 'special' dietary requirements e.g. low fat, low sugar and low salt, high fibre, lots of vegetables and fruit, as well as the allergy diets -- Egg, Wheat, Gluten Free etc. Vegetarians and Vegans were also catered for.
   Another visitor was Hugh L'Tang BM.,DIH Editor of the prestigious Practitioner Magazine for Doctors.
   Dr Graham MacGregor also came. He was researching Blood Pressure and believed substitution of Potassium for Sodium in the diet was effective. He favoured Ruthmol used as a salt replacer in cooking and at table. He had a friend with MS and was therefore interested in Alan Greer's case. Dr MacGregor (now Professor) is considered a world authority in the Blood Pressure area in 2015 and is also a leading academic against over consumption of sugar.

Blister Packing I was in favour of Blister Packing the Cantassium Supplement range. This method of packing and presentation would allow greater product security from contamination. It also permitted more wording on the outer pack to comply with regulations and better inform consumers. My brother was not in favour because of greater cost over plastic bottle containers. He was against purchasing a Noak blister packing machine seen by me at Interphex exhibition in Brighton. The question of pilfer-proof packing was also important. He claimed I was interfering with his authority regarding machines to be purchased for Charlbury Packing department, but that was the whole company's factory not just his. Dennis Hooker the manager of the packing department would be consulted by me. My brother never understood that the company needed to serve its customers and not dictate to them because it needed to use the out-dated machines and packing materials it already had. The fact is we had to keep up with the times to survive and compete successfully in business.

Diversity of product range increased with computerisation of all systems The Summer Price List indicated the comprehensive product ranges stocked by the various trading companies operating under the Larkhall Alternative Healthcare banner. The majority were produced in our factories in London and Charlbury.

Ongoing and more comprehensive computerisation of the commercial systems was enabling us to control stocks and distribution better even for the large number of items - over 450. The knowledge base for these products was dependent on me (100% General including Technical), RG (General and Food and Beauty), R.Baxter (60% Technical only) and Cyril Blau (40% mainly technical). W O'C also had some input but sadly exaggeration of effectiveness was his forte that I had to try to control.

In June we were installing a Burroughs Computer B94 our first attempt at integrating wages, accounting and stock control systems. Production needed special computer software on a separate system.

Cytotoxic blood test for hidden Food Allergy and the USM In July there was a positive article in The Pharmaceutical Journal on the new Food Allergy testing service at Larkhall. This positive step for alternative health was soon followed by problems for the facility.

After attending the NNFA convention in New Orleans I visited Physicians Laboratory in Huntingdon Beach, California and obtained exclusive rights for the UK on their Cytotoxic Test from Doug Kauffmann. On return to London I arranged for the Allergy Laboratory Manager Dr P. Fennell to visit California and train on the Cytotoxic Test. Larkhall then went ahead and fitted out their laboratory to do the test. In September the future looked bright for the allergy project. Following my return from the USA, a stockbroker friend suggested that Larkhall seek a listing on the Unlisted Securities Market of the London Stock Exchange – he was already putting companies on to that market successfully. He said a good case could be made to encourage investors in Larkhall.

However, in December Larkhall came under the spotlight with heavy criticism by The Evening Standard and 'Which' magazine was not far behind. Larkhall was one of the first to offer the Cytotoxic Test that like all other alternative methods was contrary to the Health Establishment's ideas. Since these people have the professional clout Larkhall was not able to expand the use of this test. In 2011 many laboratories offer variants of the cytotoxic test but were forced to offer them through the internet. Unsurprisingly, the manager of the Laboratory was dismissed following these articles and Larkhall never listed on the USM.

Unigreg This was a company marketing OTC specialities with formulations incorporating Vitamins and Minerals including Uniflu and Forceval (then a Vitamin fortified Protein Powder but later the brand expanded to Capsules competing with Tandem IQ). Unigreg had contacted me through the old Mark Morris company which made these and other items for them. Mr Krikorian and his brother, shrewd men of Armenian origin, had offices in Wimbledon not far from Putney. Larkhall subsequently made products under contract but soon found the work unprofitable. Unigreg proved very keen buyers – we could not compete.

Martha Hill. Larkhall attempted to supply the Martha Hill skin care range to their mail order customers but were not successful – similarly Martha's company tried to tempt their customers with a selection from Larkhall's supplement range. Neither were successful and I thought that this indicated how separate the two markets were. At one of Martha's dinners we met Mollie Parkin an eccentric celebrity from the fashion world. Martha was involved in that area too.

Garlic This was becoming a very popular Supplement. Consumers were well informed as to its benefits to heart and circulation but the odour when used in cooking was a problem for many British people. Tablets and capsules where the odour was locked in (garlic odour developed on exposure to air and moisture) became the preferred option for consumers. Standardisation was a problem and there were many varieties of material available to tableters and encapsulators. Subsequently we found an excellent standardised Garlic extract from Japan that we used in our tablets for many years.

Face Lifting by Exercise. On my annual visit to USA I met again with Senta Maria Runge the author of this book that had been in Larkhall's mail order list for some years. She was developing a range of skin care products and hoped to have them available soon. I understood that Senta Runge was a spiritualist and her idea was to prepare products in tune with her beliefs. These products never materialized but illustrated the Californian freedom of thought that had led to that US State's pre-eminence in the Natural Cosmetic (beauty) and Health Food Movements.

Lipchic USA The last call on my USA trip (1-2 August) was to Julia Page at 10 Park Avenue New York. Lipcote was not registrable as a Trade Mark in USA owing to a conflicting word already registered. Julia, with my permission, had registered Lipchic and was about to launch the product on the US market. A passionate believer in the effectiveness and value of Lipcote she started to develop a business. The packaging and advertising were designed by her for the US market. Unfortunately, her health prevented progress soon after 1983 and Larkhall and I personally (my brother refused to invest as usual) bought the rights to the mark in 1988. The product was quite successful in the early 1990s under a distributor (Ella International – the Amerrivazani family in San Diego). It passed to Matthews & Wilson after Larkhall was taken over by Royal Numico in 1999.

Concorde I flew back from USA on Concorde -- the world's only supersonic passenger aeroplane. British Airways trip time, New York – London Heathrow about three and a half hours. Amazing!

Maseur Sandals Dr Eber, Gabby Eber's brother visited regarding Larkhall distributing Maseur Reflexology Sandals that I saw in USA in July and were made in Australia. They were marketed as a healthy form of footwear. I thought the Maseur Sandal brand would fit well with Omniped Foot Cushions. We soon obtained the UK distributorship.

Tryptophan Tryptophan is an essential amino acid that occurs in many everyday foods. So may be classified as a 'Food Supplement'. Tryptophan containing foods like milk can have a very calming effect and hence it may be recommended in a diet to lower stress or help sleep.

An article on the benefits of taking Tryptophan was published in Woman Magazine – 'weaning off Valium naturally'-- was very controversial and did not please big Pharma Companies who like to control the depression/sleeping drug market. Larkhall had made Tryptophan and other amino acid tablets for sometime. (Taurine 500mg tablets were introduced in 1982) The Tryptophan Tablets 500mg soon began to sell well. As the only manufacturer of this amino acid in the UK Health Food Industry we were in a strong position. Soon it was a best seller from Health Store shelves. However, as usual, big Pharma did not like the idea of a natural essential amino acid competing with its patented synthetic antidepressant and sleeping drugs. In 1989 it may have orchestrated a great revenge in 1989 (see Chapter 17).

Trade business complaint serving two masters In the autumn RG and I produced numerous promotional leaflets and posters for use in retail health food stores. No agency was used and RG liased directly with the printers. The real problem was the dual customer base of Trade and Direct Mail.

The director of one leading wholesaler, who was also a participant in a retail Trade Federation, wrote at length to me (not the sales manager Walter O'Connell) complaining about our policy of serving the market from two directions. I suspected that this letter had been stimulated by W O'C because our own sales people did not like us dealing direct with consumers. They believed that this took business away from their retailers and so depressed their own sales affecting their bonuses. I replied to the complaints in the usual way pointing out that retailers were demanding great discounts and often paying their bills very late after costly office administration chasing payment, whereas mail order customers paid with their orders and we did not have to pass them excessive discounts. These customers also appreciated the knowledge of our in-house advisors. With hindsight, I should have concentrated thereafter on Mail Order and relied on wholesalers to service whatever demand there was from retailers. Health Food Supplements need expert advice to be available to consumers and few Health Stores have such experts long term except owner managed stores. If retail pharmacists were more committed to the ideals of wholesome diets with wholesome supplements perhaps I would have reconsidered company policy in this area.

Trade Union problem solved In December a General and Municipal Workers' Union representative demanded a meeting with me. I saw him in my office for a few minutes. He said he would be recruiting Larkhall staff to join the Union. I told him if the Unions came in I would close down the factory. He said he was expecting to recruit a large number of the staff very soon.

One of the staff was keen to get the Union going in the factory and he asked for a meeting with me and the Union representative for discussions. They chose a very odd time – 8 am. I agreed to see them in Annie's Room as it was so early in the morning. I had asked RG to be around but out of sight. Unbeknown to them she was in the kitchen adjacent, with the door open so she could hear. We were both expecting trouble and she had personal experience of how corrupt Unions could be having had problems and bullying from the NGA herself.

The two men arrived and soon got down to business with a deal. They would offer to stop recruiting or trying to get the Union into the factory if I would give the Union rep £1,500 and the employee £500 (in cash). Blackmail! In the kitchen RG was listening. She was livid and sailed into the dining room looking fierce which caught the two men by surprise.

"I heard all that and am happy to be a witness," she announced. "I'll 'phone the police right away". They both leapt up and fled the building down the fire escape, never to be seen again.

That was the last I heard of Unionisation. The employee gave notice and the Union rep never came back. It would be impossible to run a complex factory like ours with the Unions on board and more than twenty nationalities employed. We'd never have been able to make a tablet. We wondered how many companies had paid a bribe to keep Unions out.

Natural Form Vitamins   The Grow Company in the USA began to promote their Natural Vitamins. Their leaflets explained at great length how their products differ from 'Free State' vitamins and minerals. Whilst their preparations were closer to foods than most vitamins and mineral ingredients there was no convincing proof that they were more beneficial nutritionally than other products incorporated in vitamin supplement formulations. One advantage was that the concentration of the active nutrient was much lower than in synthetics and any stomach irritation caused by over concentration (especially with minerals) would be diminished. Cantassium had always tried to make their supplements, through careful scientific formulation, as close to food as possible. In any event, the Grow Company provided useful marketing platforms to distinguish natural from synthetic.

Advertisements from the early 1980s   We advertised in 'Focus' the official journal of The Guild of Natural Medicine Practitioners that showed the wide range of Larkhall services to the alternative healthcare professionals. Food Allergy teaser advertisements were used very widely in the press to obtain enquiries and add to the mailing list. Whilst Larkhall could arrange for testing for Food Allergy their Cantassium Products were formulated on a platform of suitability for food allergic consumers and incorporated the RG Symbol System on the packaging.

Lipcote and Buy-lines. Lipcote was developing into a very good brand and more space with larger advertisements was taken in print media. Larkhall were also using the BUY-line style small advertisements to carry Lipcote and often other items from Larkhall such as the Cantassium Range, Ruthmol and W5 in the same feature.

Foresight   Mangamac was a compound Food Supplement of Manganese an essential element for life made for the Foresight Charity. Foresight was a Preconceptual Care Charity that recommended both parents to undergo tests including hair analysis. This was followed by Food Supplements to correct deficiencies detected by hair analysis and risks found from analysis of answers to Lifestyle questionnaires. Adoption of the individualised regimes aimed to improve couple fertility, encourage a healthy pregnancy and baby. Cantassium made many different supplements for them. This Charity was often actively persecuted in the media because their research was not based on double blind clinical trials. Anecdotally, their system was very successful. Healthy babies were born to previously infertile couples and to those who had previously had deformed babies or miscarriages. The charity was consistently more successful than IVF and other artificial conception methods used by NHS doctors. Like Larkhall, Foresight were, so far as the establishment was concerned, enemies. This was a view, unsurprisingly, not held by the thousands of couples who benefited from using the Foresight programmes. As Mrs Nim Barnes, the founder of Foresight, said when asked about research through double blind trials "Is it ethical to have a trial when you knowingly recommend products that contain no vitamins and minerals to parents who wish to have a healthy baby and pregnancy". Is it even likely that those people would agree to participate in such a trial anyway?

112

Orchestrated Attacks on Larkhall

Computerisation - New Staff and Agency - Observer attack - Professor Sandler - Gluten Free problems - Holistic Pharmacists & Alternative Healthcare - Healthy Eating with less sugar and salt - Bigots on both sides of Balanced diet ideas - Confused Consumers - Smoking cessation and Filtro-neto - The Natural Medicines Society - Journal of Alternative Medicine - Dr Richards arrested in USA - Quackbusters and the ASA - Chiropractors unfairly vilified - European distributors - Dietmart opportunity - ABPI resignation - Media buying agency - New Medicines Inspector - Influential lunch guests - Symbol System importance - Chimney demolished - Foresight Cookbook - NACNE report -The Health Standard - Larkhall Newspaper

Computerisation meant that a data processing office was developed. We had three computer areas to be integrated- Commercial activities including Wages, Stock control with Production and Mail Order. We had a Burroughs main System but both stock control, production and Mail Order were still on individual microcomputers (Commodores) despite the original promises of our software supplier. We started to investigate a Data General system in March. I asked my brother to lead the computer department because it needed control at Charlbury - this served to keep him busy but whether it was a good decision remained unknown. I certainly made a mistake in not becoming closely involved in computers in 1983 and regretted it by 1998. However, export sales needed close management and I decided to concentrate my efforts in that area rather than computerisation.

Key Staff and Advertising Agency   Keith Etson, our mail order consultant was to leave within 2 months. He later said he would like to work for us trying to obtain contract work for a small commission. Little developed and he stopped working for Larkhall. Walter O'Connell seemed to have lost interest in the Health Food Industry – was he upset by new staff? No, it was Filtro Neto. It seemed to have taken him over. He boasted to RG that he was going to make millions and that he had been to look at expensive houses in Cheam as well as Rolls Royce cars.

There were major changes for the office. Neal Muranyi joined but was immediately sabotaged by long serving Office Manageress Mrs V. Roberts who resigned after a big fuss. In truth, she never liked the introduction of the microcomputers and did not believe we needed them. As she believed she was doing two jobs, she thought she deserved two cars in spite of the fact she couldn't drive! She was over sixty, couldn't adapt and was due for retirement.

Neil Muryani had joined from a Booker Health Foods subsidiary as mail order manager and soon became office and UK trade sales manager. W.O'Connell, despite my reservations, agreed to work with Muranyi on the UK and Irish Trade sales.

There was no-one I could trust on export of our brands beyond UK and Ireland so I decided to do this myself. Walter O'Connell had already proved disastrous in the Middle East and a brief encounter in Greece had not been good. My experience visiting the USA from 1979 had shown that I could work with overseas people successfully. I travelled to Sweden, USA West Coast and Denver and Rome, spearheading the Export Market development and in the US endeavouring to find new products and service lines. The Prodotti Naturali Italian distributor business was started.

The sales development led to Advertising Agency changes when The Media Shop became our advertising agency, replacing Hugh Winthrop's Edward Walters and David Morgan's Bray Leino.

LARKHALL GREEN FARM

Major media attacks on Larkhall began An influential academic Dr John Garrow was soon to be a founding member of Quackbusters and later HealthWatch (the scourge of Alternative Healthcare), began his press attacks on Larkhall with B17. An article by Annabel Ferriman in which Garrow was mentioned, appeared in the Observer. I answered by drawing attention to B17 having to be used in holistic dietary treatments that were totally different in concept from the drug approach of doctors and pharmacists. By the end of the year B17 was restricted by law to doctor's prescription. (It is found in bitter almonds.)

I thought that our Allergy Clinic's Cytotoxic Test would be attacked in the Sunday People Newspaper. A Sunday People journalist, came to Putney and interviewed RG and me in a shallow way. In the event, nothing was published immediately. Nevertheless, Rita seriously considered giving up writing her latest Allergy Cookbook because she thought a witch hunt was on for Larkhall and its leaders in the press. Sunday 3rd April saw both The People and Observer newspapers carry reports very critical of Larkhall's Allergy Testing. These criticisms were serious so far as Larkhall was concerned and the experience indicated that we had significant enemies. We were a small company but were being treated as if we were big players. Had we been selected for attack?

The US inventors of the Cytotoxic Test who supplied the special microplates for the test promised to come over and help us in April. Dr Geoffrey Cheung came from LA (Physicians Laboratory) as promised to put the credibility of our allergy testing back on track. Later in the year I visited the LA laboratory in USA and saw them making their own slides for the Cytotoxic Test . The process was one we would be able to do ourselves in Putney.

The Nutrient Deficiency Test emanating from USA was gaining acceptance. However, in November Derek Cooper of the BBC Food Programme (Radio) came to interview me about it. He was sceptical but I argued the case for this innovation from the USA. The programme was not favourable as regards Vitamin and Mineral supplements but followed the Garrow line — taking supplements was of no benefit to healthy people eating a 'balanced' diet. As usual there was no guide as to what a balanced diet was. Nor was there any reference to the wholesomeness of food. Did anyone know what 'the balanced diet' was?

Professor Merton Sandler from Queen Charlotte's Hospital, one of the discoverers of the chemical origins of depressive illness, came to lunch at Larkhall. He was a friend of mine but was very against Herbal Products. I enjoyed arguing with him. He considered Professor Arnold Beckett, who was my supervisor for my Ph.D., as a 'second rank researcher'. Beckett was a pioneer of the stereochemical approach to drug design as well as the originator of drug testing of athletes and sports players. I was not sure about Merton's impartiality and judgement. (I still think that academia is worse than business when it comes to jealousy, poor judgement, bias, cheating....)

In his later years Merton mellowed and discovered 'Tribulin' a complex brain chemical important in depression. He was searching for synthetic drugs to mimic or antagonise tribulin.

Coeliac Disease and naturally Gluten Free Larkhall succeeded with more Trufree products on NHS prescription whilst I continued to draw attention to the importance of a totally Gluten Free diet in the prevention of bowel cancer in Coeliacs. Their major susceptibility to the disease had been highlighted in The Lancet and another medical magazine.

The poor nutritional quality of the gluten reduced (but mislabeled as gluten free) flours not only ensured that Coeliacs ingested their poison, gluten, but were deprived of many cancer protective antioxidant nutrients that were removed from those flours during the extraction processes. I met a director of Welfare Foods (Stockport – Rite Diet Brand) at a Trade Seminar on Special Diet Foods and it was obvious that Larkhall was not popular because of its stance re-Gluten Free items being 100% Naturally Gluten Free for coeliacs. He knew the science was with us, not our opponents.

I continued to expose the sophistry surrounding **'Gluten Free'** products for Coeliacs. In November, The Chemist & Druggist published a letter from me that was quite hard hitting. There was no reply from the offending manufacturers or the Coeliac Society who were so supportive of these companies - maybe because they received funding from them.

In January, we were advertising our Special Diet Flours and The Gluten Free Bumper Bake Book in the official British Dietetic Association Adviser journal. This indicated the progress we were making in this product area.

The EEC standardises flour pack sizes   Publicity was gained for the problem of special diet flours emanating from Brussels. Trufree sold flour mixes packed specially for an individual loaf (420g) but in future it would become illegal to sell any flour in packs other than 250g, 500g or 1Kg. Consumers were forced to buy or be prescribed more than needed. How wasteful. Reasoning a rethink was impossible. Who won? The bureaucrats in Brussels, naturally.

B17 legal position clarified   In March a letter from the DHSS was received regarding a proposal to restrict availability of Amygdalin (B17 Laetrile). It would not be officially licensed as a Medicine but would only be available from Pharmacies on Prescription. I was interviewed on Capital Radio about B17. BBC2 started its series regarding the Gentle Method for Cancer treatment including B17. Subsequently, a letter was received from the DHSS on 15th December which indicated that B17, Amygdalin and Cyanogenetic substances were likely to be regulated to doctor's prescription-only, early in 1984.

Holistic Pharmacists and Alternative Healthcare   In late March I had a meeting at The Crusting Pipe, a wine bar in Covent Garden, with Mervyn Madge and Tony Pinkus, to plan recognition for the Holistic Pharmacists Group within the Pharmaceutical Society of GB. There was already a Holistic Medical Group for doctors. TP was to write to the Pharmaceutical Journal. The Chemist & Druggist took a more positive stance and publicised an inaugural meeting of 'The Holistic Pharmacist Association' in October. In the event only eleven Pharmacists attended, including those named above who were nominated; Mervyn Madge to be Chairman, me as Deputy and Tony Pinkus as Secretary and Treasurer.

Sadly, this group never got off the ground which confirmed my view that Pharmacists have closed minds as regards alternative health care, whilst the dispensing of ever more costly patented drugs ensures them a good living. The Pharmaceutical Society barely acknowledged the existence of alternative health care other than in dismissive terms. It was unlikely that members would ever be favourably disposed towards it.

Later in the year, a mailing to Pharmacists had a poor response for Gluten Free Foods, Food Allergy and Vitamins/Mineral supplements. It, again confirmed my view that there was little interest in Alternative Health Care among Pharmacists.

Healthy Eating publicity - too much sugar   In June, The Observer newspaper ran articles on white refined sugar and concluded the dietary intake should be cut because too much may be harmful. Salt was also discussed and cutting down recommended. Fresh fruit was considered beneficial. Things have come a long way since and by 2012 there was a consensus that both need close control to help reduce obesity, some cancers, heart disease and stroke. A more natural style of diet was essential for good health and wellbeing.

So, the Observer agreed with Larkhall in the healthier diet area but had correspondents such as Annabel Ferriman who appeared to support the Quackbusters.

Low Sodium or Salt Free? An ending that hardly helped the health of consumers
The Ruthmol dispute with Prewetts case continued during the year with a writ to be issued after advice from Mr Aldous QC not to pursue an injunction. Prewetts had brought out a new product labelled 'Prewett's Low Sodium Salt' implying it was low in salt (sodium). This was placed next to Ruthmol, the salt free salt, on store shelves. Prewetts contained **salt as a major ingredient** and was priced well below Ruthmol. I considered this grossly unfair competition and asked Prewetts (part of the Bookers conglomerate) to withdraw their product or face legal action from us, which they did. Subsequently Lo-Salt came on the market and prospered because Lo was not interpreted as meaning Low by the authorities and was not held to mislead consumers despite containing substantial amounts of Sodium derived from Sodium Chloride in its formula.

The legal border between Salt Free and Low Salt confuses consumers Too much Salt (Sodium) had been deemed as a cause of heart disease and strokes for many years. Consumers were told to watch their intake carefully by paying attention to food labels. Unfortunately sodium was a ubiquitous contaminant like arsenic and lead and traces of it were found in most foods. Nothing can ever be Sodium Free so governments may set limits on levels permitted to be present in Sodium Free foods. Low Sodium foods have much higher levels of Sodium present with no lower limit.

The Practitioner and Health Foods   In April this leading monthly publication for doctors carried an article "How the other half eats". This was a balanced critique of the Health Food Movement that illustrated that it was influencing the nation's diet in a positive direction. Unjust attacks on it were mentioned and the presence of bigots on both sides was accepted.

Filtro Neto   This item to help people to stop smoking was introduced at The Alternative Medicine Exhibition at Kensington Exhibition Centre in July. These filters were being promoted enthusiastically by O'Connell but they were not really a Larkhall product. O'Connell met the the Greek manufacturer when following up a Blakoe enquiry to Putney. O'Connell persuaded me to go into an independent 50/50 company (the former Richmond Order Company of Mark Morris) that would be arranged in August but Larkhall would own my share.

By October Walter O'C had found a sub distributor for Filtro Neto, John Gibson, a health store owner from Macclesfield, who believed he could develop it into something really big. The filters were being patented. They were also being researched at Huntingdon Research Laboratories who were to demonstrate their effectiveness in tar intake reduction from cigarette smoking. Our contact there was Dr Colin Roberts. A Bank of Ireland company account was opened at Walter's request.

Later the patent proved unenforceable and other similar filters appeared on the market. Once again O'Connell had made assumptions without proper investigation. The Filter was sold for several years with the highlight (according to Walter) being when the Russian President Yeltsin was said to be about to sanction a huge order for his country. Naturally the ink in his pen ran out as he was about to add his signature to the first order. Another of O'Connell's wild dreams....

RG was against this product as the advertisements showed a woman smoking.

Sweden was another different market for Health Supplements   At the end of June I visited a Swedish customer Birger Ledin in Malmo who was starting to develop a vitamin supplement business in nearby Mariestad.

They were already in alternative healthcare with a small outlet. At this time there were relatively few vitamin and mineral products on the Swedish Market and awareness of brand differences were not appreciated. Birger Ledin wanted to be a major importer and distributor to the market. Little subsequently developed with Birger Ledin and it transpired that Alternative Health Practices like to import direct so wholesaling did not really exist. Most practices operate as retailers locally and import and distribute products by direct mail to consumers outside their area.

Alternative Medicine debate   At the end of July, the British Medical Journal featured a leading article on 'Alternative Medicine'. Some doctors were favourably disposed to Complementary and Alternative Medicine (CAM) but others were worried that such unscientific (no evidence base) approaches to Healthcare were gaining ground. This had not changed by 2015 – the same arguments and divisions remain.

By September The BMJ publicity on Alternative Medicine had led to many letters to the Editor. The clear divide in the medical profession was exposed – those who were totally against and many who saw that Alternative techniques were useful but craved proof of efficacy. Many used Homoeopathy and Acupuncture in their practices because they saw them as complementary to orthodox approaches.

In October there was criticism of The Prince of Wales in The Times because he visited the Bristol Cancer Help Centre. Dr Alec Forbes, the medical Director of the charity, said doctors should open their minds to CAM as side effects of cancer drugs were terrifying.

The Natural Medicines Society.   This was a very small group within the alternative healthcare movement that was criticised on a Channel 4 TV programme in November. There was no doubt that Alternative Healthcare was still under sustained attack. I was nominated by the Pharmaceutical Society to go on LBC radio to discuss Safety of Health Foods.

Journal of Alternative Medicine (UK) was launched in the Autumn by Newman Turner (Publishers of Here's Health). In 1993 the magazine was bought by Graeme Millar (Green Library) subsequently closed 1999. Most journals on this subject were published in the USA. Interest in Complementary, Integrative and Alternative Medicine is a vast area with sources found widely on the internet in 2015. Whether there is enough demand to enable a printed magazine to thrive is doubtful.

Arrest of Dr Dick Richards in USA   In early October Dr Dick Richards, Medical Advisor to Larkhall, a long time good friend of mine, RG and her husband, was arrested in Los Angeles, accused of conspiring to murder his partner in London, the homoeopath Dr Peter Stephan. This story made front page tabloid headlines and Radio and TV news. We heard it on the 8 o'clock radio news at breakfast and were very shocked. Subsequently, his wife Pix appeared on TV to ask for help. RG and I put up a substantial sum towards the huge bail demanded by the USA Court. RG opened a bank account in Kent where Dick had a practice, to cope with loans and donations. As he was a popular GP with many loyal patients, was honest and would not hurt a fly, money poured in. So, there was more than enough for the enormous amount required for his bail and to pay for lawyers in the USA. (Eventually, everyone was paid back.) It was obvious he had been set up, but by whom? The Richards had a lovely country house and a small house in Sandwich for Dick's surgery. Due to the massive cost of USA lawyers they lost the country house. His patients lost their GP for years and we lost our qualified consultant doctor. We were as supportive as we could be to his wife and family over a situation that would drag on for years and ruin Dick's career.

Advertising Standards Authority questioned Larkhall about many products As the year progressed, the ASA became very interested in all Larkhall's ranges from Gluten Free to Mechanotherapy. They appeared overwhelmed by the complexity but were later very focused in attack. I thought that someone or a group were behind all these attacks. The Aquamaid had received a very hard time from them as had Slimswift but in 1983 the informed questions they were asking could well have been prompted by the recently formed Quackbusters.

Quackbusters This group was formed in the USA and a UK body was affiliated in some way. They were causing mayhem in the Alternative Health Care movement in the USA with extensive attacks on practitioners and products in the media. Happily there were friendly politicians and well orchestrated defences were mounted by the Alternative Health Care movement. At this moment (1983) the UK alternative lobby was weak but soon opposition became stronger when it was suspected that something sinister was afoot. The UK people broke with Quackbusters to form a charity called 'HealthWatch'. This body was a prime mover for scientific evidence based health care which they understood embraced all treatment systems including orthodox medicine and alternative systems. Unfortunately for HealthWatch they were seen as an arrogant group of western medicine men advocating health policies that many saw as against their human rights. As many of us say, "why has western medicine failed to provide 100% health to the UK population despite its treatments being 'free of charge' to patients?" The only reason alternative health care continued to exist was because the orthodox treatments were perceived to have failed. HealthWatch and its supporters had nothing to justify their arrogance.

Chiropractors unfairly vilified in the USA, a well regarded alternative healthcare method of treatment in the USA had an epic battle with Quackbuster associates that began in 1976 and ended in 1987. Here is a brief quote from the final judgment which vividly illustrates the great financial power of the supporters of 'Evidence based treatments' and how they were defeated by the Chiropractors.
"A successful anti-trust lawsuit played out against the American Medical Association in 1976 by chiropractors but the AMA continued on in their conspiracy to restrict free trade. Finally, having gathered enough evidence of wrongdoing, the chiropractors sued the AMA. The FTC agreed with the chiropractors and ruled that the AMA was in violation of monopoly laws, but the lengthy battle of Wilkes v. AMA finally landed in a federal district court where Judge Susan Getzedanner, in 1987, ruled that the AMA had engaged in an illegal conspiracy to destroy the chiropractic profession by engaging in "systematic, long-term wrongdoing with the long-term intent to destroy a licensed profession." The AMA was ordered to cease and desist. Judge Getzedanner also ordered "a permanent injunction against the AMA, forcing them to print the court's findings in the Journal of the American Medical Association".

Italy, Greece and Holland. In August Anna Maria Caudullo and her cousin Marcello Maugeri visited Putney from Bottega Del Naturista, Rome. They saw Cyril Blau and I met them briefly in the factory canteen, all three smoking like chimneys and drinking coffee. Anna expressed interest in being our distributor in Italy. She bought several items from our shop to take back to Rome for £351.00.

By December the business in Italy was developing fast. Anna Caudullo came to London and met Alan and Rita for the first time. We entertained her in Annie's Room. Her lawyer, Ugo Scuro, also visited to finalise the distributor agreement. We supplied samples and product analyses to assist with legalizing them. They were making key contacts within the many state offices. I was impressed with their dynamism and commitment.

In the same month we were contacted by a Greek Company, Vital and Naturtabs Hellas, asking for Sunflower Oil Capsules. I believed the Evening Primrose/Sunflower Oil publicity had filtered through to Athens. Things moved slowly but a shipment was made in February 1984. Maria Strofalis came to Putney in mid 1984, after the original contact from Dr J Notaras who had no commercial role in the company. Notaras was the brother-in-law of Maria and played an important part in the early years of this developing business. Dealing with the Greeks was in itself a classical education. They had the tendency to promise one thing and then do the opposite. They were all very difficult to deal with and we soon found that 'incentives' were a way of life in Greece.

Problems with the Dutch distributor We began to worry about payments from our Dutch Distributor S & A Survival. I thought the director had probably caught us. Then at then end of the month I had a visit from a Simon van de Waal who told me he was an ex-associate of S & A and would take on the distributorship after dealing with our dispute. This worked out well and Nutrivital very soon became our Dutch Distributor. He often came off the ferry early in the morning and turned up at Annie's Room for breakfast.

Dietmart offered for sale Dietmart, the mail order arm of Newman Turner Publications, was up for sale – Neal Muranyi and I visited their facility in Byfleet and had lunch with Brian Maclaughlin, their managing director, to discuss a possible takeover. However, it was not viable for Larkhall and we didn't proceed.

The First General Management meeting was held in early August. Co-ordination of sales and manufacturing was the main topic. Out-of-stock items caused considerable delays in the sales office but estimating demand was not a science and over-stocking was costly. More effort had to be made but the unpredictability of press mentions was a real problem, as was demand generated by special offers. Quality of cartons and use of more than one colour was essential but the Charlbury people did not appreciate that cheapness was not acceptable. Good quality cartons were an essential part of Brand building even if they cost more. Problems were increased by having two separate factories -- an operation in the peaceful Oxfordshire countryside, known as 'Sleepy Hollow', and one in the frenetic London atmosphere of Putney and Wandsworth. These management meetings at least achieved conversation but it was linked computer systems that ultimately enabled progress.

ABPI resignation
GO Woodward & Co resigned from the ABPI (Association of the British Pharmaceutical Industry) after some 30 years. Membership was not justified because the company had drifted out of Pharmaceuticals. Although confidential news of technical problems, particularly Medicine's Inspector concerns, was useful, we could not justify the subscription cost. We subsequently joined the HFMA (Health Food Manufacturers Association) but unsurprisingly the technical and scientific competence of that body was not comparable to that of the ABPI. After several experiences with the HFMA culminating in being asked to resign, by 1999 we still could not find any trade association suitable for us to join. (Mavericks are always out on a limb.)

International Generics   I continued to be a Director of this Tamman company and had my photo taken for their new brochure. I saw Danny Tamman, Leon's son, regarding the future but got nowhere. However, many years later after Leon Tamman's death, that contact was to prove invaluable.

Advertising agency change The change of advertising agencies would be complete by the end of the year. We were going to do our own creative and artwork or hire freelancers. Meanwhile, a Media Buying agency would advise, place and book advertising schedules. Since we had been using three Full Service agencies I received deputations from all of them. The commission and space costs from Full Service agencies were about three times what the Media Shop would charge. Neal Muranyi had done excellent work on this change.

New Food Supplements - Selenium and Glucomannan Seleniuim was coming to the fore as a vital mineral supplement. Publicity was generated by Wassen International for their Selenium ACE product. Glucomannan, a new dietary aid for diabetics and slimmers derived from a Japanese seaweed was introduced to the UK by Larkhall.

In July I was in USA again to visit the NNFA convention in Denver. The wholesaler (Brewhurst) sponsored a general trade trip and this enabled me to network with several influential people and meet potential US distributors. Wassen's Selenium ACE did well at the show. In the UK, Wassen's advertising and PR was run by Ray Matthews but soon the ASA was to be concerned. However, with the good starting momentum for the product it was unstoppable.

Medicines Inspections In the early autumn, the company was visited by our Medicines Inspector in both London and Charlbury. By now our medicinal product manufacturing formed a very small proportion of that activity. However he insisted on Medicinal Standards throughout. Whilst this was fairly easily achieved for assembly (product packing) purposes, for manufacturing of complex Herbal and Diet Supplement a completely different and more complex situation existed. The new inspector had no experience of any manufacturing outside big Pharma. His judgement of Putney was not good for us but the assembly at Charlbury was passable. Neither premises were ideal but he could see we were working hard to improve matters. After over ten years of inspections it was inevitable that box ticking was the order of the day and strictly enforced bureaucratic systems approved. We scraped through. We knew we had a battle to retain our Manufacturing Licence in London but would be all right assembling in Charlbury.

My brother, who was not technically qualified, did not understand the complexities of Medicine Manufacturing but could operate the assembly systems (Putting tablets in bottles and blisters in cartons). Tensions in the family were inevitable – one thinking the other incompetent – but not appreciating the totally different operations in the two facilities. The move from contract work to brand building needed vision – a quality my brother did not appear to possess.

Guests in Annie's Room We were still entertaining people in Annie's Room including Holland & Barrett staff; also Simon Martin and James Macdonald of the new Journal of Alternative Medicine. Journalist Suzanna Marchant Haycox came to lunch. Julia and Joe Page, who were visiting from New York, came to supper in August to discuss the progress of Lipchic in USA. Other lunch guests included David Young of Thorsons (Publishers) and Ray Matthews (Wassen International). By now Annie's Room had a reputation second to none and played a valuable part in PR for us.

Mega Supplements A congress on Vitamins in Nutrition and Therapy was held in Cartagena, Columbia in December. The publication Vitamin News covered many of the topics discussed. The general tone was very positive for the use of Vitamins in higher dosages. It is worth noting that things in this area have not moved towards general acceptance in 2015 despite many research studies favouring these ideas since 1983. There is still a call for regulation of high doses including the possibility of doctor's prescription only. Columbia is not a country much affected by mega supplements but I guess the Americans like to go there. Tax reasons?

Woman's Own magazine in its Health Update column recommended high doses of daily vitamins for extending lifespan. Vitamin C 1000mg, B6 200mg,Vitamin E 600iu, Pantothenic Acid 1000mg and more.

Symbol System   Interestingly, there was alarm in the USA about the use of up to 50% Sugar in chewable vitamin tablets for children. Artificial substitutes such as aspartame were not wanted by consumers. In the UK people were beginning to appreciate the importance of the product purity symbol system devised by Rita Greer. The new Rita Greer Symbols featured on our packs from 1983.

Boiler Chimney demolished   The factory chimney (beloved icon of Industry to International Generics) had become unsafe and began to sway alarmingly in high winds. It was sited at the side of Annie's Room. About two thirds of it had to be demolished, leaving a third at the base. RG worked with the architect and it was made into one small bathroom and one small shower room, one on top of the other. There was also room for two small bedrooms, also one on top of the other. As it made a mezzanine floor there was no internal way into Annie's Room but another front door, small hall and a few stairs meant just a few yards outside in the open to Annie's Room front door. It was a nuisance if it was raining but I now had a place to stay during the week. By 'living over the shop' I saved no end of travelling time. A walk across the flat roof and I could be in my office before the staff arrived in the mornings and I could still be there when they left at five. A definite plus.

The bathrooms and bedrooms were modest but convenient and most of it was second hand. However, this did not prevent a rumour that became a myth -- that Annie's Room had now become a luxurious penthouse flat. This was partly due to the fact it had no windows so nobody could see inside and partly because employees generally like to believe the boss was making huge profits and spending lavishly on himself. A second hand Mercedes added to this belief. The myth persisted for years.

MS and Foresight   Rita visited the dentist in Harley Street at the address where Jacqueline Du Pre visited her Psychiatrist. She chatted to her in the waiting room about her MS. They had corresponded for some time but never actually met before.

In July Ruth Jervis brought in the Foresight Cook Book for us to see. RG had illustrated it for the Foresight charity, giving them two weeks of her time free.

Radio interviews   In July I did Radio interview on Tryptophan for syndication by PR company Ellis Kopel.

RG was on Radio Brighton live, talking about Gluten Free Cookery when there was a big explosion in studio No 2 and a lot of smoke. In studio No1 they thought it might be a bomb but actually, as they discovered later, one of the two transformers had blown up. It was very frightening and the building started to fill with black smoke. The presenters, RG and the technicians carried on regardless as they were broadcasting live. RG's presenter was a trainee and went to bits. RG remained calm and went on broadcasting as if nothing had happened. A member of the crew put the 12 o'clock news script in front of her.

A few days later a 'phone link interview on BBC Wales via the BBC London had to be abandoned owing to a bomb at the studio in Wales. RG had to just keep calm and keep talking as it was going out live from the London end where RG was in the broadcasting studio on her own for the link up. She could hear the panic going on in Wales through her earphones -- staff trying to get out of the building in a panic, crashing into office furniture and screaming. Her presenter, in London, who was behind a glass panel held up a note which said "keep going". The bomb, which was supposed to have been planted in the car park under the building, eventually turned out to be a hoax. Later she went to the BBC in London again, to redo the broadcast.

Not a word was said about it on air, either at the time or in the later broadcast. The public never got to know about it. The presenter, studio technicians and RG in London had carried on as if nothing had happened, no matter how difficult it was. These were the days when the IRA was active and a bomb exploding was always a possibility.

New Blister Pack Cartons were now ready. I had asked RG to design a logo for Cantassium to go on new packs for the health food trade and chemists using an alphabet that nobody else could copy. She did a signature. I told her I wanted them to be readable at 6 feet. She spoke to several health store managers to see what they wanted. They all asked for white corners and folds to avoid scuffing. They also wanted them clearly designed to show what strengths the tablets were. RG did a crisp colourful modern range with all this in mind. The higher the strength, the brighter the colour. They were enthusiastically received and we had advance publicity in health food magazines with colour photographs of the range, taken using samples from the printer. Unbeknown to us, my brother had cancelled the cartons and supplied the printer with a large quantity of a ghastly dark olive green ink so they could all be done the same. The first I knew of it was when the olive green packs arrived in the warehouse, after we had had the publicity for the coloured ones.

RG's studio Up to now RG had been doing all her writing and artwork either at home, on the big table in Annie's Room or on a desk in my office. There was a disused womens' toilet block on the flat roof from the Cathkin laundry days, opposite a laboratory. Mark Morris had used it as a manufacturing area for Mother Brown. I said RG could have it for a studio if she paid for it to be done up. She hired a small builder and had the toilets removed, the flat roof mended, shelving put up and a lock put on the door. A quick coat of white emulsion and a large desk and it was finished. It already had a stainless steel kitchen sink unit with cold water, electric plugs and quite large windows. The light was very good. She bought window boxes for the three window-sills and planted them out with brightly coloured geraniums. This softened the view of rooftops and gave a bit of colour to a rather austere brick shed. An electric kettle meant she could make tea and coffee. The BT man came and put in a telephone, connected to the main switchboard. Voila! A studio. The kettle meant she had quite few visitors -- printers, WO'C, the architect, electrician, builders, police.....

She expected trouble from my brother and sure enough he berated her for spending company money on the conversion, especially the geraniums. So did the company secretary. She let both of them have their say and then informed them she had done it all at her own expense. Looking silly, they both walked away. Neither of them apologised.

A positive and optimistic end to 1983 – perhaps THE HIGHLIGHT of the year was publication of the NACNE (The National Advisory Committee on Nutrition Education) report. This was the subject of an excellent leading article in the Lancet on 10 December. Whilst there was widespread concern about the average person's diet, the debate had become confused. The report had taken three years to prepare and was the first statement on dietary goals from a government body for 40 years. It was noted that there was resistance in government, the food industry and in the health professions to developing effective dietary goals for the UK population. The report vindicated much of what Larkhall, RG and myself had been saying and publishing for years. RG said we should do a poster showing what 'the balanced diet' was -- something people could understand easily rather than written technical information. I agreed and she set to work on it in her little studio. (Over the coming years this poster was to become one of our most successful publicity items.)

While she was still doing the artwork RG took a phone call from a man who said he was from The Meat Marketing Board. Someone had informed him she was bringing out a vegetarian poster. In a threatening tone he told her not to. RG told him the poster had meat on it and he'd been misinformed. Who had told him about the poster? Only someone on our staff would have known about it.

The Health Standard   This was done in-house and to some extent replaced WHEN, which had been popular and done us some good. It began its life as a single sheet of advertisements for the mail order customers and expanded to 4 pages of news and comment concerning alternative medicine and new products, as a PR tool for the company. I asked for contributions from the managers. None were forthcoming so I had to rely on RG, who had done a writer's correspondence course, and myself. We collected up information from health magazines, the Lancet, the BMJ and other medical newspapers and magazines, cuttings from the daily papers and the Sundays. When we had enough to write the short articles for it, we sent it out for typesetting and layout. RG did the editing, most of the writing and illustrations and I did some of the writing and the photography, as required. It meant burning the midnight oil as it was on top of all our other work.

The first issue turned out to be far more expensive than we had been quoted as the typesetter also did the layout and did not allow for his own mistakes. There were quite a few that needed to be corrected and he charged far too much -- an extra £500. We didn't use him again as he was a bit of a prima donna and couldn't take criticism or rectify mistakes willingly. So, the second and subsequent issues would have to be done entirely in-house. In those days the typesetting had to be glued on to layout sheets and RG was able to do this as she had an architect sized drawing board with a parallel motion and very large set square. The glue she had to use was Cowgum and smelled horrible. It was eventually taken off the market classed as dangerous but it had one great asset: it enabled the user to stick the typesetting on and move it about to get the artwork in exactly the right position before it dried. Being a rubber-based glue it also allowed artwork to be peeled off and used again. Large lettering had to be drawn by hand or Letraset used. That came on a transparent backing and had to be rubbed on to the artwork in the correct place. It was also expensive to buy whole sheets of it, most of which would never be used. However, by now we had a large photocopier that would enlarge or reduce and RG found this very useful and much less expensive when she was putting the Health Standard together.

If we had used an agency the Health Standard would have cost a fortune and it would not have been viable, especially as it was to be given away free to health stores and to mail order customers. (Later on the reps were always against this publication, on principle, and didn't distribute it.) However, we kept it going, only publishing when we thought it suitable and had enough interesting information. It did not appear on a regular basis, such as quarterly, but was only brought out when we had something to say. It allowed us to print stories that nobody else would print and to report on subjects the junk food industry and the health food trade would have preferred to keep quiet about. When the media had got something wrong we could publish the correct version. It was to prove very useful as the years wore on. Above all, it gave us a voice and for a small company to have its own newspaper was a plus even if it was a PR exercise. Some health stores gave it away free and others charged a few pence. We gave it free to everyone. Best of all it gave us status.

For What it's Worth

Professor Beckett retires from Chelsea College - Quackery muzzled, all food is Healthy - Ruthmol - Coeliac Society - Dr Richards guilty - Zincold - GNC - Natural or Unnatural food - Jimmy Lee-Richardson - Diet and Depression - Opposition to Holism becomes more belligerent - Herbals threatened - Hyperactive Children Support - FRSC - Bender - Yeti Man - DLPA - Advertising Regulation - Lipcote and Ruthmol TV Commercials - Germany - The Good Nutrients Guide - Holistic Pharmacists - The British Food Fiasco – Stockbroker interest - Vitacare Science - Douglas Erskine - More Government support needed - New products - Larkhall's shop opens - B17 Saga ending

This was a significant year for Larkhall and was to be a frenetic roller coaster year of progress with highs and lows.

The first real skirmish with the opponents of alternative healthcare took place in July when I was invited to take part in a Channel 4 TV programme 'For What it's Worth' hosted by Ms Joan Shenton. On the programme was Professor Arnold Bender whom I had not known previously – he was a leading academic in mainstream nutrition – a consultant to Food Industry Companies and indirect beneficiary of their research funding largesse – he was an implacable opponent of the Health Food Movement. He had obviously singled me out for a major personal attack – other people on the programme included corporate executive Denis Bowley a director of Booker Health Foods and Anne Warren-Davis a kindly naturopath. Bender had Larkhall's product list to hand and made outrageous accusations against me and the Larkhall company founded on such ignorance that I could not believe in his credentials as a respected academic nutritionist. Nevertheless Bender's attack had to be parried and this was partially successful but afterwards, on reflection, perhaps I should have fought dirtier – especially questioning Bender's real independence and integrity as he questioned mine.

Bender had just written a book 'Health or Hoax' which was about to be published and was a deranged attack on Health Foods and Alternative Healthcare. His undeclared support from the sugar and junk food industry was never exposed as it should have been.

I was encouraged by the many letters and calls of support after the programme but critics wanted a more robust stance taken but forgot that the public can see through arrogance and a similar response to Bender's attack would have elicited no sympathy. Bullies like Bender seldom fool anyone.

Bender became one of the founders of HealthWatch (Campaign against Health Fraud) in 1988 – of course the main protagonists were working on their ideas beginning in 1983. Perhaps I should have taken it as a compliment that it was our company and not the large ones like Bookers that was seen as the real enemy of Bender and his cohorts. However, they seriously underestimated my determination and resources.

Larkhall continued to successfully fight the Coeliac Society regarding the term 'Gluten Free' and Bookers on 'Low Salt'. Unfortunately, HealthWatch would continue their attacks until 1994.

Many Tablet products were being switched from plastic bottles to blisters in cartons. Cartoning enabled more legible information to be included on the packs and provided good pilfer proofing. Many competitors were still using glass bottles for their products but these were costly to send in the post and breakage rates were unacceptable.

LARKHALL GREEN FARM

Chelsea School of Pharmacy -- my old College   After many years of evolution this was finally absorbed into King's College London. The Manresa Road building continued for a few more years. It was sold in the 90s to be developed into, at the time, the most expensive luxury flats in London. Chelsea SW3 was very desirable and I had spent several years in the basement laboratories there in the late 50s.

A retirement symposium 'Development of Drugs and Modern Medicines'. This was held at the College and there was a dinner to mark the retirement of Professor Arnold Beckett OBE. the pioneer of performance enhancing drug testing in athletes. As one of Beckett's PhD Students back in 1959-62 I attended the dinner in his honour at the Pharmaceutical Society's building in Vauxhall. All Beckett's PhD students had their signatures engraved on the silver salver presented to him. All had to give an account of what they were doing. Whilst most were or had been leading lights in Academia, I was the only one from the Alternative Health area. Not only that but I had amassed, thanks to owning an independent manufacturing family business, resources to defend and fight for those ideas.

Conversion to Alternative Health Care   AHB was very sceptical of all aspects of Alternative Health Care although supportive of me personally. He would never have joined the arrogant academics in HealthWatch. By 1991 after a chance meeting at an Olympic Sports Medicine Symposium in Barcelona I finally converted AHB to see the merits of alternative healthcare and his support in the famous Tandem IQ case was to be invaluable to Larkhall and left the bureaucrats speechless.

Whilst Beckett was to end his days as a supporter of alternatives, sadly, his insistence that convincing scientific evidence of the effectiveness and consistent technical quality of those treatments/products was possible, proved unattainable. I was to fall out with him over his certainty that calcium could only be absorbed from the human gut in acid digestive conditions. I believed that traces of that mineral could be absorbed protected by enzymes in less acidic environments that was the alternative health care opinion in the USA. I thought superiority and infallibility of science needed replacement by humility before nature. By the early 21st Century, Quantum Science has potentially transformed this situation.

The name 'Chelsea Pharmacy Association' lives on in an annual award to a Post Graduate Pharmacy Student at King's College. The old Chelsea College building did not close until after its Centenary Celebration in 1996. A Ginkgo tree was planted by the alumni in the garden of the flats in Manresa Road to commemorate Chelsea School of Pharmacy having existed for 100 years. The tree may be visited by interested people on application to the porter.

Neal Muranyi ex Newman Turner (Bookers Mail Order and publishing business) had joined Larkhall as Mail Order Sales Manager in mid 1983. He was experienced in the supplement business and had good connections within the Booker Group. He seemed good for the company but I was never really sure about him. He seemed to become angry when RG and I looked at competitors to his chosen supply sources -- not a good sign.

Quackery should be muzzled and all food is healthy   An article in the January issue of Hospital Doctor by Dr Graham Barker headlined "It is time we muzzled all this quackery" attacked the Health Food Movement and Industry for supporting special diets and supplements. It highlighted the problem that press freedom permitted journalists with no scientific background to promote 'cures' through diets.

These arguments were not new and by 1988 had led to the founding of 'HealthWatch'. Men like Barker could not see that it was the failure of free of charge orthodox medicine that was responsible for the success of what he thought quackery. He was among the first to describe 'Health Food' as a misleading term because all food is 'Healthy'. What nonsense.

The Pharmacy Health Store debate   The Chemist & Druggist ran a long article on vitamins. Whilst Chemists sell mainly products from pharmaceutical manufacturers, the Health Food store offered products preferred by those wishing to avoid synthetic chemicals. The terms 'natural' and 'vegetarian' were important. The article predicted a move from chemists to supermarkets and the rise in demand for generic vitamins where price came first. I did not see this as a threat but believed that once a consumer was buying a vitamin product there was a chance that he/she would become more knowledgeable and move to the more natural preparations for real benefit.

In August a misunderstanding was exposed in correspondence to the Chemist & Druggist between Mr Bill Draper of Pharmaton and me that arose from the TV programme in July. It was soon settled with me contending that neither Pharmacists nor General Practitioners (Doctors) studied nutrition properly during their education. Pharmaton, made in Germany, was a ginseng compound product that was exclusively distributed in Pharmacies. So, unsurprisingly, Draper favoured Pharmacists as the retailers who should advise on supplements and natural remedies. I held the view that Health Food Retailers were more knowledgeable in the natural health care but hoped that Pharmacists and Doctors would soon take more interest in this important contributor to public heath.

Ruthmol Salt Free Salt replacer (See Chapter 3, 1971 p. 24 for background to Ruthmol). Over the thirteen years that Ruthmol had been owned by Larkhall, sales had grown steadily through advertising and Doctor recommendation. It was an ethical medical product but not prescribable on the NHS. Two other competitive products were Selora by Sterling Winthrop (a multinational drug company) and Therasal by Thomas Kerfoot & Co Ltd a generic pharmaceutical company. These were both salt free products based on Potassium Chloride. Ruthmol tasted better than its competitors and was the leading brand. It was promoted to Doctors and advertised in health magazines. Public Relations methods were also used including sampling. By 1984 sales were substantial at about 300,000 packs a year. Unfortunately these sales levels attracted scientifically illiterate food companies to the salt substitute market who then introduced Low Salt products that were actually Salt (Sodium Chloride) based and certainly not low in salt.

The difference between 'Low' salt and Salt 'Free' became an issue between Larkhall and Booker Health Foods trading as 'Prewetts'. In law there was no distinction and the truly Salt Free product Ruthmol (contained costly Potassium Chloride) was greatly undercut in price by a Low Salt that was a mixture of Sodium Chloride (low cost common salt) and some Potassium Chloride. Such a mixture was not only cheaper to make but was of no proven health benefit to people following a low salt dietary regime for health purposes (Blood Pressure Reduction). The sodium would swamp the potassium in the patient's blood stream and so negate its benefit. Additionally these products were of no benefit to healthy people who wanted to reduce salt for general health benefit, particularly to prevent strokes and heart attacks. They just added to the harmful 'hidden salt' levels in processed foods. The BBC Food Programme did a feature on this problem. Publicity regarding health risks from Salt (Sodium) stimulated sales for Ruthmol. At the beginning of 1984 ASDA Supermarkets were stocking Ruthmol but the high sales soon diminished with the advent of LoSalt. These low salt products were not promoted to Doctors but their attractive prices and misleading name soon found mass consumers.

Since Bookers were a Health Food company, Larkhall succeeded in persuading them to change their packs (Prewetts) and advertising by threatening legal action that was settled amicably by me and Dennis Bowley, a Booker Director. The product LoSalt by Chemical Company Klingers remained unmoved and soon dominated the salt substitute market together with various Sea Salts that were medically useless for preventing Blood Pressure. After some 15 years the law was changed but even today it is unlikely that consumers appreciate the difference between low salt and salt free salt substitutes. Ruthmol's place in the sun faded (in May 1984 the Financial times reported that sales of Ruthmol had doubled) but still had a select but dedicated clientele in 1999.

In March there was a good report on the BBC2 Food and Drink Programme regarding Ruthmol's fight against Prewetts Low Salt. Sadly, the programme lost its way and latterly (1988) was too influenced by the arrogant academics from HealthWatch.

The Coeliac Society Relations with the Coeliac Society were still not good. Larkhall were openly criticizing them for their support for Low Gluten products by permitting manufacturers of those products to openly display the Society's 'Gluten Free' symbol on their packaging. The Society criticized Larkhall for supplying Gluten Free Vitamin Supplements that they considered unnecessary for Coeliacs. They just ignored the fact that the processing of wheat to reduce its Gluten content inevitably reduced its vitamin and mineral content too thus if any group of patients needed supplements it was certainly Coeliacs. The processed wheat endangered the coeliac patient because whilst containing traces of Gluten/Gliadin, it was deficient in the essential micronutrients that could protect their health.

The involvement of large food companies that produced the low gluten products in the funding the activities of the Coeliac Society was highlighted by Larkhall and led to legal dispute with the Society that was resolved when Larkhall finally had their Trufree product advertising accepted in the Coeliac Magazine (The Crossed Grain). RG had done bake-ups with Trufree flours that showed its excellent results and worked with a photographer to do the pictures for the adverts and the front of the packs. They were miles ahead of anything else on the market and were 100% gluten/wheat free.

Research hope for the Coeliac Society. In July a short paper in the British Medical Journal by researchers, possibly supported by the Coeliac Society, purported to show that traces of Gliadin (a component of Gluten) was not harmful to Coeliac Patients. Obviously, this research was vital to the Coeliac Society's recommendation of reduced gluten flour from Wheat as a safe ingredient in Foods bearing the society's Gluten Free Symbol. Many clinicians did not support this view despite this research.

Dr Dick Richards Guilty verdict Early in the year Dick Richards made contact about new evidence in his case regarding a supposed conspiracy to murder Peter Stephan here in the UK. A Dr Bennett reported an attack on Peter Stephan long before Dick was in LA. Dick intended to return to LA to face trial and not forfeit the bail money, much of which had been lent by loyal patients and friends. He believed US justice would be in his favour.

In August RG and I visited Sandwich to see his wife Pix. We learnt Dick was in USA defending the conspiracy to murder case brought against him. They had had to sell their country house to pay for the court case. One of the lawyers went off with the money and was never seen again. The trial was a complete farce and Dick was ultimately found guilty and sentenced to four years jail in the USA. Still on bail, he was allowed home to the UK but had to go back to America to serve his sentence in a prison near LA.

I was able to visit him twice in Chino Jail when I was in USA on business trips. He looked well and was carrying out minor surgery on prisoners in the prison hospital that kept him busy and still enabled him to function as a doctor. All those who had put up the money for his bail -- $250,000 -- were repaid in full, including RG and me. There is no doubt he was not guilty but US Law is riven with danger for foreigners. If he had not gone back to the USA to defend himself he would have remained free and not been extradited to USA. He knew this but still returned believing he would get 'justice' because he knew he was innocent, as did all his friends. If he had not returned to America to serve his sentence he would have forfeited his bail money and not been able to pay back his supporters.

Stephan died a few years later from natural causes, still dabbling in one of the less attractive areas of alternative healthcare -- eternal youth. Stephan's death made the news and RG telephoned Dick in Cyprus to tell him. The press in the UK were trying hard to find Dick and drag it all up again but friends closed ranks and they couldn't contact him.

A New Vitamin Company and Zinc   In February I met Mr Pradip Pattni who had formed a company, Vitalia, to compete in the Vitamin Supplement Market. Vitalia became a force in the trade but over extended itself by the mid 1990s and failed. Its product Zincold made excessive claims for effectiveness against the Common Cold and became involved in extensive disputes with authorities.

General Nutrition Corporation arrived in the UK from USA Ms Terry Royal visited Larkhall from General Nutrition, the UK subsidiary of a large US company which had been doing some contract business with Larkhall. They wished to expand from Mail Order to Shops soon. Co-incidentally, Pattni had been working with the publishers of Prevention Magazine, Rodales, that had passed over its UK supplement business to GNC. There could be far reaching changes in the Health Food Industry ahead if GNC, one of the largest vitamin companies in the USA decided to make the UK its base in Europe.

Italian Business was in its infancy. Legal representation of Prodotti Naturali our distributor, was through a lawyer Ugo Scuro (Hugo Dark). He thought that many of our products would do well in Italy but registration was soon to become very problematical. On a visit to London in February the Maugeris reported difficulties in importing supplements but said they would change tactics. In March, I 'phoned Anna in Rome and all appeared to be going well again. All these problems were present long before the Single Market in 1992.

Natural or Unnatural Foods. In March The British Medical Journal published a leading article on this knotty subject and it illustrated the complexity of the situation regarding the word 'Natural'. Use of this word in marketing was a potential minefield for both manufacturers and the regulators. This problem still persists in 2015.

Medicines Inspection. In March, we had an unannounced visit from our Medicines Inspector. This resulted in the company considering further reducing its 'Medicinal' Product Range. The pettiness of his criticisms and possible hidden agenda caused concern for management. The feeling was that these people just don't want the hassle of inspecting companies like ours. However, in November an inspection by him went well -- perhaps he was in a better mood.

Depression and Diet   A booklet by Dr Barrie Bartlett was one of the first to link diet with Depression and Anxiety. Food supplements containing Tryptophan were recommended and extra B Vitamins could enhance benefit. At this time, depression was one of the major illnesses prescribed daily drugs singly and in combinations.

It was a major contributor to profits for the pharmaceutical industry with many patients finding themselves prescribed tablets or capsules of potent anti-depressant drugs for life. Evidence for the effectiveness of these drugs was often weak and the side effects frightening particularly for combination drug treatments. The Pharma Industry and medical profession dismissed dietary causes and saw books like Bartlett's as a threat to sales. Nutrition was too difficult for both prescriber to believe and patients to practise. It was the familiar story of a magic one-a-day bullet being expected by most patients.

Computer system renewed and upgraded   A new Computer system was installed for general administration purposes in July. This was a Data General and replaced the Burroughs System installed in 1980. Computerisation of all Larkhalls administrative, sales, stock, wages and accountancy was now in operation. The software house involved on the DG were unable to produce a fully integrated system. Manufacturing production had to run on a separate computer, using bespoke software from an independent consultant.

Jimmy Lee-Richardson   Once again contact was made with Jimmy Lee Richardson, generally considered as the founder of the modern UK Health Food Trade. His opening letter has reminiscences which should be treasured and indicated how close Larkhall was to the trade and founder of 'Healthcrafts' in the early 1960s. Jimmy's great integrity led to his severing all connection with the company Bookers that had taken over all his companies – including herbalists Heath & Heather (to be integrated with Holland & Barrett), Newman Turner Publications (Publishers of Here's Health) Brewhurst (Wholesalers to the Health Food Trade) and Associated Health Foods (owners of several Branded Food Supplements). Bookers were now competing as Holland & Barrett with the small retailers whom Jimmy had sworn to protect from the predations of multinational corporations. Bookers were still vertically integrated in the industry as major manufacturers, wholesalers, retailers, health magazine and book publishers. I had warned him at the time of the takeover not to trust Bookers who in the early 1990s were forced out of the Health Food Industry because of their disastrous foray into the 'Vitachieve' product (see Chapter 19 p 214). We supplied Jimmy with supplements for private use.

Demand for Gluten Free foods to grow   Winston Fletcher, a well known personality in the advertising world wrote an article in Marketing Week predicting that Gluten Free foods would grow in demand amongst slimmers. This may have been more prescient than he believed because many slimmers thought 'Food Allergies" were responsible for their obesity problems and in 2010 flocked to the 'Free From' food sections in supermarkets that are heavily stocked with Wheat/Gluten Free products.

Symbol System   Medicine hunter, Christopher Kilham drew attention to the many additives/excipients contained in Supplement Tablets and Capsules. Many are undesirable in so called 'Natural' products. Cantassium's Branding had been pointing this out for many years and had recently introduced the Symbol System invented by Rita Greer on their packaging.

Cytotoxic Test   Allergy Testing article in Here's Health mentioned the Cytotoxic Test for food allergy used by Larkhall together with many other methods both medically proved (only for immediate allergic reactions) and alternative. The conclusion was left open. The problem in this area was that immediate allergic reactions sources could be readily detected but there were also delayed reactions of up to four days that were very difficult to detect and source.

Ex Minister of Health extols virtues of Holism   A report in The Lancet (July) of a lecture 'Medicine, Morality and the Market' by The Rt Hon Dr David Owen, a past Labour Minister of Health and in 1984 a leading Social Democrat.

This was an important extract from a Lecture he gave at McGill University, Montreal in April. It's view of the benefits of a holistic approach to healthcare, if it had been acted on, would have transformed the NHS by 2015. As it is, I think his really constructive ideas went into the long grass, vested interests again must have achieved suppression. A letter subsequently written by me received a reply with a copy of the full Lecture extensively amended by him in hand writing. Sadly, he never came to see us despite my invitation in August. I should have persisted more.

The opposition to Holism became more active and belligerent   After I appeared on The **'For What it's Worth'** TV programme that highlighted differing views from within the Health Food Trade and the academic world. I was on this programme on the side of vitamins and supplements but was not prepared to get involved in the 'Natural' versus 'Synthetic' debate, whilst the trade wanted someone to put forward their largely irrational approach that would have been totally demolished by Professor Bender, using dubious logic. I had recently been elected as Chairman of the Holistic Pharmacists Association and my approach had always been that 'Holistic and Wholefood' were different from 'Synthetic and Balanced'. Bender and most of the health establishment did not want to know about this fundamental difference. The main problem was that the 'Health Food trade' wanted it both ways – to claim Pharmaceutical Purity yet call their products 'Natural'. An account of Bender and his upcoming book appeared in an article in the Daily Telegraph in May 1985.

The transcript of this programme provided a valuable record of the opposition's view that has been unchanged right up to 2015. Professor Arnold Bender, writer of a book to be published in1985 by Elvendon Press 'Health or Hoax', a purported expose of the Health Food Industry, attacked me for our poisonous products and my false qualifications. All my qualifications were genuine. I was restrained in answering these unjust accusations and hopefully this restraint helped the holistic cause. Certainly Dennis Bowley of Bookers remained cool under attack from Bender as did the herbalist Anne Warren Davis. Bender displayed a certain desperation and made several false statements in his attacks. There was no rational argument but it made good Television - I was told. Bender's views, which were those of Quackbusters' (later renamed HealthWatch), were to cause Larkhall and me more trouble within a decade (1989-92 Tandem IQ case).

There was legal correspondence following the programme and many sympathetic viewer letters to me and there were countless telephone calls the following day at the office. However, I don't believe the fundamental differences between me and Bender were really appreciated -- 'Wholesome and Natural' rather than 'Synthetic and Balanced' either by the industry or consumer.

Whether Bender did his cause good by his display on this programme was doubtful. By September the show was history and I did not sue Bender for libel despite thoughts in that direction. With hindsight, perhaps I should have sued him, but court cases take up a lot of working time to prepare and cost a fortune in legal fees.

Threats to Herbals   By 1984 many herbal medicinal products had been withdrawn from the UK market but even more were facing extinction. Our Registration Manager Roger Baxter attended a BIRA symposium on this topic and reported that the area faced more product decimation from regulators. These products were lost because they were subjected to disproportionate technical rules designed for synthetic chemical drugs not natural wholesome herbs. Nothing to do with 'safety'.

Hyperactive Children's Support Charity   In July RG gave a lecture to the 'Hyperactive Children' Support Group" near Worthing, Sussex. Sally Bunday and her mother were behind this nationally growing association of Hyperactive Children Parent groups.

They were fighting against synthetic additives in foods particularly colours like tartrazine that were believed to be a cause of Hyperactivity. Many of their ideas were subsequently supported by authorities and many additives have ceased in foods thanks to their efforts. Rita's books on special diets using pure, wholesome food ingredients are still widely used by mothers cooking for their affected children. Her lecture was well received. Larkhall supplements were widely used by Hyperactive Children because they contained no additives with allergic properties. Our product Junamac was specially formulated for these children. Eventually Sally Bunday was awarded the OBE for her work.

Family Matters   A possible move of the business to a site in Portsmouth was vetoed by my brother. I wasn't that keen on the property that was a former bakery. It had a problem with 'rope', a fungal mould which is very hard to eradicate. I suspect family pressure on my brother prompted his veto to avoid leaving the bucolic life in Charlbury and Oxfordshire.

A plan to open Vitamin Shops was considered but our lack of retail expertise made viability unlikely.

'New Health' Magazine   Neal Muranyi and I visited the offices of Haymarket Publishing and were shown their new health magazine 'New Health'. We discussed the future of the health food business and possible advertising in their magazine.

I was elected a Fellow of the Royal Society of Chemistry in September. Despite my many disputes with other Chemists including academics there was no shortage of referees recommending me for this professional advancement.

More from Bender   Ironically Chemistry in Britain the official journal sent to all members and fellows of the RSC carried an anti Vitamin article by Lorna O'Driscoll. This amounted to a repeat of Bender's attack in July, Professor Vincent Marks, a supporter of Quackbusters, was quoted and his repetition of the Bender line made me believe in a conspiracy building against the holistic health movement. I sent a letter to the Editor but it was not published immediately. However, it was pleasing to see that the publication printed the response from me in the December 1984 issue but Bender also peddled his line in a letter although he appeared to have calmed down a little.

More Books   In September, RG was finishing her new book 'The Right Way to Cook' for Dents Publishers. Miriam Polunin (ex editor of Here's Health) had already written 'The Right Way to Eat'. Dents were hoping for a series. RG made several local broadcasts in the South on her new books 'Cooking with Dried Fruit' and 'The British Food Fiasco'. Her book 'Egg Free, Milk Free, Wheat Free Cooking' was published and led to several local radio broadcasts too.

Greece   An approach came from a Mr Sammi regarding distributing our products in Greece. He took some Blakoe Rings but would also be taking Supplements soon – he said. However, the previous approach from Maria Strofalis from Vital Naturtabs in Athens led to her visiting Putney when she told me that she was confident of importing more supplement products. We heard no more of Sammi.

Cantassium -- a dominant brand   The July 27 Super Marketing Magazine reported on growth of Vitamins & Tonics and judged Cantassium as a dominant brand alongside Bookers and the Health & Diet company.

Diet and Cardiovascular Disease link was recognised by doctors and government   In early September the British Medical Journal reported on the recent DHSS document regarding Diet and Cardiovascular Disease. This was the first time government had made a recommendation of a reduction of fat especially saturated fat and to increase the ratio of polyunsaturates to saturates in the diet. This was an important step on the path to a healthier diet for all - long advocated by Larkhall. This must be just the start.

Progress on Alternative Health Care   In early September, The Times carried an article 'Doctors meet to heal the rift'. This reported that the BMA had made an approach to Alternative therapists and appeared conciliatory but the Alternative/Complementary people were wary. The formation of the British Holistic Medical Association in 1983 may have helped matters but there was much work to be done on healing what appeared an unbridgeable gap between 'Alternative' and 'Orthodox' Health Care. Whilst there has been some progress since 1984 – the old positions/attitudes seem well entrenched in 2015.

DLPA 375   (DL Phenylalanine 375mg) was a very useful Aminoacid product to help with pain relief. Larkhall pioneered its use in Europe following its development in the USA. It was said to increase production of natural painkilling endorphins in the body. No overt claims were possible but anecdotal evidence from satisfied consumers passing on their experience of relief to friends ensured regular demand.

The success of DLPA led to competition. In September Larkhall threatened a competitor regarding the use of DLPA (a Larkhall Trade Mark) as a proprietary designation. It transpired that this was not our product but that of another manufacturer Reevecrest who was also in the market to a considerable extent. Subsequent correspondence with the trade association was unhelpful. I decided to stop promoting DLPA and pointed out to Maurice Hanssen, a man I never trusted, the injustice which gave companies who actually made innovations no incentive to develop because no enforceable proprietary rights were available to them.

The some time President of the HFMA, Maurice Hanssen   Hanssen was a Jekyll/Hyde character who was latterly President of the HFMA (Health Food Manufacturers Association) but also a very successful consultant to Health Food Companies. I always held that these two roles were incompatible because he had unacceptable conflicts of interest. We only joined the HFMA reluctantly and resigned when MH made me really angry in 1991. Maurice loved the high life and was often seen in expensive restaurants using one of his many Consultant Company's credit cards, instructing waiters to ensure another bottle of fine wine arrived at his table when the previous one became empty. It was rumoured that when Jimmy Lee Richardson dismissed him from Bookers he was given a top post at HFMA as compensation. Ray Matthews of Wassen didn't just give him a credit card but also a nice car, preferring to keep his friends close but his enemies even closer. MH lived really well on what people handed out to him.

Hanssen certainly associated with many of the difficult people in the industry including David Horrobin (Efamol) (who had delivered death threats to RG, John Williams and his wife) and the director of (Reevecrest). Above all he was a diplomat and had the ear of bureaucrats in the UK and Europe which proved of great value and contributed to delay of anti-health food and vitamin legislation for years. Happily, his legacy continues to this day as the industry still survives whilst its enemies have no real success.

The Yeti Man A professional Explorer, known as 'The Yeti Man', visited Putney and suggested Larkhall should sponsor his trip to the Himalayas in 1985. I said I would think about it. He claimed he found our vitamins really helped him survive high altitudes. I was sceptical as I didn't believe him and thought he might be just saying this to get a handout/sponsorship.

The TV Commercials RG had worked with Keith Godman, a TV Commercial Producer/Director, on several commercials for the British Tourist Board and for Andrex (JWT). He came to Annie's Room for lunch with Pauline Hurst in October to discuss the possibilities of making commercials for Larkhall products (Lipcote and Ruthmol). I had already decided that doing it all through an agency was out of the question owing to the astronomical costs. If we couldn't do it in-house we wouldn't be able to do it at all. By November preparations for the new TV Commercials were going well.

It required a script to be presented to the Commercial TV regulators and passed by them before we could begin. RG worked with Godman on it. They had worked together before and got on really well but even so RG submitted the script to the regulators thirteen times before it was passed as suitable. It took ages as they kept having meetings. RG offered to go to their offices and demonstrate Lipcote as they had a rule about trying everything out themselves. As it was not really a product for men we wondered how they would get on with it. The regulators were not experienced in working with a non-agency person; in fact this was the first time they had and seemed to be shocked by the idea. They gave RG a difficult time but she stood her ground. RG knew the products inside out and knew what needed to be in the commercials. Eventually, after several weeks, she wore them down and they gave their permission. Godman hired a studio, technicians, two actors and a hand model for three days.

In December, the TV commercials for Lipcote and Ruthmol were made in a studio near Drury Lane. RG had to be involved in the Ruthmol commercial as it required writing on a board with a flow of Ruthmol -- difficult. She also had to be there for the filming of the Lipcote commercial. Both commercials turned out really well. Even my brother thought they were good.

The commercial for Lipcote was used over a two year period 1985/6 in the South and North of England and London. When it was first shown on TV there was no doubt it worked as the demand for the product shot up like a rocket. After the first transmission there wasn't a bottle of Lipcote to be had in the south. However, there was no way we could be sure the retailers or the outlets kept enough stock to satisfy the upsurge in demand.

The Ruthmol commercial was only used in Northern Ireland. Costs for TV slots were high and the poor cooperation of larger retailers in maintaining stock on shelf did not encourage us to further risk on TV. We learnt the hard way that a good commercial that works is not necessarily the best route to increased sales.

Stress at Charlbury The stress of doing special blister contract work at the packing factory in Charlbury seemed to be telling on my brother's behaviour. It was clear we would lose a vital contract if this problem persisted. History indicated this was likely as it happened before in the early 70s with a bottle packing contract that became too big and difficult. I began to think my brother was really looking for a quiet life with large rewards. In the event the blister contract was lost and we also lost the tablet making for it in Putney too.

Luckily this blow had little effect because the export of our own brands was escalating. Soon we considered the possibility of moving the export distribution function from London to Charlbury and I agreed that this should take place.

Advertising regulation   There was pressure for voluntary advertising regulation by the Health Food Industry to avoid statutory regulation by the government. This threat gave rise to HFMA organised seminars on advertising and labeling of Health Food Supplements. The HFMA wanted to control its members in these areas but the dominance of large companies such as Bookers and Seven Seas in the Association meant that small companies would be forced to divulge details of new products to their powerful competitors.

This was because these companies had representatives on vetting committees. I thought this made the systems unworkable. It was noticeable that the head of HFMA Maurice Hanssen had conflicts of interest because he not only served the HFMA but also sat on the national CAP Advisory Committee. This enabled him to keep all his client companies informed and undermined the small UK companies who did not pay him an advisory fee. Larkhall would not co-operate with any of this nonsense so had few friends. The Conflict of Interest question should have been addressed by the HFMA but was very unlikely because most companies feared Hanssen.

At the informal meeting which solved the Prewetts Low Salt dispute, Denis Bowley the MD of Bookers told me that Hanssen had not passed on a letter I had written to him about Low Salt in 1983 and at their solicitor's meeting had acted dumb. If Denis had known of my offer and my view, the Prewetts product would have been withdrawn and relabelled then. This information confirmed my suspicions of Maurice as an enemy of Larkhall within the Health Food Industry. He was probably undermining me from a very privileged position. No wonder Larkhall were in for trouble with Tandem IQ and Aerobic Glasses a few years later.

Export to Germany   In October I went to Hanover to meet Obitz Pharmacy who proposed to import the Larkhall supplement range into Germany. The Obitz's give me a generous welcome and were optimistic of gaining government authorization for imports from Larkhall. I was doubtful but agreed that if they succeeded, exclusivity for Germany would be given to them. In the event after many months there was no progress but stone walling by the German officials with legalese. I contended that there was no Common Market, it was a myth. The word 'safety' is prostituted by several countries to ensure protection for their own producers. The Germans were keen to export but not import.

Another Booker ex-employee joined   Simon Martin (Ex Editor Here's Health, now editor of The Journal of Alternative Medicine) and James Macdonald, from Newman Turner Publishing came to talk to RG and me. They may be interested in working for Larkhall on Publicity. In the event James joined as our PR man later in the year.

Around this time, Chris Chope MP, Derek Cooper and John Forsyth from the BBC Food Programme came for lunch in Annie's Room for constructive conversations about Health and Food connections. More Government action was needed in this area.

Good Nutrients Guide   This book, commissioned by Dents, to be written jointly by me and RG, progressed to publication in 1985. RG had already written and been published by them – 'Allergic to Food? A Self-help Guide' and 'The right Way to Cook'. Later she would write 'Healthier Special Diets' for them. The Good Nutrients Guide aimed to provide consumers with information they could not receive commercially from advertisers. I saw books as the only way forward because product information was always being demanded from Larkhall. Customers constantly complained that we were failing to give them information that seemed really important to them. This is still a big problem in 2015 and any information must be backed by convincing scientific medical evidence that satisfies the regulator's experts, many of whom covertly worked for the pharmaceutical and junk food industries as consultants.

Holistic Pharmacists group failing to obtain real support   Pharmacists were making their living from prescription drugs and the OTC products of the Pharmaceutical Industry and so had little interest in 'Alternative Health Care'. In the following years Larkhall tried to persuade pharmacists otherwise but their increasing profits from mainstream medication made this an uphill task. The resources of the alternative industry were too little in finance and scientific expertise to prick the dominance of the modern Pharma interests. That remains true in 2015.

The British Food Fiasco   This book by Rita Greer was published by her small company Bunterbird Ltd in November and was reported in Natural Food Trader. This very controversial book caused a big stir and the junk food industry soon managed to have it off display in leading booksellers. WHSmith were too frightened to stock it, saying it was too controversial, but 'phoned up in a panic when they had an order from the Navy for 42 copies the first day it was published. As WHS had banned it, RG supplied the Navy herself. It was for two classes of naval chefs at their training college. It was not popular in the Health Food trade because she was not complimentary about its structure and dubious product claims. However, the truth is seldom good news for everyone and Rita's views are still valid in 2015. A run of 4000 copies was sold mainly by mail order and it went underground as it was very hard-hitting against the junk food industry. In 2015 it is still available second hand on Amazon, at a price.

Chain of Health Stores envisaged by a stockbroker   The Health Food Industry was developing well despite the threats from regulators and many lay people thought it a good area in which to start a new business, even if they didn't know anything about it. A City stockbroker friend asked for my advice on starting such a company. He had a member of his staff who considered herself well informed about vitamins and health foods. She was to head the project in co-operation with the broker's wife. Despite the very good lunch, I warned that it was not that easy to develop a chain of health stores in the current regulatory environment. I advised against the project. I might as well have said nothing because the friend went ahead and, of course, lost his money. I learned later that the broker had determined on the project before the lunch and thought I might open my own chain and steal the idea.

New Company: Vitacare Professional and Aquacelle   Formed in 1984 Vitacare Professional was carefully researched with a sales assessment yet it failed totally. As I had deduced when the Holistic Pharmacists Association was formed, Pharmacists were not very interested in Alternative Health Care including Nutrition and vitamins. They made a good living already from their close working with the Pharma Industry. Vitacare launched with a prestigious scientific meeting at the Pharmaceutical Society's Head Quarters in London to explain the science behind their unique Aquacelle delivery technology for Vitamins. The company struggled for about four years but then passed a little stock to Larkhall at cost. We soon closed it down.

Martha Hill   Martha Hill and her son David Hill-Brookes came to dinner again in Annie's Room. Martha was a well known entrepreneur who was in the fashion business with her own factory back in the 1930s. She now had a fashion business in Marylebone Lane and a mail order skin care company. She was always good company, very lively and on the ball regarding business. RG was, and still is, a great fan of her skin care products. Martha had researched the formulas herself, working from her kitchen. These were then sent to a chemist in Switzerland to be made in bulk.

The packaging was clean and simple. The interesting thing about her business was that Martha never advertised on principle and relied solely on person to person recommendation.

RG did an article about her skin care range in WHEN in 1978 and this started her off as they were new products. The business was run from an old farmhouse in Corby and she had a flat in the West End (London) with a shop underneath. She died in the late 90s but the family business is still up and running now, in the hands of her grandson (2015).

Douglas Erskine was a customer and a friend of WO'C, of Scottish origin and allegedly trained in Canada, who was probably a charlatan. He called himself 'Doctor Doug Erskine'. I was suspicious of his credentials but since he was an established customer and used our products in his practice I did not feel obliged to check his veracity. He was registered as an Acupuncturist but may have lost his accreditation in the mid 80s. He was a very big man who could not stop eating -- hardly an advertisement for Health Foods. He was subsequently heavily criticised in the media and suddenly disappeared abroad.

Overseas developments Our Dutch distributor Nutrivital visited Putney and we discussed the way forward. All was going well and Holland was our best overseas market.

I noted a promising future for Belgium distributor (Heelesun) in the person of Helene Wauters too.

Middle East: there was interest from Kuwait but no progress.

A Mr Atef from Saudi Arabia came to Putney and ordered 36,000 Lipcote in Arabic cartons – these were shipped and paid for but no further orders were ever received. Saudi Arabia was a difficult country as regards exports.

The Philippines proved a failure. A Mrs Fernando visited Putney from the Philippines and took carrier bags of products back with her but later, when trying to import from us into that country, these products failed to get through customs. As usual 'safety reasons' were given by the authorities - where were all these people who were keeling over as they walked out of health stores?

Future Larkhall was offering advisory health and beauty services to consumers and contract manufacturing to the trade. These were really incompatible because trade people perceived Larkhall as serving their domain. Increasingly Larkhall would move to become a Brand Service to consumers using wholesalers and retailers as distributors. We operated under many names.

We could certainly help with questions like the one from a Miss Renton enquiring about whether she should swallow or rub Hair Nutrition tablets into her scalp!

For What it's Worth controversy went further In February 1985, The Lancet resurrected the Vitamin A saga explored by the Channel 4 For What it's worth programme in July 1984. My and Maurice Hanssen's replies to Jad Adams and Joan Shenton's letter were published. I even had a request for a reprint of my letter from an academic in USA. In May 1985 Arnold Bender's recent Book 'Health or Hoax' had a review in The Daily Telegraph.

New blister packed tablets and Advertising Rita Greer designed a new presentation for Larkhall's Cantassium Range to give a more 'Pharmacy' friendly appearance. Health stores had asked for white all round the edges. The tablets (Naturtabs) were blister packed and the cartons provided plenty of space to give more information to consumers.

The 1984/5 advertisements for Cantassium. emphasised the Pharmaceutical knowledge available at Larkhall from Dr Woodward and Pharmacist Roger Baxter. The trade advertisements illustrated the consumer one within its design. Dendron, who were already distributing Lipcote to independent pharmacies, also promoted a small range of Cantassium Supplements. Seven Seas dominated the pharmacy market through their Cod Liver Oil brands and it was virtually impossible for Cantassium to penetrate profitably but we had a good try for a couple of years.

The successful introduction of Microfolic Acid 400mcg in 1992 was to change things positively for Larkhall Supplements in the professional area for the first time. There was no disputing the positive science behind Folic Acid

The Shop   Mark Morris's old office on the front corner of the building had remained empty since 1979. Before we had bought the property the Cathkin laundry had used it as a dry cleaners. RG was very keen to have a shop for our products. She had begun her working life at the age of thirteen in a shop so had some experience herself. It could double as a reception and would be very useful for showing visitors the range of our products, actually on the shelves. Our maintenance staff made a counter and shelved it out with white formica shelves. There was room for a store at the side of it. It looked like a small chemist's and as the window was large, was light and bright. We bought a till and took on a manageress, installed a phone line to the switchboard, a credit card machine and linked it to security. RG designed a carrier bag specially for the shop. An application to the Pharmaceutical Society with our Pharmacists named achieved registration as a Pharmacy.

The customers quickly built up from the Putney area and within the factory it came to be called 'the goldmine'. We knew that whatever was going well in the shop would soon show up on the mail order. It became so busy we had to take on another member of staff and open on Saturdays. The staff wore white lab coats and learnt about the products. If they got into difficulties they could ring through to other staff or RG (for Trufree) and even me, who could help. Patients who came for appointments at the Allergy Clinic, customers who wanted to buy and visitors for me or Annie's Room were all treated with courtesy and looked after. It certainly made a good, professional impression. I hung my Pharmaceutical Society Membership certificate on the wall and we became a registered Pharmacy not a Health Store.

We had many people from overseas coming to this shop who wanted to become Larkhall distributors in their country. Sometimes these visitors became very successful with our products.

B17 saga ending   The legal move against Laetrile and its synonyms was more serious than I thought but apricot kernels appeared to be all right for general sale and use in formulations. Pure amygdalin was destined for doctor's prescription on a named patient basis. Hence we would be able to dispense prescriptions from the shop.

Plate 7

New unit puts Woodward back in production

G. O. Woodward & Co Ltd are back in business for medicinal tablet production. They have been granted a manufacturing licence for the standard range of tablets —it was' failure to agree on licence conditions with the medicines inspectorate that led to the company's court appearance earlier this year, and to calls for improvement in the appeals procedure against decisions of the inspectorate.

Modernisation was put in hand in 1970 at Woodward's premises at 225 Putney Bridge Road, London SW15, and the new compression area, now completed at a cost of over £100,000, has cubicles for the tablet machines plus dust extraction for each unit.

Slimswift was taken over by our company in 1976

The new tablet compression Department built in the old wash house area put Woodward's back in medicine production as reported by the Chemist & Druggist in 1975

Mark Morris of The Richmond Order Company owner of Mother Brown Kneecaps and consultant on Pharmaceutical production. 1976

Rita Greer. artist, goldsmith, writer and expert on special diet cookery in her kitchen at home 1976

Lebanese distributor held a press conference in the Holiday Inn in Beirut to introduce the Blakoe range to the Middle East. 1975

Plate 8

The Larkhall Laboratories Building on Putney Bridge Road, London SW15 on Jubiliee Day 1977.

The small shop is on the right, used by Mark Morris as an office and later for our retail Pharmacy/Vitamin Shop.

Alan Greer paints the new sign for the Larkhall building in 1981

The Cantassium Prize awarded to the most ethical Health Food Retailer at Helfex 1980. Hand engraved by Rita Greer

Rita Greer and Dr Woodward at Helfex 1980 with Mr G Bonnevic of Birger Ledin (Sweden)

Plate 9

Rita Greer entertains in Annie's Room at Larkhall Laboratories 1981

A Health Food Store in a Los Angeles Mall 1982

'Purity of Life' image to promote the Cantassium Brand 1981

The iconic chimney at Larkhall Laboratories began to lean and had to be demolished 1983

NNFA Health Food convention Hall, Boston, USA 1983

Plate 10

Martha Hill, owner of Martha Hill Natural Skin Care. 1984

Bottega del Naturiste, via Eleonora Duse, Rome. HQ Prodotti Naturali 1983

Actors in scenes from the Lipcote TV Commercial 1984

Joe and Julia Page, Lipchic Proprietors from New York. 1983

Mr Khalik in his Health Store, Singapore 1985

Plate 11

Cantassium on display in Holland 1985.
See symbol system in Dutch.

Marcello Maugeri and Anna
Caudullo from Prodotti Naturali,
Rome. 1985

Ray Matthews of Wassen Nutrients with
Alan and Rita Greer 1985

Larkhall Laboratories stand at Herbora, Verona 1986

Gwylm Roberts and the pupils from Darland School,
Wrexham visit Larkhall Laboratories 1986

Rita Greer and Jenny Pitman at the
races. 1986

Plate 12

Rita Greer's Symbols in Greek and a picture of her with them feature in Pharmacy windows all over Athens in 1987

View over the flat roof to the new second floor at Larkhall Laboratories. RG's Little Studio extreme right 1987

Italian Distributors visit Larkhall's Charlbury factory. 1987

Prodotti Naturali & Larkhall Stand at Natura Exhibition, Basel, Switzerland 1987

NewData General Computer at Larkhall Laboratories HQ 1987

Charles W. Brown with Roy Gooch (Courtin & Warner Ltd) and RJW after lunch in Annie's Room 1987

Cantassium wins at Warwick races in February 1987

From Peak to Where?

NACNE - Arthur Chamings - Nobel Prize Winner support - Institute of Healthfood retailing - Black List - Alternative Healthcare & Human Rights - Marketing Consultant - Celsus - Here's Health Sold - RDAs - Tandem IQ - Closure of factory - Vitamin Poisoning - Amino acid supplements - unfair competition - Race Horse - Herbals still fighting for freedom - John Fingerhut - Rural Pharmacists - Omniped advertising problem

Marketing reports 1985   Anxious to build the business, I ordered two reports from market researchers Gaiman & Co and MFG Associates these followed a previous report in late 1983 to determine the way forward for computerisation of the administration activities. Integration of production had proved too difficult and so two new systems were in operation in early 1985. By the end of 1985 Larkhall should have been well placed to grow their business.

Obstacles to growth   I was driving the business with RG's help but I thought the sales team was not supporting us efficiently. The decision to put TV advertising behind Lipcote and Ruthmol had been brave but the internal and external sales people had not been able to really get behind it. Equally their understanding of the company's mission and product range was poor. I was not certain that they really knew the difference between the Cantassium and Trufree ranges and our competitor's synthetic chemically processed offerings. We were constantly telling them of the differences but their ability to communicate those differences to retailers and consumers was doubtful. The message of the premium natural purity and quality of our health products was perhaps beyond their comprehension. What really interested them was having an easy life on expenses, a car and bonuses. It came to my attention one or two were also selling for other companies at Larkhall's expense.
   A more intelligent sales staff was essential. Using the widely liked Symbol System had to be the key coupled with the right information about our product ranges.

The NACNE (National Advisory Committee on Nutrition Education) report of 1984 continued to be influential. Rita Greer's poster produced in 1985, based on NACNE and COMA recommendations, was praised in Modus Journal, demonstrating that Larkhall's ideas on the right diet were correct. We were distributing thousands of these posters free to schools, hospitals, GP Practices, with acclaim.
   The makers of Polyunsaturate rich processed foods were criticised for their booklet (Eating for a Healthier Heart) that recommended food products, also claiming to be based on NACNE recommendations. Dr Barbara Pickard (University of Leeds) said it was biased in favour of polyunsaturates and not really in line with the full recommendations of the report. **RG's poster, distributed by Larkhall, was just about eating a healthy diet -- no brands featured and no vitamin products, just healthy food.** The following year it would be fully reviewed by experts at Liverpool University. (see Chapter 14)

Garlic was becoming very popular as a health supplement. Many British people did not like the taste of fresh garlic, yet it was one of the real health boosting foods. Forming an integral part of the 'Mediterranean diet'. More concentrated garlic supplements tablets/capsules were being developed but scientifically it was proving impossible to provide specifications to meet British regulatory medicinal standards.

LARKHALL GREEN FARM

Consumers depended on brand manufacturers they could trust to prepare genuine products with reproducible benefits. I noted that brands with the largest market share varied from country to country. The Larkhall companies had been making garlic supplements as contractors to herbal manufacturers such as Pierce Arnold & Co (Croydon) since the late 1950s when a raw extract was used. By 1985 we were using a very concentrated odourless extract from Japan in our supplements. Odourless Garlic is the best source for supplements because the familiar garlic odour is actually produced by a degraded and inactive substance produced when the raw garlic comes into contact with air and moisture.

Larkhall must set itself apart   In 1985 the Company attempted to set itself apart. The Healthy Diets, Non Drug Therapies and Science Based Ideals were defined by articles and books written by Rita Greer and me. We were the spokesmen and becoming well respected within the alternative healthcare area. We were also seen by opponents as targets because of the logic of our arguments. I believed that the wholesomeness of the Cantassium and Trufree Brands was what distinguished them from the rest – particularly retailer's own brands.

Arthur Chamings life story omitted his part in Larkhall's court fights   In January I heard from my old friend Arthur Chamings, a distinguished Pharmacist of the old school, he had been one of those professionals instrumental in bringing Herbal Medicine within the orbit of the 1968 Medicines Act. He regretted this by the mid 1970s because he saw that the technical specifications that were being forced upon Herbals by the government were ridiculous. So he fought a few battles against the bureaucrats but with no positive result other than delaying the inevitable demise of a vast range of herbal medicines. These would have died anyway as the power of the drug industry grew geometrically and small businesses collapsed thanks to the regulators. Arthur wrote a piece for the Christmas 1985 Issue of The Pharmaceutical Journal 'Sixty years a pharmacist' which covered much of his life in Pharmacy but omitted his joining my side in the fight for freedom for herbals and all alternative medicines in the 1970s. I am sure this reference was deliberately spiked by the editor. Arthur was an important witness for Larkhall in the court case vs DHSS in the early 70s. Why must the mavericks always be so badly treated?

Double Nobel prize winner Linus Pauling supported Larkhall   The dust had not settled on the Lorna O'Driscoll article in Chemistry in Britain (September 1984), when Linus Pauling (the Double Nobel Prize Winner) sent me a supportive letter regarding my views on vitamin supplements expressed in a published letter to that magazine. He later contacted me and we were in complete agreement. I doubted Professor Bender would ever get a Nobel Prize winner on his side. Pauling's support heartened me greatly. Of course, the Quackbusters vilified Pauling for his views on Vitamin C but I didn't think he worried about that.

The Institute of Health Food Retailing   In February I was invited to become a Fellow of this institute in recognition of the services of the Company to the cause of Health Food Retailing. In my acceptance letter I told the Institute that despite my election, I would not be prepared to support their opinions on many topics. I never participated in the organization and resigned in 1998. I thought most of them grocers masquerading as pharmacists.

The Black list of non-prescribable products on the NHS This list was extended in February. One or two Larkhall Products were affected but we were not aware of any prescriptions for items including Herbal Quiet Life, Male Gland Double Strength. There were many other items on the list from a host of manufacturers, who must have been surprised to see their more obscure products listed. I believed that the officials had looked at many current price lists and old prescription records and dug out as many products as possible to ban. That way they might appear efficient to their political masters without moving from behind their desks.

Developments in Italy On a successful trip to Rome, I met Ugo Scuro, the Italian Lawyer working with Prodotti Naturali. Anna Caudullo was still working in her health shop, Bottega del Naturista in Rome but a new office was due to open soon.

In April I went to Verona for the Herbora exhibition where PN had taken a stand. Very well presented and I met several sub-distributors. The Maugeris appear to be putting much effort into this business. Things were going well so that in early August my brother joined me in Zurich to meet Anna, Marcello and Ugo Scuro to discuss Italian and European business development.

In September the Maugeris and Scuro came to London for more discussions. They were entertained by me and RG on both days.

Critics of Alternative Health Care were of no consequence A lecture by Professor D'Arcy was reported in the Pharmaceutical Journal. He berated the favourable media reporting of Alternative Health Care treatments and said that legislating in the area was difficult when public rights (Human Rights) count more than self-inflicted infringement of health. This is a perceptive view that is still valid, the infringement of health being, in most cases, a matter of opinion and not science. This indicated that Bender was not alone but probably of no real danger to the Alternative Health Movement -- Human Rights are politically sacrosanct.

Public relations problem In February Peter Leighton of Ellis Kopel PR advised me against issuing a press release concerning the British Medical Journal report on Alternative Health Care. I feared that the public relations agencies did not understand how we needed to strongly oppose the establishment view. I soon brought the PR function in-house again.

UK Sales progress unsatisfactory - a consultant offers help I was unhappy with progress in the UK sales. I thought it was a personnel problem. In March, by chance, an Irishman offered his services as a marketing consultant (Attitudinal Advertising) he had trained and qualified in marketing at the University of Chicago. I was not convinced but when he offered a free review survey I decided let him do it.

Which magazine to review salt substitutes? It was rumoured that 'Which', the consumer magazine, were considering a Salt substitute review. The persons involved Betty Stewart and Anna Bradley, came to lunch at Putney in April. The message from RG and I was that they must distinguish 'Low Salt' of no value in reducing salt in the diet from 'Salt Free' that was medically approved to reduce salt. The review was not published - too controversial perhaps?

TV advertising for Lipcote The campaign started in April, placed by The Media Shop, using the commercial we had made in-house late in the previous year. (see chapter 12 page 127). Sales reached over 100,000 bottles in that month, which was a record.

Interest from France. Dr Kathy Bonan from Paris visited Putney and showed great interest in the Larkhall products and services. She believed she and her father could handle a French distributorship. In the event it was a complete failure with regulations and French inherent distrust of imports from UK the main reason. It came to nothing. The Bonans were not short of finance.

Symbol system expanded RG added to her symbol system with some new pictograms. A press release was sent out about this important extension to safety information for allergic patients. As she owned the copyright of the symbols no other company could use them. She allowed Larkhall to use them for free because she knew their manufacturing methods well.

Cytotoxic Testing plates (for delayed food allergy). We were endeavouring to patent a production method for these plates. The Allergy Testing facility at Putney was hoped to have a future with investment in this area where patents were possible to protect us from copyists. By August the Allergy Testing service was going well. We were making our own analysis plates and were able to reduce the price which boosted demand.

Marketing Consultant appointed In late June, MFG Associates brought their free report. Strangely, they found Trufree Salt replacer better than Ruthmol as regards consumer awareness. I could not believe this and nor could RG who said it was nonsense. However, I was so unhappy with the current sales team that I decided to take this report on board, despite its errors. Several regular meetings were to follow and MFG were retained on a consultancy basis. Only Home and Irish sales were to be covered excepting Trufree items.

Meeting with Celsus and a review of the Good Nutrients Guide Under the auspices of Mervyn Madge FPS (Chairman of Rural Pharmacists Association) I met Bernard Hardisty MPS who was 'Celsus', the regular columnist in the Pharmaceutical Journal. Hardisty had asked MM to organize this meeting for lunch at The Braganza restaurant in Soho. Celsus had an interest in Alternative Health Care although he worked for the Drug Company Sterling Winthrop. I put him right on Evening Primrose Oil and other matters. Celsus soon wrote a wonderful review in the Pharmaceutical Journal for the book 'The Good Nutrients Guide' that RG and I had written together.

Charts used to help with consumer information A Vitamin Chart was published in Let's Live Magazine in the USA. These charts were very popular with consumers because they listed health benefits and symptoms of deficiency. Regulators do not like them but they were not unlawful either in the US or UK.

Prewetts Low Sodium Salt developments in July Prewetts (part of the Booker Health Group) launched their new Low Sodium Salt Substitute at the low price of 75p for 200g. So much for all efforts made by me to stop their previous product in 1984. Ruthmol sales would be hit by this product that was of no health benefit because it contained a substantial amount of Sodium Chloride (Salt). There was no way we could fight this because what Prewetts were doing was legal under the current food labeling laws, yet their product was very high in salt. As usual the infallibility of the bureaucrat is assumed and the consumer is not protected.

New Public Relations staff James Macdonald from Newman Turner Publications joined Larkhall staff as Public Relations executive. The previous person was Ms Kinga Johnson. Just before this time Rita Greer had been doing much of our publicity as well as her own Trufree Food brand. Her symbols were coming to prominence on our product packaging and in press releases and price lists as recommended in the Gaiman marketing report in 1984. Our PR agencies had been dismissed.

147

Netherlands business puts Cantassium at the top   In August our Dutch distributor came to Putney for lunch in Annie's Room and business discussions. A new special formula Garlic and Lecithin tablet for a healthy heart was proposed. Garlic was becoming a top selling product in Holland as well as the UK, a proposed combination with ever popular Lecithin could be successful. Later in the month I went to Holland to visit the Trade Fair in Utrecht. Larkhall's products were well displayed by our distributor Nutrivital, owned by Mr Simon van de Waal. We were the major UK company in the supplement field in Holland but Natural Organics from USA was the biggest. The European Market in Food Supplements was very different in each country with some authorities virtually banning imports because these products were classified within drug and medicines legislation. They were not considered as foods as they were in the UK.

Israeli business   Mr Muenster from Israel visited Putney again. He hoped to import Cantassium Products but was not really aware of the legislative hurdles. The supplement market in Israel was dominated by US companies which enjoyed a favourable legal position for political reasons. There had been no real progress for Cantassium in Israel since Muenster's first contact over a year ago.

Publicity matters   Here's Health Magazine was sold by Bookers to Argus Publications for £1,200,000. This made Bookers less powerful in the vitamin supplement area because they were no longer vertically integrated in the Health Food Industry as the biggest wholesaler, largest retailer, brand leader in food supplements and the number one magazine owner. They had disposed of their mail order division Diet Mart in 1983. This probably took the pressure off them as far as the competition regulator was concerned.
Sarah Bounds the new editor of Here's Health came to Larkhall for lunch to talk with me and RG.

The Good Nutrients Guide by Rita Greer and Robert Woodward This book was published in August. Several press mentions and good reviews. I wrote to Dr Michael O'Donnell the medical writer (former Editor of World Medicine Magazine) and radio personality whose interest in alternative approaches to health care was well known. He wrote a piece in the British Medical Journal. I was interviewed on London Broadcasting by Michael van Straten the health guru to talk about the book and RG went on BBC Radio with Phil Hayes. I met Oliver Gillie the health writer on the Sunday Times at LBC and had a useful conversation.

More controversy in Advertising   A review in Natural Food Trader 'Informative Advertising – an impossible dream'. I held a view that was unpopular with the Health Food Trade. This did not help the business and made me enemies on all sides. The Health trade had its roots in grocery and could not come to terms with their difference from pharmacy. They confused evidence based high-tech medicine with food supplements, thus they gave consumers the idea that their products were magic bullets like modern drugs. I said they had to realise that their supplements helped general health because people did not eat a wholesome diet and so could suffer multiple deficiencies. Advertisements that indicated a specific health benefit were illegal under the Medicines Act legislation and the ASA copy rules. Use of terms such as 'pharmaceutically pure' should have been alien to Health foods.

Another lecture to Food Allergics   In early August RG gave a lecture to a Chemical Victims Group near Southampton. Our new PR man and I supported her. He forgot, or didn't bother, to bring the all important literature about our products including Trufree.

RG was angry because it made no point in her having given the lecture. He didn't see he had done anything wrong and couldn't have cared less. This serious oversight alerted me to possible problems ahead. Why are these people so dilatory?

RG said he was very lazy and doubted he would shape up to the job. Some days he was very late coming in to work and spent much time chatting to friends on the 'phone instead of getting on with his work.

Marketing consultant started work   MFG started work as Marketing Consultants for Larkhall. They recommended pictures of Wind Surfers on packs to make products 'attitudinal'. They said this would appeal to the elderly. RG was not impressed and was very doubtful that MFG would be of use to us. She did not believe they were expert in anything but blarney and said they were not to go within a million miles of her Trufree brand. I was philosophical because the company, thanks to my and RG's efforts, had its best year ever in 1984-85. I was anxious to capitalize on that success by adding experts to our team. MFG were apparently a qualified marketing people whereas RG and I were considered hopeless amateurs by my brother, despite what we had achieved since 1979. My brother described RG and me as 'lunatics' to our faces.

Healthier Living Show   In mid August we had a stand at The Healthier Living Show at Earls Court. This was a public admission show and we hoped to sell products there. I was on the stand and so was RG. My brother never showed up on our exhibition stands -- ever.

Far East and Australasia   At the end of September I visited the Far East, Australia and New Zealand for the first time. In Sydney I visited Gabriel & Co the makers of Maseur Sandals and learned of other foot products in their range including innersoles that were later imported into the UK. In Christchurch, New Zealand I visited Wilfrid Owen & Co, the owners of the Lipcote Trademark and formula. I saw their manufacturing unit that was producing all kinds of Cosmetics and Skin Care products. The potential for exporting Larkhall supplements and special diet food ranges was low because of the customs tariffs that protected indigenous producers. In Australia manufacturers of vitamins and beauty products enjoyed subsidies on their exports that enabled them to easily compete with European makers. No such luck for UK exporters going in the other direction.
Singapore was a free port where the vitamin market was dominated by USA and Australian producers. Traditionally UK manufacturers were well represented in Hong Kong but the potential for Larkhall's products was restricted. It was a long and exhausting overseas business trip.

The RDA's situation discussed in 'Nature'   The Internationally respected scientific medical Journal 'Nature' carried an article in October that illustrated the relevance of international agreement on these important values. Progress in revising the RDAs (Recommended Daily Allowances/Amounts) for vitamins and minerals was slow. Obtaining universally accepted amounts for nutritional purposes was difficult but when safety is brought into the argument then the impossibility of international agreement could be real.

Grecian problems   There was news from Athens in October from Maria Strofalis, owner of Vital and Naturtabs Hellas Ltd., Ruthmol was being advertised in 'The Athenian' magazine where there was also an article on Health Stores in Athens. The stores were growing in number but soon most were to be closed by Government Edict because the Greek Pharmacies wanted the Vitamin Supplement business. In addition, the Government wanted to stop imports by classifying all the Vitamins and Food Supplements as Drugs, not Foods.

149

They wanted fees for Licensing the products. It was hoped that when EU law permitted any product freely sold in one country would be similarly available in all others. Yet, by invoking 'Public Safety' as a condition of importation the governments of most EU countries could prevent import of Food Supplements and Natural Beauty products for eternity despite the common market. One of Larkhall's products, Evening Primrose Oil Capsules, was impounded and confiscated by customs authorities in Pireas (Port of Athens) in 1985. It remained in the docks for over 14 years, despite many court cases applying for release. Return to UK was also forbidden on 'safety' grounds, despite evidence that hundreds of millions of these capsules were consumed in the UK every year. I thought it was likely that our distributors refusal to bribe customs officials could have been the primary reason for all this trouble in Pireas. The Greeks were never easy to deal with.

Italy progressing very well   At the end of October I went to Milan to visit Euronatura where Prodotti were exhibiting the Cantassium Range, the only UK health food firm represented there. I was told by Italian sub-distributors that Cantassium's products were considered the best vitamin supplements in the world. PN have done really well for Larkhall. I noted in my diary 'it's amazing – will it always be like this?' and wondered how long it would last. PN were planning a TV campaign for our Hair Nutrition supplement and I met the advertising agency involved. Immediately before returning to London I met Barclays Bank Factoring finance department and PN were hopeful that they could use this route to finance planned expansion. I visited some retail pharmacies and saw Cantassium products well displayed.

Marketing Consultant first strategy report. Hidden agenda?   In early November the marketing consultants, produced a report and it was decided that a Sales Supremo be appointed –- they would find candidates. Later I told N. Muranyi and W. O'Connell of this plan. Unsurprisingly they were not pleased but I said they could apply for the new post. In the event W O'C refused but NM was interviewed by MFG Associates and a director of an Irish Bank. I suspected that MFG had a hidden agenda with this bank and was on my guard.

DLPA progress   A DLPA press release was issued. Competitors had withdrawn their product and Larkhall were left on their own in the UK market. I hoped it would now succeed.

Italian set back   Early in November Mr Salvador Scuro, brother of Ugo Scuro visited me in Putney. It appeared that there were difficulties registering the Hair Nutrition product in Rome and PN had ceased to use Scuro's legal practice. Later in the month I received a commercial letter regarding payments of royalties to a lawyer who acted for Prodotti Naturali in Rome. Their previous adviser Ugo Scuro tried to come to Putney to visit me but a strike prevented him. There was obviously a serious dispute developing in Rome.

Tandem IQ story began - closure of Larkhall supplement manufacture could result.
On November 20th Larkhall issued a Press Release about the research being undertaken with a Vitamin and Mineral Supplement at a British High School in Wales. The research was designed to investigate any effect on school children's **behaviour** and **IQ test performance.** At this point results were unknown but I had promised to cease to make supplements if the results were negative. One of Cantassium's Vitamin and Mineral products had been selected for use in a trial by the science teacher at a Welsh School.

Several companies were asked to participate but only Larkhall agreed to the conditions required and agreed to supply 'inactive' tablets to match the selected 'active' supplement. Our registration manager, Pharmacist Roger Baxter, controlled the appropriate labeling and distribution of the active and inactive tablets. He also analysed the results.

Media Headline: 4000 cases of Vitamin Poisoning An important piece by Dr Carlton Frederick's in Let's Live Magazine highlighted the sophistry of the US Authorities and mainstream dieticians/nutritionists in high profile publicity that there were 4000 cases of vitamin poisoning reported annually in the USA. The fact was that there were 4000 cases of poisoning where vitamin ingestion by the sufferer was reported but there were always other substances that were ingested at the same time. These were all well documented poisons such as medicinal painkillers, sleeping agents and even narcotics. Surely, justice should have demanded that a vitamin must only be implicated in a major or lone role in any case which was reported under the heading 'vitamin poisoning'. If our opposition has to be reduced to these levels of reasoning, it was right that they should lose their credibility with consumers.

Appointment of UK Sales Manager By mid December, after having interviewed several applicants for the Sales Manager position, MFG recommended one whom I also approved. He was currently employed by a medium sized pharmaceutical company, had excellent references but was not available until the end of January. Sadly, Mark Morris who knew the company and its directors well had died in 1978, otherwise things might have progressed very differently.

RG's Books 1985 'Fast Suppers' was published by Sainsburys. They commissioned her to write it as she was well known for her work on healthy diets. A book for Hamlyns – **'Allergy to Food'**, in hardback and with colour, never got off the ground owing to the publisher being taken over. The new MD was outraged that RG retained the copyright and not Hamlyns, as she always did with all her publishers. All the books were destroyed because each copy said 'copyright Rita Greer'. That meant she had done months of work and received nothing.' **The Right Way to Cook'** and **'Allergic to Food -- a self-help guide'** were now on the shelves, by different publishers.

Pending developments from 1985 Larkhall's development showed its broad scope within the Alternative Health Care area. Sales were developing at home and overseas particularly in Europe. Two people were employed internally to handle the publicity under my direction. I had become totally disillusioned by PR agencies and believed Larkhall with its internal specialist knowledge base would be able to deal with media enquiries better. Using press releases enabled information to be given that would be impossible in advertisements. This was encouraged by the marketing consultant.

Supplemental Amino Acids Mid 1980s
Some amino acids were essential for human life and could be obtained, like vitamins and minerals, from dietary sources (usually protein). They play vital parts in body function and many have medicinal properties (Physiological effects). Their use as Food Supplements was controversial and the single aminos were classed as medicines in some countries. In the UK most were freely sold as dietary foods especially to athletes and bodybuilders. Tryptophan, one of the essential aminos, was an effective anti-depressant and sleep aid. Pharmaceutical interests achieved its banning in 1989 when the new and very profitable synthetic drug antidepressant SSRIs like Fluoxetine (Prozac) were being introduced. Many in the alternative health field thought this was a conspiracy between regulators and the powerful multinational Pharmaceutical interests.

The offending impurity in the poor quality Trytophan was not detected with certainty. It was possible that the outbreak of Eosinophilia was chance and tryptophan wrongly implicated. Although Tryptophan 500mg tablets have been prescribed legally ever since 1990, no further outbreaks of tryptophan linked Eosinophilia appear to have occurred.

Sports nutritionists often recommended amino acids to their clients because they read of their benefits in American sports training magazines and longevity publications. These recommendations and demand for many products were unpredictable. Larkhall were well placed as a genuine manufacturer rather than a marketing outfit to take advantage of these demands. Hence their wide range and frequent deletions and re-introductions because the manager of the inventory could not get his mind round the fact that the company was trying to provide the best service to nutrition specialists. L-Threonine's chequered history well illustrated arguments between me and my brother about listing new amino acid products.

Renewed acquaintance   In October the Publisher of an Arabic magazine, Arashaka, came to lunch in Putney. He reminded me that we first met in Lebanon in 1975 at the Blakoe Middle East launch party held in the Holiday Inn in Beirut. This memory resulted in good coverage of our current products and services in the magazine.

Unfair competition criticised   I continued my fight against the injustices done by bureaucrats with a letter to The Institute of Economic Affairs concerning their recently published monograph on Competition and Home Medicines. I supported their views that unfair forces were at work to preserve profitable monopolies but had noticed how little media coverage resulted. No doubt those powerful forces who spend vast amounts on advertising and their friends in government were somewhere in the background working to the detriment of consumers and small competitive companies.

First company Race Horse   The company bought its first race horse and named it 'Cantassium'. He was in training with Jenny Pitman in Lambourn – famous as the first lady trainer of a Grand National Winner (Corbiere). My brother was furious about it but it would help develop awareness of the name Cantassium, the company could set its costs against tax and the staff were enthused about it as were many customers. It also gave us the chance to investigate the possible manufacture of products for horses.

Herbal products still fighting for freedom.   Our Herbal Hayfever product was renamed Summer Catarrh in 1990 but reverted to Hayfever in 1992. The regulation of Herbal Remedies by Licensing under the Medicines Act caused endless problems for Larkhall. Ingredients were often difficult to source and specifying standards that were consistent batch to batch often proved impossible. Profitable commercialisation was rare. The Inspectorates were totally useless because they were all from the drugs industry and had no appreciation of the difficulties for herbal ingredients in consistently meeting exacting specifications. Most companies probably falsified internal records well knowing that the regulators would never detect these unlawful deviations with the analytical resources available to government. Chemical analysis of herbs was an art not a science - just try preparing the sample for analysis. I did in my youth but I doubt any inspector would have known how to start these analyses. The methods described in reference books used by analysts were often works of fiction.

More space needed at Charlbury   In August I discussed proposals for a development at the Charlbury factory to increase the product packaging areas. The company was in confident mood.

Nutrition not taken seriously by Doctors and Pharmacists In late 1985 there was a launch meeting for a new Vitacare range of professional food supplements at the Pharmaceutical Society's HQ in London. This range soon failed. Some companies thought that pharmacists would take Food Supplements seriously as health essentials. They never did and are unlikely to change. Both Doctors and Pharmacists have little involvement with nutrition during their training. They leave that to Dietitians who they consider professionally inferior because the dietitian qualification course has much lower academic demands for entry than medicine or pharmacy. The chemistry of nutrition is far too complex to be understood by Dietitians and most Doctors and Pharmacists avoid awkward questions in this area preferring the simpler chemistry of synthetic drugs.

I had correspondence from John Fingerhut, an American Pharmacist, who had been the MD of a large American Drug Company but was now practising in the Alternative Health field and acting as consultant to the Pharmaceutical Industry. Later we met for lunch in London. I enjoyed talking with like-minded pharmacists to explore ways of persuading our fellows to take nutrition and alternative health care seriously. I am afraid our deliberations failed to advance our cause.

'Balancing Vitamin Supplements for Optimum Health'. An article from an American Monthly health Magazine 'Let's Live' thought the idea of optimum health by proper supplementation was gaining acceptance. 'Supplements Replacing Drugs' by Paula Blake from Bestways Magazine (USA). Reading this might help break through to the closed minds of the health professionals but their respect for 'Bestways', probably close to zero, was likely to prevent any breakthrough.

More support from the rural pharmacists and Mervyn Madge In early November RG and I were lecturing on Alternative Medicines and Food Allergy at the Rural Pharmacists' Association meeting at The Belfry Hotel near Oxford. Mervyn Madge was the President. As usual we had a large audience and a lively question and answer session. Whilst this was encouraging professional support, it never translated into enough acceptance from the wider pharmaceutical profession.

Problems for Omniped I feared during 1984 that Larkhall were being persecuted by the enemies of Alternative Health Care. Our products were receiving unwarranted attention and this was highlighted in 1985-86 with complaints to the ASA concerning the advertising of Omniped Foot Cushions. These were upheld but I fought hard on this one and threatened Parliamentary action (letter to David Mellor our MP included). The whole matter was a bureaucratic waste of time and effort for a tried and tested product of 50 years standing with millions of happy users worldwide. A Media Week article by Mark Edwards on the ASA is included in the file at HAT. Happily, minor changes to the long standing advertisement killed the ASA complaints and the advertisements still worked.

Year of the First IQ Vitamin Trial

Homoeopathy - First IQ Trial - France - Export changes - Healthier Eating for Schoolchildren - Natural Veterinary Products - Cathay of Bournemouth for sale - Herbora Verona - NNFA Convention in Atlantic City - Cytotoxic Test - Neuform - Doubts grow about Marketing Consultant - Proxmire action in USA - Herbal progress - NACNE Poster evaluated - Chemist distribution - Alexander Schauss - Regulator for Natural Health needed - Clean Living fails - Yeti Man and the Bering Straits - An Inspection for Canada - Animal Rights

This was a year where progress was expected but did not materialize. Efforts to implement a sales strategy based around the ideas from the sales office were made and refined under our Marketing Consultant.
• Arabic Magazine Arashaka Award Certificate for Slimmer of the year was signed by me and Professor DJ Naismith of Queen Mary's College (London). Later (in 1988) he turned out to be an enemy of Larkhall with his flawed research into IQ and vitamins used to discredit Larkhall, funded by the Junk Food Industry.
• Effort to plan advertising and PR for a selected number of products was illustrated by some proposals from Neal Muranyi. These ideas were implemented in part but experience showed that obtaining retailer support outside the Health Food Trade was nearly impossible for specialist items like DLPA and the Cantamegas.
• The symbol system was effective but again was appreciated by the informed consumer who purchased mail order or from health food stores. Professional support from Doctors and Pharmacists was almost non-existent – this untapped market would continue to be tough because nutrition was not a part of their college courses. The general professional view was that its benefit to preventive care was too complex a subject and no acceptable evidence based research had been done. Larkhall had the ambition to remedy this in the future.
• Testimonials continued to come in regularly. Mrs Elaine Austin was an elderly lady over 80 who was a regular customer and always supported Cantassium's supplements following being recommended to us by her private doctor many years before. She attributed her and her husband's good health and ability to run their family business to their use. Austins was a wellknown, old-fashioned family company which owned a large general store in Newton Abbot. Mrs Austin was a great fan of mine and we had some lively 'phone conversations about health and business. Although well into her eighties, she still worked full time at their very busy store and was as bright as a button.

A Scam -- O'Connell customer went bust   In early January a company in Bristol called Fern Marketing went bust, owing Larkhall £12,000. The Sales Executive W O'Connell was held responsible as he had personally vouched for the company despite reservations from me. More than once Fern Marketing had tried to get into the factory under false pretences. RG had taken a phone call from them on a Saturday when she happened to be there. They said they had permission to enter the factory pick up an order. There was no order. This was nonsense and she refused to let them into the premises. They were abusive over the telephone. The factory was all locked up for the weekend and there was no way they could get in. Our van driver had reported back the previous week that a delivery to them in Bristol was to just a shed, not proper premises. WO'C was told about it and did nothing.

LARKHALL GREEN FARM

It turned out he had never been to see them but merely spoken to them on the 'phone and so had never seen 'their premises'. Fern Marketing scarpered abroad without paying their bill. RG and I had to make a statement to the Fraud Squad about it. However, a couple of years later the woman was caught at Heathrow, coming back into the UK on Christmas day. The police told us she refused to speak whenever she was interviewed. She ended up with a jail sentence but the man escaped. Larkhall never got their money back.

It was a classic scam and WO'C should have known better than to let it happen. He should also have taken action about them trying to get into the factory after hours and been alerted to what the van driver had said about the shed. They paid for the first few orders they placed to establish themselves as good customers. Gradually, the size of the orders increased but they didn't pay for the last one of £12,000.

WO'C's lazy attitude confirmed my decision to re-organise the home sales department. I asked our marketing consultant to achieve this. WO'C received a written warning from me.

Cytotoxic Test on the NHS? Larkhall were optimistic about the Cytotoxic Test for hidden food allergy becoming available on the NHS. This was never achieved by us or any competitor as there was insufficient scientific evidence to meet the unknown criteria, which the Ministry never disclosed. Their policy appeared to be to ask impossible questions and never publish the rules they applied at the Ministry. Larkhall were undertaking hospital trials with encouraging results.

Homoeopathic medicinal claims inconsistent At the end of February, a letter from me to the Pharmaceutical Journal was published regarding the legal position of Homoeopathy. I wrote that it was wrong that certain established companies could make medicinal claims whilst new entrants, with identical formulas, could not have similar claims applied to their products. I pointed out that Homoeopaths prescribe medicines specifically for a patient after a full consultation. In addition, Homoeopathy was ineffective when clinically tested as if it was an allopathic medicine system.

Aquamaid device discontinued The Aquamaid breast hydrotherapy device was discontinued. The problems with advertising claims and the failure to find a reliable source of the patented rotating sprays at a realistic cost contributed to this decision. This device's safety record and its beneficial effects on breast feeding made this a sad moment for Larkhall.

First IQ Vitamin Trial results publicised In early February, we announced the positive results of the first Darland High School Trial. This resulted in good publicity. Soon after there was a visit to the Putney factory by the teacher and his pupils that was very much enjoyed by the children. The Mail on Sunday headlined the Darland Trial with the words 'Vitamins improve IQ' there was no mention of improving diet – it's the pills that did it was their unprompted view. That's the problem – just like slimming – consumers wanted and expected magic pills but the truth was that lifestyle/diet were really the keys. Commercially it's good that people believe in the pills but Larkhall had to persuade them to use pills only until the diet was improved. My view was that when all children and adults were on the right wholesome balanced diet we could close the factory and retire.

Soon after this **the Tandem IQ pack** of children's vitamins and minerals started its life. In mid February, Gwylm Roberts, the science teacher who ran the Darland Trial, and his wife visited Annie's Room for lunch. Tandem IQ sales were growing well, the future of the product looked exciting and was beneficial to children.

Natural Rearing veterinary products Juliette De Bairacli Levy contacted my brother in Charlbury at the CF Abel veterinary product office. She was angry because, she thought, her range of products recommended exclusively in her books had been copied by her current distributor and sold under their brand.

Juliette was a pioneer and well known dog and animal breeder who had written books and invented many natural herbal formulations to assist animal health. Her products were promoted in her books. She lived in Greece and was financially successful. She believed her products could be sold successfully to all animal owners because of her fame. However, she was unaware that the restrictions applied to veterinary herbals were almost the same as those applied to human medicines as regards overt advertising claims and technical standards. She did not understand this and sales were never exciting because book purchase was a prerequisite for potential consumers. She had a dedicated number of followers but the products could never reach out to the mass consumer. Word of mouth, particularly breeder and farmer recommendations were the only real way to increase sales.

A marketing plan was to be written by my brother in consultation with Juliette. The products were specialist and general sale direct to consumers with pets could prove difficult and costly if space advertising and PR were to be undertaken. I got the impression that my brother thought the name Juliette De Baracli Levy associated with all products in the range was sufficient for sales promotion purposes. It was not. We would need to put considerable resources behind the range that was difficult to justify after our experience with Abel's anti-worm conditioner back in 1965.

Veterinary practitioners who believed in natural products were almost as rare as medical practitioners with that belief. Profits on the range were not as attractive as those applying to modern synthetic pharmaceutical veterinary products.

Tandem IQ Broadcast In mid March I was on LBC (London Broadcasting) with Michael van Straten, an Osteopath and very successful media expert on alternative health care. I had known Michael since 1959 when he lived in Pimlico and we were students in London. Our interview was on Tandem IQ and Michael was very positive in his support.

Favourable article on Tandem IQ In April The Daily Star national newspaper did an article on Tandem IQ that was very favourable.
All the other newspapers completely ignored it, as did other media.

French progress and language difficulties The end of March, found me in Paris to meet Dr Kathy Bonan and her associates from a company 'Herbier de Provence', who were interested in distributing Cantassium products in France. She went to the wrong airport to meet me and when I didn't turn up she phoned RG at the factory and said "Dr. Woodward, il est mort." This meant "he is dead". Unfortunately, she had already said this in English to our switchboard girl who promptly burst into tears. By the time the bad news had circulated round the factory and shocked everyone, I had phoned RG to tell her Dr Bonan had not turned up to meet me. RG used the factory tannoy to confirm I was not dead but was in Paris for a business meeting. This gives some idea of the language difficulty regarding exports. The meeting with Kathy and her associates went well.

Medical and Pharmaceutical dilemma continues   MIMS Magazine (Monthly Index of Medical Specialities), a guide to prescription medicines that is widely read by GPs, carried a series of articles on Vitamins (A,B6,C,D,K,and E) These were not very positive but not too negative either and claimed to offer 'a new perspective'. They did convey the general less than enthusiastic medical view at this time. MIMS was a highly respected knowledge source for General Practitioners. Pharmacists also read it.

Export and Staff Changes   Export sales of our branded supplements were building satisfactorily and taking the place of our previous generic medicines and wholesaling. Overall sales were remaining constant.

Later in the year, Eric Hopkins (Export Sales Manager) retired after over 20 years service. We had a farewell party for him in the picking area at the factory -- just tea, cakes and sandwiches. In future Mr Brian Morley would take over export administration and dispatch from Charlbury. One person will work on this area of the business. I did not want the home sales people diverted from the UK and Ireland despite W.O'C's offer to be "Your man in Europe". I would continue to lead export sales development myself.

Italians visit Helfex   from 19 -21 April there was the Helfex Exhibition (Health Food Trade) in Brighton. Larkhall had a stand manned by the sales manager and W.O'Connell. Anna and Marcello Maugeri came over from Italy and stayed at The Old Ship Hotel. The exhibition was well attended by UK retailers but there were few from overseas.

WO'C behaved badly after having too much to drink and serenading Barbara Cartland with loud romantic songs when she arrived, down on one knee with his arms outstretched. He always fancied himself as a singer and referred to himself as 'The Irish Nightingale'. Barbara Cartland ignored him. We didn't know where to look. It was the talk of Helfex.

Healthier Eating for School Children   Building on the Vitamins and IQ research, Larkhall brought out educational aids to help children follow a 'Healthy Diet'. One of the most important items was a booklet written by Rita Greer entitled 'Healthier Eating for School Children'. It tied in with the colourful NACNE diet poster.

We understood that it was not the vitamin tablets that were really essential but a diet that was based on 'Wholefood' principles that would include enough natural vitamins and minerals to ensure good behavior and performance at school. Children would be able to concentrate more and achieve better results. That was our message and not that all children needed a daily Tandem IQ supplement.

The problem was always that the message was usually drowned out by a misinformed and ignorant media including TV, Radio and Press who either told parents directly to give their children supplements or accused Larkhall and other companies of promoting that message. It was the media who claimed pills would increase IQ, not Larkhall.

Sadly, those against Larkhall criticized this booklet on specious grounds regarding political incorrectness of the two families depicted therein (The Healthyfoods and The Junkfoods). They claimed there was no such thing as **junk food.** All these critics were either directly or indirectly financed by the powerful sugar interests. In spite of this, we sent out thousands of copies of the booklets to schools free on request, with the poster. It was very popular when the September term began for new pupils.

Cathay of Bournemouth a Herbal Company Our Marketing Consultant brought me details of a company for sale that he and his banker friend thought we should purchase. It was Cathay of Bournemouth. He agreed to arrange an appointment. I subsequently visited Bournemouth and saw the Mittens whom I knew slightly. They had many herbal products that used to sell well by mail order. Unfortunately for the MC, I soon realized that the pressures from the DHSS Medicines Licensing department would ensure that all the Cathay products would shortly be forced off the market. The MC had no concept or knowledge of these problems and was puzzled at my negativity. I told him there would be no takeover of Cathay or their products by Larkhall. He was not pleased.

Italian business At the end of May, I went to The Victoria Hotel in Verona for the Herbora Fair. Natural products of all kinds were being exhibited. The Prodotti Naturali stand was very impressive and displayed only Larkhall Products, mainly Cantassium Supplements. No other UK Supplements were represented at the exhibition. Cyril Blau (Larkhall's Production and Technical Manager) who was on holiday in Italy with his wife, visited the show and were entertained by Prodotti. Many distributors showed interest in becoming stockists of Cantassium. The market for these items in Italy was in its infancy. PN were eager to develop the business but substantial backing from Larkhall would be required.

Orders from Italy were much larger than expected and stock levels at Putney were put under pressure. This was having an effect on home deliveries and the trade sales staff blamed this for their lower than anticipated sales. I did not accept that as an excuse but expected it from them.

American trip June 8th -14th I was in the USA for the NNFA convention in Atlantic City. I saw very few new products of interest. An Amino Acid Blood Test for athletes was being promoted and perhaps worth investigation as an add-on to our Allergy Testing. Aatron Services was the company doing the test and they were in Los Angeles where I intended going on 11th. At the International Symposium, **Neuform** of Germany gave a presentation but I doubted that all German products sold in their stores were natural as claimed or truly met the Neuform criteria. However, by applying those criteria to imported products German authorities prevented their distribution. I mentioned that it was vital for all countries to fight for a level playing field all over the world – intimating that the UK was the only country with open borders to Health Food products especially Vitamin Supplements. This situation remains true in 2015 because many countries, including the USA, enforce certain non-existent 'Safety' issues on imported products but not on indigenously produced ones.

In LA I visited Aatron Services and was impressed by the laboratory but unconvinced by the science they were using. A visit to Physicians Laboratory in Manhattan Beach indicated that they were still operating but not prospering with their Cytotoxic Food Allergy Testing. It was good that Larkhall now made its own analysis plates. I visited a Mrs Gooch's Health Store in Manhattan Beach and saw it stacked to the roof with vitamin shelves -- very different from a UK Health Food store.

The differences between UK and US markets for Herbals and Vitamins were very marked. There was, apparently, greater freedom in USA but this was because the authorities were not very zealous. Manufacturing facilities for herbals were considered low priority by the FDA and seldom inspected and if they were it was mainly for paperwork rather than the factory conditions. Slimming, Sexual Performance Enhancement, Arthritis, Pain Killing and Migraine were openly promoted on packs.

Ingredients such as Yohimbine, a herb for sexual performance and Ephedrine for weight loss were used in supplements – in the UK both were strictly controlled medicinals.

The health food retailers from the UK often went to exhibitions in the US and because of their technical illiteracy believed they could import these products into the UK. Whilst they might fail to bring in many products they were more successful with other US products and this had enabled US manufacturers to gain access to the UK market to the detriment of UK producers. Companies such as Solgar, Solaray, Natures Plus, Weider and Natren had spearheaded their advance in Europe thanks to the weakness of UK authorities. Ironically for UK exporters trying to penetrate the huge US market, the US Customs and FDA enforced a regime of supreme protection for their producers. Free Trade? – what a joke.

Marketing Consultant -- more doubts   In mid July I was invited to lunch by a Director of a Bank in Ireland. Our MC had arranged this meeting and attended. A financing proposition was made. I was immediately suspicious that our MC was acting as an agent for the bank and the marketing consultancy may not be what it appeared. By the end of the month, after meeting the directors at Dendron, the MC pressed for them to be dismissed as Larkhall's exclusive UK pharmacy distributors.

DLPA in the spotlight   A letter regarding DLPA was received from DHSS Medicines Division. I answered blandly three days later and heard no more. This was a typical fishing letter, a waste of civil service time and a disgrace. The problem for the regulator was that he could not control press articles because that would infringe freedom of speech. If a company paid for such articles to be published the article became an advertisement but without payment there was little the regulator could do except bully and frighten.

The Proxmire Action in the USA   At the Alternative Medicine Exhibition in Kensington I met Clinton Ray Miller from USA, who informed about the Proxmire action in the USA Congress. This legal action was designed to thwart the FDA's efforts against Alternative Health Care products and was important for the continued availability of Vitamin Supplements in US Health Food stores. He was very interested in the results of the IQ Tests involving British School Children and believed these trials would provide evidence to support Proxmire. We agreed to keep each other posted.

Herbal Medicine debate continued   August found me consulted by The Drug and Therapeutic Bulletin, a respected medical scientific journal, about a proposed article on Herbal Medicines. My letter was relevant to the regulatory system that operated in 1986 and remained virtually unchanged in 2015. The failure of the authorities to grasp the fundamental technical and philosophical incompatibilities of herbal (naturally derived) and allopathic (synthetically derived) medicine continued to lead to costly problems for both regulator and herbal producer. Much to the blinkered regulators disgust, consumers still wanted herbal medicines and politicians insisted that their voters were placated. Hence, real issues were ignored and uncertainty continued.

The NACNE colour Poster by Rita Greer is reviewed by experts   In September (1986) Modus Magazine, a respected publication for teachers and lecturers, examined Rita Greer's colourful illustrated poster in detail and found it a valuable tool for instructing lay people on the right approach to diet, based on the findings of the official NACNE and COMA reports. The work was carried out at Liverpool University.

This was an excellent appraisal and vindicated Larkhall in printing and distributing it as widely as possible, free of charge. It carried the Rita Greer Symbols and a reference to Larkhall but did not promote any supplements. It was widely distributed until 1999 when our successors just ignored its existence to save costs. RG believed in the project wholeheartedly and had given her time and services free. No other company produced such an informative poster to help promote the 'Health of the Nation'.

RG had a telephone call from Modus asking her what computer programme she had used to construct the poster. The truth was she hadn't used one, merely a notebook, a pencil, common sense and her brain. They were nonplussed.

In October Larkhall exhibited at the Health Visitors Association Conference in Scarborough. The colourful Healthier Diet Poster by Rita Greer illustrating the NACNE report weekly Diet Recommended Food Intake was given to virtually all attendees and well received.

Public relations for Tandem IQ Our recently appointed publicity manager had continued to be a disappointment. He had failed to get his act together. When he took over The Health Standard, our little newspaper, he just didn't bother to write anything for it. Publication day arrived and we had no newspaper to send out to mail order customers. RG had to spend a weekend writing and putting one together and still he came up with nothing. He couldn't have cared less and just shrugged his shoulders. Dismissal was inevitable.

By September a new Publicity Executive had been appointed to succeed him. She issued a press release about the Trufree Tandem IQ supplement, the product that was to give Larkhall a much higher profile than ever before.

More bad advice from Marketing Consultant As advised by the MC, Dendron were given notice to quit their distribution of Lipcote, Vitamins and Ruthmol to retail pharmaciies. In hindsight, this was a big mistake. They were doing a good job but I failed to realize what a very tough market for natural vitamins the pharmacy trade was. Pharmacists were trained in dispensing prescriptions for drugs. Dietary approaches to healthcare were alien to them and the profit on drugs was far greater and less hassle for them. Lipcote was a very good product but cosmetics were not vital to most pharmacies. The main outlets for Lipcote were the multiples Boots and Superdrug. Whilst Larkhall could probably cover those outlets quite easily through their head office, they could not possibly cover the independent pharmacy trade as well as Dendron did. We should have continued with Dendron and tried to make the vitamins work better for them. Meanwhile we should have concentrated our sales team in the independent retail health food trade. In the event, as will be seen in later years, Larkhall were constantly looking for and trialing other distributors who, without exception, were not as worthwhile as Dendron.

An Irish tale An Irishman, previously a manager of a Health Food Store in Jersey, approached his fellow Irishman Walter O'Connell, who had by now been demoted to a sales representative at Larkhall, with a proposition to travel overseas and find distributors for Cantassium. I was slightly amused by this man's set up but did not tell Walter of my suspicion that this was a totally fake project where Larkhall were sure to lose money. His friend would produce a story of how hard he had worked but with no immediate success and ask me to just wait for the big break in six months. Similar to our Lebanon experience in 1976. Despite talking big, he was a small time operator with a West Midlands Regional Office in a Manor near Burton-on-Trent (not far from the brewery?).

A visit to Jersey by me, RG and her husband, WO'C and the agent was called off at the very last minute. WO'C had spent several days in a recording studio, singing a song, copied from someone else. The plan put forward by WO'C and his friend was to release this record as part of the PR campaign. What nonsense. WO'C would do anything rather than get on with his work. Perhaps he believed the record would be top of the hit parade and he would be a star overnight! He would make a million. Another of his dreams. As it turned out his plagiarism was spotted and 'Beautiful Isle of Jersey' starring WO'C never made it to the hit parade and we never made our visit to Jersey.

School teacher to write book on nutrition and IQ   At the end of October Gwilym Roberts visited us again and told me about his plans for a book on Diet for Children, including the Tandem IQ research. This book would be called 'Boost Your Child's Brain Power - How to use good nutrition to ensure success at school'. It was ultimately published by Thorsons in 1988 after the second Darland Trial ended but before the World Sugar Corporation's sponsored trial that contradicted the Tandem IQ results but using a very different formula tablet with synthetic ingredients, and a different IQ test and timescale.

Sales boost unreal   A sales report for November and December 1986 appeared to show that the new sales staff recommended by the MC were succeeding. Sadly, the success was less to do with the new staff and more to do with the previous organization. Considerable extra selling expenses were being incurred and the successful distributor (Dendron) was about to cease working with Larkhall. The new staff believed that the costs of Dendron service would be better used directly by a Larkhall Sales Force. This proved a bad decision because the new manager and our consultant were unable to build an efficient well trained sales force, at even treble the Dendron cost. By the end of 1987 their inadequacy would become crystal clear.

Research on Dietary inadequacy of American Children ridiculed   In mid November Dr Alexander Schauss from New York came to London and gave a talk to the Health Food Manufacturers Association about his research (1983/4) into School Children's Diets. Very positive results in performance and behaviour were found when a Healthier Diet was adopted generally. Schauss compared two school year's performance in IQ tests – first year the regular diet, second year (Same age group but different children) following more wholesome dietary recommendations. No supplements were used. I listened but did not speak. The next I heard of Schauss was that his research had been questioned and then heavily criticised by US academics with known connections to the sugar interests. So Schauss was successfully discredited in USA by the junk food industry.

Rumour that a large Health Food company was for sale   At the end of November the MC came to see me with the director of an Irish Bank. They said that a very successful Health Food Company, was for sale. They proposed making more enquiries and coming back to me with a proposal for Larkhall to bid. I knew the owner of the company well and he had been to Annie's Room for lunch on several occasions. I was doubtful about this proposition and continued to wonder about the MC's real agenda. We did not make a bid.

Alternative Health Care under pressure   The December issue of the Journal of Alternative Medicine had several articles of direct interest. There was wide dissatisfaction with the regulatory body (Medicines Control Agency). Evidence for efficacy was only anecdotal. This stimulated the Natural Medicines Society to try to set up a regulator for Natural Health Care. This was an ambitious idea that proved impossible for cost and qualified personnel reasons. The competence of the regulator of allopathic medicines to assess 'Natural Medicines' was a live issue that still existed in 2015.

Clean Living Products   This range of beauty products was introduced to test demand for this type of product based on naturally derived ingredients. A Clean Living shop had been opened in partnership with David Gaiman in East Grinstead earlier in the year. It was competing with Body Shop and many other similar ranges. The shop closed in July 1987 because the prices and margins did not provide a viable future. I agreed to take back all stock and then the range was subsequently sold to a Saudi Arabian trader in 1988. Larkhall ceased sale of the range in 1989. RIP Clean Living.

The Yeti Man   Our publicity executive, who had been dismissed earlier in the year, had been approached by a Scottish explorer who had recently been on an expedition to the Himalayas in search of the Yeti, the mythical beast supposedly on the prowl there. He had not found the Yeti but had written a book entitled 'The Yeti Man' about his experiences which was submitted to publishers but with no success. He planned a new adventure to unite the Eskimos from each side of the Bering Straits. He wanted sponsors for this undertaking and saw our publicity executive as a man to persuade Larkhall to help. In June and July he had had contact with the explorer and Larkhall paid some expenses including the expedition notepaper. I set a limit of £3,000. It was agreed that he would mention Cantassium vitamins as much as possible and ensure that the book manuscript was updated to include several mentions.

  The adventure was an ambitious project with the idea that high ranking Russian and US representatives would be present when the two tribes of Eskimos met. I was always doubtful but the promise of the man to really push Cantassium with his current book and associated publicity (including on the popular BBC Wogan show), gave reason for very cautious encouragement. The executive left Larkhall in July to join another company and continued working with the explorer as his agent, but by November had been dismissed from that company.

  At Christmas the explorer came to see me and asked for £5000 to continue his Bering Straits project. He was off to Sweden to see an associate and I advised him to see one of our Swedish distributors 'Sesame International' and obtain support from them. If he failed, he was to come back to see me. Despite all his efforts the Yeti Book was never published, nobody would sponsor him and no more was heard of him.

More bureaucratic waste   Our Principal Medicines Inspector wished to carry out a two day inspection of the Putney Factory early in 1987. This was to be on behalf of the Canadian Authorities. We had a possible customer in Canada who wished to import about 10,000 PEROIDIN (Potassium Perchlorate) tablets at a cost of £2000. Originally this had been a popular anti-thyroid medicine but was no longer a licensed medicinal product in the UK. It was permitted for sale only on a named patient basis. We hardly sold any and obtaining a full licence would not have been commercially worthwhile.

This principal inspector proposed to waste two days of his time carrying out an inspection of a manufacturer of very few medicinals whom he knew well. I indicated that I thought this a waste of resources but the principal inspector probably fancied an expenses paid trip to Canada on the taxpayer so it all went ahead and we met him in February. As far as I recall we never saw him again. No business in Canada resulted, but lots of taxpayer money went up in smoke. There was plenty of lost executive staff time for our small company into the bargain.

Animal Rights Campaigners severance of support. A Group of these people were foolishly introduced by the previous Publicity Manager. I decided on reflection and his departure to cease any connection. Supporters had been involved in violence. One had infiltrated the staff at Larkhall and was found nosing around on the roof by RG's studio, looking for rabbits and rats in cages that she was sure we were using for experiments. There were no rabbits or rats in cages or animal experiments. RG told her the only animals used for testing at Larkhall were the staff and that we had a professional pest control officer who dealt with rats. The woman gave in her notice.

Later she approached staff on our stand at an exhibition, still convinced about animal experiments at Larkhall. She had a quite mad look about her with staring eyes and was extremely aggressive. The police advised us to drop the 'laboratories' part of our name at the front of the factory as this encouraged animal rights campaigners. It would also discourage drug users from thinking we were producing drugs on the premises that led to break-ins. We took note.

Unsettling and Difficult Year

Problem consultant - Second IQ Trial - Reputation building - Dietitians & Nutritionists - Computerisation and a Judas - Ideal Home Exhibition - Cantassium wins first race - Inspections - Filtro Neto - Mixed Publicity - British Standards Man agrees with me on the EU safety policy - Natura Exhibition in Basel - Additions to Veterinary range - Press releases - FAX machine - Marketing blunders - People need more vitamins - French prospects - Drugs problem - Medicinal claims law - New Staff - Fad and wholesome diets - Hidden Food Allergy - Lipcote disappointment in Germany - IQ diet BBC programme - Opposition to Committee on Safety of Medicines - Blacklisted Placebos - Edwina Currie - Professor floored by Homoeopathy - Second IQ Trial's positive results known - Depressing Sales staff - Actors to promote Lipcote - Retailer seminars illegal - Organic Germanium - Healthmark symbol of Excellence

Home sales force built/Marketing Consultant dishonesty After the great success of 1986, 1987 was to be a year of change for Larkhall. Having dismissed Dendron, the pharmacy distributor of Lipcote, Food Supplements and Ruthmol on the MC's advice, we brought all sales administration in-house. A sales force was gradually built but the strategy began to falter mid-year, after an encouraging first few months. This was to such an extent that in late October the Marketing Consultant was dismissed and by the end of the year we were seeking a pharmacy distributor once more. This experience illustrated the old maxim that the work done by immediate predecessors often benefits their successors more than they admit, giving a false initial impression of their new policies.

Second Tandem IQ trial The most important development was the second nutrition trial of Tandem IQ formula at Darland High School, Wrexham. The trial was directed by Dr David Benton of Swansea University. He had challenged the results of the pilot study carried out in 1985 and agreed to direct a repeat trial with a larger number of children. The junk food industry and its academic followers appeared to be unaware of the pilot study so the new trial proceeded without problems.

Lipcote TV advertising of Lipcote continued but ceased mid year when the commercial value became uncertain. This advertising boosted sales but sales people basked in that effort believing they were responsible and were quick to blame faults at the production end for subsequent decline.

Reputation building A press release covering aims of the Company was issued in January and was directed at Pharmacy. It was endeavouring to build its reputation as 'Alternative Health Care Specialists'.

Dietitian Licensing: Against or 'Who is the Real Nutritionist'? The Journal of Applied Nutrition Vol 39 No 2 covered the dispute in the USA between registered dietitians and the non-registered Nutritionists. This dispute also applied in the UK. One of the main tenets of the dietitians was that there was no general need for diet supplements since people obtained all their needs from a 'balanced diet'. Nutritionists, on the other hand, were sure that there was a place for supplements because the balanced diet was a myth -- nobody knew what it was - it was not clearly defined.

LARKHALL GREEN FARM

In addition, general pollution of the environment not only depleted food of its micronutrients but the stress associated with modern living increased dietary need for these vital substances. Dietitians insisted that because they were registered professionals they must have control of all dietary and nutrition science because they were the qualified experts.

This was not accepted by governments but the dietitians lobbied strongly, without success. However, Nutritionists needed to continue their fight to maintain the status quo.

Computerisation became of increasing importance and a Judas character appeared
A new member of staff joined the management team at Charlbury to co-ordinate stock control/packing/service levels. He was computer literate and had experience of stock control and commercial computer systems. His previous company had been selling CDs and gone out of business. My brother became very dependent on this man and I had to ensure his ideas, such as 'close down Putney and outsource tablets', were not adopted as company policy. The well known opinion of my brother "We never make mistakes at Charlbury", became a legend. He perceived this employee to be infallible. Doubts about the man's honesty were ignored as complaints came rolling in from suppliers, particularly printers. He covered up his over-ordering of cartons by having burn-ups after hours behind the Charlbury factory.

RG complained that orders she fulfilled for The Bumper Bake Book that she sent down on the weekly lorry to Charlbury did not arrive at that end. As she supervised their putting on the lorry herself every week but there was no satisfactory explanation given. Hundreds went missing but the man denied they had ever arrived. She just had to keep replacing them. (A full picture of what the man had been up to had to wait until he eventually left under a black cloud of dishonesty.) It made the situation very difficult for Dennis Hooker, the manager, and it made him ill. The employee became ever more bold and boastful. He threatened to steal my brother's Filofax and get away with it and he did.

My brother would not have a word said against him so he got away with more and more. The cover-ups went on. A whole pallet load of Lipcote 'disappeared' --13,000 bottles. No wonder it could be bought from market stalls cheaper than the cost of production. He left under a cloud after stealing all the product formulas off the computer system. My brother took out an injunction against him to prevent their use.

Computer Systems The present Computer System's 100 mb disc space was succeeding but development was limited. More staff were becoming involved and using it. A decision was taken to look at a new system an MV7800 (780mb disc space) using software from Trinity Computers based in Cheshire. It was hoped Production, Accounting, Mail Order and Trade Sales and Stock Control could be integrated. In the event production could not be integrated owing to the mathematical structure of our formulations from grammes to microgrammes which meant a separate bespoke specialist system would be required. The Mail Order Address list was to continue to be contracted out.

Exhibition The company exhibited at the Daily Mail Ideal Home Exhibition opening on 10th March in London (Earl's Court). This was the first time we had exhibited there and our publicity department actively mailed our customers and issued several press releases covering the items to be exhibited. The new IQ nutrition trial was announced together with the positive results from the pilot study in 1985/6. Our stand was very busy with enquiries from overseas visitors and the public looking for special offers and freebies, especially our free Canatassium carrier bags. Attending as an exhibitor is costly, not just in money but in staff time. A repeat performance was unlikely but it helped build consumer awareness of Larkhall.

Cantamega 2000 -- the strongest Vitamin and Mineral Supplement in the world was made available in quarter size tablets called Cantamega 2000 Divided Dose. Marketing using Trial Packs was proving popular for the Cantamegas 2000 and 1000 tablets. Some people just could not swallow the larger size of tablets and much preferred them in the smaller size.

Cantamega 2000 & 1000 were spearheading the Vitamin & Mineral range whilst Lipcote was leading the Beauty product range under the Aquamaid Brand.

The Food Allergy services and special 'Free From' products demonstrated Larkhall's wide interests in the 'Alternatives to Orthodox Medical Healthcare'.

Racing win for Cantassium. In late January 'Cantassium', Larkhall's Race Horse, won his first Hurdle Race at Leicester at odds 14/1. The staff were over the moon. I received a letter of congratulation from Forbes Publications, the Publishers of Nutrition and Food Science magazine. Even the Bank Manager was pleased and continued to help us with finance. This horse was building precious consumer awareness that my brother sadly did not appreciate -- good PR for Trade and Mail Order Customers, many of whom followed him. When the horse won or was placed 'Cantassium' went out over the airwaves free to millions as the racing results were reported.

Our horse wins again On 11th February Cantassium won again and a press release gave news that a Larkhall Supplement was given to him (5-10 Cantamega 2000 as a powder mixed into his feed). This was not doping but merely improved his diet with a concentrated food. Every horse that wins was tested for drugs immediately after the race. This was a standard procedure for horse racing in UK.

More Inspections and request for a 'sweetener' In late January we had a Medicines Licence Inspection by two inspectors by appointment that took place at Putney. This produced copious criticisms and questions, the majority were nit-picking, probably to justify their jobs to office-bound bureaucrats. They seemed determined to recommend refusal of Licence renewal. One of the inspectors, who was subsequently moved away from inspecting, was very critical but this was him showing off to the junior man.

On a previous visit an Inspector had demanded a 'gift' for a favourable report -- a free painting by RG -- in front of several witnesses. He wanted her to paint him as a dormouse in a teapot and was quite serious about it. He had appeared to be the worse for drink although it was only 11 am. I think that her adamant refusal, in spite of his repeated demand for the 'gift', was probably responsible for his attitude on his next visit, although nothing was said about it. A further inspection by a different inspector on 30th April appeared to resolve matters and Larkhall achieved its licence renewal.

A useful overseas trip In early February I spent a week travelling to Greece, Singapore and Malaysia to visit customers. In Athens I attended and spoke at a seminar followed by a reception and dinner for Doctors. I also talked with retail customers of Vital Naturtabs at the Caravel Hotel in Athens.

Filtro Neto progress W.O'Connell was visiting Athens to see the manufacturer of Filtro-Neto and he suggested I meet Mr Lolas the owner of the product and see the filters being made. I had been suspicious that these filters were not being made in Greece at all and believed that what I subsequently saw was a specially arranged demonstration. Larkhall distributed the product for W. O'Connell's company in which our company had taken a 50% share. O'Connell was spending far too much time on this project and there was little benefit to Larkhall's image. However we linked the filters to our Herbal Anti-Smoking Tablet and general advice to give up smoking so there was a justifiable reason to stock them.

Important meeting with a man who worked for the British Standards Institute
In February I visited Holland to see Nutrivital in Leeuwarden who were, at that time, our largest overseas customer for Supplements. I also saw Sonia Jensen a new Lipcote distributor who whilst enthusiastic was not financially reliable -- not an uncommon problem. At my hotel, I happened to meet a man from The British Standards Institute who told me that there would never be any agreement between Common Market (EEC) countries on safety standards because this was a good way of preventing imports – just as I had always thought.

Notable publicity for Larkhall. Natural Food Trader reported that 'Larkhall's hitting the headlines'. Cantassium, our horse, had won at Leicester. The Independent newspaper published an article that was favourable to Larkhall's Cantamega 2000 and Foresight Mineral supplements.

Allergy Laboratory criticised after 'Which' testing Our Allergy Laboratory was heavily criticised by 'Which', the consumer magazine, which wrote that our allergy test was no use. They had used an underhand trick by not asking for a RAST allergy test when they sent someone under cover to our allergy lab for testing. Larkhall could have performed the RAST test but used its own Cytotoxic test which detected masked allergies, not the classical instant allergies. The problem was then compounded by further unfairness.

We normally insisted on taking blood samples ourselves to ensure that the blood sample was fresh for testing. However, one day, our laboratory manager was contacted by people who pretended to want tests done in large quantities but insisted on taking the samples themselves. Our laboratory Manager should not have agreed to do these tests but was assured by the sender that they were fully conversant with sampling blood and would ensure that these would be taken, stored and delivered to us according to our directions. They emphasised that they would be requiring many tests in the future that, of course, made our manager more willing to break the sampling rules he should have enforced. Several purportedly fresh samples were received a week or two later and the results sent back. In fact, our manager had been entrapped by 'Which' representatives. No more samples were received as promised and an article trashing us was published.

Following this experience and the adverse publicity, I wrote to the press about 'Which's' behaviour regarding its 'Testing methods' relating to our hidden food allergy service. That was a waste of time 'Which' was perceived to have God-like perfection as the consumer's champion.

Usual mixed publicity Prima and Fitness magazines published articles on Vitamin Pills being ineffective and a waste of money. Whilst Fitness was negative, Prima was more balanced. These articles would still be apposite in 2015 because the science of supplementation has hardly moved, it was enough to convince the converted but not the opposition. It still is.

Natura Exhibition in Switzerland Mid March, I was in Basel in Switzerland for 'Natura Exhibition', to see the Prodotti Naturali Stand. Several European Companies expressed interest in Cantassium but no real business resulted as there were too many bureaucratic obstacles. It was the usual problem -- Diet Supplements equate to, or were treated legally, as Medicines. Having an Italian base made no difference from a UK base.

New products for Natural rearing range My brother was pressing for new products for the Natural Rearing Veterinary range but I agreed with R. Baxter (Registration Manager) who thought there were legal hurdles akin to those associated with human medicines and the company should seek to adapt from the established formulas found in the Larkhall ranges and sell food supplements for veterinary use. No product licences would be required.

Dene's, the previous manufacturer of the Natural Rearing ranges, had made the products for several years and had licences of right that they could continue to exploit for a few more years. That gave them an advantage over us and Mrs Bairacli Levy failed to realise or understand this from her idyllic home in Greece.

Eventually, my brother asked RG and me to produce a catalogue for the range but sadly we could not find a format that we thought would work, without great publicity and substantial unjustifiable financial resources.

The Veterinary Products list in 1987

Abels Anti-Worm, Anti-Eczema All in one Conditioner (Veterinary Medicines Licence of Right continued until 1989) but could not be advanced to a full licence. However, with re-labelling it became a Food Supplement Conditioner with no reference to its anti-worm and anti-Eczema actions. Of course, old users knew of its medicinal value - so sales were maintained but reduced over time. An excellent safe product lost by overwhelming bureaucracy and the determination of the synthetic medicine interests.

Other products were Birth Aid Tablets, Seaweed Calcium & Vitamin D Complements (Full Diet Supplement), Daily Health Tablets, Garlic Plus Gruel (Tree Barks) powder, Super Vitamin E 100 iu., Yeast 500mg Tablets Zinc Compound, Herbal Compound Tablets and Seaweed Mineral Food Powder.

Examples of publicity releases for pregnancy, Alzheimers prevention and aid to slimming In April we issued press releases for Foresight Vitamins and Minerals where we hoped to build on the positive article in The Independent Newspaper. For Aluminium Free Indigestion tablets we hoped provide an answer to the adverse publicity on Aluminium in most indigestion remedies that recent research had found contributed to the development of Alzheimer's Disease. G.Ps B-Slim showed Larkhall had a product to assist Grapefruit Dieters – one of the latest fad diets for losing weight.

FAX arrived at Larkhall to spell the end of Telex During 1987 Facsimile Transmission machines were introduced both at Putney and Charlbury. The Fax method of communication was better than Telex and was run on ordinary telephone lines. The Fax process machines were soon integrated with 'phones and the telex mode of communication ceased. There was concern about the durability of fax messages because they faded after a few years to become illegible. Later advances with digital processing would soon eliminate the durability problems associated with fax messages.

RG was delighted about the fax machines as they would enable sending of handwriting, drawings and diagrams as long as they were in black and white. She said their use would be invaluable for communicating with our printers and typesetters regarding corrections.

Computer Technology Microcomputer systems were becoming more powerful and so Larkhall were upgrading to an MV 7800 (a so called 'MiniComputer' System) which was accessible at both sites. There were many software companies setting up in the IT business and finding reliable ones was difficult. This would be the third system used by Larkhall over the last 7 years. These installations saved on clerical staff but the costs were substantial. Work grew to fill the memory capacities quickly. Minicomputers had memories measured in megabytes - in 2010 Gigabyte capacity microcomputers were available as laptops.

More blunders by the MC   At the end of April, I went out to dinner at a very good Chinese Restaurant in Victoria, hosted by the MC's director. Larkhall's chief salesman came too. A pleasant evening, plenty of talk, but little in the way of constructive plans for a way forward. Sadly, soon after the dinner, The Home Trade sales report for April came off the computer and made interesting reading for me but not for the MC. It showed that Lipcote was seen as a spearhead to develop the beauty side of the business. W5 Cream had been introduced in late 1986 and the large Lipcote 14ml pack, followed by the Aquamaid Range. All but W5 Cream had been at the behest of the MC. In the event, the large Lipcote was not successful and we should have gone in the reverse direction and introduced a smaller 4ml pack leaving the 7ml as a standard pack. The 14ml pack lasted users far too long and its presentation in a new white opaque bottle specified by the MC was ugly and pathetic -- surface coating on the glass peeled off when in contact with the Lipcote liquid. It was a disaster. The MC had had the Lipcote commercial changed to include it, which ruined it. This was expensive and a total waste of money.

More Vitamins needed by UK consumers   The May edition of Here's Health Magazine carried a long article entitled 'Vitamins are you getting enough?' This excellent account clearly made the case for most people in the UK to supplement their diets. It quoted authoritative sources concerned as to the adequacy of several vitamins and minerals in the 'Balanced Diet'. The RDAs (Recommended Daily Amounts) were often too low and based on incorrect information. The estimation of intake based on raw food items was a wrong approach because cooking and storage soon reduced concentrations of Vitamins in food. The situation has changed little from 1987 to 2015.

Prospects in France   In mid May, I went to visit Dr Kathy Bonan in Paris again and met with her associates who were expecting to import large quantities of Cantassium Supplements. However, I had learned that an American Supplement company had recently opened a retail outlet and had soon been closed down by the authorities for selling unlicensed and dangerous medicines. So, I could not share Kathy's optimism.

Chance Meeting with the MC's friend   I visited an exhibition of Health Products in Paris and met a friend of the owner of our MC, who asked about their work for Larkhall. I realised he was fishing. I said they were OK. Although I really had some private doubts. I had the feeling that whatever I said would go straight back to the MC. They did learn of this contact and I believed it gave them a sense of extra security at Larkhall.

Drug dealing at Larkhall   We had to get in touch with the Drug Squad regarding what seemed to be a drugs problem among staff at Larkhall. It had come to light in May and was getting worse. It was obviously impossible for us to sort it out in-house. Sniffer dogs couldn't work in the factory as there were too many conflicting odours. A local undercover plain clothes police officer was taken on as a new member of staff in the factory. One person had to coach him on how to fit in and had to keep an eye on him and help him if required. It was imperative his cover should not be blown and the only two people who knew about it were that person and myself. The undercover policeman hadn't been in the building for more than twenty minutes before he was offered all sorts of drugs by several of the staff, quite openly in the canteen. None of these could have come from Larkhall as we only made vitamin and mineral supplements. Nevertheless the whole factory had to be searched overnight. Nothing was found so it was a question of sorting out the pushers and where they were getting their supply of drugs.

A couple of days later there was a sting and arrests were made in the park in Putney Bridge Road, opposite the factory. Four members of our staff were involved with dealers.

Subsequently, more police came and carted off the staff from the canteen in the lunch hour, by bus to the police station, for questioning and to be searched. Officers came into the factory and searched from top to bottom again, including the drains. Nothing was found. The four who had been caught in the act in the park were arrested, stood trial and were jailed. So far as I was aware the problem had ceased. None of our products had been involved. It had been a worrying time and it was good to have it cleared up. The police were pleased with the way we had called them in, cooperated with them and with the resulting convictions. Everything settled down and there was a much better atmosphere in the factory now the pushers had left for prison.

Retailers warned about laws surrounding medicinal claims. I wrote to 'Natural Food Trader' about the legal constraints surrounding the advertising and medicinal recommendation of Food Supplements. I warned retailers about verbal advice too, noting that most of the successful products in the area had gained their popularity by breaking the law. Perhaps this was because authorities were either too lazy or ignorant to prosecute marketers and manufacturers, many of whom were based overseas especially in the USA. Seminars for practitioners and retailers were widely used to provide illegal medicinal messages.

Performance of Marketing Consultants questioned At the end of June I had a serious dispute with the MC over the appointment of a new Mail Order Manager. The MC's chosen two candidates interviewed badly but a woman from a local Putney Staff Agency was much better. When I decided that she was to be appointed, the MC got no fee for the appointment but thought he should. This experience made me even more wary of the MC and added to my doubts. They had already received several payments for obtaining new staff who had proved unsatisfactory. One had been for the Dispensary and their director assured me he was qualified. He turned out to not even have O-levels, let alone suitable qualifications. Another one was put in charge of mail order. Again the MC director, chose a man he knew himself, assured me the man had experience and was qualified. It turned out he had only worked in a mens' outfitters previously and, like the MC, knew absolutely nothing about mail order. His work performance had unsurprising and expensive consequences. A mail out's postage bill was £9,000 more than it should have been because he had no idea about his target weight for each envelope. The MC had no idea either.

DLPA surprise In Late June, unprompted by Larkhall, 'Chat', a weekly newspaper format publication, highlighted DLPA for curing arthritic pain with a note of the supplier of the tablets and reference to a Book on DLPA by Dr Arnold Fox, published by Thorsons. This article produced good sales for the Mail Order department. Michael van Straten was the writer of the article. He was Chat's Natural Medicine Man. This surprise DLPA publicity in CHAT Magazine made this product number one very quickly but production was insufficient to satisfy the totally unpredictable flash demand. Since this publicity could not be repeated in paid for space advertising, for legal reasons, the demand died quickly. However, Larkhall was able to benefit long term through word of mouth recommendation. Holland & Barrett, the UK's largest health food shop chain, stocked DLPA in all stores as a result of the CHAT publicity.

Balanced and FAD diets Vogue, the major fashion Magazine carried a long article 'The Fads, the Facts, the Truth about Nutrition Now' -- a useful account of the controversy surrounding fad health diets. The basic balanced diet should be wholesome with emphasis on fruit and vegetables with whole grains - less animal fat, refined carbohydrate (white flour and sugar) and less processed food.

Only when that failed to help should specific supplements and exclusion diets be undertaken. I told staff that this was what Cantassium had been advocating since 1970 and they must communicate that message to our customers.

Hidden Food Allergy   July 3rd, Action Against Allergy (AAA) held their annual meeting in London's West End. The Chairman of AAA was Amelia Nathan Hill who had suffered severe Food Allergies for many years. Her condition was treated successfully with exclusion diets and she used supplements by Cantassium too. The meeting was visited by Dr Mackarness and the guest speaker, American Dentist Dr Hal Huggins, talked about health problems caused by mercury amalgam fillings. He had written a book on the subject entitled 'It's All in Your Head' - Mackarness's book 'Not All in the Mind' was surely a close companion volume.

An interesting time in the USA and Dick Richards still detained in Chino.   Mid July, I took my annual trip to the USA where I attended the NNFA convention in Las Vegas and visited various suppliers including Weinstein Nutritionals in Irvine, Los Angeles. Anna and Marcello from Prodotti from Italy came to Las Vegas to investigate market trends. I went on to Los Angeles to visit Mia Rose (Air Therapy) in Costa Mesa. Air therapy was a unique natural citrus based non-aerosol air freshener that we had recently added to our product range in the UK. It was popular with allergy sufferers.

I visited Chino (California Institute for Men) again where Dr Dick Richards was held in prison. After some delay I managed to see Dick where he was serving time in prison for something he did not do. I found him looking well and cheerful. He signed some papers for me, as a UK medical expert, relating to the Licensing of Herbal Medicines for maintaining Product Licences of Right. He was still allowed to work as a Doctor, doing minor surgery in the prison hospital and so was kept busy. I think he was even managing to enjoy the experience of his stay, being the sort of man who could always adapt and make the best of everything, and, he was a very good doctor. His wife Pix had been out to see him a few times. By now they had had to sell their lovely Kent country house to pay the lawyers, one of whom had disappeared with Dick's forward payments. So, they had lost almost everything and the disappearing lawyer eventually ended up in jail himself.

We were still no wiser as to why the case had been brought against him for something that was supposed to have been planned but never carried out in UK, not USA. RG wrote to the US President about it but did not receive a reply. Dick paid back everyone who had put up money towards his huge bail amount, including RG and myself. Each time I went to USA on business I continued to make a detour to visit him in the prison. Eventually, with his sentence served, he came back to the UK and had to start again. Who had done this awful thing to him? And why? What did it achieve? I still keep up with him and his wife in 2015 and so does RG.

Aqamaid beauty range.   In July, as suggested by the MC we were actively testing consumer reaction to the Aquamaid beauty range - loved for quality but uncompetitive regarding price in a crowded market. In September the drive for the beauty range was continued with more press releases but with little result. Growth relied on using Lipcote retailers and enquirers to consider the range.

Lipcote demonstrated the European Common Market was a myth.   We learnt that Lipcote was not allowed importation into Germany from the UK. This was strange because it was formerly produced in that country without a problem, albeit sales were much lower than UK despite similar population numbers. Now we were looking to supply the product from the UK to the same formulation. Registration was to prove impossible and we could only supply small quantities to single stores so there was no wholesaling possibility.

This was more evidence that the EEC level playing field was a myth. Most EEC countries still protect themselves from imports ex UK but were happy to export their own products into the UK. Hopefully things would change in 1992 when the market was supposed to become totally open. In the event nothing changed for Lipcote but if we had opened a German factory things would have been quite different.

The first contact with BBC TV QED programme about Vitamins and IQ On 12th August, Tony Edwards a presenter on BBC2 QED programme came to visit Putney to talk about plans for a TV programme about School Children's Diets and the results of food supplement trials including the Welsh (Darland High School) and similar trials in the USA supervised by Professor Stephen Schoenthaler.

Publicity for the opposition to the Committee on Safety of Medicines (CSM) policy towards CAM At the end of August, The Pharmaceutical Journal column written by 'Celsus' (Bernard Hardisty) was critical of the DHSS and the Committee on Safety of Medicines. Referring to a recent book 'Medicines in the Market Place' by Dr David Green, Celsus developed the argument against the 'Safety Committee' in a new way. His cogent argument was later backed by my friend Mervyn Madge in a letter to the Pharmaceutical Journal. I attempted to put the point too and my letter was published in the October 3rd issue. Unfortunately, little had changed since 1987 but the authorities remain unwilling to enforce action against CAM that would prevent its availability. No doubt the opponents of CAM had its ear but apparently without support. I am sure that Human Rights issues surrounding CAM have always been and remain of overwhelming significance as regards government policy towards alternative health care.

A doctor wrote that Blacklisted Placebos have a role in medicine The 11th September issue of 'General Practitioner' magazine carried a letter entitled 'Placebo does have a role in Medicine' from Dr Tony Keable-Elliott arguing, as I did, that placebo has a place in medical treatment. Yet twenty-eight years later in 2015 things are unchanged. Keable-Elliott was stimulated to write on the subject following the loss of 'ineffective medicines' under the recently introduced blacklist rules for NHS prescribing. Since Health Supplements were blacklisted as ineffective they deserved consideration as placebos for treatment.

Professor Beckett intervened on Complementary Medicine. How to analyse a Homoeopathic product that contained no molecules of active ingredient In mid September the Pharmaceutical Journal published Professor Arnold Beckett's intervention regarding Complementary Medicine. He accepted that Homoeopathy and other alternative treatment practices had a role to play but was concerned about the methods of production being to high standards. He showed little appreciation of the philosophy behind treatments and products. I asked him how can you measure content of a homoeopathic product that contains no molecules of 'active' agent. Strangely, he admitted he did not know. Is quantum science involved?

Allies of Alternative Health Care were ready to help but not the Health Minister Edwina Currie In early October I received a letter from Dr David Green of the Institute of Economic Affairs Health Unit. He was pessimistic as regards early legal changes regarding Alternative Health Care. Public opinion must be more informed. The population was still besotted with the NHS and orthodox medicine especially because it's perceived as 'Free'. A huge task awaited the Alternative Health enthusiasts.

172

I sent local MP David Mellor a copy of my letter to the Pharmaceutical Journal regarding the problems for alternative medicines. In mid November I received a copy of a zero interest reply from Edwina Currie (A minister of Health) that demonstrated her ignorance of and ineffectual attitude towards the real world of Alternative Health Care. The widespread distrust of the orthodox medicine scientists by the Alternative specialists was unknown to her. Her blind obeisance to the bureaucrats was unbelievable, but look at her record on salmonella in eggs that was a disaster for excellent small egg producers. Similarly she was totally hopeless for the Alternative Health Care movement. Polite comment on her attitude was impossible.

Larkhall's Health Education programme was publicised to Health Teachers spearheaded by the Healthier Eating for School Children Booklet following its review in 'New Home Economics' in May 1987. The Healthier Diet Posters in two sizes were also available. All free. The A4 poster was designed for children to take home.
It is especially **worth noting that this education programme was ongoing before January 1988 when the Lancet paper concerning the improvement in non- verbal IQ when children's diets were boosted with the Tandem IQ formula supplement was published.** The accusation by our enemies (TV Productions for the BBC) that Larkhall just got on a bandwagon regarding improving Childrens' Diets was untrue and evil. The denigration of the Lancet Diet/IQ research by all those academics, journalists and junk food manufacturers (World Sugar Research Corporation) meant millions of children had a bleaker future.

Marketing Consultant dismissed On 27th October, the MC was dismissed as Marketing and Sales Consultant following poor performance and evident dishonest commercial practices.
RG, who had always refused to let the man anywhere near her products, had reported that he had tried to blackmail her into stealing the **Lipcote formula** for him. She refused point blank even though he bullied her. He had gone to her studio when she was alone and told her he could prove she was having an affair with someone in the factory. He said if her family found out, and he would make sure they did, there would be all sorts of trouble. At that moment she saw her husband walking across the roof towards the studio with a tray of tea so she said, 'Well, here comes my husband now, why don't you discuss it with him?" The MC saw him coming towards the studio and went off like a scalded cat, back into the offices, all red in the face. RG's mysterious lover was actually her husband. She told her husband what had happened and they both had a good laugh. Nevertheless, she reported it to the police since blackmail was a criminal offence. The MC never managed to get hold of the Lipcote formula.
I had hired a consultant I knew I could trust to evaluate some of the MC's research. The MC's son was studying at a London college and had used a few of his student friends to cobble up 'market research'. The consultant asked to see it. It was absolute rubbish, purporting to have been serious research using hundreds of people to fill in forms. The handwriting did not vary. It was by the same person and on torn scraps of paper, not proper forms. The MC was outraged that he had been found out and made a scene in the boardroom, balling and shouting. RG happened to be next door in her bookstore at the rear of the shop and came to see what all the noise was about. The shop girls were frightened. He was purple with rage, roaring and threatening violence. He left immediately via the front door.
When I dismissed him he threatened to sue me for 'breach of contract and substantial damages' and later on he tried and failed.

The Sales department had to adapt to the new situation quickly when he left. The Sales Manager remained and the other representatives continued to cover their same areas. The November sales Meeting outlined the proposed 1988 programme. The minutes of this meeting (in the Archive) provide an insight into the ongoing growth plans. Increasing office space, personnel and systems illustrated the positive ambitions of the company, all without our old MC and his 'attitudinal marketing' disasters.

Positive results of the Schoolchildren nutrition trial known   The results of the School Children Nutrition IQ trial became known to me in November. These led to Tandem IQ (two different tablets one of Vitamin C and the other a Multinutrient) becoming the major product for spearheading sales efforts from January 1988. Radio and National advertising was planned but unfortunately Advertising claims were greatly restricted by the code of advertising practice rules. Nevertheless the brilliant but courageous name 'Tandem IQ' carried a powerful message itself. I warned all staff that any media opportunities on publication of the Lancet research in January should not mention the name Tandem IQ in Radio, TV and press interviews and prevent easy criticism from the expected opposition. Whilst I adhered to that, members of the sales staff did not and, of course, consumers, journalists and retailers often went over the top in their excitement.

Good report revealed fallibility   Reports from a particular sales representative were always interesting. He, like others, emphasised the negative aspects eg moaning about out-of-stocks, competitor activity and errors at the sales office. I always read these reports and constantly complained at their negativity. Ironically he praised the recent introduction of a 14ml (Double capacity) Lipcote pack but, in fact, this was a disastrous move by the company instigated by the old MC. Sales people should always be positive and optimistic and remember that management disliked constant bad news and excuses from them.

Sadie Nine had a Lipcote proposal   I met actors Peter Willis, Sadie Nine, Paul and DJ Bear who were interested in promoting Lipcote on national TV using PR methods. Phyllis Rounce, of a theatrical agency office in Regent Street, was the manager behind them. They made a good presentation but after a short trial, results were very disappointing.

Advertising threats from the ASA   W5 Skin Treatment received ASA censure of small buy-line advertisements in 'Sunday Shop' a feature in Sunday Magazine (a National). Well illustrated that it was best to keep controversial claims out of 'Nationals'. I enquired about competitor advertising without response.

ASA attacked our Health Examiner, a mail order item designed and written by the mail order sales team. I defended my new sales staff but copy was amended later. In September 1987 I was pretty despondent about a letter from ASA regarding the 'Health Examiner'. In the event they soon lost interest and we never submitted copy to them but modified claims and received no more letters on the matter. New staff at Larkhall were always stretching claims but I insisted that I vetted in-house from then on.

Marketing ideas without the Marketing Consultant   An internal staff meeting generated some more ideas for 1988. The Sponsorship of the Cambridge University Lightweight Rowing Crew was discussed as was the introduction of Seminars for training retailers in Larkhall products. Many companies used this route but it was dangerous because any medicinal claims for unlicensed products at these seminars could lead to prosecutions. Many US Companies were using this method and were known to be in trouble with the authorities. New enthusiastic staff just did not understand the difficulties in this borderline area and most representatives, including Larkhall's, regularly strayed into the illegal claims area.

I knew that any national seminar project would be dangerous for Larkhall because they were constantly being scrutinised by Trading Standards and the Medicines Authorities. It was only the excellent relations that RG and I had fostered with our local TSOs that had boosted our credibilty with authority in recent years. Our internal publicity department had not performed well and we were to look for an agency again.

Tandem IQ advertised during 1987 A regular advertisement in Here's Health Magazine during 1987 featured Tandem IQ but always with a Healthier Diet emphasis. It should be noted that this was before the great publicity generated by the BBC QED programme in January 1988, after the Lancet Paper was published. This proved Larkhall were strong on Children's vitamins and nutrition before all the controversy started. The Tandem IQ tablets had been used in the pilot study in 1986.

Cantassium Organic Germanium tablets Organic Germanium, which was introduced in low strength tablets in 1987, was a form of the mineral originating in Japan. There were many brands of raw material and there were doubts about the purity of some. As a result all germanium was banned in the UK towards the end of 1989 after adverse safety reports from Japan concerning one particular chemical form of Germanium were publicised in UK media. Germanium was still permitted in most countries. Larkhall still exported tablets because it knew that their source of Germanium was not the one implicated in the problems. Larkhall had used Germanium in some 'Complete Vitamin & Mineral' supplements and the unjust orchestrated publicity was to greatly harm their Cantassium Brand in 1991. Cantassium Organic Germanium tablets were made from a Germanium yeast and contained organically bound germanium.

Healthmark -- the HFMA Quality Mark for Healthfoods   In 1987 the Healthfood Manufacturers Association introduced a special Quality Mark (Healthmark) for products sold in Health Food Stores. This was to enforce high 'Natural' standards on manufactured products that were not fresh. Larkhall became one of the first companies to have a product (Crunchy Malt Flakes) awarded this Healthmark. Unfortunately the scheme did not find favour with retailers or manufacturers because as soon as strict standards for Naturalness were applied to 99% of the manufactured products they failed to comply because of the widespread use of synthetic additives as aids in production processes. The Healthmark appearing on just a handful of products on the retailer's shelves would give rise to customer concerns as to claims for 'Naturalness' used by Health stores and perceived by their customers on all the other products on the shelves.

Year end reflections By the end of 1987 the Marketing Consultant's general marketing ideas had failed and they had been dismissed. In the period 1986-7 awareness of Larkhall had grown through the ongoing IQ/Children's Nutrition research rather than any of the consultants' ideas. Larkhall was becoming well known but failed to realise what enemies they were making. Study of several of the PR releases, in the Archive, indicate why they soon faced problems with the junk food industry and pharma interests. By mid 1988 the success of the IQ trials on schoolchildren was troubling authorities, junk food manufacturers (World Sugar Corporation) and the Pharmaceutical Industry. The blatant attempted copying of Tandem IQ by the largest supplement company, Seven Seas with their Boost IQ product (a totally different formulation from the Larkhall product used in the IQ research) indicated to me that not even my own industry understood what Larkhall was really about. Scientifically proving the modern diet was nutritionally poor and educating populations on how to make lifestyle changes and ultimately have no need of Diet Supplements, other than in special health circumstances.

175

Year that changed Larkhall forever

MP lets me down - Vitamin supplement threatens vested interests - Bioflavonoids carcinogenic says Professor - ASA attack Tandem IQ - Pointless Inspections harm Britain - Visiting Saudi Arabia for business - Largest Supplement Company copies Tandem IQ - Sugar interests behind denigration of IQ/diet research - Good Nutrients Guide - Medicines Inspection Test Madness - Ayurveda - PR Agency Blunder - Herbals not suited to the Medicines Act - Common Market a joke - USA retailers' knowledge poor - Cytotoxic Test banned in USA - Exporting hidden realities - Professor's poor research received unmerited praise - Sylvia Meredith agency to inform Doctors - Romanian Olympic expert to research Supplements - Lipcote sales efforts - Medicine should incorporate Nutrition - General Drummond dies - Consultant claims for unlawful dismissal - Animal Testing difficulties - Books imported - Cambridge Rowers - Royal Jelly

MP fails to keep appointment   In mid January RG and I went to the House of Commons to meet David Mellor the MP for Putney, by appointment regarding prescription of Gluten Free Foods. He failed to turn up and could not be found. No apology received. I was not impressed and nor was RG as we waited for several hours.

Portugal and Belgium   I visited our distributors in these countries -- Vitalsil in Lisbon and Heleesun in Antwerp. Both countries were developing an interest in Cantassium products. Portugal was a much smaller market and the partners in the distributor were in dispute. Mrs Helene Wauters and Rita Scheepmans of Heleesun in Antwerp operated in the mail order health area and were successful with a limited range of Cantassium products.

The Vitamin supplement that should have led a revolution   On January 22nd the scientific paper on Vitamins and IQ was published in The Lancet (considered one of the premier world publications for general medical research). Much work was done by the sales department in anticipation of the interest generated by the positive research and the BBC2 Q.E.D programme that publicised the results from the UK study and similar research in the USA. We provided for large demand for our Tandem IQ (Ideal Quota) product but in the event there was much greater publicity than expected and media distortion of the conclusions reached by the scientists proved an enduring problem for Larkhall. The publication 'The Tandem IQ Story' related these problems in detail. My attempt to keep a low profile for the brand failed for the following reasons:-

1   The fundamental aim of the research, to prove the **general diet** of school children was inadequate, was always excluded from press reports despite the emphasis on diet being the headline subject of the Q.E.D. programme.
2   All press reports indicated to the lay person that Vitamin Supplements alone would improve a child's IQ. **This was not our message but one the press and media concocted.**
3   Improving the diet with healthy foods was never mentioned despite me always talking about that when interviewed. I even went to the extent of saying the Larkhall factory would cease to make the tablets when children were consuming the healthy diets that had featured in Larkhall publications for many years previously.

4   The junk food industry and refined sugar producers used their financial and media power to ensure that the healthier diet message was not effectively communicated. According to them the idea that a vitamin pill alone could increase IQ was a myth (It certainly was, although not claimed by Larkhall but merely an invention of the media). They also claimed recent research was flawed and not credible.

5   The many academic researchers who depended on the junk food and sugar interests to fund their departments quickly wrote apparently authoritative independent letters and even performed 'trials' to rubbish the original UK and USA science revealed on the QED programme.

6   Other Vitamin companies launched general low cost multivitamin/mineral products to compete with Larkhall's Tandem IQ and promoted them as formulated for IQ without any background educational material referring to Healthy Diets. In other words they jumped on a bandwagon.

7   Big Pharma did not have a pill that would improve IQ (any more than we did). They were not happy about that.

During 1988, much of Larkhall's business involved their efforts to improve the diets of schoolchildren; not just in the UK but in USA, Netherlands and Italy.

Latterly, between 1989-1993, Larkhall had become enmeshed in Trading Standards disputes and whilst their competitors were fined heavily and criticised, Larkhall were fined minimally for abstruse technical labeling errors and congratulated on their contribution to the research.

Sadly, the Media again failed to report the correct messages. The junk food and sugar interests ensured that the message from Larkhall that 'a wholesome healthier diet was essential for all children' did not reach the public. Larkhall continued to promote their ideas through schools and health professionals. Gwylm Roberts the schoolmaster who started it all, lectured to schools for a few years funded by Larkhall. In the early 2000s Jamie Oliver, the celebrity chef, tried to improve school childrens' diets but with questionable success. I am sure he faced opposition from those same vested interests.

A good supportive article by Miriam Polunin (former Editor of Here's Health) appeared in She magazine. It said the IQ Trial by Benton and Roberts was hard to dismiss.

Trufree Tandem IQ report. The high Trufree standards were chosen by the schoolmaster who directed the IQ trial because, unlike all competitor products, the Trufree brand used no synthetic chemical additives in the formulas. This point, whilst a considerable positive for some people, was not generally accepted by scientists who thought untested cocktails of additives were as safe as single additives. As a chemist I could never understand this view as chemicals have a potential to react with one another and perhaps produce harmful reactants when ingested. None of the tablets/capsules used in trials after Larkhall's by others met the high Trufree standard and thus the results could never be fairly compared to those obtained with the original tablets. **Different formulas were used for much less time and trials were not carried out properly. They were tailored to fit the demands of the media.**

Most of our critics were not chemists and so could not comprehend our arguments but some had 'Professor' in front of their names so carried disproportionate credibility as far as media reporters were concerned. One Professor, Donald Naismith actually criticised the Trufree formula for Tandem IQ because it contained bioflavonoids that he said were carcinogenic -- utter nonsense. If bioflavonoids were cancer producing why was marmalade on the UK breakfast menu? It is full of bioflavonoids.

Tandem IQ attacked by ASA. By 19th of February, correspondence started with the ASA about a single (yes, a single) complaint they had received about Tandem IQ. This was disingenuous. The member of the public was obviously a puppet of someone but the arguments against Larkhall were unchanged over the years leading to the prosecution in Shropshire in 1992. The really significant point was that the Lancet article was published on 23rd January and this attack from the ASA letter was dated 19th February -- the 'member of the public' must have been very quick off the mark. This was quite likely to have been a set-up by the Junk Food Industry who were to manipulate the opposition to Larkhall for many years to come, despite the fact that this initial skirmish was settled by May 1988.

Medicines inspections In late January, some new Medicines Inspectors visited our Charlbury factory. A report on the visit by my brother painted a picture of two nasty self-important men acting officiously. As the facility only devoted under 2% of its throughput to medicines, this exercise was hardly a useful cost effective way to spend a working day. The nit-picking comments recorded would be used to ensure these men continue to justify their existence to their superiors in the Licensing Authority. I am sure third world low cost producers are encouraged by these people whose actions ensure UK production is transferred to them.

A medicines Inspection took place at Putney in early May. Larkhall's involvement in Licensed Medicinal Product manufacture was a very small percentage of our total involvement (less than 2%). Nevertheless these inspections were useful as a guide to our staff and kept them up to the mark. No one could ever satisfy these power crazed individuals. I hardly ever met them but always replied to their nit-picking letters.

Saudi Arabia In late February I travelled to Riyadh (Saudi Arabia) to visit a Saudi entrepreneur whose Royal Family contacts in UK had arranged for my travel visas. Since I had visited Israel I had to obtain a new Passport with no Israeli stamp therein. Whilst I was treated with great courtesy and generosity by my host, I saw that business in Health Food Supplements would be very difficult in Saudi Arabia because a consumer knowledge base and demand for products was non-existent. Perfumes and Beauty products were more likely to succeed but marketing techniques seemed unknown to my host. An agreement for sole distributorship of Larkhall products in SA was signed - great importance was attached to the document by my host and an order for £5000 worth of the Aquamaid Beauty products was obtained and ultimately shipped and paid for.

The following day I attended the offices of the company and met the all male ex-patriate staff (mainly Pakistanis) that looked after all its commercial affairs - no female staff were employed. Coffee and soft drinks were served constantly and there was a continuous stream of visitors to the office. I was ignored much of the time. I asked to visit a shopping Mall and saw retail outlets for supplements did not exist. All Pharmacies were independent and obtained their supplies directly from overseas manufacturers. Saudi Arabia seemed an unlikely place for a UK company offering Larkhall's range to gain worthwhile business.

On my last evening in Riyadh, I attended a party at my host's home and was introduced to his wife that, in itself, was a great honour for a foreigner in Saudi Arabia. A party with just his male friends then took place and we sat round a properly ritually slaughtered sheep that had been spit roasted. A sheep's eye was given to me, another great honour, which I ate with gusto, sitting cross legged round the feast wearing an arab head dress. The guests consumed many bottles of Johnny Walker Scotch Whisky (illegal in Saudi Arabia) and appeared intellectually juvenile. The TV boomed out news of the King's doings but little else. After the party I was taken to Riyadh airport in pouring rain and flew to Bangkok at 3 am.

At least I had learned the truth about the business prospects in Saudi Arabia. In contrast to the very optimistic picture reported to me in 1975/6 by the Lebanese distributor friend of O'Connell's brother (Mustafa El Jundi). I guessed that a similar situation existed in the Gulf countries like Bahrain, Kuwait, UAE etc. where prospects had been similarly exaggerated in 1976. The £5000 order at least paid for my trip thanks to the great generosity of my host as regards Hotel and Taxis. Nothing was heard from him after his order had been shipped and received in Riyadh. Full payment was received. Honest traders like him must be all over the Gulf Countries but their business etiquette was totally different from ours.

Going on to Bangkok and Singapore I found the traders more Westernised. I had a successful time in those countries.

Largest supplement company attempts to copy Tandem IQ and consequently set back the Health Supplement industry many years.   At the end of February, Seven Seas, the largest supplement company in the UK, launched Minadex Boost IQ. with a hard hitting national advertising campaign. The IQ stood for 'Increased Quota' because it was stronger in content than their ordinary childrens' supplement Minadex. Price (£1.99 for 30 capsules/one months supply)) was far below Larkhall's Tandem IQ (60 Tablets, one month's supply £4.99) and the formula was totally different from the ones used in IQ Trials in UK and USA. Their product launch letter to pharmacists gave an impression that they had something to do with the recent research that was nonsense. Unfortunately, their marketing platform soon alerted the authorities and they were ultimately fined many thousands of pounds in the Shropshire Court on multiple charges. They avoided most costs by pleading guilty. The stupidity and greed of Seven Seas almost certainly helped set children's dietary improvement back many years. (In 2015 it is little better.)

That they pleaded guilty made things impossible for reputable manufacturers like Larkhall who understood that, at last, there was scientific evidence in support of supplementation to correct poor diets. My hopes of educating consumers to adopt better eating habits in the medium term were dashed. When it came to Larkhall being prosecuted in 1992 the Seven Seas admission of crimes gave the Shropshire Authority an unfair advantage, although the magistrate did appreciate the differences between Tandem IQ and Boost IQ (and by that time several others), he was able to convict us on minutiae of labeling which could be found on countless packs of health supplement products. Such trivial matters, if discovered by trading standards, were customarily settled by agreement with the producers to change packaging/labeling, not in courts of law. However, this did not seem to have been an option for Larkhall in this case.

Trade sales expansion   The Trade sales department moved upstairs to new offices which had been built at the front of the factory, on the second floor of 225 - 229 Putney Bridge Road. These were immediately above the Administration and Mail Order offices. The expansion came just at the right moment because the Tandem IQ publicity produced more interest in the whole product range. We now had six sales representatives and whilst sales were going well, thanks to Tandem IQ, overheads were rising. Lipcote stlll dominated overall sales as this product had a solus position in the market but was failing to take the general Aquamaid range with it.

We had recruited an American Rabbi, who had good knowledge of the nutrition health professional market in the USA. He was popular on his travels to retail stores in the UK but I feared that he was exaggerating product effectiveness and wondered if his enthusiasm could be dangerous when authority saw him in action. He was doing small seminars in store but his benefit to sales was not continued when he left the retailers to their own devices. His use of expenses was eye-watering.

Reports of sales activity and advertising plans indicated the beneficial effects of the Tandem IQ publicity on the whole Larkhall range. A letter from Bob Sims, the MD of the Media Shop agency, indicated the enthusiasm pervading the company at this time. By early July we were using Tandem IQ as the lead product, concentrating effort on the chains of Health stores with training sessions and lectures by myself and our Rabbi.

The Sugar industry orchestrated a campaign against Larkhall Unfortunately, our plans were soon curtailed for commercial reasons not least the great opposition generated against the IQ research from powerful interests (Junk Food and Sugar Industries). They co-ordinated supportive and dependent academics to spearhead a public relations and media backlash using their huge financial clout and advertising power. I was unprepared for the ensuing orchestrated campaign against a small family business and one man -- me.

Italian Beauty range Mid March found the Maugeris in London to see me and visit Hampshire Aerosols regarding their proposed beauty range, AntiOxyd (Antioxidant) skin care. They intended to introduce the range to the Italian Market soon. They asked Paul Younger, the MD of Hampshire Aerosols, for advice and showed him the products they wanted.

Gluten Free brand made a takeover In the spring, Chemist & Druggist reported on Cow & Gate (a Nutricia owned brand) taking over a gluten free food manufacturer G.F. Dietary Group. Nutricia already dominated the Gluten Free market through its different brands so this gave them even more clout. The owner Mr Ward soon departed from Nutricia's employment and after five years returned to the market with his new company Gluten Free Foods. (It was Nutricia that were to takeover Larkhall and Trufree Foods in 1999.)

Italian progress for Larkhall In May I went to Verona to the Herbora Show where PN were exhibiting. There was a very good display and products were doing well. Larkhall was now a leader in Health Supplements in Italy. Very few UK producers were exporting there successfully. The distributor was working close to the legal edge, but winning.

Ayurveda the traditional Indian medicine The Chemist & Druggist published a recommendation by a London based PR company, McAlpine,Thorpe & Warrior, that companies should enter the herbal drug market. These people were well known to me for representing the Ayurvedic Traditional Medicine producers from India. Mr Warrior attempted, via friendly entertainment, to involve Larkhall in importing these products for sale to Ayurvedic Practitioners in UK. When I saw the formulations and that payment was required before shipment, I declined further interest having spent many hours investigating the commercial possibilities. In fact, I discovered later that all the practitioners imported their own supplies direct from their Indian contacts so it would have been a complete waste of time and money.

Madness evident in Edinburgh Inspectorate The Medicines Inspectors had an ongoing system of surveillance and had selected Larkhall's Galegae Herb Tablets for examination by their laboratory in Edinburgh. This product had sales of less than 100 bottles of 60 a year. I considered this surveillance a total waste of taxpayers money. According to the Potter's cyclopaedia of Herbals (1988) Galegae (Goats Rue) was a traditional herb that had been used for many years as a milk-inducer, diuretic and anti-wormer (vermifuge) medicinally. Since it was held to be helpful to breast tissue Larkhall sold the product in conjunction with the Aquamaid Bust device. The product held an historic Licence of Right.

Should the Medicines people really concern themselves with products in such low demand and likely to be outlawed soon by impending technical regulations totally inappropriate for herbals? The registration manager dealt with the Medicines Laboratory and nothing was heard again. I wonder what they did with the sample bottle?

Representatives offer excessive discounting Business was continuing to grow especially on the Home Trade side. Much investment in Advertising and representative support had been made. The Helfex Exhibition in Brighton in March had been successful but retailers were more concerned with the discounts on offer rather than learning of the real implications of the Tandem IQ research in lectures. I was still concerned that sales people were concentrating on discount trading to gain easy sales. If the representatives could embrace the message that Larkhall was supporting retailers by advocating proper supplementation and having research projects well ahead of all their competitors, the need for discounting would diminish. In the trade there were many discount traders operating and reps continually quoted ludicrous examples to me. I gave them short shrift. Computer programmes were becoming more sophisticated and the reps who were over- discounting could be detected easily and reprimanded if their excuses were considered inadequate by the sales manager. This never happened.

New PR agency didn't last long The success of the Tandem IQ Trial had to be capitalized on. Advertising proved difficult because the Advertising Standards Authority followed the accepted rule that a balanced diet provided sufficient Vitamins and Minerals, in spite of the fact nobody knew what this mythical balanced diet was. According to the ASA no one, except members of particular groups, needed supplements to maintain good health.

The fact that it was difficult to know whether you were eating a balanced diet or even what that diet was, was ignored. Certain categories of person such as the elderly, pregnant women and children could be targeted by advertising but claims were restricted. I saw the only way forward as being awareness and availability advertising. Radio and TV were planned on that basis and magazines too. The main thrust had to be PR so I selected a well known PR Agency that was part of a large group to work with us. It all worked fairly well with many articles in the press.

However, on May 26th a Press Conference and Luncheon was held at the Hilton Hotel in Park Lane. The agency invited top journalists including Dr James Le Fanu of the Daily Telegraph.

Gwylm Roberts and I spoke and answered some tricky questions. I explained that **Tandem IQ was a food supplement not a magic pill for IQ.** It could improve the child's Diet immediately, enabling better concentration and better learning but medium term the children would need to be persuaded to eat wholesome food instead of junk food. When this approach had been tried in the school where the Welsh trial had taken place many of the children would not eat the healthier food particularly vegetables, despite the heroic efforts of the kitchen staff.

Unfortunately, the food served for the journalists' lunch at the Park Lane conference was a bad choice (by the agency) and afterwards I questioned them about it, intimating that it should have been healthier, on the lines advocated by Larkhall in their publicity and educational booklets.

RG noticed that the lunch served to agency staff was quite different and healthier than the one served to us and the journalists. Most of the journalists enjoyed the free lunch but Le Fanu saw it as an opportunity to knock Larkhall in a long article in the Daily Telegraph. He rubbished our research and criticised the lunch he had eaten. RG said he was quite right about the lunch that had been far from healthy. She had left hers on the plate after one look and taste.

Three journalists sitting around her gave her a hard time about the cars we owned, looking to make something of it. They didn't get satisfaction as she herself drove an old mini van so her husband's wheelchair could be easily transported and my Mercedes was second hand. (This explained why photographers had tried to photograph us arriving in my car outside the venue.) They believed the whole IQ story was a scam, that Larkhall were crooks and I had made millions. They were more interested in cars and money than the truth of the situation. There was never any interest as to who had put up the money for the research -- our small family company. We had received no research grants from anyone.

Larkhall (and me in particular) had dared to blow the whistle regarding the poor state of nutrition among schoolchildren because they were being fed so much junk food. The junk food industry was out for revenge via the media.

It was too late to undo that bad publicity. The agency obviously did not understand what Larkhall was really doing after three months on the PR. RG would have done a superb, healthy lunch at our own dining room and the journalists could have been shown round the factory but the agency advised against it and said that top journalists were unlikely to come out to Putney. This was hardly the outer reaches of civilization. The agency's choice of the Hilton Hotel in Park Lane was hardly a help. The majority of journalists who had turned up were just there for a free lunch. Some of them had been really aggressive. It had been an expensive PR disaster that would have been far, far better done in house and for a fraction of the cost. I dismissed the agency.

BHMA (British Herbal Medicines Association) On May 15th I attended the annual meeting of the BHMA (British Herbal Medicines Association) at the Connaught Hotel (Bloomsbury). Many products had already been lost but I was a lone voice in calling for a boycott of the whole herbal licensing system being operated by the DHSS Medicines Division. I told them that Arthur Chamings agreed with me that we should never have agreed to have anything to do with the Medicines Act because the criteria suited to synthetic drugs could not be applied to Herbals. The Act was designed for the pure single or perhaps three active ingredient combination products of the modern Pharmaceutical Industry. I said it would all end in tears. No one was listening because the few technical people present were employees making a living out of producing registration documentation for company owners who were technically illiterate. I doubt anyone present had done practical herbal analysis let alone obtained consistent results.

No Common Market By July export sales were developing well but whilst Italy and Holland were expanding steadily, there was no business in France and Germany. The export dispatch manager could not understand this discrepancy between large countries. I explained that the European Union was not really a free market and France and Germany were notorious chauvinists when it came to importing. Greek customs officials were still causing problems with imports of food supplements and our distributor said it was because she would not pay bribes. I agreed that this was the correct policy because once you had paid one bribe future bribes were expected.

In mid July a Mr Brant from Austria visited Larkhall with a view to importing Gluten Free products. Nothing resulted. I added Austria to Germany and France on the list of protected markets for indigenous producers.

American food supplement retailers disappoint   In July I was in Las Vegas to exhibit Tandem IQ at the NNFA convention on a joint stand with Mia Rose Air Therapy products. Larkhall had distributed Mia Rose's Air Therapy sprays in the UK for several years and were grateful to Ms Palencar (owner of Mia Rose) for her help with Tandem IQ. Many enquiries were received which I followed-up after the show on the West and East coasts. However no distributor was appointed.

The Tandem IQ video was played on the stand but the audience of American Health Store retailers failed to understand the significance of the research. I was not impressed by the basic knowledge of the US retailers that seemed well below the standard of the UK Health Store proprietors. Unfortunately, all these folk were looking for magic pills for illnesses as substitutes for pharmaceutical drugs. I didn't believe they really understood what nutritional supplementation was about.

This perception of Food Supplements replacing Medicinal Drugs was the prime reason for regulatory pressure that frustrates the Health Food Industry even in 2015. The proposed Health Claims for Food products could yet devastate the trade. It was the Shropshire IQ Case that alerted me to what the future could hold for food supplements if handled incorrectly by the supplement industry that, sadly, it has been.

Cytotoxic Allergy Test banned in the USA After the NNFA Show I went to see Physicians Laboratory in Huntingdon Beach. The office was closed. Doug Kaufmann had vanished and Geoff Cheung was moving on but he informed me that the cytotoxic test had been banned in California and New York.

At the end of my trip, I visited Dr Dick Richards in Chino Jail again where he was acting as Prison Doctor, still managing to enjoy life. He was due for release in March 1989, the following year -- to be immediately deported to UK. His US lawyer was apparently still in jail.

Export market penetration required special skills The suggestions of Brian Morley our Export administrator, who had recently been on holiday in the USA, in his report dated 5th July were enlightening. Remote from the markets he saw possibilities but had no appreciation of the real difficulties of entering the US and several European Markets. Only by my personal visits could these be seen and accurately assessed on the ground. Regular home trade sales staff could spend years, as O'Connell did in the mid 1970s, in these markets and have no explanation for certain failure. There were over-optimistic local distributors with no in-depth knowledge of the legal situations surrounding Food Supplements and 'Natural' Beauty products for non-indigenous manufacturers. Most countries operate import regulations to protect their markets from foreign invasion not least the USA.

In early August I issued a memo regarding the unfavourable international market in supplements. Whilst we accepted substantial imports from Canada, Australia, New Zealand, Germany and Denmark, the imports from UK manufacturers to those countries faced impossible hurdles. The situation was similar in the USA but as the largest world market for these products, the competitive pressures, including immediate imitation would deter most exporters.

Germany again In mid August I flew to Berlin (before the wall came down) via the low fly zone. This visit was to see the of the sweetener Hermesetas who were considering taking over a UK healthfood/herbal company. Talks were inconclusive but seeing the Hermesetas micro tablet factory and their top selling herbal liquid product was very interesting.

French Freedom in Medicinals could offer UK an opportunity In September, an interesting letter in The Lancet pointed out the possible problems ahead for Medicines Regulation in the EEC. There were differences in basic philosophy between Britain and France. France was said to offer more freedom of choice than the UK. Later these differences extended to most nations and the Complementary approach was more acceptable in the 'Free' countries that did not include the UK.

The flawed Naismith research   A letter to the Lancet containing the apparently negative data derived from the 'Naismith' trial on vitamins and IQ was published in July and widely publicised. This proved disastrous for Larkhall and its ramifications were fully discussed in 'The Tandem IQ Story' booklet. Suffice to observe that this trial was suspect and far from a replication of the original Benton and Roberts trial although it pretended to be so. It was financed by Junk Food interests in co-operation with The World Sugar Corporation. Importantly, it was vigorously publicised by a large public relations agency with huge funding. It is impossible not to regard Naismith's research and its subsequent publicity as very suspicious. Its sophistry and inadequacy was beyond belief and reason.

As a 'Professor' Naismith (a chain smoker) assumed immediate supremacy on the subject of IQ and nutrition in the journalist's and consumer's mind. All evidence was slanted to suggest that Larkhall was seen as the consumer's enemy. A stony road lay ahead. Ironically, Professor Garrow of The Rank Department of Human Nutrition at St Bart's Hospital, later to join the anti-Larkhall brigade, was apparently planning a trial assisted by Larkhall. This trial never materialised, Naismith had presumably just done what was needed from the academics they funded and seemed to serve the Junk Food producers well.

In a few weeks I was in Holland to discuss the marketing of Tandem IQ and help our distributor overcome the effects of the Naismith flawed research. I am certain that the tentacles of the junk food industry were behind the problems. It is sad that our distributor could not overcome those powerful interests. He quit the market.

Was there a way back?   In early August, a managers' meeting discussed the way forward for sales and marketing with a new catalogue as the main publication to set out Larkhall's way ahead. The appointment of Sylvia Meredith Health Education Advisory Service, an agency, was likely. This agency would spearhead Larkhall's aim to be seen as a reliable source to medical professionals who might then recommend and prescribe their products. I was still optimistic that the Larkhall IQ diet research could soon regain credibility because the 'Naismith' trial was scientifically flawed yet could have been positive if the scientific statistics had been interpreted correctly.

Holism in health care had a future   In August, Journalist, Christine Doyle (who was well known to me and had been lunched at Larkhall) wrote an article for the Daily Telegraph on the chances of Holism being accepted by mainstream medical professionals. An in-depth piece which is probably relevant in 2015.

Romanian nutrition research   A letter from Maria Strofalis, Vital & Naturtabs Hellas, was received about research undertaken by Professor Joan Drangan of the Sports Medicine Department in Bucharest, Romania. Drangan was a member of the International Olympic Committee and an enthusiast for his Elite Athletes to use nutritional supplements to aid performance. Larkhall supplied supplements to help his research work. His 1988 study was on a Selenium product and was positive and showed the possibility of antioxidant effects of Selenium in human metabolism. Mrs Strofalis was building a good rapport with Drangan. Greece, as a fellow Balkan Country, was ideally placed to deal with the Professor. I knew that the British Scientific establishment was unlikely to favour results from an Iron Curtain country such as Romania. In reality Drangans' results were useful to Larkhall because consumers had more open minds than British Academics in cahoots with the multinational junk food interests.

Petition against the proposed Pharmacy Only distribution of food supplements In early September, Larkhall planned to mount a petition against government proposals that sale of Food Supplements should be restricted by law to Pharmacies. An inappropriate idea since most Pharmacists did not understand nutrition. Additionally, they had an innate bias from their education to the expansion of synthetic medicines produced by big Pharma. This petition produced excellent publicity for Larkhall with the final result being taken to Downing Street. Later in the year, Natural Food Retailer reported that Larkhall were organising a petition regarding the effect of threatened legislation coming from Brussels. This made Larkhall's contribution exceptional in the market place.

Sales in the UK flatlining The home sales were progressing but promotional costs were exceeding estimates. Radio advertisements had shown a poor return because of their weak messages that were enforced by the authorities. Representatives were costly individuals and it was becoming increasingly apparent that covering the country was commercially too costly. Business in Health Foods was restricted to the prosperous areas including London and the South East, Birmingham and close suburbs, Manchester and close suburbs, Bristol and Bournemouth, scattered areas in Scotland, Yorkshire, Wales, N.Ireland and the West Country. Independent Health Stores were, at best, just maintaining numbers because of increasing legislative threats that were planned for supplements and herbals. Most consumers were taking the cheap synthetic Vitamin supplements sold in supermarkets. To persuade those users to change their choice to the naturally prepared and more costly supplements needed more than awareness advertisements. I was still convinced that only professional recommendation, despite previous disappointments, could work long term and so I proposed changing advertising strategy.

Practitioner marketing Mail order to Alternative Practitioners and consumers was becoming increasingly attractive. Unfortunately, the media were exploring dubious practices in the professional supply route because practitioners were making secret arrangements with manufacturers to receive commissions from orders received from their named patients. Whilst Larkhall did not participate in these schemes they had to compete in other ways to maintain market share. Several promotions with the retail chain (Holland & Barrett) and wholesaler (Brewhurst) were ongoing as were discount incentive deals with independents. Whilst I did not really back all these schemes I was aware that in the real world they were needed.

Lipcote new Wing Pack This pack was produced for use by supermarkets to decrease risks of pilferage by making the pack of this small product bulkier. We hoped all retailers would appreciate the change because the new pack enabled us to provide more information on packs. But of course they didn't and we had to retain old type packs too.

Lipcote was the number one lipstick sealer in the UK but since the TV advertising campaigns more competitors had arrived in stores, encouraged by Larkhall's spend on advertising. Lipcote was an important product for the company but there was now fierce competition so sales schemes and promotions were important to maintain market share. These involved Gondola End Promotions in Boots and 14-for-12 wholesale deals with a free counter display to hold 24 bottles for Chemists and Beauty stores. Despite extra sales generated by TV advertising, promotions were essential to maintain retailer loyalty and the crucial shelf positioning. Ironically, Larkhall still failed to obtain agreements with major multiple outlet stores to display Lipcote within their lipstick area. Undoubtedly, this was because lipstick makers perceived that extended life of lipstick depressed sales of lipsticks. This was nonsense. Most users ceased to use a particular lipstick for fashion reasons not because the product had run out.

Mainstream Medicine should incorporate nutrition including food supplements. 'Medical thinking must incorporate Nutrition' was an interesting article from Health Foods Business (USA) in October 1988. The views of Dr Murray Susser many of which agree with mine that orthodox (evidence based) medicine and nutrition are complementary and should be seen as a continuum. He was alarmed at what he called the brainwashing by the medical establishment against nutrition because there was no evidence base. He added that it was a myth that everything in medicine was proved to be effective by double blind clinical trials, the truth was that it was about 20%. I doubt that's changed much since 1988.

In February there had been some apparently encouraging news from USA in Bestways Magazine that the American Medical Association might be taking a more positive approach to supplementation. I was not optimistic since the only supplement mentioned was Magnesium to relieve asthma attacks.

Multiple benefits from one supplement reported An interesting September letter from a member of staff at a Hospital in Stockport showed that use of Cantamega 2000 could have differing beneficial effects on health. The writer had overcome menopausal problems and her daughter had overcome mood swings. There was an interesting point about Guar Gum that the writer believed to have been banned in the USA. This gum in large dose capsules/tablets (500-1000mg) may swell quickly in the throat but if dosing instructions are followed (to take with a glass of water) there was no problem - the tablets/capsules are swept to the stomach in seconds. The same applied to Glucomannan made from the Japanese Konjac seaweed. In Cantamega 2000 there was very little guar gum and it was used to contribute to making the formula a sustained release nutrient product.

Korea -- a strange market for Tandem IQ In mid November Mr Paik of Myung Moon came to visit Larkhall to enquire about export of Tandem IQ to South Korea. Larkhall eventually met all the documentary demands for import and a large order was shipped. However, as previously with a Pollen Supplement, further orders were never received but the tablets were made in Korea, with promised royalties. The product may still be available today. No royalties were ever received.

Chairman of International Generics Sir Alexander Drummond's death in September received coverage with an obituary in The British Medical Journal. An appointment in his retirement that was not mentioned by the BMJ was his long connection with the Tamman family. Having known Leon's father for many years he accepted the Chairmanship of his son's pharmaceutical enterprise, International Generics in 1962. He helped Leon network in several African States to gain large government contracts and also had excellent relations with key bulk drug suppliers and producers in Yugoslavia and Pakistan. He lived on the north side of Clapham Common in The Chase and frequently visited the Putney Laboratory to discuss business when I became a Director of IG in the early 70s.

Claim for unlawful dismissal issued by our ex-Marketing Consultant The marketing consultant dismissed by Larkhall in October 1987 lost his contract for many reasons including his lack of knowledge of the rules surrounding Health Product advertising in the UK. This was demonstrated by his insistence on Radio Advertising because the messages in the ads were weakened to comply with the code of advertising rules. Equally, he praised the ads of a competitor, which I refused to copy because they contravened the law and the code of advertising practice. That company was subsequently fined heavily under trading standards law. With my solicitor, I began to fight the dismissal case. RG agreed to make a statement because the marketing consultant had tried to blackmail her.

Gradual change to our trade sales In early Autumn, one representative left our employment and her territory was passed to the remaining six that included the Sales manager. Telesales from HQ rather than direct representation with face to face customer meetings was expanded. Larkhall attempted to enter the bulk supplies chain by using a representative, a loquacious Welshman who had resigned from a leading supplier. His boast of obtaining large sales within months failed to materialise and he soon departed.

Animal Testing A Beauty without Cruelty registration was used by some companies in the Health Food trade. This was operated under the auspices of the anti-vivisectionists (BUAV). My view was that this was a waste of time since the BUAV lacked the technical skills to properly enforce this standard. Testing on animals was ubiquitous in the cosmetic industry and most countries insisted that all ingredients used in cosmetics must be tested on animals by law. This meant that no company could guarantee this standard but could claim that they, themselves, did not test on animals.

Book supplies To ensure Larkhall could supply reliable information to consumers we intended to import Books from USA (Keats Publishing) to add to Roberts Publications small range. This was not successful despite considerable marketing effort. Consumers always complained about lack of information on product packs, in leaflets and catalogues but reading books did not have wide appeal. These people did not understand that there were legal reasons for lack of information on packs and in advertisements.

A 'Better Health' Booklet written by me with recommendations of dietary regimes for specific health problems was welcomed by retailers as an educational tool. The title was copied from the dietary/biochemic booklet first published by Cantassium in 1921

Sponsorship of Cambridge University Lightweight Rowing Crew In November we officially sponsored the Cambridge Lightweight Crew with Vitamin supplements. We had close contact with Fitzbillies bakery in Cambridge. RG designed a new cake for them called 'Eight Cake' especially for the crew and it went on sale to the public at the bakery. Later, RG and I visited Jesus College Cambridge to dine in Hall and discuss the sponsorship of the Lightweight Crew. That night Pan Am 103 crashed over Lockerbie. We heard the news on the car radio as we drove back to London.

Arthritis and Royal Jelly In April the leading company in the Royal Jelly market reported a fall in profits. This was a company that had grown rapidly on very favourable tabloid publicity generated by **Public Relations.** The company claimed cure-all properties for Royal Jelly via their clever PR programme that caught the imagination of many consumers. Whilst they said they were doing research that was doubtful because they relied on testimonials and could not use effective advertisements because they had no scientific proof of efficacy. Unfortunately, expensive showy packaging of the their range was not enough to ensure long product life and the company went bust a few years later. Royal Jelly has no defined combination of ingredients nor a credible written analytical specification. It had a magical name and was the food of the Queen Bee that enabled her to have a wonderful life. Barbara Cartland never recommended it and said 'it was fattening'.

In September, I complained to the ASA about claims for a branded Royal Jelly that included arthritis and pointed out that no scientific evidence existed. I referred to Dr Barton Wright's arthritis research back in the 1970s where Royal Jelly connections were envisaged but stability and specification problems had precluded its use in clinical trials.

Looking forward Commercially   In late September, Noel Hodson, an accountant friend of my brother, from Oxford Business Planning, visited me in Putney. His company proposed to draw up a plan to prepare the company for the future. In fact, their proposals led me to see a possible practical route to sale of the company. It was essential that the properties were split off into another separate company that was already existent in the group. Since the takeover of Blakoe Appliances Ltd, a branded product company, in 1969 the trading income had gradually transferred to it from GO Woodward & Co Ltd that owned the properties. So, a clean break could be made at little cost. Protection from the effects of political decisions might be obviated.

HealthWatch/Quackbusters Aggression

Health Professionals - Off Prints - Mervyn Madge - Channel Island competition - Garlic - Green Lipped Mussel - The Health Standard - Tryptophan Disaster - Coeliacs and Gut Cancer - Lipcote threats - Lipchic - Slow Mag and Selenium rich Spirulina - Whither Health Freedom - The NHS negative for Health - Food Act - Germanium ban - Scottish children's Diet - European Market - Greek Drama -- Abolition of Alternative Health care suggested - Professor Brian Josephson - Too many bodies for alternative medicine - Symbol system flourished - Legal fight with Consultant continued - Natural anti Cholesterol products angered big Pharma - Royal Jelly - State of the vitamin Industry - Hilda Cherry Hills - Dibencozide irrelevant research pitch - Ignorance exposed with Tablet Crusher

The year began well internally for Larkhall with better stock control and service improvements to their customers. Overseas business was holding up well. However the general mood in the Health Food Trade was overshadowed by adverse publicity emanating from Quackbusters (Now HealthWatch) and a freelance investigative journalist with a strong bias against the trade was becoming very active. He was closely connected to HealthWatch and BBC Food & Drink Programme produced by Bazal Productions.

A new Trade Price List was issued which listed forthcoming products. This was an ambitious list and indicated that the final year of the 80s should be special for Larkhall and its customers.

Vitacare Professional Late in 1988 Larkhall had the Vitacare Range available to Health Professionals/Practitioners only. These products were claimed by the originators to be technically superior and more acceptable to Pharmacists because of their scientific education and background knowledge. In reality this was a dream and a negligible number of Pharmacists were interested despite great promotional efforts including scientific seminars exclusively for these Professionals. The lack of Medicinal Licensing, being blacklisted for NHS prescribing as well as general disbelief in nutritional supplementation contributed to Vitacare's lack of credibility to Pharmacists. The products failed to appeal to the alternative practitioners because these people did not have the science based training or knowledge. Nor did they like Vitacare's use of synthetic ingredients.

One member of Larkhall's staff (Ms Julie Madden) had worked on the launch of the Vitacare range and it was she who put me in contact with the originators. She was not pharmaceutically trained and had no in-depth knowledge but a layman's enthusiasm that was seldom enough. The American Rabbi, who had just joined our staff was knowledgeable as regards Vitamin and Mineral supplementation. He was successful in persuading a few health food retailers to stock the products but he had to keep revisiting the shops and act as a staff member to obtain sales. As soon as he left the stores to their own devices sales would plummet.

Sylvia Meredith Health Education Advisory Service Larkhall pursued the mainstream health professional route through the appointment of the Sylvia Meredith Service to send information to General Practitioner Practices for distribution to patients through practice nurses. I knew that until nutritional healthcare approaches were accepted by the mainstream medical people that food supplements would remain classed as 'alternative'. Sylvia Meredith produced and distributed to GP practices leaflets including one entitled 'How good is the case for dietary supplements'.

LARKHALL GREEN FARM

Larkhall invested heavily over three years and distributed hundreds of thousands of leaflets for display and use in NHS GP practices. It had little effect and was abandoned in 1990.

In 1992 the proof that Folic Acid supplements could prevent spinabifida presented Larkhall with a golden opportunity in the professional area thanks to my design of Micro Folic Acid. The awareness created by the earlier Sylvia Meredith campaign probably helped Larkhall's credibility when Micro Folic Acid became available. As so often in the past, Larkhall was ahead of its time.

A more direct but less acceptable approach to information The public's demand for information about Alternative Health Care was insatiable, yet the authorities waged a continuous war against the alternative health movement to prevent this. Many devices were used to overcome the problems and one of the boldest was 'Off Prints' reprinted from various sources about alternative healthcare approaches by Green Farm Library. These 'Off Prints' were originally marketed by a mail order company in the mid 1980s. They were used to make 'illegal' medicinal claims for products. Although a price was printed on each offprint, they were usually given away and so infringed the Medicines Act advertising regulations. The company was threatened by the authorities and so offloaded them to Green Library that, although attached tenuously to the Green Farm Supplement business, was less likely to be attacked by the Medicines Act regulators. Green Farm supplied these offprints to companies at special prices so they continued in use. When Larkhall took over Green Farm (1993) they did not take over Green Library that was retained by Graeme Millar who published the offprints and the Journal of Alternative Medicine for some years before its demise.

Mervyn Madge the driver behind the 'Rural Pharmacists' was a good friend of mine and like me, a Pharmacist who believed in the alternative approaches to healthcare. He was also a realist and advised that we must not antagonise pharmacists. He believed we should extol our virtues and persuade them in the long term. Mervyn supported my policy of advertising to professionals including Pharmacists but thought greatest emphasis must be on doctors and practice nurses. Hence the Sylvia Meredith appointment.

Unfair direct mail competition from off-shore Channel Islands The Larkhall Mail Order department was developing but competition from sales companies in the Channel Islands (avoiding VAT) and flagrantly ignoring advertising rules, made life difficult. We researched our lists and found the best way to grow was through our established customer base. We bought in lists of claimed current consumers with a connection to health problems. These were disappointing in response quality, and I doubted the validity and age of these lists. Use of Free Sample offers in PR generated national newspaper and magazine publicity were equally disappointing. Consumers just didn't value free items and better response quality was obtained if a postage and packing charge was included in the offer. Making these offers in paid for space advertisements was successful.

Garlic This herbal food was still growing in popularity but consumers wanted tablets or capsules rather than fresh garlic from the greengrocer. The claims that garlic had a beneficial effect on blood cholesterol levels as well as decreasing platelet aggregation (blood clotting) that contributed to heart attacks and aneurisms were hotly disputed by Doctors. Large amounts (7 fresh cloves daily) seemed the right amount but was more than the average British consumer could stomach. Supplements could not approach this level of intake and used aged garlic including modified ingredients.

Many consumers were using these products with some brands promoted on the basis of pseudoscience which the authorities had difficulty contradicting. One of the most successful supplements in Europe was Kwai and the manufacturer invested much money in research and advertising. The spin off to generic garlic products was substantial and throughout Europe Garlic Supplements boomed. Invented in Germany, Kwai was declining owing to adverse publicity, yet the Garlic market remained buoyant and became very competitive with generic products dominating. Popular brands in the USA included Arizona and Kyolic, a fermented garlic tablet made in Japan. Larkhall had been making garlic tablets since the late 1950s and currently specialised in odourless products using a special organic extract.

Green Lipped Mussel   This extract from a marine source in New Zealand had been popularised by John Croft. He visited the UK regularly to talk about this extract and an Oyster Extract. Claims that it was very beneficial to Arthritis sufferers ensured success for brand and generic copies. Publicity for Croft's ideas were widespread in the UK Media but no medicinal licence was authorised so advertising with claims was illegal. Nevertheless, by use of clever naming of products and the publicity generated by paid PR, it ensured that Green Lipped Mussel based supplements achieved successful levels of sales. Proof of efficacy to satisfy the authorities never materialised despite some confident predictions from New Zealand. Arthritis is an affliction that is frequently misdiagnosed and could sometimes respond to placebo treatments. By 2012 Glucosamine became the most popular placebo for arthritis and muscular/rheumatic problems. Green Lipped Mussel was still freely available and Mr Croft was actively publicising it.

Health Standard   Spring issue 11, edited and written by RG, carried many interesting pieces and covered activities at Larkhall. It was a very popular publication with both mail order and trade customers. The continuing fight surrounding vitamins and IQ was reported. A petition organised by Larkhall to protect availability of dietary supplements from Health Food Stores was taken to 10 Downing street. As there was no publicity in the pharmaceutical press, Pharmacies would have been the only retailers stocking supplements had the Brussels bureaucrats succeeded. Happily, all in the alternative healthcare field were supportive and pleased with Larkhall's stance. In the event no changes were made in the distribution chain. However, in 2012 other rules surrounding health claims were threatened that might have an adverse effect on Health Store viability.

The Health Standard recorded that there were several break-ins at the Putney Laboratories. Perhaps this was indicative of the upcoming difficulties with HealthWatch and the investigative journalist, who was not averse to employing underhand methods to attain his ends. He had apparently been trained by MI5, very sinister.

The Larkhall racehorses' progress was brilliantly reported to the delight of many of our customers and trainer Jenny Pitman herself, who applauded RG's accuracy in reporting.

General difficulties for Health Food retailers   An article in Health Food Business (UK) previewed the upcoming Helfex Exhibition and gave an accurate picture of the state of the market. Uncertainty about the future of supplements and the general paucity of consumer and retailer product information was highlighted. Retailers appreciated face-to- face meetings with company representatives but wanted these to gain extra discounts rather than knowledge. The manufacturer therefore had more expense for less return. No wonder few had representatives and preferred to show at exhibitions and concentrate on direct telesales. Few, if any, retailers appreciated the constraints on health claims but expected forceful advertisements with words like 'Cure' and 'Arthritis' clearly stated. This was impossible.

The Tryptophan disaster began During January, Tryptophan the essential amino acid caused the industry great problems. Many people in the USA had been affected by Eosinophilia Myalgia and there had been seven deaths associated with the syndrome. The cause was thought to be a contaminant in the Tryptophan ingredient emanating from a major Japanese manufacturer. Larkhall had not used this supplier or their distributor as their source of Tryptophan. NNFA monitor in the USA put together a useful summary of the situation as of January 1989. Banning of all Tryptophan containing food supplements by authorities soon followed. It was more than twenty years before the bans were lifted. Meanwhile millions of people had been prescribed powerful synthetic anti-depressant drugs who, otherwise, might have helped themselves safely with around three 500mg Tryptophan tablets a day and adopting a wholesome balanced diet. The Wall Street Journal, 31st January, covered the position well.

Lipcote copied by Boots In early February, David Owen, the owner of Lipcote visited the Basil Hotel, Knightsbridge. RG and I met him to discuss Lipcote future business. Owen was from New Zealand and owned the Lipcote formula and trademark. There was concern because Boots had introduced a new product they had named 'Lipcoat'. As the patent holder for Lipcote I insisted that Owen funded a legal case but this had to be be done diplomatically because Boots currently retailed some 40% of Lipcote sold in the UK. After several months of correspondence, Boots copy (Lipcoat) was gradually withdrawn from sale.

Cambridge rowers In mid March the Lightweight Oxford & Cambridge Boat Races took place at Henley. Cantassium sponsored the Cambridge Crew with an aluminium boat 'a Tin Fish' for the coach, finance and vitamin supplements. RG and I went to meet the crew and coaches, watched the races and were entertained to refreshments.

The Gluten Free scandal returned to show I was right I contacted Dr Thomas Stuttaford, the writer of a weekly Medical Briefing in The Times after I read 'Wheat Germs' in Stuttaford's column. I sent details of the Trufree Products and many other items in Larkhall's lists suitable for Coeliacs. The reference in Stuttaford's column to a Dr Geoffrey Holmes was particularly interesting because he had discovered that Coeliacs who did not adhere to the strictest Gluten Free diet had a greater disposition to gut cancer. This was something that I had long suspected after reading that Coeliacs had an above average positive diagnosis of gut cancer. I used this as an argument for the government forbidding Wheat Starch based foods for prescription to Coeliacs. Those foods were poison for Coeliacs and it was wrong to allow Wheat Starch to be used in Gluten Free Foods of all kinds.

As expected, my view was never accepted because there were large financial and government interests in continuing the use of a cheap nutritionally worthless ingredient in Coeliac Foods. Not only were the Coeliacs ingesting what was to them poisonous gluten but they were also deprived of the essential fibre, vitamins and minerals naturally present in Wholemeal Wheat Flour. Many of those micronutrients were proven to contribute to the protection of humans from developing cancers.

Italy progressing but Dutch business threatened In mid May, I went on another quick trip to Italy and Holland taking an evening off in Venice to go to a wonderful Vivaldi Concert in his Church on the Grand Canal. I travelled from Venice via Milan to Amsterdam by rail (7 hours), stopping off in Verona for the Herbora Exhibition where Prodotti were showing Cantassium Supplements. I saw they were doing very well. In Holland, I visited Nutrivital in to discuss future business. However, they were developing their own supplement brand -- Optimax -- with bulk imports of tablets from Australia.

They were too low in price for Larkhall to compete, despite the high cost of shipping the product from Australia. I learned that the Australian Government was encouraging exports with large subsidies. I expected more copying of our products soon.

Lipcote threatened by former distributor   Dendron, Larkhall's long time distributor of Lipcote, who had been dismissed at the request of a consultant in 1986, introduced a copy called 'Liptop'. This was at a lower price and vigorously marketed by their sales force to all the major Lipcote stockists in the UK and Ireland.

RG helped test the Liptop product and found it very inferior to Lipcote in quality and efficacy. Larkhall had a winnable battle on their hands to hold on to our number one position in the Lipstick Sealer market. Our sales team did an excellent job. We used a contract sales force to visit retailers countrywide and our own sales team to cover the major distributors and by offering incentive discounts and deals we managed to see Liptop off by the middle of 1990. I was glad the consultant firm had gone because it was their director who had recommended us withdrawing Lipcote from Dendron in the first place. The consultants were currently in the process of suing Larkhall for breach of contract. They lost totally but Larkhall's legal costs of fighting them were over £15,000. I thought this cheap at the price.

USA trip   In Mid July I flew to Las Vegas for the NNFA convention at the Hilton Hotel. I met many regular contacts and agreed to distribute in the UK, Richard Hau's spirulina based Selenium Supplement, made in Germany.

Later I flew on to Indianapolis to visit Servaas Laboratories producers of 'Slow Mag' a product that had caught my eye in a US Health Magazine. Magnesium was an essential mineral and through this unique formulation good absorption and assimilation was guaranteed. I proposed to make the product under licence in the UK and Europe. Talks went well but demands for considerable guaranteed sales were made by Servaas who did not know the difficulties of advertising likely to be encountered if over claiming was undertaken. I do not believe 'Slow Mag' was ever successfully distributed in Europe.

Lipchic, the Lipcote of USA   By chance in early June, Susan Pemberton a UK national living in San Diego, came to visit Putney to discuss a plan for Lipcote distribution in the USA. I told her that Lipcote was not available for US distribution as the trade mark could not be registered. However, I had negotiated with the owners of Lipchic (Julia Page Inc). and hoped to be able to make an agreement with a new US distributor soon. I expected to be in LA later in the year and would be pleased to meet her associates and listen to their proposals. After seeing several potential distributors in LA, I met Susan Pemberton's associates in July, the Amerrivezani Brothers (Reza and Ali), and thought they seemed capable of doing a good job with Lipchic. They were much the best of those I had seen so far.

I flew on to Roanake (Virginia) via Cincinatti to see the most successful Lipchic distributor in USA who was a person working from home and distributing through the mail. She had worked with Julia Page from the start in 1982 but I could see that overall USA distribution would not be possible with her. Larkhall owned the Lipchic Brand because I had agreed to purchase it from Julia whilst my brother refused to participate. I had to use my own money to make the purchase. This was the second time that my brother refused to back a Brand Name purchase. I thought that Lipchic could do much better under my guidance than it had done with Julia. Sadly Julia's health was not of the best and this had hampered her progress with marketing.

I went on to Miami (Florida) and had an appointment with another potential distributor. Although her application had been credible my face to face visit proved how vital an actual meeting was in this sort of commercial undertaking. The weakness of her proposals and inability to go outside Florida clinched a decision that Ella International (Susan Pemberton and the Amerrivezani brothers) would be appointed. They went to exhibitions throughout the States and could cover the country through their contacts.

Whither Health   In early August, The Sunday Times carried an article by David Selbourne which highlighted the observations of a GP practising in the 1938 -1952 period. He said that only a small minority of British Citizens knew how to keep themselves fit. The writer thought little had changed by 1989. Maybe there was a general lack of interest in health even in the early days of the NHS. People believed that health was free, provided by governments and not their own responsibility.

   Some research at The Medical Research Council's unit for lifelong health and ageing in 2012 indicated that the generation that had grown up in the era of the NHS was less healthy in its later years than the previous generation. Much more Heart Disease and Diabetes. Such a situation reflected the view that most citizens believed health is free and provided by government. If this continued we were likely to experience insoluble problems in the near future.

Was there Health freedom in USA?   The August issue of Let's Live Magazine in USA published an article by Mark Blumenthal, a leading advocate of Herbal health care, entitled 'Is there Health Freedom in America?' This article discussed the arguments put forward by the Quackbusters and exposed the weaknesses in them. The situation has changed little since then and persecution of alternative healthcare people continued yet the movement in favour of Complementary Medicine still grew.

A Food Act was threatened   In August I wrote to the editor of the Sunday Times, David Green ((Institute of Economic Affairs) and Norman Macrae (Sunday Times contributor) regarding the proposed Food Act. This act would result in the Food Industry coming under bureaucratic control and would threaten the existence of many companies with little benefit to consumers. In the event, the Food Act did not become a reality until the late 90s and the resulting Food Standards Authority was a bureaucratic behemoth that moved very slowly with little discernible benefit to the public. Of course, by then, there were similar bodies in all EU countries so there were lots of conferences and jamborees for politicians and officials to attend annually. In 2012 a directive about Health Claims for foods threatened the Health Food Industry but the Trading Standards Departments across the UK had already intimated that enforcing the provisions of the directive was not a priority for them because there were so many really dangerous matters to absorb their officers. So what is the point of the legislation? The resources for enforcement were unaffordable.

Germanium   Time after time Larkhall was picked on by the media as an example, and set up, causing trouble and expense. A classic case was Germanium, a mineral found in many foods, especially garlic. There were two kinds available for manufacturing tablets – synthetic and natural. Larkhall used the natural version. There had been a problem in Japan where people were taking ridiculously large amounts of the synthetic version. In the UK this evolved into Princess Diana taking 'Killer Germanium Pills', although she probably never took a germanium pill in her life. The media went into a frenzy of stories and there were articles in newspapers, magazines and on TV programmes.

The truth was that very small doses of natural Germanium, as in garlic, were harmless. However the government stepped in and put a ban on all germanium after a civil servant declared, "Unequivocally all forms of germanium are toxic". All Larkhall's formulas had to be changed, stock recalled and perfectly good stock destroyed. The public was hoodwinked, especially regarding the arithmetic surrounding germanium concentration. Larkhall had germanium tablets and multi vitamin products with traces of germanium in them. **No other major country banned it, just the UK** so Larkhall was still able to export it. (It was a miracle all garlic eaters in the country hadn't dropped down dead and all the population hadn't been killed as the average intake per day, in the UK per person was about 1 mg). There was never any risk to consumers who had taken Larkhall's germanium products – quite the opposite of what the media said. However, we could do nothing about it. Germanium looked nasty by name to most lay people so that wasn't a good start.

The point of all this was to try and close us down. Our enemies failed. They had another go with Tryptophan, an essential amino acid and natural antidepressant and pain relief remedy. After another ban we were still able to sell it but only for animals. By coincidence the ban materialized when SSRIs, a new class of antidepressant medicine (drug) appeared on the scene. A natural product such as Tryptophan presented a threat to that market.

Critique of Scottish School Children's diet   The September issue of 'Health at School' a teacher's magazine carried an article by Anne Curr an Assistant Head Teacher entitled 'What Infant School Children Eat: Some Observations from Scotland'. She had not read about the Darland High School Trial but her observations on the children's diets were similar to those of Gwylm Roberts the Welsh Science Teacher. She noticed that those on what she perceived as inadequate daily diets were more sickly, concentrated less and were restless. She offered some ideas for improvement of diets but it was a real battle to get movement from colleagues. As she stated 'The idea that an adequate diet promoted good health was nothing new or original' yet authority seemed to be blind to the benefits of real policy in this area -- why? I am in no doubt that the malign influence of the junk food/sugar industry and its dependent yet elusive academics in colleges throughout Britain had governments under their spell.

New Public Relations company appointed   In early September I asked Stuart Pocock, our Market Research consultant, if he knew of a PR consultancy that could work with Larkhall. He recommended Morris Media owned and managed by Sue Morris. Their office was not far from Putney, in Earl's Court. I had become disillusioned with PR companies but after a meeting with Sue Morris it seemed to be worth a try again. Many meetings took place over the next few months and several initiatives with Lipcote and Tandem IQ were pursued successfully.

Italy and Europe   In early October, Anna Maugeri visited Putney to discuss current Italian Business and the upcoming 1992 free market in the European Union. This should have made exporting Supplements which are legal in one country (UK) easy but in the event little changed because each country could protect its market by enforcing its own safety rules and standards on imports. The indigenous producers were unaffected. Germany and France were notorious users of these protective measures. It was probably a major reason that Germany enjoys huge trade surpluses. France hinders supplement imports but permits local companies to make and sell copies of UK and USA brands.

Greek dramas In early September, I learned that Maria Strofalis, MD of Larkhall's Greek Distributor, had had a serious heart attack. Professor Joan Drangan from Romania was in London and we entertained him to dinner, took him to the Science Museum and discussed the upcoming Balkan Sports Medicine conference in Cyprus. Maria Strofalis came to London and was in poor health, I thought this visit was prompted because she had learned that a Mr Spiros Stavriniades was to visit Larkhall to discuss possible business in Cyprus. She probably feared that he would try to take the whole of the Greek and Cyprus Larkhall distributorship business for his company.

When I met Mr Spiros he talked big but I was unimpressed by him. He was not a Chemist but a property man. His knowledge of the difficulties of importing supplements into Greece was zero and his idea of using Cyprus as a staging post for goods on the way to Greece in order to overcome import problems was naive. This occurrence made me more wary of the Greek market and the character of Greek business people. The feuds and difficulties were to get worse over the coming years.

Later in the month I was in Cyprus. The quarrel between Mrs Strofalis (Athens) and Spiros Stavriniades (Cyprus) was heated. Mr Spiros picked me up at the Airport (Nicosia) and drove me at night through rough terrain but at least I arrived safely at the Hotel where the Balkan Sports Medicine Conference was to take place. I lectured on Antioxidant nutrients and this was a success. However the feud between Maria and Mr Spiros became worse and I had to negotiate the situation that ensured continuation of the current arrangements for supplying Greece and Cyprus.

The calls for the abolition of Alternative Health Care became really serious In late October The Sunday Correspondent (a National Sunday newspaper that had a short life) published an article inspired by Caroline Richmond the Chairman of the Campaign against Health Fraud (now HealthWatch). 'Beware of the new Quacks' was its title and was the usual over-the-top rant against Alternative Health particularly the 'New Age' therapies which were becoming popular in 1989.

At the end of October, The Chemist & Druggist reported the dispute about Herbal Medicine safety, nothing new about this. Disingenuously, a leading Herbal medicine manufacturer was prattling on about the safety of licensed herbals compared with unlicensed. The NPA director Tim Astill had questioned the old chestnut that natural meant safe. The fact is that no medicine is 100% safe whether it is natural or synthetic. This whole 'Safety' issue was emotion based, just one minor accident was all that was needed especially if it was a journalist's grandma coming out of a Health Food Store - let's have an "Vitamins Dangerous" headline.

By the end of October media and government pressures on the Vitamin and Health Food Industry were growing at an alarming rate. New stories were appearing regularly and I began to think that these were orchestrated. It seemed likely that the 'Campaign against Health Fraud' could be the driving force but I believed that the costs of the anti publicity were being met from hidden sources probably big Pharma and the Junk Food Industry (Sugar interests). The crucial happenings had been:-

4   In 1988 The Naismith trial on Vitamins and IQ (performed at, but not declared anywhere, a secondary school where his wife was Headmistress). RG had been told by Naismith that getting the children to take the supplements had been a problem. The 'Vitamin trial' was funded by the World Sugar Corporation. This set out to sabotage all the work done by Larkhall over three years.

5   In 1989 the safety of Tryptophan was questioned following a contamination problem in Japan. Tryptophan was a major Larkhall product.

6 In 1989 the safety of Germanium following deaths in Japan from ingestion of very large doses. Whilst Larkhall produced three germanium products none were high dose and none were made from the particular ingredient used in Japan.

One letter (27.9.89) from Mark Robinson of Larkhall's agency Sylvia Meredith Health Service was very relevant. This concerned a conversation with the editor of 'Health at School' that had carried an article about nutritional adequacy concerns pertaining to young primary school pupils in Scotland (see Critique of Scottish School Children's diet above). A probing telephone conversation had been most disappointing yet enlightening. Mark was really shocked by her attitude and views on the Darland Trial and the word 'discredited' as regards the research was used. Coincidentally also on November 7th the Daily Telegraph published an article by Judy Sadgrove which used the word 'discredited' in connection with the 1988 IQ and vitamins research. It was obvious that all opinion formers and journalists in the health area had been targeted by an organised anti-Darland Nutrition trial publicity campaign. Mark Robinson drafted a letter to the Telegraph about this article but it was not published. It was probably a mistake to send it under my signature. After this it became very difficult to obtain positive publicity for nutritional approaches to improving school pupil performance anywhere in the media.
   It is relevant to mention here the current (2016) views of **Nobel Laureate Professor Brian Josephson of Cambridge University** regarding the problems for scientific heretics. These are all scientists who work in areas that are not acceptable to the mainstream of science such as Homoeopathy, Cold Fusion, Alternative Health Care and others. Such people find it impossible to get their research published anywhere and have 'reputation' problems. Their progress is totally blocked by powerful interests including Sugar, Learned Scientific Societies, Medical Establishment, Media etc. Often these researchers are banned from lecturing or presenting their work at specialised conferences too. Undoubtedly the IQ research sponsored by myself and Larkhall was affected by these mafiosos.
   By the end of 1989 there was evidence that I and Larkhall had a very serious enemy - probably intent on our destruction. However proving such suspicions was beyond our resources because we were not a large player in the Vitamin Supplement market and myself and RG were Larkhall's only sources of real knowledge in the area. My PhD (London University) and Fellowship of the Royal Society of Chemistry were already under scrutiny with deliberate hints by academics such as Professor Naismith saying the FRSC was false and the PhD from a mail order outfit in USA. By 1992 it was Naismith's research that was shown to be fatally flawed but by then tremendous damage had been done to me and Larkhall from which recovery was nearly impossible. So having seen real growth in business in 1988 by the end of 1989 things had changed dramatically and this was to continue for the next few years. Indeed the overall Vitamin Supplement market had grown 24% in 1988 (the year of the Darland Trial) and 1989 had been expected to grow another 34%. It did not.
   A letter from a Dr A.H. Hodson to the doctor's magazine 'General Practitioner' made a point about HealthWatch - Quackbusters that their motives for rubbishing Alternative Health Care was really to curry favour with their peers in orthodox medicine.

Natural Health Care had no unified body to represent its interests In early November The Journal of Alternative & Complementary Medicine issued a questionnaire to suppliers of dietary supplements to Alternative Health Care Professionals. Larkhall replied but the project could not be completed because so many suppliers failed to answer and the questionnaire was too complicated. The Alternative Health Care Movement felt under attack from the Quackbusters/HealthWatch and were struggling to defend themselves but fearful of going on the attack. There was no single body representing the Movement and this was a serious problem.

Larkhall and I had no confidence in any of the industry bodies and resolved to fight back on its own.

Around this time the BHFTA (The British Health Food Trade Association), of which Larkhall was not a member, demonstrated their weakness when challenged by quackbuster journalist Duncan Campbell regarding their strong response to articles in the Mirror and New Statesman on Germanium. They withdrew certain points from their statement and he then knew he would be on easy street with them in the future. The Quackbusters must have been delighted.

Meetings abroad   In mid November I visited Athens to attend a meeting with Importers, Regulators and International producers concerning Diet Supplements being classified as Medicines in Greece. These products were restricted to Pharmacy sale because all Healthfood/Herbalist shops had been closed. Larkhall's distributor Maria Strofalis gave a talk explaining her difficulties and asked for help from the central EEC department in Brussels. As I expected, this meeting produced nothing apart from stimulating further intergovernmental discussions. Meanwhile importing of many of Larkhall's products continued but many unorthodox means were used to achieve this. I met some academics from Romania who hoped to do research and help importation of diet supplements into that country.

The problem in Greece had its ramifications in the UK because there were moves by our authorities to restrict Diet Supplement sales to pharmacies as in Greece. This threat was reported in The Daily Mail on 20th November. Happily nothing resulted and general retail sale of supplements was not restricted in the UK. Undoubtedly, Larkhall's petition to be presented in 1990, played a part in this outcome.

There were problems for the industry in the USA too. Tryptophan contamination had first been reported in USA. It was a costly material to produce and most was made in Japan. It was a particular producer Showadenka whose lower cost processing was suspected to be the only contaminated source. Recently, in the USA the NNFA Trade Association had issued an alert concerning Germanium, Orotates, Wheatgrass Juice and Hydrochloric Acid. This alert was indicative of the zealous efforts to discredit the Health Food Industry by Quackbusters in the USA.

Alternative Health Care supported by popular demand and a medical man   In late November, The Times carried a piece 'Natural remedies supported' which reported that Mintel (a market research organisation) had found more and more people were using natural approaches for healthcare. Twenty million alternative practitioner consultations in the UK were taking place each year and these were forecast to grow 10% annually. It was this sort of report that encouraged the opposition like Quackbusters to call for more legislation in the alternative medical area and to discredit the commercial leaders like Larkhall and me. These criticisms were supported by Pharmaceutical interests. In mid December the Daily Telegraph carried an article by Dr Michael O'Donnell, former Editor of World Medicine the medical magazine, looking at the progress of Alternative Health Care during the 1980s. As a medical man he was far from dismissive of the treatments available outside the mainstream and expected further expansion in the 1990s. He was clearly not a Quackbuster and maintained an open mind.

The Symbol System proving its benefits.   Our December product list painted an optimistic picture of the company and the areas spearheading expansion. Rita Greer's Symbol System on the packs was really benefiting sales and confidence in the Cantassium Brand with its trademark signature. It was controversial because it was not generally approved. However, Larkhall never received any complaints from authorities because all products carried the legally required details too.

It was also vitally important that all products were manufactured in-house and authorities knew Larkhall could be totally confident in the symbol claims. Most companies were contracting out manufacture and could not be sure of the total integrity of their ingredient lists. It should be noted that when the brands were sold to Nutricia in 1999 the symbol system was discontinued because the new owners used contract manufacture so did not purchase the rights from RG. Those standards were of no interest to them.

The ex-marketing consultant still caused problems. The ex-marketing consultant, was still vigorously pursuing a claim for breach of contract against Larkhall. Rita Greer made a statement for our solicitor regarding many matters. This was very enlightening and indicated, in hindsight, that perhaps the director may have worked closely with an organisation that might have hoped to acquire the Larkhall company for a client. I knew he was close to top people in an Irish Bank who were anxious to become Larkhall's bankers. I met one of the Bank's Directors who was plausible but I was happy with Barclays Bank who had acted for the company since 1946. In her statement at the solicitors, RG painted an alarming picture of the consultant's lack of knowledge and extraordinary behaviour, including attempted blackmail. This ultimately led him to withdraw his action against Larkhall in 1990 before the case reached Court. He had to pay all his legal costs.

The director of the consultancy was a strange man who seemed capable of misleading on a grand scale, a man whose veneer of knowledge found him out. Looking back, I cannot understand why it took me so long to see through him but I was keen for Larkhall to expand and good advice from a consultant on the marketing side had seemed the way forward in 1986. My brother thought Larkhall lacked expertise in marketing and new product development. In reality the company had done well and did not need consultants in either area. I believe these consultants learned more from Larkhall than vice versa. Nirvana seldom exists is a lesson for all would be entrepreneurs.

Big Pharma reacted to another threat from alternative preparations The introduction of new tablet products, Sustaniacin and Oat Bran, were directly linked to the growing awareness of the negative health effects associated with high dietary Cholesterol. Sustaniacin was widely recommended by Doctors for patients with high cholesterol because it was very effective. However, the Pharmaceutical interests did not like the idea that an unpatented ingredient like nicotinic acid (vitamin B3) should be prescribed instead of a very profitable patented drug. As with Tandem IQ and Tryptophan, they soon generated an anti-niacin campaign that led to the banning of sustained release niacin products like Sustaniacin. Instant release niacin tablets, although effective, caused unpleasant hot flushes but a sustained release formula overcame that effect so was a threat to the synthetic drugs used to combat cholesterol. In 2012 the Statin group of anti cholesterol drugs was worth billions of pounds every year in the UK and was an important profit source for big Pharma. Patients lower their cholesterol but there are rare unpleasant side effects which, if caused by a natural product like niacin, was unlikely to be tolerated by the medicines control authorities.

In 1990 there was a panic in the Health Food Trade about side effects of this type of product – in fact the leaders of the trade associations were so ignorant of clinical data interpretation that they just capitulated to demands of the regulator without reference to the only company affected (Larkhall). I was angry but because the top people in the association's companies were unaffected, they found it simple to agree the quiet life to save them work and cause problems for maverick Larkhall. Larkhall resigned from all trade associations over this and other equally stupid actions against Tryptophan and Germanium by these people. Having been instrumental in the only convincing positive scientific research on a Diet Supplement (Tandem IQ) in 1988 and cleared the retail shelves of all Children's multivitamins in a weekend (January 1988) our company was always at risk from its rivals.

199

Sustaniacin enjoyed small but steady sales over the coming years despite becoming a 'prescription only' product. It was probably more effective and safer than the drug industry's synthetic chemicals.

Cholestastop was another supplement to fight Cholesterol (Betasitosterol) that was targeted by the authorities. Sitosterols were soon added to spreads and health drinks and so supplements were not in demand. Also legally these were possibly medicinal, Statins were big business for the Pharmaceutical Industry and those powerful companies would try to ensure that products similar like Cholestastop would not prosper.

Royal Jelly an easy target for Quackbusters   Royal Jelly was a very popular supplement but adverse publicity had a devastating effect on all Royal Jelly items. Outrageous exaggerated unproven claims were overtly made and these were exposed leading to many prosecutions particularly for a mail order company associated with the Sunday Sport newspaper. Regina Royal jelly was a brand that had been promoted very successfully on claims of widespread health benefits. Exposure destroyed the company.

Year end thoughts on the Industry   The year end sales report was optimistic but clouds were gathering as Tryptophan was returned by retailers. The Liptop threat from the previous distributor was overcome with Boots declining to stock that particular product. Our effort with an auxilliary sales force had been costly but had helped secure Lipcote in most independent stores despite large discounts being offered by the competitor. It was known that Liptop was not a good experience for Dendron but equally these sort of commercial battles leave neither side without scars. Larkhall could have done without the lost sales and the expense of the successful fightback.

Over the late 1980s Larkhall had become a real force but their high profile Tandem IQ product and highly successful Lipcote had made them enemies. The vigour of their fight in the Vitamin Supplement area, with the very controversial successful research on diet and IQ, combined with their involvement with Tryptophan was making them unpopular with establishment academics and their media associates. The 1990s were uncertain in this climate. Yet, despite these problems and others, Larkhall managed, miraculously, to sell out by January 1999 just before the new millennium, as I had hoped in 1980.

It is worth noting that outside Larkhall other companies faced problems. Reevecrest, (who had just taken on distribution of Naudicelle GLA capsules) soon went out of business; Kerfoot Pharmaceuticals (an old competitor of Larkhall when we were involved in generic pharmaceuticals) was struggling to survive in that market long abandoned by Larkhall; Creightons (an Unlisted Securities Market quoted natural beauty product company since 1986) was destined for extinction because of its exposure to the contract manufacturing area. All this proved the 1980s had been a fast changing era for the health and beauty trade that faced an uncertain future.

When Larkhall took over Green Farm in 1993 we found they had had many problems with the ASA, Trading Standards Departments and the Medicines Control Agency in 1989. I was sure this was a watershed year for the Vitamin industry but there was little coordinated effort made to fight these mostly unjustified attacks. Nearly thirty years later, regulatory efforts to outlaw products continued yet loopholes to maintain freedom still cannot be closed.

During the year our Bankers had pressed for Larkhall to expand and we had discussions on a possible public floatation. I said that I felt the marketing and regulatory climate was not right. Indeed the 1993 takeover of Green Farm revealed that there were city investors who saw a quick gain in the alternative health area at this time and burned their fingers.

Hilda Cherry Hills   In May, I received a very nice letter from Cherry Hills's husband Lawrence informing me of his wife's illnesses at 93. She cannot write anymore but has a young Danish contact who may be able to update her 'Good Food, Gluten Free' book which currently had very poor sales. I replied releasing the copyright and wished Cherry and Lawrence better health. I was always grateful to HDRA (The Henry Doubleday Research Association) and the Hills for co-operating with me back in the early 1970s on Special Diet Books. Cherry Hills had been a pioneer in Gluten Free Cooking. I asked her to co-operate with us in formulating special diet foods to go with her books but she declined. Soon after I met the Hills, I had learned of Rita Greer's 'Extraordinary Kitchen Notebook' (Gluten Free) and made contact with the author. Her approach was more commercial and practical regarding special flours and food mixes.

Little was heard from the Hills after this contact in 1989 but we continued to send royalties on Cherry's books to HDRA for many years thereafter.

In November, Hilda Cherry Hills died. The author of Living Dangerously, Good Food, Gluten Free, Good Food Grain Free and Milk Free, and Good Food to Fight Migraine. She was a pioneer in the wholesome food area and very concerned about ubiquitous synthetic chemical use including pesticides, herbicides and synthetic food additives. She was always, in my view, over optimistic on winning over orthodox medical practitioners to her ideals. She wrote for them rather than the ordinary mortals who, sadly, she felt beneath her. She was very different from Barbara Cartland, who was brilliant in communicating with the ordinary folk, who loved her and was as sincere as Cherry about what she wrote.

Exaggeration by a sales person proved   A supplement of Dibencozide 5mg was proposed for introduction by one of our salesmen. It was never prepared because I thought the research from USA was suspect. Bodybuilders and sportsmen would probably not gain muscle mass and strength as the babies had done in the trials. The sales rep had said it would be a best seller but when we listed it before making it no orders were taken, yet another example of exaggeration by the sales people.

Tablet Crusher. A device imported from the USA, which enjoyed success in helping elderly people take tableted products by crushing them in this well designed little device. It was not for use for Sustained release tablets such as Sustaniacin (see warning on pack), yet copyists soon offered competitive items. Being ignorant, Health Food Mail Order Companies left off the warning and so got crushers a bad name with health professionals.

Lucky start to the New Year at the races   Just after Christmas our new horse Cantamega won a hurdle race at Stratford-on-Avon. In January, I received a pleasing letter from a customer who saw that Cantamega had won the race. Her congratulations were appreciated as was the awareness value of race horses to a brand.

Sadly, Cantamega was slightly injured at Stratford and was unable to race for some time. When he returned to race in 1991 he was not successful and retired from racing to work at a good home on a sheep farm.

Frightening end to the year augurs troubles ahead

Far East Exports - Shropshire bide their time - Health Club - RDAs - Science and Healthfood Industry - Danish law made a difference - Filtro Neto - Regulators causing angst for the trade - Pharmacy sales plan not adopted - Contrary Licence ruling - Takeover proposal - Trade press article - Petition to Downing Street - Self regulation of Advertising - Tandem IQ denigrated in National Magazine - Disproportionate standards enforced on Herbals - Cantamega 2000 worked - Hair Analysis - More tribulation for Tryptophan - Hugh Sinclair, The NHS and Nutrition - Health Heroes - Gypsies less cancer prone - Medicines Inspections no threat but product licencing different - Food Fiasco - Consultants not needed - US industry still prospered despite regulators - Unreasonable requests from HealthWatch - Greece and Romania Vitamin Markets - Threonine (an Aminoacid) offered Licencing opportunity - Scare stories a Turning Point - Homoeopathy moved Centre stage - Going Green - Safeseal vindication too late - Major Media attacks - Placebo effects ignored - Mystery Intruder - Ivan Illich (health Hero) - Tandem IQ criticised on BBC TV - Shriopshire start their attack - Naturalness of Body Shop - Management do not understand Larkhall's mission - Unenforceable Patent - Coeliac Society peace - Garlic contains Germanium - Doctor's Death blamed on Alternative Health Care supporters - Break ins and more - Campbell's programme slated

The successful shipments of a large quantity of Tandem IQ tablets to S. Korea and Ruthmol to Taiwan gave a new dimension to the export sales prospects. Unfortunately, both were one-off orders and the products were either not successful in their new markets or copied/modified locally. This was not unexpected since a previous large order back in the mid-eighties for Phallen (Pollen) tablets was a one-off to S.Korea.

The legal action by Shropshire Trading Standards against Tandem IQ lost momentum and the zealous officials were seeking a new approach against the supplement. It seemed obvious that they would take the law to its limits to convict Larkhall of something -- anything. They seemed to be close to the academics and journalists who had been pursuing Larkhall so vigorously since 1987 and as it turned out, the BBC TV Food and Drink programme, despite the fact that they denied this.

Larkhall started their Health Club for mail order customers to encourage loyalty. A new style of list was introduced 'Look good and feel good with Larkhall Natural Health', with a membership card.

The Recommended Dietary Allowances for micronutrients continued to be debated. The Health Food Industry were in favour of higher levels than the scientists. Arguments regarding absorption capabilities varying from person to person of all ages were never likely to be resolved. In my opinion, the variables were so many that health assurance levels of vitamins and minerals in supplements should be well above officially advised doses and most importantly formulated on a wholefood (natural) basis.

In April 1988 Health Foods Business (USA) had carried a critique of the calculation of the US RDA values. These were the Daily Amounts of Vitamins and Minerals applied in the USA. These were not necessarily equal to the UK or EU quantities. International Units (iu) were also variable from country to country. - many US manufacturers operate in the UK and EU and mislabeling is usual - *Caveat Emptor* - always check what a USA produced product claims on its label.

LARKHALL GREEN FARM

Poor grasp of science was a major problem for the Health Food Industry
I highlighted that a major problem for the supplement industry was the continued fundamental lack of basic scientific knowledge at all levels from Chief Executives within the industry through to retail personnel and store proprietors. An article from the medical publication Scrip entitled 'Healthy appetite for Food Supplements' indicated that there was an interest in researching supplements and giving sound advice before a sale but I doubted that these views were indicative of the general situation.

A Danish Company commercially exploited a complex regulatory loophole
A Danish Pharmaceutical company had just gained a foothold in the UK Health Food Industry. However, any UK Health Food company that attempted to open in Denmark needed to become a Pharmaceutical Company in the UK -- a change that would be nearly impossible. The quirk of the EEC was that most countries, including Denmark, classed food supplements as medicinal products and demanded product licensing. This company had entry into the UK market where their products were classed as foods and a UK medicinal licence was not needed or mentioned. In spite of this, claims were made according to their Danish licences. They claimed medicinal properties for their products but most authorities did not accept their evidence for efficacy. Their licences in Denmark enabled access to many European markets.

Filtro Neto was a health product The addition of the Filtro Neto cigarette filter product to Larkhall's range had been controversial in 1988. A testimonial received in early 1990 gave some justification to the argument that when smokers saw the amount of tar that the filter collected from just 10 cigarettes then they were put off their unhealthy habit. In practice the product was never a success for Larkhall. The patent protection that the Greek manufacturers claimed to have did not prevent competition from very similar devices.

Industry chiefs urgent meeting on current problems In mid January, I attended an interesting meeting of HFMA member company executives who were concerned about the current problems with Tryptophan, Germanium and high strength supplements. The Tryptophan - eosinophilia link was still a mystery. A Japanese manufacturer appeared the likely source. The problem was that US manufacturers audit trail records were poor and whilst a contaminant appeared the probable culprit, no samples of raw material were available for analysis. Even if they had been, the identity of the offending substance was unlikely to be found. Until it was identified with certainty, all Tryptophan products would remain under a cloud. This was unscientific but inevitable in our safety obsessed world. I, and many others in the alternative health care movement, believed it possible that this had been a deliberate act of sabotage that could have been perpetrated by big Pharma, using industrial espionage.

This problem with Tryptophan was similar to the recent contamination of some Spanish Cooking Oil that caused Eosinophilia in some consumers. That problem still remained a mystery. A mycotoxin was the possible cause was surmised by some people.

Later, in some published Trytophan notices from USA, it appeared that the contaminant still remained a mystery. The problem was confined to products produced in the USA using a Japanese L-Tryptophan that had many trace contaminants present - one or more of which could have been linked to the Eosinophilia outbreak.

Officialdom puts up fees for licensing Herbal Medicines At the end of January the Chemist & Druggist and the British Medical Journal reported the disproportionate increase in Licence Fees relating to Herbal Medicines. This was likely to increase cost of product to consumers and drive more herbals off the market for reasons other than 'Safety'. The regulatory authority was now led by an ex-pharma industry man seeped in synthetic medicines and with little sympathy for natural medicines.

Trouble with exporting In February a large order for Tandem IQ tablets from Myungmoon in South Korea had nearly been completed after many months of work on registration and production in special packaging. As I feared, analysis of the samples of tablets led to disagreement between Larkhall and Myung Moon, the importer finding fault. These arguments were common place when companies were looking for substantial discounts at the last moment. The importer knew that the exporter had produced the tablets and by questioning the analysis, hoped for a substantial cost reduction. Vitamin Supplements often have a relatively short shelf life (2 or 3 years) - so each day is precious. In the end Larkhall shipped the product, got paid on the Letter of Credit but refused to supply Myung Moon again.

A sad tale but a warning to others. It is not known whether Myung Moon made the next lot of tablets themselves or cut their losses too.

Pharmacy sales proposal rejected. In mid February, we received the pharmacy trade sales promotional proposal that had been prepared by Boss Advertising. This report was strongly in favour of Cantassium Vitamins being used to spearhead the promotion. Cogent reasons were given regarding the exclusion of Lipcote and Fltro Neto. This was an interesting approach but was not favoured by the Sales staff. Based on this report no promotion could be undertaken until we had developed a successful evidence based supplement (MicroFolic Acid). Concentration on Mail Order sales development was probably right.

A decision by the Medicines Licensing Authority overturned in February
My continued interest in Medicines Act activities caused me to question a recent court ruling where the DoH had lost a test case because they had restricted a product licence owing to a side effect that was not unique to that antidepressant drug whilst other similar drugs with those side effects had not been similarly restricted. The antithyroid substance Potassium Perchlorate (Peroidin) had lost its licence for similar reasons of side effects that also affected competitive antithyroid drugs - Peroidin did not warrant an appeal on commercial grounds but it would have been interesting had we pursued it through the courts rather than hoping a letter would reach the eyes of an influential official.

A takeover proposal received from Green Farm In mid March Graeme Millar the owner of Green Farm Nutrition came to see me with a proposal for takeover of the whole of Larkhall including Lipcote. Millar's contact was through a mergers and aquisitions expert in the City of London. Millar had taken over Green Farm, a Vitamin Supplement supplier, in 1989 and was financed through Lazards Bank with the aim of a stock exchange listing within 5 years. He had to grow his business by acquisition. His experience in the industry was not extensive but his wife was a good PR person with useful press contacts. The founders of Green Farm had emigrated to the USA but had not yet been paid in full for the business. Millar's offer was of no interest to us and he broke off negotiations. I knew he also approached other companies at this time.

Major press article on Larkhall   In mid March, the Chemist & Druggist published a full page article on Larkhall Natural Health. This outlined plans for developing sales of Cantassium Supplements in Pharmacies where sales growth continued to be disappointing. Our tablet crusher was given a positive recommendation. A picture of myself and Rita Greer in the Pharmacy at 229 Putney Bridge Road headed the article. This pharmacy did not dispense NHS prescriptions but offered dietary products restricted to pharmacy distribution or doctor prescription. My controversial views were well covered in the article.

An Official Dietary Supplement Investigation   In early March, I had correspondence relating to an official investigation into Dietary Supplements of Seaweed (Kelp) that contained Iodine. Iodine was an essential dietary mineral associated with the thyroid gland and was often used by slimmers to speed up metabolic rate. The final outcome of these investigations was not revealed. I wondered what its purpose had been?

Larkhall Petition for Downing Street   This was well reported in the Health Standard that gave good coverage of this Petition to fight restriction of supplement and herbal sales to Pharmacies, including pictures of me and the sales force members with the petition outside No 10 Downing Street. This Petition was done independently and did not please the industry bodies such as HFMA and their people. This explained why the Health Food Chains and other manufacturers shunned it. However, the small business people, often one person firms, felt that they were bullied by the large companies and were grateful for the effort Larkhall made on their behalf. Over recent years Larkhall had moved to the fringes of the Trade Bodies and were ready to resign from them all because they did not think that they represented the small traders real interests. The domination of the large firms gave them an unfair advantage that they were pleased to use, to drive the small competitors out of business.

Later, a letter from the Medicines Control Authority indicated that the Petition by Larkhall to ensure that Pharmacy would not monopolise supplement distribution had been successful.

Self regulation of supplement advertising   Advertising of supplements with claims for effectiveness was a difficult issue for the Industry and Regulators. The largest health trade body HFMA, in co-operation with the very powerful PAGB (The Proprietary Association of Great Britain representing over the counter drug suppliers), agreed with the Advertising Standards Authority that they would oversee the marketing and promotional items of all companies operating in the health and herbal area outside the prescription medicine producers.

Small companies were to be compelled to submit their materials to a body set up by HFMA and PAGB. This was manned by people from the large companies and their advisors. It meant that **any new products or new marketing platforms** envisaged by a small company **were exposed to their biggest competitors** and so they lost any advantage in the market -- totally unjust and unacceptable. Just remember what Seven Seas did to Tandem IQ in 1988. Larkhall refused to submit anything to this phony body. If the authorities wanted to challenge Larkhall's advertising and packaging they could do so in Court. The area was surrounded with complex legislation and sometimes it's best if it is sorted out at the highest level. One loss or even moral defeat for the zealous bureaucrats would usually silence them and luckily they were often foolish enough to make their attacks on firms they underestimated.

HealthWatch inspired article in a women's magazine denigrated Tandem IQ
In April, an article in the popular women's magazine Bella took a critical look at diet supplements. It quoted Professor Bender, the author of 'Health Hoax' and a leading member of HealthWatch. He did not have an open mind about Health Foods. The article mentioned Tandem IQ in a derogatory way and lacked any attempt at balance. Its line was that 'Experts dismissed the claim as ludicrous nonsense' was pernicious. It referred to an international study that was currently being conducted to find out what is going on. This international trial later, in 1991, proved positive (known as the DRF study) but received no positive publicity from Bella. At the end of the Bella article, Maurice Hanssen of the HFMA replied to the critics but his remarks, as expected, were not really useful or constructive.

Homoeopathics would not have such disproportionate standards as herbals
In mid April, the Chemist & Druggist carried a leader commenting on the licensing of Homoeopathic and Herbal medicines. It appeared that there was a fear that some proposed regulations would substantially reduce the number of products in these categories available to consumers. The regulations would be coming from Brussels but it would appear that Homoeopathic items would have a lighter regulatory framework. Sadly, consumers would be given less information because claims would not be permitted. If herbals had disproportionate standards to meet by 1992 the UK market would have been decimated whilst the Homoeopathic market would be unaffected.

It was worth noting (in same C&D issue) that some naive pharmacy students at a conference in Manchester were convinced that tougher regulation of herbals was appropriate. I am sure none of these students had ever tried to analyse raw herbs. Their naivete was emphasised by their assumption that these items were very profitable because of the lack of regulation - total nonsense. Competition is fiercer in unregulated situations and that keeps profits and prices low. Regulation always increased prices and tended to result in monopolies to the detriment of consumers.

The controversy in these areas is unresolved in 2015 despite all the new regulations introduced in the intervening years. Herbals include many items used for culinary and medicinal purposes, unlicensed herbals abound on the remedy shelves because authorities are unlikely to win court cases. If parsley powder is put in a capsule and sold as such, is it for use as a diuretic or for cooking?

Comprehensive properly formulated supplements work   During April one of the testimonials for Cantamega 2000 was very interesting. The lady had received Larkhall's catalogue by chance and appreciated that the Cantamega 2000 formula offered a really comprehensive range of micronutrients. Having tried many prescription remedies she thought her many problems could be diet related. All her symptoms, including persistent urinary infections and tremors cleared after taking Cantamega 2000. So many health problems were diet related that it is only with a blockbuster type formula that they can be conquered. Larkhall always emphasised that supplements were not drugs and that their use must be combined with a naturally based balanced diet, like the Cantassium Dietary system devised in the 1920s.

Hair analysis in Italy and UK.   In early June I was in Italy over a weekend supporting the endeavours of PN in Milan with a morning lecture on Diet Supplements at a seminar for practitioners that introduced a new application for Hair Analysis. The new Mineralogramme system with special supplement formulas was the subject of for the afternoon presentation by Dr David Watts of Trace Elements Inc., from Dallas USA. Hair analysis for detecting dietary deficiencies and levels of toxic minerals such as Arsenic, Lead, Mercury and Cadmium was becoming popular amongst the naturopaths.

Several Italian Companies were promoting this approach and it proved successful for PN in the next few years. In the UK any connection between health and Hair Analysis was considered nonsense by the medical establishment but had not been made illegal.

The UK based Foresight Charity used Hair Analysis in its parental assessments. Despite excellent results from the subsequently recommended dietary and supplementation regime, the authorities never accepted its ideas. At this time it was experiencing problems with adverse media comments. I thought that the HealthWatch Charity was behind this adverse publicity for another Charity - a strange situation for two health charities.

More trouble for Tryptophan The ongoing Tryptophan contamination problem was highlighted in The Lancet. Reports from the USA confirmed that just one manufacturer was responsible for the problem. It seemed that the pure Tryptophan had found its way to Germany, France and Switzerland where all Tryptophan was licensed as a medicine and more closely controlled than in the UK where it was mainly supplied as a food supplement. Perhaps licensing did not provide as much patient protection as its supporters claimed. I was not surprised.

Genetic modification of Trytophan processing really the cause of the problem
Showa Denko's Trytophan was very much cheaper than other manufacturers and had been prepared using a new synthetic route using genetically engineered/modified bacteria. This processing had produced a highly toxic by-product that could not be readily extracted or identified in analytical laboratories. Analysts generally have to know what they are looking for before they can detect it. That's why this Tryptophan problem proved so difficult to solve. It set natural approaches to conquering depression, anxiety and stress back for years but opened the door to Prozac, mirtazapine and the antipsychotic drugs like Resperidone. These added to Pharma profits and side effects including patient suicides.

The unpatentable tryptophan plus vitamins supplement, Tryptokalm made by Cantassium, would harm no one. Adoption by the medical profession of the principles outlined in Dr Barrie Bartlett's booklet 'Anxiety, Depression and Nutrition' published by Robert's Publications might have revolutionised the treatment of millions of sufferers but would have decimated big pharma profits.

In 1993 Vitamin Research Products published an article 'The truth about L-Tryptophan' by A.S. Gissin. This article exposed the inefficiences and perhaps sophistry of the FDA in the USA as regards L-Tryptophan. The synthetic Tryptophan that was responsible for the problem was produced using genetically modified bacteria. The process produced very pure pharmaceutical grade L-Tryptophan yet had very toxic spectrum of impurities present in those micro amounts and it was these that caused the Eosinophilia side effect. The FDA had welcomed the new method of production and were impressed by its purity of 99.65% - considerably better than the normal 98.5%. They must have concluded, with fatal results, that the 0.35% was insignificant and would play no part in harmful side effects. The fact that the L-Tryptophan was bioengineered probably, delighted the officials at FDA who supported use of this type of production process. Of course, the natural health movement deplored use of genetic engineering in food production. Pharmaceutical companies, on the other hand, often have interests in those methods of processing and even own subsidiaries in that field of manufacture. One can see the huge problems facing the FDA and it is no surprise that these matters have been papered over for years. Bureaucrats all over the world had acted against the essential amino acidL-Tryptophan but persuading them to admit their error would be very difficult and take years.

NHS could save millions with changes to diet In mid May, I wrote to a lady who had successfully kicked a drug habit (in this case 22 years on the Librium antidepressant drug) by supplementing with Cantassium's Full B with C tablets. She gave permission for us to use her letter anonymously.

I am convinced that the current antidepressant therapies are of little benefit unless accompanied by dietary improvement towards wholefood and additional supplementing using a comprehensive formulation of B Vitamins with Vitamin C. If doctors put their depressed, stressed or anxious patients on such a supplement first together with a dietary plan, vast savings could be made - but who will pay for the proof of efficacy to be determined to the satisfaction of the bureaucrats? Patients expect 'Free Drugs on Prescription' and would not accept paying extra for supplements. Doctors cannot win here but it is the patients and the taxpayers who fund the NHS who really lose.

Health Hero Hugh Sinclair dies On 22nd June the death of Dr Hugh Sinclair the eminent nutritionist was announced. Sinclair was a maverick and eccentric who made many enemies in the academic and medical establishment. He had concluded in the early 1930s that the biggest health problems had nutritional causes but targeting specific ideas and writing elegant scientific papers eluded him. His apparent lack of selfdiscipline led him to lose academic posts and he never became a professor.

In 1956 he expounded the Sinclair Hypothesis in a long letter to the Lancet. He theorised that ageing and degeneration was related to low intakes of the Linoleic and Linolenic polyunsaturated fatty acids. This was not a welcome revelation as far as most medical men were concerned. Evidence to satisfy them was never established by Sinclair. This reminded me of the rejection of Dr EC Barton-Wright and Pantothenic Acid and of John Williams's Evening Primrose Oil research.

When in 1985 Sinclair's letter of 1956 was hailed in the much respected scientific reference publication 'Current Contents' as a 'Citation Classic', his peers were not amused. The academic row over his 1956 publication meant he had to strike out on his own. This was a bold move and cost him greatly financially. However his 1980 experiment when he put himself on the Eskimo Diet was his greatest hour. After putting himself in mortal danger when he lost two stone in weight and his blood clotting time went from 3 minutes to an hour, he concluded correctly that ingestion of the long chain fatty acids of fish were of great importance in diminishing the prevalence of coronary thrombosis.

Sinclair continued his research and was convinced that proper nourishment - not the dietitians balanced diet was the key to health, quality of life and longevity. It was a pity he did not reach 100 himself. I remembered meeting him at the Athenaeum Club in Pall Mall in the 1980s but the vagueness of the conversation could not be capitalised upon. Nevertheless, **Hugh Sinclair stands with Richard Doll, Ivan Ilich, Thomas Cleave and Dennis Burkitt as one of my health heroes.**

Gypsy lifestyle meant reduction in cancer The Appleby Romany Survey - written by a Mr Christopher MacNaney showed that incidence of cancer was lower in Gypsies who travel every few days than in those who put down roots. This was a typical example of natural healthcare theories where because there had been no scientific method applied the results were given no credibility. However, it is merely confirmation that those with less sophisticated and more natural lifestyles generally fare better and develop less degenerative disease.

Medicines Inspectors no threat In mid June we had a Medicines Inspection at Charlbury that indicated the zealotry of the Inspectorate was waning and the premises were considered 'Low risk' by the MCA. The faults found were trivial but it was always important that these people could justify their jobs to their superiors.

Typical of inefficient bureaucracies set up by naive and ill informed politicians, The Medicines Act passed in 1968 after the thalidomide tragedy of 1962, had perhaps become mature and dull.

Pharmaceutical Journal highlighted regulatory problems   Towards the end of June The Pharmaceutical Journal carried a report about Aminophylline Suppositories 'Failing' a licence review. I wrote protesting about the word 'fail' because I believed it was economics that worked against the product. It was just not possible to make this very small demand product to the standards enforced without incurring vast unknown levels of cost. The word 'fail' was inappropriate in this instance and many products had been lost on review for the same reasons. The reality was that bureaucrats were driving products off the market to serve their purposes and please the big Pharma interest by ensuring them more of the market. My ally, Michael Ivens, at 'Aims of Industry' was included in the correspondence because his organisation was always fighting for small companies. Aims appreciated the huge obstacles that the small company faced when ignorant regulators picked on them. The Pharmaceutical Journal published my letter and hopefully it caused some discomfort in the Medicines Regulator's offices.

I liked the quotes from Richard Crossman's diaries regarding how he found Civil Servants 'Second rate and unimpressive', 'extremely good at working the procedures of the Civil Service' and 'They lack a constructive apprehension of the problems with which they deal and any imagination' as reported in Pharmaceutical Journal p 780 June 30 1990. Crossman was the Minister of Health 1968-1970 during the time that the Medicines Act was going through parliament.

Rita Greer and the British Food Fiasco   To mark the anniversary of the end of wartime food rationing on July 3rd 1954 Morris Media issued a press release using RG's ideas. Food rationing produced healthier consumers and this stimulated interest in the dietary recommendations of RG and the views expressed in her 80's book 'The British Food Fiasco' where she pointed out the dangers to health of the High Saturated Fat, Salt and Sugar, Low Fibre, low vegetable and low fruit based diets of 1990. Her comment, "We have the knowledge, the facility and the produce to be the healthiest nation on earth but something has gone horribly wrong". Her views were not acceptable to the food industry, big Pharma or the bureaucrats and undoubtedly contributed to the clouds gathering around Larkhall and its products and educational materials. Rita's writing and illustrative skills were annoying our enemies like HealthWatch, the snack industry, the sugar lobby and even the media who worried about losing advertising revenues from junk food manufacturers and supermarkets.

The July issue of 'Prevention' the USA health magazine carried a short article on health - wise eating -- relevant to RG's book.

I wondered about need for consultants   In mid July I noticed a report in The Chemist & Druggist that referred to a Pet Health product company Marc & Chappell. This firm was managed by the Marketing Consultant dismissed by Larkhall in 1987. Ironically, Dendron the old distributor for Larkhall who he had advised dismissing, was the appointed Chemist distributor for this new company. M&C had some of their product brand names using the endings -ium -um. I wondered if these were chosen because of his past connection with **Cantassium** a major brand of Larkhall's? Later Marc and Chappell was delisted by Boots and had great trouble with their advertising as it had not complied with the CAP Code. By 2012 they appeared to have products available only on the Web by mail order. The consultant had recommended the Pet Trade as a fertile area for Larkhall but I had had experience of this field from 1963 with Abels anti-worm anti-ezcema all-in-one conditioner for dogs.

I knew it was a crowded and difficult market so had not acted on the marketing consultant's advice. It seemed I was right. (Years later I discovered he had registered Cantassium in the USA as his own trademark!) Did I need this type of consultant? No. They learned more from me than I did from them.

In the USA for the annual NNFA convention in Boston. At the end of July I travelled with UK Health Food Trade representatives to Boston USA for the annual NNFA Convention. This instructive trip was organised by Colin Tophill a well known personality in the Health Food Trade working for Bookers (Brewhurst). I met some more interesting contacts in the USA and continued effort to gain interest in the Tandem IQ research.
An International Symposium was held and the problems for the industry were almost identical everywhere but authorities were frustrated by the strength of the US Industry and its ability to maintain much freedom for claims with a vast range of pharmaceutically styled products. The FDA (Food and Drug Administration) had difficulty in obtaining state wide controls because many States, especially California, insisted on independence in the Vitamin Supplement area. Most of the US Health Food industry was based on the West Coast. The Lecture programme for the convention was interesting reading. Two items were of more than passing interest. The Metabolic Holistic Medical Centre brochure. This clinic and business, run and owned by Robert Bradford, was based just over the border from California in Tijuana, Mexico. It would have been an illegal operation in America.
An article headlined 'Pycnogenol' appeared in Let's Live about this controversial health food supplement. Larkhall introduced it to the UK market in the 1980s It was a concentrated extract from a Maritime Pine Tree Bark, rich in anti-oxidant flavonoids.

More unreasonable criticisms for Larkhall's competitors from HealthWatch In early August HealthWatch issued a position paper on two products produced by Wassen International - Confiance and Magnesium-OK - which the campaign against Health Fraud, aka HealthWatch, believed made dubious claims on their packaging but more specific claims in a recent Press Release. They challenged Wassen to subject these products to independent clinical trials which some of their 'Expert Members' would be prepared to design and, if successful, would endorse. Of course, no right thinking supplement manufacturer would agree to such terms when the prejudice towards supplements of HealthWatch was well known and questionable. This was amply illustrated by their unwarranted attacks on Larkhall and Tandem IQ. Their association with Professor Naismith and the Scottish group of Dr Crombie being covert but clear to any impartial observer. It was easy for the HealthWatch experts to issue their views on what constituted adequate trials when only they knew what that really meant. However, the lay public and most journalists didn't understand that what HealthWatch demanded of unpatentable vitamin and mineral supplements was technically impossible and could cost vastly more than any trial of a patented synthetic drug. To write such a position paper was unworthy of intelligent persons but deliberately made the Health Food movement look shady. The HealthWatch people took sophistry to a new level. Their demand for alternative health care treatments to meet criteria set for pharmaceutical drugs was analogous to asking a bicycle as a mechanised mode of transport to comply with emission and other standards enforced on cars and lorries.

Professor Drangan and Romania In mid June I received a letter from Professor Drangan (Romania) regarding Larkhall sponsoring him for various visits to International Sports Medicine conferences. I was aware of Drangan's status on Olympic Committees but also wary of spending substantial sums that would not help Larkhall.

The problem was food supplement product classification as medicine in most countries meant that importation and distribution of UK made supplements faced great problems in many small end user markets with little sales potential. However, I agreed to discuss Drangan's request for money with our Greek distributor. In the event we did not sponsor him for these trips.

European Union Market for Food Supplements   On 9th August I wrote to Maria Strofalis, Larkhall's energetic Greek distributor, about Professor Drangan and a general meeting with the European Health Food Association at the end of September in Athens plus an International Sports Medicine congress in Barcelona.

My view on Drangan's Cantamega study was clear. Whilst it was acceptable for private correspondence, it would not be approved for publication in sports medicine publications. The continuing problems with supplements was evident with a proposed meeting sponsored by Vital and Naturtabs Hellas. The leaders from EHPM were to be entertained by Vital and would include people representing the various national health trade organisations (Maurice Hanssen (UK), Mr Reinsch (Germany) and Mr Huggon)

I travelled to Athens for the meeting between EU and Greek Officials and the EHPM. Several Greek Traders were also present. Little progress was made because the Greek Authorities insisted that supplements were medicines and needed legalisation for import and distribution. It was only the impending 'EEC Free Market' that enabled the fairly restricted trading in supplements to continue in Greece. The authorities knew there were no real safety problems with vitamins but the products currently paid no fees to government and were therefore impeded as much as possible in the market place.

A press release from Morris Media was issued in October regarding the Athens meeting this gave full details of the meetings and the personalities involved.

Up to 2015 the situation regarding supplements in the EU remains the same but, as always action from Brussels was 'expected soon'. How many deaths from supplements have occurred in the last 25 years? Perhaps none is the answer and explained the continued procrastination. Meanwhile many of the personalities and companies of 1990 no longer exist.

The visit of the top people from EHPM was useful because of the impression it made on Greek and European bureaucrats but I had serious doubts whether there was long term sustainable business for these products in Greece

The European Market was far from free for supplements. Italy was currently doing very well but our exports were going via Yugoslavia. What the reasons were was unknown. One store in Germany was doing well directly importing from Larkhall but a major wholesale distributor could not be found. Small supplies to pharmacies were not yet blocked, Sweden and Holland continued to be worthwhile.

Invitation to apply for NHS prescription status for an essential amino acid   In mid August Larkhall was invited to apply for borderline prescription status for L-Threonine tablets and capsules. This was a surprise but I thought that the paperwork required for a submission was unlikely to achieve prescription status for the product and its production would cost more than the likely profit over many years. There were no patents available on L-Threonine because it was an established amino acid occurring naturally in the human body. The correctness of this decision was confirmed when the Borderline Committee secretary wrote a long letter to Larkhall on 11th December that rejected Threonine for listing for NHS prescription but encouraging an appeal against that decision. These people cannot be in the real world or they would realise that no sane company would waste precious resources in appealing for L-Threonine to be on NHS prescription. The ways of bureaucracy never ceased to amaze me.

211

A turning point month for Larkhall September saw much of the progress made from 1985 wiped out. The scare stories on Tryptophan, Germanium and Niacin coupled with the capitulation of the Health Food Manufacturers Association and the National Association of Health Stores following the demands of bureaucrats was catastrophic. The technical illiteracy of the people running these trade organisations was exposed and this contributed to many future problems.

HealthWatch and their allies saw the weakness and exploited it to the full. The trade was defensive for fear of profit loss. Attack should have been the policy but they had no courage and too few companies, mainly Larkhall, were really affected.

Happily, the difficulties were restricted to the UK and Irish Pharmacy and Health Food retail trades. Unbeknown to most people Larkhall had commercial strength in UK, Ireland, Europe and the USA including direct export to overseas distributors throughout the world, their Lipcote product was the leader in the UK Lipstick Sealant market and the special diet foods Trufree and Ruthmol were strong while their marital aids range was significant.

The sales report for September from the manager, written by his office assistant, was relevant and informative. It painted a biased internal picture blaming influences outside the control of the Manager and his team for a decline in business. I found this report disturbing but reading it in hindsight I can see it presaged the problems to come. Were there enemies within? The dismissal of some sales representatives had been seen as a threat to the manager's empire and malicious rumours of the imminent bankruptcy of Larkhall were probably encouraged from within. What happened in 1991 and 1992 definitely implicated at least three disgruntled employees and ex-employees as possible accomplices of Larkhall's enemies.

Homoeopathy moved centre stage but still placebo In September the Journal of the Royal Society of Medicine carried an article entitled 'The homoeopathic conundrum' that provided a backdrop to the September paper in the leading scientific journal 'Nature' from a French Group (Benveniste) that purported to prove effectiveness and provide a working research model for 'Homoeopathy'. Controversy about Homoeopathy then reached a height not seen for many years. After much excitement and debate in 'Nature' and elsewhere, the Benveniste experiments could not be replicated in other laboratories and were therefore discredited. Homoeopathy reverted to its place as a placebo method of health care that was not equivalent to useless or ineffective. Homoeopathy could not meet scientific criteria designed for modern pharmaceuticals nor would it ever.

Larkhall went greener In early September I issued a memo that would revolutionise the tablet manufacturing process at Larkhall's Putney facility. The old fashioned wet granulation process was to be cut back to less than 5% of production. This would save over 50% of energy requirements and represented a greening of Larkhall's processing. This had taken several years effort and funding to achieve.

Late vindication for 'Safeseal' after 20 years As often happened, an idea from Larkhall proved to be ahead of its time. The Pharmaceutical Journal 20th October published a letter questioning the security of Blister Packs for capsules and Tablets after a child had died following accidental poisoning following eating tablets he had extracted from blisters. This interested me because in the early 1970s I had introduced 'Safeseal' packs, for some prescribed sugar coated tablets. The idea was to have a secure pack to which inquisitive youngsters could not gain access even if a careless parent had left them lying around the house. At the time I said that only safeseal strips could provide this security and blister packs that had just become available would not give the same degree of protection. It seemed I was right. Safeseal was never approved for NHS use since a doctor could not prescribe the packaging - that was a matter for the pharmacist.

A bureaucratic rule in the interests of whom? Certainly not accidentally poisoned children. The cost of safeseal packs was not excessive perhaps the answer was simply 'NIH -- not invented here'.

Major media attack began   In early October Larkhall issued a press release regarding Niacin. This aimed to answer the expected criticisms of Niacin supplements likely to appear in the media. It put the defence case very well. A couple of weeks later I sent a copy of Larkhall's medicinal product licences for three niacin products to Maurice Hanssen, the HFMA President. This was important because a TV programme 'Watchdog' was about to broadcast an anti-vitamin feature highlighting the side effects of Niacin in high doses (not known at the time but probably 250 mg and 500mg Nicotinic Acid).

Whilst Larkhall were members of the Health Food Manufacturers Association, yet because of their Pharmaceutical heritage they were technically far more knowledgeable than the other members who had their heritage in the food and grocery industries. Hence the HFMA were not really suited to be our trade association, but there was no other. In hindsight we should never have joined that body but fought the enemy on our own. I was alarmed when the health trade associations just capitulated to a media manipulated by HealthWatch 'Experts'.

Germanium, Tryptophan and Niacin were used to spearhead the attack. Significantly, Tryptophan was seen as a threat to the growing highly profitable pharmaceutical market for prescribed antidepressant drugs (**Prozac**), Niacin to those hugely profitable prescription drugs for lowering Cholesterol (**Statins**), while Germanium sounded nasty so was easy to disparage to a receptive public. HealthWatch were guaranteed support from the rich and powerful drug companies through these attacks. Even a word like germanium was easy to use against the Natural Health Food Movement because it didn't sound at all nice. Tryptophan, an essential amino acid found in nearly all protein foods, was easy to rubbish because to lay people it sounded as if it was a 'Nasty Chemical'.

The hot flushes associated with Niacin were considered unpleasant as a side effect even though harmless and natural in the menopause and other life situations. A little extra blood flow in the skin can, in fact, be a tonic and helpful. A few yeast tablets could also produce this effect.

My experience of having sat on committees of the Pharmaceutical Industry Association in the early 1970s had given me an insight into how ruthless the large pharma companies could be. At that time, generic competition of various kinds was seen as the enemy and preventing those companies achieving total monopoly of the prescription drugs market was a priority. Denigration of generics was successfully engineered by questioning product quality and efficacy so that patients demanded the proven effective patented products from their GPs.

By the late 1980s government action had ensured widespread generic drug acceptance. However the industry then perceived a new threat to their proprietary drugs from Diet Supplement and Herbal health products whose growing market and healthy food ideas were causing their friends in the junk food industry headaches too. Tryptophan threatened the lucrative antidepressant market whilst special cholesterol lowering diets with extra niacin could adversely affect the rapidly growing sales of Statin drugs. It was certain that big Pharma and junk food producers would be ruthless in trying to overcome these threats. They could afford the best Public Relations agencies and use their allies in academia whose laboratories were in receipt of their research grants to help them. Academics were interviewed on media such as BBC TV's Watchdog and Food & Drink but never had to declare 'commercial' interests such as their industrial benefactors. They appeared as neutral and unbiased experts to listeners, viewers and readers. This was a corrupt alliance that still needed attention from authorities in 2015.

Placebo effects not mentioned In mid October the Daily Mirror carried an article in its Mirror Woman section regarding the controversial use of Vitamin B6 Supplements to alleviate the discomforts associated with Pre Menstrual Tension (PMT).

A fairly balanced article but a conclusion that alleviation was achieved by the placebo effect should perhaps have been mentioned. Magnesium supplements were also said to help but again placebo effect was just as likely as it was with Evening Primrose Oil.

Strange visitor On 18th October I went out in the evening at 6pm and RG reported a mysterious break-in at the Putney Factory around 7pm. The alarms went off and the police came with the warehouse manager. They found no one, reset the alarms and left the building. As they walked up Putney Bridge Road the alarms went off again and they returned. RG watched the new CCTV monitor and observed the back of a person exiting the front door who looked suspiciously like an employee from the Charlbury factory. After another search nothing appeared to be missing but with hindsight this was probably the time when samples of Tryptophan, Niacin and Immunomega were taken from the back area of the shop and passed to investigative journalist Duncan Campbell.

Ivan Ilich Future of Medicine and side effects On 20th October the Economist Magazine published an article "The Future of Medicine". Leading in with Ivan Ilich's 'Limits to Medicine', this excellent article looked closely at the likely costs of continuing on the present path of Medical treatments. Having done a good job in this article it would seem that nothing had changed up to 2015. What happened? I had long been a follower of Dr Ilich's ideas as regards the over chemicalisation of treatments. Sadly, his ideas had no following among opinion formers. Side effects were a big issue for Ilich and coincidentally with the Economist, a report in the British Medical Journal indicated that ibuprofen, the widely used over the counter anti inflammatory painkiller drug, could cause colitis. The author believed all non-steroidal anti-inflammatory drugs had the potential for this side effect.

Attempt to enforce a patent for Evening Primrose Oil in cosmetics. Martha Hiil skin care had been attacked for using Evening Primrose Oil in its creams without permission from a patent holder (Bio Oils). I advised them that Larkhall had used EPO in creams since 1974 and had never paid Bio Oils anything. I suspected the patent could not be enforced and advised Martha to ignore the complaint. She did and heard no more.

BBC2 broadcast a programme on Tandem IQ At the end of October The 'Food & Drink' programme on BBC2 TV carried a very critical item on vitamin pills that they said purported to increase a child's IQ. Three products were examined: Tandem IQ, Boost IQ and Top Marks. Tandem IQ was attacked in the most trivial way. No attempt at balance was made by the programme makers and I had refused to be interviewed for the programme because I feared distortion. The producers refused me a live interview. It was well known that the man behind all this was Duncan Campbell, who regularly cut recorded dialogue to suit his ends. Several highly critical pieces had been made on alternative health care industry and movement practices with no attempt at balance. The quote given on the programme from me was taken totally out of context. I always emphasised that it was dietary improvement that produced the benefits and that the only way to scientifically improve the micronutrient quality of a diet was with properly formulated supplements of known concentrations. This was far too complicated for Campbell to understand and he just passed his ignorance on in this programme with a simple, critical script. Larkhall had been behind the research and I had said that if the experiment did not work I would close the factory.

Importantly, the programme also distorted Dr Benton's 'phone conversation with them. The studies by Naismith and the Benton Belgian trial had not been repeats of the original Darland trial as was indicated by the programme – they were very different.

The programme's presenter said it was going to refer the products to **Shropshire Trading Standards,** a council with a zealous chief officer, David Roberts, who was famous for stating 'Health Food' constituted a criminal trading standards offence. This body was in close contact with HealthWatch, as was Campbell. Since most of Shropshire is agricultural, its trading standards budget was available for use by zealots like Roberts and his henchmen Henshall and Walker. They were ideal people to assist HealthWatch in their mission to destroy the Food Supplements Industry. Legally, Trading Standards convictions are criminal but not necessarily fraudulent, this fact would eventually catch out HealthWatch and cost them dearly.

We had a very good relationship with our own local Trading Standards officers and always consulted them. Why was their opinion and advice ignored in favour of Shropshire -- miles away?

A piece in Private Eye about "The Food and Drink Gang", meaning The Food and Drink Programme, indicated the triviality of some of the journalism associated with that programme.

November 1990   This was the month that Shropshire started their cases against Larkhall and Seven Seas who had brazenly copied Larkhall with a completely untrialled formula 'Boost IQ'. They soon pleaded guilty and paid substantial fines which, of course, encouraged Shropshire in their pursuit of the innovators -- Larkhall.

The term 'Natural' on products was questioned   Early in November, The Sunday Times carried an investigative report concerning the 'Body Shop', a multi-million pound public company with hundreds of beauty stores all over the world. Their products were not as 'Natural' as they always claimed. This was a situation that I had long been angry about but the boss of the chain, Anita Roddick, a person with no proper technical knowledge, was a superb self publicist who had created a perfect aura around herself which ensured consumers believed in the perfection and naturalness of her products. The article exposed the truth so I sent a letter to the journalists supporting their attack.

Top management did not understand Larkhall's mission   A memo received from my brother regarding Natudophilus -- a recently introduced Larkhall product that was superior to Acidophilus Tablets. The sales had not been as high as hoped but the critical nature of the memo indicated his shallow understanding of the supplement business. Products needed marketing spends to succeed but £8,100 was a trivial sum in this context. Natudophilus was not introduced as a blockbuster product but to penetrate the Probiotic Supplement market with a more technically advanced source of live friendly bacteria. Such products were aimed to show Larkhall as an innovating company and stimulate interest in their whole range. Sadly, my brother did not understand this perhaps he had been on too many courses and listened to marketing theorists rather than practitioners of the art.

Coeliac Society dispute resolved at last   The Coeliac Society was continuing to refuse Larkhall advertising space in its magazine 'The Crossed Grain'. They had never come to terms with the criticism that was spearheaded by Larkhall regarding them permitting use of their unique 'Gluten Free Symbol' a Crossed Grain on packs of products made using Wheat Starch. Wheat Starch always contained gluten because no system of extracting it was 100% effective.

In addition to extracting some of the gluten this process also removed nearly all the naturally occurring vitamins and minerals therein, so making the wheat starch a very poor source of nutrition for the already seriously deprived coeliac patients - no wonder they were more prone to cancers than others.

Disallowing Larkhall's advertising constituted a **restriction of trade** that was illegal. RG had spotted a declaration by them in a publication that said anyone could advertise in their magazine. She took it up with them and was refused again. She then complained to the appropriate advertising authority that later led to a solicitor's letter to the society. As if by magic, this achieved 'reconsideration' by the Coeliac Society and at last, after years, Larkhall could begin to advertise Trufree successfully, in the best medium available for Gluten Free items. The Coeliac Society was not pleased but we were delighted. It would mean giant bake-ups of food made with Trufree for RG for use in photography, a new mini catalogue and a general shakeup for the brand. Hooray!

Garlic contained natural Germanium This month's issue of the USA Health Magazine 'Let's Live' carried an article on 'Garlic's Natural Medicinal Qualities'. A classic illustration of the difficulties legislators had in their attempts to control natural medicine. Garlic was indisputably a foodstuff but it had well researched medicinal properties -- where was it to be classified by the bureaucrats? No doubt they would try to establish obscure specifications to meet their criteria but the lay consumers would take no notice and continue to buy ordinary garlic. Ironically it appeared that garlic contained Germanium that may contribute to its beneficial properties - whither the Germanium ban?

Devon Expansion for Larkhall? In November I spent a day going to Axminster in Devon to look at an industrial development site. The idea of possibly moving the company to Devon was an option worth considering. Having two sites was not really proving economical. The Axminster site was very good but the problems with moving were too great and we reverted to consider consolidation in either London or Oxford.

Death of HealthWatch doctor blamed on supporters of Alternative healthcare.
Many Alternative Health supporters and practitioners had been suffering grievous injustices at the hands of HealthWatch and its followers. In mid December the journalist Julie Burchill in the Mail on Sunday reported her opinion that Professor Timothy McElwain, a leading light in HealthWatch, following an attack of acute depressio had been hounded to death by supporters of the Bristol Cancer Help Charity. Burchill criticised those Alternative Health Care people for their actions but she did not balance that with a word about the totally unjustified and underhand practices of McElwain's associate Duncan Campbell, that had caused heartbreak and more to his victims. When would both sides see sense? Widespread dissatisfaction with orthodox medical practice was the real reason that Alternative Healthcare grew. McElwain would not be the only HealthWatch supporter to commit suicide, Dr Thurston Brewin a war veteran who had suffered serious wounds left £10 for a parlourmaid who found his body in a hotel room on the South Coast.

Break-ins at the Putney Factory During the Autumn, a series of break-ins began at the Putney factory. RG offered to deal with the police permanently so that they dealt with the same person each time there was trouble. The break-ins were puzzling as usually only documents were disturbed in the filing cabinets -- as if the burglars were searching for something. Each time the alarms would go off and the police would arrive to search the building. Sometimes they brought dogs. On police advice we had had CCTV installed but the break-ins continued. Scotland Yard were puzzled and gave RG a special number to ring if there was trouble. It would bring a special squad to the factory as quickly as possible.

Duncan Campbell (of Zircon satellite and Official Secrets difficulties) telephoned to ask how much we had paid the BBC QED programme for featuring our product Tandem IQ. The truth was we had not paid them anything and we had certainly not tried to influence the programme makers in any way, but it was like talking to a brick wall. In October a man rang the goods inwards entrance bell so persistently, that the cleaners, who were the only ones on the premises, felt obliged to answer it. The man said he was delivering stationery. He wasn't. He was merely trying to get into the factory after hours. The following night a man tried to break down the gate to the yard at the rear of the factory. When he saw the cleaners were aware of him he made off smartly in a big car. After a break-in when nothing was taken, the police concluded it was someone spying on or investigating us.

A few days later Tim Hinks, Campbell's side-kick, telephoned to say he was working for the BBC Food and Drink programme as an 'unbiased consumer affairs researcher'. There followed a tirade of accusations about Tandem IQ that were all ridiculous. He revealed that their story would require us taking Tandem IQ off the market out of fear of the BBC. Their threat did not work so they tried something else. We had a nasty 'phone call from a Trading Standards Officer. It wasn't our local one but one from Shropshire. He threatened arrest, imprisonment and lawyers. He told RG she had better get a good lawyer as she was going to need one. We had to take legal advice. The Shropshire TSO officer was told we would abide by normal TSO procedure (which did not involve threats) but he did not reply. He denied any connection with The BBC Food and Drink programme. However, on the programme the presenter gaily admitted they had asked the Shropshire Trading Standards Office to investigate us. The officer said he was now going for a straight summons "because of the Asil Nadir case. Nobody had any idea of what this meant and we had had nothing to do with such a case".

When the feature was broadcast it was biased and inaccurate. It had a disturbing part at the end when patients who were ill were waiting in a doctor's surgery. They were frightened and distressed by the camera team.

Just before Christmas a man in a BBC TV car was been seen making notes and watching the side entrances at Putney and generally at the Charlbury factory. We warned staff there was trouble brewing. RG had been on TV enough times to know how they researched prior to making a film. She tipped off the police who had given her a special number to ring and they advised her how to cope. They seemed to know all about Campbell and his tactics and were very helpful. We didn't have to wait long as it all came to a head in the new year.

Building up the pressure on Larkhall Just after the Tandem IQ BBC Food and Drink programme we experienced several worrying occurrences. Which, in hindsight, must have been connected to the programme makers for 'Food and Drink' who, we knew were making more programmes against the Health Food industry.

'Phones hacked long before scandals of the early 2000s One evening, after all the staff had gone home, I decided I'd go to a restaurant for a meal with RG. She 'phoned and booked a table. When we got there RG went into the restaurant on her own while I parked the car. A man was outside the Restaurant with a film camera. I walked into the restaurant at the same time as some other customers. We had a quick meal and as it was raining, I left on my own to get the car and picked RG up outside the restaurant. The man with the film camera was there again. He was trying to film us both together but failed as we had arrived and left separately. How did they know we had booked a table at that restaurant? He was there before us so could not have followed us. 'Phones were hacked at Larkhall by the media long before those scandals exposed in the early 2000s.

RG thought that her 'phone was probably being tapped since no one else could possibly have known about the restaurant booking. The police said they could not intervene but she got a telephone engineer to take her handset apart and he produced what looked like a small, flattish button. He said that type lasted about 6 months. It was a 'bug'.

RG recognised the man filming at the restaurant as the one who had previously come into the factory shop, with a tape recorder under his blouson jacket. He tried to hide the film camera, which was much larger than the tape recorder, and had difficulty getting into a car that arrived, driven by his mate. RG said if it wasn't so sinister it would make an Enid Blyton story.

Suspicious Burglaries There were several break-ins at the Putney and Charlbury Factories during the autumn. The two serious break-ins at the Charlbury factory resulted in the loss of thousands of pounds worth of equipment including a computer and discs holding confidential information. The computer was found by police but the discs were lost. I wondered who would find these useful?

No actual thefts were found after the Putney break-ins. At the Greer's house in Hampshire which I shared with RG and her husband we were burgled twice while we were not there. Valuables were missing but the police were unable to trace the missing items.

Non-stop pressure made life very stressful. RG's husband became very ill as he couldn't take the stress of all the break-ins at Putney or the house. His MS relapses now occurred more frequently and after each one he failed to make a good recovery. After many years out of a wheelchair he now had to use one again. The last thing someone with MS can cope with it is stress and at the Putney factory it was wall to wall, without any sign of it abating. The police were helpful but mystified.

The staff felt under siege, just as we did. I wondered whether I should close down the shop as this seemed to be a magnet to Campbell. There were frequent 'phone calls from his team and sometimes he phoned himself, trying to trap staff into making statements he could use against us. Working at Larkhall was becoming a nightmare.

Campbell boasted he had access to Larkhall's computers. On TV Campbell said he had inside information about Larkhall from someone who 'knew our systems' and described this person as "a senior member of staff". He also claimed he had confidential information from 'an executive. (Could this have been the employee who had been recently asked by RG as to why he had two identical brief cases? He had told her one was a 'special'. Showing off, he had opened it to show her. Although apparently empty it had a built-in recorder that was worked from the handle of the case. Shades of MI5?)

This backed up what the police had told us right at the beginning of the trouble -- it involved one or more persons on the inside at Larkhall passing information to Campbell. Was somebody or some organisation trying to close us down? Was the idea to make us sell the company for next to nothing? Who were the informers Campbell referred to? It was all a huge worry. If I had challenged and dismissed an employee about this, the legal consequences could have been very costly at a Tribunal.

Over the Christmas period I was contacted at home by Peter Bazalgette the producer of the "Food and Drink programme' who wanted to know how our Immunomega Tablets had been found to contain Germanium. I explained that these were probably the export formula tablets which could have been packed in the wrong cartons but they did not contain the synthetic Germanium Dioxide but an organic form of Germanium. The actual amount of Germanium was minimal and not in the form that was being questioned by the UK authorities. Bazalgette just did not understand what I was saying because he seemed to have little knowledge of chemistry.

The technical points would be difficult for a lay person to grasp and he confirmed that a live TV interview with me on his programme would not be permitted under any circumstances. I was sure Larkhall was about to be stitched up by him and Campbell. One day, Just before the BBC2 Food & Drink Programme on Germanium, Niacin & Tryptophan was broadcast in January 1991 a film crew struggled up to the Oxfordshire factory along the riverside at Charlbury so as not to be seen. RG had tipped off Dennis Hooker, the manager, that they might be coming as she had seen Campbell and his crew in Putney and they had tried again and failed to get into the Putney factory, demanding an interview with me. At Charlbury, Dennis Hooker told them what RG had told them in Putney -- that I'd gone to the Witney Office. We had no Witney Office but off they went in hot pursuit. Actually, I was abroad at the time on business which told us they were not that well informed.

Local Manufacture in Italy soon   In January I had been in Rome to visit PN for business discussions. Their interest in expanding to manufacture the supplements in Italy was a possibility but they would need to takeover an indigenous producer. In early December, I was in Rome again to visit PN for discussions. They were seriously considering a move to Genoa to enable local manufacture of the Cantassium Supplements that were by then the leading brand in Italy. They intended to takeover the Winter Company that produced a large range of Herbal products that they made in a factory in Genoa.

Year End Pressure after very busy 1990   In spite of the behaviour of the media, our enemies, and our troubles with Campbell and HealthWatch, life at Larkhall went on. I had had to make quite a few trips abroad.
   A note here about those trips. The UK staff always regarded these as holidays and they had no idea of them being business trips. They were always very hard work and meant staying in various hotels which the staff also deemed as holiday behaviour. Business meetings would start early in the morning and continue until midnight on some days. Each time I returned to the Putney factory I would have a pile of work on my desk as well as the follow ups from my visits.
   As will be seen from the above, Larkhall and myself were facing a bleak 1991. We were alone although there were some friends but they were afraid of contamination if they openly supported us. Could we survive? Yes, because our cause was right.
   Should we have taken out a temporary injunction in the Courts to prevent the Food & Drink programme broadcasting their damaging programme? - Perhaps, but I remained confident that we would weather the storm because what appeared, at first sight, serious matters, in fact, amounted to nothing more than misleading media hype.

Plate 13

New development at Larkhall's Charlbury Factory 1987

Larkhall's HQ in Putney showing the start of 2nd floor 1986

Map of Putney in 1980. Larkhall shown a 'laboratories' surrounded by houses in Wadham Road, Putney Bridge Road and Bective Road. Note Underground railway to Wimbledon & Central London.

Dr Kathy Bonan at a Health Show in Paris 1987

Dennis Hooker manager of Larkhall's Charlbury Factory in Oxfordshire 1987

Mia Rose Palencar and assistant on the Air Therapy stand at the NNFA convention in the Las Vegas, Hilton. July 1987

Dr R.Woodward with Maria Strofalis at a meeting in Athens at the Caravel Hotel 1987

220

Plate 14

Dr Robert Woodward shows Barbara
Cartland Tandem IQ at Helfex Exhibition
1988

At Ali al Kohil Office in Riyadh and a feast at
his home. The meal was eaten sitting on the
floor around the food. I was given a sheep's
eye - a great honour. 1988

Putney Warehouse ready for
inspection in June 1988

The 1988 Cambridge University Lightweight
Crew sponsored by Cantassium

A competition winner with her prize
presented by Dr Woodward and Jane Yates
(Mail Order manager)

Plate 15

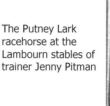

The Putney Lark racehorse at the Lambourn stables of trainer Jenny Pitman

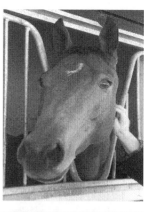

Dr Dick Richards with his wife Pix

Cantassium at the races in the company silks 1987

Arthur Chamings FRPharm Soc

Mia Rose Palencar, owner of Air Therapy brand

222

Dr Woodward presents the petition on the open distribution of Vitamin Supplements to Downing Street February1990

Plate 16

Pharmacy in
Bologna stocking
Cantassium
Supplements 1990

Prodotti Naturali exhibit their new Antoxyd skin
care range at Cosmoprof, Bologna 1990

The 'Winter' herbal product factory in
Genoa bought by Prodotti Naturali 1990

Prodotti Naturali stand at Herbora in Verona May 1990

Dinner with Maria and Tasos Strofalis, Athens to attend meeting
with the EHPM & Brussels officials. September 1990

Plate 17

Prodotti Naturali and Winter Laboratory in Genoa 1991

Cantassium delivery van in Athens 1991

an in

Maurice Hanssen, President EHPM, at Herbora in Verona to report on progress with EU single market in Supplements. 1992

Norman Cox (Solicitor), Professor Stephen Schoenthaler and Professor Arnold Beckett OBE personalities defending Larkhall in the Tandem IQ case in Shropshire 1992

Prodotti Naturali stand at Herbora in Verona 1992

Rita Greer is welcomed to Athens Airport with a bouquet to meet our distributors and doctors 1993

Plate 18

National Association of Boys Clubs, Cross Country Championships held at Keele University and sponsored by Cantassium Vitamins September 1993

Dr Woodward and Rita Greer at the Prodotti Christmas party in Camogli near Genoa. 1993

Spina Bifida week

The first Spina Bifida Week was launched August 15-21 by the Association of Spina Bifida and Hydrocephalus to create greater awareness of the association and the benefits of folic acid supplements.
Leaflets on the condition have been produced with Cantassium and Larkhall Natural Health and have been sent to 2,000 family planning clinics. The leaflets are also available direct from Larkhall.
Cantassium has developed micro-vitamin supplements in the form of small, easy-to-swallow, concentrated tablets. The range comprises Micro-garlic (90 tablets, £2.95; 200 tablets, £3.95), Micro-multi (90, £2.45; 200, £3.95) and Micro folic acid (90, £3.95).
● Folic acid, given before or after conception in a controlled study in California, has been implicated in lower incidence of cleft lip and palate defects.

A cheque for £25,000 was presented to Gina Broughton, ASBAH south east region co-ordinator, by Dr Robert Woodward, managing director and chairman of Larkhall. The money was made up from the contribution of each sale of Cantassium folic acid and the damages from the libel action against Healthwatch. Also pictured are Juliet Iveson and Ronnie Harding, both born with spina bifida

£25,000 Cheque presentatiion to **ASBAH** Spina Bifida Charity in 1994

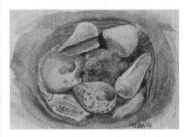

Water Colour painting by Rita Greer used on the cover of the "Health Leader" in 1994

The Old Windsor Gas Boilers were sold 1994 and removed by Harry Hollis our independent contractor

Microvitamins were first exhibited in the USA at the NNFA convention in Las Vegas in July 1994. Professor Stephen Schoenthaler attended the show and stand organised by Ella International our distributor.

225

Larkhall versus BigPharma, JunkFood Industry andBBC

Larkhall under threat –Resignation from Trade Association - Visits from BBC TV- A few favour Larkhall - Germanium - Niacin - Anti-inflammatory Medicines serious side effects - Call for control of Herbals by orthodox experts - Dirty Medicine - Health Trade knowledge deficient - Inspectorate Closing UK companies - More positive research on Diet and IQ - Advertisements by Competitors were not following the ASA Code with impunity - Journalist in trouble - The DRF IQ Supplement Trial - Larkhall range too comprehensive? - Greece still in problems - Hypocritical Competitor - Aerobic Glasses - A Staff Resignation letter - Placebo support - Government reviewing nation's Diet - Evening Primrose Oil on NHS - Health Trade leaders under fire - No funds for Pharmacist education in Nutrition - Surprise in USA - Prisoner behaviour and diet research - Garlic - Trouble for supplements in Holland - Nutraceuticals - Charities for better diets - Professor Arnold Beckett - Adverse Drug reactions - The Blacklist updated - Year ends with Positive and then Negative press coverage

Duncan Campbell seemed to be determined to destroy Larkhall The year started badly with the investigative journalist Duncan Campbell attacking and vilifying Larkhall and its brands on the BBC2 TV programme 'Food and Drink'. His methods were similar to those of MI5 where I understand he had once trained. He thought nothing of misleading to achieve the result he wanted and he had infiltrated staff at Larkhall with the help of a disgruntled ex-member of staff, as he boasted on TV programmes. These persons endeavoured to cover up their association with him but I was certain who they were and was on my guard. The letter to the trade issued by the trade sales manager about Germanium in December was probably a smokescreen. Could he have been involved in all this possibly colluding with the aggrieved ex-marketing consultant? Sadly, I think our PR consultancy Morris Media was probably being duped by the disloyal staff too.

Resignation from Trade Association Larkhall were asked to resign from the Health Food Manufacturers Association over their policies on Germanium, Niacin and Tryptophan. We did this with alacrity. I believed that without the interference of Maurice Hanssen, the association's President, Larkhall could have fought a more successful battle against Duncan Campbell instead of just caving in. Hanssen was very friendly with Peter Bazalgette the 'Food & Drink' programme maker. I thought Hannsen had little or no technical knowledge and relied on bluster -- a great weakness for a leader endeavouring to represent Health Food manufacturers, who needed scientific expertise to successfully defend themselves against the attacks of their critics at HealthWatch. I implored Hanssen to stay out of Larkhall's problems but he interfered and unfortunately only made matters worse. He totally overlooked the fact that our shop was a 'Registered Pharmacy' and therefore subject to the Royal Pharmaceutical Society rules not the HFMA's.

Although Larkhall had been praised and thanked by the HFMA for their IQ research success in 1988 it was through other members, including Seven Seas and Lifeplan, the belief was promoted that it was primarily pills that produced the results, not dietary improvement. It was the old problem that the consumer was always looking for 'the pill for every ill' and industry offered them accordingly.

226

LARKHALL GREEN FARM

Revised mail order list   A revised style of Mail Order Price list for 1991 was designed using codes for prices. This was for regular customers but most Mail Order business was generated using direct response advertisements in national press publications and in-house special mailings using the Health Examiner 3 - 4 times a year, to our full customer list. Larkhall used an outside mailing company to update the list and rent it to specified non-competitor companies when requested. Larkhall's own computer systems were fairly restricted in memory -- one gigabyte memory was quite usual at this time.

British Diet improving?   According to a National Food Survey Committee the British Diet was improving. Fifty years of reporting was showing an encouraging trend. Perhaps Larkhall's messages with the diet posters and booklets were contributing?

Two visits to Larkhall from a BBC TV Film Crew   Campbell wanted to film me as part of his anti-Larkhall film for the BBC Food and Drink programme and when he arrived on January 2nd with his film crew, the entrances to the factory were locked to keep them out. As soon as they showed up RG alerted the managers and staff. She phoned the police, who were waiting not far away so enabled them to arrive within two minutes. Campbell and his crew were taken by surprise as three squad cars appeared in Putney Bridge Road, outside the factory, in front of the shop.
   I sat it out in Annie's Room which had no windows, while RG kept me up to date by 'phone on events. She tucked up her invalid husband in bed in the flat, safely out of the way of any film crew, and went down to the shop to talk to the police. They were very supportive and promised they would not go until they were sure Campbell had left the area. They were absolutely determined he would not get into the factory. Campbell argued with them about his rights and said that as he was from the BBC it meant he could go anywhere he liked to film, including inside the factory. The police put him straight on a point of law and said he couldn't. Campbell was livid. Just to be on the safe side, the police had asked for the fire hoses to be put ready as a last resort. Having tried all the entrances, including the back door in the factory yard, and failed to get in, eventually Campbell and his crew cleared off, looking miserable. It had taken the best part of an hour. They had no film of either me or the inside of the factory. Some of the staff had been frightened by the episode, production had suffered and customers had not been able to go into the shop but Campbell and the film crew had not got into the production area. RG thanked the police as without them Campbell and his crew would surely have got in.
   A few days later they returned again. There was an Auction House opposite the factory, the other side of Putney Bridge Road. RG didn't need to 'phone the police this time as the Metropolitan Police were delivering lots for the auction that day and the place was surrounded by squad cars, unloading. Campbell and the film crew took one look and beat a hasty retreat. He had failed to film me yet again but I was actually abroad on business at the time. Campbell's Achille's heel was definitely his poor research. It was pathetic but then he seemed to invent something if his research let him down and the BBC didn't seem to mind in the least.
   RG wrote it all up in detail in the Health Examiner (No. 14). Campbell was grasping at straws to get us bad publicity. He decided the Trade Order price list was a form of advertising as it listed RG's prescription products. Ridiculous. (Prescription products were not allowed to be advertised to the public.) He seemed obsessed with the shop at the front of the Putney factory and used to send his side-kick Tim Hinks in to try and buy things and get advice from the staff.

RG would go down to shop and intervene as the staff couldn't deal with it. One man came in with a tape recorder under his blouson jacket. It was so obvious as to be laughable. Campbell described our small shop (registered as a pharmacy with counter service only) as a 'self-select' (supermarket type) shop. What rubbish! He put in other nonsensical complaints about us to various authorities that all had to be investigated. They all came to nothing but wasted our time and taxpayers' money.

Others attacked by the BBC Food & Drink programme The Food & Drink programme attacked the ION (Institute for Optimum Nutrition). The programme criticised practitioners and the ION courses and qualifications. Dr John Marks a nutritionist and former director of medical studies at Girton College Cambridge came to the defence of ION and questioned the validity and truth of the Food & Drink programme.

A sinister conspiracy? Yes Ray Hill, a well known and respected Health Store owner and writer took the BBC 'Food & Drink' programme to task over Duncan Campbell and his totally biased attitude to the Health Food Industry. He refuted Campbell's claims and asked why not ask the authorities to ban alcoholic drinks that were proven as dangerous, rather than harmless vitamins? The pressures building up against the health food producers were undoubtedly orchestrated but the question remained, who was really behind all this? These attacks cost money and Campbell and the Food and Drink programme makers must have been receiving largesse from someone. I thought my conspiracy theory might be right. So did the police.

We knew that Professor Naismith's IQ/Vitamin/schoolchildren research was funded by the World Sugar Research Corporation and that his research laboratories probably enjoyed funding from the Snack Industry. These organisations used sophisticated, costly and subtle Public Relations methods to support their industries. They were very successful. The Tobacco, Drinks and Pharmaceutical industries used similar publicity generators to promote their views. These industries have tremendous financial clout and could influence media by withdrawing advertising if they persisted in criticising their products. Many anti-vitamin stories were receiving publicity way beyond what was expected but who ensured this took place? Most good news about the benefits of a natural style of diet or modest supplementation was countered within days by a hostile 'Safety of Vitamins doubted' stories in all national newspapers - such articles were often dug out of old archives. The positive work of Cleave and Burkitt on fibre in the diet in the 1960s was systematically discredited with PR promoting their 'flawed' research.

Larkhall had been fighting for the natural approaches to healthcare for years and enjoyed such success that those opponents were now determined to stop them - no wonder many were surprised we were still in business in 1991. Tandem IQ, Tryptophan, Niacin, Germanium.....could there be more blows to come? Indeed, how could any small company survive such an onslaught? It was strange that all the products selected for adverse publicity and extra control by authorities in the UK were in Larkhall's lists. I believed this was no co-incidence but directed specifically at me and my company by outside interests who had infiltrated the Larkhall workforce. Perhaps they were using financial inducements to select the products and draw attention to possible weaknesses. This information was then used to pillory Larkhall in the UK. What seemed strange was that our products were available in many overseas countries but nothing ever appeared against them in the media there and sales were unaffected.

Duncan Campbell actually boasted on the Food and Drink Programme that he had inside information on Larkhall. He said the primary informant was an IT man who had recently left the company but was well informed on the company's computer systems. He was aided by certain Larkhall staff whose duplicity kept them in with me (through apparently supportive memos and letters).

A mail order manager who had left in late 1990 was known to be close to the IT man. The warehouse manager had reported to RG that he had seen the two of them in a local cafe in deep conversation with Duncan Campbell.

The Germanium programme that set out to destroy Larkhall   On 2nd January when Duncan Campbell and his film crew had arrived at Larkhall's shop, the shop manageress served him appropriately with Niacin after he had asked leading questions regarding its supply. He was obviously trying to set her up. Two days later Campbell informed Maurice Hanssen (President of the HFMA) that he had obtained Niacin from Larkhall's shop where it was on self-selection (help yourself like a supermarket). All lies, designed to have Larkhall thrown out of the Trade Association, so he could boast to viewers about what he had achieved, on his forthcoming programme. Campbell was not aware that the shop was a registered pharmacy and not a Health Food shop and therefore not subject to HFMA directives that had no legal basis at all.

The programme was broadcast on 15th January and was an attack specifically aimed against Larkhall and me, lasting about 12 minutes. We watched in silence. I was horrified by Campbell's script but amazed at the poor understanding of the real facts displayed by Morris Media, the PR agency, and our sales staff. The arguments to defend Larkhall were just not understood because these people had little in-depth knowledge, despite their employment with the company.

The first claim made by the programme was that Immunomega tablets contained dangerous amounts of Germanium was untrue. They contained traces of Germanium and it was definitely not the unsafe form. Indeed, Campbell had had the Immunomega tablets analysed by a trace element analytical laboratory which could not distinguish between natural and synthetic forms of Germanium.

The second claim was that Sustaniacin had been supplied freely in our shop. It had not, because the customer had been questioned about his knowledge of the product when he asked for it. It was only available from behind the counter. Niacin tablets could be legally sold by pharmacies. Because I was a qualified pharmacist, technically the shop was a pharmacy and my professional certificate was on the wall. Campbell did not know this.

Thirdly, he said Tryptophan containing supplements had been purchased at the shop. They had not, because they were not available on sale. It was likely that the products mentioned were supplied to Campbell by disloyal members of staff who were in league with him. Campbell took his complaints to the Pharmaceutical Society who confirmed the freedom of Larkhall to offer many products for sale that were not permitted for sale in Health Food Stores.

Following the programme we managed to answer all the 'dangerous' matters to the full satisfaction of all authorities. They were all nonsense. Campbell's expertise in the Food Supplement area was not good. There was no correction or apology on the next TV programme.

Another anti Niacin TV Programme   On January 28th the BBC TV Watchdog programme carried on its opposition to Dietary Supplements with a further attack on Niacin. It was well known that the Nicotinic Acid form of Vitamin B3 caused flushing in most people and that was why Nicotinamide was the preferred form of the vitamin in supplements. However, for people expecting cholesterol reduction when using supplements of this vitamin, the only form that works is nicotinic acid. Larkhall, unlike all the other manufacturers, had a Product Licence for 500mg Niacin tablets they were therefore fully entitled to make these available for general sale unless stopped by the Department of Health. Watchdog had no power to stop this but they were probably being manipulated by the HealthWatch lobby.

I said Cantassium's sustained release Niacin had not been implicated in the only reaction reported by Watchdog nor had their Licensed product. Of course, Maurice Hanssen represented the general health trade and I refused to obey his association's request for withdrawal because I saw this as a deliberate move against Larkhall, by a trade association that had no other members making 500mg Niacin tablets. As usual, the fact that Larkhall had a licence for the product was ignored by the HFMA, its President, the BBC, Watchdog and HealthWatch.

More serious side effects of ordinary over the counter medicines On 5th January the British Medical Journal carried a letter which indicated that the popular anti-inflammatory drug Ibuprofen might cause stomach and colon problems. These were closely associated with side effects from the whole anti-inflammatory drug class. Now that a commonly used 'safe' over the counter anti-inflammatory had come under this cloud I believed the case for the natural style of diet and associated products became more urgent but no doubt the Pharma Industry's PR operation ensured nothing changed.

Call for control of Herbal medicines but Pharmacists not trained in them properly
An academic pharmacist from the Chelsea School of Pharmacy (Kings College London) wrote in the Pharmaceutical Journal (5th January) calling for efforts to be made to ensure all herbal remedies were legally controlled with licensing. Pharmacists should be trained to deal with plant material but that part of their education was well behind that in Europe. He wanted herbals controlled as medicines but realised that UK pharmacists were ill equipped to adequately deal with the technicalities in this area. That inadequacy was still evident in 2015 when herbal regulation from Brussels was in operation. Enforcement of The THMPD (Herbal Directive) was poor because the MHRA employed scientists used to dealing with synthetic drugs to apply inappropriate criteria to natural medicines.

I had always argued that only persons trained and experienced in the fundamental philosophies of herbals should set the criteria and enforce law applied to herbal health practices and products. Pharmacists who were generally ignorant and inexperienced in the natural product area should not be permitted to set and enforce standards for those products. The MHRA gained no respect from the herbal movement by relying on experts from the big pharma area to act for Herbals. That was not only unjust but foolish.

Support for Pharmacists suffering from biased criticism of the Consumers Association
In early January I wrote to the Pharmaceutical Journal regarding the Consumers Association recent report on Pharmacy. I described the CA as misguided, politically motivated misfits and busybodies. I dismissed their report as worthless and was not surprised that real consumers had taken no notice. Regular customers usually find retailer's services good but the strangers from 'Which' acting suspiciously were generally unwelcome and as a result failed to be served considerately.

Recall of Sustaniacin against consumer choice Towards the end of January a Sustaniacin recall letter was sent out by our sales department on the advice of our PR agency. This indicated that Larkhall were complying with some trade bodies' requests. I thought that was unnecessary because I had zero regard for the decisions of those ill qualified bodies, whose main concern seemed to be to maintain commercial viability of most members, at the expense of safe healthcare consumer choice. Many in the Health Trade supported me and thought it courageous to fight the misinformed media like the Food & Drink and Watchdog programmes, manipulated by our enemies at HealthWatch.

'Dirty Medicine' author came to visit   At the end of January, the journalist Martin Walker visited me to talk about his forthcoming book, which reported on the activities of the Quackbusters (HealthWatch) and Duncan Campbell. The book would contain a considerable amount on Larkhall's and the Greer's experiences at the hands of these people. Walker had written extensively on contentious subjects including the Miner's Strike of 1984. His book 'Dirty Medicine' should have made an impact as soon as it was published. Walker expected serious legal opposition and dirty tricks from Campbell and his associates. When it was ready for publication it was driven underground as bookshops were afraid to display it. We had copies at Larkhall and had to take great care even giving it away.

Health Trade criticised for lack of scientific expertise. Health Food Business carried a letter from me regarding Germanium in Supplements. This letter discussed the merits of Germanium in the diet and explained that it was regularly ingested in foods/herbs like Garlic and Ginseng in very small quantities (1-1.5 mg). Larkhall had used 0.5mg, 4mg and 10mg strengths but Immunomega only contained 1mg, way below the 250mg offered by other supplement companies. This letter criticised these companies and added that too little basic scientific knowledge was the curse of the Health Food Industry. Too many were selling dreams to their customers and recommended products of which they knew nothing, apart from the price.

Competitor closed down by the Inspectors   In mid February I read that Steinhard Ltd a generic drug manufacturer in Acton had had its medicinal product manufacturer's Licence suspended by the Department of Health. This firm had been a competitor of Larkhall back in the 1970s and I was surprised that it had survived the Inspector onslaught at that time. As a company owned by Asian immigrants it may have had some advantages over the likes of historically English Larkhall. Several more generic companies followed Steinhard and it seemed a final clean-up was taking place. No doubt most of the products were now being made in Asian factories in China, India, Pakistan and Bangladesh where DHSS reciprocally recognised and local inspectorates operated. Whether this protected UK consumers better was questionable. Anyway, British jobs were lost and there was less work for the growing UK inspectorate - the expected outcome of excessive and disproportionate UK regulation by bureaucracy.

More positive IQ research from Dr Benton   In early February, Benton and Cook's paper on Supplements and IQ with six-year olds was received. This was subsequently published in Personal and Individual Differences Journal and concluded that taking supplements could help school performance in children consuming a diet high in sugar. Larkhall had sponsored the research and provided the placebo and supplement tablets.

Threats from Advertisements from competitor companies.   In early March I met an advertising agency who were running very successful mail order advertisements for some of Larkhall's competitors. I believed these ads contravened the ASA Code but they denied it. Soon after, these advertisements were withdrawn but appeared again from new companies. This agency was at the root of many of the 'Medicinal Claims' issues in the coming months.

Duncan Campbell lost a legal action to Institute of Optimum Nutrition
In March, The Correspondent Sunday newspaper paid libel damages to the Institute of Optimum Nutrition. This arose because they published a scurrilous article by Duncan Campbell about the Institute and its director Patrick Holford. The claim had been that vitamins and nutritionists were worthless and fraudulent. The ION was also suing Campbell himself over the article but he was being evasive.

231

Campbell in trouble again At the end of March, Duncan Campbell was in trouble again but this time it was concerned with Olympic gold medallist Chris Brasher and his London Marathon. Brasher was suing Campbell regarding very serious and damaging accusations of financial fraud. Chris Brasher eventually won the case that had been a scandal but not before considerable time and expense and a great deal of worry which had sadly affected his health. The BBC and New Statesman Magazine were also successfully sued. This all added to the evidence of injustice to myself and Larkhall by Campbell and his accomplices in the Media. Campbell refused to believe he had lost.

The DRF Study on Vitamins and IQ was published and generated a great deal of publicity in the national press. The impressive list of scientists involved included Professors Yudkin, Schoenthaler and Eysenk which coupled with the number of children involved in the trial made it, on the surface, the conclusive validation of the theory that many children were not receiving a wholesome diet and their school performances were thereby compromised. The administration of scientifically formulated supplements with guaranteed amounts of micronutrients overcame this dietary problem. The study had been funded by the independent 'Diet Research Foundation' but the healthfood company Bookers (Healthcrafts) were involved too and immediately launched a supplement product 'Vitachieve' with a multimillion pound advertising campaign and royalties on sales for DRF. The BBC2 QED programme were also involved throughout the research project. That was distinctly different from their involvement in the Tandem IQ research which had only started when the trial was completed. The journalist covering the programme was Tony Edwards who had directed the programme on Tandem IQ.

After the Tandem IQ success, instead of listening to my advice that recommended caution with further research, Edwards and Schoenthaler involved themselves with multinational company Bookers, who were a great many times larger than Larkhall. I am sure DRF went with them because it believed there were fortunes to be made. Larkhall was totally ignored and my counsel not even sought thereafter. Benton and Roberts may not have been high powered academics but appreciated that low profile had its advantages in the highly emotive area of children's IQs. The DRF study generated plenty of publicity including that Vitamins were the key to youngsters' IQ on the front page of the Sunday Express on February 17.

Foolishly, the DRF press conference at the Pall Mall Gentlemen's Club, (The Reform), coincided with Bookers launching their Vitachieve products. Unsurprisingly, journalists were immediately sceptical. Duncan Campbell was present and ridiculed Eysenk and Yudkin as past professors and deluded old men. Schoenthaler was a huckster if not a cowboy from the US -- all terrible accusations. Although there were some good headlines there was an immediate undercurrent; other trials had not been as positive and even the DRF study, which was supposed to have been replicated in the US and Israel as well as the UK, was incomplete. Those other countries never produced results to match those in the UK.

I suspected that commercial pressure from Bookers was probably responsible for this debacle. As a Health Food company they did not have sufficient technical/clinical knowledge to understand the dangers of a less than scientifically convincing presentation. They were soon involved with Shropshire Trading Standards and capitulated, just like Seven Seas, yet they had at least sponsored the research that was more than Seven Seas had. So Larkhall and I faced an uncertain future with our product and ideas because competitors trespassed on our land, driven by greed and served by ignorance. A golden opportunity for the whole Health Food Industry was lost and Bookers went out of the healthfood business soon after. I was disillusioned but pressed on.

232

Diet not magic pills should have been the constant message. The important point that was always overlooked was that this IQ research was not into pills but into DIET. The presenter of the first QED programme in 1988 said 'Your child's Diet on trial' and Diet was mentioned all the time and in neither programme was there mention of 'Tandem IQ' or 'Vitachieve'. Viewers and journalists latched on to the tablets because the vast majority of people see no difference between a Vitamin Pill and a prescribed one from the GP. Vitamin Pill for IQ and Antibiotic Pill for infection - it's obvious to the average consumer. I had always said the food supplements put the nutrition back into the diet in a scientific way. Properly formulated and made products were the only way to guarantee improvement in the diet nutritionally in a scientific trial. Consumers should use supplements in the interim period whilst correcting their diets. Correct the diet in line with wholesome principles and then throw away the pills. All the vitamin supplement manufacturers should take that approach. Sadly that would only happen in dreams.

Unrealistic criticism of the nutrition IQ trials must have arisen from those with a special agenda. Opponents of this nutritional research said that, to gain real credibility, blood levels of all the nutrients used in the proposed test tablets must be measured in all participants before the start and during the trial. They never specified how many times and you could be sure that once would not be enough - probably ten at least - never mind the costs or the discomfort of the participants. In addition the trial must be performed by others and gain identical results. Yet for the 'Experts' on the Food & Drink programme that would never have been enough to satisfy them and HealthWatch - they would find faults unless the trial was negative and performed by their friends such as chain smoking Professors. Let's ignore the fact that it was well known that many vitamins affect the brain and foods lose vitamin content during storage and cooking.

Common sense dictated that supplemental benefit must be positive in the modern world where junk foods were the reality. Additionally, childrens' behaviour and performance at school would inevitably improve. I believed that only those with a special agenda would attempt to argue against this.

Comprehensive product range was essential In early April my brother circulated a memo to managers because he was desperate to reduce the range of products stocked by Larkhall. A new computer system was producing what he thought was good data to prove the rightness of his case to drastically reduce the range. Several of the products were already marked for deletion but many were essential to the business with potential. For instance Folic Acid 500mcg which by 1993 with its strength slightly reduced to 400mcg then sold in millions of tablets per month and spearheaded the Microvitamin Range. Sadly, he demonstrated by this memo that he knew little about the philosophy behind the Larkhall business but his attitude could drive us to foolish decisions if we became beholden to the 'System'. I fought this memo aided by the sales staff at the sharp end. It was because of our comprehensive and relevant range that Larkhall had credibility and a service that was appreciated by its retailers and consumers.

Problems in Greece persisted In mid April I had correspondence with the EU in Brussels regarding the ongoing problems with diet supplement distribution in Greece. I helped Maria Strofalis with the dispute but visits to Mr Mattera the head of the EU department in Brussels dealing with 'Elimination of restrictions on the free movement of goods' were never successful. The safety and technical issues associated with medicines were applied to diet supplements by the Greek Authorities because they did not legally recognise 'Diet Supplements' as existing as a product category. A Directive on Diet Supplements was promulgated in the late 90s but its implementation was still delayed in many countries in 2015 because of safety issues.

Criticism of the IQ research from competitor rejected as hypocritical I wrote to Health Food Business regarding the criticism of the IQ/Vitamin research by a competitor. This company marketed the supplement product Zincold that was a very controversial and poorly researched product to treat colds. I considered it was very hypocritical of this company's director to 'preach to others from the heavenly heights'.

Aerobic Glasses threatened with legal action In mid May Mr Martin,a Trading Standards officer from Birmingham, visited Larkhall and intended a prosecution against the Pin Hole Glasses that we imported from USA. The USA trade mark was 'Aerobic Glasses' which were used for exercising the eyes by the well established Bates method to help overcome specified eyesight problems. If used successfully they enabled many people to see without prescription spectacles. 'See better Naturally' was the headline of the advertisement with which the officer took issue. I thought I could answer satisfactorily but the man made it all official - he was out of order because he had not discussed his visit or complaint with the local TSOs in Wandsworth as he should. I am sure this was yet another set-up against Larkhall with the Opticians Professional Organisation behind the scenes. I had made a serious error seeing Martin. However another company, using advertising agency, Lavery and Rowe, offered these glasses and were being taken to court by Birmingham TSOs. They lost their case. I foolishly decided to fight because I believed that the Aerobic Glasses were useful and effective and knew that the Optical Profession was concerned that they saw these natural approaches to eye health as a threat to their monopoly. At first, I was guaranteed support from some optical professionals but as the case progressed most of them timidly vanished. I took the blame for the marketing copy we used because I would not have any of our staff or agency implicated - the buck stopped with me.

Happily, on 19th July we received a very positive testimonial for the Aerobic Glasses, which had come under scrutiny of Birmingham Trading Standards, goaded by the optical profession who were deeply opposed to the use of these exercise glasses. Larkhall were singled out for attack and were to be engaged in a costly dispute with the authorities despite the harmlessness of the glasses and their undoubted benefit to many people.

A suspicious letter of resignation received. I early June, I received an interesting letter from a sales representative who was resigning. On first reading this seemed a genuine letter but in hindsight it was very different. The lady concerned was working in Scotland - a large area with few healthfood shops. Sales were never exceptional and the overhead costs in car wear and fuel were heavy. She probably calculated that declining sales were not likely to help job retention. She wrote the letter to me not her immediate boss, it was two pages long written in biro with no corrected errors. It was effusive in its praise for her boss and his office manager. However she made a case for declining sales blaming 'adverse media publicity'. Overall, the letter made such a wonderful case for her boss and his department as to be unbelievable. With benefit of later experience of the trade sales department, I thought this letter was probably written under duress from her boss to cement his hold on his position at Larkhall. The points she made would be excellent to support his defence should he be dismissed and also work to his advantage in retaining his job, which happened.

Placebo debate going mainstream The Journal of the Royal Society of Medicine published a paper by Alfred Tauber (Boston University School of Medicine) regarding physicians and placebos. The placebo debate had raged for many years and there was still no adequate reason to condemn placebo treatments except that medical training made them impossible for doctors to prescribe because they were taught that placebos were ineffective. To prescribe something they 'know' to be ineffective would be a betrayal of patient trust and contrary to their professionalism. Such a problem did not arise for alternative practitioners who had total belief and trust in their treatments.

Government said to be reviewing UK diet In mid July, The Sunday Times reported on a new government review of the UK diet. This indicated that too much sugar/starch and saturated fat was harming the nation's health. However the food industry reacted quickly with the Sugar Bureau planning a positive view of its products in an advertising campaign. Meanwhile the Meat Industry blamed the Dairy Industry's products for most of the extra fat. Larkhall continued its efforts by continuing to give away its Diet Posters (Approved by an independent body) and its 'Healthier eating for School Children' booklets. The Cantassium Dietary System had advocated a balanced wholefood diet since 1921. Rita Greer's book 'The British Food Fiasco', which highlighted these problems in 1984, was still in print but had had a rough ride from the Junk Food Industry who 'persuaded' booksellers such as WH Smith not to stock it. She still managed to sell all 4,000 copies, including a few to government departments, dietitians and the Royal Navy. (it is still available second hand from Amazon, on the Internet.)

Evening primrose oil on NHS prescription In mid June I wrote to Dr A Li Wan Po, a lecturer at Queen's University Belfast, who had been writing a series of articles for the Pharmaceutical Journal on Dietary Supplements. I agreed with Po's assessment of Evening Primrose Oil was the only true diet supplement to have gained a Medicinal Product Licence from the Department of Health. This had given the licence holder Scotia Pharmaceuticals a boost to their finances and I suspected that pressure of some sort had been applied to officials by Dr Horrobin the owner of Scotia and the man RG had reported to the police for threatening her with a concrete overcoat when she wouldn't take a bribe from him. His name had cropped up since 1976 in connection with EPO and its medicinal properties. Efamol, one of his companies, had marketed it aggressively in the late 70s for PMT (Premenstrual Tension). This upset many in organisations similar to HealthWatch and when the medicinal licence was issued for Breast Soreness and Eczema, most doctors/GPs prescribed it for PMT. This was technically illegal since that was not a permitted claim on the licence. Many generic EPOs such as Gammolin by Larkhall became available on prescription because Gammolenic Acid was the generic substance equivalent to the licensed Epogam/Efamast. Evening Primrose Oil (King's Cure All) lost its medicinal licence when reviewed in the early 2000s because it was considered ineffective and so was no longer permitted on NHS prescription. It may be remembered that EPO first reached prominence in the mid 1970s as helpful to Multiple Sclerosis patients but was rejected for NHS prescription.

Health Trade leaders criticised Towards the end of June I wrote to Health Food Business Magazine criticising the Health Trade leaders who were welcoming a government report on supplements from the Denner committee. I also castigated some old established Herbal companies who had been fortunate to obtain licences for their products and had attempted to obtain monopolies.

A fairly long established company had an attitude that dismayed me. Newton's Traditional Remedies used an advertisement, in National Media, for its licensed herbal slimming product that was illegal. It broke many rules in the CAP Code and in its defence the company stated that it could do this because its product was licensed. This did not protect Newtons because they had not submitted their advertisement to the Department of Health's licensing authority before use. The rules of the licensing authority were stricter than those of the CAP code. The advertisement was withdrawn.

Athens and Rome At the end of June I had attended the Latin and Mediterranean Group of Sports Medicine 17th Congress in Athens. Invited by Greek Distributor Maria Strofalis. It was much the same as the Balkan congresses I had attended. The Greek Prime Minister was present. Afterwards I travelled on to Rome to discuss expansion of the PN business in italy.

Representational problems The reduction of our UK Trade Sales force stimulated a look at the broker/representation possibilities. A Sales and Marketing Brokerage were approached. They claimed to visit 2500 Independent Chemists on an 8 weekly cycle by 8 representatives equating on a five day week to 7 calls a day. All seemed OK but I wanted to incentivise them to increase the business. We were already doing core business with independents and if we gave them this at the full rate of commission we could lose out. Experience showed that new business was difficult to obtain but the core just went on and on with little representation other than a friendly 'phone call. No way could such a deal be accepted by the broker but in desperation we went ahead anyway. A couple of years later no progress had been made by this company. I believed the range of 10 products was too complicated for the quality of representatives they used, later we found these salesmen were not actually employees but freelance agents who often did not divulge all their interests to their managers. I thought the sales manager had not researched their capabilities. Was this an endemic problem with all these brokers? Yes probably, yet stupidly we still persisted.

Our sales people had asked for the introduction of bulk packs of some of our products such as Dolomite, Yeast, Kelp and popular vitamins. These would greatly help overall sales they said, and gain business in gyms and sports clubs. In the event it was another failure. Why did I listen to these people?

Government report on Diets welcomed but did it do any good? Mid July and "Eating for a healthier life" was the headline in the leading medical journal 'The Lancet' to report the publishing of a new COMA report from Government. This report ranged over many important aspects of nutrition and health. Sadly, the dietary intakes of vitamins and minerals were presented in consumer confusing RDAs (Recommended Daily Amounts), DRVs (Dietary Reference Values), EARs (Estimated Average Requirements) and RNIs (Reference Daily Intakes). As a professional document this report should have proved useful in producing sound dietary advice to the population.

The Pharmaceutical Journal also welcomed the report and quoted the Government's Chief Medical Officer "This report is a recipe for a whole diet for a population, nutrients in it derived from an infinite variety of different foods.....prescribed the nutrient composition of a range of diets..... expected to reduce the burden of illness and death from a number of diseases related to diet... including coronary heart disease and some cancers".
Looking back it is disappointing that so little progress has been made in the twenty plus years since this report was published.

No funding for nutrition education of Pharmacists At the end of July, I reacted to a small note in the Pharmaceutical Journal that noted no funding was available to add 'Nutrition Education' to a Pharmacist's post graduate training.

In my letter I bemoaned the lack of nutrition education in undergraduate pharmacy courses. I now hoped this would change but suspected that dietitians would oppose pharmacists taking an interest in what they deemed as their specialist area. Dietitians were not expert in chemistry and feared that pharmaceutically trained chemists could pose a threat to them. Unfortunately many pharmacists believed that improving nutrition of patients might diminish their commercial dependence on OTC and prescribed medicines, so threatening the pharmacy business.

There was too much professional rivalry in Healthcare, often not understood by politicians or patients. I went on to take the example of bran in the diet lessening sales of traditional laxatives and hinted that bran is the tip of the nutrition iceberg. Proper knowledge of nutrition could transform the health of the population. Doctors may have been the worst offenders.

Take the example of Larkhall's product Ruthmol as a pharmacy product not sold in supermarkets because retail pharmacy was thought better suited to sell a genuine salt substitute after, hopefully, Doctor recommendation. A nutritional product beneficially used by patients with high blood pressure who might ask for the professional advice to reduce their dependence on blood pressure lowering tablets with unpleasant side effects. Subsequently, in September, the secretary of The Nutrition Society wrote to the PJ agreeing with me and intimated they were doing something positive in the area. What?

The PJ, surprisingly, published this letter on August 24 but over twenty years later little has changed. Pharmacists persist in selling drugs and take little interest in nutrition. Of course Doctors lead the way with their pill-for-every-ill prescriptions and extra pills prescribed to counteract the side effects of the first prescription. A crazy situation that costs patient's health and taxpayers money.

A surprise ending to my annual USA trip   In late July I went to Las Vegas for the NNFA Convention where I was joined by Anna and Marcello Maugeri from PN. I flew on to Los Angeles where I met Allen Jensen from Gold Stake in Pasadena. His company claimed to be mining an extensive area in the hills for a comprehensive mineral refined carefully to provide a unique consistent balance of essential micronutrient minerals. The Gold Stake product was being researched and had properties that Jensen said might help sufferers from various degenerative ailments. A booklet was available. I asked to be kept informed of progress in the clinical trials so that claims could be made.

I met Madame Runge author of 'Facelifting by Exercise' a book that Larkhall sold successfully in the UK. She was interested in marketing her new skin care range in Europe. I offered help but this range was never developed for overseas markets. I never even saw samples. RG met her a few years later and said she was the most wrinkled woman she had ever seen -- no advertisement for skincare.

Lastly, I visited David Jenkins, the British Olympic Athlete who had set up a sports supplement business in the USA. He was apparently doing very well and hoped to export to Europe. Soon after my visit, there was a scandal surrounding his company's involvement with anabolic steroids and synthetic boosters for athletes. Fortunately, I came away unscathed.

Hyperactivity and prisoner behaviour research continued   Early August saw an article in The Times by Liz Hodgkinson about the connection between hyperactivity in children and diet. Several academics were interviewed and the complexity of the theories became apparent. I knew Dr Brostoff, Professor Bryce-Smith and Bernard Gesch who were using food approaches to the problem of hyperactivity. Brostoff researched allergy/sensitivity to foods and was very concerned about synthetic food additives. Natural fresh foods with no additives or pesticide residues were best.

Bryce Smith believed in mineral deficiency of zinc and chromium as major causes of hyperactivity whilst Gesch was working with Bryce Smith on a good diet and supplementation to help young criminals and prevent re-offending. Over twenty years later we are no nearer to a solution to these problems but there is little doubt that poor diet with too much sugar and additives aggravates matters. It seems probable that there is no single diet that will work for all those affected but the more naturally based and wholesome diet is better for all.

Coincidentally, a Police Superintendent Peter Bennett was interviewed on Breakfast TV about improving behaviour of young offenders through diet. This research on nine children was seeking authority support in 'Nutritional crime prevention' and was described by interviewer Angela Rippon as innovative. At least the Superintendent admitted this was all very complex.

I read the transcript of the programme (4 minutes) and agreed that the work was innovative but doubted whether nine children who would all be treated individually with various dietary exclusions and supplements would produce results of scientific significance. It seemed all too scatter gun and the number of participants too small. Bernard Gesch at Natural Justice was involved with this work and later contacted Schoenthaler and me to help him. He obtained some support from the Home Office but never produced definitive significant results. I heard little more from him - funding his research caused problems. The finances required for this research would be millions of pounds and funders would need assurances regarding the researchers and their proposed methods. I tended to believe no one would succeed in this apparently worthwhile endeavour.

The ideas are simple but biochemical individuality has to be taken into account in this area with treatments individualised - probably impossible in the real world. Much better to put these children/young offenders on the additive free plus a low sugar regimen and see they stick to it. That's far from impossible.

Garlic latest In mid August Garlic received a guarded review of its benefits in the British Medical Journal. Whilst it had a long history of herbal medicinal use going back to 1500BC, modern science had not found convincing proof of effectiveness. Quantitative variability of ingredient content and stability were proving difficult hurdles to surmount. Germany had the largest market where garlic items were the best selling over the counter herbal products. The social problem associated with the odour of allicin and other breakdown substances derived from Garlic was often seen as a problem by consumers. The German company that owned the top selling garlic product Kwai added some very positive research details in the BMJ of 28th September. This was commercial research and had a credibility problem with academia. However, it was likely to ensure continuing consumer demand for garlic as a preventative for heart problems.

Marketing problems for Larkhall distributor in Holland At the end of August, I was in Holland to visit Nutrivital and the Health and Beauty show (Indro) in Utrecht. I met Mr Pol (a multimillionaire entrepreneur) from Monaco who was marketing a specialist range of Diet Supplements with Nutrivital. He was using TV commercials to promote his products (examples are in the archive at HAT). I thought the content of the commercials was too medicinal and was surprised they were permitted for broadcast. I was right, this project started well but the Dutch Authorities were soon actively fighting against the products. They became non-viable and Nutrivital experienced a set back.

Nutraceuticals In August, The Times carried an article looking at the market for Nutraceuticals that it described as functional foods or psychoactive drinks that fall in a category between drugs and food including dietary supplements.

I preferred to define Nutraceuticals as ingredients of nutritional value but neither drugs nor vitamins/minerals. The area was a grey one. Authorities were evasive about them and one, the Advertising Standards Authority, would not answer questions on Nutraceuticals. ASA referred people to the Pharmaceutical Society or the Medicines Regulator, neither of which would give definitive replies. Grey areas are always fruitful commercially because regulation required that a definition existed in order to apply legalese.

Charitable and self funded bodies in the better diet area. In September an article in Marketing Magazine highlighted the efforts of pressure groups opposed to many aspects of the Food Industry especially junk food, high sugar and fat. There were several independent groups at work including:-
'The Coronary Prevention Group' promoted a healthy national diet.
'Parents for Safe Food' unadulterated food for all,
'Compassion in World Farming' against factory farming and live export of animals,
'Action and Information on Sugars' cutting refined sugar in the diet to prevent tooth decay and obesity (why not diabetes too?).
'National Food Alliance' the well known food writer Geoffrey Cannon headed this general organisation against cheap foods marketed as good.
'Baby Milk Action' promoted breast feeding,
'Food Commission' sprang from the GLC funded London Food Commission and was close to government in its efforts to empower consumers and look behind the marketing hype.

Some of these groups survive in 2015 but the advent of the Food Standards Authority in 2000 had made them less known.

Adverse reactions from OTC remedies On 12th October, The Pharmaceutical Journal carried information about Iatrogenic (drug induced) Disease as a cause of Hospital admissions. Adverse reactions to prescribed and over the counter remedies were common but in this article it was calculated that 3.3% of such reactions led to hospital admission. This was significant because the research had been carried out in a government establishment in Cambridge.

Black List updated with more alternative products permitted. The Black List of products banned from NHS prescribing that was set up in 1985 had been updated again. The Daily Express carried the news under the headline 'Beans are what the doctor ordered'. This referred to baked beans having been prescribed by some GPs but it appeared that only a few tins had ever been prescribed. Most herbal medicines and nutritional supplements were already banned but in this review three more herbals and four supplements were now permitted (excluded from the list).

Norway In mid October, I went to Oslo to meet with technical experts at a company that wished to import Tandem IQ tablets. Their demands for information made me suspicious that they were seeking details of our manufacturing methods. A product copy was likely and I abandoned the idea of exporting to them. This illustrated the importance of me acting as the export sales representative. A salesman with little technical expertise would have spent weeks or even months trying to set up Tandem IQ in Norway with no chance of success.

I met Professor Arnold Beckett at the Olympic Sports Medicine Congress in Barcelona At the end of October I went to Barcelona for the pre Olympic Sports Medicine congress with Maria Strofalis and Professor Drangan. By chance Professor Arnold Beckett was a participant and I sought him out. Beckett had been my PhD supervisor at Chelsea College, London and was the founder of many organisations involved in Drug Doping in Sport.

Beckett was supervising Dr Michael Beaven when he discovered that the metabolites of amphetamine could be separated and analytically quantified using paper chromatography. It was this discovery that led Beckett's research department to worldwide recognition and fame. I took Beckett out for dinner and found that in his retirement he had become somewhat sceptical about the future of big Pharma. He knew of my business in alternative healthcare and my advocacy of an open minded approach to its many aspects; the efficacy of placebo, vitamin supplementation, holism and many herbal areas. Beckett confirmed his interest in all these so I told him about all I had been through this year with the Food & Drink Programme and Trading Standards with Tandem IQ. He was very interested in the Tandem IQ case and I invited him to Putney to view the evidence and recordings of the critical TV programmes.

Beckett's enthusiasm for alternative health care successfully kindled Soon after our meeting in Barcelona, Professor Beckett came to Putney. He viewed the TV programmes. After seeing them he was very angry at the injustice suffered by Larkhall and offered his help in fighting what he said was the ignorant opposition. He also accepted, for the first time ever, that vitamin and mineral supplements could be of real benefit to the health of apparently well nourished individuals. He telephoned Professor Naismith from Larkhall and challenged him to a TV debate to defend his negative research on Vitamins and IQ. Naismith refused. I offered to send Beckett to the USA to meet Professor Schoenthaler, help work out a strategy for the future and hopefully defend Larkhall in the pending court case in Shropshire.

I had ignited Beckett's enthusiasm in the Natural Healthcare area but sadly he was soon to become allied with other health food companies, one of which later claimed, quite wrongly, to have been the first to kindle Beckett's interest in the area and used his name to spearhead their brand. Even after he had died they kept on using his name and photograph in their advertisements. Another used him to back the use of propolis (Bee Glue) in the licenced medicine area. I told him they would never get a licence for propolis because it could not be standardised or scientifically specified to the satisfaction of the Medicines regulators. He took no notice.

Medicines Manufacturing Licence received On 6th November we received a Medicinal product manufacturer's licence over 5 years after the application. It was still not correct but nothing changed for Larkhall who continued to produce its product range. I was convinced that the inefficiency of bureaucracies was endemic yet unrecognised by the political class that continued to call for more regulation, despite the bureaucracies being unable to deal with the laws already enacted.

Lipcote branded within Aquamaid This autumn, Lipcote was still progressing and the emphasis on Aquamaid branding for the product associated with a Boots promotion was aimed at range development. Advertising of Lipcote was increased and point of sale counter/till displays holding 24 packs enabled competitive pricing and attractive deals for retailers. Commercially Lipcote was still our leading product but making it spearhead our beauty range diversification successfully still eluded us.

Positive press articles   The December issue of 'Woman and Home', an up-market women's magazine, carried a comprehensive guide to supplementation by a well known nutritionist, Kathryn Marsden. This was a useful article and had a balanced approach that would appeal to many consumers. There was a list of mail order suppliers given at the end of the article and Cantassium Supplements were in the product montage photo heading the piece. A not dissimilar article appeared in the Magazine 'Top Sante' indicating the increasing interest in vitamin and mineral dietary supplementation.

On 26th December, a leader in The Times headed 'Red Wine with Everything' was apposite. It highlighted cholesterol and a Finnish study that indicated high cholesterol was not a cause of heart disease if high levels were accompanied by protective dietary micronutrients. The benefit of the Mediterranean diet was not its lack of cholesterol but its high levels of protective antioxidants Vitamins C, E and Betacarotene (Vitamin A precursor) that prevented its oxidation. Looking objectively, the writer then went on to consider genetic illness and diet. Darwinism indicated that genetics favoured survival and reacted to lifestyle changes that threaten survival. Hence, if no drugs were administered to sufferers from heart disease caused by cholesterol then soon genetics would ensure that was overcome through natural selection of those on the Mediterranean diet. Drugs that lower cholesterol interfered with natural selection and evolution. That must apply to all illnesses and so all medical treatments interfere with evolution and weaken the gene pool. No wonder cancer, heart disease, diabetes and allergies rise all the time.

The writer of this leader believed that genetic engineering could be used to overcome this problem by artificially adapting the human genome to enable survival on the synthetic fatty/sugary junk food diets. It seemed to me that we had boarded an everlasting treadmill, adapting our bodies to artificially made hazards. Nice work for the boys in the lab for sure. The new science of 'Epigenetics' could be the future.

Top doctors condemn alternative medicine 29th December, The Sunday Times published a piece by Neville Hodgkinson, its Science Correspondent, under the headline 'Top doctors condemn alternative medicine'. Apparently the Royal College of Physicians, one of the most respected and prestigious medical colleges, had produced a wide ranging controversial draft report in response to the increasing public disillusionment with orthodox medicine. This was so critical of alternative treatments that the draft had been withdrawn because of protests from many people associated with those treatments including Homoeopaths, Acupuncturists and Physicians who use alternative approaches to complement orthodox practices when treating patients with allergies, ME etc. One Doctor stated that "the report was so negative about everything, it made it all unbelievable. I am not against people trying to root out unacceptable practices, but this report goes far beyond that".

The report was withdrawn but appeared sometime later considerably toned down. No doubt HealthWatch supporters were likely to have been involved in all this. I had always opined that that body was totally biased against the alternatives and blinkered as regards its own fallibility.

Forced Out   The Police had advised Rita Greer and her husband Alan to move away from the Putney factory as they couldn't guarantee their safety. They had made efforts to protect the couple but couldn't keep on doing that. So, the Greers went to live in Hampshire. This made difficulties with RG's Trufree QC work and enquiries but there was no alternative. The flour samples for testing had to be posted to her and it meant she was not on hand at the factory for problems with its manufacture or see customers who needed help. It was over a year before they ventured back when things seemed to have quietened down.

A Health Food retailer reviewed 1991   A final piece by Harry Masterton-Smith on the trials and tribulations in the Health Food Business. He mentioned many things but Larkhall had a mention that was sympathetic and echoed my views on the trade associations.

Courage and Courts

Principles before profit - Gluten Free Standards still in doubt - Probiotic problems - GP to Media guru - Supplement range reduced - Brighton Pharmacy School introduce Nutrition module - Time magazine highlights Vitamin power - Paracetamol danger I am proved right - Inspectors threaten close down - European and International supplement threats - Research Medical men fall foul of HealthWatch - Boom time for vitamins in Holland - Upgrade for Putney production facility - Evening Primrose Oil Licensed as a Medicinal - Dr Hans Eysenk - Aerobic Glasses Case Key Witness Deserts - Two court cases within a month - Sympathy and dismissal - Cross Country running races sponsored - New Consultant - Nanny State - Italian takeover - Balanced diet not well defined - School Dinners and Hyperactivity - Supplement research in Elderly discredited - Regulatory pressure from Europe - Garlic defined as a Nutraceutical - Duncan Campbell faced a Libel action - Health Foods backed by US Senator - TUA for Passive Exercise - Nutritional Integrators - Magic Mushrooms

This was another interesting year for Larkhall. The Shropshire and Birmingham trading standards cases took up much of my time. I was determined to fight both cases because they were important for the future freedom of alternative health care. Larkhall could have saved money pleading guilty on agreed terms as other companies did but that would have been cowardly and put **profits before principles**. I felt the battle against injustice had to be fought.

Auberon Waugh and the Literary Review   In early January, I wrote to Auberon Waugh, the Editor of The Literary Review and Way of the World columnist on The Daily Telegraph, regarding a recent piece he had written, "More Medical Notes", concerning the excesses of the NHS. His views coincided with mine.

Let's Live   Let's Live magazine in the USA started the year with an editorial indicating that preventive health care principles had come of age in 1991. Time Magazine (USA) had a story in November 1991 entitled **'The New Age of Alternative Medicine'**. This article said the emphasis on crisis management in Health Care with the prescription of Drugs and Surgery must be changed to preventive ongoing lifestyle practices including diet aided by supplementation.

Overseas companies have unfair advantage over UK ones   Health Food Business published several letters regarding the inability of manufacturers to make medicinal claims for unlicensed products. One from me but another from Ray Hill who rightly castigated 'Training Digest' for publicising a treatment sponsored by a USA supplement company. It was a company who frequently used their USA promotional pieces in the UK. They hoped this was a way round the law, and because they were an overseas company they were not prosecuted. Presumably they said, "sorry, but our staff used the legal in US items in error". A UK company would not get away with it. This made for very unfair competition.

I rejoined International Generics   In January I lunched with Leon Tamman at his office in Portland Street. Some years before I had been a non-executive director of Tamman's pharmaceutical company International Generics but had resigned. I agreed to rejoin and help Tamman with product licensing.

LARKHALL GREEN FARM

The Gluten Free market still suspect   At the end of January The Chemist & Druggist published letters regarding 'Gluten Free Diets and Coeliacs'. One from Rita Greer supported the use of 100% Gluten Free flours and breads, she pointed out that doctors and pharmacists permitted many Coeliacs to be supplied with 'Low Gluten' products without them realizing. Yet ingestion of even traces of gluten by a coeliac could have devastating consequences for their health.

The Parliamentary Group on Complementary medicine   At the end of January I attended a regular meeting of the Parliamentary group on Complementary Medicine. Many MPs were present with various alternative health representatives but nothing constructive resulted. This group was a talking shop with little clout so far as the authorities were concerned.

Former GP moved to media guru and industrial employment   In early February 'You' the magazine published with the 'Mail on Sunday' carried an article by a former GP that extolled the benefits of supplements. It covered ten items such as multivitamins and minerals, garlic and fish oil - then looked favourably at Ginkgo, Ginseng, Blue Green Algae, Royal Jelly, Aloe Vera and Propolis. This doctor subsequently became a vitamin guru in the media and worked exclusively for a supplement mail order company on the Channel Islands.

HealthWatch and probiotic supplements   Problems were experienced in the trade when HealthWatch took an interest in Probiotic capsules and tablets. Many products were analysed by a hospital laboratory, found to contain few bacteria and often the incorrect species. Our supplier was prompted to advise labeling changes on Natudophilus capsules that Larkhall also applied to their Cantassium Acidophilus tablets. These products had not been criticised by the testers.

Greek distributor in Brussels again   I wrote to Mr Mattera at the European Commission to support our Greek Distributor, Maria Strofalis, following my visit to Mattera's department with Maria on 15th January. We had seen a member of the department but made no progress. Maria still failed to appreciate that officially Greece did not want to import supplements. It classified Diet Supplements as Medicines so that it could prevent import unless a medicines licence existed for the particular product. Some of Larkhall's products had licences, but not all. Sadly, some of the most successful -- for example Evening Primrose Oil, Hair Nutrition, Cantamega 2000 -- did not and those gave Maria problems with the authorities in Greece. She would not give Greek officials an'incentive' and that didn't help her. I thought it unlikely that Mattera could change the situation because Europe wide agreements would be required and negotiations would take years.
 An example of the difficulties surrounding supplements in Greece was Super HN (Hair Nutrition) that was the best selling Cantassium supplement in Greece. However, the regulators were always trying to prevent its success because our distributor Vital Hellas, owned by Maria Strofalis, continued to refuse paying incentives to officials. Unfortunately, the regulations in Greece were so incomprehensible that many meetings in Brussels were needed to maintain Cantassium's market in that country. Frequent formulation changes were necessary to keep the product on the market.

Food Supplement range threatened   I answered problems arising in the retail trade caused by Larkhall reducing its product range.

Whilst the matters ostensibly emanated from the Northern England sales representative, it was probably drawn up in close co-operation with the sales manager. Several US firms with very large product ranges were trying to penetrate the UK market. However, they all experienced problems with their labeling not being compliant with UK regulations and soon withdrew low demand items. In my reply I emphasised that our sales people must make retailers understand the legislative burden that surrounded supplements. It meant the viability of many products no longer existed. The company had a long term plan to ensure its future in a trade that was becoming evermore competitive.

Deleting items had its hidden costs but I was confident that our computer system analysis of monthly data would accurately assess these. Unfortunately, you cannot please all the people all the time and our sales representatives were almost impossible to please at any time. They were always looking for excuses as to why they could not sell up to target and not qualify for bonuses. As Monty said when he took over the eighth army in the desert, "I'll have no bellyaching". I felt the same at Larkhall.

MPs show interest   By the end of February, the efforts of Larkhall to protect the Health Food trade from oppressive legislation seemed to be producing results when MPs Tim Sainsbury and Paul Marland became interested. A later letter indicated that a draft directive on food supplements had been proposed and sent to Brussels for consideration. It is worth noting that a directive was partially agreed in 2009 but is still under debate in 2015. A unified European market for supplements appeared as far away as ever and was not a priority for bureaucrats. The overriding problem was interpretation of the word 'safety' in each country and would probably never be solved by any law.

Action against Allergy   The spring issue of Allergy Newsletter published by AAA (Action Against Allergy), the small charity run by Amelia Nathan Hill, well known to me. The Newsletter was typical of its genre and supported alternative treatments. Amelia's support for Dr Richard Mackarness the author of 'A little of what you fancy' was legendary. The Newsletter was dependent for survival on advertising including Larkhall's.

ICP   The March issue of 'The Independent Community Pharmacist' carried an article on Vitamins & Minerals including my views on the intransigence of pharmacists in not embracing nutritional approaches to health including use of supplements. My efforts trying to change this situation through a link with Brighton University Pharmacy School were noted.

University Pharmacy Course on Nutrition   I agreed to give the occasional lecture and support some relevant research project. On 6th March I visited Brighton University School of Pharmacy to lecture on vitamins and supplements. This was part of the newly introduced nutrition education module for undergraduate pharmacists.

US Media liked supplements   US magazine Let's Live published a piece 'What to look for in a Multivitamin'. It noted that a lay person could be confused by too much technical jargon. Health Foods Business, the trade USA publication, carried an article for consumer education talking about the compound formulations. Although not easy for a consumer to follow, there was a pay off line 'Spending a little today on supplements for maintenance may save you much in reduced health care costs later, just as doing maintenance on your car keeps it running efficiently'.

In early April, 'Time' Magazine of USA published a very favourable cover story with a six page article entitled 'The real power of Vitamins'. a secondary headline read "...more important than Doctors thought in warding off Cancer, Heart Disease and ravages of aging......and you might not be getting enough.......in your diet".

This article in this prestigious weekly magazine caused a furore from the opposition but was certainly pertinent to Larkhall who were due in the Shropshire court in six months. The International version of Time still had the story on the cover.

In early December the UK version of Reader's Digest magazine informed me that it would be carrying a condensed version of the TIME magazine vitamin article. This was very positive and would make a constructive contribution to the supplement debate.

Exports threatened by inspectors This was a typical example of how inspectors could waste time with unnecessary red tape. Their ignorance of business and sensible procedures was legendary. On 28th of April a two days inspection at our Charlbury facility had angered my brother when the inspectors said that printing only the product code rather than a batch number for a non-medicinal product on individual blisters was insufficient and contrary to the Guide to Good Manufacturing Practice which they had to enforce for medicines. We were asked if there was a copy at Charlbury but there was not. It was kept in Putney and used by the laboratory there. They then wrote a few days later that the matter had been referred to the Licensing Section officials. No doubt they expected us to be closed down but nothing happened immediately or subsequently, presumably because the product involved was not a medicinal. Our product names varied from country to country but the product code remained the same - it was impossible to pack very small quantities to please every overseas market. A batch number could always be found on the carton enclosing the blisters.

I had a letter published in National media. On 21st April a letter from me was published in the Daily Mail where I put my favourite argument for alternative medicine - The Royal College of Physicians had just reported on the dangers of alternative treatments. I argued that it is the failure of orthodox medicine, even when free, to satisfy patients that led them to the alternatives which exist on meagre resources, whilst the NHS absorbed colossal human resources and costs tax payers billions.

Anadin and paracetamol dangers In April I wrote to the Pharmaceutical Journal about the recent grant of a variation to the licence for leading analgesic brand 'Anadin' to enable extension to a family of products. I castigated the officials for permitting this because it would lead to consumer confusion. Anadin was associated with a unique formula of particular chemicals and line extension, using different chemicals or even different strengths, should not be allowed. I sarcastically observed that I had no doubt the bureaucrats had examined technical minutiae but had missed the real problem with this product extension proposal. (published May 9)

Incredibly, in July there was a coroner's report on an **accidental death** caused by confusion arising from one formula of Anadin becoming five different products. Common sense and I were right, bureaucrats wrong. They now had a death on their hands -- disgraceful, but how many officials involved were sacked? None.

An article by Dr J Spooner regarding Paracetamol overdose dangers was of interest in connection with the Anadin error by officials.

Classification of food supplements as medicines in Europe may become reality after December Threats to vitamin supplements were referred to by the 'European Magazine' at the end of May. The article highlighted recent pressure on the distribution of Vitamin C pills. Pharmacists insisted that they should be the sole retail source for Vitamin C because of its many dangerous side effects. No reference was made to the situation in France where supermarkets were selling Vitamin C supplements very successfully and depriving Pharmacies of their monopoly.

The attack from pharmacists was totally unjustified but court cases were in course of resolution. France had always classified supplements as medicines to increase their tax-take and would continue to fight for this to apply throughout the single market after the December opening of that 'Free' market.

Seminar in Verona highlighted the supplement dilemma in Europe In early May I went to Verona for the Herbora Exhibition to see PN. I attended the EHPM (European Health Products Manufacturers) meeting where Mrs Strofalis made a presentation about her problems with the Greek authorities. She was very unwell and was only in Verona for two days. I endeavoured to help her as much as possible.

Publications helped provide independent information for supplement users. Let's Live Magazine published a column by Dr Earl Mindell which covered benefits from specific supplements such as Selenium, Garlic and Vitamin E. Mindell was the author of the USA best selling 'Vitamin Bible' that had monographs that covered most of the supplements on the American market. This was a useful reference book for retailers and consumers. RG and I had written our Good Nutrients Guide (Guide to Vitamins and Health Supplements) for the same reason. Consumers were desperate for information on supplementation but the law prevented essential communications, especially claims on product packs and in advertisements. We received a letter from a Larkhall customer that expressed the fears of many regular and committed supplement users about threatened European legislation on food supplements. It mentioned Linda Lazarides the founder of SPNT (The Society for the the the promotion of Nutritional Therapy). She was an author and leader in the fight for freedom for nutritionist practitioners in the UK and Europe.

Pressure from the anti vitamin lobby grew on both sides of the Atlantic. The June issue of the International Journal of Alternative and Complementary Medicine reported an FDA armed raid on a Natural Health Clinic in Washington State. This clinic was run by a Physician Dr John Wright, a staunch defender of Alternative Health Care who was horrified at this action. The report also referred to the actions of Trading Standards Officials in the UK against a major supplements company (presumably Larkhall). The reactions of the American public to the FDA attack were wholly supportive of Dr Wright. Dr Alexander Schauss the Director of a USA voluntary group 'Citizens for Health'(CFH) witnessed the FDA raid and was horrified. Schauss had done some research in 1983/4 on schoolchildren's diets in New York and had concluded that better diets without junk foods led to better performance in school - this research had been rubbished by academics. Schauss had been vilified too.

It seemed that pressure on Health Food and Alternative Treatments was building up in both USA and UK. This was because of the efforts of the Campaign against Health Fraud (USA) and their associates HealthWatch(UK) fostered with financial and general resource assistance from vested commercial interests, whose profits were threatened by use of the alternative approaches to health care.

In the UK a letter from a pregnant Larkhall customer, dated 4th June, indicated the success of the anti vitamin lobby. This lady had been told by her Doctor not to take anything containing Vitamin A because that could harm her baby. This was a great exaggeration. Only about two instances had ever been recorded where vitamin A could have been implicated in a birth deformity. The amounts of vitamin A ingested in those cases was from eating large quantities of liver derived from animals who had eaten animal feeds enriched with extra Vitamin A. The lady who wrote to us had been taking Foresight Vitamins that contained the normal RDA (recommended daily amount), so even if she had been eating a diet containing sufficient Vitamin A she would only have doubled that with a supplement.

The cases of danger involved about twenty times RDA for weeks. Some ordinary medicines harm thousands of people a year as do alcohol and smoking. Vitamins had a safety record unequalled, even by water. This hysteria probably generated by sources close to HealthWatch and its cohorts was total sophistry and not in the interests of patients/consumers.

Meeting for retailers sponsored by our Dutch distributor Nutrivital In mid June I was in the Netherlands, in Utrecht, to attend a meeting for Dutch Retailers and practitioners on Tandem IQ and the Cantassium range of products. This was a whole day, which included playing crazy golf, and I gave talks on food supplements. It was a success but the Dutch Authorities had begun to take an interest in Tandem IQ using similar arguments to those in the UK against supplementation helping school children.

Key Staff matter At the end of June I wrote to SHJ (John) Rugless, who had worked for the company since 1946. Sadly, he had suffered a stroke and was not fit for work, although in contact with the office to give help on the 'phone. His faultless hand written working formulas, experience of tableting and raw materials was legendary. Unsurprisingly, his skills were not appreciated by the medicines inspectors. He would be missed because he was never able to resume his post again and had to retire.

Registered Medical practitioners fall out with HealthWatch Towards the end of June, I had correspondence with a leading authority on Complementary Treatments, Dr George Lewith. He was one of a trio of Doctors who were qualified Medical Practitioners with deep interest in Complementary Medicine. They had practices in Southampton, Hampshire, Guernsey Channel Islands and Harley Street, London. They had published the Complementary Medical Research Journal and had a friendly approach to HealthWatch. However, HealthWatch soon fell out with Lewith and criticised his research ideas, despite their publicised aim of wanting 'Evidence' to validate complementary practices. The Complementary Research Journal was closed and a letter that I wrote to it was never published. Ostensible patient care was always integral to HealthWatch's approach to alternative health - so they claimed!

Alternative Health Care was offered a life line 'Which Way to Health?' (June issue), a magazine published by the Consumers Association, carried a balanced article with some apparently constructive ideas for progressing research into alternative health care. Putting the ideas into practice when no patents were possible and huge resources in manpower and money were required was very difficult -- some might say impossible. The medical maxim 'First do no harm' was appropriate.

Not for long In the August issue of 'Which Way to Health?' that had published the balanced article on Alternative Health Care in June, now tackled Multivitamins. Unfortunately, the article followed the usual media approach that the 'balanced diet' was all most people needed to obtain sufficient vitamins and minerals so supplements were a waste of money. The people at risk of deficiency and could use supplements were the elderly, pregnant women, faddy eaters (children), vegans, menstruating women, convalescents, those with digestive problems. The supposed dangers of overdosing were highlighted. Terms such as Time Release, Chelated Minerals and Food State Vitamins were criticised for no evidence of benefit.

As usual, there was no attempt to define the balanced diet or reference to the possibility that many foods were depleted of micronutrients, owing to overcooking, long storage or having been grown on poor soils.

247

Labeling confusions were a problem but no reference was made to manufacturers who tried explain these anomalies to consumers. That was government's role and they were waiting on European agreement -- still unresolved in 2015.

It was a disappointing contribution to the arguments about supplementation, unworthy of Which. No doubt their 'experts' were the usual crew from academia far removed from common sense but arrogant with closed minds.

Fortunately, there were open-minded doctors too. One such was Dr Bruce Charlton from the University of Glasgow who wrote in the August issue of The Journal of the Royal Society of Medicine an article entitled 'Philosophy of Medicine; alternative or scientific'. He saw the impossibility of the two coalescing and co-existence with a very clear division was essential for the protection of the public. In other words he acknowledged that there were two distinct strands of Health Care; the scientific evidence based and the alternative/belief based. I had held this view since 1962 but went further and said they must be regulated separately. Many of the problems that have arisen in healthcare were because the evidence base followers had used regulations suited to their practices to attempt to eradicate the belief base -- impossible and a great waste of resources. Until this fact is grasped by governments there will be no progress in this area.

Cantassium led the way again   The USA NNFA Monitor publication referred to recent research in the New England Journal of Medicine that highlighted the importance of the nutrient inositol in fetal development and infant growth. I pointed out to the sales department that the Foresight Vitamin formulation had always contained inositol (since 1980) whereas it was absent in competitive products. This research was an important plus for Larkhall and the Foresight charity and was publicised by Larkhall.

Rita Greer was asked to help dietetic students   In mid July RG visited Bristol Medical School to demonstrate gluten free cooking to dietetic students. The increasing acceptance of practical cookery's importance to dietitians was encouraging. She was disappointed with the students' cooking skills. Some of them didn't even have a clue how to mix ingredients in a bowl using a spoon.

USA visit   At the end of July I travelled to the USA via New York, and took the opportunity to see Dr Stephen de Felice, the man who coined the word 'Nutraceutical' for substances and food products with pharmaceutical/health promoting properties but which were sold as foods. He had many interests in health foods but was determined to have clear distinction from medicines. His book 'From Oysters to Insulin: Nature and Medicine at Odds', and an interest in L-Carnitine had led me to want to make contact with this standard bearer for alternative health care. We had an interesting meeting and discussed matters of mutual interest. He had many contacts in the US vitamin industry. I thought his Italian connections might be of interest to PN.

The following day I flew on to Nashville for the NNFA annual convention to meet overseas customers, suppliers and competitors from many countries. These contacts have always been invaluable. The vitamin supplement business started in the USA and the world looks there for the future. That is why the NNFA conventions were such a magnet for all those interested in alternative healthcare.

The upcoming Shropshire case on Tandem IQ was at the forefront of my thoughts whilst in Nashville but my primary task whilst in the USA was to make contact with Professor Stephen Schoenthaler in California. I reached Turlock close to the UCLA campus on 27th July and had three days of discussions with Schoenthaler. He taught criminology and it was the benefit of supplements to young offenders that had drawn him into the nutrition IQ area of research. He was a statistician too. He had seen the Naismith research and said it was flawed and he could prove it.

He had studied the Benton/Roberts research and was prepared to come to UK to stand as a witness for Larkhall. He thought we would win but his experience of English Law, in practice, was nil.

From Turlock I travelled on to Los Angeles and then Pasadena. Once more I met Allen Jensen who owned Gold Stake - the natural mineral supplement. The clinical studies were still not definitive. Jensen was a nice man who entertained generously at the Ritz Carlton Hotel. His knowledge of medical research was inadequate. The future for Gold Stake supplement in Europe, with no good evidence of benefit to patients was likely to be poor.

The Society for the promotion of Nutritional Therapy led by Linda Lazarides were undertaking a 'Save our Supplements' campaign to fight the feared interference of Brussels Bureaucracy on the free availability of vitamin supplements and other alternative healthcare preparations.

Boom in Vitamins and supplements in Holland At the end of August I was in Holland again, this time to visit the Drophar exhibition in Utrecht. This was for retail pharmacy. The Pol Vitamins were featured very heavily on the Nutrivital Stand to the detriment of Cantassium. I believed that the future for Cantassium in Holland was compromised. Nutrivital was a one man company (Simon van de Waal). He was a man with an agricultural background (mainly tomatoes) who might have been out of his depth in the proprietary pharmacy area. Gross profits were high but sales promotion and advertising took a huge slice if products were to succeed. Mr Pol was a wealthy man with no background in nutritional or herbal health, based in Monaco who was using Nutrivital as his agent and I realised there was probably trouble ahead. The TV advertising commercials for Pol's products featured Dr Christian Barnard the South African pioneer heart transplant surgeon. I noted that Dutch TV advertising, unlike in the UK, was not tightly controlled but this would not last with new regulations coming. Sales were booming but for how long?

Plans for upgrading the Putney factory At the end of August I met with our new Architect (Grahame Berry) who was working on plans for further upgrading of the manufacturing areas to ensure compliance with the demands of the Medicines Control Agency, Fire Brigade and Environmental Health departments. Often these official bodies want opposites. They do not seem to co-operate so Larkhall needed an architect working with them. George Messervy, the previous architect had tragically died -- a very sad loss because he was a supreme handler of self important officials. I always thought he should have been a diplomat.

Gammolin and Lingam Capsules. Two Gammolenic Acid capsules that were branded forms of Evening Primrose Oil were promoted to Pharmacists and Doctors to fill prescriptions for the newly NHS prescribable Evening Primrose Oil. The decision to permit NHS prescription was very controversial. The illness for which it was prescribable was 'Benign Breast pain/soreness' but Doctors truly prescribed it for Pre Menstrual Syndrome (technically not permitted but this grey area was the sort of minefield that lawyers loved). Scotia, the company who gained the licence, had no patent protection apart from their Brand Names 'Epogam' for childhood eczema and 'Efamast' for benign breast pain. Hence, copyists with unlicenced branded 'Food Supplements' openly competed without legal attack because the Medicines Licence that Scotia held was insufficient protection for their monopoly. Since the competitors were selling foods, Evening Primrose Oil Capsules were legally Food Supplements, the grounds of safety were not open for attack and as to efficacy, they dared not open that can of worms because efficacy was not clear cut.

The Royal Pharmaceutical Society tried to stop Pharmacists dispensing generic EPO by claiming that they breached professional standards when filling prescriptions with an unlicensed product. However, the commercial advantage to the individual pharmacy, not necessarily owned by the pharmacist responsible for dispensing, was great. As to Doctors prescribing generically 'Gammolenic Acid Capsules', that was Government policy and the availability of the generics forced what the pharmacy was paid for dispensing the Evening Primrose Oil capsules ever lower. This was the usual result when proprietary prescription drugs lost their patent protection and generics became legally available. When a new patented synthetic chemical drug came on the market it had both a proprietary name and a generic one. Whilst patent protection operated the drug could not lawfully be substituted with generics by pharmacies even if the product was prescribed generically by a doctor.

The Scotia products lost their licences a few years later when they were reviewed by the Medicines Control Authority and EPO was placed on the black list and banned from NHS prescription. This was a blow for all producers but none more than Scotia that closed down soon after.

Preparations for the Trading Standards case in Shropshire   On 9th September, I visited Dr Hans Eysenck at the Department of Psychiatry in the Maudsley Hospital on Denmark Hill (Dulwich) to seek his help as a defence witness for Larkhall in the Shropshire Case. He was a world authority on IQ who headed the Psychiatry department at the Maudsley and edited a leading medical journal 'Individual and Personal Differences'. He had been a lead researcher in the DRF (Vitachieve) study with Schoenthaler and was totally convinced regarding the positive effects of supplementation for children. Eysenck accepted the task on a no fee basis, Larkhall to pay modest hotel and travel expenses for one day only. He was used to controversy and quite a maverick, like Professor Arnold Beckett. The other witnesses for us were to be Dr David Benton and Professor Stephen Schoenthaler who had flown over from USA. They were all really positive characters when compared to the dour three prosecution expert witnesses, all charging huge fees for their shallow contributions particularly one who charged treble the others and admitted in Court that he had not even read all the papers.

Work on the Aerobic Glasses Trading Standards case in Birmingham progressed   On 10th September I attended a meeting with Counsel and our expert witness, an optician, on the Aerobic Glasses case due to be held in Birmingham at the end of the month. I was not optimistic of the outcome because the prosecution emanated from the Opticians Professional body who were powerful and respected by most people. Lay magistrates were unlikely to accept Larkhall who were perceived as business people on the make and appeared to offer an alternative method of eye care to that offered by qualified opticians. Our witness, who was charging outrageous fees for his expertise, was a poor defender of Larkhall. Unfortunately Dr Stanley Evans who was an outstanding optical authority who advocated dietary aids to eye health (the Ocutrien supplement was his invention) and supported the use of eye exercises, including the Bates method, let us down when he refused to stand as a witness although he admitted the merits of the aerobic glasses. I had supported him with generous royalties on the Ocutrien product for many years but as so often in business it is only when you are up against it you find out who your real friends are.

Two Trading Standards cases courageously fought by Larkhall   Larkhall and I fought for our lives in two Trading Standards cases that had been looming for over a year. The first was in Shropshire a rural county with a zealous anti-health food Chief TSO aided by his Deputy an officious character whose place as a commissar in communist Russia would be assured. (His department had told RG on the phone she had better get a good lawyer because she was going to need one.)

The second in Birmingham where another zealot had been strongly influenced by the Registered Opticians Professional Organisation (Trade Union?). (Coincidentally, a year later I was, personally, swindled out of £800 by a mail order trader in the Birmingham area but the TSOs didn't want to know.)

Shropshire Between 21st and 25th September I attended the Court in Shropshire, staying in a hotel. The TSOs there had already successfully prosecuted Seven Seas and Bookers regarding their IQ products and both were fined heavily. Neither of them had vigorously defended their cases and pleaded guilty to save costs. I despised them because they had no courage and their managements, who had attempted to climb on what they perceived as a bandwagon, were not conversant with the real issues that surrounded supplementation. (One executive, when asked what the calcium/magnesium rich Dolomite was replied, "It's a tablet".) Such incredible technical ignorance was normal in the industry --- most were food salesmen with no background in chemistry or pharmacy.

Larkhall pleaded not guilty and had to wait a couple of weeks for a **conviction on three technical labelling points**. We were fined on only two -- £500 each with no imprisonment as expected by the TSOs. **The magistrate praised Larkhall for its research**, adding that he could clearly distinguish our case from others -- presumably Seven Seas and Bookers. However, Larkhall had to pay costs, including the fees of the prosecution's 'experts', one of whom admitted in court he had not read the papers on it. Although they had claimed a great deal more, costs were set at £35,000.

Trading Standards had set out to stop Tandem IQ and take it off the market. The media were hoping Larkhall would be prosecuted for fraud and I'd go to prison. The BBC Food and Drink programme wanted a big story for their programme as they had made the complaint to Shropshire Trading Standards specially. Neither succeeded. Actually the case was about the technicalities of labelling, not science or fraud. The prosecution could not produce a single witness, only their so called 'experts'.

Although the magistrate had actually praised Larkhall, the Tandem IQ pack had been seen as possibly misleading as probably only a million children could benefit from the tablets as opposed to all. A disclaimer had to be added to the pack. This was not a problem and when the pack was changed few people could see the difference. (Christopher Booker did a piece on it in the Daily Telegraph, showing the two packs in a photograph.)

The press, who were like a pack of wolves, went off at a tangent, saying the link between IQ and vitamins was wrong. This wasn't what the case had been about at all. All the Food and Drink Programme could do was to announce the verdict -- hardly a riveting feature. The magistrates referral to an obscure court case that had gone to court in 1972, Dobie versus David Greig Ltd, which was about a 4p deposit on a bottle, was not much to go on.

Regarding the fine and costs, Shropshire Council agreed that Larkhall could pay off the debt to the court on a monthly basis of £3,000 from March 1st, 1994.The documents were sent to us and put on file. As the small Shropshire court did not have the facilities for our monthly payments and we were based a long way away, it was transferred to the South Western Magistrates Court. In the event, SW Magistrates Court's facilities for our monthly payments turned into a nightmare situation -- see chapter 22 1994 for the details.

Larkhall's case was reported in all national media with interviews with the interested parties. Strangely, all the defence experts remained silent. The press were fixed on the idea either pills would improve IQ, or they wouldn't, and anyway it was a scam. Meanwhile, the children we had been trying to help were ignored.

Years later the diet of schoolchildren was even worse than it was when the research was done by Larkhall in the 1980s. It has probably improved a little in recent times (2010s onwards) thanks to the efforts of TV Chef Jamie Oliver but the Benton & Roberts research has never been repeated or widely praised for its ground breaking results.

Aerobic Glasses in Birmingham   On 30th September I went to Birmingham to defend myself against the criminal charge of writing an advertising headline 'See better naturally' in connection with pinhole glasses and the Bates method of eye care through exercise. 'Aerobic Glasses' was a branded product that Larkhall imported from the USA. Aerobic in USA version of English meant 'Pin Hole'. These glasses were used for short periods to aid the effectiveness of eye exercises which were often recommended by opticians to help strengthen vision and make the wearing of prescription glasses unnecessary. The US makers had countless testimonials and studies to validate effectiveness.

The case against Larkhall centred on a couple of optical experts who said that wearing the glasses hindered sight. The fact that these glasses were not recommended by Larkhall as a substitute for normal prescription glasses was ignored by TSOs and their experts. As expected, after two days of argument in Court, Larkhall and I, who admitted to writing the strap line to protect our agency copywriters, were convicted of an advertising crime. It was a cruel decision but businesses are seen as fair game and legal specialists in this area are difficult to locate. The defence witness, who was an optician, cost Larkhall more than all the lawyers, fines and prosecution costs. We did not appeal because of the complexities of the case. However we continued to sell the Aerobic Exercise glasses for aiding with the Bates method successfully without use of the offending strap-line for many years thereafter without officious interference, as did our competitors. The copywriters who had written the strap line got off scot free.

Doctors using supplements in treatments   The September Issue of USA Magazine Let's Live carried an article by Jack Challem about the advance of vitamins in health care with many doctors using them in treatments.

The vitamin IQ connection with diet   The September issue of The Psychologist carried three articles headed 'Fact or Fiction' which discussed the role of supplementation in children's IQ. Hans Eysenck who participated as a lead researcher in the DRF study and whose journal published the scientific paper resulting from that study held to the view that there was a positive link. TAB Sanders gave an academic nutritionist's view that the positive effects of supplementation were misleading. David Benton, at one time a total non-believer, and who was the lead researcher in the positive Darland School Study held to the view that there was too much emotion in the negative camp for objectivity to prevail.

I would add that the vested interests whose tentacles and influence on resources reached deep into academia and the media, effectively made sure that any positive results were deviously rubbished and disregarded by the establishment, whilst any trace of negative effects were hailed as correct and so justify the comment "the research on the benefits of vitamins to children's IQ is discredited". Nonsense, but more importantly, extreme sophistry.

The treatment of a relatively insignificant company like Larkhall was probably unique in the annals of science - why? Let's hope that one day all those opponents will be put to the sword.

Was there life after the TSO cases?   By the 13th October Larkhall had been congratulated by the Shropshire Stipendiary Magistrate for their part in the research into the connection between diet and IQ. They had received the lowest fines possible on just three technical labeling errors. One of them was a contention by the TSOs that we had claimed the benefits of Tandem IQ were general and widespread - this was not on the pack but just deduced by the TSOs. It appeared that they meant the product was of universal benefit - no product existed that could meet such a claim but why was not every health product served with summonses by the Shropshire TSOs?

252

Shropshire TSOs were made to look foolish for bringing the case but sadly they were awarded outrageous costs to pay their 'experts'. One of whom admitted to not reading his papers for the case, another whose research had been part funded by Larkhall and the third whose research had been funded by the World Sugar Corporation and had been proved worthless in Court. Thought was given to appealing these costs but it would have been expensive for Larkhall and our solicitor advised that what we had achieved by defending the charges had been worthwhile as regards our reputation.

The Aerobic Glasses case was disappointing but, at least, we had stood up to the vested interests of orthodox healthcare and stood tall in the alternative healthcare world.

Many interviews on TV and Radio as well as countless press articles on the IQ case did us no harm but gave the **public impression of a good company wronged by an overweening bureaucracy.** The Aerobic Glasses case achieved zero national media attention.

I determined to continue the fight for freedom for alternative and complementary health care but needed to concentrate on the commercial viability of Larkhall as my priority. I remained disillusioned with the Health Food Industry leadership and held many of the leading companies in contempt.

Vitamin Company sympathised I received a sympathetic letter concerning the Shropshire case from G&G Vitamins. They reported on a recent trade meeting about legal threats from Brussels to suppliers of supplements to European Practitioners. G&G representatives attended and they concluded that there were two schools of thought. Those who would go along with the bureaucrats and others who favoured using consumer power to stop advancing regulations. A professional PR company were advising the trade body and doing well for themselves but achieving little - probably a good thing since all questioning always added to delays. This is a situation that continues to 2015 and will probably be indefinite. Why not grasp the nettle and demand belief based as a classification for the alternative Health Care practices and Products?

I recalled the January personal view of Paul Barker that perhaps heroic surgical operations were not really better than Homoeopathy.

The World Health Organisation Expert dismissed useless supplementation In October Health Food Business had an article by Sheridan Stock putting a lucid case for supplementation to contradict an earlier piece reporting the view of WHO scientist Dr Elizabeth Heising (on the same wave length as TAB Sanders from London University). Heising believed supplements were not needed by anyone in the developed world because they all enjoyed the 'Balanced Diet'. "None suffered the imaginary poor absorption or low micronutrient content foodstuffs so beloved of the marketers of Health Foods and Vitamins" she stated.

Sponsorship of The finals of Cross Country races for young people Our PR agency, Morris Media, arranged our support for this event. The final races took place in the early autumn on a Saturday in the Midlands and drew competitors from qualifying races that had taken place throughout the UK. The National Association of Boys Clubs Cross Country Races had been established for many years but now embraced girls too. This was very successful event that created positive publicity and involved our sales staff who entered into the spirit of the races well.

A new government approved Marketing consultant's report At the end of December, I had a meeting with Ken Doidge in Putney to discuss his marketing report on Larkhall which would have a commercial influence on Larkhall in the next couple of years.

Nanny state In an issue of Marketing Week in October their regular coluumnist, Iain Murray, a polemicist, looked at the Nanny State and its many departments. He was very much against the way it held that people must be protected from themselves and that regulators always knew best. He finished by quoting Auberon Waugh's view that it was best for the UK to be ruled by Brussels, where moronic and unpleasant Sun Readers, whom he considered represented modern Britain, had no influence. In contrast Murray wrote that he would rather have Nanny here within kicking distance than far way in Brussels. I agreed.

Larkhall's Italian distributor took over a competitor, a herbal manufacturer
On 28th October I visited PN who had moved from Rome to Genoa. I saw over the factory that they had taken over from the Winter Herbal company. I met some of the Cantassium distributors who were enthusiastic about the takeover. However, I could see a threat to Larkhall from the ability of the Winter Company to manufacture Cantassium Products in Italy.

The term 'Balanced Diet' is too simplistic and not properly defined The November issue of Vegetarian Living Magazine carried an article on Vitamins and Minerals. This had been written with the aid of books written by Celia Wright, one of the founders of Green Farm Nutrition, and Patrick Holford the founder of the educational organisation 'The Institute of Optimum Nutrition'. It was sensible from the supplement angle and actually used the phrase 'a varied,fresh and balanced wholefood diet' rather than 'a balanced diet' when it described the situation when there may be no need for supplements. I had always said the simplistic approach encouraged by the ubiquitous term 'balanced diet' was very misleading without amendment. There had never been a survey to show that lay people knew what constituted or is meant by a 'balanced diet'. I believed its adherents were mainly dietitians.

School Dinner Quality and Hyperactivity I wrote a letter to Mrs ID Colquhoun the Chairman of the 'Hyperactive Children's support Group'. It referred to an article in 'Which' magazine regarding School Dinner quality that made no reference to the help that supplements could provide. I expressed my frustration that press hype of the IQ trial in Wrexham had made things worse because supplements were reported as if they were magic sources of intelligence rather than interim aids whilst diet was improved with real foods. Meanwhile, Larkhall had worked behind the scenes to try and ensure that the UK diet was being improved. The HASG had been very successful regarding the removal of many food additives that were causing hyperactivity. The use of drugs to treat hyperactive children was seen by HASG and Larkhall as a serious problem. A recent press article regarding a pharmaceutical firm "Medeva's" expansion was alarming Mrs Colquhoun as this company was making 'Ritalin' a drug for hyperactivity which could have devastating side effects.

New 'research' indicated Supplements helped older people On 7th November some research by a Dr Chandra was published in the Lancet. This was a landmark paper that reported modest dietary supplementation of the elderly improved their immunity and decreased the risk of infection in old age. It met with much opposition and unfortunately by 2002, after Chandra claimed to have done more research concentrating on Children's nutrition, a whistleblower revealed that his research was fraudulent. As a result his 1992 paper could not be considered valid because he resigned his post in Canada and appeared guilty.

Pressure on Food Supplements growing in Europe   By mid November the pressures within Europe regarding registration of diet supplements was being felt in Italy. I asked the Greek distributor to give me copies of registration documents they had received from the Greek authorities. Of course, none were received and all that had happened in Greece was that our distributor sent in applications for licences using the details supplied by Larkhall's registration department. Imports were permitted on the basis of that action but no official licences were ever issued. They were forever 'pending'. How could they be issued when 'Diet Supplement' was not an accepted Product Class in Greece and therefore in Greek Law did not exist?

Garlic still of interest as a healthy food and Nutraceutical   Garlic was still a very popular supplement/herbal health foodstuff and was claimed to have widespread benefits in heart and circulatory illness. There were many positive articles including one in a December issue of the Chemist & Druggist that attempted a comparison with Fish Oils and Aspirin. There was also coverage in Chemistry in Britain by Dr John Emsley entitled 'The Curse of the Cure All' that put garlic in perspective and was fairly balanced in approach. Chemistry in Britain also carried an article entitled 'Future health of the food industry' which predicted a growing market for nutraceuticals and the use of foods as medicines.

Duncan Campbell still under pressure from a libel action.   On Christmas Eve I was contacted by Patrick Holford of The Institute for Optimum Nutrition regarding a libel case he was pursuing against the investigative journalist Duncan Campbell. Holford was trying to find helpful witnesses and I agreed to be involved. In the event Holford abandoned the case but the correspondence was informative about characters involved with Campbell. It included at least one whom I formerly regarded as friendly and on Larkhall's side. I discovered that person was probably helping Campbell.

US Senator backed the Health Food Movement in his country   At the end of 1992 a sponsored USA publication 'Special Vitamin Report - The latest on supplement science' gave a useful picture of the dietary supplement industry in that country. Pressure from the FDA and politicians was incessant. However, the market in the US was fairly mature and industry was well prepared to do battle with the aid of its vast population of healthy Americans who valued the easy availability of supplements and herbals without interference from Doctors and Pharmacists. Importantly, Senator Orrin Hatch wrote convincingly about the problems in this publication.

Significant new products in 1992

• **Tua Electronic unit for passive gymnastics** was introduced to the UK market. Imported from Italy where it was a great success. Larkhall decided to sell TUA exclusively by mail order. However, as soon as the first advertisement based on those used in Italy appeared in a UK Magazine it was criticized and banned by the ASA. The copy had to be revised to such an extent that sales soon dwindled and we discontinued TUA in 1994.

• **Nutritional Integrators**   These were introduced in two formulas Female and Male. This was a new product grouping used initially and exclusively by Cantassium in an attempt to position products within the grey area between 'Food' and 'Medicine'. This was a difficult concept to put across as the legal noose tightened but we would await a challenge from the regulators and fight. I reasoned that since the European authorities did not recognise 'Food Supplement' that the new class of 'Nutritional Integrator' would add to their dilemma.

255

• **Magic Mushrooms** Reishi Mushroom 300mg Introduced following encouraging publicity in the press about 'Magic Mushrooms' benefiting immune response. No claims were permitted and soon interest in the product was lost but in USA it remained popular as did other dried mushroom capsules.

• **Micro Folic Acid 400mcg** the most significant new product in 1992. The idea came to me when I saw the tiny Folic Acid 500mcg tablets being compressed. I asked the packaging buyer to obtain samples of elegant one-at-a-time dispenser packs similar to those used for sweeteners like saccharin tablets. He found such a pack in France. Attractive packaging was designed and an eye catching product was produced that over the next few years would become Larkhall's top selling supplement.

Commercial pluses and minuses (swings and roundabouts) Overall the Export business was driving Larkhall forward with record months at nearly £200,000. Italy & Greece were the main markets although Spain was now showing signs of real life. In early July, I lunched with local directors of Barclays Bank at their offices in Richmond something to thank us for paying them an Interest rate on overdraft minimum 9.5%?

Commercial observations on possible frauds Memos regarding costs of leaflets from a supplier who may be giving kickbacks to Larkhall staff. Suspicions increase as regards the agency supplying artwork, design and finished sales promotion items to the trade sales department. Was this overpricing with kickbacks to Larkhall staff I wondered.
In November I wrote a memo regarding the value of Christmas gifts to customers. No more than the value of a calendar/diary was acceptable. Protests from representatives did not change my mind. Larkhall's Largesse was beyond belief and made me very suspicious of the trade sales staff.

Alan Greer RG's husband was diagnosed with a Brain Tumour. He was in his late 50s and his health had gradually been failing ever since the Duncan Campbell problems. He had major surgery. Although at first it was thought he had been wrongly diagnosed with MS he had not. This left him very disabled and blind with both the brain tumour, which grew again, and the relapsing MS. It would be four years before he could come home from hospital and nursing home. He did not recover his health but was an invalid until he passed away in April 2007.

The Right Honourable David Mellor MP In June I wrote to David Mellor MP for Putney concerning a new government initiative including a subcommittee on Health policy. I asked that RG and I be permitted to send some relevant information for consideration under this initiative. At this time Mellor was on the ascendancy and had been appointed Culture Secretary in the Cabinet. I heard nothing and had no idea what happened about this promising initiative. And then in October 'Marketing Week' published a piece about David Mellor the MP for Putney who was in trouble with the media and had resigned as a Cabinet Minister. Mellor had tried to help Larkhall with their various problems but got into more problems himself.

Mrs Elaine Austin Just before Christmas a longstanding customer Elaine Austin sent news of her family and large general store business in Newton Abbot. Her husband, a first world war veteran, had attended the 75th Anniversary of the battle of Ypres in France. His continuing good health was attributed to supplements.

Year of the Single European Market

Holding our own - Lipcote threats - California attempts enforcing taking supplements on prisoners - Sales forecasting - Greek Government orders customs officers not to heed Brussels rulings on Supplements - Green Farm takeover hazardous - HFMA directs Health Claims for supplements - Help from Cabinet Member - False optimism for supplements on prescription - IQ Nutrition Trial still misunderstood and media message distorted - Romanian and UK research pleased Greeks - Academics question the Balanced Diet - Junk Food advertising harming Children - Plant medicine is a problem - Adding vitamins to Junk foods no help - ASA toothless - Lipcote had trade and technological threats - Impossible research demands by HealthWatch - Was the official view on Supplements changing?- Folic Acid microtablets - Civil servants failed to save money - Optimism for supplements soon extinguished - Oncology Congress in Athens - A sad sponsorship - Forecasts easily missed - Way forward as Green Farm was assimilated - Homoeopathics and small companies - Paid for knowledge unwanted - Natural Beauty products

'Larkhall Natural Health' became 'Larkhall Green Farm' In early 1993 Larkhall took over **Green Farm** and **Natural Flow** which led us to publishing a magazine and expanding our Mail Order sales, using a membership scheme. Having lost sales in Italy this enabled immediate replacement of sales levels but expenses were increased substantially. Organic growth was proving difficult with many new companies entering the market both in the UK and Europe. Microfolic Acid transformed Larkhall's position in the UK market.

Holding its own position A new Mail Order Price list was issued for 1993, before the takeover of Green Farm. This showed the continuing comprehensive product list -- still the most complete of any UK company in this field. Export sales were falling slightly owing to more manufacturing in PN's new Italian factory in Genoa. The Spanish market for Cantassium was developing well and was rapidly making up for the losses in Italy.

Lipcote leads and fought positively for its market share Lipcote continued to be our largest selling product but equally enjoyed the most national advertising, PR and sales promotional effort, with discounting and special packs. It was Larkhall's only product available in the larger retailers such as Boots, Tesco and Superdrug. It was the generic 'Lipstick Sealer' but vulnerable to new technologies that were producing lipsticks with long lasting formulations. The problems with these products were the excessive 'Drying feeling on the lips' engendered and the persistant staining of clothes that was often encountered. Larkhall devised advertisements to persuade consumers that the extra effort in applying Lipcote could overcome those problems, whilst continuing with use of ordinary and less expensive lipsticks.

California attempted to legislate for supplement use   In February the California State Legislature brought in a Bill that would require Vitamin Supplements to be administered to young offenders. This became bogged down in the legislature and has not been made law in (2015).

Legal asides In January we abandoned the trademark of a boy and girl used on the Tandem IQ pack because we did not want any more trouble from power crazed TSOs. I wrote to David Mellor the Putney MP but he could not support the early day motion regarding opposing the threatened legislation from the EU on Vitamin Supplements. He was now a leading Government minister in the Cabinet so could not sign these motions.

Sales forecasting dispute The trade sales staff presented optimistic estimates of sales of Evening Primrose Oil Capsules following Larkhall's introduction of Gammolin for prescription. A memo to show how the buying department was reacting with a very competitive contract supply indicated there would be no problem with vast increases in sales. In the event, the estimates of quantities needed were wildly over optimistic and no great gains were made. Predicting sales accurately was seen by my brother as our greatest problem but I always insisted that there were too many variables involved and that it was better to look at historic demands rather than gaze into crystal balls. If a system to forecast sales accurately existed then all companies would be successful and managements could retire to the golf course.

Greek customs officers ordered not to follow the new European Free Market. The Greek government was disciplining their own customs officials for obeying the new laws from EU regarding imports from other EU countries. This meant that restrictions on supplement product imports continued despite what the EU directed.

Soon after I wrote to Mr A Mattera, a leading bureaucrat in Brussels, regarding the problems surrounding importation of Dietary Supplements that were freely available in the UK, into Greece. I was asked to do this by Maria Strofalis. I am sure that whilst these approaches engendered little reaction from the EU HQ in Brussels they effectively prevented more drastic action by the Greek Authorities, who were acting in their country's self interest by cutting down on imports and using all means at their disposal. All this without prejudicing their treasured membership of the exclusive EU Club. Perhaps this was shades of the EURO problems in 2015.

Green Farm acquired from the Liquidator. Although Graeme Millar had tried to sell me Green Farm Nutrition as a going concern he had failed. This made the takeover difficult because the sales figures were suspect, the previous two year's trading remained unaudited and recent sales had been reduced by shortage of stock. I asked our own accountants to look at the records and they thought the risks involved were containable.

The Green Farm takeover was supported by staff but I was concerned that our sales representatives were still not selling the Larkhall company and its ideals but just looking for the odd substantial order for Lipcote or a top selling vitamin line such as Evening Primrose Oil capsules, to ensure their bonuses. This attitude had to be overcome because the payment through sales for bonuses was not working for the company. The representatives just didn't have the in-depth product knowledge. It was my own efforts in overseas markets that were saving everyone. It was fortunate that I had insisted on doing overseas sales myself, back in the mid eighties, when O'Connell had tried to convince me that he should do it. His previous failures in Lebanon and the Middle East at least prevented me repeating the dose. Strangely, O'Connell was probably our best salesman but his foibles could make life difficult for me. (Alan Greer composed a comic song about him -- 'Make me your Man in Europe'.)

259

Green Farm had good educational and training materials and hopefully these would really help Larkhall succeed. The signs at the front of the factories were changed to 'Larkhall Green Farm'. The Green Farm Magazine was used to spearhead our drive for spreading real knowledge. Many American firms had infiltrated the UK Market and used USA methods, many of which were illegal in the UK but they were succeeding.

When Larkhall Natural Health took over Green Farm it used the name 'Larkhall Green Farm' as a trading name. The Supplements/Herbal Treatments/Beauty Products/Diet Foods were then sold under several headings Aquamaid, Blakoe, Cantassium, Green Farm, Natural Flow and Trufree with agency lines Nature's Plus and Annie Marie Borlind. They were selling to Trade, Export and Direct Mail consumers. Efforts were made to rationalize the ranges to minimize overlaps and most new products concentrated on Cantassium and Natural Flow. The Green Farm Magazine was seen as a mainly promotional publication but had to adhere to the strict advertising rules surrounding the whole "Alternative Healthcare area". Outside advertising was sought but unsurprisingly none materialised.

Many products were deleted if there was a Larkhall product very similar but popular items were often sold under another Larkhall Brand too. Duplication was minimal but did exist. New products were often introduced under the Green Farm Brand 'Natural Flow'.

Notable Green Farm Products past and present   Green Farm had been involved in the Germanium controversy in 1989 but, unlike Larkhall, had offered 250mg tablets which they immediately withdrew when the trouble came. They sold this product through alternative health practitioners who had received handsome commissions on what was a very expensive preparation. This was a practice that I considered irresponsible and the root cause of much of the poor publicity the supplement industry experienced at that time.

Animal Fun Chewable Supplement Tablets for children were made in the USA in the shape of Animals (Teddy Bears, Dinosaurs etc). I was not really in favour of these because they were too attractive to children but on tasting they were not really pleasant, despite the claims of the US manufacturer.

Caprylic Acid Plus was a very popular product amongst Candida sufferers and frequently prescribed by nutritional practitioners to combine with a yeast free diet.

Calcium Special Delivery was a well established Natural Flow tablet formula which claimed the best availabilty (delivery) of Calcium to the body.

Eyebright Gelee it was a popular product that fitted into the Aquamaid beauty range.

Joint Nutritional Complex was the first Natural Flow formula devised by Larkhall. It had started life as Jointactin but never sold as such. It was probably the first Glucosamine/Chondroitin formula and was successfully patented, with a full formulation including Calcium Pantothenate and DL Phenylalanine with Shark Cartilage. Glucosamine was becoming a very successful supplement product used by joint pain and arthritis sufferers. I had the Joint Nutritional Complex tested in a double blind crossover trial but its effect did not reach significance statistically. This confirmed my view that arthritis and joint pains respond well to placebo treatments. Health stores and pharmacy shelves were and still are loaded with these placebo or health integrator products. Competitor Companies showed their hands with many copycat formulas.

An enemy in the Health Food Industry was exposed in a letter received from a Green Farm customer that indicated that a named company had been saying that customers were unlikely to receive their orders because of Larkhall's troubles. Of course, when this lady received her order safely she was delighted and sympathetic towards Larkhall. The insidious situation exposed by this letter was indicative of the below the surface rumours being exploited by Larkhall's many competitors. Much jealousy was generated by the recent takeover of Green Farm and the company named had been a major creditor of the bankrupt Green Farm Company.

Trade body published list of approved health claims for food supplements Health Claims that could be made about Vitamins and Minerals were listed and had been drawn up following advice from the HFMA. There was no government authority listing available. Even with this list it was still accepted that only the Courts could decide definitively on illegal health claims. This was hardly reassuring for people wishing to invest in supplement marketing. The problems surrounding claims have still to be resolved in 2015 despite recommendations that emanate from a Brussels Directive.

A copy of the letter to members of HFMA about these claims reached me and I issued a memo that took a pretty jaundiced view of this nonsense. It was noted that the Larkhall range was hardly affected and no action was necessary. These matters provided an ongoing excuse for bureaucrats to collect wages and pensions and have long holidays at vast cost to taxpayers, with no discernible benefit to them.

Help from the Putney MP In early February, David Mellor tried to help Larkhall with their problems regarding Tryptophan, Nicotinic Acid and Germanium. The letters he received from the Parliamentary under secretary for Health were enlightening and illustrated how successful the anti-supplement lobby had been in establishing serious doubts about vitamins (nicotinic acid Vit B3), aminoacids (Tryptophan) and minerals (Germanium). These vastly exaggerated problems were muddying the waters and made progress to recommendation of developing a really healthy diet with interim use of supplements, nearly impossible. A single isolated incident concerning Carrot Juice (Vitamin A) had been a bugbear for decades but now three more totally exaggerated 'safety' issues had arisen. EU wide unhindered distribution of supplements remained a pipe dream.

An Optimist about supplements in the EU existed In early February I replied to Nim Barnes of Foresight's recent letter. This made pertinent reading about the supplement controversy in the EU so that Nim expected it to go on the back burner, because of more pressing matters. However, she was vastly over-optimistic about the NHS permitting the 'Foresight Healthy Baby' supplements on prescription, because of her charity's updated research that was about to be published with a publicity drive. This research was uncontrolled and anecdotal, it could never satisfy the scientific evidence criteria demanded by the medical professions and experts. Nim proposed new formulations but I did not believe these could be justified merely on the expectation of positive action by the NHS, that I considered very unlikely. Doctors and Pharmacists who opposed both supplementation and hair analysis were many and powerful. Nim's supporters were nearly all alternative practitioners so users paid for all tests and supplements themselves. The Foresight programme was quite successful but the selection of trial subjects was very different from the criteria essential for credible clinical trials. The fact was that 'Foresight' was alternative healthcare as was homoeopathy -- not ineffective but unproven using the scientific methods acceptable to the NHS and Medicines assessors.

The outcome of the Tandem IQ trial in Shropshire misunderstood In early February Dr Trivizas of Reading University approached Larkhall offering to carry out a nutrition trial that could be helpful should Larkhall appeal the Shropshire Tandem IQ verdict. I replied stating that we had only lost the case on **labeling technicalities,** not on **nutritional trial data**. Distortion by the media of the outcome of the case had led to as much misunderstanding as had the positive effects of the original nutrition trials on Tandem IQ. Newspapers publish 'stories' not factual explanations.

Romanian research approved in Athens   Towards the end of February, Professor Joan Drangan wrote to Maria Strofalis requesting support for his attendance at the upcoming European Sports Medicine Congress in Nicosia where he was to present a paper on his research into the benefits of Inosine to Elite Weightlifters. Maria Strofalis was enthusiastic in her support for Professor Drangan and proposed to help him with funding his travel to and hotel accommodation in Nicosia.   I was becoming less enamoured of the value of this research and its use by Drangan in enabling his travels to world sports medicine congresses. Drangan was an important man in Romanian Athletics but it seemed that he used research on products for personal reasons. The credibility of Romanian research in the UK scientific community was low. I knew that the sample sizes in Drangan's trials were insufficient to have significance but probably would not be questioned by the alternative medicine community in Athens.

Mainstream Cancer research congresses   In the middle of February I received a letter from Maria Strofalis regarding a Seminar to be held by the Therapeutic Centre of Cancer in Athens at which the new advances regarding use of Carbogen (Gas) and Nicotinamide (Vitamin B3) in the potentiation of the effectiveness of Radio Therapy would be discussed and a paper from the researchers at Mount Vernon Hospital would feature. An invitation to one of the scientists (Dr Rojas) at Mt Vernon was to be issued. Mrs Strofalis was anxious to become involved because she was selling Cantassium's Nicotinamide 500mg tablets in Greece. She believed that there would be an increase in those sales following this congress. I had already agreed with Mt Vernon to sponsor a symposium later in the year at that hospital because the newly named and licensed Arconomide was a Larkhall Product and the only one that had a licence from the Medicines Control Agency in London. This was a big gamble but all publicity should be positive for Larkhall and enhance the company's reputation in the medical community. There was also the problem that the research was ongoing and not yet widely accepted or applied.

Were academics changing their stance on the Balanced Diet?   The April issue of 'Health Food Business' carried a column by Ray Rice who had recently attended a meeting when papers were read by three eminent academic nutritionists from London University. Two were from the same college as Naismith and Nelson, Larkhall's adversaries in the Shropshire IQ Case. The conclusion was that the 'Balanced Diet' was not really satisfactory because it was ill understood by consumers and evidently not adequate anyway. Sadly, no mention was made of the importance of 'Wholesome Foods' but surprisingly the use of supplements was favoured.
   In the USA, the magazine 'Let's Live' looked at the current controversy over the RDAs and RDIs for micronutrient daily quantities. (A = Allowance and I = intake). The new RDIs were the same as the RDAs but the article warned that the authorities were likely to lower some of the figures. The whole area of daily requirements had been a minefield for years with persuasive arguments against acceptance of suspect calculations. These disagreements persisted but unfortunately, bureaucrats in places like Shropshire would always enforce the gospel according to 'experts' of dubious ancestry.

Junk Food advertisements were undermining children's diets   A Daily Telegraph article in early May carried that headline. The efforts of Larkhall were perhaps bearing fruit with the acceptance that poor diets that might be theoretically satisfactorily 'balanced' for energy requirements, were not suitable for long term good health. Publication of a White Paper **'The Health of the Nation'** set out the way forward yet even in 2015 there is a very long way to go.

The message from the Tandem IQ trial still distorted in the media An article, around the this time, by Annabel Ferriman on Vitamin Pills was published in a colour supplement within a daily newspaper 'You and Your Family' made the usual errors about the Tandem IQ case. Ferriman claimed that the TV programme stated that pills could increase IQ. Nonsense! What the programme actually said was that a better diet achieved with supplements enabled the children to score better in IQ tests owing to improved concentration. The pills were supplements within the diets that were not essential but for **scientific** reasons **had to be used in the research** to guarantee the diet used by the participating children provided the minimum daily amounts of the essential micronutrients.

The judgement against Larkhall was that only children with deficiencies were likely to benefit, all that was needed was a mention on the pack to that effect. Logically that would apply to all supplements, since it was a generally accepted that people only used supplements if they believed that they had a deficient diet. Such minor labeling changes could have been made in consultation with TSOs without any need for costly legal cases. This poorly researched and written article just added to consumer confusion. Confusion that still persists in 2015, but no further cases convicting supplement companies for such offences have occurred.

Professors Diplock and Sanders were quoted as in favour of supplements and even Garrow of HealthWatch, who was previously opposed to their use.

Plants have much to offer or do they? In the middle of May, The Pharmaceutical Journal published a cogent article 'What can higher plants offer the industry?' by an academic biochemist. She drew attention to the problems regarding isolation of 'Active' components from complex herbal extracts. A particular herb may be known for its traditional benefits to illnesses but attempts to isolate and make the active single ingredient/molecule synthetically had seldom proved successful. Nature's mixture works but cannot be reproduced synthetically or analysed definitively. This situation does not lend itself to pharmaceutical regulation and licensing because of the significant variation batch to batch. Lateral thinking is required and the pharma industry needed to rediscover its common roots with herbalism and ask "not what plants can offer the industry but what both traditions can offer plants."

The Soil Association confirmed junk foods with added vitamins remain junk foods Living Earth Magazine published by the well respected 'Soil Association' carried a short article on Food Fortification entitled 'Junk with added vitamins'. Whilst some long established fortified foods were justifiable, it seemed that many junk foods were being fortified with micronutrients to encourage consumers to believe they were therefore 'healthy'. Such was not the case and the practice must be deplored because it's a marketing ploy with hidden dangers of overdosing, said Living Earth.

Danish Vitamin Company attacked by HealthWatch The HealthWatch Newsletter No 12 attacked the Health Food Industry advertising policies. It was interesting to see a Danish company's Bio series of products were highlighted. They were using translated reprints of a Danish Alternative Health Magazine. The articles made blatantly illegal medicinal claims for their products. The company was building a very successful business on the back of this sort of advertising. Because it was Danish and in the EU it had, as yet, experienced little interference from UK regulators. This appeared to expose ASA as a toothless organization.

Lipcote's ongoing dispute with Boots Chemist supermarket In early June I wrote to our trademark agents, regarding the way that Boots were ignoring their promise to remove **'Lipcoat'** (a deliberate copy of Lipcote) from their stores within a year. This product had been displayed near the lipsticks in their stores, although Boots had always refused to display Lipcote, the original lipstick sealant, in proximity to lipsticks. They said that Lipcote was not displayed in the lipstick area of their shops because 'it depressed their Lipstick sales'.

Lipcote faced a real threat to its market In early September, there was a significant front page article in the Femail section of the Daily Mail which heralded a significant threat to Larkhall's top selling product 'Lipcote'. Scientists in the USA had developed a long lasting lipstick formulation and versions would be launched in the UK soon. The lipsticks would be costly and limited in colour range. RG and I worked with the current advertising agency on how to limit the damage to Lipcote from these products that would be sure to depress its sales. Competitive pricing allied to retailer margin improvements would be used. Long lasting lipsticks were likely to have considerable points against them including high price, limited colours, drying effects on lips and long lasting/indelible stains on clothes.

Concentrations of micronutrients in the blood of School Children in IQ and Diet trials Neville Hodgkinson, a Larkhall friendly journalist, was asked to consider certain items of current importance. I referred him to the confirmatory blood analyses results to be published soon, showing that many of the children benefiting from supplementation had low blood levels of some important micronutrients affecting brain function, prior to taking part in the IQ trials. In the event this analytical work did not convince our opponents to change their minds. They wanted it all done independently, on regularly taken samples and before any results on IQ were known to the researchers. As usual, the anti lobby demanded impossibly costly tasks for us and to have their friends in the sugar industry involved too. Common sense alone dictated that most children eating junk foods were likely to benefit from a wholesome diet. Whilst most laymen would appreciate that fact, researchers benefiting from sugar industry funds would not agree with Larkhall under any circumstances. After all, we had blown the whistle on the poor nutrition of UK schoolchildren and it had gone global.

Newspapers could be changing their views on Supplements At the end of June, The Observer newspaper carried a substantial article on Vitamin Supplements that was not totally positive but moderately in favour of particular supplemental items, such as Calcium with Vitamin D for brittle bones. Following the Annabel Ferriman article in June, this could be seen as a move away from what used to be a very hostile attitude taken by the National Press in the UK. The HealthWatch view might be on the retreat.

Micro Folic Acid success and ASBAH The success of the introduction of Micro Folic Acid tablets in 1992 had been exceptional. Importantly, folic acid medical research funded by the charity ASBAH was now officially accepted as proving that Spina Bifida could be prevented if mothers planning a baby, supplemented their daily diet with 400mcg of Folic Acid preconception. Since ASBAH (The Association for Spina Bifida and Hydrocephalus) had expended funds on the research, Larkhall offered to donate 10p to that charity on every pack sold. As expected, no other company selling Folic Acid 400mcg products made any contribution to ASBAH. ASBAH fully endorsed the Larkhall product thanks to the efforts of Paul Wootton of the charity and myself.

In early October, an article in a health magazine described the 'Foresight' approach to preparing for pregnancy in the best possible health.

The article carried an adjacent advertisement for Cantassium's Micro Folic Acid - the leading brand of folic acid in the UK. The tie up with ASBAH featured on the ad and the pack.

Over the next few years many packs were sold and the charity enjoyed a substantial reward. However, as soon as Larkhall were taken over by Multinational Nutricia in 1999 the donations ceased. (Sadly when my relatives purchased the Cantassium Trade Mark back from Nutricia in 2003, they refused to consider re-instating ASBAH's donation and by 2012 had destroyed the brand.)

The Microvitamin concept and Trade mark registration attempts   On my recent trip to the USA, the microvitamin product range was introduced at the NNFA convention in Las Vegas. Prospects for Cantassium and the microvitamin range appeared very positive, so much so that I proposed registering the necessary trademarks. In the event, import restriction soon became evident and only two orders were ever completed for the USA market. As in many countries it is better to produce locally but that inevitably leads to copyists because companies have to divulge technical knowhow to the authorities and the local staff who are often less than scrupulous.

Similar problems surrounded Tandem IQ exportation. I had hoped to register Tandem IQ as a trademark but in the event this was not worthwhile, owing to so many closely related marks being extant. I concluded that since we had sold products using this name for six or seven years without any problems we had common law rights to our marks and would continue without official registrations. RG had designed the pack with a boy and girl logo and that design was her copyright.

By mid October the registration of Micro-vitamin and Cantassium in USA was becoming difficult. The Cantassium mark had just been registered by an Irish Company, probably the one owned by our dismissed marketing consultant, trying to hinder our progress in the USA. The Microvitamin mark was too close to the already existing Microvites mark to warrant further outlay in fees. I remained un-phased by these findings and intended to proceed gradually without official trademarks. In addition, export business was hampered by the EU rules that were achieving little as regards a level playing field for supplements. Germany enforced rules that permitted indigenous manufacture but prevented large imports from UK. A similar situation prevailed in France.

Trufree confusions   In mid August, I was advised that certain 'Trufree' products had been removed from the blacklist of items which were banned for NHS prescription. Larkhall had asked the Department of Health for these to be deleted from the list because they had all been **deleted** from our own ranges many **years** ago. Their previous listing had caused confusion for prescribers because their names were similar to the numbered Trufree flours (1-7) that were permitted for NHS prescription. Of course, the reason that deleted items continued on the Black List was because the civil servants liked a large list to justify jobs and impress their political masters with their efficiency in having perhaps saved the NHS millions. In fact they had not saved one penny on Trufree but it looked good on paper.

Positive findings on Cancer prevention and microntrients   In mid September, The Times reported research by US Scientists that a vitamin supplement containing anti-oxidant nutrients Selenium, Vitamin E and Betacarotene was cutting cancer deaths in China. This controversial finding was to be subjected to further research and within 10 years it was largely discredited. The usual arguments developed that the synthetic nutrients used by the new researchers could not be expected to work -- it was the natural ones that were active. Undoubtedly, dietary research results are seldom universally accepted because too many vested interests are against such findings – for example the IQ diet research.

Oncology congress in Athens. At the end of September, an Oncology Medical Congress was held in Athens. One of the major topics was the Nicotinamide/Carbogen treatment in conjunction with radiotherapy. A scientist Dr Hodgkiss came out from Mount Vernon to participate. This caused great excitement for our distributor Maria Strofalis who went to great lengths to welcome him and see to his needs in Athens. RG and I went out to Athens to attend part of this congress but did not participate. We spent a few days in Athens and had discussions and visits to Tavernas (during which plates were smashed!) with the Strofalises. Business was building again in Greece but problems with parallel imports continued and gave the distributor excuses for non-payment of invoices. The participation in the Oncology congress was important for the credibility of Cantassium and its distributor with the medical profession in Greece. Dr Hodgkiss was a minor player at Mount Vernon and no senior people from there were in attendance despite Maria's efforts to persuade them to come. Congresses of this kind are held all over the world and are good for the host country's economy but many are not taken seriously by UK researchers whose funds for junkets are tightly controlled by the authorities.

Meanwhile Maria received a fax from the EU advisory services (a private consultancy) in Brussels that seemed optimistic about the Greek import regulations but I believed the bureaucrats were just procrastinating and remained fearful of the future for diet supplements in Greece. The EU Advisory services was a consultancy working as go betweens for many companies and trade bodies in Brussels. It was in their interests to be optimistic and hopeful of a continuing dialogue with the bureaucrats because that provided their livelihood.

Sad outcome to sponsorship of an Arctic Challenge car rally In mid October, Cantassium sponsored a team from Welwyn Round Table in the Arctic Auto Challenge '93. Tragically, one of the team's cars crashed early in the challenge and the driver was killed. The sponsorship was arranged with Steve Unwin, whom I had known for many years, as well as his father Ron. They had a successful ingredients business importing into the UK. Sadly, the sponsorship was the saddest we had ever made.

HealthWatch president Nick Ross bared his teeth At the end of October Nick Ross the journalist, TV presenter, self important individual and President of Quackbusters (HealthWatch) wrote to the Chairman of BT regarding a Larkhall Advertisement in a BT publication 'Call for Action'. Whilst he admitted to being a member of HealthWatch, the letter was undoubtedly constructed in consultation with their experts. He made himself and HealthWatch look silly as our advertisement had actually been vetted by the ASA. His letter was quite threatening and he told BT to regard it as a 'shot across their bows'.

I replied to the complaint succinctly with information that obviously floored Ross because no more was heard from him or HealthWatch on this subject. Larkhall were about to sue his organisation for libel. The persistent anti-Larkhall behaviour from HealthWatch was probably motivated by grievance and prejudice. All being well, the libel suit could put a stop to all this harassment from this arrogant lot.

Sales forecasts still cause my brother concern Towards the end of November, my brother pointed out that sales targets for Gammolin Capsules were a fraction of the Sales Manager's estimates when the product was introduced. He was unaware of the methods being used by Scotia to protect their position in the market. They had a Product Licence Larkhall did not. The issue was that it was unprofessional for Pharmacists to dispense an unlicensed generic product when a licensed one was available. Prescriptions for Generic Gammolenic Acid had to be filled by dispensing Efamol brands owned by Scotia Pharmaceuticals. This dispute continued until Scotia went bust soon after losing their licence for Evening Primrose Oil because it was considered ineffective. In the event, most of Larkhall's EPO poducts did sell well over the years to 1999.

My brother was constantly asking for accurate sales forecasts but never appreciated the real world where sales people invariably exaggerated what they could achieve, whilst I had to be more realistic because what my experience had taught me of the fickle market in which Larkhall was involved and where advertising was so closely regulated.

Ways forward The takeover of Green Farm had presented Larkhall with new opportunities but we needed to be realistic. By the end of November the Green Farm business had been assimilated and I had received the marketing consultant's report on the possible way forward for the UK. This was known as the 'Ken Doidge report' and it called for concentration on the direct sales and the appointment of a sales supremo. I was aware of weaknesses in the sales team and Doidge was retained to implement his recommendations. I believed he was interested in becoming the new supremo himself but this was not on my agenda.

The former Green Farm directors were working as consultants to Larkhall. Graeme and Tricia Millar, unsurprisingly, had their own ideas as to the way forward for the 'Larkhall Green Farm' business. Green Farm had already gone bust when they owned it. I listened to them but knew that their previous policies had not been successful. The attraction of Green Farm to Larkhall was its heritage with Alternative Practitioners, The Green Farm Magazine and excellent mail order business in Supplements and other items. The expertise in selling this range was needed by Larkhall and employing Graeme and Tricia Millar as consultants ensured that the heritage was not totally lost, beyond what had already been destroyed by the mismanagement and over optimism of the Millars during their ownership.

The Green Farm Magazine together with Natural Flow Supplements, the Nature's Plus distributorship and AnneMarie Borlind beauty products were key items in the portfolio we purchased from Begbies Liquidators. The previous owners of Green Farm (Celia & Brian Wright) had gone to the USA to seek further fortune but when the business went bust under the Millars they returned to live in their Burwash home adjacent to the factory and bought the property back and re-built the business successfully as Higher Nature.

Larkhall took the Green Farm business but were unaware that the Wrights had not been fully paid out by Millar. Their return took me by surprise. They had a faithful following in the Alternative Health and Beauty trade and Higher Nature soon became the major competitor of Green Farm. The Wrights were not scientists but perhaps close to scientologists and thus had an affinity with the Natural Health fraternity that I could not match because I was a scientist. Sadly, Celia Wright died some ten years after returning from USA.

Tricia Millar was good at PR but for a company to grow, PR was an add-on. We needed regular repeat paid space advertisements to raise awareness and solid sales. No more than six products would feature in advertisements with the brands Cantassium and Green Farm being the main features in all advertisements. PR is too hit and miss. The Millars had failed to grow Green Farm despite their protestations to the contrary.

Larkhall really only benefited marginally from the takeover but learned some useful lessons.

Magazine style house publications such as 'Green Farm Magazine' were not cost effective but could provide status for a company. RG was astonished to find its articles were mostly plagiarized with a mere 10% of the copy changed. She discovered this when Tricia Millar showed her some articles she had 'written'. Ninety percent of the text was copied from published work written by RG herself. Her attention had been drawn to what was going on by the editor of a magazine which regularly published articles by RG.

She confronted the culprit who just shrugged her shoulders, laughed and said it was quite legal. RG had to give up writing for the magazine owing to TM's plagiarising as she refused to stop. So much for copyright!

RG found them a strange couple. They lived many miles away in a fine rented house near Lambourn in Berkshire. Instead of coming into work together in one of their expensive cars they came singly, racing each other all the way. Although Graeme was married to Tricia he suddenly became engaged to a rich Australian lady. RG described the Millars as 'dreamers'.

As consultants to Larkhall, I deputed the Millars to cover many areas to ensure the takeover had a good chance of success. Unfortunately, there were soon clashes with current staff and comparisons made with their old Green Farm personnel. I reasoned that if the old GF staff had been so good why had the business failed? No answer was forthcoming from either person. The truth was that the overheads had been excessive and the profits meagre if they even if they truly existed.

Hair Dyes and Cancer In September there was news of Australian research regarding cancer being caused by synthetically derived hair dyes. This was a disturbing finding. I later insisted that the 'Tints of Nature' dyes that Green Farm were marketing should be reformulated with protective antioxidant nutrients added to aid user's health. This had been accomplished and gave the products an important advantage over competitive brands.

Policy of the Medicines Control Agency towards small companies and Homoeopathics was questioned In early December Christopher Booker's column in the Sunday Telegraph highlighted the problems being experienced by Homoeopathics and developed his article to question the whole ethos of the MCA (Medicines Control Agency). There was a sign of disproportionate regulation affecting the existence of small companies. The UK government was using the EU as a reason for its over zealous gold plated rules while other countries enforce EU directives in such a way as to preserve the small operators. In my opinion, the assumed infallibility of bureaucrats was crushing and use of half-truths, evasions and lies scandalous.

Alternative Practitioners wanted to be spoon fed Clinical Pearls News was a newsletter published in the USA to inform Professionals of research in Nutrition and Preventive Medicine. Its comprehensive coverage of International research was very useful. Larkhall imported many copies every two months to distribute free to Practitioners in Alternative Health Care. We tried to achieve regular subscribers but this was a lost cause - people liked it when it was free but as soon as they had to pay, even a subsidised price, they lost interest - sad but true. Clinical Pearls was a credible publication that could have been really useful to spread positive research based news on the natural methods for Healthcare.

Larkhall Involvement in Natural Beauty range questioned The monthly report from Tricia Millar showed the breadth of the areas in which Larkhall was now involved. Comprehensive catalogues for the Beauty and Health products were being prepared.

AnneMarie Borlind was a brand from Germany near Stuttgart and products were made using spring waters of the Black Forest. UK Distributorship came to Larkhall following their takeover of Green Farm. Borlind had many products but they were expensive. Our customers were not enamoured with either the product nor cost and despite spending on promotion – trade stockists failed to materialize. The Principal gave us little help for advertising.

The effort we put into Annemarie Borlind was probably over the top when I looked at the margins available on this range. RG was sceptical of it because she believed the formulas were more suited to German women whose winters were much colder than those in the UK.

In her opinion the German products were not as acceptable as the much less expensive Martha Hill range, which we had not successfully added to our list some years before. I think she was right.

The very smart catalogue we produced did not really work because prices were very uncompetitive. Few retailers were interested in stocking the range. I questioned whether products were really 'Natural' but more likely as 'Natural' as most products sold under that banner in Health Shops. A trip to the Black Forest area factory of Borlind (paid for by Larkhall) was planned by Tricia Millar. Take-up from journalists was disappointing but Larkhall picked up the bill for empty seats on the 'plane. Not surprisingly, with such lack of interest, we lost the distributorship in 1995.

Several distribution companies in the UK had failed with this particular brand that is well protected in Germany by rules that permitted the 'natural' claim, whilst the products were not totally natural and not dissimilar to 'natural' skin care ranges generally available in UK shops.

Vitamin Safety was not an issue   I was sent a competitor's bulletin on 'Vitamin Safety' that was written by academic Dr John Marks. The margin of safety for most vitamins was in excess of 100 times the RDA said Marks. The only vitamins where caution was recommended were the oily ones Vitamins A, D and K. I wondered if Vitamin A was really a great problem because much of the anti-opinion was always quoting the man who drank ridiculously large quantities of carrot juice that turned his skin orange. However 25000iu as a single dose once a month was quite safe because the liver could store this vitamin when dietary sources were inadequate. There was no issue surrounding the safety of essential micronutrients - the opponents of vitamins continued to exaggerate to suit their own agenda that was against the need for diet supplementation.

Promising new products?   Amongst our promising new product ranges were Cantassium's Microvitamins spearheaded by microfolic acid and a One-A-Day group that had export demand. The one-a-days were the result of attempts to by-pass the stifling regulations surrounding Food Supplements. We devised the titles with the judgement from the Tandem IQ case very much in mind. The leaflet described the range and no challenges were received from Trading Standards Officers although the Advertising Standards Authority were opposed to these products. Many manufacturers followed these ideas but by 2015 proprietary designations like this for food supplements were likely to be outlawed. Product names for the initial range in 1993 under the 'Cantamega' heading included **Cold Winter, Premenstrual, Pregnancy, Hair, Clear Skin, Vitality, Osteo, and Slimmers.** Plans to expand the range in 1997 were abandoned because the aims of the initial range was still not grasped by retailers and consumers - the message was obscured thanks to the law, despite copywriter skills.

Battling the Bailiffs

New Marketing Manager - Appeal withdrawn and Bailiffs arrive - Ten years with one Agency - Green Farm progress? - FDA hounding the Vitamin Industry in the USA - Magazine introduced an own brand Supplement range - Top US Doctors take supplements - Garlic under threat - Licence fee a tax on supplements in Europe - Health Channel and Microvitamins - Greek Drama - Dirty Tricksters - Children of Chenobyl - Vitamin used in Cancer treatment - Inside Information - Public Analyst error - Ideal Home exhibition - Cantassium dominated - Evidence based prescribing under scrutiny - Suspect Clinical trials - Knowledge base for natural health professionals - Professor Ernst and Complementary Health Care - Parallel Exports - Pleasing Inspection surprise - Accused of Fraud - Larkhall's stand against HealthWatch approved - Amygdalin Inspection - Kickboxer Doctor - Green Farm contacted at their old address - Great Future predicted - First Spina Bifida Week - Green Farm owners had misled on sales in 1991-2 - Consultancies lost - Australian Government subsidies for exporters - Herbals and Supplements threatened -Trade associations did not help - Greedy Man - Coeliac Food Symbol - Buy-lines - Supplement company based in Luxembourg - Most Herbals exempted from Medicines legislation - Sales agents dilemma - Microvitamin range extended - W5 under scrutiny - A new competitor the du Natra brand from Scotland

This was a year when emphasis was on development of the UK market following the Doidge Marketing report of 1993. The general problems for vitamin and mineral supplements caused by threatened EU laws had not abated. The Greek market, where there was little attempt by Government to permit a special classification for these products, continued to be difficult. Happily, the general export market was still good but the regulatory environment continued to mitigate against worthwhile growth. Certificates of Free Sale were still required for many overseas markets and the holding of a Manufacturer's licence under the UK Medicines Act and Inspectorate was very useful to Larkhall. Since the authorities in countries which did not recognise Food Supplements as a legitimate product category, were often prepared to permit import of such products, when presented with a Medicines Manufacturing Licence Certificate held by the exporter and applying to the source address in the UK.

OTC Sales and Marketing ceased to distribute Larkhall Products and were replaced by a team of independent sales agents who were to cover the areas of the country that our own sales people could not. The Sales Manager was responsible for these agents.

Efamol Research Institute, whose Evening Primrose Oil products had achieved a Product Licence, were sponsoring research into other plant oils at a Scottish Agricultural College. Preliminary results were encouraging in several treatment areas including reversal of ageing, maintenance of eyesight and reduction of wrinkles. Their research efforts led to small trials in Hyperactivity and IQ with equivocal results that were positively exploited with Public Relations campaigns. Latterly, the Equazen range of supplements were introduced but advertising claims were curtailed by the ASA. Efamol had mainly worked in fringe areas of treatment where small studies could impress lay persons but the mainstream scientists were never persuaded on efficacy. The exception was Evening Primrose Oil that was once licensed successfully but on review a few years later, lost its licence and was blacklisted.

LARKHALL GREEN FARM

Marketing Manager appointed   In early January a new Marketing Manager was appointed. I asked Ken Doidge to train him. The new man had experience in the marketing of Health Food Supplements. KD arranged a comprehensive one month induction programme for him so that he would be fully conversant with the company's ambitions. Sadly, things did not work out very well. He achieved some success but moved on after about a year. I had not accepted his ideas for concentrating the company's efforts on a foreign brand that was not manufactured by Larkhall. This range was too brash in concept and advertising to be acceptable to UK regulators. I insisted that Cantassium was the future for Larkhall, not overseas made brands that had been used to fill a few gaps in the range taken over with Green Farm.

Appeal withdrawn and without any notice Bailiffs arrived   In mid January, after we notified that we would not be appealing the decision of the Shropshire Court as it would have proved far too costly and time consuming. Instead, it had agreed to accept payment of the costs and fines outstanding by **monthly instalments of £3,000** until the court fines and costs had been paid. However, it then transferred collection to our Local Court in London, who, without any discussion or notice, sent in Bailiffs with a **distress warrant for £36,000 plus £8,600 Bailiffs charges** on Friday 11th February. The first instalment was not due for over three weeks but they refused to listen or read the arrangements we had made regarding the instalment payment agreement with the Shropshire authorities. They said **if we could not raise the money within the hour they would remove all our computers, some of our stock and put us out of business.** Outside on the pavement, at the front of the building, they had parked their empty lorries ready to remove our property.
   This was undoubtedly an orchestrated set-up by our enemies, who thought I would be away from the Putney Factory on that day, as planned, and also knew Larkhall's solicitor was away too. Unfortunately for them, both RG and I were unexpectedly at the Putney headquarters and easily rose to the occasion. The staff would not have been able to do so. The funds -- forty-four thousand, eight hundred pounds in cash -- were raised within the hour so their vans went away empty. It was not so good for the local court who should not have issued the warrant to the bailiffs. I took legal action against them for the way they had acted. This resulted in a refund of the charges and costs of their action to Larkhall. Our enemies had lost again. (It made the newspapers.)
   Who was behind all these troubles since 1989? Surely this had all been a conspiracy?

Ten year celebration   At the end of January a lunch party was arranged at the Media Shop to celebrate ten years of our association with that advertising agency. Usually they took clients out to a restaurant but on this occasion it took place at their offices in Adeline Place. They didn't have catering facilities so had hired a small firm to bring in food.
   Their Managing Director, Bob Sims, and I had become good friends during those years and the company's involvement with National Hunt Racing was one result. Many of Larkhall's customers and staff took real interest in the successes of Cantassium, Cantamega, The Putney Lark and Vitaman. This was a bonus for establishing loyalty and bonding for Larkhall. Bob Sims was to be a part owner of the Grand National Winner, Earth Summit, a very successful handicapper.
   The efforts of the Media Shop played a major part in the marketing successes enjoyed by Larkhall. They were happy years to be savoured. By 2013 both companies had ceased to exist, under the leadership of our successors who all, perhaps grossly underestimated what Bob Sims and I had contributed to our companies.

Green Farm progress questionable   Tricia Millar submitted her monthly report. Its general content remained as before, with many tasks being undertaken by the two experienced people from the Green Farm business. Much work was being done but I could not assess its commercial success after one year. Were we trying to do too much? Was PR of individual products achieving the object of increasing awareness of Green Farm and Larkhall? Would free sampling from regular paid space national advertisements be better? The Micro Range might be a way to go I thought. That would not appeal to TM who liked to do PR. RG would not let either of the Millars near her Trufree brand.

Legal position of supplements and herbals in the USA   The Food and Drug Administration (FDA) in USA had issued new proposed laws on Diet Supplements that included: 'High Potency' banned on all labels; Manufacturer provided safety data was not acceptable; All herbals must be fully analysed; term 'Natural' to be defined by FDA etc etc. These rules, many of which were impossible to meet, were not accepted by the industry. The disputes continued and sales expanded.   In July, an article in 'New Age Journal' in the USA indicated that FDA was still fighting the US Health Food Industry aggressively.

Saga magazine introduced its own range of supplements   SAGA, the over 50s and retirement monthly publication, brought out its own brand of supplements and used its magazine to promote the range with articles making outrageous medicinal claims. This was soon exposed as illegal by many companies that had been advertising successfully in the magazine before Saga decided to try and take the business from them. The Saga range did not last long but did not help the growth or reputation of the general Diet Supplement market. The range was only supplied by mail order but Saga broke so many rules and had given more ammunition to the opponents of supplements. Saga were probably the worst offenders, but companies with bases in the Channel Islands were making illegal claims for unlicensed food supplements and selling VAT free to customers on the mainland. That was definitely unfair competition but the authorities appeared to be taking no action.

Top Doctors taking supplements   The February issue of Prevention Magazine in the USA carried an article entitled 'Why Top Doctors take Supplements' which reported interviews with Medical Doctors in the USA that supported the views of Larkhall and me. The 'balanced diet' was a myth; Calcium Supplements supported bone density and prevented Osteoporosis, the risk/benefit ratio for vitamin supplementation was impressive (health benefited with no adverse effects). Cardiovascular disease was reduced and prevented by supplementation, less incidence of cancer of the stomach for supplementers and much more.

Garlic under pressure In February, 'Let's Live' the US health magazine reported on Garlic and the obstacles put in its way as regards claims for health benefit. A new USA law obliged products to pass four apparently straightforward criteria from the FDA - Garlic failed three and so active promotion to the consumer was hampered by impassable barriers. Of course similar unreasonable criteria were used by bureaucrats all over the world to stop imports. It was hoped that a new bill before the US Congress (Orin Hatch and Richardson) would change matters.

   According to Health Food Business Magazine (USA) Garlic had been found to be antibacterial but the research appeared to be '*in vitro*' not '*in vivo*' thus would not be helpful to its case.

Economist Magazine looked into Garlic   The prestigious Economist Magazine published an interesting article on Garlic in its Science and Technology section. This article highlighted the difficulties surrounding assessment of clinical efficacy data. Consumers were confused when the various brands competed as regards benefits - there was doubt in their minds and this had an adverse effect on demand for all garlic supplements. The conclusion that plenty of the herb garlic in the diet made supplements redundant, was probably correct. After all, the Mediterranean diet with its olive oil and garlic was clearly linked to better cardiovascular (heart) health. Since garlic was a herbal ingredient, I never thought that a specific single chemical molecule within the mix was the effective entity or prime importance. It was more likely the balanced ingredient mix that was essential to gain benefit.

Governments take tax from non efficacious supplements   The Lancet (12th February) published a letter concerning the registration of Medicinal Products in France and Italy when 'there was no evidence for efficacy', according to the licence. The reasons for such products being permitted for registration and prescription was a mystery but was possibly because many doctors in those countries had found the products efficacious despite the views of officialdom. On the other hand, by issuing official licences for such products these governments were able to collect 'Licence Fees' as extra tax revenue. I wondered if that was the real reason? This was not an isolated occurrence and indicated how difficult the area of 'efficacy' was in medicines legislation. The evidence based medicine criteria cannot be applied to the belief based and there should be distinctions in law to recognise that fact. I had been saying this for decades.

Health Channel   A sales promotion agency thought the 'Health Channel' service in Doctor's waiting rooms should be considered for use by Larkhall for Microfolic Acid. It was intended for use as a service to advertise approved health products in this pivotal promotional position. In the event, we used the Screen alternating display service but on checking various operational sites we discovered that the screens were frequently out of service and concluded that whilst the potential was excellent the local operators were unreliable and inefficient. Larkhall did not continue to use 'Health Channel' after the initial contract period expired.

Microvitamin ideas criticised   One of our sales representatives criticised the introduction of the Microvitamin product range. He failed to understand that these products were not designed for vitamin aficionados and Health Food Store customers but for people just beginning to be interested in supplementation. Their strengths also appealed to medical professionals who believed people only needed the RDA levels of supplementation to correct likely deficiencies. Hence Larkhall's drive to persuade Doctors to recommend these products to their patients. Folic Acid 400mcg was the ideal starting product because it had excellent positive medical research to back its use. Using product sampling to GP practices, the Health Channel service (initially used then discontinued see above) and medical direct mail promotion had to be right. Health Food stores sold high strength supplements and Folic Acid was not a product on their radar in 1994. Whether the sales team ever understood my reasoning seemed doubtful - *c'est la vie*. Patience and perseverance would be pre-requisites of this important microvitamin development for Larkhall.

Greek dramas Late in February, I received a letter from Greece regarding new legislation on fines for contravening the pharmaceutical product laws - many of which were unique to Greece despite the apparently 'open EU market' from 1992. These fines were directed at importers of fringe health products such as diet supplements. Most violations would, no doubt, be settled by incentives for officials. These regulations made the life of exporters from the UK more difficult and had a negative commercial influence.

Nigerian Fraud and Greece, in June, I wrote to Maria Strofalis regarding an approach she had received from Nigeria. I advised her that the offer was fraudulent and if she went to Nigeria (as she intimated she would on the 'phone) it was unlikely she would ever return. I sent an article from a UK Newspaper on this topic of Nigerian fraudsters to Maria to try and make her see sense.

Dirty Tricksters by Duncan Campbell At the end of February, an article in the fringe publication 'Time Out' reported a secret meeting of 'Quack Doctors and Businessmen' under the headline 'Dirty Tricksters'. This meeting was organised to hear from Martin Walker whose recent book 'Dirty Medicine' had carried detailed factual accounts of how many alternative health practitioners and producers had been pilloried and harassed by the press. A concerted effort by opponents of Alternative Medicine had sought to have Walker's book banned. Many writs had been issued but the book had been distributed to several people. This article in 'Time Out' formed part of the attack on Walker and those who had given him information about their persecution. Duncan Campbell, the journalist who wrote the article, had fronted many of the attacks reported in the book and his friends in the HealthWatch Charity were still helping him. He used a well-known legal firm to handle any actions taken against him following this scurrilous article. It was strange that both Walker and Campbell were from the political left - yet it was Walker who fought for freedom whilst Campbell was for the establishment. I believed that this showed how very difficult the alternative versus orthodox healthcare dilemma would be to resolve.

RG, who had been attacked in the article, which included a photograph of her, had gone to a city solicitor and began a legal case against Campbell. This seemed to protect her from further onslaughts from him and served as a warning to the member of Larkhall's staff who she believed kept passing Campbell duff information. The case rambled on for years and was to cost her eventually over £20,000 in lawyers' fees without getting anywhere. However, he did leave her alone after this. Her main worry was always how this kind of thing badly affected her husband's health. A man with the worst kind of MS and a brain tumour did not need stress. His wife was an easy target as he would not be able to fight back for her.

Children of Chenobyl Larkhall were helping Mary Gabl in the Austrian Tyrol in her efforts to improve the health of 'The children of Chernobyl'. Some of the children visited her home for a holiday away from Russia/Ukraine in the summer and she gave them vitamin supplements to take home after their stay. Nutritional deficiency was seen as a major continuing problem for those children and vital help was given by using supplements. Import in bulk to Austria was difficult and into Russia impossible, because of drug laws. Mrs Gabl achieved supply by using friends who visited the Tyrol to bring packs of the free products from Larkhall with them. I had regular contact with Mary and continued to supply supplements until 1998. In 2015 she still helps the children.

When the Chernobyl disaster occurred Larkhall had offered the Russians a large quantity of supplements from factory stock, for free, for the children. They refused the offer saying the supplements were too near their expiry dates. Actually, they weren't. Fortunately, Mary Gabl was only too grateful for our help and Larkhall supplements did get to help the children of Chernobyl, via Austria, year after year, in spite of the Russian bureaucracy.

Vitamin B3 Cancer research In early March Larkhall sponsored a seminar at Mount Vernon Hospital on the Carbogen/Nicotinamide/radiation Cancer research. We had a display including samples of our products and the licenced Nicotinamide 500mg tablets called Arconamide. We hoped to have overseas interest but in the event nothing really developed. However, involvement in the project gave Larkhall an image as a professional supplement company. Some appropriate publicity resulted. A trip to the Theatre in London (Mama Mia) was arranged for delegates and Larkhall representatives attended. The PR agency Morris Media made all the arrangements for our participation in this event very competently.

Inside information I was sent some very revealing correspondence between an advocate of Complementary Health Care and a journalist who was helping HealthWatch and others, to rubbish and persecute people in belief based health practices. The tenor of these letters was alarming. The journalist was quite open about his intention to use legal means to fight against the likes of Patrick Holford, Linda Lazarides and me. He was apparently self-funded and there was no evidence that he was paid by Pharmaceutical interests. It was known that legal actions cost a great deal of money and extra funding paid to an outsider could be a very effective cover for the really powerful vested interests fighting the alternative health care movement. Already, Larkhall had experienced the effects of what I considered a campaign of vilification and hatred out of all proportion to Larkhall's size. Powerful interests wanted me and the Larkhall company destroyed. Perhaps that journalist provided them with what they wanted? Were HealthWatch aware of what was going on behind the scenes?

Another Trading Standards error In early March, a complaint from Kent County Council TSOs about 'Caprylic Acid Plus' was received. There appeared to be a serious deficiency but I pointed out that the analyst had made a technical error and that the tablets had been analysed by Larkhall's own QC Laboratory and were perfectly satisfactory.

This kind of complaint was frequent and often demonstrated the inadequacy of the Public Analyst service. Cyril Blau, Larkhall's Technical and Factory Manager, and I had both served time with a Public Analyst back in the 1950s and with our knowledge were well placed to deal with these complaints. The payment for samples submitted by local authorities was meagre so that complex assessments of products such as Caprylic Acid were probably not done thoroughly. (In this case the analyst had not realised that both Caprylic Acid and Undecelynic acids were oily liquids and it was as crystalline salts that they were formulated and declared on the label.) No more was heard from Kent -- not even an apology -- although the complaint had been ridiculous and wasted our time.

Attack on new Marketing Manager In March a nit-picking memo concerning profit calculations on special offers from the Sales Manager was designed to disparage the Marketing Manager. Perhaps he saw the new man as a threat to him. This was not the first time for him to exaggerate someone else's errors to demonstrate his own prowess. I was not fooled.

Ideal Home Exhibition From March 23rd Larkhall exhibited once more at 'The Ideal Home Exhibition' at London's Olympia. Hoping to build awareness of our services and products. The Green Farm Magazine was promoted with a special subscription offer. The hours were long, including weekends. Maintaining staffing on the stand with knowledgeable people was a problem too. The exhibition was open for four weeks, take up of the subscription offer was poor and the whole exercise was not thought worthwhile. It would not be repeated.

The Guild of Health Writers In March, Tricia Sabine (aka Millar) told me about the formation of a new group of journalists to be called 'The Guild of Health Writers'. These specialist journalists were courted/lobbied by interested companies and provided the information supplied is of good quality there was the prospect of publication in mainstream media. Larkhall's liason with this group will be managed by TS.

I was sceptical of the group and wondered how much money would be required by members and who would judge the quality of the information? RG, who was a published health writer, was also sceptical and wouldn't have anything to do with it. She said it should be called the 'Guild of Health plagiarisers'

Green Farm marketing effort There was considerable marketing activity generated through the Green Farm ranges and development of the Green Farm Membership who were all subscribers to the Magazine. The Millars were important in this area and I hoped that the introduction of new products branded under 'Natural Flow' and 'Green Farm' could be advantageous so far as mail order sales were concerned. However, Cantassium was still the dominant trade and export product range. Green Farm was very weak in export markets and little interest in the brands could be generated. All our export distributors wanted 'Cantassium' which was a well respected name in European Countries. The name Cantassium seemed right as a universal branding. The building in Putney was now named 'Larkhall Green Farm' from which emanated closer to nature supplement products. I often referred to it as 'my farm in Putney'.

Evidence Base used by prescribers was questioned In early May, the British Medical Journal carried a leading article entitled 'Clinical Freedom and scientific fact'. This illustrated how lofty ideals about treatments were compromised in the real world. The area of everyday prescribing by GPs was far from the clinical trials environment. The evidence base for those treatments was often unsatisfactory and moving forward as regards science took years whilst NHS treatments were needed today. Most of the time doctors had to rely on clinical judgement based on experience and on-the-job learning. Is it any different in 2015?

Clinical Trial results were often suspect In mid June, The Lancet reported problems in the USA surrounding a flawed clinical study on Breast Cancer. One participating researcher had falsified patient records to bias his results in favour of the preferred outcome of the study 'that lumpectomy was as effective as mastectomy for treating early breast cancer'. When this was discovered, after publication of the results, it was found that by eliminating that researcher's results did not alter the positive outcome for lumpectomy. That a medical researcher had falsified records was hailed by the lay press as a real problem but, in this case it was not. Yet public perception of, and confidence in, any medical trials was undermined. This sort of situation was not unusual and that was why replication of results independently was essential. However, if the replicator was biased against a particular finding, as in the case of Tandem IQ in 1988, where can trust reside? In the USA this situation is leading to persecution of alternative products and practices.

The August issue of Health Foods Business (USA) carried a commentary entitled 'Over-protected and Under-served'. This short article described two Bills before the US Congress. One was 'The Dietary Supplement Health and Education Act' that aimed to give greater consumer freedom to choose supplemental approaches to their healthcare whilst the other 'The Access to Medical Treatment Act' advocated freedom to choose alternative health care treatments. There was evidence in the USA that consumers trusted the alternative practitioners and products more than they did the FDA who were seen to be in cahoots with the big Pharma and Medical interests despite their protestations that they were protecting consumers. This divide was causing many problems and was far from resolved by 2015.

Clinical Pearls News and UK Alternative health care professionals Clinical Pearls News, the USA newsletter that reported on recent research into health and nutrition was still distributed by Larkhall to Health Professionals in the UK. However, successful attempts asking these people to subscribe with a payment were proving impossible. I thought we should continue to fund its distribution to a few professionals who we thought worth the effort. It was difficult to persuade other managers of the value of Clinical Pearls but market surveys always showed that people wanted 'information' on supplement products and the only legal way of disseminating that information was generically through independent publications such as CPN. It was a hard road to sales and its effectiveness guess work. Unlike our competitors Larkhall always refused to pay hidden commissions to practitioners and that probably hindered our progress in this market.

Optimistic USA magazine article 'Let's Live' carried an article by natural health consultant Betty Franklin which took an optimistic view about the future of supplements. Research was moving the right way but with little impact on the leading opinion formers and authorities. Health freedom was still threatened but consumers were on our side and the medical professions were no closer to achieving their goal of making supplements prescription only items. Even in the EU the authorities liked the idea of self-help health care that kept the cost of socialised systems like the NHS lower for taxpayers. If consumers were happy with what doctors considered ineffective placebos - so be it. With 100% of the market what would Doctors, Pharmacists and the Industry charge the NHS for their monopoly service?

Alternative Health Care and Professor Ernst of Exeter University A UK Pharmacy Trade magazine 'The Independent Community Pharmacist' carried a useful feature entitled 'Alternative means' which covered the growing interest of Doctors and Pharmacists as well as governments in complementary treatments. Claims by some people in the industry tended to over estimate real progress. Much of the market research into the total alternative medicine market included 'fad products' like Royal Jelly, Evening Primrose Oil, Ginseng and wonder slimming products like Chitosan. These fad products cause huge distortions and researchers were seldom aware of their existence. Evening Primrose would be accepted as a natural herbal when, in fact, it was thought by many women to be a cure for PMT whilst Royal Jelly was a wonder youth restorer for looks and virility.... It was best to take these market figures with a good pinch of salt. The author of this article also believed that the opening of a Complementary Medicine faculty at Exeter University would make a big difference as regards credibility of CAM Practices. This was wildly inaccurate because Professor Ernst who led the faculty proved to be as hostile to CAM as HealthWatch because he was an evidence base man. He had absolutely no time for the belief based concept advocated by me.

Parallel Export and Import   Export business was still prospering with the reduction in Italian demand off-set by increases in Spain where Cyril Blau and I were regularly visiting to give lectures to interested practitioners. Photos were received of seminars for practitioners held by our Spanish distributors in Madrid and Barcelona. There were some 140 attendees at both meetings. However, there had been disputes between the owners of our sole distributor that would soon be resolved successfully.

Greece was marginally our largest overseas market but beset with licensing and parallel import problems.

In December a Christmas card arrived from a Turkish customer who had collected items on his visit to London in the summer. Unfortunately direct export to him in Turkey was impossible because of restrictions on supplements and alternative health care products. He will visit London again to replenish his stock.

I was suspicious that some UK trade customers were selling product to Greece against Larkhall's terms. It seemed likely that our sales representatives were co-operating with these customers and boosting their sales commission effortlessly. There was no doubt that parallel importing was a well established and a legal minefield so far as supplies to the EU countries were concerned. Nevertheless, it gave the distributor good cause for complaint and excuses to delay payments to Larkhall because the parallel importer was a parasite. The official distributor invested his own resources in marketing and distribution but did not receive the proper rewards.

The European Commission was really responsible for the problems of local official distributors of branded products. It had decreed that all EU citizens should have access to the lowest possible prices in their shops. Hence, all branded products should be on sale throughout all countries at similar prices. It was illegal for brand owners to overtly attempt to prevent this price arragement. RG and I had to make a flying and unexpected visit to Greece to try and sort out what was going on regarding Maria Strofalis and parallel importing because she was quite rightly very angry about it. Larkhall reps were involved in it with one of the UK main distributors. They would wait for me to be out of the country on an overseas trip then produce a very large order from a wholesaler in UK to be delivered within 24 hours. From there it would be shipped to Greece, where Maria Strofalis had done a lot of work in publicising Cantassium and Larkhall, at her own expense. The Greek wholesalers had spent nothing but gained the benefit. The Larkhall reps involved enjoyed the commissions on the large orders because ostensibly they were UK sales.

Medicines Inspection all clear   At the end of June, we had a satisfactory Medicines inspection of the Putney facility. A new inspector who was really encouraging to Larkhall staff was a revelation. He would not be back for a couple of years. A fax communication relating to this visit was received on 21st September. It appeared that his letter of 29th June had gone astray in the post, so was not replied to by me until 3rd October. I wondered if that original official letter had been intercepted and destroyed by disloyal staff.

Lipcote owner visited London   David Owen from New Zealand came to London and visited Putney in June for discussions on the Lipcote business. I had several meetings with him and hoped we could sign a new agreement regarding Lipcote distribution in Europe. This was achieved some months after his visit. Lipcote continued to be Larkhall's major product but for various reasons was never an ideal fit within the range of health products. I knew we should extend the Lipcote brand to a group of products but we had failed thus far and Owen, whose father had created the product, had found no successful extension in nearly sixty years. A sealant for eyebrow make-up had been proposed but was rejected for safety reasons.

Larkhall sued HealthWatch for libel   HealthWatch reached new depths. In their newsletter they intimated that Larkhall had been guilty of fraud in the Shropshire case. We had not. The case concerned a minor labelling offence and was brought by Trading Standards. It was not fraud. HealthWatch also accused Larkhall of collaborating with the BBC QED TV programme to publicise Tandem IQ, bringing it on to the market to coincide with the programme in 1991. In fact Tandem IQ was already on the market in 1986 -- five years previously. I got in touch with my solicitor. He read the newsletter and said as they had accused me of fraud this was not only serious but wrong. They could be successfully sued for libel as it was an open and shut case.

   HealthWatch capitulated and settled out of court. It meant costs, damages and a full apology as well as an undertaking not to criticise Larkhall or its products in the future unless they had thoroughly checked their facts. They also agreed to send one of their 'experts' to the Putney factory to be shown over the premises and have lunch in Annie's Room to discuss matters. It was time the whole tissue of lies, myths and bad stories concerning Larkhall were sorted out.

Libel case against HealthWatch successfully settled out of Court   In early July, a press conference at the London Hilton Hotel (Park Lane) was arranged to present details of Larkhall's successful libel action against HealthWatch following their **accusation of fraud** after the Shropshire TSO case. Many journalists attended and HealthWatch sent one of their leading doctors, Thurston Brewin, to present their views. The meeting was a success for Larkhall and achieved much favourable publicity in the Health Press. Many retailers thought we had beaten Shropshire Trading Standards Department. An exaggeration, but maybe we had because without the HealthWatch input the Tandem IQ case would probably never have reached court. After all, RG had been threatened with imprisonment by TSOs in Shropshire.

   At the start there had been much argument at Larkhall about the way to proceed with this libel case. Although the accusations of fraudulent action by Larkhall and of conspiracy with the BBC QED programme in their newsletter were very serious, our solicitor advised caution. He felt that because HealthWatch was a charity that claimed to be protecting consumers from fraud, they would therefore have the public's sympathy and Larkhall could be seen as wicked commercial exploiters of such perfect people. On the other hand RG, who already had a case going against Campbell, thought Larkhall should have no mercy on HealthWatch. There seemed to be nothing charitable about them. They had deliberately started a vendetta against Larkhall and her by their 'experts' providing misleading information to the BBC Food & Drink programme and the Shropshire authority. That had cost the company untold expense and great personal stress for me. Their experts had even accused me of having bought a PhD degree by mail from a US company. The truth was that my PhD was from London University in the faculty of Medicine and RG had already put Professor Naismith right about it. Some of their supporters, including Professor Naismith, added that my Fellowship of the Royal Society of Chemistry (FRSC) was imaginary. It certainly was not and I had a certificate to prove it.

   RG was keen to stop them in their tracks as we had had years of trouble from them but, assembling the case would have been very costly, maybe several tens of thousands pounds, for Larkhall. I knew that HealthWatch was in no position to ever pay the resulting fines and costs. To annihilate HealthWatch may have been gratifying but would have achieved little more than the abject apology that they agreed to publish in the July 1994 issue of their newsletter.

   Naturally, Larkhall's success was not reported on the BBC Food & Drink Programme (produced by Peter Bazalgette), unlike the result of the Shropshire Case that they had totally distorted, without reference to the magistrate's comments. And nothing was ever reported about the payment HeathWatch agreed to make Larkhall, which, after the libel case, was all donated to the ASBAH Spina Bifida charity.

After the libel case, Larkhall had no more serious problems from HealthWatch and I believed that after the case I was no longer perceived as the devil incarnate by them, and, that they now knew I would take action against them in court instead of turning a blind eye. The exception was media star Nick Ross who was the figurehead at the top of HealthWatch. He seemed to have a personal vendetta against me for some reason and a strange closed mindset against Alternative Health Care that I believe continues to this day (2016).

In early July, Professor John Garrow, from HealthWatch, met with Professor Arnold Beckett over a healthy lunch prepared by RG, at Putney. I hosted the lunch in Annie's Room. This meeting was a part of the terms of settlement in the libel action. It went well and Garrow toured the manufacturing and laboratory facilities at the factory that were to pharmaceutical manufacturing standards. He was totally surprised to find that Larkhall were not a company to be dismissed as cranks and crooks and that we had qualified pharmacists on the staff. He was astonished at the cleanliness and professional way the factory was working with over 50 staff. It was not what he had expected at all. Who had brainwashed him?

Praise for Larkhall's action against HealthWatch   Retailer and columnist on Health Food Business Harry Masterton-Smith in his August Column gave me a pat on the back for my efforts to defend vitamins against HealthWatch. He was right about the cowards at the top of the Health Food Industry who always cave in to unjustified attacks on products by press and authorities. Profit preservation was their concern not the well-being of the consumers. I wrote to Harry on 15th thanking him and drawing attention to the demise of a rival company 'Vitalia' owned by a Mr Pattni whom I criticised strongly when he denigrated the IQ Vitamin research.

Amygdalin on prescription only   At the end of July, B17 became prescription only but remained an unlicensed medicinal product. All products containing Amygdalin/B 17 were only available through pharmacies. Larkhall's retail outlet at 229 Putney Bridge Road was registered as a pharmacy with myself and Roger Baxter named as pharmacists in charge. Hence we could legally supply patients who presented a prescription from a registered doctor with these products.

One morning when I was out on business and not able to return until late afternoon, a Pharmacy (not a Medicines) Inspector called, unannounced, and spent the whole morning checking every single prescription we had ever had for B17. The records went back years and tied up Cyril Blau and Roger Baxter when they had other urgent work to get on with. As I was out they asked RG to help and so she acted as a go-between. Much to his disappointment he found everything in order and it was obvious he had been sent on a fool's errand. The Inspector then wandered round the store at the rear of the shop, asking RG about products, especially the Blakoe range of marital aids. RG, who had also wasted the whole morning and had nothing to do with B17, had had quite enough of him. When he asked about the effects of taking too many Royal Jelly capsules she flapped her arms up and down and made a buzzing noise like a bee. He then left hurriedly, but came back to the shop/reception a little later to see if she would like to go for a drink at the nearby pub. RG declined emphatically and said her husband would not approve. When I returned I found her angry and asked her what the Inspector was like. She said, "a creep of the first order."

Kick Boxer American Doctor   At the end of July, RG and I flew to Las Vegas to the annual NNFA convention at the Hilton Hotel. Larkhall's US distributor Ella International of San Diego exhibited the Microvitamin range for the first time. The interest was great but turning the enthusiastic enquiries into business was difficult. Dr Eddie Andujar a doctor and champion kick boxer from the East Coast proved a difficult customer. He tried visiting me in London in an attempt to by-pass Ella, something I would never even consider.

He wanted me to take him and his wife out to dinner at an Italian restaurant. I booked a table at San Martino in Knightsbridge and asked RG to come as company for Mrs Andujar. They turned up with their tiny new baby that was only a few days old. Dr. Andujar insisted on ordering **every** starter on the menu. The table was covered with them and he made his wife try each one and say if she thought it was something he would like. If she said yes, then he ate a mouthful of it. Most of the food was wasted and the waiters taken aback. The bill was astronomical and the baby cried until Mrs Andujar breast fed him. RG held the baby in her arms for a while to give the wife a break as she looked exhausted. It was very bizarre. We didn't get up from the table until nearly midnight and then he insisted I drove them (including the tiny baby who should have been in his cot) round London to 'see the sights'. It was a cold, dark,wet, winter night -- rather a long evening which went on until 2 am. RG dismissed him as a 'cowboy bully who liked his own way'.

After two years struggle with this man I gave up on him. He tried many tricks of the trade but experience had taught me to be ready for every one. I think he tried to copy the microvitamin idea but found that more costly than he had anticipated.

US Doctor Eddie Andujar tried another approach on Microvitamins
At the end of November, the USA Micro Vitamin business, started at the NNFA Convention, with Dr Eddie Andujar was not yet closed. He requested exclusivity in the USA for the one-at-a-time dispenser packs. The makers would only agree if Andujar guaranteed three million packs a year and that Larkhall were the sole packers. In the event Andujar never replied. What was he up to?

In early December, the Ella Company in San Diego sent me the contract details relating to the supply of large quantities of Microvitamins to Dr Eddie Andujar. I saw great dangers in this contract because experience had taught me that as soon as the buyer has the right to reject goods on an analysis performed by his own representatives, then the risk is totally with the supplier. Analysis of multivitamin products is a specialist area and arguments between analysts are not unusual. I insisted that the warranty was given by Larkhall's quality control department, and, provided the buyer approved their analytical certificate prior to shipment then there could be no subsequent dispute in that area. I refused to sign this contract and awaited developments. Having recently met Eddie Andujar in London I was wary of the 'Champion Kick Boxer', mainly because he proposed that he dealt directly with Larkhall and so bypassed Ella in San Diego, who had acted for Larkhall in all the preliminary work in the USA. That was totally unacceptable business practice and I wouldn't hear of it. I trusted Ella to look after Larkhall's interest in the minefield of US commercial law.

Medicines control agency wrote to Green Farm's old address   At the end of July, Joint Nutritional Complex came under the spotlight of the Medicines Control Agency because of an article outlining benefits in the trade magazine 'Health Food Business'. This was an article developed by the magazine without direct input from Green Farm. Hence there was no problem for them. Equally, Green farm had left the address to which the letter was sent over a year before. No further correspondence was received from MCA when these points were passed to them. Very strange I thought but guessed it was for legal reasons. Life must have been as complicated for the authorities as it was for companies.

National Newspaper foresaw a favourable future for Alternative Health Care   On 3rd August the Daily Telegraph published a special report on Healthy Living. It covered diet and supplements as well as indicating that alternative medicine was gaining official recognition as regards effectiveness. There was even a move for some doctors to recommend patients to alternative professionals such as Chiropractors for back pain and other muscular problems.

Whilst the tone was optimistic, I doubted the Evidence Based Criteria that would be demanded for real recognition could ever be satisfied by Alternative Practices and Products. On the whole this was a constructive feature. Well done the DT.

Earlier, the Sunday Mirror carried a long article which was helpful to the supplement cause and gave the views of Professor Diplock (Anti Oxidants) and Tom Sanders who was now more in favour of the idea that RDAs might not be right for maintaining optimal health. His boss Professor Naismith might not have agreed!

First Spina Bifida week 15-21st August the first ever "Spina Bifida Week" organised by Larkhall's PR Agency Morris Media in conjunction with the charity ASBAH was held. Larkhall made donations to ASBAH based on the sales of microfolic acid. This had started in 1992 when Microfolic Acid was launched. Chemist & Druggist reported that £25,000 had been donated to ASBAH by Larkhall. The cheque presentation photograph was also published.

Demise of Vitalia revealed former Green Farm company had hidden a problem with sales Following the recent demise of Larkhall competitor Vitalia Ltd, I obtained figures from the liquidator which showed how their sales had declined from 1991 to 1993. Green Farm had experienced a substantial fall too, but G Millar had disguised his figures by excluding constant discounts in his reports. The fact that that Green Farm went down was evidence of true declines in the supplement industry. Larkhall had survived because of their much wider product ranges outside supplements (Lipcote), excellent exports and constant vigilance by management. The boom after the Tandem IQ research had been general in the vitamin trade and had encouraged supermarkets to take the area more seriously. It had also made companies take their eyes off the ball.

Green Farm directors lose consultancies I decided that the consultancies of Tricia and Graeme Millar had to be terminated by 1st January 1995. Their reactions were, as expected, less than understanding. The demise of Green Farm had been as a direct result of their mismanagement and failing to understand the fundamentals of the supplement business. Whilst the scattergun public relations approach could be helpful in generating interest in a company it will not produce constant sales growth of profitable product -- that needed regular paid-for space advertising. The Green Farm Magazine was expensive to produce but obtaining outside advertisers to help with costs was impossible.

I decided to try something new in the New Year, using more in-house resources. Subsequent correspondence from Tricia Millar was long and informative. The surprise return of the previous owners Celia and Brian Wright to the Burwash premises where they had founded 'Higher Nature' was crucial. The development of a small supplements business relying on personalities into a larger one was difficult, because growth invariably meant loss of the personal touch. This personal involvement was vital in an area where imparting reliable information to customers was fraught with regulatory constraints. A large business must ensure that the information given, even over the 'phone, is legal. If staff were incentivised with commission on sales then restraining enthusiasm regarding medical effectiveness of supplements was nearly impossible and could lead to trouble.

Despite TM's protestations I was convinced that Green Farm was mismanaged financially by the Millars. GM was a car dealer before taking over Green Farm with finance from Lazards Bank. He was probably dazzled by the very high gross profits generated by 'healthcare products' in comparison with cars. He and Lazards failed to realise either the very substantial cost of advertising that had to be paid out of those profits or the legal climate in the area. It should be noted that both he and his wife Tricia still had had their luxury cars to go around in -- two cars travelling separately from Newbury to Burwash daily (over 200 miles return).

Unfair Competition could be encouraged by Governments As usual, at the end of August I went to Holland, to the Health & Beauty exhibition in Utrecht. Nutrivital, Larkhall's sole Dutch distributor, was exhibiting but were now concentrating on their own ranges imported from Pan Laboratories in Australia. Unfortunately, Larkhall could not compete on prices offered by Pan Labs because they received huge tax incentives from the Australian Government on manufactured goods for export. Ironically, soon after 2000, Pan Laboratories were out of business owing to serious deficiencies in their manufacturing facility after an Australian Medicines inspection. I think that their demise caused problems for many European companies who were just marketers not manufacturers.

Threats to Herbals and Supplements from regulators continued. The Natural Medicines Society newsletter reported the threat to herbals from the EU. The threat was subsequently averted but by 2010 more legislation came into effect but its enforcement so far appears to have been limited. Many EU countries ignore directives or just pay lip service to them. Hence the UK authorities cannot justify zealous adherence.

This NMS newsletter carried an advertisement for the Mail Order service from Larkhall Green Farm. We were trying to use the Green Farm Magazine as the leader to our sales but this was hazardous legally. We had to ensure that the editorial was independent of our sales department. This was a major problem for its future viability.

A colourful promotional flyer was used in mailings and orders to stimulate requests for catalogues and books to help teach people about products. The flyer itself demonstrated how little product information could be legally imparted by Larkhall to its customers. Larkhall never had problems with authorities when using this type of flyer although a book by me did come in for criticism from the Medicines Control Authority but no prosecution was ever threatened because the advice in the book was generic.

Regulatory situation could further deteriorate helped by Trade associations In early October, I learned from the EHPM (The European Health Product Manufacturers group) of proposals to further regulate herbals and supplements by the EU. This news caused me alarm. These included the introduction of a negative (banned) list of herbs based on the ideas of certain industry associates. I immediately asked Maurice Hanssen of the HFMA for more information and expressed my dissatisfaction with this list and the open admission that the UK group HFMA was a prime mover in its development.

Linda Lazarides of SPNT was also very concerned. If officials at the EU considered a herbal unsafe then it was up to them to consult with stakeholders selling that herb. The last thing the industry needed was for trade associations, whose members and leaders were not representative of all stakeholders, being proactive in this area. In the event this idea never came to fruition but continued vigilance on the actions of trade associations as well as the bureaucracies was essential.

The cosy relationship of people like Hanssen with both UK and EU Officials was dangerous. I was glad not to be contributing subscriptions to these trade bodies because most of the activity of these people was only generating 'Jobs for the boys and girls'.

Excessive behaviour Maurice Hanssen (Trade body President, Trader, Secretary, Chairman...) always carried a large wallet with him. Inside were many credit cards. Each one had been given to him by various health food manufacturers, distributors and exporters many connected with the HFMA. He lunched frequently in different restaurants, using a different one of the credit cards. Everywhere he went he would instruct the waiter to keep an eye on the wine. As soon as the bottle was finished another one should be brought to his table. He seemed to be a very greedy man.

Once, when invited to Annie's Room with other people from the trade, RG gave them all a good three course lunch. However, Hanssen was not satisfied with this and asked for cheese. No one else wanted cheese but him. RG produced 6oz (150g) of Stilton and cheese biscuits. Hanssen devoured the lot. Everyone was astonished.

Coeliac Society withdraw their symbol   The Coeliac Society withdrew its gluten free (crossed grain) symbol and by the end 1995 all producers would not be able to use it on their packs of Gluten Free Food Products. RG had designed a symbol years previously that had been used exclusively by Larkhall on their packs for many years. The loss of the Coeliac society's symbol, that they had allowed to be used on products containing wheat gluten, was not a problem for us or Trufree, RG's own brand.

BUY Line advertising in Reader's Digest was proving satisfactory especially for W5 Skin Supplement. I was interested in developing this style of advertising but Reader's Digest rationed space available to keep the Buy-line feature manageable and reader friendly. These advertisements were never as successful in other magazines because the readers of the Digest were probably the prime target group for this style of advertisement.

Supplement company based in Luxemburg opened in the UK   Early in November I had sight of a letter from Mr Peter Verney the director of a recently founded company Vita Natura to the PR company Ash Associates that I believed was significant. Larkhall were soon to be in negotiations with Mr Verney to possibly takeover this company. It was noted that this appeared to be a distributor acting for a German company with supplement products possibly made in Germany to high strength formulations that would be illegal in that country if exported from the UK. This probably indicated that the Germans, as I always suspected, were not acting within the ideals of the EU Free Trade Market either in supplements' or Natural Skin Care/ Cosmetics. Germany had always been a keen exporter but never a willing importer and the EU made little difference to that basic chauvinism. They protested their ideals for a free market but were not true to them. No wonder the Euro is in such trouble as I write this in 2015.
   The correspondence from Sue Ash, the owner of the PR company, was indicative of the coming demise of Vita Natura in the UK.

Section 12 exemption for Herbals   In mid November after several appeals Herbal Medicines were exempted from medicines licensing provided they were not 'industrially' produced. This was a major victory for consumers and those in the herbal movement. I could not understand how a tablet or capsule could be produced non-industrially but decided not to argue with such a rare outbreak of commonsense from government. The authorities seemed in no doubt that most herbals would be exempted from licensing.
   This was a Section 12 of the Medicines Act 1968 exemption and before many more years had passed the authorities had changed their mind and the THMPD (The Traditional Herbal Medicinal Product Directive) was enacted for European countries to adopt. It was expected that herbals would all become licensed as medicines. This was a futile piece of legislation that still left most herbal health products on the market because interpretation of the law in this area was a minefield for the enforcement authorities. All we awaited was a major health scare proved to be caused by herbal products and if that never happened the law might die a natural death.
   As can be seen from some of the articles published this year, a Dr Simon Wesseley was very antagonistic towards herbals. As might be expected he was a leading member of the HealthWatch organisation. Happily, many journalists were well disposed towards herbals including Christopher Booker who wrote highly regarded articles in the Daily and Sunday Telegraphs.

I had criticised the local MP's non-participation in the recent early day motion regarding Herbal product availabilty. He said he had helped to a greater extent by going through Virginia Bottomley, the Health Secretary, and enclosed a letter from Tom Sackville that confirmed the situation as reported above.

Sales agents value to the company questioned On 30th November there was a Home Sales and Marketing meeting to review progress and aims for 1995. Whilst sales were growing the promotional costs were increasing considerably especially following the appointment of sales agents on commission. They were paid on total sales and not on their real achievement that should be new business that the individual generated. I continued to doubt their worth but the sales manager was very supportive of them. I wondered why?

We needed to target the advertising spend and concentrate on the core products. The new computer system was improving the information available by monthly sales analysis and this was very important if progress was to be achieved.

Microvitamin range extended A separate computer generated trade sales report made interesting reading. The growing importance of Micro Folic Acid in the vitamin supplement range was highlighted. The connection to ASBAH and wide acceptance of the presentation by Doctors and Pharmacists was proving successful but growing competition from generic Folic Acid tablets under their own label by Boots and some wholesalers was a threat to Larkhall's dominance. I believed that Micro Folic acid should spearhead other micro supplement products (Micro Multivitamins, Vitamin C, Smoke Screen antioxidant etc) from Larkhall and new introductions were taking place. All these products offered 'Free Sampling' opportunities with professional recommendation.

Defence of Alternative Health Care using Martin Walker's book A report in the December issue of Nutritional Therapy Today by Linda Lazarides covered the arguments put forward by HealthWatch and the defences by Martin Walker in his book 'Dirty Medicine'. Linda approved of what Martin had done and advocated that all supporters of Alternative Health Care referred to this book when confronted by the Quackbusters/HealthWatch. In 2015 it is impossible to obtain copies of this book because it has been subjected to legal attacks that have ensured its elimination and killed free speech. The costs involved must have been vast and could only have been funded by powerful interests in opposition to alternative health care.

Nutraceuticals as active foods Chemistry in Britain (Royal Society of Chemistry Magazine) reported on Nutraceuticals - active foods. It quoted the ideas of Dr Stephen De Felice who I met in New York in July 1992. It drew attention to the situation where claims for health benefits were not permitted for Nutraceuticals but only for licensed medicinal products. De Felice had asked, in a lecture to the American Chemical Society, that Nutraceuticals needed their own economic and regulatory environment that would then encourage research in the area.

The trade magazine 'Food Processing' carried an article entitled 'Honey -- Nectar or Nutraceutical'. This illustrated the continuing dilemma that surrounded natural foods that have curative or preventive healthcare properties. Manuka honey came from New Zealand and was claimed to be different from other honeys because it had superior health promoting properties - it was claimed to be antibiotic. Authorities must be confused - was Manuka Honey a medicine or a food?. How was it chemically different from the rest of the honeys? Were its clinical trials valid? The UK importers made claims in PR releases but not on labels or advertisements for fear of criminal convictions. Manuka Honey would probably pass into folklore as a cure for infections. No wonder that in 2015 no laws exist that can prevent the availability of the natural antibiotic Manuka Honey - nor will they ever.

Suspicious request from our Sales Manager Proposals for W5 to compete with Imedeen, a skin supplement from Scandinavia, were drawn up by the trade department. However, I saw there was a potential problem. W5 had been a very successful low profile Mail Order product since the 1960s and building it into a retail health food brand could be difficult because of the product's heritage as a preparation from rabbit serum (non vegetarian). Sadly, this became a reality in the following year (1995) when adverse publicity involving W5 Cream and the Princess of Wales appeared in the national press. It concerned her going into a London shop and buying one of our W5 products in a carton I had never seen before. RG, who did the designs for W5 products, had no knowledge of it either. It was a plain carton in a particularly brutal mauve -- quite ghastly. Where had the shop obtained it? (The proper carton for it featured a lily for which RG had done a pretty watercolour.) If we had followed the proposal from the sales manager there would have been serious unjustified adverse publicity for Larkhall. What was behind all this? Could the enemy within be plotting a surprise for Larkhall?

New competitor from Scotland A new brand of supplements was launched by a competitor of Larkhall called 'du Natra', based in Scotland. Very limited in scope but very elaborate carton packing with plastic bubbles containing a daily amount of several Tablets and Capsules for three specific groups Men, Women and for boosting immune system (Defenders). Seven daily cartons of bubbles and 4 weekly cartons of bubbles. I suspected this business had been launched with a large grant/subsidy from Scottish Government. Only one trade advertisement was seen by me and these packs were sent free for use in Larkhall's shop. There was no follow up and the business must have failed very quickly. Unsurprising because the product was too expensive and there was little demand for these daily packs of several items – consumers prefer single daily tablets/capsules like Cantamega 2000 or to make up their own specific regimen of single nutrient ingredients.

End of 1994 Business at Larkhall was continuing to grow because of the impact from adding the Green Farm range. However many new companies were entering the supplement market and the restrictions on imports of supplements into important markets such as Greece, France and Germany together with more indigenous production in Italy did not bode well for the future. There was still no sign of proper supplement rules being established in the EU. Larkhall's expensive overhead to ensure keeping their medicine manufacturing licences from the DHSS was still a cost problem because main competitors did not possess these licences. Green Farm had had no internal quality control systems or laboratory and nor did the vast majority of Larkhall's direct competiton.

286

Plate 19

Cantassium Hellas SA formerly Vital and Naturtabs, New Entrance and Office in Athens 1994

Display at Mr Khalik's Heath Store in Singapore with Tandem IQ prominent. 1994

Nutrivital, our Dutch distributor brings a party of retailers to visit Larkhall Green Farm in 1994

Plate 20

Larkhall's Stand at Helfex 1995

Mrs Belinda (Nim) Barnes, the
Chairman and founder of the
Foresight Charity in 1978

The Cantassium Tin Fish presented to the Cambridge
University Boat Club as sponsorship 1995

Granulation and dry mixing area for
making small batches of tablets at the
Putney facility 1995

Dr Robert Woodward in the Vitamin Shop at the
Putney factory with manager Nina. 1996

Plate 21

The Children of Chenobyl with Mary Gabl in Pfunds, Austria 1999

The vitamin supplement shelf in a Health Food Store. Los Angeles 1997

The HQ Building of the Larkhall Companies in Putney, London. 1998

The Listed Door in the front of the building. Over three centuries old.

The canopy and original name of the building.

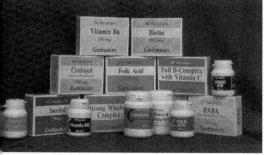

Selection of Cantassium Supplements from 1986

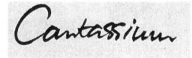

Cantassium signature after 1987

Plate 22
Unique symbol system by Rita Greer available to Larkhall for use on Larkhall's own manufacture products, also translated for use in overseas markets Italy, Greece and The Netherlands

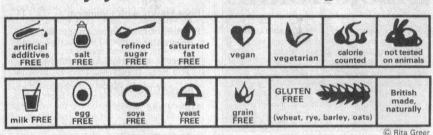

15 reasons why you will say yes to Cantassium products

artificial additives FREE	salt FREE	refined sugar FREE	saturated fat FREE	vegan	vegetarian	calorie counted	not tested on animals
milk FREE	egg FREE	soya FREE	yeast FREE	grain FREE	GLUTEN FREE (wheat, rye, barley, oats)		British made, naturally

© Rita Greer

Only Cantassium products carry the unique "Symbols of Purity and Health"
– the immediate guide to the contents of your diet supplement.
Your guarantee that only the ingredients shown in the formula, on the pack,
are used when manufacturing Cantassium Naturtabs,
there are NO HIDDEN EXTRAS!

Dr Robert Woodward in the Putney Laboratory

Rita Greer in the Putney factory.

One of Rita Greer's colourful packs for the pilot range of her 'free from' foods. 1982

Loaves, rolls and breadsticks
baked with Trufree Flours
Nos. 1,2,4,5 & 8. 100% Wheat-free,
Gluten-free and Milk-free.

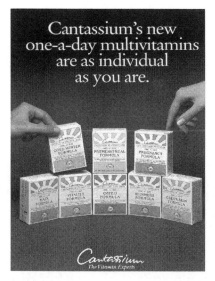

New pack designs for Cantassium Supplements
1995. Note the original Cantassium signature
at the bottom of the advertisement.

A 1995 Italian advertisement using old
style packs with Cantassium signature
large and bold.

Plate 24

Rita Greer's poster based on the NACNE
report recommendations of 1984 page 122
and verified by Modus Magazine page 160

292

Revitalising Year

Positive and Negative publicity - Propolis (Bee Glue) - Safety issues - Crisps or Apples - Conflicts amongst Alternative practices - New UK sales manager's challenges - Cosmetic product threats from EU - Questions for HealthWatch from the House of Lords - Larkhall's London Headquarters had possible buyers - Charities promoting good nutrition supported - US companies' research - Injustice exposed in Daily Mail - Vita Natura - Prominent bias against Complementary Health - Drugs and processed food threaten health - Parallel importers stopped - Philip Barker - Second Spina Bifida week - Bron Waugh and the Princess of Wales - Dr Gillian McKeith - Supplements perceived as medicines by users - Challenges for Supplements - Foresight supplementation regimes commercially doubtful - W5 critics silenced - Royal Pharmaceutical Society showed Larkhall had been correct - Stone age dismissed - More Greek drama - Positives after six months - Poor diets blight Longer lives - Academics often out of touch with reality

This was the year when the implementation of the Doidge report became a reality with the appointment of a General Sales Manager who had experience in sales management in the Pharmaceutical Industry. I hoped he would develop the UK sales on a firm basis and implement necessary changes.

The Media Shop continued to be our Advertising agency. The MD Bob Sims had become a good friend of RG and me. His staff were experienced in several areas of advertising but were specialists in Media Space Buying with considerable advantage to their customers. His horse Earth Summit was 2nd in the Welsh Grand National on 31st December 1994, run at Newbury. He went on to win Peter Marsh Chase at Haydock on 22nd January.

Our new General Sales Manager projected a 12.5% increase in UK Trade Sales but I was doubtful of its achievement with the current hit and miss promotions policy. A natural Hair Dye range was to be launched in February but this was a very competitive area and our prime retailers, Health Food Stores, seldom stocked them.

A worrying start   As the year began, export sales continued to hold up well despite the loss of much Italian business. Spain and Greece were going well but Holland was beginning to demand more regulatory information on products.

On the home trade side I expressed concern that the staff were bonusing brand name items like Joint Nutritional Complex and the Cantamegas, on which we were spending greatly on space advertising, but ignored the generic items like Vitamin C, E and B Complex. I put this down to the laziness of our sales representatives. More effort was needed with new management -- perhaps a Messiah?

American positive and negative publicity In the US, 'Health Food Business Magazine' published an important article entitled **'Chilling Proof'**. This highlighted the fact that the Norwegian Team that beat Captain Scott to the South Pole in 1912 used a more natural style of diet on their expedition. The biscuits used by the Norwegians were based on wholemeal flour, raw rolled oats and yeast as the leavening. Scott's biscuits were white flour with sodium bicarbonate as leavening. There were other factors influencing the Norwegian success but better nutrition should be counted as a positive for them. This was before the discovery of Vitamins. I reflected on the following: Scott's team died of starvation, disease and exposure while Amundsen's team returned home safely with no injuries or illness.

LARKHALL GREEN FARM

A book entitled **'Vitamin Pushers'** was published in the USA. It was written by the leading Quackbusters Victor Herbert and Stephen Barrett and was similar to the book written in the UK 'Health Hoax' by Quackbuster/HealthWatch leader Arnold Bender. The Vitamin Pushers was a vindictive book with a diatribe against the manufacturers of supplements as fundamentally dishonest and 'a form of organised crime'. It received great support in the US media including a Dr Gott who described the book as "a refreshing resource that counsels its readers about nutritional responsibility". Happily there were plenty of influential supporters of supplements to counteract the over-the-top views of Herbert and his allies. One such was Dr Michael Colgan who believed that supplements were likely to become the medicine of the new millennium.

New General Sales Manager appointed   In early January Neil Wright came to be interviewed by me and Ken Doidge for the proposed General Sales Manager position. On 10th February I announced his appointment as General Sales Manager. The memo issued to staff was comprehensive and in line with the strategy outlined in the Doidge report. Earlier, the trade sales manager had issued a rambling memo on his ideas for **not** appointing a general sales manager but this was not accepted by me or Doidge. He had had his chance and failed. It was beyond him. In early March, Ken Doidge came to induct Neil Wright as General Sales Manager.

Propolis not licensed as a medicine   Private Eye published an article about Propolis (Bee Glue) which criticised the Sun newspaper for exaggerating the effectiveness of propolis on various medical conditions. The Sun had been doing this for about a year and was colluding with a UK Health Food company and carrying advertisements for propolis. I had been aware of this problem for some years, indeed, I had warned my friend Professor Arnold Beckett to steer clear of that particular company but was ignored. Beckett told me that propolis would soon receive a full product licence from the UK Medicines Authority - I replied "in your dreams Arnold". That company went ahead and spent much money on the propolis licence project with no success in obtaining a valid licence with commercially useful claims. This problem highlighted, yet again, the need for separate regulation for 'Alternative Health'.

Export issues   The export manager reported continuing requests from EU countries for a Certificate of Free Sale for each product. The UK authorities refused these requests because they said the unified market meant that safe products should be available throughout the EU with no need for Certificates of Free Sale. The Spanish authorities were not satisfied but requested more bureaucratic documents from Larkhall that we provided. This was happening throughout the EU and was used by the various countries to try to prevent imports. Germany was probably the most protective of its market but France was not far behind. They made a mockery of the 'Free Market' using the smokescreen of 'Safety' an issue for imported products.

In early February, I flew to Athens to attend the opening of the new Offices of the Greek Distributor Cantassium Hellas. This went very well with a large attendance from friends, customers and family. A Greek Orthodox Priest gave a blessing. They were certainly into all things dramatic.

The Spanish distribution of Cantassium Supplements was taken over by the Nutrinat Company that was owned by the most dynamic partner of Iberonat, our previous distributor.

Romanian research by Professor Drangan of Bucharest University led to that country permitting import of Cantamega 2000.

"Crisps are better for you than apples" said a Professor   In the middle of March a letter in The Times Magazine from Geoffrey Cannon of The National Food Alliance, exposed the ridiculous claim of The Snack, Nut and Crisp Manufacturers Association that crisps were better for you than an apple because they contained more Vitamin C. Apples had never been considered a rich source of Vitamin C but, at least, they don't contain lots of saturated fat and salt like crisps. That old enemy of Larkhall, Professor Naismith, was the originator of the crisp/apple comparison. He was a consultant to SNACMA and his university department had probably enjoyed research funds from their members. Naismith's flawed research into Vitamins and IQ was discredited but was still used to generate media antagonism towards Larkhall. The media were hardly likely to take up swords against the junk food industry who spent big money on advertising. I wonder if 'experts' would come out with such daft information if they were compelled to state who was paying for their research and words of wisdom.

The Institute for Complementary Medicine   Towards the end of March, I visited Michael Endacott at ICM (Institute for Complementary Medicine) in Greenwich to discuss ways forward. Basically ICM was looking for sponsorship from Larkhall. I told Endacott that the conflicts within the many different Complementary Health Practices made that impossible. It was agreed that I would take part in a presentation at the Alternative Health Exhibition in July.

Parliamentary Group for Alternative and Complementary Medicine   Later in the year, I wrote to Lord Baldwin about the Parliamentary Group for Alternative and Complementary Medicine. This group was not well funded because it was trying to represent such a wide diversity of organisations - industrial, retail and others who were practice based. These groups were not really closely associated but competitive, so achieving funding was impossible. The opponents of Complementary Health Care were pleased to observe those divisions and exploited CAM with a divide and rule approach. Larkhall supported the group with a subscription payment but awaited them making progress. Although the meetings were well attended and the audiences enthusiastic, the organisation was underfunded. When you observed the resources of the multinational Pharmaceutical Industry and Junk Food Producers on the other side it was easy to get depressed.

Investigative Journalists from a National Newspaper   In November, we were visited by two journalists from the Sunday Times. Their reasons for coming were unclear although ostensibly they claimed to be friendly towards alternative health care and Larkhall. Bearing in mind that it was the Sunday Times that recently, in September, published a misleading W5 article, I was on my guard and they departed after an hour in good spirits but nothing good or bad resulted. RG said they were probably spying and went away disappointed. Perhaps they had heard rumours about me from my enemies and wanted to see if these were correct. Who knows?

Overview as the General Sales Manager started his task   The General Sales Manager was having an effect. Questioning the regular monthly sales report and asking for more details from computer generated information. The sales representatives were already putting him at a disadvantage by exploiting their long experience in the company and dealing with its customers.

I assured him that he was in a position not to tolerate their behaviour and that he must learn quickly. Advertising was exposed as not his strong point and I, who by now had long experience in that area, continued to keep tight control.

The strategy needed to run Trade and Mail order sales operations needed constant attention. Retailers were said to be very anti Larkhall because of their mail order involvement under-cutting the stockists. What these customers failed to understand, because they didn't want to, was that the many discounts, offers and deals for retailers all the time gave them the edge on pricing, if they passed on those price advantages they enjoyed from Larkhall, to their customers. The problem was that they usually pocketed the price advantage, making extra profit themselves. Representatives loved to bring their 'customer's price moans' to me and I noted them. Larkhall had to survive and only top management could see the whole picture. Larkhall had a very good mail order service backed by a customer advice service that could never be equalled by any retailer. There was little doubt that mail order customers were appreciative of the personal service offered and hence were the backbone of Larkhall sales. The retailers who stocked our products benefited from Larkhall's reputation and direct service but didn't want to see it. Naturally, the sales representatives wanted us to abandon mail order because they saw any mail order sale reducing their commission on what they believed would otherwise be retail sales. Keeping the peace and increasing overall sales was a challenge. The dynamics of media advertising was always changing and everlasting vigilance and constant analysis was vital to success.

Export trends continue to cause concern   Export sales were declining owing to regulatory differences in EU countries and the Italian Market was now self sufficient in own manufacture. Spain was a growing market. The parallel import problem into European Markets was real. Greece, Spain, Belgium and Holland were particularly affected. I suspected that many of the fringe wholesalers, particularly those run by Asian Traders, were largely responsible but all our UK sales representatives denied this. I noticed some products popular on the continent, but with little UK sales, were increasingly being sent to these UK customers. I was very suspicious because I knew that the UK sales people were not well informed about these particular items and would find selling them for genuine consumption by UK consumers very hard.

Cosmetic trade threats from Europe   A new EU directive on Cosmetics was causing concern. However, I was in contact with the Ministry involved through David Mellor MP. It would seem that things were likely to grind on slowly and there were no immediate problems facing Larkhall's products. Lipcote was still a major brand for but its distribution channel was different from diet supplements. Consumers expected to find Lipcote widely available in retail shops. Larkhall's sales force could not cover all the little retailers directly so agreed to supply sundries wholesale traders based in cash and carry warehouses, where small traders obtained their stocks of goods like Lipcote. One such customer was Wallace Wholesale with a head office in Mitcham. This company had become major distributor of Lipcote to the retail trade including Superdrug. It took care of the marketing to their many cash and carry customers and was very active in promoting Lipcote in this specialist distribution channel. The extra discounts Larkhall gave Wallace and other similar sundries wholesalers saved us from supplying the very small retailers. Some of these companies supplied European countries at prices below our sole distributors in those countries because European Law encouraged competition. This led to parallel export problems for Lipcote. Only by producing a unique style of packaging for every country could these problems be reduced. Commercially such action was not warranted.

HealthWatch Charity accused by a Peer in the House of Lords of acting inappropriately   On May 10th, Hansard recorded that The House of Lords discussed 'Registered Charities; Accountability'. Countess Mar brought attention to the actions of the HealthWatch Charity against complementary medicine practitioners, hospitals and companies. It transpired that the Charity Commission had the right to investigate these complaints and had not found HealthWatch accountable as accused.

   After reading this record I commented that it was well known that the Charity Commission was biased. It was often politically in favour of charities manned by left wing sympathisers. Justice did not seem to exist in these matters.

   In 1998, I wrote to The Countess of Mar. It was possible that her efforts against the HealthWatch organisation could have lost them Charitable Status. We both opined that it was often acting as a lobbying organisation as a Charity working in the public interest. My letter had the important statement about my experiences with HealthWatch. This was tabled by the Countess and, at least, brought the attention of legislators to the methods of HealthWatch. The injustices suffered by Larkhall at the hands of powerful media interests were a disgrace and I was sure that without HealthWatch efforts that input would not have occurred.

Takeover of Larkhall in London proposed   At the end of May, Mr Theo Baal a Mergers and Aquisitions Banker offered his services in the possible sale of the Larkhall businesses. This was an out of the blue approach but with the current problems of expansion I was not averse to at least hearing what he had to say.

   Coincidentally, in September, I was visited by Property Developer James Pollard who expressed interest in buying the Putney Site for development. I agreed to keep in touch. So this year we have had unprompted interest in the sale of the company (Theo Baal) and a London property outfit.

Association with Charities promoting good Nutrition   Early in June correspondence with the ASBAH Charity noted how successful the association has been for both parties. I told ASBAH that a new Public relations agency would take over organisation of 'Spina Bifida Week' after this year.

   Larkhall were also working with 'Foresight', the first 'Preconceptual Care Charity', and were advertising the Foresight Supplements and a booklet emphasising that other micronutrients beside Folic Acid can be taken at this important time of life for parents and baby. This charity would soon be supported with a donation per pack.

   The Government recommended Folic Acid supplementally as essential for the mother. Hence Larkhall's microfolic acid received most of their advertising and publicity supplement resources. Government support for folic acid was unique in the supplement area. Everywhere else it contended that the 'Balanced Diet' supplied all vitamins and minerals people needed. Still nobody stated what this mysterious diet was in spite of it being the apparent answer to everything.

USA Competitors in the UK   In mid June I wrote to Howard Weinstein, a supplier of raw materials to Larkhall, in Irvine California about a Research Centre in New York which appeared to be attached to a Vitamin Company. This company was making rapid headway in Europe and had a good reputation with health food retailers. They were considered a really scientific company and employed as their research manager a man described as a 'Doctor'. I knew that this man was not a scientist but had obtained a PhD by mail from Bernadean University that was not a recognised academic institution. It seemed that this Research Centre was not a reliable source of evidence based information.

UK retailers enjoyed good discounts, free trips to the USA and training from the company so it was difficult to persuade them not to pay attention to marketing ploys generated by their research department. I had believed that they did not abide by the advertising rules in the UK and their US labels were also suspect. Nevertheless most US vitamin supplement companies were similar including a brand that was currently distributed in the UK by Larkhall, following the Green Farm takeover. I thought that this association should be reconsidered but before I could act the rights were withdrawn by the USA and an office in London was activated.

I realised that this situation must have been a reason that the HealthWatch people suspected me of obtaining all my qualifications from dubious institutions in the USA. They should have checked their facts and made sure they had the right doctor before attacking me so aggressively with the aid of media and Trading Standards departments.

More on Evening Primrose Oil In mid June I wrote to the Legal Department at the Royal Pharmaceutical Society regarding its recent policy decision regarding Evening Primrose Oil Capsules prescribed by a doctor on the NHS, having to be dispensed as a Licensed medicine, not a food supplement. This was a policy of the Society not the Government so had no legal force. The authorities were saving money by tacitly permitting Food Supplements on prescription so were unlikely to defer to the RPS's policy. Ironically, the licences for all Evening Primrose products were later cancelled because of lack of evidence for effectiveness. Soon after, the products were all black-listed for Doctor's prescription on the NHS.

The October issue of Pharmaceutical Marketing featured a review of the progress of smaller Pharmaceutical Companies. Scotia (the Evening Primrose Oil company) was featured. Setbacks were reported but the stockbroker predicted sunny times ahead for the company that had never paid a dividend. In the event the company collapsed within a few years when all the pipeline products failed the final regulatory hurdles.

Later, Scotia's founder Dr David Horrobin died. I had mistrusted him back in 1976 yet he reached the Sunday Times Rich List in the 1990s. Horrobin was another failed optimist in the annals of alternative health care. He, like others, had tried to join the big Pharma club but obtaining acceptable evidence based research defeated him. There were others like Arnold Beckett (Propolis), Irene Stein (Royal Jelly), Richard Dixey (Herbals) and more.

The point that Foods must be safer than Medicines is a major one - if a food helps the patients and was available cheaply in a supermarket, let the Doctor tell the patient and by-pass the pharmacist. No wonder I had no fans at the RPS.

Death of Leon Tamman Later in June, I received the sad news that my friend Leon Tamman had passed away. We had done business together since 1964. He was a very gifted businessman and one of the richest men in England. He only envied me one thing and that was my scientific degrees and professional qualifications. He said, "Money couldn't buy them". At one time I considered joining Leon's international company but felt my independence was my most valuable asset. That scientific advantage may have counted for Leon but in dealings with most academics a businessman can seldom be acceptable. It was a lonely furrow for me.

Injustices to Larkhall exposed in The Daily Mail and Daily Telegraph Towards the end of June the 'Red Tape Alert' column in the Daily Mail, written by Christopher Booker, covered the Tandem IQ case. It drew attention to the injustices done to Larkhall and illustrated how a trivial labeling change, offered by Larkhall before the case was brought to Court, could have saved officialdom and Larkhall a great deal of time and money. I had always hoped for such media interest but had been told by my agency it was impossible. Had they been put off by somebody?

298

After the agency's admission of defeat and ineptitude RG said she would get me some free publicity herself in another of the national papers to show that yes, it was possible. She 'phoned Christopher Booker and had a chat with him. A photographer came to photograph me with the packs at the factory the following day. A few days later the article appeared with the photo in The Daily Telegraph. The agency was livid but I was delighted and so was RG.

Jimmy Savile made a proposal In early June, RG and I attended the annual Church Service and Reception at St Bartholomew the Great and afterwards at Butcher's Hall for the Knights Bachelor. Sir Austin Bide was our host and HM The Queen was present. Jimmy Savile was there as he had been made a 'Sir', looking completely out of place, like a fish out of water. After the reception he made a bee line for RG, whom he had never met. She was in the hall, putting on her cloak. He went down on one knee and asked her to marry him. She refused him saying, "Sorry Jim, I'm already married." He swore, stood up and went away. RG perceived him to be completely mad and so did I. The Bides were just embarrassed and the whole incident was quite bizzare.

Vita Natura In mid June Mr Peter Verney of Vita Natura visited me to discuss a possible takeover of his company and a week later he came again. It appeared that his company was finished. We could probably pick up the pieces.

The company had been set up in the UK in late 1994 was rapidly declining and soon in liquidation. I had previously offered to buy the assets based on verbal assurances from Verney but these had never been validated. Whilst the company claimed to have two leading supplement products 'Vitaminus Rex' and 'Selenium 14' and had had large stocking orders from Boots and Unichem, there had been no repeats and it was obvious that no viable advertisements could be designed to comply with ASA rules. A Public Relations campaign including an ambitious Road Show for the children's chewable dinosaur shaped Multivitamin Formula 'Vitaminus Rex' was apparently ready to go. All this was nonsense because there was no money available from Vita Natura.

We bought the office furniture from the liquidator and employed, on Neil Wright's recommendation, Melissa Tuffley (Marketing Director of Vita Natura) to be Larkhall's new Marketing Manager, replacing the previous one who had given in his notice. Her job description was comprehensive but her ability to do this task was suspect, despite her position at Vita Natura that had gone bust in a very short time. The Supplement market in the UK was very competitive and new companies such as Vita Natura were offering no USP to the market.

It appeared that the source organisation for the Vita Natura Company was Nutritional Molecules International SARL of Luxembourg. This company was used as a convenient base to supply supplements to the EU but had failed to develop because of the medicines regulations enforced in EU countries.

Distribution only agreements Considerable resources were being put into Borlind Skin Care but the margin was too small to warrant greater effort. The new natural hair dyes, 'Tints of Nature', were priced competitively but demand was difficult to increase in this very overcrowded market without better margins from the principals. The owners of the formulas were soon dissatisfied with Larkhall's progress as sole distributor and decided to end the association except for direct mail to consumers. No offer was made to compensate Larkhall's substantial costs in the launch of the new brand. I soon concluded that sole distributorships were of little benefit to Larkhall and reverted to concentrating on our own brands.

Complementary Medicine in 1995   In early July, The Times devoted its Focus feature to Complementary Medicine. Articles within the feature included Homoeopathy, Acupuncture, Eating Properly (no qualification of the balanced diet towards fresh fruit and vegetables) and herbal medicine. These articles were useful as a guide to professional thinking in 1995. Little has changed in 30 years - the pros and cons remain the same. The anti brigade peddled its usual nonsense about 'The balanced diet' that laymen cannot understand. It called for research to gain evidence without estimating what the cost would be and who would foot the bill. It never accepted that nothing would change the establishment view, because they would always find one of their scientists to rubbish the research with blockbustering resources. In fairness, orthodox medicine research can usually be similarly disparaged but the fighting funds for those practices are overwhelmingly better resourced to win any battle.

An interesting quote:- The National Poisons Unit at Guy's Hospital, London had received 5,500 inquiries about side-effects of alternative medicines, herbal preparations and food supplements in recent years. Dr Virginia Murray of the Poisons Unit, said, "There was no need for people to panic but they should be aware that these products can sometimes cause adverse effects".

This seemed to be an apparently fair short statement but just look at the loose language. The word Poisons occurred twice, 5500 in recent years (how many years three, five, ten?) side-effects/adverse effects twice and a Dr's name used for the quote. This was not a fair statement and was deliberately constructed to sow doubt rather than confidence in readers' minds. This was the constant battle that Complementary Health Care has to contend. Bias was endemic in this area.

Public Relations   In early July, I had meetings with the two PR agencies working with Larkhall. Morris Media (run by Sue Morris) and Field Communications (run by Gina Field). Field were concentrating on the professional side with Ruthmol whilst Morris did Lipcote and the Food Supplements. We still had Tricia Sabine (Millar) working on Green Farm. I realised that this was not ideal, but with ever growing advertising restrictions surrounding the alternative healthcare area I had to keep all options open. Dr Mike Smith, a TV Doctor, came with Gina Field and offered his help because he was favourably disposed to what I was trying to achieve. RG had helped Gina Field to cope with a relation who had a serious terminal illness by giving her specific information about diet. The relative was doing much better and it gave her extra time.

Drugs and Processed foods a threat to health   In the middle of July, The Pharmaceutical Journal carried an article on Drug and Diet interactions. This paper illustrated the great chemical complexities surrounding drugs and food. Many scientific investigations have been done but the problem was that one result inevitably triggered the need for more research. Certain drugs represented threats to every patient's nutritional status. Food additives were proliferating and as chemicals, these posed problems for the body's metabolism. Whilst single additives could cause health problems - cocktails of several additives could have unknown hazards. The latest chemicals found in new drugs potentially present many biological challenges. The message to patients and prescribers must be that taking more medicines and eating more processed foods for very long was unwise. Chronic use of either had to be avoided if good health was the aim.

Direct evidence that Parallel Importing distorted UK sales   On 15th July I received a panic 'phone call from Maria Strofalis in Athens regarding the activities of a parallel importer. I decided I would have to go to Athens forthwith and took RG with me as she knew Maria well, the likely perpetrators on our staff and the problem.

We left on Sunday 16th to spend four days with the Strofalises and to visit several importers who had stock of Cantassium products. There was no way the sales force knew we had gone to Greece so they could not contact any of the Greek wholesalers and tip them off that we were coming. This was a wise move.

At one warehouse we took the MD by surprise in his office, having been told he wouldn't see us. Maria Strofalis came with us but didn't get involved even though her own livelihood was at stake. She just pretended to be our interpreter.

RG was dressed in a black overcoat with a black Fedora and sunglasses, black gloves and black boots. She looked like someone out of a crime movie about the mafia. She said what the Greeks were impressed with was drama and this was sinister power dressing. It was no good looking like pathetic little people from England -- that wouldn't get us anywhere. We needed to take him by surprise and get a look at their stock of Cantassium products.

I had to look after Maria Strofalis as she wasn't too good on her legs so RG led the way up the MD's office stairs and confronted the man. He stood up and she saw that he was a tall man of over six feet. RG was only 5 feet tall, nevertheless he seemed quite nervous at her sudden appearance. RG ordered him to sit down and he sank back into his chair like a lamb. He did speak and understood basic English so we did not need an interpreter. She demanded politely to be shown his stock of Cantassium Supplements and without a murmur he took us into his warehouse. It was like Aladdin's Cave as his Cantassium stock was substantial. RG took batch numbers and made a list. This wasn't much use to us but it looked official and purposeful.

He was taken aback by RG's firm approach which also impressed Maria and we came away convinced that the products must be emanating from a wholesaler or large retail customer in the UK. Also, there was a possibility that one of our other overseas distributors was also involved.

Other wholesalers had much smaller stocks and we had meetings where the interpreter relayed what we had to say to the staff. It seemed a waste of time and the expense of a trip to Athens.

The parallel import problem was real in EU countries because health products were often price controlled by government edicts. This could lead to extreme distortions in cash margins at all distribution levels from country to country. The EU authorities were not interested because they wanted the lowest consumer price possible everywhere in the EU. Maria did not understand this, or, more likely did not want to understand that fact. I promised to look more closely into the problem when I returned to London.

Later it appeared from analysing the computer reports that certain retailers/wholesalers in the UK were ordering products for their shops/customers which were not generally popular in the home country but had good sale in Greece. I immediately challenged the sales department and received, as expected, evasive answers including the tales that these customers have developed exceptional sales for these specialist products because of the excellent product knowledge that the representatives had provided to these particular customers. All lies, because they knew that the parallel exporter whom they were supplying was giving them large orders that boosted their sales towards bonus targets and required minimal effort from them or the office based sales staff. To prove this was impossible because their customers were in cahoots with them and enjoyed extra discount on the very easily boosted sales.

Since the parallel export poblem was exclusively in the Cantassium Brand, I insisted that the customers I had selected as parallel exporters should be supplied mainly 'Green Farm' brands to replace the Cantassium ones and enjoy greater discount on those products whilst getting less discount on any Cantassium products.

These rules proved difficult to implement but did make the Greek Importers less of a threat to the authorised distributor (Maria Strofalis) without contravening the EU laws.

This situation with the trade sales team certainly undermined their standing with me and encouraged me to look more closely at Larkhall's whole business future.

Philip Barker, a fighter for Alternative Health Care visited Larkhall with his Shri-lankan wife Gillian who was an alternative health practitioner. He was one of those involved in the Duncan Campbell/BBC Food & Drink investigations and was heavily criticised by Campbell. He had been employed as a director by Brownings. The account of his travails was reported in the Martin Walker Book 'Dirty Medicine'.

In November I learned of a pending court case against the BBC by Philip Barker that concerned the activities of journalist Duncan Campbell. This news encouraged me to write to the Health Food Trade Media about the case that might help the credibility of health foods and alternative practices. Olympic champion athlete Chris Brasher who was behind the highly successful London Marathon had recently won his libel case against the BBC and Campbell, so things were not going well for the journalist/troublemaker. Philip Barker had discovered Campbell had a criminal record that dated from his student days.

Chris Brasher had sent RG an encouraging post card when he heard she had started proceedings against Campbell. His case, which was much bigger, had taken up four years of his life. Chris was a member of 'The Travellers Club' and I joined their racing syndicate that owned a good flat-race horse 'Telemachus'. Sadly Chris passed away before we enjoyed modest success with the horse. There was no doubt his four years of worry and stress and the BBC's attack regarding Campbell's accusations had helped to destroy his health.

Second Spina Bifida Week 31st July - 6th August organised following an idea from Morris Media by ASBAH and sponsored by Larkhall's Cantassium Microfolic Acid. Dr Miriam Stoppard did Radio Interviews. The Foresight charity was not involved – Nim Barnes was not in favour of Folic Acid as a single nutrient but only in compound supplements.
Spina Bifida Week - features included "New concepts for the Nineties" The Independent, Prima Magazine, trial packs of MicroFolic Acid and Spina Bifida Week – Daily Mirror, also Our Baby Magazine, also Woman & Home Magazine, also CHAT Magazine
Folic awareness failure – Cantassium campaign . Chemist & Druggist Trade magazine – typically telling Pharmacists the edict only to dispense a Licensed product was not a legal requirement merely advice from the Royal Pharmaceutical Society – most Chemists have to live in the real world so Cantassium maintained a huge lead over competitors in the prescription market – Licensed products were more costly to NHS and Chemists than Cantassium's microfolic acid. Licensing restricts advertising and promotion of products and for a "Food Supplement" was inappropriate – why volunteer for a marketing straight-jacket when you can be lawfully FREE?

Changes to Marketing with new PR agency appointed August 1995 was an important month because the new General Sales Manager and the newly appointed Marketing Manager were trying to move business forward in an organised way. A new PR Agency, Ash Communications, which had handled Vita Natura's PR was appointed to act for Larkhall Green Farm from September. The new Marketing Manager had worked with this agency, I was impressed by their presentation and knowledge of the UK Natural Health Market.

Auberon Waugh, Editor and Columnist On 1st August, Auberon Waugh, the Daily Telegraph 'Way of the World' columnist and Editor of the Literary Review, came to supper at Larkhall with a lady Doctor. This followed an earlier contact when I was in Santa Margherita and read that the magazine was looking for a sponsor for their monthly Poetry Competition. 'Bron', as he was known, was a supporter of small scale private enterprise and of individual freedom. We got on well with him and his friend and agreed to sponsor the Poetry Competition under the 'Larkhall Green Farm' name. This continued, despite objections from my brother, until 1999. This sponsorship provided an awareness of Larkhall to a select population of intelligent people. Bron also helped with PR from time to time in his many columns. We had both been born on the same day in 1937 & 1939 and he would come to Annie's Room to celebrate with me. RG used to cook us grouse which we both liked and Bron would bring a good bottle of wine to go with them. One year, the Princess of Wales came to the Literary Review's annual lunch to present the winner of the Poetry Competition with their prize in the cellars of the Cafe Royal in Regent Street. RG and I attended this intimate affair.

Marketing proposals presented At the end of August, I received a memo that Neil Wright had sent to the new Marketing Manager. It covered several opportunities for marketing to consider. It should be noted that W5 had been selected by the new manager for special effort. This product was soon to receive adverse publicity which could only have been generated from an inside Larkhall source. I now believed that this was a deliberate act of sabotage by the old sales staff to undermine the new management.

A marketing proposal was put forward by members of the sales staff who had been effectively demoted following the appointment of the General Sales Manager. It contained a re-hash of many previous ideas and for the old sales team to present it was laughable. It certainly covered the right direction but I was doubtful that its authors could implement their proposed programme that had previously failed. This indicated that the old sales team were confident of their position despite the appointment of Neil Wright. One of the staff in particular dedicated himself to ousting the newly appointed man. Employment regulations made it virtually impossible for me to do anything about it. It did not augur well.

The possible use of Microfolic Acid to spearhead interest in the comprehensive Foresight range of preconceptual supplements with direct involvement of Nim Barnes the founder of that charity was proposed. Ash Associates were in touch with the Government's 'Health Education Authority' regarding their promotion of Folic Acid pre-conceptually. It seemed unlikely Larkhall's Microfolic acid would obtain any special mention. However, we agreed to work with them as far as possible. The HEA was axed in 2000 and other bodies have since arisen.

Dr Gillian McKeith might possibly become an advisor through the new PR agency Ash Associates. She later, in the 2000s, became a TV Diet guru but was subsequently exposed as having a Ph.D (Doctorate) qualification by mail order from the USA like so many others. She was still on the way up when she worked with Larkhall.

Sponsorships of Wimbledon Football Club and The Aerobics Society of GB were seen as worth continued effort. The connection of the marketing manager's father with the RFU in Twickenham was to be explored, to hopefully enable Larkhall to provide nutritional advice and support for the England Rugby Team.

UK Market for Food Supplements an Autumn overview The September issue of the Trade Magazine, Pharmacy Products Review carried an interesting article on the Vitamin and Mineral Supplement (VMS) market in the UK. Growing competition was coming from Supermarkets with own brands of the most popular formulations.

The fad part of the market was noted, particularly Royal Jelly where sales had slumped from an annual peak of £50 million to £1 million in a very few years. The fads had been enough to sustain the overall market at around £250 million but there was no consistency. Consumers were fickle.

One-a day Multivitamins, VItamin C and Cod Liver Oil still formed the backbone of sales. Lack of good reliable information was a problem as was threatened legislation from Europe regarding strengths of nutrients permitted in unlicensed supplements. To add to producers problems, most consumers perceived food supplements as medicines.

Fortunately for the company RG and I were able to write books about food and supplements, although it meant an extra workload for us. (For a complete list of these books see appendix.)

Foresight Preconception Charity a commercial conundrum In July I telephoned Nim Barnes regarding developing a one-a-day Foresight supplement tablet. However, Nim was adamantly against the idea so I abandoned the project and resigned myself to the view that awareness of Foresight would remain restricted and development of the preconceptual nutritional ideas would need to be within either Cantassium or Natural Flow. Confusion within Larkhall's customer base would need avoiding -- probably impossible. I thought it was best to leave things as they were.

By mid September, I was negotiating with Foresight to attempt a scheme for donating to the charity based on sales of the Foresight branded products. Mrs Barnes was in favour of a scheme but there were side issues including press coverage and promoting the Foresight books to health professionals. Unfortunately, many of the health professionals working with Foresight were naturopaths or homoeopaths who were not registered medical practitioners. Credibility with mainstream doctors was difficult because the evidence for the effectiveness of the Foresight health programmes was not of sufficient scientific quality, but Mrs Barnes did not understand this. I said there was scientific credibility for Folic Acid 400mcg daily preconceptually, so why not link Foresight with Cantassium in some way? That idea was unacceptable to her because multi supplementation was essential and folic acid alone was not appropriate for her followers.   Whilst I agreed a donation scheme it was not really useful to Larkhall. For instance, Boots wanted the Vitamin A present in the Foresight Vitamins to be derived from Betacarotene rather than as pure Vitamin A. Mrs Barnes would not allow this and so the Foresight Vitamins were delisted in Boots and Larkhall lost out building more products on the well established micro folic acid product in Boots stores. This was a very costly decision because our competitors developed their brands instead. I tried to persuade Mrs Barnes as late as December to change her mind -- to no avail.

Coincidentally a customer wrote a testimonial praising the Foresight range. The male partner had used them to reach a very satisfactory nutrient profile that had assisted a successful conception at last.

Microvitamin range in Belgium In September I was in Belgium to meet a company interested in distributing a Micro Vitamin range under their own label in that country and Germany. This business produced an excellent opening order. Considerable resources had been put behind this new brand but unfortunately only Microfolic Acid succeeded.

W5 article a damp squib On 17th September, The Sunday Times published its anti W5 attack. Larkhall produced a rebuttal Press Release which took the sting out of the scurrilous story. A letter from me to a customer who had been misled by the article covered the situation well. I considered a libel action but later dropped the idea because the story proved to have had little or no impact. W5 was not a large brand and had been selected for an attack on Larkhall by our enemies with the usual lack of detail.

Cranberry Tablets produced by Larkhall made a difference I received a letter from a Consultant Urological Surgeon telling of his success with a patient taking Cantassium Cranberry Tablets. This tablet was made from the best powdered cranberries. Competitor's were marketing products that were weaker, not made properly (without *Secundum Artem*) and failed to work. The problem was that accurately assessing the strength of cranberry tablets/capsules was currently impossible analytically. Efficacy was dependent on the integrity of the producers of product and their suppliers. Such quality was appreciated by consumers but would never satisfy regulators.

In June we received a very interesting testimonial for Concentrated Cranberry Tablets that highlighted their benefit and zero calories compared with taking cranberry juice.

October Trade overview The dominance of Lipcote (cosmetic) sales persisted and I continued to be concerned that the relatively easy sale of this item was, as before, distorting sales peoples' efforts and adversely affecting the future of the health side of the trade business. This was nothing new but considering the extra resources deployed on the supplement side over recent years and the increase in mail order sales of those products was perhaps supportive of the recent Doidge report that advised Larkhall to concentrate on mail order and leave the retail side to its own devices.

Retailers were not passing on the favourable discounts given to them to their customers. We would try to use value added packs in 1996 but these types of promotion were costly in new packaging materials and made sales administration more complex. The hair dyes Linea Natura were growing but 50% of sales were generated by one very experienced sales agent who had been passed to Larkhall when they took over distribution. In 1996 this business would be lost except for mail order sales. Larkhall lost out but I had suspected the principal's goodwill from the outset and been cautious with Larkhall's investment in the brand.

The trade sales people thought that obtaining a medicines licence for our Gammolin Products (Evening Primrose Oil Capsules) would boost sales. They backed this with unsubstantiated estimates of the markets in UK and the EU. I argued against this idea because it would be extremely costly and uncertain, owing to the lack of evidence surrounding medicinal efficacy. There were many competitors in the area and only one apart from Scotia, Norgine Ltd, had a licence. Norgine were already involved in litigation with Scotia regarding their licence. Despite Pharmacists apparently being in favour of licensed products most would always accept a lower cost item to boost profit provided quality and safety were not in doubt. Evening Primrose Oil was generally regarded as safe because it had been on the market for over 20 years as a food supplement. I thought long term profitable sales for Larkhall were unlikely. Certainly any professional marketing to achieve doctor's prescriptions for a licensed 'Gammolin' would be very costly.

I was certain that Microfolic Acid's continued success was sure to lay the foundation for the future of Larkhall's health/vitamin business in pharmacies. More Doctors were recommending Microfolic Acid to patients because of our promotional activity with sampling of a 30 tablet professional sample pack to practice nurses. The introduction of further professionally acceptable micro supplements was sure to build credibility with orthodox health professionals who had patient confidence. Unfortunately, the Health Stores and the alternative practitioners only served a small minority of people and Larkhall needed to concentrate its efforts with orthodox professionals and use less resources on the others. The direct mail business was already supplying many 'Vitamin Freaks'. The long term future lay with the mainstream professionals. A bonus was that the sample packs of micro supplements could be used to generate sales leads to consumers and perhaps some of them might become 'Freaks' too.

Concentrating on the Micros and using Lipcote as a lead into retail stockists might work. It was worth a try. A new Micro Garlic product was to be launched into Boots. So 1996 looked interesting.

A Telesales agency could be tried to add to development of Micro Folic Acid sales. This method was less costly than employing a contract sales force for a short period but lacked face-to-face opportunities.

Royal Pharmaceutical Society and the Department of Health confirmed Larkhall had been in the right In late October, The Royal Pharmaceutical Society sent me a letter that confirmed that Sustained Release Niacin could be freely sold in Pharmacies and this was confirmed by the Medicines Control Agency.

Just after the Christmas holiday I received a letter from Department of Health that confirmed **Germanium Supplements were never banned** from sale and any ban had been voluntary. Hence Larkhall, who had never sold high strength germanium dioxide supplements that were the only ones implicated in safety issues reported in Japan, were not affected in any way.

This all meant that the **criticism of Larkhall by the BBC Food & Drink and Watchdog programmes had been wrong** and the Health Food Manufacturers Association had been mistaken in their censure of Larkhall - our shop was not a Health Food Store but a Pharmacy. Our overseas customers had correctly never stopped using our Germanium Supplements.

Hence Larkhall had suffered a great wrong and injustice but the technical complexity of the issues so far as Health Store Owners, our advertising and PR agencies, most of our own staff including my brother and regular customers led me to not to publicise this news or pursue the BBC for damages. The programmes had been broadcast several years before and a reminder of those dark days was not warranted. Larkhall had moved on.

Stone Age Diet recommended but The British Nutrition Foundation supported the modern way At the end of October, reverting to a Stone Age diet was advocated in a report in The Times newspaper. The British Nutrition Foundation the important sounding organisation that is effectively a front for the Food Industry replied that, "modern food was still essentially nutritious". A bureaucratic cop out for modern food processing as would be expected from the BNF, to protect its powerful industry sponsors.

Greek drama continued In early October RG and I went to Athens again to make a film for local TV -- all in Greek, but we spoke in English and there were subtitles. It went well according to Maria Strofalis.

Later we went to see the 'Organisation for Drugs' the Government body interpreting and enforcing the rules surrounding import and distribution of food supplements in Greece. Maria intimated that bribes were needed which she refused to pay, unlike other importers. I thought it was all Greek drama -- part of the culture in Greece. They were particularly interested in photographing and filming RG as she had beautiful, unwrinkled fair skin, blue eyes and dark hair. (Greek women are dark haired, brown eyed, olive skinned and are very wrinkled because of the hot climate so are fascinated by the opposite of this.) As well as the little film, posters and hoardings soon appeared all round Athens with an image of RG pointing to a pack of Cantassium tablets, with Greek advertising.

UK Sales positive and negative after General Sales Manager completed six months At the end of November I drew the attention of Neil Wright to the good business relations I had with the director of Company which owned several Health Stores. This was to counter the misleading statements of the trade sales manager that I am positively disliked by that person. Negatively, the trade sales manager had made this an excuse for his failure to achieve good results in those stores. The company had been taken over by one of the largest vitamin companies in the USA. Pressure was on the trade sales manager to be more accountable to Neil Wright but I was becoming suspicious that he was seeking a dismissal with compensation. Building a business with teams seemed more difficult than ever. When Neil Wright had been appointed, the trade sales manager had boasted to RG that he would have him out in three weeks and was going to find out everything about him.

On the positive side, the General Sales Manager was putting pressure on the sales teams regarding forecasts and product knowledge. He was working on the supermarkets but no firm commitments for stocking, apart from Tesco with Microfolic Acid and Micromultivitamins, they already stocked Lipcote in some stores. Positive Mail Order sales boosted the overall position of Larkhall.

The General Sales Manager had examined the commissions being paid to our sales agents. Our subsequent conversations increased my concerns regarding corruption within the sales team but proving these matters to satisfy an employment tribunal could be very costly. Neil was obviously causing worries for one in particular who four years later was dismissed for fraudulently taking payments from the agents for himself. I was also concerned about the activities of an ex-employee who might be involved in industrial espionage. He could have a contact in Larkhall, but who? I prepared a letter for my solicitor but thought better of it and didn't post it. My experiences with Duncan Campbell and his associates between 1988 and 1992 still haunted me.

Longer but poorer quality of Life at the end of 1995 In early December, The Daily Telegraph published a story headed 'Longer Life is blighted by years of ill health'. Better treatments were having a beneficial effect but lifestyles were not improving enough. Hence many were living with ill health especially blindness and arthritis.

Academics were in a parallel universe. I wrote to a Professor at London University regarding his views on Herbal remedies and their regulation. His opinion that herbals depended on a number of herbs and ingredients for their efficacy inevitably made validation of specifications for products virtually impossible. Yet he advocated strict technical specifications for these products costing companies maybe millions of pounds to devise and replicate batch to batch -- how did he square that circle? No reply received as expected. **Like so many academics he was out of touch with commercial realities.**

The Prince of Wales hosted Reception for Alternative Health Charity In mid December, I attended a Reception with RG, hosted at St James's Palace in London by The Prince of Wales to support the Bristol Cancer Help Centre. This was a fund raising event. All the guests had some connection with cancer. The invitation came to us came through Philip Barker who was currently working with the Centre.

News from USA I received a letter from a Dr Hoffer of Victoria BC regarding the recent USA Government Act that proposed to take the power to legislate against Vitamins away from the FDA. The Dr said that this should become a message to the rest of the world.

Vitamin News, a USA publication that gave information on the latest vitamin research, reported that Jeffrey Blumberg Ph.D., a well known expert in this field, found that many diseases caused by viruses could be controlled with proper nutrition.

Apple Macs In December, RG and I visited Z2 Repro in Thetford for the final typesetting and design work on their computer for our Health Leader Mail Order publication. They were among the first to have Apple-Mac Computers in the UK. RG said they were the best ones for designers. She wanted to buy one for her studio but my brother would not give permission for the line to come in, even if she paid for it herself. He had no vision. This meant we have to keep going up to Thetford, hours away by car, leaving very early in the morning and working all day with their staff to put the Health Leader together. The little company was run by Phillipa Inskip and was thriving. Their main account was the Ann Summers catalogues.

Supplement Labelling differences gave US the advantage. Vitamin A strength declarations in UK and USA and Betacarotene equivalency to pure Vitamin A.
The problems with Vitamin A (Retinol) and Betacrotene was discussed in detail in memos from our registration Department. The technical problems in this area were serious commercially because there was confusion as regards conversion equivalents between USA and the rest of the world. Use of the US system gave higher perceived concentrations for identical material inputs that gave a competitive advantage to the US manufacturers. Not popular with UK producers and put them at considerable disadvantage in the eyes of many UK retailers.

Export is such fun In December a Czechoslovakian company 'La Boheme' visited Putney to discuss Lipcote importation. They brought us sparkling wine and bought a small amount of Lipcote but never developed the business. Nice people but Lipstick Sealer users were rare in that country.

Year of The Nutrition Task Force

The Larkhall Natural Health Service - HealthWatch attack another Supplement
Company - Naturtabs - Herbals must be Wholesome - Scientific deficit in
Communications agencies - Probiotic problems - More Supplement users - Growth
but US takeover rejected - Training consultants - Press bias - Nutraceuticals need
regulating - Marketing Manager difficulty - Literary review Poetry sponsorship -
Propolis - Matthias Rath - Technical adviser - BSE and Gelatin Capsules -
Testimonials a double edged sword - Junk Foods not guilty -
Doctors in control - No Free Trade for Supplements in the EU - Evidence Base Dogma
- Bioflavonoids unsafe - Clinical Ecology pioneer - Diet and supplements experts clash
- Losing patience? - Parallel Export again - Hair Dyes - Sports Supplements - Shark
Cartilage - Dr Gillian McKeith - Folic Acid and the Health Education Authority -
Medicines Inspections - Complementary Health Care - More patience needed - Junk
Food power kept Children nutritionally deprived - Herbal research under funded -
Media man sees anew - Trufree steams ahead - Supermarket observations - A Years
Public Relations progress - Internet Marketing attempt - USA export difficulties -
Vitamania - Professor Schoenthaler in London - Autism helped by Gluten exclusion -
Little funding for Complementary Health care - Multifactorial illnesses don't exist -
Chelsea College Centenary - USA research confirmed brain power was diet related -
Supplements help patients on medications - HealthWatch not infallible - Folic Acid B4
idea - Arrogance of the Marketing Department - Delisting concerns - Symbol System
updated - Phytopharm - Reflections 1996

In 1992 'The Health of the Nation' publication had been issued by the Government. This
set out the way forward for educating the population in healthier eating. The earlier 1980's
COMA report had set out much the same ideas with the vision of people really taking their
food intake seriously and so improving general health that, in turn, would cut the cost of the
NHS.

Unfortunately, there were powerful industrial interests who, whilst on the surface
appearing in favour, were actually against these proposals and used well constructed
schemes to keep resources both academic and financial from genuine support of a healthier
population based on really healthy diets. The opposition included the pharma/medical
interest which thrived on sickness, and the junk food producers/marketers who made huge
profits from low basic cost processed foods and ingredients.

1996 saw formation of the 'Nutrition Task Force' under Dr Michael Nelson, who had
been one of the 'experts' used by Shropshire Council in their prosecution of Larkhall in
1992. His research, funded by the World Sugar Corporation, had been exposed as fatally
flawed. This Nutrition Task Force certainly had the right ideas to educate people in
adopting healthier diets by improving cooking skills and selecting fresh fruit and
vegetables. As expected, Dietary Supplements were derided as a waste of money, whereas I
advocated their use whilst the diet was being improved. They should be the crutch to be
discarded when consumers were healthy again.

An editorial in a Nutrition Magazine 'Down and out in 1996' illustrated the dilemma well.

LARKHALL GREEN FARM

The Larkhall Natural Health Service   Microfolic Acid was still seen as the spearhead for the Supplement range at Larkhall. A media advertising proposal was put forward by The Media Shop and the marketing plan agreed with certain specific aims. The HEA (Health Education Authority), a government body, was undertaking a large educational programme from February and Larkhall wanted to capitalize on this initiative. The PR agency (Ash Communications) were on good terms with people at the HEA working on this project.

Publicity concerning supplement users and professional advice was shown to be preferred. Pharmacists and Doctors were not enthusing patients about vitamin supplements and most positive approaches were generated by practice/counter assistants. It would seem that Larkhall's policy of using the professional route was likely to benefit the company long term but little immediate result could be expected. The important finding was that doctors were the most trusted source of health information.

The Larkhall Natural Health Service was launched with a new type of direct sales colour leaflet on quality paper. This aimed to appeal to the less committed supplement user. Information to comply with recent advertising codes on Larkhall's Natural products were given under headings Hair, Feet, Joints, Skin, Eyes and Men. This leaflet also led people to the whole range if they followed up with an enquiry.

Larkhall brand for children wins   The magazine 'Here's Health' tested Children's Vitamins and Natural Flow's 'Animal Fun' won with four stars and **best buy** award.

HealthWatch fight another Supplement producer   HealthWatch continued its fight with the supplement and alternative health movement with an attack on a PR company acting for Wassen Nutrients Selenium ACE product. They pointed out that the Press Release made claims for medicinal benefit in Arthritis that would be illegal in advertisements. This was a continuing problem for unlicensed products that look like medicines but seldom led to action by the authorities. They considered publicity generated by press releases very difficult to prevent by legal action in Court because finding the culprit was close to impossible - who did they sue? The publisher, the agency, the company - could they prove it with an audit trail that would stand up in Court?

Naturtabs and Microvitamins   In early January I drew the new Marketing staff's attention to the 'Naturtab' branding once used by Larkhall on those Cantassium Supplements that reached the highest 'Natural' standards. They agreed that it should be re-introduced and that the term was self explanatory. I wondered why the sales people who joined us in 1986 never appreciated what Cantassium was really about. RG's symbol system and the naturtab branding were probably our best assets in the food supplement market yet not enthusiastically promoted as positive attributes for our products.

Ash Communications were working on a press release for 'Micro Garlic'which had been accepted for stocking by Boots. The release emphasised the benefits of Garlic to health and the advantages of the microtablets being concentrated without odour.
Hopefully, Naturtabs and Micro Supplements with Symbol System were to be core attributes in the future. Reference to our heritage of Secundum Artem should be used too.

Herbal products must be wholesome.   I made contact again with a retired academic Emeritus Professor at the School of Pharmacy in London. He was at Chelsea School of Pharmacy with me back in the 1950s. He was currently concerned about the way legislation was moving against Herbal Remedies but could not take the possibility that academia itself was largely responsible because of its fixed 'Evidence Based' view.

I firmly believed that this intransigence could effectively only result in the purest herbal extracts being able to comply with enforced technical criteria. This ultimately meant that only single chemical entities which matched the molecule found in a specific herb. He proved to be less persuaded on these difficulties than Professor Arnold Beckett or the late Professor Joe Shellard.

Ignorance amongst Marketing agencies staff and directors The 20th January issue of the British Medical Journal carried a short piece in its 'Soundings column' about Market Research and PR agencies. It drew attention to the ignorance of medicine and chemistry of many staff and executives in that business. I had experienced this several times and a marketing consultant in 1985 had proved typical of the breed. Several PR agencies were equally inept. I believed the problem was endemic with communicators including journalists and TV pundits.

I mid February I wrote to my old adversaries at the BBC Food & Drink Programme about a feature in a recent show on BBC2 TV that concerned the negative results in a nutrition trial where the supplements used were made from synthetic ingredients including Beta Carotene. This letter put the argument in favour of Natural rather than Synthetic micronutrients in supplements well. As expected, there was no response from the biased F&D Programme to defend their report nor was any comment made on their subsequent programmes. Such ignorance from influential journalists was disgraceful and the tragedy is that it persists to this day (2015).

Probiotic supplements had problems Natural Flow Acidophilus was one of two probiotic supplements that tested satisfactorily for species and concentration by a Professor at the Royal Free Hospital. Health Which Magazine (Consumers Association) featured the results of all the products tested and several were revealed as 'empty food supplements' including some of the most popular American Brands. Health Which ran an article highlighting what it deemed serious errors by producers. The repercussions did not affect Larkhall but several companies lost consumer credibility.

More food supplement users last year Chemist & Druggist reported that 750,000 new users had joined the supplement consumer population in 1995. The demand for higher strength supplements was increasing. The actual report on which the magazine relied had been produced by Seven Seas a leading supplement supplier to Pharmacies through their ever popular Cod Liver Oil range of products. In recent years they had widened their range but they were usually copyists rather than innovators. This report was considered a biased commercial document drawn up for PR purposes to try and increase business for Seven Seas through Chemists & Supermarkets.

Larkhall still growing overseas Export sales were growing again. Supplements were sent to Greece, Spain, Sweden, Belgium, Portugal, Holland and Ireland. The Veterinary Products sold under the Natural Rearing Brand were confined to one customer in Canada - these products did not command any marketing spend and sales were generated by Mrs Baraclai Levy's books. Veterinary products were highly regulated in most countries and because this range was herbal, obtaining licences was costly. The trademark holder (Mrs Levy) was responsible for licensing not Larkhall. A serious approach from Brazil regarding Lipcote was expected to result in orders soon. Hope sprung eternally.

New countries with exchange rate control laws made things difficult. Croatia was increasing slowly but Romania seemed to be erecting barriers against supplements despite the influence of Professor Joan Drangan their sports medicine expert. A large order from Belgium for micro supplements was shipped. Although four products were supplied only Folic Acid was to succeed in the longer term. This highlighted the importance of scientific credibility in the development of markets overseas.

Takeover approach from USA   In mid February, a man came to see me regarding an American Sports Supplement company 'Amerifit' being interested in purchasing Larkhall. This was a fairly new company that had expanded rapidly in the USA. I did not think they had funds available for the venture and knew little of the differences between US and UK regulations in the food supplement area. I thought that our recent efforts with Microvitamins in the USA may have prompted this approach. I did not expect another visit but on 24th April one of the owners of Amerifit visited Putney to pursue the possibility of the takeover. He wanted my brother and I to continue managing Larkhall under their ownership. We were not interested.

A Freak weather accident at Annie's Room On 20th February there was an accident on this very cold, windy day, everything iced-up and snow. The temperature was -6°C that morning. In a freak gust of wind that morning the heavy lid of the water tank on the roof was blown off, went up in the air and crashed down on to the skylight immediately above the dining table at 9.30. Luckily no one was in the room at the time. A large tarpaulin had to be fixed over the skylight, which was now a gaping hole, open to the elements. Owing to the icy conditions it was several days before it could be repaired properly by a roofer. The dining table was covered in shards of glass, some of which were stuck into the wood. A local firm later repaired it. The insurance investigator said it was one of several freak accidents in Putney that day, owing to a sudden squall. RG had been sitting at the table working a few minutes earlier and had only just left to collect her mail at the office and then go her studio on the roof. She had had a lucky escape.

Sales training consultants to change culture?   A sales training company, was contacted in March and made proposals for carrying out internal staff training tailored to Larkhall's requirements. It was anticipated that these training courses would address many of the problems I had seen following re-organisation of the sales department. The firm undertook an initial appraisal of Staff in August/September. Their service looked good but maybe tailored for larger companies than Larkhall.

   Coincidentally, I issued a memo because I had spotted a letter in the Pharmaceutical Journal regarding a Tablet Crusher, sold without a warning regarding its use with sustained release tablets. This item was sold by a Larkhall competitor who had been copying our products with cheaper versions for several years. This time they had been caught out by professionals. Larkhall's crusher was always labeled with advice about **not crushing sustained release products.** I used this memo to point out Larkhall's professional and responsible approach to the sales staff that many of these people always seemed to find difficult to appreciate. Could the training company change that attitude?

Biased press story on Vitamin C.   At the end of March, The Pharmaceutical Journal reported on recent research regarding high strength Vitamin C Supplementation interfering with oestrogens by increasing the levels in the blood. There was a warning regarding contraceptive pill use and HRT too. Overall, I thought the press coverage was probably orchestrated by the anti-vitamin lobby. As usual an anecdotal story for a supplement causing harm was deemed important but similar reports on drugs were brushed aside as of no concern. How many people died each year from overdosing with Aspirin?

Nutraceuticals controversy   The Lancet carried an editorial on Nutraceuticals (functional foods) with suggestions for draconian regulation including assets of manufacturers being seized when false advertising claims had been made. The borderline between foods and drugs is not well defined and this controversy still continues in 2015. This article was useful because it covered the arguments concisely and well. It even mentioned the fortifying of food with folate to help prevent Spina Bifida - still not adopted in the UK (2015) but enforced in some countries with doubtful benefit. Whilst Spina Bifida is reduced there are health problems for those who are not females of childbearing age.

Bailiffs Case in the Daily Mail   Tandem IQ case against the Bailiffs was won early in the year and they had to pay back their fees to Larkhall, after long fight. A long article about this case by Christopher Booker was published in the Daily Mail where I was pictured **in defiant mood.**

New Marketing manager posed a problem   Larkhall's recently appointed Marketing Manager, had serious disagreements with our long serving Advertising agency (The Media Shop). I was concerned about this and wondered if there was a hidden agenda with her trying to undermine the Media Shop, to prepare the ground for the appointment of an agency favoured by her. She had worked for one of the largest agencies Saatchi and Saatchi (for a short time) and was, perhaps, confident that she would be listened to. She had no idea that I had been involved with several advertising agencies since 1965 and knew something of their ways. The Media Shop report of these occurrences was clear - I waited to see what action the general Sales Manager Neil Wright would take.

Literary Review sponsorship raised awareness of Larkhall amongst opinion formers
The recent Health Leader (in house) publication demonstrated how the direct mail side of Larkhall was developing with many satisfied and supportive customers. A letter to the Literary Review about the rural idyll at the Charlbury facility was reprinted in the Health Leader. Perhaps that is why so many people at the Head Office in Putney called Charlbury 'Sleepy Hollow'. The packing work done there was crucial to Larkhall's success but no imagination was required to run it and the connection with the Literary Review Poetry Prize was entirely with RG and me in Putney. (We frequently entertained the editor, Auberon Waugh, as a guest in Annie's Room.) Charlbury management were opposed to this sponsorship but I always said it put Larkhall at a different level in British culture. I met many intelligent people who were supportive and aware of Larkhall's ideals.
  This issue of the Health Leader was lively, informative and enjoyed by many. Produced, designed and written by myself and RG there was no outside agency or staff input. Who else would have had our knowledge to draw on?

Propolis (Bee Glue) as a licensed Medicine   In mid March Professor Arnold Beckett came to Dinner in Annie's Room. He was very bullish about Propolis (Bee Glue) obtaining a medicines licence from the Medicines Control Authority. I was very sceptical and surprised at his naivety. The officials would appear friendly and co-operative and take money for the application but the end was certain to be nothing doing because they wanted scientific consistency based on the strict criteria they applied to synthetic chemical drugs impossible for propolis.

Dr Matthias Rath   At the end of March, Dr Matthias Rath a qualified medical doctor from Germany but based in the USA, visited Putney for discussions about marketing his natural health programmes. Rath later became notorious and a target for the anti-alternative health care lobby. I listened to his sales pitch but was not persuaded or impressed by his brash American manner.

313

Expertise requested by International Generics   I had been asked for help in connection with a large export order for multivitamin tablets that had deteriorated very quickly in West Africa. International Generics, Leon Tamman's old company, provided me all relevant documents and samples. I discovered several irregularities in the production records that enabled lawyers acting for IG to gain compensation without a court case. It was pleasing to find that I had not lost my eye for the technical side of tablet making. That must have been the result of youth spent on the manufacturing floor.

BSE and other drug problems   In early April the Daily Telegraph carried a piece on the hazards surrounding the very popular anti-osteoporosis drug Fosamax (Alendronic Acid). This type of publicity was an aid to patients looking at the possibilities supplements and diets (eg Calcium,Vit D, Magnesium) helping without resort to powerful drugs like Fosamax. Even the long established (1921) 'Cantassium Dietary System' had a role to play here.

The Independent on Sunday referred to Sugoids with antiviral properties being researched at Oxford University but by 2013 an internet search indicated that this was a dead end. This newspaper also investigated 'Functional Foods' and heavily criticised the hype surrounding products like branded yoghurts.

In mid April, the Medicines Control Agency continued to be concerned about BSE contamination from the gelatin used in Medicines, especially capsules. I thought this was a total waste of bureaucrats time since common sense science dictated that the chances of any consumer contracting BSE/CJD via bovine purified gelatin in capsule shells were zero. Anyway, Larkhall's technical services manager replied to their request correctly.

Testimonials cheer me up   At the end of April two testimonials from customers made happy reading. One lady had used Joint Nutritional Complex formula with amazing results. Ibuprofen, the anti-inflammatory drug, caused nasty side effects but JNC was perfect and unsurprisingly to her GP's amazement. The other from a male district nurse praised so many of Larkhall's products used by his family and friends. Unfortunately, he requested free supplies if we used his testimonial for publicity purposes. No doubt this letter was genuine but the likes of HealthWatch would just emphasise that final request and so denigrate Larkhall if we used that letter.

Junk foods not responsible for Obesity said its lobby group   In early May, an article in the Daily Telegraph illustrated the efforts of the Biscuit, Cake, Chocolate and Confectionary alliance, a Junk Food industry group, to promote the benefits of their products. Their denial through an expert Doctor from Mars (sic) of any connection of cakes, snacks and biscuits with obesity was laughable if it wasn't so serious for public health. The expert said obesity was primarily a genetically derived health problem. No wonder Larkhall and I have been so regularly attacked over the years by the Alliance and their many associates and dependent researchers in academia.

Doctors are the real masters of medicine   The Independent on Sunday drew attention to allergy blood tests being offered by branches of Supermarket 'Safeway' that have pharmacies *in situ*. As expected the medical interest was against this move. Since time immemorial, doctors have been very protective of their professional superiority over pharmacists.

314

Free Trade in supplements and the experts showed their hand   I attended a meeting of The European Health Food Trade Association at the Institute of Directors. The concerns about the reality of 'Free Trade' in Supplements and Health Foods was the main topic with many countries preventing imports on the grounds of 'Safety' despite those same products being freely available in other countries. I asked the panel of experts about the evidence for higher death rates and other health hazards in the countries in which supplements were freely imported and was answered with a long silence.

Evidence based dogma   In mid May, the medical journal 'The Lancet' carried a short account concerning the term 'Evidence-based Medicine'. This illustrated the concern that dogmatic adherence to science based concepts by policymakers was adversely affecting Doctor/patient interactions to the detriment of patients. The Sydenham Society - (Clinical Epidemiology) supported these concerns about the current path being taken by authorities. Has this changed by 2015? I think not.

Bioflavonoids safety issue   In early May, Nim Barnes of the Foresight Preconceptual Charity was worried about the inclusion of 'Bioflavonoids' in some of their formulations owing to a member seeing a reference in 'Superimmunity for Kids' that Bioflavonoids break down to Quercetin, which that author considered unacceptable for ingestion during pregnancy. I dismissed that opinion saying that Bioflavonoids used in Foresight Supplements were safe. I intimated that the research quoted was on animals at very high dosage and of no relevance to Foresight's supplements. This type of scaremongering is not unusual and extensively used by the anti-food supplement lobby. Sadly, health food producers often quote beneficial animal research in their promotional efforts and so undermine their defence against opponents.

Death of Dr Richard Mackarness the Food Allergy pioneer   In May, Amelia Nathan Hill of Action Against Allergy, privately published a tribute to Dr Richard Mackarness who died on 18th March in Australia. Mackarness had worked closely with me and I had met him several times. He was a pioneer of Food Allergy in the UK and followed the teachings of Clinical Ecologists in the USA. The term and science of 'Clinical Ecology' had been developed over the past several years in the USA.

Diet and supplements - experts clash   On June 2nd, The Sunday Times Style section published a general article entitled 'Supplementary benefits' which showed the difference in approach between the experts Patrick Holford and Amanda Ursell. Holford sponsored many formulations and ran 'The Institute for Optimum Nutrition', a controversial nutrition education set-up. He had written books on the subject and was a strong promoter of supplementation including high doses where the borderline between food and medicine met. Holford was disingenuous in the quotes attributed to him in this article. Ursell believed in diet before supplements as can be deduced from her article for the Sunday Telegraph on 23rd June.

Company sale contemplated   In early June, Martin Kimber a mergers and aquisitions accountant came to see me on the recommendation of Oxford Business Planning Consultants. He may act for us if he can find a purchaser. He came for more talks at the end of the month.

Continuing UK sales problems I voiced my fears regarding the sales team after a general trade sales meeting on 5th June. There was a personality problem and this made progress for the company very difficult. It appeared that the regime developed since 1994 was failing. I was not prepared to hold these people's hands indefinitely - already the Export Trade was carrying home trade whilst it should have beeen the other way round. Later, there was evidence of the dissent in the sales team - the former trade sales manager had spent advertising money with a wholesaler who was not stocking the product. Apparently he had agreed to that expenditure before he received a customer order that was contrary to company policy. He was reprimanded but had a barely plausible excuse which would have been sure to satisfy any employment tribunal to find for him should he have been dismissed.

Parallel Export still going on The suspicion that certain home trade salesmen were encouraging their customers to pursue parallel export sales where the sales efforts of myself and the chosen distributors overseas were doing well. This was certain because I had noted particular home customers were buying items that were mainly in demand in Greece. Of course, there was a legal problem with EU countries where all borders must be open and Brussels wants the lowest prices for all consumers. Distributors in some countries were making great efforts at huge cost to them only to find parallel imports undermining their prices. Larkhall sales staff enjoyed sales bonuses too having made effortless excessive sales to their dishonest customers. Meanwhile Larkhall's overseas distributors had excuses for late payment and insisting on more discount. Nothing had changed.

A UK customer called Panfold had been ordering excessive amounts of Hair Nutrition tablets. We stopped his account.

Tints of Nature distributorship further news A Complimentary letter was received regarding the 'Tints of Nature' Linea Natura range. This 'natural' hair colourant range was made in Britain and incorporated antioxidants (at my suggestion to perhaps offer cancer protection). After the successful launch Larkhall were promised long term exclusivity but the manufacturers reneged as expected because we failed to reach their hoped for sales level in Health Food Stores. We continued to distribute the range by mail order. However, sales soon dwindled when the Healthfood wholesalers stopped buying from Larkhall.

Sports Supplements Towards the end of June, the Sunday Telegraph's Sports section carried an article by dietitian Amanda Ursell (see above), a known sceptic as regards supplementation. She deplored the surfeit of sports supplements on Health Store shelves. She claimed most were of unproven benefit and well over strength as regards dietary requirements. The hype in this area had been developing since the mid 60s and most of the product lines emanated from the USA. Magazines for body builders were proliferating and most were published by supplement suppliers who also sponsored tournaments. Recently, more UK manufacturers had joined the party and authorities were beginning to clamp down on the exaggerated claims. Generally, Pharmacies had not been stockists of these products because they were considered as strictly food based. Health Food retailers and Gymnasiums were the centres for retail sale and the lack of technical knowledge helped manufacturers make wild claims that were passed on to the gullible athletes/bodybuilders. Many of the successful retailers picked up their sales pitches from visits to the USA where exhibitions had large spaces devoted to sports supplements with demonstrations from successful bodybuilders who often had their own brands. These persuaded consumers both male and female that a supremely muscular body was readily achieved with the right supplement programme and some exercises.

Larkhall had never specialised in this product area although we had worked as contractors to some of the marketers.

Mid year UK Sales review   A general UK Sales Report from the sales manager was useful. It highlighted several ongoing concerns that would need attention. Lipcote was the most successful item in our range and this was reflected in advertising and sales effort over the last twenty-five years. It had few competitors but was now threatened by the advent of long lasting lipsticks that were being heavily promoted by the leading cosmetic companies. The Microvitamins, apart from Folic Acid, needed more marketing input and Tesco seemed likely to delist soon. The contract business was dying -- unsurprisingly since our own brands competed with companies likely to need our manufacturing expertise. Such potential customers inevitably believed their products would receive less priority in our production programmes. There was also the suspicion that if we saw one of their products succeeding then we would add a more natural version of it in our lists.

Incentivising retailers with special added value packs and promotions were far from a guarantee of extra long term sales.

Neil Wright was trying to ensure that the UK Trade sales staff budget their promotional activity in a memo in June. I said I would be interested to see whether this memo had any effect.

The activity reported indicated that the company was exploring new opportunities particularly with information to interest consumers. The health claims rules made this task very difficult in the UK. Sadly, the American based competitors seemed to be bringing their brash and aggressive advertising and sales techniques to our market that encouraged bureaucrats to call for more regulation for the health food market. Defending the indigenous law abiding companies in these circumstances was impossible.

Lets Live magazine in USA published "Ten Vitamin Truths" by Jack Challem. Larkhall obtained permission to re-print in UK and use it as a promotional leaflet to retail stockists and mail order consumers.

Shark Cartilage   In early July, Dr Holt from USA visited Putney representing the Shark Cartilage proprietary company 'Cartilade'. He was enthusiastic about their unique product and its prospects in the UK and Europe. I told him that the regulations surrounding miracle food ingredients in the UK would make claims impossible other than through PR. In the USA, Shark Cartilage was very big business following the publication of the book 'Sharks don't get Cancer' by Dr Lane. Lane was fronting for Cartilade but I doubted his credibility although, having listened to him, admitted he was a persuasive lecturer to lay people. The product never gained a market in the UK that did not lie in shark infested seas.

Gillian McKeith   In early July, Howard Magaziner, the partner of Dr Gillian McKeith who gave press talks for Larkhall at the PR Agency (Ash Associates) came to see me. He wanted to promote G McKeith as a health guru with her own range of products. He promised Larkhall considerable beneficial publicity for a regular payment. Having already paid Dr Gillian to do some press briefing meetings I agreed to continue with that for the time being. I soon realised that the Doctorate that McKeith used to enhance her credibility was one of those from a USA institute and not a real University. I thought it best we should keep her at arm's length.

Health Education Authority meeting on Folic Acid   I joined a meeting at The Agency with Ash and representatives of the HEA (Health Education Authority) regarding monetary support for their upcoming drive to reach women preconception with the Folic Acid supplementation message. There was much pressure on the Government to make the addition of Folic Acid to bread and baking flours compulsory. Many doctors said this would cut the incidence of Spina Bifida babies.

However there were many medical experts who were against compulsory 'Medication' of foods. Since too much folic acid masked the presence of low levels of Vitamin B12 in the blood test for pernicious anaemia there was a major problem in this instance. So like Fluoridation of Water the idea had a long road ahead and I believed Folic Acid would never be compulsorily added to breads and flours in the UK. There was no progress by 2015.

Medicines Inspections   In mid July, we had an Inspection by appointment at Putney by two inspectors from the Medicines Control Agency. This went well but the report and their follow-up letter indicated the typical attention to minutiae that the bureaucracy has spawned. It was pleasing to note that our general manager's report recorded that the lead inspector said "This is a brand new world for Larkhall and it is a revelation". But nothing is ever all right for these people. I thought that this was probably a key moment in my future plans whichever way they went because, after over twenty years of steady investment, we now had a very good manufacturing facility that the right commercial buyer would appreciate. It was also essential to ensure our continued success in export.

In mid August, there was a Medicines Inspection at the Charlbury facility. There were no critical problems to be addressed but many nit-picking comments that would be looked into. Business could continue but the output lost by these inspections was of no commercial concern to the inspectors and their masters. Any patient benefits accruing from these bureaucratic affairs would be hard to find especially when key production personnel and the facilities remain unchanged from year to year.

Complementary Medicine in the British Medical Journal again The July 20th issue of The British Medical Journal carried an article under the headline 'Complementary medicine is booming worldwide'. The complexity of the area was discussed and some progress in regulation was reported. However the overall situation remained a minefield with most funding private and 'evidence' for effectiveness of the treatments sparse. Many Doctors indirectly support CAM (Complementary and Alternative Medicine) and used it in their practices so that the NHS was helping developments. Co-operation between CAM and orthodox treatments was a way forward according to the British Medical Association.

Observations on the current UK supplement market   Activity in the UK trade was higher and progress was discernible but the caveats seen in June have not gone away. All supermarkets have been presented with the Microvitamin range but only Tesco have stocked. Boots propose to do Microgarlic but the upfront cost to Larkhall was high and unavoidable. Management was attempting to control the promotional budget but some areas were perhaps underfunded. Hopefully, we would know more by the year's end. Direct sales were threatened through competition and the declining number of Green Farm Members. Whilst Larkhall had a large range of products the popularity of just a few items - Vitamin C, Joint Nutritional Complex, Evening Primrose, Microfolic Acid led to calls for range reduction -- a view long opposed by me. Although the agency line Linea Natura (Hair Dyes) was progressing well the sales effort diverted from our main ranges was not without cost. Happily this distributorship was soon lost.

Neil Wright had reported on his visits to customers accompanying the sales representatives. There seemed to be progress but the key product range (Microvitamins) was seen as a pharmacy line not a Health Food one. I hoped the possible imminent introduction of threatened EU rules banning high strength supplements would favour the micro range. The value-added promotional packs were going well. The sales reps did not appear to be giving the office team enough support but NW intended to address the problems at the next sales meeting.

False reporting of the IQ vitamin link continued   The Nutrition section in the August issue of the magazine 'Maternal and Child Health, carried an article on the 'Diet of Schoolchildren' by a chief dietitian. Whilst the adequacy of micronutrients provided by school meals was unsatisfactory, the use of supplements was dismissed as not worthwhile since Professor Naismith's research had enabled dismissal of Benton and Roberts' positive findings (Larkhall's funded research). The facts that a Court case had elucidated that Naismith's research was flawed, was not a repeat of Benton and Roberts work and that there were many other positive results recorded in the scientific literature, were totally ignored by the author. I wrote to the PR agency about this article but nothing helpful followed. It was very frustrating but not unexpected because of the powerful opposition in the Junk Food industry that seemed impervious to attack, despite their misleading information.

Science for Herbals possibly too demanding   The August 3rd issue of The British Medical Journal devoted a leader and a long research paper to the herb St John's Wort (Hypericum) that emanated from Germany. This was a useful appraisal of the herb through the eyes of a leading world Medical Science publication. However, it demonstrated the great difficulties facing herbal medicines in the future - resources for research into non patentable herbs were scarce and it was unlikely that wider acceptance of herbals would ever materialise.

TV programme maker change of mind   In Mid August, the Sunday Times carried an article by the maker of the BBC Food and Drink programme that had reported adversely on Larkhall without checking facts. In this article he criticised 'scare stories' about chemicals where harmful effects could be detected in very high concentrations and no effects when the substance was present in minute quantities. What a huge change of mind he has had since 1991. I wrote to him, without receiving a reply, about the error made by his 'Food & Drink, programme where the journalist had grossly misled viewers concerning Germanium in a Larkhall product. It's a great pity that this man was not prepared to admit to his error five years later. I included references to Tandem IQ and Salmonella/BSE illustrative of the media's power to cause unjustified havoc.

Trufree advertising at last!   The Coeliac Society publication 'Crossed Grain' carried Larkhall's first ever advertisement for Trufree No 1 Flour for Crusty White Loaf (not 'Bread' since trade description enforces a wheat content if the term Bread is used). The advertisement carried a direct response possibility -- a feature much favoured by RG and me. Trufree was particularly difficult to advertise as it comprises prescription products and legally they should not be advertised to the general public, it was permitted in the case of the Coeliac Society's magazine.

RG began a series of enormous bake-ups in Annie's Room kitchen using her Trufree flours, for future advertisements. She worked with Chris Christodoulou, a photographer, arranging the food herself. He was the same photographer she had employed to take the photographs for her Bumper Bake Book. The photos of the bake-ups were stunning and put us years ahead of any other gluten-free brand -- Trufree left them standing.

In September The Chemist & Druggist reported **140% increase in sales** for the Trufree range of special dietary Flours. When it is permitted, advertising can be magic. The Larkhall sales team had nothing to do with this hike, just RG herself, and everything in the photos was genuinely made from Trufree flours and not faked-up with ordinary wheat flour items -- a favourite agency trick.

319

Tesco and other supermarket listings   Tesco were proposing to delete the microvitamins both Folic Acid and Multivitamins. This was because they only stock products from suppliers with an average of at least £2000 per month total invoice value. Lipcote continued because it was sold under an umbrella with other cosmetic products from a variety of producers. The General Sales manager had to try and find a way to get this proposal rescinded or find a partner to handle the products through Tesco. I thought this typified the problems for small companies being listed in supermarkets.

Ash complete a year as our Public Relations agency   Ash Associates had completed a year as Larkhall's PR agency and presented a report on the past year and on proposed activity for 1997. This showed the success of Ash's work and the grasp that they had of the business, its philosophy and products. They had made Larkhall more targeted in the specialist areas but resources have to be eked from the total promotional spend. The £60,000 budget for 1996 was difficult for management to justify and unlikely to be increased in 1997.

The total promotional spend was running at around £1,000,000 a year: increasing PR would have had to be at the expense of other areas. Attempts to analyse media spend/effectiveness were being made by the sales manager but I still believed that advertising was more intuitive than scientific. It was thought that 50% of advertising spends were wasted but the problem was knowing which 50%? The current advertisements often incorporated a direct response mechanism so theoretically there was a trade and direct sales benefit from such advertisements. Trade advertising was often dismissed as not worth it yet large export customers had come to Larkhall that way. PR in Trade magazines incorporating a colour picture (paid for) was perhaps good for sales too.

Ash had prepared an article for Green Farm Magazine following Professor Schoenthaler's October visit to the UK. This would be published in the Magazine in early 1997. It concentrated on diet and brainpower with the proven connection to Children's IQ but went on to develop the research's findings and implications for the whole population.

Internet Marketing a sorry tale   At the end of September, my brother introduced me to Mr Shiner who was apparently an expert in marketing products on the internet which was then in its infancy. He wished to add a popular supplement to his portfolio and I agreed with him that a special formula Vitamin C currently available in USA would be a good test product. Shiner was confident that his web site would sell this very successfully and asked for prices. The product would be branded 'Cantassium'. Shiner was an enthusiastic salesman but I was wary as regards costs and responses. It later transpired that Larkhall would have considerable upfront costs including stocking Shiner with product.

I still thought this would be a good test of the power of internet selling but needed to know more about Shiner and his enterprise that he claimed was world wide but strongest in the USA. This all fell apart early in 1997.

In late February 1997 my brother was sent a letter (dated 26th but arrived in Charlbury 3rd March) by Leo Shiner of Global Market Ltd regarding his proposals for selling Larkhall's Vitamin C Tablets on the Internet that was first mooted in September 1996. In the letter he stated that I had agreed the proposed arrangement on the 'phone on 25th February 1997. This was not true1[but unfortunately I had gone to the USA on business on 1st March. My brother took Shiner at his word and agreed to this business without checking with me or waiting for my return from the USA. There was a thought that this was a unique opportunity for Larkhall to test the Internet route to sales and my brother was keen on the Internet and believed the US market was where it was all happening -- it wasn't in 1997.

Shiner was going to produce a book and set up the website. His idea was that Larkhall would pay £10,000 in two tranches before any internet sales of the Vitamin C Tablets had been made. All this was an impossible dream and hardly any sales ever took place. My absence had cost Larkhall £10,000. I would never have agreed to this but might have risked £2000 which would probably not have appealed to Shiner who was looking for a bigger sting. In the event, a very little business in the Vitamin C tablets was done but Shiner soon disappeared.

USA progress?   In October, after intensive negotiations by our US distributor, a major US multilevel direct sales company ordered nearly £60,000 worth of Lipchic (the USA version of Lipcote). This was a major breakthrough into the USA market for Larkhall. However, as expected in the next year, a change in management personnel at the multilevel company took place and the business soon died for no good reason. We had refused to supply them with bulk Lipchic for them to have specially bottled because that would have enabled them to copy our product. As usual the Americans wanted extra profit and would try to copy our product by hook or by crook. Exporting was such fun as Prime Minister Harold Wilson had always said.

Supplementation was too complicated   The October issue of Let's Live, the US Health Magazine, carried a letter from a reader that complained about the many different approaches to supplementation. There was much confusion and frustration amongst consumers. Good advice was given "Take a good multi formula with perhaps 50 ingredients and then add a little extra VItamin C", after that consider special nutrients allied to the symptoms you are experiencing say Pantothenate and polyunsaturates for rheumatics. Do not just take any new item as many were pure fashion and hype.

A new book **'Vitamania: Vitamins in American Culture'** by Rima Apple was reviewed dispassionately in the leading science journal 'Nature'. Whilst the extreme claims made by manufacturers had been curtailed by law the industry still thrived because the ubiquitous processed food had shortcomings that could not be good for the human diet. This made supplementation justifiable or perhaps a necessity for many.

Professor Schoenthaler in London   In mid October Stephen Schoenthaler came to London to lecture on his recent research into supplemental benefits entitled "Nutrition and Behaviour" He had been working with the Californian Justice agency helping young offenders. Radio interviews arranged by Ash Communications were very well received. Schoenthaler was at his best in those interviews. Ash Associates arranged a press meeting at The Agency in St Martins Lane that was a great success

Autism could be helped with diet   In early October Paul Shattock, who was a Fellow of the Royal Pharmaceutical Society, visited Larkhall to discuss the Gluten Free diet's application to autistic patients. He had an autistic son who was following a dietary regime excluding gluten and Paul appreciated RG's books and her Trufree range of flours. He had been in touch with Dr Andrew Wakefield from the Royal Free Hospital and was much in favour of Wakefield's research work on the MMR Vaccine having a connection to autism. Shattock had a theory that large intestine leakage was aggravated by the MMR jab and necessitated a Gluten Free Diet to prevent autism developing, equally that where autism had developed then a GF diet could be helpful in treatment. Shattock was sceptical about the diet IQ (Tandem IQ research) connection but I persuaded him otherwise.

Shattock asked us for research funding for his Autism Unit and I said we would consider that. After the visit things went awry for Shattock and no funding took place. The controversial MMR research of Wakefield was heavily criticised by establishment scientists. Wakefield suffered huge problems and was discredited professionally. That cannot have helped Paul Shattock. It was ironic, that Shattock should suffer much as I had done with the IQ diet research that had been similarly attacked by the establishment.

At lunch with us in Annie's Room RG told Shattock that patients with MS harboured measles virus in the gut and showed him a book that contained the reference. He was absolutley shattered to discover this. RG knew about it because her husband had MS and she always kept herself informed about MS research. RG had known about it for years and was surprised Shattock had not. She gave him the reference book to take home.

Low funding for Complementary Health Care   The Pharmaceutical Journal reported that low funding for Complementary Medicine possibly led to weak research in the area. Who is to fund it to levels equivalent to that spent on patentable orthodox medicine? I have always said no sane company or individual would. The PJ also reviewed a recent publication 'Toxicological problems resulting from exposure to traditional medicines and food supplements' published by the government. This research found no public health problems associated with food supplements or herbal remedies other than those that emanated from the Far East. However the authorities were not satisfied and intended to widen their investigations, so wasting more tax payer's money. If the claim that complementary treatments were growing apace was true then these findings indicated that benefits to consumers must be considerable and saving the NHS money.

Degenerative and Multifactorial illnesses 'Pulse', one of the leading weekly Medical Magazines for GPs published an article 'How diet can help fight degenerative disease'. Larkhall ordered reprints of this paper to distribute to its customers, practitioners and stockists because its relevance to antioxidant supplementation was authoritative and credible.

At the end of October The Pharmaceutical Journal reported under the headline 'No such thing as multifactorial disease?' that a Professor had postulated that there was always a single cause for a disease but until it was identified people would term the illness multifactorial. Often it could be a single nutrient deficiency but the difficulties in measuring intake of a nutrient and its interactions with others was probably 'an impossible task'. The best way of approaching a perceived multifactorial disease such as coronary heart disease was to recommend patients to follow healthy eating regimes and lifestyles. Good, that was just what Larkhall had been saying for decades.

Sales Consultants report The training and consultancy company (see March p.288) carried out their Staff Motivation Workshop to assess the Sales Department in August/September. Their report was received by our consultant Ken Doidge in November. As I expected this failed to move things forward but recommended more workshops to 'hopefully' correct the shortcomings detected. The failure of both Doidge and the Trainers to come into the open on the endemic personality problems that I saw as the root cause of poor staff morale was disastrous. I saw little point in more workshops when any progress would be sabotaged by leading staff whose disloyalty to me was well known and deep seated. It had been hoped that Doidge and Neil Wright would have, by now, isolated these people and recommended their dismissal.

The Marketing Manager had been dismissed in October but not at the suggestion of consultants. My brother and I had just failed to see what she was achieving. NW took the decision as it was his responsibility.

All Consultants that I had employed since 1984 had failed to recommend bold decisions but were eager to recommend more research and reports. In hindsight and cynically, I should have employed no consultants but acted on my gut feeling about the staff whom consultants protected because they probably knew these people were their lifeblood. It was a fact that one of the staff who was still in our employment in 1999 proved to be a criminal who had insidiously stolen from a sales agent and bullied staff to ensure their loyalty to him rather than top management. Small companies are all at risk from these individuals who know their rights and are well protected to pursue their evil ways by the law. One of our consultants who worked for Larkhall told me in 1999 that he thought the man a criminal but dared not tell me when he delivered his report.

The Centenary of Chelsea School of Pharmacy and Personalities   Early in November, the Centenary of Chelsea School of Pharmacy was reported in the Pharmaceutical Journal. It was an extensive article about this school and its many distinguished Alumni. I was there 1956-1962.

A college contemporary of mine was, at one time, an inspector of Larkhall and was overheard to say that he was out to get me because I had been born with a 'Silver Spoon'. That seemed to be the start of Larkhall's deep troubles with the Medicines regulator.

Professor Arnold Beckett was my supervisor for my PhD research - he proved a good friend to Larkhall when confronted by the Medicines Licensing authority and latterly Shropshire Trading Standards Officials. He saw immediately that I had been deliberately targeted in areas where many others were technically acting unlawfully. The problem for small English family companies was that they were often chosen as the examples by the bureaucrats seeking to enforce new laws. Inspectors like that man, know these companies are fair game and bully them unmercifully because they want to wield their power. Challenge these people and they probably callously drive you out of business with impunity. I remembered how inspectors were considered experts by their officials despite the fact that much of what they said was nonsense and some forgot to sign their letters, whilst if they find an unsigned document in the records of a company they wish to close all hell would break out.

More Scientific Evidence that a healthy diet might not be adequate for Children
On 19th November, the Daily Express reported that Children who ate a healthy diet might not be obtaining enough Micronutrients for Brain Power. Research at California State University showed supplemented children had the best results in IQ tests. More confirmation of the original Tandem IQ research in Wales back in 1987.

Supplements could help patients on medications On 23rd November 'Over the Counter' a Chemist & Druggist supplement publication, carried an article 'Meeting your requirements?' which discussed possibilities for supplements benefiting patients with various ailments and who took certain medications. A useful comprehensive article that described many approaches for Pharmacy counter staff to adopt.

Criticism of Quackbuster (HealthWatch) rationalists who were not infallible   At the end of November, The Independent on Sunday carried a two page article headlined 'Quackbusters under Siege'. It covered many of the cases in Martin Walker's recent book 'Dirty Medicine'.

In reporting the HealthWatch versus Larkhall dispute it omitted to state that when HealthWatch supporters tested the Larkhall sponsored IQ positive research they used a different formula for a much shorter time and that the test was performed at a school where the wife of the lead researcher was headmistress.

Latterly this research was dismissed as useless by independent assessors of the raw data that was only given up after the Court case in Shropshire. The research results had been released prematurely and great publicity generated throughout the media thanks to the resources of the junk food and sugar industries.

HealthWatch came out of this badly but refused to tone their message down and arrogantly insisted on their infallibility.

The 'Fraud' libel case lost by HealthWatch to Larkhall was mentioned. This situation was analagous to religious disputes and exactly replicated the James Randi (atheist) vs Uri Geller (Psychic). Some people believed absolute political support for the rationalists was vital but it was actually politics that ensured the debate remained open. I always found the rationalists unreasonable people who were often prepared to outrageously mislead to bolster their cause.

Professors with commercial interests   On 28th November, I wrote to a Professor at St Bartholomew's Hospital, regarding the naming of Folic Acid. As a professor of Preventive Medicine he was keen on the term B4 so that the phrase 'B4-you conceive pill' had relevance for public awareness of Folic Acid's benefits. Folic Acid was sometimes known as Vitamin B4. I was destined to meet the Professor and his son later to discuss the Polypill that they believed could transform prevention of Heart Disease. Larkhall also assisted his son with research at St Richard's Hospital, Chichester to determine an optimum dose of daily Folic Acid (see Chapter 25 /1998). I warned them that their ideas for a daily polypill containing Folic Acid, Aspirin with a Statin and Blood Pressure lowering Drug would likely fail to obtain regulatory approval for a variety of technical reasons. They, of course, took little heed of what I advised and went ahead with patent applications. In 2015 the concept was still not a reality but from time to time some publicity was generated - including a clinical trial in India that was apparently positive but unlikely to cut much ice with European Regulators.

Ideas from outside the marketing department ignored   At the end of November, I sent a memo to Neil Wright regarding my ideas for some new advertisements that were drawn up in October and given to the marketing manager, some time before she was dismissed. It appeared that the ideas had been deliberately ignored -- a kind of sabotage? The continuing problem that the sales staff believed top management knew nothing about marketing prevailed. How did they think we ever got started in this business? After 1999 an exactly similar attitude prevailed with the new managements. Is it a disease?

December Trade Sales, delisting and other concerns   In early December, Tesco confirmed delisting of the microvitamins. A failure for the General Sales Manager whom I thought was losing interest in his position with the loss of his marketing manager and the ongoing problems with the sales staff on the road. The prospects for growth in 1997 were not encouraging.

Stuart Pocock (Market Research) visited me to discuss a research project for Lipcote. Sales had plateaued and I wanted to explore possible routes to growth even in the age of the serious competition presented by long lasting lipsticks.

The Independent Marketing Company that held our direct mail customer list on their computer had been questioned as to the efficiency and security of their systems. Development of this database was very important going forward and Larkhall would need to have regular meetings with their executives to ensure they were serving us well. We must take advantage of the greater analyses these computer based listings offered in developing marketing priorities.

Advertising Note   It appeared that one of our competitors was making a new drive for Mail Order via a loose insert of their new catalogue in 'Good Housekeeping' magazine. I heard that it was not a success. 170,000 Good Housekeeping Magazine readers were not necessarily interested in Supplements. The Mail order area was already very competitive with companies trying to penetrate all the time. I still believed test sample ads using Microvitamin products with a postage cost included was the best way forward for Larkhall in this area. Larkhall were using Folic Acid, Microgarlic and others in their direct mail development and awareness campaigns.

In September RG and I attended the Annual Literary Review (Auberon Waugh) Poetry Prize Lunch at the Cafe Royal in Piccadilly in the basement, amidst the wine stock. A small celebration with a few celebrities and interesting people present. The commercial value of this sponsorship could not be dismissed as worthless.

Successful Professional marketing and its opposite   On 19th December, I had lunch with Paul Abrahams of Communications International who distributed regular packs of reply paid cards to Pharmacies and GP Surgeries. We had used these cards including their wrappers as marketing aids for several years. They stimulated further enquiries from GP surgeries and provided leads to interested pharmacies. Lipcote and Microfolic Acid were Larkhall products that used this service quite successfully. I still had direct contact with Paul and had not had confidence to pass him over to the new sales staff. I am sure that after what happened with the recently dismissed marketing manager that was a right decision. It would have been classed as old regime stuff and of no interest to her and considered as of little benefit to the company.

That manager had seemed to show interest in expenses, trips out of the office and long weekends but never got to grips with what Larkhall was about. She dropped the use of symbols in the Larkhall manual as she found them too much trouble. This did not help the health stores who needed the manual to advise customers. Once she tried to trespass into Trufree territory that was RGs. and from which she was banned. Her idea for a 'shoot' for foods baked with Trufree (gluten/wheat free) flours was to use ordinary baked up foods bought from a supermarket. Her excuse was that nobody would know. RG was disgusted. The manager had been very keen on shoots that involved the rent of a studio, cameraman and equipment, catering, transport and other expenses. There did not appear to be any thought as to the costs.

Just before Christmas 1995 she interfered with the Health Examiner, which RG and I did together with the typesetter in Norfolk. It was finished at our end and sent off to have the chromalins made for the printer in France. He would have printed it over the Christmas period (something impossible using a UK printer) and it should have been delivered to us to send out on January 1st. This year it did not arrive ready for the staff to do the mail-out. There was no sign of it. MT, who had no business to concern herself with it, had decided she would alter it to her own satisfaction. All without RG's or my knowledge. She telephoned the typesetting company in Norfolk to say it was on hold but she would do the alterations and get it back to them before the Christmas break. She didn't and disappeared on her Christmas break. The result was the chromalins didn't get made or get to the printer in France and so he couldn't print it ready for us by 1st January. We were 10 days late getting it into the post to the customers and no alterationsneeded to be made. Not a good start to the new year and the mail order department underemployed for two weeks.

One morning when I passed her on the stairs she was off out with the Wimbledon Football Team for a morning meeting. I told her to get back to her desk and get on with some work as the sales were down too much.

One day, when I was out, she asked RG for the key to my flat and said she was moving in. RG knew this was nonsense and refused to hand over the key. As she had told several of the staff this extraordinary tale I had some very funny looks from them.

When eventually she was sacked, she refused to believe it and would not leave the building. The company rule was that anyone who was dismissed left immediately before they could do any damage. After several hours I had to threaten her with the police as she just would not leave. RG asked me what planet the woman was on as she had been giving the staff the impression that Larkhall was her own company, of which she was the boss, and she could do as she liked.

Outrageous artwork cost An example of expensive spending on advertisement artwork. We had the idea of showing just ONE tablet of Cantamega 2000 that pointed out its content. The work was put out to a designer for the typesetting but there was the question of a photograph of the single tablet. The estimate was for £2000 that would include the hire of a studio, photographer, equipment etc.

RG was in my office when I received the estimate and saw how angry I was at all this expense for a photograph of just **one tablet.** She went over the roof to her little studio and got out her watercolour box. Within ten minutes she had produced an actual size painting of the tablet with a perfectly matched colour. I couldn't tell it wasn't a photograph and nor could anyone else. The difference in price was amazing. She only charged £1.50! I was very pleased with the final advertisement.

Symbol System updated In late December, the very successful Rita Greer Symbol System with its emphasis on natural purity for allergy sufferers was expanded with the introduction of 'Nut free' and 'Citrus free' symbols. (She had copyright of all the symbols and never charged Larkhall for the use of them or let anyone else use them.) An article on the system from a Jewish magazine was relevant. Larkhall were far ahead in their thinking and the author of this article appreciated that, with his remarks on products which claimed low fat but then had lots of sugar instead, lots of Fibre but plenty of Salt, low Salt but plenty of Sodium etc.

Larkhall published a new Symbols Booklet and a Purity guide.

Oldie on Supplementation The Oldie magazine's medical contributor Dr Tom Stuttaford wrote an article extolling the benefits of vitamin supplementation. The Oldie readership was appreciative of Stuttaford's open mindedness in this area of healthcare.

Stock Market newcomer Phytopharm At the end of December the founder of a Herbal Company Phytopharm, was the subject of a City Profile in the Sunday Telegraph. He believed that some Chinese Herbal Medicines to which his company had rights would become Prescription items and obtain Licences. I had told my City friends who were investing and promoting Phytopharm on the stock exchange that this was an impossible dream and no profits would be made or dividends paid, but the chief executive, would be paid handsomely. After a chequered history with no return for investors, Phytopharm, no longer employing the founder, in 2013 was about to cease to exist. Its founder had rightly been judged by the author of the article as a dreamer - what was amazing was that he got away with it in the hard nosed financial world. He was not unlike Dr David Horrobin of the failed Scotia Pharmaceuticals but was probably a much nicer man. As for the founder of "Regina Royal Jelly PLC" she, at least did not pretend to be a scientist, so her investors can only have bought hype and they certainly paid the price. Many private companies in this area have succeeded modestly but were never subjected to the commercial pressures of the stock market.

Reflections on 1996 This had been a difficult year and I was not optimistic about achieving constructive growth of the company. However all options were open with no financial threats to the family. As usual, regulatory pressures were excessive and disproportionate. These were likely to get worse for family owned businesses of our size. For a man who valued independence more than anything else I knew time was running out. I had failed to build a good team but did not want to see the foundation destroyed.

Testimonials continued to pour in from a devoted customer base. Many of these anecdotal stories including one from a Macular Degeneration sufferer cheered me but the constant denigration of alternative health care by Quackbusters was evil. These efforts which were probably funded by powerful financial interests were an overkill that would hopefully one day produce a rebound of great intensity. In 2015 it maybe that the Anti-sugar lobby is now unstoppable.

Excessive salt and sugar in our diets were always seen by Cantassium and Larkhall as similar to tobacco smoking for their harmful effects on public health. This can be seen from reading our publicity archive.

Light at the End of the Tunnel

A real Offer - Commercial Concerns - General Sales Manager showed that he understood the Larkhall Mission just before he resigned - Computer information not being used - Advertising design returned to in-house - EU confused on Gluten Free - German Company acted properly - Food Standards Agency gestated - Free sampling - Diet cures better than Doctor's - A reflection on the birth of the Health Food trade - Nicobrevin - Sir Richard Doll - Foresight ideals - New MP for Putney - New Chemist distributor - Italian Herbal supplements - New Weight Loss supplement - Backwards trend - Homoeopathy still under fire - Coeliac Society accept Larkhall - Cantassium Diet of 1920s is the Government's anti-cancer one too in 1997 - Synthetic vitamins were drugs - Progress in USA stalled - Athena Pheromones - Treachery? - Vitamin B6 ban? - Foresight Hair Analysis - Trial of comprehensive Supplement proposed - Shark Liver Oil - First meeting with the company that proposed to take us over - Polyphenol Tea - EU threat to health claims - Doctor questioned Validity of clinical trials on drugs - Medical Go-Between - The Skenar Black Box an acupuncture point instrument - Natural fighters of Breast and Colon Cancer - High Strength Vitamin Supplements - The Placebo dilemma - More on Glucosamine - Lateral thinking for Folic Acid sponsorship - B6 a stitch-up by Drug Industry? - Supplements for 97% of population - Michael Ivens (Aims of Industry) backed Larkhall on B6 - Trade sales concern continued

This was a decisive year for the company. It received a serious approach from a multinational food company to purchase the food supplement and special diet food product ranges. All staff would be absorbed by the new owners but the directors would not be required but given short term consultancy contracts. The company's Lipcote product and its Blakoe ranges would not be part of the deal. Most of the stock, plant, machinery and IT equipment with its specialist software would be purchased. The two factories at Putney and Charlbury would not be included in the deal. We owned these outright. This broad outline was acceptable but no price had been proposed. The Multinational was in the process of purchasing many supplement companies in Europe and had ambitions to enter the US market through a major takeover.

Commercial concerns Early in the year I again voiced my concern regarding Larkhall's representation in the leading Health Food Chain. I felt that it was the fault of our sales staff over many years that our products were so poorly present in these stores. Excuses can no longer be accepted -- the staff must make more effort. Differentiation of our supplement formulas from the rest was vital but needed more in depth knowledge than sales people appeared able to gain and hence communicate to their customers.

Neil Wright understood the company mission In early January Neil Wright wrote to a journalist providing comprehensive details for Pharmacy Products Review on Larkhall's mission and the overall view of the supplement market in the UK. This was a good letter and indicated how Larkhall hoped to progress. Sadly, Neil had left the Company by the end of February. So the company never benefited from Neil's successful move from synthetic pharmaceutical health products to naturally based ideals.

LARKHALL GREEN FARM

Healthy Heart through diet   In March The Daily Express carried a headlined front page story about the benefits of the correct diet for Healthy Hearts. This was good educational stuff but how many of the general readership would actually do it? Not many I guessed.

Thoughts as Neil Wright left the company. The loss of Neil Wright, the general sales manager, in the spring, for personal reasons, was not unexpected. He had been successfully undermined by his senior sales staff. What those people did not realise was, that as a man of nearly sixty, I had already decided that if Neil left -- thanks to their continuing efforts -- I would agree with my brother to **sell the company and retire**. My brother although 5 years younger than me, had been wanting to retire since the early 1980s. The expected Labour government would likely make businesses such as English family owned Larkhall even harder to run. Any new sales manager/supremo would be unlikely to succeed under the prevailing circumstances. The business was probably too complex to be run by a new person and a takeover by a company with a similar set-up was the best option. RG said, "There are no Messiahs out there for you -- just leave something for the other man." Like me, she had also had enough. The next step forward with Trufree, which she owned, would be to manufacture and sell baked-up gluten-free food, which required a dedicated bakery. She too was coming up to sixty and retirement and we didn't have the facilities at Larkhall for a bakery, the specialised distribution or investment funds to do it.

The current senior sales staff and the general manager proposed to me that they would carry on without a sales supremo and work as a team. This was accepted and if they really succeeded then perhaps I would change my mind, but I did not stop talking to the multinational whose approach would probably take two years to come to fruition. Other approaches would also be encouraged. I was very doubtful that those senior staff would produce what they promised -- UK sales expansion. Neil Wright had drawn up a Sales and Marketing Plan in December 1996. This was used by the new regime and was focused on the core ranges.

A private advertising budget drawn up by me for reference purposes indicated my thinking for 1997. My thoughts in January indicated continuing concerns on the home trade side.

New Computer information not being applied by the sales department   The computer system installed in 1994 had made analysis of sales trends possible. However, the trade staff had not made use of this data and lack of IT skills among its senior staff was a serious weakness. I was not IT literate but studied the monthly printouts of single month and cumulative figures very carefully and thought others were doing likewise. I expected that Neil Wright would have made good use of the data and was surprised that little mention was ever made of the benefits of these monthly reports. The Charlbury office was diligent in producing reports for everyone.

Over the Christmas period 1996 I analysed the figures and found that the Trade Sales had marginally declined in 1996 from 1995. This indicated that the new UK trade regime established in 1995 had basically failed despite the investment in staff and promotional spend. There was little doubt that the parallel exporting had been done by three major trade customers that I had detected in 1995 and the support of these customers by the senior staff had been total. They had denied that these companies were exporting Larkhall products but said they were supplying small retailers by wholesale dealing.

An interesting statistic indicated that one sales agent was doing better than any representative with retailers. It transpired in 1998 that a senior representative was actually adding his own customers to that agent's list and then taking the commission from the agent after their receipt from Larkhall. He was dismissed without compensation in March 1999 by the new owners whom I had informed of my suspicions. Due diligence required this.

The main problem was the lack of comprehensive product knowledge by all the trade sales people. This hindered their effectiveness in the field. Mail order staff were more knowledgeable and that showed in the success of any new products sold by that route.

My workload becoming excessive   My Brother (an equal financial partner with me) was happy to have me deal with all sales responsibility as well as running the overall business from new product formulation to advertising, PR and export. He had no concept of the complexity of this work and failed to appreciate what a burden it was for me. I had that vital professional responsibility load to carry too -- my brother had no qualifications but unlike me had attended many computer and management courses that seemed to have been of marginal benefit.

Advertising design back in-house   Work began in-house on some new style advertisements. RG and I created these and the final artwork was done by the Media Shop's own production man Mike Washer, with photography by independent Chris Christodoulou. The costs of a full service advertising agency could not be justified. RG's Symbol System was still seen as a major feature for Larkhall. Most were dual purpose advertisements with both trade and consumer having provision for a reply coupon.

EU interest in Gluten Free labeling   In early January there was new EU legislation on food labeling for Gluten content that appeared confusing. It seemed that they assumed starch derived from any plant material could contain gluten. This was nonsense. Initially, an attempt to obtain clarification from the UK authorities was fruitless. A more practical reply was received by the end of the month.

Borlind end agreement properly   Annemarie Borlind met their obligation to Larkhall as regards return of stock at the ending of our distribution agreement in a proper way as expected from a German family company. I was not surprised to lose the distributorship but Larkhall had learned much.

Wonder Drugs still expected but at great tax-payer cost   An article by Christine Doyle in the Daily Telegraph examined alternatives to wonder drugs. This piece showed how little the arguments on this subject have changed in the last 17 years (up to 2015). The pill for every ill was bad news then and it is worse in 2015 with many more chronic 'illnesses' discovered by the drug industry requiring 'cures'. As usual, minor lifestyle changes would often suffice with no need for costly tablets/capsules.

EU threat to Health and Food   At the end of January, Dr James Le Fanu was in fine anti-EU form in the Daily Telegraph regarding a proposal for a super regulatory agency covering Health and Food. He saw this would become a huge, ineffective bureaucracy and a waste of resources.

Free Sampling   At the end of January, an article in The Health Guardian (a free publication from National Association of Health Stores) on 'Going Gluten Free for Better Health', offered Trufree samples to readers if they sent 50p in stamps to Larkhall. Note the 50p charge for samples. I had deemed no totally free samples because Larkhall had found, that whilst totally free combined with free postage obtained vast numbers of enquiries, the conversion to customer status was not viable commercially.

An example of this was a Trufree advertisement in Here's Health and other publications with no charge but requiring a letter to be posted to Larkhall -- another deterrent for the freebie professionals.

Diet cures better than doctors   Jack Challem wrote a useful article in Let's Live (USA) 'Diet cures more than doctors'', a short history of the micronutrients with future predictions.

Ginseng and Glucosamine - Medicines or supplements?   The magazine Pharmacy Products Review presented the case for supplementation and illustrated the increasing acceptance of these products in Pharmacy. Importantly, a well known olympic swimmer was featured presenting an award on behalf of Pharmaton Ltd. Pharmaton were manufacturers of a Standardised Ginseng product which was a medicine in Germany but not in Britain. Many claims were being made for this product through press articles.

This Olympian had recently started his own company marketing a Glucosamine product that could make no overt claims. However, by use of press releases about clinical studies had got the message through to consumers that his brand of Glucosamine was effective in some forms of Osteoarthritis. In addition, it was very helpful to sports people and the elderly in maintaining healthy joints. These claims were medicinal but no licence was granted to the company. The product was considered a placebo by the authorities. His company grew rapidly and he sold out successfully to a famous established herbal pharmaceutical manufacturer. This was just before trouble started for glucosamine products as they were considered ineffective by government authorities. The term 'beneficial to joints' began to be applied by some companies but was beneficial the same as effective? In 2015 Glucosamine was under close scrutiny and its future as a supplement uncertain.

Optimist offers distributorship for hair loss remedy   In early July, I met a Doctor at the Royal Society of Medicine to discuss the possibility of marketing what he claimed was a natural clinically proven 'Hair Loss' lotion. The research appeared to be valid but I noticed that there were no corroborating trials. I doubted that a large market could be created because only limited PR would be possible. Our sales representative who had recommended me to meet the Dr was very optimistic and called the product 'Samson's Secret'. It failed for the usual regulatory reasons. W O'Connell went over the top regarding this product and began dying his hair badly, to the amusement of the staff. Bluster, boasting and imagination does not equal sales.

Scotia Pharmaceuticals problems continued In mid February, the Daily Mail carried a scathing financial report on Scotia Pharmaceuticals (the Evening Primrose Oil specialist) on its City pages. It should be noted that Dr Horrobin dismissed the criticism as 'just silly'. I had always been sceptical about Horrobin since the mid 1970s. Eventually Scotia went bust.

Genetically Modified ingredients In the mid nineties, customers were increasingly aware of the possibility of genetically modified ingredients entering their diets through supplements. Larkhall did not use such substances in their products but stated that the likelihood a processed material was prepared using such ingredients was not impossible. We investigated all our ingredients carefully and no traces of GM had been found. It was suggested that a GM Free symbol be added to the Rita Greer symbol system but this was an idea for the future.

At the end of February, concerns about Genetically Modified Soya Beans were giving the Food Industry plenty of problems. I replied to one company stating Larkhall's position on this topic emphasising that purchaser control was very difficult. Lecithin and Vitamin E were two food supplement ingredients derived from Soya used by Larkhall. It was not possible to guarantee that GM Soya Beans were not in the starting soya powder used to produce these products. Most Soya comes from the USA where GM Food growing is permitted. Most Lecithin and Vitamin E emanated from the USA. When Larkhall used soya flour directly in their products they were careful to ensure non GM derived soya was used. The same applied to Trufree flours.

Sir Frank Hartley Frank Hartley's obituary was published in the Times. He had examined me on my PhD thesis in 1962 when he was a leading academic at London University, a success for me. After he retired from academia he chaired the Tribunal for GO Woodward & Co's dispute with the DHSS in 1974 that was a disaster for the Company but kept Hartley's standing in the DHSS high, enabling him to chair more of these tribunals. He was an Establishment man by then, soon to have the accolade of a Knighthood.

Cookery preferred by Medical Professor A Medical Professor, Gertrude Mingrone, was interviewed by the Lancet for 1st March issue and said her alternative profession of choice would have been "Innovative cooking -- it is like research: you need an idea, basic knowledge, sound methodology, imagination -- and persistence." No wonder RG is a practitioner of that skill, an unexpected accolade.

USA trip for a first with a reflection on the past In the first week of March, I flew to the USA. First to visit Athena the makers of a human pheromone preparation that had been positively researched in Philadelphia. Male and Female attractants were available and I was intrigued to explore the possibilities for marketing in the UK and Europe. I remained interested in Athena's products although they were experiencing scepticism in many States in the US. At this time, direct sales using the post avoided difficulties from the authorities.

I went on to California and in LA I visited the Annaheim West Coast Natural Products Expo for the first time. This was the largest annual show for Health Foods in the USA and it was here back in the mid 1950s that Jimmy Lee Richardson discovered that Vitamin Supplements were becoming very popular with US consumers. He came back to the UK with the agency for Natural Organics Inc and the UK Health Supplement Industry was born through independent Herbal retailers. Initially, Jimmy obtained some of his marketing ideas from the USA but soon developed his own brand 'Healthcrafts' that was set to dominate the UK market for nearly forty years.

The Microvitamin range was exhibited by our distributor Ella International of San Diego. I met many contacts and was entertained on the 'Electra' for a Harbor Cruise at Newport Beach by Weinstein Nutrients. Wonderful Southern California weather too.

Wonderful Zinc? In mid March, at the R.A.F. Club in Piccadilly, I met with my neighbour, Wing Commander Paul Cormack and an associate, to discuss a Zinc product that was claimed to cure the common cold. I expressed doubts that such a product could be marketed without much costly research that would satisfy the MCA. These very nice people knew nothing about the regulatory restrictions in the health area and were probably suspicious of my truthful but not encouraging advice. They did not realise that zinc versus the common cold was an idea that had been knocking around for several years. UK Companies had experienced great problems with those health claims.

Nicobrevin Towards the end of March, Reginald Loftus who was well known to my father GOW many years ago came to see me regarding the distribution of an anti-smoking remedy 'Nicobrevin' originating from Germany. This had been a very successful product in the past but had been in decline for several years. The proposition offered by the owners was not attractive and I saw problems ahead for a combination formula containing camphor, quinine, menthol valerate and eucalyptus oil. The MCA would likely find reason to ban it soon - in the event it took until 2011.

Sir Richard Doll a coeliac The British Medical Journal carried a feature on Sir Richard Doll the renowned Oxford epidemiologist. He discovered the lung cancer - smoking link and was angry that promotion of tobacco was still permitted by governments. Interestingly, he had contacted Larkhall about our gluten free range and used Trufree flours himself because he was a coeliac. He was enthusiastic about them.

Foresight ideals Nim Barnes of Foresight was concerned about her formulations leading to headaches in some users. As always, she wanted to try and change these to prevent chances of headaches because she believed this stopped users taking the products she recommended following hair analysis results. Foresight tried to individualise the micro nutrient regime to each person/couple. I made some suggestions which could be adopted in future manufacturing batches. I noted that Nim had reprinted a chapter from veterinary scientist's book on Vitamins in Endocrine Metabolism for dissemination to her followers. I believed such publications were probably beyond the understanding of those people and matching veterinary results to humans was unwise.

MP change in Putney In early April, I had been in touch with the Putney MP David Mellor about the dispute with the Brussel's bureaucracy concerning Vitamin Supplements. He had not signed the early day motion and argued that these motions were not as useful as direct Ministerial contact that he said he always employed. This correspondence ceased after the May General election when Mellor lost the seat to Tony Colman. Colman soon contacted me by calling in at the factory and we developed a good rapport. He surprised RG and me by telling us he had read all RG's books avidly and thought they were great. The Vitamin Supplement situation had not moved in the last sixteen years despite great efforts by the anti lobby. I wonder whether the threatened restrictions will ever be promulgated to have sufficient force to stop the marketing of these products in the UK.

Ceuta Healthcare appointed our pharmacy representatives In early April, I wrote to Edwin Bessant the MD of Pharmacy distributor Ceuta Healthcare regarding the launch of Micro Folic Acid into the chemist trade. Ceuta had been chosen to spearhead a new drive by Larkhall to break into the Pharmacy Market more effectively. The cost of this was not peanuts per month but guaranteed direct visits by sales representatives to 5000 retailers every 8 weeks.

I decided to take on this project directly without involvement of any Larkhall Sales Staff. Initially this should ensure that there was no interference from the Trade Sales staff who I believed had been undermining Larkhall's progress. The recent loss of Neil Wright stimulated the new approach. Ceuta were to concentrate on the microvitamin range which I believed had good potential.

Italian change of emphasis In mid April, I was in Genoa to see Prodotti Naturali to discuss progress of the Italian Supplement Market. The Maugeris were making headway with new products. I proposed to import products from them to sell on our mail order list. The problem was that the Italian advertising rules were very different from the UK and although products were registered by the Italian Ministry of Health, many of their claims were disallowed in the UK. PN's main interests lay in Hair, Slimming, Cellulite and general 'beauty from within' supplements/herbal formulations. The Common Market was still a myth.

Citrimax for weight loss In early May, 'Citrimax'(HCA), a US ingredient recommended for weight loss, was to be aggressively marketed in the UK with public relations by the American manufacturers. The company thought that this would help supplement marketers develop their proprietary preparations containing HCA. Their representative came to visit me to discuss the possibility for more business in view of their publicity drive. I was sceptical because I thought it likely that the authorities would put a stop to the PR proposed. Nevertheless, I hoped it would succeed. Fat Control was the supplement in the Larkhall range that contained HCA.

Dr Mike Hudson made contact On 22nd May, following correspondence with RG, Dr Mike Hudson (His PhD was awarded by Imperial College) came to see her in Putney. He had sent her a letter about her Gluten Free Foods and had recently worked in the medical diet product area. He was interested in marketing the 'Trufree' gluten free range of flours under his own label. He had wide experience of the pharmaceutical market and thought there was room for new range of Special Diet foods. He was currently approaching several companies about his new range.

By July he had joined the multinational food company Nutricia in Holland, who were already interested in Larkhall and was instrumental in their subsequent take-over of our company. RG had already convinced him, when he came to see her about Trufree, of the great synergy of special diet foods and vitamin supplements that could be exploited much better by a large multinational than small company such as Larkhall. Trufree was on prescription and mainly sold in pharmacies. Like the supplements Larkhall manufactured, it was made in a licensed laboratory to high standards. She had told him she believed the way forward was bakery gluten-free food and that was beyond her and Larkhall. It would need a large investment. Nutricia already had industrial sized gluten-free bakeries and distribution for such products, although nothing of the quality or diversity of food baked with Trufree.

Hudson spoke fluent Dutch which gave him a great advantage when he joined Dutch Multinational food company Nutricia. This company aimed to be the largest vitamin supplement company in the world and were on a takeover trail.

New Trade Sales structure reverted the company to its old ways During April and May I continued my pressure on the restructured trade sales staff. I used examples of success in Mail Order that was not reflected in retail shop sales. This was an endemic problem. The use of Mail Order to test product acceptance had worked well for many years but the trade sales staff took no interest. Much more effort was needed so I looked for a response but failed to get it. Just as I thought, the departure of Neil Wright returned the company to its old problems once more. A successful sell-out would surely shake the trade sales staff out of their torpor.

I was in direct contact with Larkhall's North of England sales representative regarding company policy on Foresight and Microfolic Acid supplements. This exchange showed that the old attitudes were running deep. It was very useful when considering the direction of Larkhall in the market and the possibilities that Micro supplements offered.

The general manager was insisting on controlling minor advertising spending by the sales representatives. Many retailers used their local newspapers to advertise their shops and run events locally. This could be useful sales promotion but needed control centrally to prevent the salesmen agreeing excessive advertising subsidies with poor value accounts.

Pointless criticism of Homoeopathy and Alternative Health Care At the end of May, The Lancet published two letters that opposed its recent unfavourable review of a recent book 'Wheat and Chaff in Alternative Medicine'. Still going round in circles with pointless criticisms of Homoeopathy, the Establishment believed its attacks on Homoeopathy and Alternative Medicine were fully justified and that one day it would all be outlawed. Happily that was a forlorn hope.

Coeliac Society open day In early June, RG and I attended the Coeliac Society open day in Regents Park and made useful contacts with group leaders and members. We were now accepted as useful suppliers to the Coeliac Market after many years in the wilderness because of our insistence that wheat starch with its reduced gluten content was unacceptable as a food ingredient in medically prescribed gluten free diets. Owing to this long running dispute we were unable to attend any of their meetings/open days but we now we could advertise in their magazine 'Crossed Grain' we were able to have a stand at the open days. Response from the coeliac members was excellent but the committee was different. The Chief dietitian who was a fan of wheat starch and the companies that funded them tried to stoke up a public shouting match with RG who told her, quite calmly, she wasn't afraid of her like everyone else. And she wasn't which somewhat deflated her.

Bad diet the major cause of Cancer 8th June, the Sunday Times reported this in a news headline. It was likely that the government would begin to take steps to implement dietary improvement in the UK population. The emphasis would be to increase the consumption of fruit, vegetables and fibre. This was hardly news to Larkhall whose Cantassium Brand was founded on the researches of Dr Forbes Ross in the 1920s. In 1939 Cyril Scott wrote a book 'Victory over Cancer' where the diet long recommended by Cantassium was advocated - perhaps better late than never. I had written a book with RG titled 'Antioxidant Nutrition' with information and recipes for a healthier diet to fight cancer. RG had been writing books for years to encourage healthier eating, so we were no slouches in this area.

Publicity emanating from vitamin based research was unfair and biased The 21st June issue of The Lancet carried a letter from Caroline Wheatley in Switzerland. Caroline drew attention to the unfair adverse publicity emanating from opponents of vitamin based health systems. A recent trial involving supplemental use of synthetic Beta Carotene, Vitamin C and Vitamin E was negative but as Caroline pointed out it was trialing those micronutrients as if they were drugs. She wrote that natural and wholistic principles were needed in Vitamin researches and proper balance in the nutritional formulations was essential. As in the famous Tandem IQ trials in the 1980s, the opposition gained great publicity for the anti story that was created by academic opponents, funded by powerful financial interests such as sugar manufacturers.

Progress in USA would need more investment In early July, I went to the USA for my annual visit to the NNFA convention in Las Vegas where effort was continuing to promote the 'Micro Supplements'. Ella International from San Diego were leading the effort helped by discounts on their orders from Larkhall. There was still a lively interest in the micros but much more investment would be required to successfully penetrate the USA market. Hopefully, if Nutricia were to take over they would put money behind these products.

Treachery suspected A senior salesman objected to being excluded from memos and accounts of PR agency activity. I answered his memo appropriately and indicated that he was not excluded from relevant PR details. He had lost much of my confidence following reports of serious misconduct that would eventually culminate in his dismissal in early 1999. He could not be trusted with confidential information between me and the PR agency. He was suspected of leaking our new commercial plans to competitors and media enemies.

Vitamin B6 supplements might be banned in the UK by the new Labour Government In July, the recently elected Labour Government had decided to pick the issue that Vitamin B6 supplementation was hazardous when the daily amount ingested in supplements exceeded 10mg. The minister who was to handle this 'problem' was a wellknown vitamin industry enemy, Jeff Rooker MP. All supplements that exceeded the 10mg quantity would be banned by law. At great cost, the health food industry quickly fought back with a consumer campaign and expert opinion in favour of larger doses of B6, including a leading scientist Professor Arnold Beckett, whom I had introduced to the Vitamin Industry via the Tandem IQ case. Many meetings and some years later the threat to B6 was lifted and nothing further has been heard up to 2015. Maximum Permitted Levels (MPL) of Vitamins and Minerals in supplements still awaits European decisions despite a European Directive on Food Supplements being introduced in the early 2000s.

Foresight Charity Hair Analysis Laboratory moved to Putney At the end of July, The Foresight Preconception Charity laboratory moved into rented space at the Putney site. Mrs Barnes used these facilities to bring and install the charity's analytical instruments for carrying out Hair analysis that was used to determine what supplements were needed by parents to achieve a healthy baby. At that time, using the lifestyle recommendations and supplements made by Larkhall for Foresight had achieved over 90% success with parents who had previously had fertility problems and miscarriages, with no abnormalities. Follow up over many years had demonstrated that 'Foresight' children were well above average achievers at school. Of course, whilst the number of couples was many hundreds the success carried no weight with doctors because the variables had not been controlled and never could be. Its opponents would have liked to ban Foresight. They preferred costly IVF techniques that had a poor success rate and were unlikely to produce better than average achievers. IVF is accepted as scientific evidence based. Foresight's successes were dismissed as anecdotal.

Nonsensical Vitamin Test proposed A report in The Times on 21st July was timely. A critic of the vitamin industry was to test 'magic bullet' diet supplement pills. The proposed trial was very limited in scope and would cost £200,000. It was criticised by Professor Tom Sanders (Naismith's successor) who believed short term trials of four weeks were unlikely to have significant results. I considered it a total waste of money especially because it was to be funded by Roche, a leading producer of synthetic vitamins. The supplements would be synthetic and in no way comparable to the 'Foresight Formulations', nor those of Cantassium/Larkhall such as Tandem IQ. So far as I am aware this research was never published. I wonder if it ever took place?

Shark Liver Oil a new immune booster supplement The August issue of Let's Live the US Health magazine carried an article on a new supplement 'Shark Liver Oil capsules'. This oil contained Alkyl Glycerols and was harvested from Sharks, a fish species that had an excellent immune system. Hopefully this supplement would boost human immunity and perhaps protect from cancers. Many new supplements in the US were launched on this platform but few ever obtained mainstream acceptance. It seemed likely that a similar fate awaited Shark Liver Oil.

A Multinational Company with ambition On 11th August my Brother and I had our first official meeting with Nutricia arranged by advisor Theo Baal. We learned that Dr Mike Hudson who had met with RG earlier in the year, had now joined Nutricia to help co-ordinate their proposed development into the international vitamin supplement market.

Antioxidant Teas with Polyphenols The Pharmaceutical Journal had a brief report on the protective health properties of teas. Whilst black teas had little virtue there were claims that green teas had positive health benefits including to heart disease and cancer. The polyphenol molecules in green tea were claimed as the reason for its benefits. Polyphenols are anti-oxidants and there were countless different ones occurring throughout nature, many new supplements were being marketed on this basis. The chemical separation of the countless polyphenols that are naturally present in herbs made them a fruitful area for 'Antioxidant nutraceuticals'. I believed the whole spectrum of polyphenols in a herb was what was really important not an isolated chemical extracted from the whole herb's mixture.

A new regulatory threat from government MAL8 In early September I wrote to health Store Proprietor and writer Harry Masterton Smith and drew his attention to the ramifications of the new MAL8 government directive on 'unsubstantiated' claims. American manufacturers work under less legal restriction than the UK yet use their American promotional approach in the UK with apparent impunity. I told Harry that although I had many excellent formulas in my head - MAL8 meant they would never see the light of day. Our recently introduced 'Folic 29' with ingredients offering excellent cardiac protection could not even obliquely refer to that property in media.

EU delay and obfuscation on Food Supplement regulation Towards the end of September, I went to Brussels for the European Health Products Manufacturers meeting regarding the regulations being proposed by the EU Officials. Maria Strofalis came over from Athens to attend this meeting. As usual, there was little progress but much hot air talked. Maurice Hanssen from the UK was a leading light in the EHPM and still a master of delay. He believed, probably rightly, that by being on friendly terms with the officials he had gained their confidence. They were just civil servants with no specialist knowledge of diet supplements. Confusion was rife and this combined with the obfuscation from the industry side meant that vast delay at reaching decisions was normal. Officials were called on to do so many diverse tasks that their workload meant that after meetings delays of three months before the next were agreed without question and then became six.... after holidays intervene that can easily become a year or more. Meanwhile no EU citizen had died of supplement overdose -- so there was no priority.

Doctor questions validity of clinical drug trials   In the Sunday Telegraph on 28th September, Dr James Le Fanu questioned the efficacy of some modern medicines which had been clinically trialed with positive results. He drew attention to the influence of bio-individuality and expressed concern about the accepted orthodox treatments when compared with those found scientifically ineffective. He declared that the situation was unsatisfactory.

In the same issue, Robert Matthews wrote about the misleading ways clinical trials were reported by the Drug Industry. This was a hard hitting, disturbing article. The Drug Industry was quick to rubbish the natural approach therapies but its products have a protected status in law to which their right is questionable. Too often the 'Wonder Drugs' of today become the nasty products of tomorrow.

Perhaps, more encouraging was an article, 'Broccoli sprouts join war on cancer', where a new strain of Broccoli in the USA had been found to contain a greater concentration of the cancer protective substance sulphoraphane.

Princess Diana's go-between doctor   In 5th October issue of the Mail on Sunday, Dr James Colthurst, who had been to lunch in Annie's Room, was exposed as the go-between in the sensational book by Andrew Morton entitled 'Diana her true story'. Colthurst was very interested in Alternative Medicine and involved with Philip Barker who was importing and distributing the Russian **'Skenar'** device - a mysterious electronic black box that was said to work on acupuncture principles. I was somewhat sceptical and was not surprised when Colthurst fell out with Barker and started up independently. I advised Barker to be wary of the Russian alternative medicine inventors and their treatments.

The Lancet emphasised Natural ingredients protected against Breast cancer
In October, the Lancet (the respected International Medical Journal) carried a research paper that indicated that Phyto-oestrogens were protective against Breast Cancer. These substances were found widely in foods -- soya was rich in them. This research stimulated the journal to carry a leading commentary on what it believed were important findings for public health. The paper even mentioned the general benefits of isoflavones (a family of Phyto-Oestrogens) in degenerative conditions. This showed that the value of 'natural ingredients' was recognised - isoflavones were not pure synthetic substances with precisely defined pharmaceutical and chemical purity standards but a group of substances occurring naturally in some foods. Larkhall generally included wholesome ingredients in their supplements to make them as much like 'foods' as possible. We were criticised and pilloried by academics such as Professor Naismith for doing this. Maybe I might be right after all and natural ingredients did have special properties to promote health.

Protection from Colon Cancer aided by antioxidant supplementation   In mid November, The Lancet carried a small piece that reported some US research which indicated a protective effect from the antioxidant vitamins A, C and E in Colon Cancer. This had been a constant concern for many years but there was no consistency. The authorities were not yet persuaded beyond recommendation of better diets with plenty of fruit and vegetables. No supplementation is yet advised (2015) - in fact this was a reasonable attitude because no single supplement formulation had ever been proved effective. The variations of formulations on the market was infinite, so, stick to the dietary advice but be free to choose a supplement if you think you need one, was my advice. Health journalist Christine Doyle reported on the above and other antioxidant nutritional research in The Daily Telegraph. The New England Journal of Medicine warned of overdose problems yet the daily protective levels of some vitamins like E and Betacrotene (A) were far higher than could be obtained from food so supplements were the logical aids needed.

It should be remembered that synthetic vitamins are significantly different from the natural ones that the Heath Food lobby rightly said contain concomitant factors that boost their effectiveness. This remained controversial (2015) because it is currently impossible for science to arrive at consistent natural formulations that can be researched to meet the evidence base criteria demanded by regulators.

High strength Vitamins and B6   Early October and the Vitamin B6 saga continued. Mrs Barnes of Foresght had a letter from the bureaucracy about this. Later, I wrote to Nim indicating that I had been in contact with the bureaucrat whom I described, maybe unfairly, as a 'Eurocratic Nutter'.

The saga regarding Higher Strength Supplements had been ongoing since the late eighties and was set to go on for a very long time because member states could not agree. Some wanted to licence the high strength products as medicines because they wanted the product licence annual fees for funding their bureaucracies. High strength products were available in most countries but some inspection systems turned a blind eye whilst others occasionally tried officious tactics. France had closed stores down and stock was confiscated, only to be replaced by further imports soon after. I guess that the odd bribe paid to some officials could be very useful in avoiding trouble.

At the end of the month, The Times newspaper carried a balanced article on Supplements that put the case for use of the products favourably. The evidence pointed to greater acceptance of supplements by Doctors and the evidence for a government banning of Vitamin B6 was founded on discredited research.

Placebo prescribing and a dispensing dilemma   The November issue of 'Pharmaceutical Times' carried an article by Dr Phil Hammond that described the effects of placebos termed as 'Smarties'. On the whole this was a favourable piece that gave food for thought. Whilst medical students were taught that placebos may make patients 'feel' better they do not 'make' them better - only a doctor can achieve that. Thus the doctor's ethical standards did not permit him/her to prescribe something that he knew was just a sugar pill. As the placebo had been banned so the side effects of orthodox treatments became a real problem. This was a common dilemma for the Doctor at the sharp end who 'deceived' a patient with placebo treatment. Hammond thought the ethical placebo existed but I had not seen evidence of this and Pharmacists were also forbidden to use placebos by their professional body on pain of being struck-off the practise register. No-one had yet had this happen to them but threats were commonplace.

In the Chemist & Druggist on 15th the regular columnist 'Xrayser' covered the placebo situation but had certainly been persuaded to keep clear professionally. Nevertheless, he admitted that commercially he stocked items like supplements (considered placebos by the controlling professional body) because of consumer demand, not because they have had the pharmacist's advice on their benefits.

Tabloid publicity boost for supplemental Glucosamine for Arthritis   In early December, The Daily Mail carried a story headlined 'Arthritis: does this spell a cure?'. This was derived from a public relations release from a review of an American Book 'The Arthritis Cure'. The recommendation of Glucosamine and Chondroitin supplements was not new but such stories were sure to boost sales of those products.

The fact was that Arthritis often responded to placebos and was a good generator of countless special dietary treatments on offer in the health food market. Anti-inflammatory drugs were the Pharmaceutical Industry's cures but their side effects could be devastating for patients. Hence the great appeal of 'safe' natural alternatives despite their lack of 'scientific' evidence of efficacy.

A sponsorship stimulated by lateral thinking. In mid December, I attended a Larkhall sponsored House of Lords reception for ASBAH hosted by Lord (Jack) Ashley on the fortification of flour with Folic Acid. Whilst ASBAH had always been in favour of fortification I had always thought that it would not be achieved for scientific reasons. Nevertheless, sponsoring the event meant that Larkhall continued to enjoy ASBAH's support for their 'Microfolic Acid' that was still the leading supplement brand of folic acid on the UK and Irish markets.

By 2015 there was still no government authorised fortification with folic acid but the successors to Larkhall failed to keep 'Microfolic Acid' at the top or sponsor ASBAH with proper marketing investment and it is now lost without trace. All the other micros were lost too. In 2003 I recommended to my nephew, whose company then owned the Cantassium Brand, to make a Vitamin D micro product because I foresaw there would soon be huge demand for Vitamin D supplements. Of course, as an accountant and stranger to the vitamin market and current research he ignored my recommendation. In 2015 Vitamin D was among the best selling supplements on the market. The Cantassium Brand had been destroyed and was no more.

Another stitch-up by the drug Industry? At the end of December, Private Eye magazine waded into the Vitamin B6 controversy. It carried a small piece headlined 'The Glaxo Gang' and showed that certain members of the committee recommending reduction in strength of B6 preparations had connections with the drug companies. These companies make patented products at high margins that help the conditions for which B6 is recommended. In addition, the brother of the public health minister, Tessa Jowell, was head of medical and regulatory affairs at Glaxo. Could B6 be another orchestrated stitch-up similar to Tryptophan back in 1988?

Supplements needed since only 3% eat healthily On 28th December, Hazel Courtney in the 'Style Section' (Sunday Times) wrote a very supportive and wide ranging hard hitting article outlining the health benefits of diet supplements. The threats from regulators were discussed as was the contrast between the regulations in different countries - she highlighted that the herb Ginkgo was a licensed medicine in Germany but had been refused a licence by the UK authorities. The dietitians and doctors who said we are all consuming a healthy diet were put in their place by Hazel. She wrote that perhaps only 3% were eating healthily and their idea of the 'balanced diet' was not a healthy diet at all.

Michael Ivens was a friend of Larkhall During December, I was corresponding with Michael Ivens, now a consultant formerly the Director of the Business pressure group 'Aims of Industry'. Larkhall had been long time supporters of this independently minded group driven so well by Ivens. Ivens said he would cover the Vitamin B6 saga in one of his columns. He enjoyed the copy of Green Farm Magazine I sent him.

Trade sales still depressed me as 1997 ended The new regime set up following departure of Neil Wright was not working as planned. This did not surprise me. In June, I had discovered that the trade sales staff were not keeping the important retailers bible, known as The Chemist & Druggist price list, updated. There were the expected not guilty pleas from the department so in desperation I transferred the duty to the Charlbury site. Management's continuing concern that trade sales were not working efficiently stimulated further computer analysis. I had appointed Ceuta Health Care as Chemist distributors with sales representation in Pharmacies because our own staff could not cover the country adequately but this was unpopular -- why? We still had some independent sales agents working with us but their contribution to expanding sales had been negligible. Like our own staff, their product knowledge was poor. They were not able to digest the information provided by the company apart from the discounts on offer.

At the end of December I noted that the annual increase of about 3% in home trade sales was distorted by excessive discount trading in core items such as Lipcote in December. There was evidence that the sales people had boosted December, not with Christmas sales, but by forced overstocking of a few wholesalers. It appeared that overseas distributors were experiencing competition from parallel importers served by UK wholesalers and Asian owned 'retailers'. I believed this would have a serious effect on sales in January and February1998 and that was exactly what happened. Large bonuses to sales people for exceeding annual sales targets in 1997 meant next year would not be good for them unless they found reserves of skill and competence. In the event they did not. No surprise there.

New advertisements for Cantassium and Green Farm were designed. The aim was to obtain a reader response for 'Free Fact Packs'. The Green Farm advertisment was oriented towards Mail Order supply whilst Cantassium was aiming at the retail outlets. The sales of supplements to retail continued to disappoint whilst export and direct mail were growing well. I was convinced that our sales reps were still not effective because of poor product knowledge. Perhaps they just did not really understand what we were about. I imparted good product knowledge to all the export customers and the mail order side was well supported by RG, our nutritionists, technical staff and me - a 'phone call to the Putney HQ enabled consumers and stockists to get the right answers to all questions. Reps were inclined to tell retailers that each knew all the answers and failed to use the expertise in the office. How could this be overcome?

Last Full Year

Food safety and the EU - Food Standards Agency - Holistic Cancer Treatment on Trial - Third generation - UK sales down but Export up - Charity delighted - B6 fight went on - Tesco interested in Free From foods - Folic Acid a factor in preventing Heart disease - American Prevention magazine strange mix - Direct response advertising - More on Scotia - Burger consumers maybe Ostracised soon - Antioxidant nutrient lecture at the Royal Society in London - Bright future for Lipcote if nettle grasped - Good prospects for Nutricia - Greek business declining - UK Supplement Market in the doldrums   - USA not as buoyant - Resveratrol a new antioxidant nutrient - CAM treatments have a better press - Foresight Vitamin A rightly received support but remain isolated - A tragedy for living healthily - Let me out of here - Dr Rob Hicks - The old chestnuts from anti-supplement lobby regurgitated again - Foresight supplements far superior - Cod Liver Oil still top - Pharmacy staff get a training guide on Supplementation - Proprietary Designation can be an implicit claim - Cancer situation in USA improving with attention to Diets - Borderline products - Award for Foresight supplements negated - Sponsorships unwanted - Breast Cancer prevention Diet Book backfired - Aims of Industry best supporter for Larkhall - Long suspected staff criminal exposed- CHC to fight for Health Products against Medicines bureaucrats - Supplements for cancer prevention diets must not be pharmaceutically/chemically pure - Business as usual

This was the last full year that the company, which had started in 1946 under the name GO Woodward & Co Ltd, traded under the direction of the Woodward family. In early 1999 (January 31st) most of the products together with staff, manufacturing data and some machinery were taken over by multinational Dutch food company Royal Numico trading as Nutricia. Included was Trufree that was owned by RG but had always been manufactured and marketed by us.

After a very good trading year in 1997 the sales, particularly UK Trade, took a downward path in 1998. The pressure on supplement companies was intense with the new Labour Government determined to follow the policy advocated by leading members of organisations such as HealthWatch, Big Pharma and Junk Food industry. The attack on Vitamin B6, with a threatened ban on daily supplemental doses above 10mg, cost the supplement industry vast resources to fight and blighted growth because all supplements then seemed suspect to many of the UK public. The cloud still hovered over the vitamin industry for three more years after which Jeff Rooker, the responsible minister, lost his job and the B6 threat was lifted with weasel words from the thwarted bureaucrats.

Larkhall's position was not aided by the poor performance of the trade sales team, one of whom was finally exposed as a crook who was doing, and had done, immense damage to staff morale by engendering an atmosphere of fear and even used blackmail. He had encouraged outright disloyalty to me by spreading false rumours and lies. He foolishly believed he would be the next MD of Larkhall under the new owners but was going a strange way about it.

Food Safety threats from Brussels In early January, The Lancet reported that European Union legislators were eager to bring in many new regulations regarding 'Food Safety'. Genetically modified food ingredients were a major concern but lack of technical competence probably meant delay. It appeared that Diabetic Foods, Low sodium and Gluten Free might soon be subjected to EU scrutiny and control.

LARKHALL GREEN FARM

Opinion leaders entertained   I entertained Sir Austin Bide (Past Chairman British Leyland and Glaxo) and Tony Colman the newly elected MP for Putney (Labour) at the Travellers Club in Pall Mall for lunch. A lively meeting with all three of us enjoying some good conversation on Government and Industry.

Food Standards agency bureaucracy proposed   In mid January, the new Labour Government announced that it proposed to establish a 'Food Standards Agency'. This would introduce many more uncertainties for businesses, especially the smaller ones. As usual the politicians seemed to believe there was an ocean of competent regulators ready to take on the important tasks selected by them. I believed this agency would generate many jobs for the 'boys and girls' and cost the taxpayers evermore, every day. It was very unlikely to be effective in protecting the public from rogues but its staff would enjoy life at meetings and consultations in Europe plus exotic destinations abroad. I thought that the only reason for forming this agency was to mirror similar institutions in European countries. Currently, the industry and public were well served by the Ministry of Agriculture, Fisheries & Food (MAFF). I felt a new army of bureaucrats would just add to unproductive overheads for Britain's taxpayers to meet.

Holistic Cancer treatment on trial   In January, 'Nature' the world's leading scientific journal and the 'British Medical Journal' reported on another case of unproven therapy for Cancer. This time it was in Italy. Driven by emotion, drama and court decisions 'somatostatin', an expensive untrialled treatment, was transferred to free prescription by the Puglia regional authority. This forced the Italian government to fund a clinical trial during an interim period. The trial proved the substance ineffective. The promoter of the treatment was a Dr Luigi Di Bella who actually prescribed a complex mix of natural substances, which included somatostatin, so that substance alone was not expected to be effective anyway. I believed it was impossible to clinically determine scientifically whether any of the many multi element natural treatments could be effective using criteria applied to known medicinal chemical molecules.

Third generation Woodward wanted to takeover Lipcote   Late in 1998 Ben Woodward (my nephew) and his fiancee were entertained for supper by RG and me at Putney. He was interested in joining Larkhall and find outside investors from his City contacts after the Nutricia takeover. He proposed to develop the major product Lipcote that he saw as a spearhead to great success for himself and his City associates. He was not interested in the nutrition side. I thought, as a Chartered Accountant and Business Studies graduate from a top accountancy firm he could be successful if he dedicated effort to a difficult task. My brother was much in favour because he wished to retire but my mother, now in her 89th year, was not.

UK Trade sales nosedived yet General Manager optimistic   The situation I predicted had occurred. Trade sales had nose-dived because of serious overstocking by Larkhall customers in December 1997. Lipcote had suffered really badly. Subsequently, February and March proved equally disastrous. I thought these three poor months were unlikely to be made up in the next nine. Happily, Export sales were going well with Spain and Greece outstanding. Unless our home trade representatives could do better, a re-think on policy seemed inevitable. A computer sales analysis on Vitamin C 1000mg Naturtabs demonstrated the problem with just two export customers topping the list by a long way.

343

However, the general manager was optimistic so a sales bonus scheme was implemented. I believed the representatives would fail to achieve these targets despite the incentives offered by the bonus scheme. By July things were continuing to deteriorate.

ASBAH appreciative of our work with Microfolic Acid. On 9th February, I received an appreciative letter from the ASBAH charity regarding the donations made by Larkhall based on sales of the Microfolic Acid product in 1997. The very successful promotion with 'First Response' pregnancy testing Kit was really appreciated too. This idea and its negotiation came from Ash Communications, Larkhall's PR agency, who had done a first class job for us.

Spina Bifida Week, sponsored by Larkhall, was successfully held from 14-20 September, organised by Ash Communications and ASBAH.

Vitamin B6 fight continued In February, the Vitamin B6 battle continued. The Vitamin B6 Scientific Task Group headed by Professor Arnold Beckett became the major force against Jeff Rooker (an MP and minister) and his acolytes. The government advisory group behind the threat, 'Committee on Toxicity', maintained its arrogance in a letter to the Task Group in mid February, however, Beckett's reply castigated them with carefully presented arguments. Their use of a toxicity factor at 300, applied by them to known toxic chemicals against the essential nutrient factor B6, was crazy logic and could be a sign of desperation. Non technical journalists could use this sophistry as a cosh in their reports. Distortion of scientific data with use of inappropriate multiples was a well-known ruse, eg the use of mcg, ng instead of mg and iu, where fixed quantities could distort reported quantities by factors running into 1000s. It all helped to confuse the layman. Nevertheless, there was optimism in the media that Rooker would back down soon with a face saving statement.

April saw the Vitamin B6 fight continuing. Larkhall made a submission at the request of Consumers for Health Choice a pressure group based in Bristol. They were continuing to spearhead things as consumer representatives but coordinated by Health Food manufacturers, wholesalers and retailers.

On September 5th, a letter from me on Vitamin B6 was published in the Pharmaceutical Journal entitled 'Change in direction needed'. This letter not only criticised the Royal Pharmaceutical Society for its stance on B6 but stated that that body was running true to form like the Consumers Association, Medicines Control Agency and many others. I called for an awakening of all these groups to the fundamental differences between Food Supplements and Herbals, including their total distinction from synthetic drugs. This problem persists to 2015 with little sign of a rethink despite the setting up of apparently independent committees to examine alternative health care systems. Most of the membership of those groups have, of course, been recruited from the bodies in favour of the Status Quo with salaries and pensions dependent on those same bodies. The public are conned so easily -- big Pharma continued to laugh all the way to the bank as do bureaucrats all over the world.

Supermarket interest in 'Free From' food products In March, RG received a letter from Tesco's company nutritionist who enquired about 'Grain Free' food items. (Trufree No.1 Flour was grain free.) In her reply she put the case for Trufree well. No reply received from Tesco but their letter indicated that Tesco was becoming interested in 'Free From' special foods suitable for supermarket sale. RG said they were 'just fishing'. By 2013 the supermarkets had become major suppliers of these items and many had 'own label' ranges. The seeds of this were sown back in the 1970s by RG and Larkhall. At that time such foods were usually medically recommended including Ruthmol 'Salt Free' salt substitute and naturally 'Gluten Free' flours and baking mixes.

Folic Acid may prevent heart disease   The 21st March issue of the British Medical Journal published a paper analysing many randomised trials involving Folic Acid reducing Homocysteine (an aminoacid) levels in human blood. This indicated a positive role for the vitamin in heart disease. This has remained controversial because Folic Acid was not a patented drug substance. The amount of validated independent research needed to convince authorities was unlikely to be reached. The authorities will always nit-pick the natural approaches and readily accept 'synthetic drug' trials where patents guarantee high prices and profits.

American magazine 'Prevention' was a monthly magazine published in the USA. There used to be a UK edition but this closed when JI Rodale's in Berkhamstead ceased trading in the early 1990s. The US publication contained advertisements from the OTC Pharmaceutical Industry but also promoted Supplements and healthy living lifestyles, strange but true. There was an article in the April 1998 issue that aimed to guide consumers through the maze of Diet Supplement products; a fairly balanced view.

Sale of Larkhall   In March, Martin Kimber, an M & A accountant, came to see me regarding negotiating with potential buyers of Larkhall. I subsequently had regular meetings with him. In August, Alan Wilson from our accountants Alliotts came to talk about the takeover that began to look as if it really would go ahead. Confidential talks with our professional advisers continued and became serious in September when Nutricia agreed to take on all staff on a rights protected basis. The ramifications of TUPE regulations were agreed. I had a special private fax machine installed in Annie's Room at Kimber's request so information could not leak.

Direct response advertising   The Spring Edition of the Coeliac Society Magazine carried a Trufree advertisement. They had been forced to capitulate regarding never allowing Trufree to advertise. RG had caught them out when they wrote to an authority saying any company with gluten free products could advertise in its magazine. In practice it had meant any company except Trufree (Cantassium).
   The free sample of Trufree No. 7 S.R. offer was very successful. There was enough of the flour to make 6 sponge buns with the recipe for different flavours. It should be noted that there was a polite request for a postage contribution that most enquirers sent with their sample request. RG answered all the enquiries herself so they were dealt with properly and there was no delay.
   A direct response advertisement for Bio Release Glucosamine was being used successfully by Larkhall in the Daily Mail. I had found that this was the best national newspaper for gaining response to Supplement advertisements. The copy had passed the ASA rules and no challenges from the likes of HealthWatch were received. The Daily Mail also regularly published articles on supplementation and Health Foods, most were favourable including one about the Great Vitamin Debate by Dr John Briffa their regular columnist. He was a supporter of supplementation and the answers he gave to his questioners were balanced and constructive.

A professional view on Vitamin safety   On April 11th The Pharmaceutical Journal published an article by Pamela Mason advocating regulation of daily amounts of each nutrient which could be taken as a supplement up to a maximum permitted level based on safety rather than accepted nutritional need. She believed the EU would agree a universal regulation on this basis within 2 years. In 2015 the MPLs have yet to be published despite being threatened for over 15 years! The fact is that certain countries want to regulate levels marginally above RDA whilst others advocate safety as being the only criterion.

The difficulty was that above RDA levels could still be available if licensed as medicines and therefore subject to Licensing with Annual fees as medicinal products and for their manufacture. This would increase prices and drive smaller companies off the market. Ms Mason's and the Pharmaceutical Journal bias was probably towards the big Pharma interest because that was and is where the power lies. Little to do with safety but all to do with good returns for big Pharma and their allies throughout the EU.

A Trade Mark dispute involving Larkhall achieved nothing My old adversary Dr David Horrobin's company Scotia Pharmaceuticals attacked Larkhall's 'EFA complete' product through a solicitor's letter from their Technology Solicitors, Lochners. I asked our Trade Mark agents to handle our defence. Their letter dated 5th May was answered succinctly on 15th. Further letters were subsequently exchanged and correspondence finished at the end of August with Larkhall agreeing to change the name of the product to 'Complete EFA'. Ironically, Efamol (not Scotia) and Larkhall were soon taken over by Nutricia so little changed anyway. Scotia went bust within a few years. Cost to Larkhall had been negiligilble but Scotia's legal fees must have been many thousands of pounds. Well done the technology lawyers! Horrobin and his associates, including paid retained advisors, specialised in bullying small competitors and had affidavits ready to use in their attacks. The continuance of 'Complete EFA' and withdrawal of 'EFA Complete' as an outcome defied reason. Well done Larkhall and their Trade Mark agents.

In 2000 Scotia Lost their product licences for Evening Primrose Oil Capsules (Efamast and Epogam) so the NHS prescription business was lost. GD Searle no longer acted as distributors. Despite encouraging words from 'Questor' in the city pages of the Daily Telegraph, on January 13th 2000 Scotia never broke even and went out of business early in the noughties.

Folic Acid research in Cardiovascular health. In early May, a Professor, attached to the Wolfson Institute of Preventive Medicine part of St Bartholomew's Hospital in London, asked me to provide varying strengths of Folic Acid tablets for a cardiovascular research trial. The research was to be carried out at St Richard's Hospital, Chichester by his son. This became the last major nutrition trial in which Larkhall participated.

Fast Food outlet customers maybe ostracised in the future Towards the end of May, The Sunday Telegraph carried an article that exposed the poor nutrition currently provided by many fast food outlets. It speculated that perhaps eaters of burgers would be as ostracised as smokers in the near future.

Antioxidant Nutrition On June 4th I attended a seminar entitled 'The role of dietary antioxidants in the human immune system, with special reference to the ageing process' at The Royal Society in London. The leader of this seminar was Professor Jeffrey Blumberg from the Tufts University in the USA. Blumberg was one of the world's leading academics advocating antioxidant nutrition. The makers of Vitamin E (Henkel) sponsored the meeting that was well attended. I attempted to mention the book 'Antioxidant Nutrition' which I wrote with Rita Greer. Hopefully Blumberg would like it and take news back to the USA. The subject was still very controversial and considered unproven by authorities in most countries. Anti-aging claims were banned in advertising for antioxidant supplements in Europe but in the USA there were many companies offering eternal youth with special supplement regimes including anti-oxidants.

Lipcote future   In June a wonderful testimonial for Lipcote was received. This indicated the importance of developing a large range of beauty products so that customers who loved one product could try others, expecting similar joy. This news could be helpful to my brother's family in providing confidence to expand the Lipcote brand after the sale of the supplements and diet foods to Nutricia.

Mail Order sales   This was one of the prime interests for Nutricia when buying our business. The continuing success of 'Strong Bio Glucosamine' in June was very encouraging for them and more products with the 'Strong Bio' prefix would be worth exploring. Direct response advertising could be the way forward but ASA rules could threaten progress if HealthWatch suspected any success for Larkhall. Soon the company would be Nutricia and likely to be left alone because I, Dr Robert Woodward, would no longer be involved.

European threats   The problems with the authorities in Greece were depressing business. Our distributor's debt was not being paid. Spain was our most successful market but I foresaw difficulties lurking. Long term progress seemed unlikely because of pressure from the big Pharma lobby to outlaw higher strength supplements. By October the difficulties of the Greek distributor prompted Maria Strofalis to try to obtain a sterling loan using her property in Thessalonika as collateral. I was aware of her money problems and hoped she could obtain help from Barclays Bank. In the event, the situation got worse and Nutricia might become involved.

Trade sales problems   Senior trade sales staff continued to ignore company rules regarding the purchase of advertising space in the media. I had decreed that all advertising must be done through the Media Shop agency not direct with publications. This was to ensure control of the budget and restrict advertising to specific products. A letter from Sue Croft was a classic example of malign influences at work in our sales team. The case against them was building fast. I knew of their objection to the appointment of Ceuta Healthcare but niggling queries regarding Ceuta's performance were noted. I thought most of these were being generated by our own trade sales staff in an effort to undermine my faith in our pharmacy distributor.

On August 22nd a report in the Chemist & Druggist indicated a substantial sales decline for many companies in the diet supplement market owing to the Vitamin B6 situation. Heavily advertised items (Centrum) and current vogue products including garlic had bucked the trend. This article would provide us a good defence in the coming takeover talks.

News stories not all positive   The Summer edition of Vitamin News from Takeda had some useful positive articles. One headlined 'Harmful Report on Vitamin C' indicated that this was probably a false conclusion generated by the opponents of Food Supplements. Will this crazy war ever end? I wondered. As usual, there were positive articles too, including one on Folic Acid and Heart Disease, Vitamins C and E reducing Sunburn damage, poor antioxidant levels influenced pre-enclampsia, Vitamin B2 and migraine.

USA trade in turmoil too   In mid July, I went to San Antonio, Texas for the NNFA convention to visit the show and help promote the Microvitamins which were hopefully to be stocked by a major Drug store chain. However there was trouble for herbals in the USA with the FDA banning Cholestin, a natural yeast grown on rice, that had been consumed as a harmless food in China for over 2000 years and had been found to have a beneficial effect on blood levels of Cholesterol.

Big Pharma was encouraging the FDA ban to protect its substantial number of Cholesterol lowering drugs including Statins. There was widespread concern within the natural health food industry. Cholestin was just one item on Health Store shelves but there were countless more at risk of attack in the USA.

Coincidentally, I met Richard Edges in San Antonio. He wished to distribute the Blakoe Ring in USA but I wondered if his connections in the FDA would be as supportive as he imagined. He believed in the Energising Ring but did not understand the obstacles to importing such a device for sale in the USA. The ring was a good substitute for the many drugs prescribed for male impotence and threatened big Pharma as did herbals - so attacks would be certain.

Although USA was seen as the most developed market for Supplements there were great differences between States, Texas being notably less enthusiastic compared with California.

Resveratrol a new nutritional antioxidant factor   In August, USA publication 'Vitamin Retailer' carried an article on Resveratrol (an antioxidant found in grapes) that had been found to be effective against the initiation, promotion and progression of Cancer. I had included a food concentrate of this substance in the recently introduced 'Cantamega New Millenium' formulation. It was the first supplement in the UK and Europe to contain added resveratrol. Sadly, consumers were unlikely to become aware of its health benefits owing to advertising restrictions. I predicted that it would be well into the 21st Century before there was any acceptance by the authorities - so in 1998 only the really informed people would be aware of this important nutrient factor.

Progress of Complementary and Alternative Medicine after a decade   The August issue of European Pharmaceutical Contractor carried an article entitled 'Complementary and Alternative Medicines gaining acceptance in the West - Recent developments in the United States'. This discussed the changing environment for CAM over the previous decade. Despite the claim of gaining acceptance, little real progress had been made and CAM was very much underused and often abused in mainstream health treatments. One factor apart from cost of research was the difficulty in replicating clinical trials because natural ingredients were never truly identical from batch to batch - tight specifications written for synthetic chemicals were usual but herbals could never have these sort of specifications that are considered essential by regulators. The complexity of vitamin supplement formulations made analytical reproducibility virtually impossible - so a similar regulatory stonewall existed for those products too.

Helpfully, in the August issue of The Lancet a letter drew attention to the use of Complementary Health Care by patients and advised Doctors to be more sympathetic and less aggressive with those patients.

In the USA, Prevention Magazine had an article 'Can Herbs fight Cancer?'. A useful example of Alternative approaches used to treat sufferers with Herbs. A host of Herbs were potentially helpful but magic herbal formulas were to be avoided. Professional Herbalists treated patients as unique individuals and prescribed what they perceived as a balanced treatment regime.

Foresight Vitamin A controversy - a tragedy for Health   A report from BASF, a multinational company producing Vitamin A, indicated there was no harm to pregnant women from pure forms of Vitamin A below 10,000 iu per day which was well above the normal concentrations in Supplements. The strange UK view that Betacarotene was the best source of Vitamin A in supplements, as advocated by Boots in their recent decision to delist Foresight Vitamins, was not supported by this research. Mrs Barnes had never considered Betacarotene as an effective source of Vitamin A in supplements, and would not change her view to please Boots! She was right but she carried no influence with authority.

In mid October, The Foresight Vitamin A saga was explored in some correspondence. Mrs Barnes had submitted research supporting use of pure Vitamin A in pregnancy but I explained that the view of the Royal Pharmaceutical Society remained unchanged and Boots had chosen to obey because this was a 'Safety' issue and was therefore surrounded by legal threats. To require a product specifically formulated to aid the formation of a healthy baby to carry a warning of danger of use in pregnancy was plain crazy -- but that was the world in which we endeavoured to live healthily.

This was the sort of issue that made me look forward to selling the business soon and working in a environment where the law was not an ass.

Adhering to Foresight's principles costly   In mid September, I composed a letter to Nim Barnes regarding the source of Vitamin A used in Foresight vitamins. Before sending this letter I had a long conversation with her and she rejected all suggestions for a change in her formula. She did not appreciate the legal problems that could arise with Trading Standards who were constantly being pressed by Larkhall's enemies to take action. This effectively killed all the advertising for Foresight Vitamins and de-listing by Boots was a formality. This was a real blow to Larkhall since progress with Foresight in Boots had encouraged consideration of adding further products in the near future. Mrs Barnes's decision would be certain to negatively affect the sale price of Larkhall that was now entering its final phase with Nutricia. I was feeling exhausted by the takeover problems but determined to see it through. Unfortunately, no one else at Larkhall understood all the facets. I never attempted to overrule Mrs Barnes regarding the use of Pure Vitamin A because I was aware that her charity's successful results in producing so many Healthy Babies free from birth defects for parents following her regimes was too precious to put at risk by adopting the insane demands of bureaucrats. I was reminded of the Tandem IQ product that in 1989 had been criticised by a Professor because it contained certain Bioflavonoids that he said, quite erroneously, were carcinogenic.

Trufree problems with Trading Standards   RG was having a difficult time with our local Trading Standards department. She had spent months working on a new flour -- Trufree No 8 -- which was in effect a mix, to use with a sachet of yeast (supplied) that would make a small loaf of bread, suitable for anyone on a gluten/wheat free diet. The photograph for the pack had been done and showed the lovely golden loaf of real **bread.** However, the new local Trading Standards officer was a woman who knew absolutely nothing about cooking/baking. When she saw on the ingredients list that the mix contained sugar (about 3 pinches) to activate the yeast, (normal in bread) she decided the product had to be called a **cake mix**. As it was clearly for **bread** and not for a cake, which would have required about 150g of sugar (not 3 pinches), margarine and eggs that were not in the mix or the recipe, this was ridiculous. The trading standards officer would not back down and so Trufree No 8 for a loaf of bread could not be brought to the market, except as a cake mix. The product had to be scrapped including green bins containing a quarter ton of bulk mix ready for packaging into colour printed cartons showing the loaf of "bread" it would make. What a terrible waste.

349

RG said it was the straw that broke the camel's back. She really had had enough. A TSO officer who didn't know the difference between a loaf of bread and a cake was an impenetrable brick wall. Like me, she had found this was the sort of issue that made her want to sell off Trufree and get out. RG said it was the straw that broke the camel's back. She really had had enough. Her patience had run out.

Vitamins in the dock On 11th September, The Daily Telegraph headlined an article 'Vitamins in the dock'. As usual, the British Dietetic Association had been consulted by investigative journalist Barbara Lantin when she wrote the article singing the usual song 'you get all the vitamins and minerals you need from a balanced diet'. There were safety issues with high doses of the old chestnuts -- Vitamin A, Iron, Zinc, Selenium, Vitamin C (diarrhoea). The dietitians were always complaining about supplement manufacturers probably because nutritionists, rather than dietitians, were considered the experts in the field and were the usual spokespeople used by supplement producers. Dietitians were the profession traditionally involved in the medical diet treatment area. Nutritionists were not acknowledged to exist as a profession by dietitians and were generally dismissed as part of quackery. There was a war on and it continues to 2015....

Choline a vital nutritional substance in Pregnancy 'Foresight Vitamins' contain Choline - dietary component that is difficult to formulate within compound multiformulas because of its inherent property of absorbing moisture. Larkhall had been able to successfully incorporate Choline in their formulations. Recent research published in Science Compass Journal indicated that Choline was vital in brain development and should be taken during pregnancy. I sent memos to sales staff and wrote to Mrs Barnes on Choline to emphasise Foresight's superiority in this area compared with competitors.

Cod Liver Oil for ever At the end of September, the Chemist & Druggist looked at the most popular Over The Counter (OTC) preparations in the UK. Interestingly, Seven Seas Cod Liver Oil topped the list with nearly £50 million sales - no other supplement exceeded £12 million. Whilst this list was true for 'Single Branded Items' -- products such as Royal Jelly, Evening Primrose Oil, Garlic and Glucosamine, both as brands and generics, have recorded very large sales at particular times but these have seldom been sustained like Cod Liver Oil. The market for 'new supplements' was always unpredictable owing to advertising restrictions on the sales messages.

Training guide for Pharmacy staff A chemist trade magazine published a training guide on Vitamins for use in Pharmacies to educate staff. This guide was not restricted to Vitamins and explored healthy diet and exercise regimes much on lines long advocated by Larkhall. This was a useful reference article but no specific nutritional treatments were reviewed - Gluten Free, Low Salt, Low Protein recommendations were for specialist dietitians or even nutritionists to specify.

Health claims implicit in a proprietary name. In mid October I questioned the Medicines Control Agency regarding medicinal claims made for certain food supplements. The proprietary designation 'Memory Plus' seemed totally unacceptable as a name for a food supplement because it implied improvement to the memory -- a physiological effect. The bureaucrats wrote back and emphasised the confidentiality of their subsequent actions. Nothing more was heard but the product was soon off the market. Many companies were coming into the food supplement market with little or no knowledge of the laws surrounding the products.

Established supplement companies policed the area searching for these competitors. Hence few of their products survived to thrive. New laws were being promulgated by EU regulators and health claims for food supplements were being restricted (2015) throughout the EU.

Cancer situation improved in America. In October, The Lancet carried two optimistic short pieces that reported about dietary aspects surrounding cancer. Education of the US public about healthy diets had led diet to become less important as a cause of cancer. Long term intake of multivitamins seemed to reduce the risk of colon cancer.

Last Medicines inspection A report from an inspection by two Medicines Inspectors in September was nit-picking but we easily survived. All the minor issues had been cleared by mid November and the manufacturing facilities at Putney continued to be approved. A vital 'due diligence' factor in the upcoming takeover by Nutricia.

Borderline products not substances In mid November, I requested a copy of a new European Directive MLX249 from the Medicines Control Agency regarding the legal status of Borderline products. New rules in this area meant that health claims would be closely scrutinised by the MCA to ensure products - particularly new ones - did not require licensing as Medicinals. (Note: Borderline Products should not be confused with Borderline Substances which were foodstuffs like Gluten Free Flours, not diet supplements).
 Soon after, the Chemist & Druggist reported that MCA was aiming for openness in 'Borderline' decisions. This was a further threat to advertising and promotion of Health products where in truth, the MCA would be judge and jury regarding the status of a product and classifying it as medicinal subject to licensing. The legal jargon in the area was already a minefield and few cases would ever reach a court but companies would be scared off by aggressive letters from the MCA and capitulate. Larkhall had fought for freedom on Tandem IQ and the sophistry of the authorities was exposed but few companies had the courage to fight these in 1998. Just relabel and relaunch would not become unusual. Only by having legal limits on the doses of items such as minerals or vitamins would things change because the authorities could then direct that if the amount of a nutrient exceeded the amount permitted in a supplement that would ensure the product was defined as a medicinal. (Maximum Permitted Levels which were still being debated in 2015).

Zest for Life award for Foresight to be thrown away. On 18th November, the new "Zest for Life Awards" organised under the auspices of Cosmopolitan's Health Magazine ZEST awarded Foresight Supplement formulations the premier place as a Winner in the supplement group. This was good news and should have pleased the new Larkhall owners Nutricia, since they would be able to major on this award in their advertising programme. In the event, they elected to substitute their own formulation that had no award and was very different in ingredient contents and strengths. Mrs Barnes rejected this substitution and I despaired of what the new owners intended to do with the Larkhall ranges when they finally took over in February 1999. The winning of the award would be instantly negated -- totally unexpected and unbelievable.

Sponsorship had raised £100,000 At the end of November, ASBAH representatives including Paul Wootton, who was retiring, came to lunch in Putney to see me.
They informed me that total donation by Larkhall to the Charity had reached £100,000 ; most gratifying to both parties. When Nutricia took over this sponsorship it was cancelled as was the one to the Literary Review monthly Poetry Competition. Why did these people undo years of really useful promotional sponsorships?

Did they really want our supplement business? Perhaps it was the Trufree Special diet foods that were wanted so that they could close the competition. Who knows? Larkhall's involvement with the National Association of Boys Clubs via their annual cross country running event was also abandoned and the annual help for the Children of Chernobyl too.

Breast Cancer Prevention Diet   On 28th November, The Lancet carried a critique of a book recently published in the USA and written by a well-known doctor and media personality Dr (Bob) Robert Arnot. Entitled 'The Breast Cancer Prevention Diet' it appeared to be promoting benefits of 'Flaxseed' as a dietary constituent. Huge controversy had resulted in the USA owing to the positive publicity generated because Arnot was so well known. There was little science behind the claims for Flaxseed apart from an animal study in rodents (probably mice). This was a typical example of the methods used by the USA Health Food Industry to gain awareness of products -- there were no patents for flaxseed. The credibilities of Arnot and Flaxseed had not been advanced by this book.

Aims of Industry were true friends I continued the company's support for Aims of Industry and Michael Ivens CBE. In my view, this group represented the interests of Larkhall better than all trade associations like the CBI or HFMA. It was truly business friendly and a fighter for freedom too.

Probable criminal actions detected at last   The suspicions surrounding one member of the sales staff were confirmed with a problem concerning an account for one of Larkhall's sales agents. It appeared that the suspected member of staff had set up some convoluted arrangements that had by-passed rules set up by the accounts department. This permitted free goods/disputed deliveries/credits to take place. The individuals involved had been caught out and were in a state of panic. The evidence was presented to the probable new owners as part of **due diligence** and they agreed to see it through by a thorough investigation after February 1st 1999. Whilst the evidence gathered already that included past records could be challenged, it was felt that cross examination of the sales agents would prove decisive and save the new owners substantial costs which had been previously expected.

Consumer body fighting officialdom   In early December, Susan Croft the director of Consumers for Health Choice sent a reply to the MCA's consultation letter MLX 249 regarding reform of the marketing rules that surrounded Food Supplements. She made many valid points and rejected the ideas put forward by the MCA. It appeared that the MCA wanted to become a total dictator in the area and to be advised by persons who were already working with the agency or acting as consultants. No experts from the natural food movements were to be involved. Sue saw the dead hand of bureaucracy and big Pharma in all this. She was right.

Supplements used in cancer prevention diets should not be Pharmaceutically pure   In December, The British Medical Journal published an extensive positive article 'Diet and the prevention of cancer'. The introduction stated that up to 80% of bowel, prostate and breast cancers were related to dietary factors. Other cancers were probably partly diet dependent too. Larkhall's Original Cantassium Dietary system dated from 1920s and was based on similar principles. The company had been developing those ideas for years. I found much to agree with the BMJ about.

Whilst the BMJ said there was no evidence that vitamin supplements helped prevent cancer, I would have said that basic formulation of supplements needed more attention in order to be worth testing in the clinical environment. Designing acceptable trials was almost impossible. It was better to formulate supplements as foods so that they complied with the ideal diet for prevention. This necessitated the use of food bases for tablets and capsules and not attempting to reach pharmaceutical purity and that would be the right way to go.

These ideas were covered in a talk I gave to the Ceuta representatives in Bruges. I also made predictions on the Larkhall ranges for 1999.

The Takeover looms but it was business as usual In mid December, a staff meeting highlighted many problems and the measures that were being taken to address them. The New 'Tetra' computer system seemed to be seen as good but more training would be required. It was unfortunate that much of this would be wasted. Although Nutricia had seen the potential of the system and agreed to pay Larkhall's outlay when they purchased the company, as a large multinational they soon abandoned it.

Ash Communications Towards the end of December, our PR agency, Ash Communications prepared to release news of Larkhall's success in the Zest for Life awards. The Foresight Charity was set to benefit from sales of the supplements. Their activity report for November and December showed the wide remit they had continued to undertake for the Larkhall range from Lipcote - Konnyake - Blakoe - Foresight - Folic Acid etc. The Green Farm Magazine production, Practitioner Briefings and follow-up were controlled by Ash. The agency were probably one of the key reasons for Larkhall's continuing high profile in the media and contributed to the company's credibility in the UK Market. The knowledge of Ash staff was also invaluable. I felt sure that Nutricia would retain them after the takeover but how wrong I was.

Past Competitor lost its Manufacturing Licence Just before Christmas I learned that a long standing competitor of Larkhall (Regent Laboratories) had had its medicines manufacturing licence withdrawn and faced great problems. A few months later the company ceased trading. Regent had been formed from two companies B&P Laboratories and Medopharma that had existed back in the 1960s. B&P Laboratories used to make spherical soft gelatin capsules using 'Globex' processing machines whilst Medopharma was a generic and contract tablet maker. Regent were involved in contracting to many Vitamin Supplement and Herbal marketing companies. The herbal company 'Modern Health Products' was owned in the 1980s by Peter Briess who had also owned the UK rights to the 'Globex' encapsulating process in the 1960s and was a friend.

353

Final year of the Family Business

January the last month - ASBAH - Positive Folic Acid trial results - Transfer of Foresight brand licence impossible - MMR and Autism - Takeover day - Agencies dismissed - ASBAH donation questioned - Folic Acid statistics incorrect - Putney facility to be closed - Highgrove - Negotiation with Greek distributor - Theo Baal - Foresight and the future - New Herbal law proposed - Folic Acid supplementation problems - Nutraceutical regulation - Herbal and Complementary health care threats - Fate of Trufree

January was the last month of the Larkhall business under my family's control. I wrote to customers about the sale of the company and expressed the wishes of Royal Numico (Nutricia) to continue supplying the existing product range with extra items from their other subsidiaries. In the event, they ceased supply of Cantassium and Green Farm Brands except Microfolic Acid. In addition, much of the stock was destroyed by them -- burned. The shop at the front of the factory was closed down. They opted not to continue to use the symbol system on products. Customers were let down and I was unable to prevent this. I thought that I had been misled by the representatives of Nutricia. The reasons for this change of mind could have been a new policy from the top management in Holland. Nutricia had purchased all the secret manufacturing data but left Larkhall's computers in Putney, after destroying the records. Perhaps they never wanted the supplement business but only the Trufree Foods brand? The quality was superior to any of their own gluten-free products. More likely, they found themselves out of their depth in multi-formula tablet-making to food standards and decided to cut their losses and integrate the special diet foods into their established ranges in view of their very large upcoming takeovers. I would never know.

A year of consultancy for Nutricia   As part of the takeover I, my brother and Rita Greer had agreed to be on hand and be available for consultation. RG was on hand for testing each batch of Trufree that continued to be made in the production area until Nutricia took it to their main factory in Wiltshire. After that she had no contact with them at all.

Difficulties with the sales force   A few days after Nutricia's takeover and the sales staff were already finding complying with the new management's requirement difficult. Ironically, one of our salesmen sent me a memo regarding a sales promotion that he claimed was arranged by Ceuta, our pharmacy distributor. In fact it was he who had booked this promotion but had not told me or his immediate superior Mr Nobi, the company secretary. As nothing had been heard from the executive by Unichem when the time came for the promotion I asked Ceuta to look after it. The executive was attempting to undermine Ceuta as expected. He got a flea in his ear from me who hoped his day of reckoning would come after Nutricia assembled their case against him in February.

One of the sales staff sent a job application letter to a company applying for a job as general sales manager. His description of his role at Larkhall was enlightening and fanciful with no mention of the disciplinary proceedings against him currently being pursued by Nutricia.

Granada lecture   in March, I went to Granada in Spain for 3 days to lecture on the Larkhall products for Nutricia at the request of the Spanish Distributor (Pozo-Naturnat).

LARKHALL GREEN FARM

ASBAH donation abandoned but had the regulator really changed?   The agreement with ASBAH in connection with Microfolic Acid was soon abandoned by Nutricia despite assurances they had given me. According to the Nutricia manager, there appeared to be a problem connecting the ASBAH Charity with Micro Folic Acid. He said the problem had arisen with the MCA. I doubted this because the regulator had acknowledged, several years before, my argument that ASBAH deserved recompense for the financial contribution it had made to the clinical research that had fully confirmed the link between dietary folic acid deficiency and Spina Bifida.

This was a moral matter - Pharmaceutical Companies obtain huge rewards/profits for their research into successful patented drugs whilst unpatentable molecules like folic acid yield no return on any research. ASBAH's agreement with Larkhall was totally right. Sadly no other manufacturers paid ASBAH anything. A mean lot! Look at Larkhall's reward from the School Children's diet research - being unfairly copied by competitors and then letting Larkhall take the flack and be put to the sword by HealthWatch, the BBC and the Shropshire TSOs. Every good deed deserves its own punishment!

Perhaps Nutricia saw this problem with MCA as an opportunity to deny ASBAH their cash and so save the company money for a donation based on packs sold. The ASBAH donation had been made for many years on packs and advertisements without any comment from the authorities. In the event the donations to and mention of ASBAH ceased as did any advertising of the product itself. What were Nutricia up to? How did they propose to progress the Larkhall business? Did they intend to progress it at all or merely remove it from the market? What did they intend for Trufree?

I concluded that multinational businesses invariably had nothing in common with the smaller operations such as Larkhall. They often takeover businesses that they see as a threat to their market and then destroy them.

Good review for RG's new book   The Journal of Dementia Care reviewed Rita Greer's new book, 'Soft Options' very favourably, as did several other publications. One called it 'a labour of love.' It was a complete healthy cuisine for people who cannot chew, with new ideas and imaginative recipes. Like all her books, it was written to help people with food problems and it was for better health.

Folic Acid, the Professor and the Polypill   The research into Folic Acid proved encouraging with a scientific paper published in 'Archives of Internal Medicine' in March. Sadly, I had ceased interest in Larkhall by then and it was unlikely that Nutricia would put anything behind publicising the research, despite making encouraging noises when I had discussed ongoing research efforts involving Larkhall with them in late 1998.

There was never any chance of patenting the microfolic acid tablets and the researchers were more interested in a so-called 'Polypill'. They saw it as wonderful opportunity and took lunch with me at my club in June. Indeed, soon after the lunch I saw much publicity was obtained regarding a polypill product being widely recommended to all patients over 40, to prevent heart disease. It was originally envisaged to be a compound formula that would possibly include Folic Acid, Aspirin, a blood pressure drug, a cholesterol lowering drug and a diuretic. The researchers intended to clinically trial a product and patent the formula.

I warned them that the MCA regulator was unlikely to award such a product a licence even for clinical trial only. Regulatory opposition to compound formulas was well known and the technical analytical criteria demanded were likely to be impractical and impossible financially.

Undeterred, the polypill concept has continued for over a decade with differing formulas but no regulatory success in the UK. It appears that folic acid has been left out as has aspirin - some Indian trials took place but their credibility has been questioned. Mass medication with licensed formulas of this kind are very unlikely and there is even opposition to a single low dose Statin being prescribed to everyone seen as 'at risk' because of age alone. I believed such scepticism would continue for a very long time.

I asked the researchers to acknowledge the old team at Larkhall who had made the original folic supplement used in their research -- Dr JM Thomas, Baldeo Ramsarran and myself.

Transfer of Foresight - an insoluble problem with ramifications A major problem arose with transfer of Foresight Supplements and use of the trademark from Larkhall to Nutricia. Mrs Barnes had a fundamental objection to Nutricia. I had not realised her antagonism towards this company that she considered totally unethical because of their record on baby milk substitutes. I soon understood that there was very little I or Nutricia could do to save the situation. My brother dismissed her as unreasonable and wanted to demand compensation. I was totally opposed to this because I fully appreciated her concerns. It was now apparent that Nutricia were a multinational food/pharmaceutical company and had no intention of following the healthy diet concepts that had always guided Larkhall's manufacturing methods. They didn't seem to appreciate how different Larkhall was from other vitamin supplement manufacturers. I began to wonder why they ever came to be interested in buying the company. To leave the deal at this point was not possible and Foresight were confident that they could find a new manufacturer. Happily, all was resolved amicably with Nutricia agreeing to make the Foresight products to Larkhall standards at the Putney operation for at least six months whilst I helped Mrs Barnes find a new manufacturer who could work to her standards as Larkhall had done.

After this experience I privately thought that Nutricia were unlikely to succeed in expanding and developing the Cantassium and Larkhall product ranges which they had bought outright. I was proved correct sooner than expected when Nutricia withdrew and sold out of the vitamin supplement industry in late 2003. By 2010 the whole company had been taken over by French company Danone. A new Trufree range of baked special diet foods was introduced. These were commercially successful but did not conform to the standards followed by Larkhall and RG before 1999.

MMR, Dr Wakefield and Paul Shattock and Autism In early January, I replied to a letter from Paul Shattock of University of Sunderland. He had first contacted me when he was working with Dr Andrew Wakefield at the Royal Free Hospital in London on Autism and the MMR vaccine. Wakefield's research was under fire from the medical establishment and government because it appeared flawed and its publicity had reduced parental demand for the Triple Vaccine (MMR). The worry was that measles would soon rear its head again as a serious threat to child health. This happened by 2012. Parents did not want their children having the triple vaccine (Mumps, Whooping Cough and Rubella - measles) but single disease vaccines instead. The single vaccines were available privately but the NHS only permitted and used the triple. Many doctors, professionals and laypeople thought that the triple vaccine was too demanding on a baby's immune system whereas the single vaccines were easier on the body. In addition, Wakefield thought he had found autism to be connected with the triple vaccine.

Shattock, who had an autistic son, was now implicated with Wakefield and his credibility had also been questioned. I had warned him long ago that the Establishment would never accept the MMR and Autism research any more than they would the Vitamin Supplement and IQ connection. Shattock had been very disparaging about the latter when he first met me, but later changed his mind when he learned the truth from me and later David Benton.

Another buyer for Larkhall -- too late   A director of a Yorkshire based mail order company wanted to purchase Larkhall but I had to tell him it was too late because the contracts for the sale had already been exchanged with Nutricia (Royal Numico) in Brussels.

Takeover day   On 1st February 1999 Nutricia took over control of the Larkhall Vitamin and the Trufree special diet food businesses. My brother and I went to Bristol, to Nutricia's solicitors, to sign the final documents.

I soon received kind letters from many people in the Health Food movement including one from a Kinesiologist Julia Wolfreys, saying the company would be missed. She had realised how different the Cantassium Supplements were from all the others on the market. Unfortunately, Nutricia still didn't appreciate this despite being told about the philosophy behind Larkhall's products. I would have thought that the experience with Foresight would have told them something was very different about Larkhall methods and the way their subsidiary Swedish Pharmaceutical company made and formulated food supplements.

Marketing agencies dismissed   Soon after the takeover, Sue Ash from Larkhall's PR agency reported that she had had a useful meeting with the new management. Unfortunately, this optimism was short lived as Nutricia dispensed with the services of both old Larkhall marketing agencies (Ash - PR and The Media Shop - Advertising) apparently totally ignorant of the valuable knowledge they possessed about the business from several years close involvement. What were they going to do to progress the business they had bought? I planned to recommend both agencies to my nephew (Ben Woodward) to act for those parts of the business (Lipcote and Blakoe) that he had verbally agreed to take over with an investment partner (as yet unknown) because Nutricia did not want these brands. Ceuta also ceased to act as distributors.

Folic Acid statistics incorrect   At the end of February, The Chemist & Druggist carried an article on 'Supplementary Benefits'. It covered the 1997 and 1998 Sales levels of Folic Acid supplements but omitted to mention Microfolic Acid by Cantassium. It would seem Nutricia omitted to refer to it but did permit Cow & Gate Folic Acid that they were going to concentrate on in the future. (For the record, Larkhall's Microfolic Acid had sales of over £600,000 in both years -- so it was the top branded seller.)

Putney Factory to close completely   In early March there was an internal meeting of staff at Larkhall with new management that indicated closure of the Putney facility would not be long delayed. Most staff would be made redundant at the end of April and the rest at the end of June. I was very surprised by this news but it confirmed my recent suspicions that Nutricia took over the company with the intention of transferring all products to their own existing formulations and switching Cantassium/Larkhall consumers from the old formulas to new ones, re-labelled under the Cantassium designation. I thought that decision was a bad one but since Nutricia were now the owners there was nothing I could do. As for the Trufree Food brand items, I suspected a similar fate awaited them. They would soon discontinue them but make new products under the Trufree trademark.

On 25th June, Nutricia quit the Putney premises at 225-229 Putney Bridge Road. All Larkhall staff had now been made redundant. A couple of the maintainence staff were retained for a short period to help clear up the remaining items in the factory.

Visit to Highgrove In early May 1999, I was invited by the Bristol Cancer Centre to join their party at Highgrove Garden to meet the Prince of Wales. This was a fund raising event held at Highgrove because the Prince was President of the Charity. I spoke to POW about Foresight and their work - he appeared very interested. He was certainly a supporter of Complementary Health Care but his lack of in-depth knowledge made difficulties with his credibility when opposed by organisations like 'HealthWatch'. They played the 'Crank' card very successfully through their very influential media members. Anyway, I had an enjoyable afternoon and met some interesting people who were deeply grateful to the BCCC and their dedicated workers. I found the gardens at Highgrove inspiring and the Prince of Wales very welcoming.

Nutricia meet Maria Strofalis In early May, I went to Athens to assist Nutricia in taking over 'Cantassium Hellas'. Maria Strofalis was dramatic but was possibly interested. I feared 'no' would be her answer. After long talks nothing was decided. We met the Greek companies handling Nutricia business in that country and I was not confident that they would be able to handle the 'Cantassium' concepts. I wondered if Dr Hudson had learned anything about Cantassium ideals yet?

Theo Baal Towards the end of May, I met Theo Baal for lunch in Putney. We discussed the current situation regarding the Nutricia takeover. I thanked Mr Baal for the major effort he made in achieving the sale. I always thought that Baal had encouraged Nutricia more than Martin Kimber admitted.

Foresight and my view of the future In its June issue, Health Food Business reported that Foresight Supplements would **not** be licensed to Nutricia and that Mrs Nim Barnes disagreed with the company policy exemplified in the Cow & Gate brand. The magazine also reported that the threatened Food Supplement Directive from the EU would be delayed.

I wrote to Nim Barnes, assuring her that I was not retiring completely, but would now be free to express an independent view on Vitamins and Food Supplements without 'commercial taint'. I hoped to be listened to by the media. A forlorn hope as the media thrived on controversy and using the word 'profit' in a story was always good for publicity. I intimated that I would still be temporarily associated with 'Lipcote' and my family. (In the event, the association, which turned out to be most unsatisfactory, lasted 6 years.)

Herbal product law meeting Towards the end of June, I represented the SPNT (The Society for the promotion of Nutritional Therapy) at a meeting on proposed Herbal Product laws held by The MCA in Market Towers in Vauxhall. The meeting was chaired by Mr Woodfield who had been appointed as the bureaucrat to represent the MCA. Several luminaries of the Herbal trade were present including Professor Arnold Beckett who was now a trusted advisor of the Health Food Manufacturers Association. After listening to the deliberations and offering my views on the unworkability of the regulatory framework on offer, I left the meeting pleased to have no more commercial involvement with herbals. The naivete of some of the experts round that table was unbelievable and would ensure that when promulgated the new laws would be ineffective and probably penalise genuine manufacturers. Consumers would undoubtedly hate losing their favoured remedies and their objections would ensure the continuance of the herbal trade, whilst many marketers, manufacturers and retailers would get round the regulations with impunity. I was sure Woodfield himself would prosper. In the event, a new law 'The Traditional Herbal Medicinal Product' Directive was introduced in 2011 and proved ineffective in Europe. Many governments appeared to take no notice, believing their own current rules already met the Directive's requirements.

Folic Acid supplementation not working   In September, The Pharmaceutical Journal reported that a letter in the Lancet from a research group had found no reduction in the incidence of Spina Bifida babies in the UK population, despite the publicity campaigns on the positive effects of Folic Acid in the diet. The view of the authorities was that it was too early to take the finding as definitive. There were too many variables at work including taking supplements too late in the pregnancy. More education was required.

Nutraceutical regulation   In October, Pharmaceutical Marketing magazine carried a report 'Nutraceutically Correct'. This covered progress on the MLX249 regulatory paper from the MCA. This was not a new problem for the health food industry but was failing to have a marked effect because the area was still a legal minefield. Advertising, PR and sales promotion were likely to come under attack from officials but defences would be successful and the authorities would not have the resources to justify fighting companies in Court.

Cantassium's future   At the end of June, I joined Mike Hudson in Italy to visit Prodotti Naturali in Genoa. I introduced Hudson as a representative of Nutricia who were interested in acquiring PN. Things went well and further talks were to be held. The Cantassium Trade Mark used by PN made the interest greater since Nutricia were expecting to use this branding throughout Europe, where they hoped to dominate the food supplement market. Similar use of the mark in Greece meant that Cantassium Hellas, owned by Maria Strofalis, was still negotiating with Hudson. In the event absolutely nothing materialised and the Cantassium Trade mark was only used on one product, Microfolic Acid, from 2000. This was bought back by Matthews & Wilson in 2003 when Nutricia cut their losses and withdrew from vitamin supplement production and marketing all over the world.

September auction   Most remaining bulk stock of raw materials went to G & G Supplies of East Grinstead. They were long standing customers of Larkhall. The plant and machinery not sold to Nutricia was auctioned in September but made little money. The sale of used industrial machinery is a specialised area and prices at auction seldom achieved book value. The utensils and office equipment made enough to meet clearance costs. The idea that machinery was a better investment than advertising proved untrue and it was as well that the company's founder, George Orange Woodward, who so strongly held that view had passed away.

The Putney Factory sold for redevelopment   In December 1999 the Putney premises were all cleared out and finally sold to developers for the purpose of building Town Houses and Flats (around 30 dwellings). Demolition was inevitable.
  Christmas Eve, after receiving a letter asking for help from Nim Barnes at Foresight, I wrote to her and gave my private reasons for the sale to Nutricia. After 31st January 2000 I would be free to take on consultancies but would concentrate on helping charities and other independent alternative health organisations. However, I no longer had the means of manufacturing the supplements that she needed for Foresight. My days of running a factory were over and so were my days of making pills/tablets.

The final months in Putney   Nutricia vacated the Putney factory and offices in June. Ben Woodward continued to assist me with the final tidying up of the premises including the sale of many raw materials not wanted by Nutricia. Surplus plant and stocks were sold at auction on the premises. Ben moved to the Charlbury factory near Oxford in the autumn. I joined Rita and Alan Greer later, in Hampshire, after the factory had been sold to developers in December. I began to look for a detached country house with a decent sized plot, for a butterfly garden. It was time to begin a new chapter - retirement.

Retribution   As part of due diligence I had been obliged to inform Nutricia of our troublesome salesman's conduct. He was now in their employ. The young woman who was part of the salesforce (an agent) had at last decided to come forward and complain about him. RG had tried to help her and had been to the police about the matter. They could not intervene as the woman had not complained directly to them, being too frightened of the salesman.

Everything was done by the book by the lawyers from Nutricia's Head Office. After the man was interviewed in front of witnesses and one of his colleagues, he was immediately dismissed, his car and 'phone taken away; his salary was paid up to that time but he was given no redundancy, compensation and no holiday pay. He was asked to leave his keys on the table, given his taxi fare home and escorted out of the factory. He was lucky not to have a criminal action brought against him as what he had done was certainly criminal and involved theft and blackmail. The sales agent lost her little cottage as she had not been able to keep up her mortgage. The salesman was made to pay her back most of the money he had taken from her - over £20,000. In his office desk a pile of visiting cards that he'd had printed stated he was a director of Larkhall - which he never was.

The fate of Trufree   Rita Greer had sold Nutricia her formulas, registered Trufree brand and logo. She had always seen to customers' enquiries herself by return of post with a poster, product booklet and details of The Bumper Bake Book. The Trufree logo was abandoned, likewise the poster and the cookbook and, for a while, the booklet with products. Enquiries were left piling up in the office, unanswered. Nutricia produced a new products leaflet but it was pathetic. A demolition job for Trufree! Later, a few baked products such as biscuits were put on the market under the brand name and in uninspiring new packaging. Eventually, Nutricia sold on Trufree to Danone.

As a help to existing Trufree customers, at the time of the takeover, RG had produced a large booklet with new recipes and sent each customer on her mailing list a free copy to go with their Bumper Bake Books. It meant there wasn't anything that couldn't be made with Trufree flours. She offered the few left to Nutricia (free) and the copyright. Their employee said they were not interested as 'it was only a job'.

After Larkhall, Rita Greer continued her work on special diets and published several more books with HarperCollins and Souvenir Press before becoming a history painter, specialising in the 17th Century scientist Robert Hooke. Oxford University put her history paintings on Wikimedia, making them free images for use worldwide. Her husband Alan died in 2007 at the age of 72, after many years of fighting MS and a brain tumour. **In 2011 the Open University gave Rita Greer a rare Honorary Master's Degree for her work in Education and Culture.** She had had over 30 titles published for special diets and healthy eating and much acclaim for her work on Robert Hooke that had brought him from relative obscurity back into history again.

The end   By the end of 1999 I was completely exhausted, both mentally and physically. I had no regrets about getting out because I had had enough. Larkhall, after the takeover, was in shreds and in another company's domain. (RG said the wheels had come off.) The family business my father had started in 1946 had flourished until the end of the century. We had seen it through recessions, the three day week, court cases, fights with the local authorities, the ASA, the media, bailiffs, mindless bureaucracy and control from Brussels. What had begun with one machine making saccharin tablets in a small shop in Larkhall Lane, Clapham and had morphed into two factories, one in Charlbury and the other in Putney, making supplements -- alternative medicine. Over the years we had given employment to hundreds of people of many nationalities. Our products were the best of their kind and were exported worldwide.

My brother did not retire after all despite wishing to do so since the 1980s. Instead he went into business with his son at the Charlbury Site using the oldest trading name in the Larkhall portfolio Matthews & Wilson from 1894, taking the Lipcote and Blakoe brands that Nutricia had not wanted.

They developed part of the site to rent to a childrens' nursery and another part to a haulage and storage warehouse for renting out. The Cantassium brand was bought back from Nutricia in 2003 but not developed by them. As my brother said that would have been "Too much like hard work".

My mother Mary Woodward died in 2001 aged 89. She had seen our family company from start to finish.

The factory in Putney was demolished and smart town houses and flats built on the site. The huge listed, wooden front door and canopy was put on one of the houses. The little shops around closed down without their regular clientele from the Larkhall staff - Grocer 'Indian Joe' (Pak Fruiterers) and the paper shop. The Cedar Tree pub next door was revamped to become a restaurant. Apart from the Listed front door and canopy no trace of Larkhall remained in Putney. It was as if we had never existed.

I indulged in a house with a butterfly garden in the country, several hobbies and gave my services to a large charity for a few years. My three children married and had children - my grandchildren. I kept up with a few of the staff and customers and continued to campaign for Alternative Health Care guided by the ideals of Ivan Illich and other health heroes.

Plate 25

HEALTHIER EATING for Pregnancy

Rita Greer

HEALTHIER EATING FOR SCHOOLCHILDREN

Rita Greer in Putney and four of her

Books and Booklets

The Gluten-free & Wheat-free
BUMPER BAKE BOOK

Rita Greer

The British Food Fiasco

–a practical reply
by Rita Greer

Plate 26

Beautiful lips?
The secret is
Lipcote

Lipcote seals and fixes
your favourite lipstick
all day. Lipcote keeps
you looking your best.

From Chemists & Beauty Stores

Examples of artwork for
our various promotional
items produced in-house
using Pencil, Watercolour
and Photography instead
of images purchased from
general commercial studio
selections. No royalties
payable but all copyright
Larkhall. Popular with
consumers but not
agencies or new marketing
staff.

363

Plate 27

Demolition of the Putney HQ of Larkhall Green Farm in 2001. The end of a family company and workforce as well as a dream of 1969 thanks to officials, bureaucrats, politicians, journalists and crooks.

Plate 28

Mouliniere Place town Houses in Bective Road, Putney 2001.
On the site of Larkhall's warehouse and packing areas

Flats and a Town house in place of the Larkhall HQ Offices at 225-229 Putney
Bridge Road,London SW15 2PY in 2001. Note the listed door and canopy – all
that was left of Larkhall.

Appendix I
ANNIE'S ROOM
Director's Dining Room with a Difference
Edited by Rita Greer

This was a room for business entertaining at the rear of the factory, on the first floor. It was adjacent to the experimental/testing kitchen for Trufree and joined eventually to the tiny flat (two bedrooms, a bathroom and a shower room) that I used when I was staying overnight. The room, a dining room and lounge combined, was very private as it had no windows and was on the end of the building, no conversations could be overheard. It was ideal for business entertaining. It had a certain mood as it had been made out of part of the laundry where Victorian London had had its shirts starched and ironed. Before that it had been the hayloft over the stables where the miller had kept his big Shire horses and carts that brought the grain to the mill in the 17th century.

RG ran it, doing all the cooking herself. As it was within walking distance of Putney High Street she had access to a large Sainsburys, M & S and Waitrose so fresh produce was readily available. Because she wrote books for healthy cooking and articles for health magazines she had to be seen to be practising what she preached. Food was basically low fat, sugar and salt, with plenty of fresh vegetables and fibre, fresh meat and fish. Vegetarians and guests with allergies were catered for and meals ranged from breakfast, elevenses, lunch, teas to dinners - whatever the guests required depending on the time of day.

We did not expect visitors to eat British type food if they preferred something else. Different nationalities liked different foods, very often what they were used to in their own country. Some guests were shy of eating healthily - it just didn't interest them. RG still served healthy food topped up with unhealthy food if they particularly requested it. She took the view that eating in Annie's Room should not be a crusade but rather an enjoyable experience that would help the business - and it really did.

We didn't know of any other company that had a directors' dining room such as Annie's Room so it was something of a plus for us. It knocked spots off taking people out to a restaurant, was ten times cheaper and with excellent food served. The only experience RG and I had of a directors' dining room was the Bank. Their dining room was as dull as dull could be. It was a time when 'cost cutting' was in progress. We were not impressed, especially by the flutes of water served with the miniscule portions of smoked salmon. We had roast pork with the crackling served separately in a small bowl with a teaspoon - one small bowl for the whole table of ten! Consequently, when the directors of the Bank came to lunch in Annie's Room they relaxed and tucked in to what was to them lavish food. Cost cutting? Not allowed in Annie's Room. Lunch would begin at 12.30pm and they would still be sitting at the table by 4.30 and looking forward to tea, freshly baked scones and jam. Once they didn't leave until 7 pm!

Most firms took customers out to lunch in a nearby restaurant. A few, who had the premises, would get in caterers from outside to do a lunch but this could be hit or miss especially if there was no kitchen to work from. The food was usually cold, having travelled from the kitchen where it had been made. The starters and sweets would have been bought in from a supermarket. (RG said it was an insult and cost cuttingly mean.)

People from the Health Food Trade would stay all afternoon but journalists would eat quickly, making notes at the table and be gone in two hours or less. Overseas agents would eat heartily and then accompany me to the boardroom or my office to do business or see round the factory.

366

Basically, we gave the impression of a company doing well and flourishing. If we were particularly trying to impress we would start with freshly made fruit juice or champagne, served on a silver tray with homemade nibbles, crudites (raw vegetables) with a dip and toasted almonds. I always served good wine appropriate for the food we offered. Coffee was freshly ground and served in small cups. Tea was always offered as an alternative.

Presentation Annie's Room was a cross between home and a very plush hotel. The presentation was never over the top but RG liked everything to be spotlessly clean and shining, nicely laid up, welcoming and comfortable. The only people entertained in the kitchen were the police and the fire brigade and they had their tea/coffee/cocoa out of mugs. They were always offered biscuits/sandwiches. This occurred mostly at night and was always appreciated, particularly if the weather was wet and cold.

The large dining room table was black and chrome (from Conran) and could be laid covered with a big tablecloth or with linen placemats. RG had a red tablecloth for Christmas or a honey coloured one for most times. Each had matching napkins. (She never used paper ones.) In what we called 'The Marble Room', which was a kind of large hall that joined up the small living accommodation and the dining room/lounge, there was a round table, also from Conran. It was only used in summer in hot weather as the room had a tiled floor with big glass sliding doors opening on to the roof garden. For this we had a pink tablecloth and matching, large, napkins. Cutlery was from David Mellor (the cutler, not the MP). It had black handles and stainless steel in a simple modern design.

On the roof garden there was a white table and chairs and a big sun umbrella. Unfortunately, it was quite a way from the kitchen and we only used it in hot weather, in the summer. The tubs for the flowers were made out of containers used for raw materials that would normally have been thrown away.

China was Wedgwood, white bone china with gold rims. For the not-so-posh meals we had a patterned porcelain design. All of it went in the dishwasher.

Silver and glass. I had a few pieces of silver, family heirlooms of my own. The salver was useful for serving flutes of champagne and I had a large silver bowl for fresh fruit which looked good in the centre of the table. For formal meals we had cut glass goblets and tumblers and for less formal, plain glass from Conran -- simple but beautiful.

Flowers. There were always fresh flowers on the dining table but only in a small vase. If we had someone coming for a meal who had allergies RG always checked to see if flowers were OK. The tubs on the roof garden would usually supply the miniature bouquet.

Candles. We always had candles on the table for evening meals, in simple china holders.

Menus. Having checked with the guests beforehand regarding likes and dislikes or allergies, RG would plan the menu. This would be shown to them on arrival. She usually typed it out and kept it for reference. Greatest worriers about the menu were strict vegetarians and people with one or more allergies. (Meat eaters would panic at the thought they might be given vegetarian food.) As RG had written books about it and she did the cooking they were able to feel they were in safe hands. Everything was homemade as far as possible and leftover freshly baked bread rolls, especially gluten-free ones, would be given to the appropriate guest to take home.

Guests. All sorts of people came to eat in Annie's Room - people from business, customers, MPs, doctors, chairmen of companies, printers, agencies, journalists, bankers, broadcasters, overseas clients, suppliers, accountants, architects, engineers ...
Derek Cooper from the BBC, Sir Austin Bide (Past Chairman of Glaxo and British Leyland), David Mellor (the later disgraced MP), Chris Chope MP, Tony Colman MP,

Joe Nishide from Japan, Bert Schwitters from Holland, Dr Kathy Bonan from Paris, The Maugeris from Rome, Auberon Waugh, Leslie Kenton (Harpers & Queen),The Media Shop, Barclays Bank Directors, Martha and David Hill etc.

Food In the early 1980s the nation's favourite foods were prawn cocktail; steak, chips and peas followed by black forest gateau. RG never served that particular meal. It was more likely to be a light starter, main course with meat or fish with vegetables and a light dessert, usually with fruit. For vegetarians the main course would be an egg or nut dish with several vegetables. Bread was always homemade, usually freshly baked rolls, served in a wicker basket.

Nibbles: Homemade cheese straws, toasted almonds, matchstick vegetables (all vegetarian)

Starters: Vegetable crudites with pink mayonnaise dip V
avocado and orange slices with sesame seed oil vinaigrette V
mushroom pancakes with a cheese sauce V
homemade chicken liver pate
mushroom pate V
melon and Parma ham
stuffed mushrooms
green salad with toasted almonds V
smoked salmon with lime and chives, brown bread and butter
nut pate V melon V prawn cocktail (by request)   asparagus V garlic bread V

Soups: (all vegetarian)
watercress
red pepper and tomato
mushroom
parsley
pea and asparagus,
vichyssoise (cold) or hot leek and potato
tomato with basil
minestrone
vegetable (thick) or broth (thin)
pea
lentil or split pea

Main courses: Poached salmon and parsley sauce with hot veg and Jersey Royal potatoes
cold salmon, mayonnaise and two salads (red and green), boiled new potatoes
cold ham or chicken and salad with jacket potatoes
cannelloni
pasta with a ham sauce and salads or hot vegetables
pasta parcels with cheese and spinach filling in vegetable broth (very popular) V
baked fish with savoury rice
braised beef with carrots, mushrooms and vegetables with jacket potatoes
cod, leek, red pepper and tomato casserole with boiled potatoes
Devonshire pasties (cold with salad or hot with veg)
roast grouse with bread sauce, redcurrant jelly, game chips and vegetables

sweet and sour pork with crispy noodles, rice and prawns, stir/steam vegetables
roast leg of lamb with garlic and rosemary, roast potatoes and vegetables
roast topside of beef with Yorkshire pudding, roast potatoes, parsnips and hot vegetables
roast pork with apple sauce, crackling, vegetables and roast parsnip and potatoes
leeks in cheese sauce with hard boiled eggs   V
spinach quiche with hot vegetables or salads   V
breast of chicken with fresh herbs, lemon and mushrooms, vegetables and rice
spaghetti with meat sauce and green salad
spaghetti with a nut sauce and salad or hot vegetables   V
homemade pizza with a salad
Everything was home made, even the pasta. A green vegetable was served with each main
course. Good gravy was made without stock cubes. (V = vegetarian)

Desserts: (all vegetarian)
exotic fruit salad on a plate with fresh raspberry sauce
baked apples, plain or stuffed
tart du jour
autumn fruit compote
spiced apple pie
apricot pie
plum tart
fruit crumble
prune souffle
fresh fruit such as raspberries or strawberries
summer pudding
dried fruit pie with cinnamon and wholemeal pastry
apple or raspberry snow (low calorie for slimmers)
baked bananas with passion fruit
Single cream served by request, also custard, freshly made (very popular with the men).

Cheese: This was rarely served as it is very high in fat, but if requested, the cheese board
would have Stilton, strong cheddar, goats' cheese and a soft cheese such as Camembert or
Brie. Always served with celery and grapes, and homemade cheese biscuits or bread rolls. If
available, UK produced cheeses were the choice.

Chocolates: Charbonnel and Walker or homemade, little homemade almond macaroons or
nougat.

Annie's Room Specials: These were only served if RG could be persuaded as they were
not in line with healthy cooking.

Bookie's Eye Pie. This was shaped and decorated like a fish, made from puff pastry.--
quite spectacular. Inside was a layer of cream cheese, a layer of watercress and fillets of
salmon.(RG called it 'Heart Attack Pie'.) Very popular with the racing crowd.

Millionaire's Starter -- golden fried bread topped with cream cheese, smoked salmon, black caviar, chopped chives, a squeeze of lemon juice and a thin slice of lemon.

lemon meringue pie (high in sugar)   V
treacle sponge pudding (high in treacle/sugar)   V
profiteroles (high in double cream)   V (Popular with the MD of Wassen International as the word 'profit' was part of the name.)

Overseas customers would arrive for breakfast, off the ferry or early 'plane. The Dutch would require pizza (lots) and the Italians fresh pastries with coffee. They were all homemade. The Italians were particularly fond of a yeasted fresh fruit plait which RG would make herself. It was out of one of her books. What was left over would be given to the office staff - very popular.

If people came for tea RG usually made scones and little buns. There was always a big bowl of fresh fruit on the table. Sometimes she made little fruit tartlets. If RG had been testing Trufree flours there would be special buns/biscuits etc as well.

For quick, light lunches RG would make soup and bake rolls. They were filled with whatever the visitors asked for. i.e. they were asked to choose when they arrived. were Seasonal food: Hot cross buns, mince pies and Christmas cake, both with wheat flour and Trufree gluten-free flour.

Special diets and allergies: Visitors who required a slightly different kind of food were accommodated. One MD was on a low cholesterol diet. A womans' magazine journalist had several allergies and once changed them all half way through lunch. One of the Italian visitors had a severe allergy to garlic. Vegetarians were easy to cater for. Some visitors were completely put off vegetarian food so RG only served it if it was required. The meat eaters regarded it as an insult, especially those from the health food trade.

Overseas visitors were inclined to be curious about English food, celebration food or our food in general. This didn't always work out when they asked for samples. RG admitted she made the worst mistake ever when a Korean businessman came to lunch and asked to be given English food as he 'wished to experience it'. We were having poached salmon with boiled new potatoes, steamed carrots, peas and spinach. RG laid up the table in the usual way with knives and forks. The man couldn't use either and she offered him a spoon instead of the knife. He couldn't use that either. The size of the portions (normal) horrified him so RG had to take his plate to the kitchen, remove half the food, chop it up and put it into a bowl. Fortunately, we did have some chopsticks in the cutlery drawer. He was then very happy and ate up. He refused the pudding and said he was totally full, astonished that there was more food to follow the salmon dish. The dinner plates fazed him as he was used to only bowls and our normal portions seemed enormous to him.

Italians have a huge regard for Italian food that is regional, simple and healthy. They had no respect for English food and smoked liked chimneys right through the meal. Consequently, RG served Italian food to them, even pasta (homemade of course). They liked several courses with plenty of protein served separately from the vegetables. The one English meal they really did enjoy was roast beef and Yorkshire pudding with not many vegetables. RG served plenty of Yorkshire pudding with plenty of good gravy as a starter, several slices of beef (double portion) as the main course (and seconds) and a small plate of vegetables (without the roast potatoes as they were not used to them) as the third course. They were not that bothered about a dessert but in particular liked pastries. The meals would take about three hours or longer as they liked conversation, enjoying themselves and wine. Champagne meant nothing to them as it was French. They preferred Italian wines and to finish - grappa.

They were fond of expensive food such as smoked salmon in double helpings and went to the best restaurants when they were over in UK on business. Good presentation was important to them so whenever they came we used the silver. They took this as a great compliment. It was unusual for them to entertain at home in Italy so Annie's Room was rather a novelty. A meal for the Italians was always something of an event especially as they expected RG to be dressed to the nines as the hostess, not just the cook. Dinner in the evening would go on until long past midnight.

The Swedish business people liked English food and were easy to entertain. They would come in big groups to look over the factory and would have elevenses in Annie's Room. The first time they came RG made a huge amount of coffee and just a little teapot of tea in case anyone would prefer tea. They all wanted tea! They were very into biscuity things and not interested in bread and cakes at all.

The reputation of British food was universally poor. Visitors expected it to be awful and were pleasantly surprised at what they were served in Larkhall's dining room -- Annie's Room. It was a big PR asset.

CRIME

An ongoing battle

Shop assistant's fraud. We had two middle-aged women working in the shop at the front of the factory in Putney. They got on well with each other and did a good job. That is they did until one of them left her husband and took up with a petty criminal. We had a deal going on W5, an expensive beauty product in the form of tablets. If the customer wasn't satisfied with the improvement in her skin they could bring it back and get a full refund. This was a good offer but it was on a very good product. Beryl's new boyfriend encouraged her to steal the product. He then came into the shop on Beryl's day off and asked for a £50 cash refund, returning the empty packs. It happened more than once. The other member of staff reported going to a nightclub in Wimbledon and being offered W5 at half price but not in the packs. Beryl admitted the thefts and was sacked. A notice about it was posted on the canteen door for all to see.

New Year Damage   The Police 'phoned me at 3 am one New Year's Day. A drunk had been making his way up Putney Bridge Road and smashed the shop plate glass window. The shop was shelved out with stock. I had to go down into the cellar and find some boards, nails and a hammer to board it up. Not a good start to the year!

The Police suggested a smaller window might be a good idea instead of the smashed one which was floor to ceiling. So, I had the bottom half bricked up and a half sized window above it. Fortunately, it was never smashed again. The police were pleased I took their advice.

Studio trashed, spring 1990   RG's little studio on the roof of the Putney Factory had the lock forced. It was trashed and took her 2 days to sort out. Nothing was taken but the person who did it was obviously looking for something. It was not on the alarm system so the bells had not gone off.

More break-ins, more security   In spite of the new high tech alarm system we were still getting break-ins. There were eight in six weeks. Not surprisingly the police were as fed up as we were.

The roofs of the factory by now were lead free owing to thieves stealing it at night. One year they tried to break into the factory through the roof. They destroyed a large quantity of roofing felt and only gained access to the hatch containing a large motor for one of the extraction fans. They had fled, leaving a trail of destruction which all had to be repaired. After this the roof lights had to be left on overnight, wasting electricity and a nuisance for the people who lived in the flats and houses around the factory. However, this had the effect of reducing the number of would-be burglars on the roof.

Prowlers still tried to come into the factory during the daytime. The police advised us to make the front door more secure. This necessitated an inner door being erected with an entry system and buttons for staff to press with a code number. This number was changed each month. Anyone who forgot their code number would come in through the shop where they were known to the shop staff. It now meant staff could get in and out of the big front door but not the public. All the other entrances were exit only. Anyone who managed to get in at night would (and did) set the alarm bells off. Visitors to the factory had to go in through the shop, who would phone through to the MD, RG or the appropriate manager who would go to the shop to escort them into the factory. Visitors arriving by car in the small car park at the back of the factory could go up the fire escape and ring Annie's Room doorbell.

There was now no way straight up on to the roof as a new room had been built on between Annie's Room and the boiler house, blocking it off. However, more and more security did not stop the intrusions.

Car Stolen In March 1990 my Mercedes was stolen from the single garage at the front of the Putney factory. It was taken during the lunch hour. When I had gone to drive it out at 2 o'clock all I found was a pile of glass on the floor. The police were not hopeful I would get it back. However, someone reported seeing it about 5 miles away a couple of days later. Two men were changing the number plates in the street. The police were tipped off and quickly recovered it. I sent the person who had reported it a cheque towards her family holiday. She was delighted and so were the police.

Shop crime One afternoon a man came into the shop and in spite of alarms and CCTV cameras he robbed the till. The staff were terrified. Fortunately, the takings had already been put in the safe in the company secretary's office on the first floor, so he only got away with the float -- £30. However, the staff were quite shaken up.

Break-ins 1989 A man was caught trying to break in to the Putney factory. The police put him in the cells and charged him. Our extra vigilance and security measures had paid off.

The police were called to the factory again in a few weeks later. They searched the building with dogs but found nothing. However, in April there was another break-in when cheque books, £3,000 of mail order banking, the ansaphone and tapes were stolen. This caused chaos in the mail order office. Customers had to cancel their cheques and check to see why their orders had not been delivered. The cheques were found scattered in Battersea Park, under bushes. The following day all the locks had to be changed.

Police came with a Warrant RG reported an officer from Scotland Yard had come to see her in the boardroom about Walter O'Connell. He had brought with him several large files that contained photographs taken covertly of Walter and a small, dark haired woman. The police had been watching them for some time, even following them to Ireland. A businessman had reported them, suggesting they had been stealing products from his new, small chain of health stores with the intention of setting up a health store of their own in Ireland and stocking it with the goods they had been stealing.

The detective asked RG about Walter's character and she was shown a warrant for his arrest. He was always getting into scrapes but this was serious. He also showed her some of the photographs. They looked a ridiculous couple as Walter was a really big man and she was a tiny little thing. WOC had been divorced by his wife for his drinking and behaviour. This had caused a major fallout with his family as they were Catholics, and his father was an ex-policeman. The girlfriend, who was manageress of one of the stores, was still married and the detective said they were worried by threats about what her husband was going to do to WOC when he caught up with him.

RG said it would take a couple of lorryloads of stock to start up a store in Ireland and there was the added problem of getting it over to that country. It would take years to steal enough stock and most of it would by then be over date. WOC had stock in the boot of his car. The police had seen it. RG said that was perfectly normal for a Larkhall rep as it was used to top up small shops who had run out of things.

The detective asked RG to describe WOC. She told him he was a big Irishman who had swallowed the blarney stone. His head was full of dreams and he did little work.

RG suggested some details of the businessman who had reported him and his girlfriend might come up with something as Larkhall supplied him with goods for his few stores.

She went to the trade department and it appeared that the businessman owed Larkhall over £12,000 and had refused to pay, for months. It had nearly got to the Bailiff's stage. A pity he had forgotten to tell this to the police as it put a completely different complexion on the matter.

The detective went away, taking the warrant for WOC'S arrest. It would not be used after all. The police dropped the case. WOC refused to discuss the matter with anyone, especially RG.

Problems with the womens' toilets owing to fraud There were complaints about the toilets not flushing properly. The maintenance men looked into it and found not enough water was refilling the tanks after the toilets had been flushed. When they took the lids off the tanks they found all sorts of stock, stolen from the packing area, wrapped up well in plastic and hidden in the water. These were being collected by the thieves and taken home. A search of the female staff as they left the building caught the two of them red handed and they were sacked on the spot.

Fraud using the mail The postman who collected our mail by van every day spoke to the mail order manager. He asked him why we didn't deliver some of the mail ourselves as it was going to an address just round the corner. The mail turned out to be parcels of goods stolen from the picking area by one of the packing staff and packed for posting to herself.

Police and blood In the allergy testing laboratory at the front of the factory, for a time we had a blood testing service. The man I hired to be in charge had worked in the army blood unit. One day when I was away, RG was called down to reception. Two very sinister looking men in navy blue overcoats and trilby hats were demanding to see me. They turned out to be from Scotland Yard. There was a scandal about soldiers selling blood at the time and they wanted to interview the man in charge, the ex soldier. (Later he denied they had ever come to interview him.) RG described the two detectives as a pair of bullies in nice coats and hats as she had had to cope with them. They were quite rude to her when she told them they couldn't go into the factory unless they were wearing white coats and hats. She stood her ground and they decided not to go into the factory, merely into the Allergy Laboratory.

Signatures RG had agreed to deal with the police for me when they came as I was often away, up to the eyes with work or out on business and the staff were likely to be frightened and would clam up. She had three places in the factory where she could be interviewed -- her studio, the boardroom or Annie's Room. She also knew how the factory was run, who the staff were and she knew her way around the building and where everything was. I had enough to do without dealing with the police and RG didn't mind.

One morning a plain clothes officer arrived unannounced from Scotland Yard. RG saw him in the boardroom and made him a cup of coffee. He had several files of papers with him and wouldn't say immediately what the call was about. I was abroad on business and not due back for a week.

The detective asked RG if she would recognise my signature. She said yes, of course, as she worked closely with me and often handled confidential documents. When asked, she would act as my PA. He asked her what my signature was like. RG said, "mad but very strong, unreadable and impossible to forge". He took a letter out of a file and showed it to her. She saw it was from an Australian Company also called Larkhall. At the bottom was a weedy little signature, in my name. Along the bottom in print was a list of directors. She noticed it included my name. The detective asked RG if this was my signature. She laughed and said it was nothing like it. She phoned through to the company secretary and asked him to bring a couple of letters - any document would do - with my signature on it.

He was reluctant, (as always), to help so RG told him it was for the police. This made him slightly less reluctant and he sent one of the office staff down to the boardroom with two signed letters from the files.

RG verified the signatures as mine and showed them to the detective. He laughed and said he saw what she meant about my style of signature. They were not remotely like the signature on the Australian letter. RG pointed out, that the Australian one was made by someone left handed and that I was right handed. This was something the police had not yet realised. She also said Australia was not the sort of market that would interest me and that I was not the director of any Australian company.

The detective then relented and told RG what it was all about. The Australian police had been watching a gang of fraudsters who had copied our stationery, packaging etc and used our business name so it all looked 'kosher'. Now the Australian police had asked Scotland Yard to investigate in UK and to see what our part was in the fraud. The answer was no part at all. I went to see the CID when I returned and was horrified to be told RG and I would have to go to Australia for the court case, paying our own lawyers and expenses and that the case could take months. This would be to prove we were innocent. If we did not agree to go then a warrant for our extradition would be served.

Fortunately, the case didn't get as far as court and it just petered out. RG's husband would have had to be put into a nursing home and the case could have gone on for months. Neither of us would have been able to run our businesses. It was a very worrying time and all for something going on over the other side of the world about which we knew nothing. Later we discovered the partner of a friend of the Prime Minister's wife, was thought to be involved in the fraud.

Pension fraud with signatures One weekday evening when I was abroad, RG was called over to the office by the company secretary. It was after all the staff had gone home for the day. He asked her to sign something but didn't say what. He was in his office with one of the sales team and there was a bit of an atmosphere. They wouldn't tell her what the document they wanted her to sign was about but just demanded that she sign it. It was several pages long and she was not authorised to sign anything for the company as she was not employed by the company, being a separate entity. RG was immediately suspicious they were up to something as they refused to explain. She suggested they wait until the following day when I would be back and could sign it myself. She refused to sign point blank, especially as they demanded that she must. The two of them then became threatening, particularly the salesman, and said she would be very sorry if she didn't sign. The salesman began to get physical about it. RG suggested she would like a word with the police about it, which took the wind out of their sails somewhat, and she beat a hasty retreat, running over the roof to Annie's Room, to which she knew neither of the men had a key. As she was spending that night there with her disabled husband, she was anxious about what the two employees were up to and so did phone the police, who gave her a special number to ring if she needed assistance.

The following day when I returned from abroad, neither of the employees said a word about this document that had urgently required a signature. Years later I found out what the scam was. Unknown to me or my brother, the company secretary had awarded himself an extra 9% on his company pension. This was not discovered until we had sold out. The document that RG had refused to sign had later been signed by one of the office staff. She had signed it once in her maiden name and again in her married name. So, it appeared to be signed with two different signatures but actually was signed twice by the same person.

Fraud   One of the men working in the production unit had thought up a scam. Everybody knew about it and it was much talked about in the canteen. He said he had a bad back owing to the work he had been doing at Larkhall and took it up with a solicitor to try and get compensation. Everyone knew he was faking it, trying to get Larkhall to pay up and taking life easy on sick pay. The case dragged on for months with solicitor's fees mounting up on both sides. RG discovered the man was able to pick up and carry his full dustbin from the back of his house to the pavement at the front with no trouble at all - so much for his bad back. She let it be known Larkhall had proof of this on a video and that he would get nowhere with his claim. When this news spread, the case was suddenly dropped. (Actually, there was no video.) - end of story and two solicitors dragging the case out to their own advantage.

Warehouse accident   One of the warehouse men was a very lazy character. To get up to the top shelves a strong set of steps with a platform was used. It could be moved around as required because it had wheels. It also had a brake to make it stable when it was parked. The man didn't bother to use the brake and fell down on to the floor below. He was just bruised but made a great thing of it. He wanted compensation for this accident that he had brought on himself and was prepared to lose his job. He was given just over £1,000 and gave in his notice. Larkhall's insurance paid up and the warehouse manager was glad to see the back of him. The man was lazy and didn't want to work.

Attack on a camera   After we had CCTV installed for security, one of the cameras, high up in the warehouse stopped working. Someone with a very long ladder had tried to remove it in the lunch hour.

Warehouse break-in   One night a van pulled up at the side of the warehouse. Two men broke in through the window, setting off the bells. The only goods they stole were boxes of Lipcote.

Lead stolen from warehouse roof   Usually the police did a great job but sometimes things went wrong. An American couple had rented the house next door to the factory. One night they saw men on the warehouse roof removing the lead. They 'phoned the police who took over an hour to arrive. By then the men had disappeared. The police went back to the station. After another hour the men came back and began again. The Americans 'phoned the police again. By now it was raining. This put the police off and they didn't want to come out a second time. Two and a half tons of lead were taken from the warehouse roof. The roof was now leaking badly, letting in water on the packed goods. Police enquiries in the area took place the following day and one neighbour reported a large green van labouring up the road, heavily loaded down with the lead. They were never caught. All the lead on the warehouse roof had been stolen by then and it had all had to be replaced with zinc.

A week later RG and her husband and myself were staying in the flat over the weekend. On Saturday morning RG was in the kitchen and heard someone walking about on the roof. She went outside and saw a man trying to steal the lead. He made off when he was discovered. We thought we had caught him in time before he could have stolen it but rain in the afternoon caused cascades of water down the kitchen walls. The man had stolen the lot and cracked many of the slates. The roof was leaking like a sieve.

Thieving at trade shows   There was a particularly troublesome overseas customer who used to turn up at trade shows. He was obviously quite well off as he used to fly over to the UK in his own 'plane. He always came with a large sports bag and would go round to each stand pinching stock off the shelves. By the time he had filled the big bag he would exit to the car park and unload his haul, then return with the empty bag and continue to go round thieving even more. Rather than make a scene, staff on the stands turned a blind eye to his activities.

Complaints to the organisers and security fell on deaf ears. He continued for years, flying back with his stolen goods to sell in his own country. Each time he came back to another trade fair he stole more and more. He came to the Larkhall stand and started to put packs into his already quite full bag. Unfortunately for him, RG was manning the stand with one of the reps. When he wasn't looking RG took the packs he had stolen out of his bag and put them back on the shelves. He was enraged by this. Eventually, at another trade fair, he was arrested and escorted out of the exhibition as the exhibitors got up a petition about him. It was quite a scandal. (RG said she had the idea of writing SWAG on his bag in big letters because that is what he used it for.) The man was refused admission to any more trade shows.

A new Larkhall employee was put in charge of the Larkhall stand at Olympia. At the end of the show he tried to sell the **till** to someone for cash. As it was on hire, he got caught and had to be dismissed.

Break-in at the front of the Putney factory   In full view of Putney Bridge Road, a man climbed on to the roof of the phone box at the front of the laboratory and broke in at night, through the window. He left black sooty handprints everywhere as the roof of the phone box had never been cleaned. The forensic man came from the police and took prints etc. From these they were able to identify him. Alas, he was of no fixed abode and so a summons could not be sent to him.

Rep's Petrol scam   One of the managers showed RG four receipts from a petrol station. They were all dated the very same day and were for varying large amounts of petrol. They had been handed in as proof of expenses by one of the reps. On that day he had been in the area where he lived. The amount purchased would have enabled the rep to do thousands of miles. Friends and family had been filling their cars themselves at Larkhall's expense. The receipts were all from his local garage.

Visits by reps?   A complaint was made by a large health store in the south that had not been visited by one of our sales force for two years. This turned out to be the tip of the iceberg. Unbeknown to the sales team, a questionnaire was sent out to many stores on our books asking about the visits from our reps they were supposed to have visited regularly. The sales team was outraged when the results of the questionnaires showed a dearth of visits. (The completed questionnaires mysteriously didn't make it to the HAT Archive.) The 'phone is no substitute for a call and no contact at all is a disaster for sales. It had been going on - or not going on - for some time and been covered up, or even encouraged by poor management.

One of the reps always had a tan, even if we had a poor summer for sunshine. (RG said he looked like someone who worked out of doors.) It transpired that instead of doing his work for Larkhall he was in fact running a car park in a field near one of the airports, chauffering his customers to and fro and patrolling the cars.

Car boot selling   As the reps were allowed to have a small stock in their cars it could lead to dodgy deals and pocket money. Basically it was thieving. A friend of mine reported that he had been told by two of them that, "it was normal, went with job and everybody did it," - especially at Larkhall it seemed.

Thieving   There are some staff who would never steal anything from the company and others who cannot seem to stop themselves. Stealing from the office can take many forms. At Christmas staff would put their Christmas cards through the franking machine. Paperclips, pens, packets of printing paper, elastic bands, envelopes, etc used to disappear a little at a time, putting up the office bills. Time when they should be working they can go out of the building and do shopping, especially if other employees cover for them. Private phone calls can knock up the telephone bill and making copies on the photocopier can cost too. If the office manager was up to it so were the rest of the office staff.

Police arrest   A police officer was in the boardroom when a call came through to him. His suspect had just entered our shop. The officer ran through the rear of the shop and leapt over the counter, apprehending the man. Brilliant!

Intruder   RG caught an intruder in Annie's Room and marched him across the roof to the office. She went back to the dining room and laid the table as we had a visitor for lunch. In the office the man said he had to go and put more money in his parking meter. Off he went and did not return. RG was furious.

Gang warfare   RG was called down to the warehouse. A gang of three men had marched into the factory and were looking for someone. Staff were frightened and hiding in the canteen under the tables. RG approached the three men, looking fierce and asked them their business. She told them they could only come into the factory if they were wearing white coats and hats and they were not welcome anyway. Amazingly, they just turned tail and fled.

A machete   One of the production staff, an Indian, had brought a machete to work with him and put it in his locker. The other production staff were terrified. RG sent him home with the machete and told him to come back without it.

Appendix III

MISCELLANEOUS ANECDOTES

1987 Storm   After a night of high winds the first sign of trouble was the silence at 6.30 am. The big gas boilers did not go on because the maintenance man could not get in to work. The radio and TV didn't work either so there was no news. There were no lights on anywhere. I had breakfast and prepared to go across the roof to the office. On the way across I saw the debris -- branches off trees, dustbin lids, bricks, slates off roofs, guttering, fencing etc. Nobody had come into work. No cars were parked outside, the office was silent until the 'phones began to ring. The switchboard operator turned up because she lived within walking distance. Half a dozen of the manufacturing staff struggled in, having had to walk as the underground trains were not running nor the trains and buses. In Wandsworth Park opposite, huge trees had fallen, uprooted. Roads were blocked with more fallen trees and branches that had been ripped off by the great storm that had hit during the night. The electricity was off so RG boiled up a big saucepan of water on the gas stove in the Trufree kitchen and took it down to the canteen to make tea and coffee for the staff that had managed to get in. Only a handful had made it. It was very weird.

There was no way the factory could run that day so I sent those who had managed to get in home except the maintenance man and a couple of the production team who didn't mind helping to clear up. One of them collected up the dustbin lids and took them round the local houses. Each one had the house number on it but not the road name. It was some time before we had electricity again and could listen to the news. Their main trouble was that their broadcasting staff couldn't get in either. It was chaos. 'Phones rang in the office. RG took one call from a really irate shopkeeper from the north. He had 'phoned several times to give an order, had got no answer and wanted to know what was the matter with the company. She explained about the overnight storm and the state of London. It was all news to him.

It was some time before I could get through to Charlbury which hadn't had it as bad as Putney, but with same problem of travel as there were many trees down over the roads. The south of the country had had it worst, losing electricity for days, or in some areas weeks.

It took several days for things to get back to normal. The post was erratic and days late. Our maintenance men were able to cope with all the repairs, including the one roofing panel that had been torn off the packing floor roof. RG said it was a good job I had had the big chimney taken down when I did or it would surely have crashed down into the factory.

A Big Storm   A big storm on 25th January 1990 took its toll at the Putney Factory. Putney Bridge Road was closed owing to flying scaffolding and at lunchtime a really strong gust ripped off the first floor door at the back of the offices that led on to the flat roof. This allowed the wind to get into the factory. The roof over the quality control laboratory began to be torn off in large pieces. Guttering and a drainpipe parted company over the shop at the front and took off up the main road. The maintenance men managed to anchor the shop blind before that broke loose but missiles rained down on the factory all day - dustbin lids, roof slates, pieces of fencing, greenery from gardens etc. There was a good deal of structural damage over a wide area.

There was less damage at the Charlbury factory as the storm was not so severe there but the lean-to where the bins were steam-cleaned was ripped off and ended up on the factory roof. It was a difficult day for staff trying to get on with their work and they had problems getting home because of train cancellations. The good thing was no one was injured in spite of the severe and very frightening high winds.

Change of Air at the Putney Factory 1990 - We were conserving energy and had been recycling air through fine filters. As this did not have to be reheated this was a saving. The unit cost over £20,000 to install and was very successful as well as being good for the environment. However, new Government regulations changed all that. Suddenly, it was no longer permitted to recycle air in this way. From then on we had to take air from Putney. This had to be heated, filtered and returned to Putney. Much more energy was required and would be adding to the greenhouse effect. Worse still, the new equipment cost us another £20,000. Bureaucrats and politicians, the greenhouse effect and the green revolution? New rules and regulations made a nonsense of it all and left us well out of pocket.

Music while you work Music was played over the sound system used for the tannoy until PRS rules were enforced. Royalties had to be paid to the performing rights society how ridiculous. After we stopped it the staff in production brought in their own transistor radios and played them all day.

The Tango One of the ingredients used in sugar coating for tablets was ether as it dissolved the bees wax that made the tablets shine. Only a tiny amount was used. One of the staff in the coating room developed a liking for the ether and used to sniff it. He was caught putting his head into the big coating pan as it was going round. He had become an addict and was getting high on it. RG was in the warehouse one morning, checking Trufree stock and there was a tango playing on the radio. The man came towards her and took her in a dancing hold. RG could do the tango and saw the funny side of it. Anyway, the man was determined. Together they tangoed up and down the aisles of the warehouse, which had woodblock floor, until the record finished. RG said he was high as a kite. It did not take much to find out why. He eventually left when he was put into another area to work, away from any contact with the ether.

An unwelcome visitor One morning an animal got into the factory through the yard and into the production area at the rear. Staff chased it out with a broom believing it to be a brown dog. It wasn't a dog, it was a fox!

The Crusher My brother had an idea to save money on the number of skips at Putney. He bought in a crusher. Staff were instructed to use it to crush the empty containers of raw materials. This enabled much more to be put into the skips. There was a problem. When the skip man came, the skip was so heavy it couldn't be lifted on to the loader. The crusher was returned to Charlbury where it rusted away and was never used again.

Fire There was a plastic litter bin on the landing of the stairs into the office. One day somebody threw in a lighted cigarette. It caught fire and soon the stairwell was full of acrid black smoke. I put it out myself with a fire extinguisher.

The staff were always told to report any smell of burning. The tenants who lived in the little houses in Wadham Road, at the side of the factory, had small gardens at the rear. They thought nothing of having burn-ups against the factory wall. We could not do anything to stop them.

The big worry about a fire in the factory was the sugar used for coating. It was quite flammable. We had regular fire drills and kept to the regulations with regular checks on the fire extinguishers and hoses. A fire drill meant everyone must vacate the building and assemble in the yard at the back or on the pavement at the front and be counted. Fortunately, all the years we were there, there was never a serious fire.

When the little flat over the shop was gutted by builders they were allowed to burn up the wooden beams on the premises as they had woodworm. This was legal. They burnt them in a large metal drum in the yard during the morning, supervised by the warehouse manager. When it was all burnt it was hosed with water. That evening the fire brigade arrived as someone in the neighbourhood had reported a fire on the premises. They sent two fire engines with crews. There was no fire but they would not go away and stayed hanging around for about 3 hours as they couldn't go away until the police had been. RG made them cups of tea and commiserated with them. She said one of them was wearing make-up!

One Christmas it was my turn to be on duty as caretaker since we didn't have one at that time. The factory could not be left unattended for several days. RG had called the gas board on Christmas Eve as she could smell gas in the kitchen of Annie's Room and so could her husband. A man came to inspect and could find nothing. However, later a pan of oil on the stove caught fire. RG heard it ignite and then saw 3ft flames. Strangely, The gas under the pan was not lit. She calmly covered the pan with a wet tea cloth that put the flames out immediately. The strange thing was the pan continued to heat. Another man from the gas board came as an emergency call out, furious at being summoned from his Christmas break. The pipe to the gas hob had split and was alight even though the gas tap was turned off. The pan obscured this. He disconnected the complete stove and told us not to move the pan for several hours, keeping it completely covered with a wet cloth.

Being Christmas, it took a week for the gas people to repair the faulty pipe.(If we had not been there, there would have been a big fire.) Fortunately, we had two stoves in Annie's Room kitchen as it doubled as the experimental kitchen and was used for testing the Trufree flours.

Larkhall part of local history One day RG walked to the High Street to collect her glasses from the optician. He wasn't quite ready with them so while she was waiting she called in at the local museum to have a look at their exhibits. To her amazement there was a showcase devoted to Larkhall and in particular there were the old patchwork packs of her original Rita Greer Foods (with her photograph on them) as well as Cantassium packs. They must have bought them from Larkhall's shop. We had had no knowledge of it.

When I had first bought the factory in 1968 there were several small factories around in the area. In Deodar Road opposite, the other side of the busy Putney Bridge Road, there was an iron foundry, a fur cleaning business, garage, picture framers, a very large architectural antiques yard and an auction house that had previously been another laundry. By the time we left, Larkhall was the only factory still working. Everything had been pulled down and built over with houses and flats. The area had changed from mostly industrial to mostly residential. When the business was sold in 1999 the factory and site was sold separately and two years later was a complex of new houses and flats.

Parking When we first moved to Putney there was ample parking for cars in the side streets and few of the staff had cars. By the time we sold up in 1999 parking had become a nightmare. By then the female office staff were the ones with cars, not the manufacturing men. RG got together with the architect to sort out the small yard at the rear of the premises. Right in the middle it had the old petrol pump that had been used for the laundry vans and underneath was the petrol tank. To remove the pump required planning permission. The tank was too dangerous to remove so it had to be filled with sand. This meant there was now parking for 5 or 6 cars. Wider gates made easier access.

At the side of the warehouse was a path for the forklift truck which went from the warehouse door to the yard. It was sealed off from the pavement in Bective Road with tall railings. By removing the railings, parking for 6 or 7 cars was made possible. It meant cooperation by the staff as it was a bit of a squeeze but it was very popular. Alas, it wasn't popular with the council.

After a while they came and put oak bollards all the way up the side. Then one day they came and put in another bollard to stop the cars altogether. The transport manager took the workman round the pub while our workmen took out the bollard and ensured it was loose fitting. It looked perfectly set into the concrete but could be lifted out and put back. This enabled the parking to continue and it was about two years before the council realised this. Their workmen returned one weekend and hard-set the bollard into the concrete.

This coincided with new by-laws about the exclusion of large lorries in the area. Their idea was the lorry went somewhere else to unload/load and we would have to use a fleet of small vans to ferry the goods in and out to the lorry. What planet were they on? We just ignored it. There was a pretty severe campaign against industry in Putney. The council wanted it all as residential so they were forever thinking up new ways to make life difficult. As some of our deliveries were by vehicles from Europe, the drivers had a really impossible job to park and unload.

When cars parked illegally on the ramp into the warehouse, thinking they had found a free parking space for the day, they had to be removed on a low loader.

Important visitors were offered parking in the yard when they came. One day Mr Ray Matthews came from Wassen International in his very expensive brand new, top of the range, white Mercedes. He came to lunch in Annie's Room. One of the warehouse staff asked for the key to move it because of a delivery. He smashed it into the warehouse wall.

One evening a foreign lorry driver (nothing to deliver for Larkhall) was looking for somewhere to park for the night and saw the empty yard. It had 12 feet high gates with barbed wire on top and a huge padlock. He tried to back his lorry to break the gates down. RG saw it on the CTV in Annie's Room kitchen and heard the noise. She went down the fire escape to the yard and tried to sort it out. After a tirade of abuse from the man because she wouldn't unlock the padlock, she ran back up the fire escape, locked the door and phoned the police. They were not busy and enthusiastically set off to find the man in his lorry. They kindly sent a WPC round to make sure RG was OK. She had been out of breath from running up the fire escape when she had 'phoned the police - they had taken this to mean she was afraid of the man.

Celebs From time to time celebrities came to the shop to buy supplements. Roy Plomley (Desert Island Discs) lived opposite in Deodar Road and was keen on the 50p basket of special offers, kept on the counter. Vera Lyn (known to us as Mrs Marks) often came in to buy Trufree flours, Martin Shaw was a frequent customer. Terence Stamp was a fan of RG's work and wanted to bring out wheat/gluten free baked up foods on to the market. He called it 'The Stamp Collection'. He came to the factory for advice from her and was given a guided tour. Margaret, the Irish lady who worked the switchboard, asked if she could meet him. When RG introduced her, her legs buckled and she was overcome and out of breath. She said afterwards it was the most wonderful day of her life.

Derek Cooper from the BBC, MP Chris Chope, MP Tony Colman, MP David Mellor, Sir Austin and Lady Bide, Auberon Waugh and Lesley Kenton all passed through the shop on their way to Annie's Room. Visits by celebs were always exciting for the staff because it gave them a lift out of the ordinary day, and it was something to talk about in the canteen.

Long Christmas break W O'Connell went to Ireland one Christmas in his company car. After a month he had still not returned to work. The first I knew of it was when his wife telephoned to speak to him. She had not heard from him and had no idea where he was, nor did Larkhall. He never liked the company to know where he was and failed to put in any receipts for expenses. He eventually turned up to resume work with no explanation. I thought how different my Christmas had been with just Christmas Day and Boxing day off then I had had to open up the factory and go back to work with a skeleton staff immediately.

Mothers and babies One year, eight of the office staff became pregnant. They were baby mad and only one was married. Owing to the law I couldn't replace any of them with new staff other than temps. All the staff expertise in mail order went missing for that year and the wages bill went rocketing up. When they returned after their maternity leaves -- all except the married one - they asked for a creche. I said no.

Questionable Practice by large companies The largest producer of wheat starch kept Trufree out of the coeliac foods market for years. One of their ploys was to run a bus in rural areas to take customers free to a presentation in a village hall. Only coeliacs and their families were allowed on the bus and they had had to prove they used the producer's product on prescription. No surprise, uptake of Trufree in that rural area was nil. A customer had tipped off RG at a trade show.

Multiplication Someone from social services called one morning and asked for an interview with one of the production staff. He was originally from the West Indies. They had tracked him down after several years. By this time he had fathered nine illegitimate children by nine different women who were all on social security benefits.

Sleeping on the job One of the production staff managed to construct himself a hidey-hole behind a wall in the coating department with a kind of bed. It was here he hid and went to sleep instead of doing his work.

Staff from many nations One day we had a count up of all the different nationalities who worked at Larkhall in Putney. It totaled 23, including employees from Russia, Poland, The West Indies, China, South America, Canada, Granada, USA, India, Pakistan, Arabia... One of them was half Eskimo and several were Irish. Religions were Roman Catholic, C of E, Bhuddist and Muslim. My policy was if an employee could do the job it didn't matter where he or she was from. At the Charlbury factory only English staff were on the payroll, mostly local people whose families had lived around that rural Oxfordshire area for generations.

Communication On a trip to Hong Kong I went to the largest restaurant I had ever seen. Indeed, it was so vast the waitresses communicated with the kitchen by walkie-talkie. The food was amazingly good including wonderful fresh fruit.

Agencies, Bow Ties and Interviews One PR Agency I employed for a while took offence to my wearing a bow tie. They said it made me look like a cat. They made a great thing of it so I gave up wearing one. After they had left I went back to wearing a bow tie and have worn one ever since.

The same agency, at great expense, organised a media interviewing techniques session in a studio and I was required to attend and be judged. I was the least successful and one of the salesmen was judged the best. The agency suggested he should in future do all the interviews on radio and TV. They rather missed the point as his knowledge of products and alternative healthcare was poor. A good example of an agency wasting Larkhall money on a pointless exercise. I also lost a day at my desk. What planet are these agencies on?

Asbestos When we first moved to Putney and had to get the building up to standard for fire risk. The law made us put in asbestos based partitions. The alternative was a huge fine or a jail sentence for the directors. In the late 1990s we were forced to take it out. This was done at the weekend when the factory was closed. Part of the offices were screened off. Men came in special protective suits with masks and removed the asbestos to be taken away in a special vehicle. It cost an arm and a leg. There was no compensation.

Crocodiles   A Middle and Far East Export trip found me in Bangkok, Thailand to visit a young businesswoman called Mrs Rengsangboom who had a health and beauty store. She was very hospitable and took me to lunch near a crocodile zoo. The smell of the animals was appalling. Lunch was eaten in a restaurant overlooking them – rather unnerving as there was only the window between us and the snapping jaws. The possibility of business was low and sadly the young businesswoman died in a car crash a couple of years later.

A special kind of branding   Inspection of Kosher products during the packaging process at Charlbury was obligatory. A Rabbi had to be present and one was sent from Manchester. Packs of potato flour, one of our naturally gluten-free products, was popular with Jewish people for Passover. The packing factory was alongside the tiny country station of Charlbury and the Rabbi came down by train. He worried that nobody would be able to pick him out on the station platform - a man with a large beard, a big black hat and black clothes. The secretary assured him there was nothing to worry about. He would be met off the train and could walk the few yards to the factory.

Once in the factory he was given a white lab coat to wear and a cover for his hair, as the law required. His job was to sit in a comfortable chair provided and watch the production line with the packets of potato flour passing by. Having seen them he could then make sure they were stamped with his own Beth Din stamp which would certify their correctness and suitability for use during Passover by Jewish people.

However, it was extremely boring and he fell asleep. The production line continued with the packing and stamping. At the end of the afternoon the Rabbi went back to Manchester on the train taking his Beth Din stamp with him. The packs of potato flour went off to the warehouse for distribution.

The personal trial of Vitamin B3 (niacin) by Walter O'Connell   WOC appeared one morning at RG's studio in a rage. He had sold Vitamin B3 to an Indian shopkeeper who said our tablets didn't work. They were supposed to cause flushing as tiny blood vessels dilated. The man had demanded his money back and returned his order. WOC was furious and said he would prove they didn't work as he would try them out himself. "I will prove it with my own body," he roared.

RG provided him with a glass of water and WOC proceeded to take several (far too many) of the B3 tablets. He then strode up and own on the flat roof outside RG's studio flapping his arms about as he proceeded to turn red and feel very hot. The lab staff were watching out of their window opposite wondering what it was all about. This continued for the best part of an hour as the B3 dilated his blood vessels. By now he was purple in the face and sweating but still shouting about his experiment to prove the tablets didn't work. He wanted RG to sign a statement to that effect. As WOC had taken far too many tablets it could hardly be described as a serious experiment. He went off to see the shopkeeper to 'sort it out' with him. He set off across the roof and down the fire escape to the car park, still roaring about how he had experimented with his own body. RG said he should have been a clown and tried to catch up with her work.

Waste not want not   Old leaflets, out-of-date advertising and price lists etc could be put through the shredder to make fine packing for mail order goods. Magazines we had advertised in were also used. A complaint came in from a lady customer. She said it had taken her six hours to piece all the shredding from her parcel back together and she was absolutely disgusted. As we advertised Blakoe products in Penthouse she had received a shredded 'saucy lady'. A letter of apology was sent to her with a free pack of vitamins. We heard no more about it but Penthouse was not used again to make shreddings. We admired her patience and dedication!

384

One short   A customer complained more than once about being one short in his Cantamega tablets. They were packed by machine and there would have been more than the 30 stated on the pack. He demanded another pack free each time. RG sent him just one tablet in an envelope instead of another pack of 30 with an apology. He didn't try it on again as he realized we were on to him.

The USM   Some executives arrived from Barclays Bank head office to see if the company was suitable to be put on the USM (Unlisted Securities Market attached to the London Stock Exchange). They were invited to lunch with me in Annie's Room. RG put on a splendid lunch including an apricot pie. The senior man was most impressed. However, this was about all he was impressed with. I was asked a lot of questions including what were my brother's qualifications (none) and why wasn't RG on the staff (she was self-employed). The racehorses would have to be sold, the flat would have to go, why did we have two factories instead of one, etc, etc. A couple of days later a letter arrived from him, mostly about the apricot pie. It was obvious they thought we didn't have the slightest hope of going on to the USM; end of story.

RG followed   One morning RG went out of the front door of the factory into Putney Bridge Road with her wicker shopping trolley. She was going to do shopping in the High Street. As she came on to the pavement a man opposite shouted very loudly, "There she is". He was with another tall man and they were both wearing dark overcoats and wide brimmed trilby hats. They both looked sinister. They began to cross Putney Bridge Road a very busy road, towards RG, looking purposeful. While they moved towards the factory RG had the presence of mind to cross to the other side. The men crossed back to follow her so RG dodged the traffic again and returned to the factory side. They were not giving up so while they tried to cross the road again after her, she legged it to the pine shop where she knew the owner, Mick. She asked him to hide her as she was being followed so he put her trolley inside one half of a pine wardrobe and RG into the other. One of the men came into the shop and rudely demanded to know if a woman had just come in with a trolley. Mick was impressively calm and said as he could see there were no customers in his shop and if one had come in his dog would have let him know. The man looked around while Mick stood in front of the wardrobe. Inside it RG was as quiet as a mouse. The man had a look around and then left. Mick went into the open doorway and lit a cigarette, watching him go up towards the High Street while his mate went all the way up on the opposite pavement. They were still looking for RG. When they had disappeared Mick opened the wardrobe and RG got out. Mick asked who the men were. RG said she had no idea. Mick advised her to go back inside the factory as it wouldn't be safe for her to go to the shops. They might come back.
   Later that afternoon RG did go to the shops but with a minder. She went and returned in the back of a company car, covered with a blanket.

Bumper Bake Books   RG always sent out her TRUFREE Cookbooks by return of post, using postage stamps, via the factory post but not put through the franking machine. There was a spate of complaints from her customers who had not received their books. The Post Office investigated but could not come up with an answer. One of the factory staff was putting rubbish in the skip when he found a carrier bag full of RG's cookbooks, ready stamped for posting. Somebody was removing them from the office post room and throwing them away. Who? A complaint to the office manager and the company secretary drew a blank. RG had to take her post to the local post office rather than let it go out through the factory as there was no way of finding out who the culprit was.

Germanium Time after time Larkhall was picked on by the media as an example, and set up, causing trouble and expense. A classic case was Germanium, a mineral found in many foods, especially garlic. There are two kinds available for manufacturing tablets – synthetic and natural. Larkhall only used the natural version. There had been a problem in Japan where people were taking ridiculously large amounts of the synthetic version. In the UK this evolved into Princess Diana taking "Killer Germanium Pills", although she probably never took a germanium pill in her life. The media went into a frenzy of stories and there were articles in newspapers, magazines and on TV programmes.

The truth was that very small doses of natural Germanium, as in garlic, were harmless. However the government stepped in and put a ban on all germanium after a civil servant declared, "Unequivocally all forms of germanium are toxic". All Larkhall's formulas had to be changed, stock recalled and perfectly good stock destroyed. The public was hoodwinked, especially regarding the arithmetic, Larkhall got a bad name as we had germanium pills and multi vitamin pills with traces germanium in. No other country banned it, just the UK so Larkhall was still able to export it. (It was a miracle all garlic eaters in the country hadn't dropped down dead and all the population hadn't been killed as the average intake per day, in the UK per person is 1 mg). There was never any risk to consumers who had taken Larkhall's germanium products – quite the opposite of what the media said. However, we could do nothing about it.

The point of all this was to try and close us down. Our enemies failed. They had another go with Tryptophan, an essential amino acid and natural antidepressant and pain relief remedy. After another ban we were still able to sell it but only for animals. By coincidence the ban happened when SSRIs, a new class of antidepressant medicine (drug) appeared on the scene. A natural product such as Tryptophan presented a threat to that market.

Harassment regarding the new healthy eating poster RG was in the studio finishing off the artwork for the NACNE poster when she took a phone call. It was from a very angry man who said he was from the Meat Marketing Board. He said he had been informed that she was doing a poster about what everyone should be eating to stay healthy and that she was not including any meat on it. He then made a few threats. This was complete nonsense and RG told him so. She said she would send him a poster when it was printed and on it he would see bacon, beef, lamb, pork and poultry. He wouldn't say where he had obtained his 'information'. As the poster was on RG's drawing board and as yet unfinished, we could only assume it was someone from the Putney or the Charlbury factory. It was disturbing to think we had a mole in our organization working against what we were trying to achieve and making trouble for us. We went ahead with the poster.

Healthier eating for pregnancy This was a free booklet for expectant mothers. RG wrote it for us, based on government recommendations, rules and regulations. When it was ready to be printed our agency got hold of it and decided to make it more exciting, regardless of the nutrition. They added Brie, Camembert and soft cheeses – these were not allowed by 'Foresight' for pregnant women. Fortunately, RG was able to stop the print run. This was a typical example of lack of knowledge and arrogance from an agency. If the printer had gone ahead it would have meant thousands of booklets would have had to be destroyed. Our reputation would have taken a severe hammering, we would have been well out of pocket and incorrect information would have been sent out to pregnant women.

Company Racehorses Our four National Hunt racehorses were all with trainer Jenny Pitman. Their names were Cantassium (our brand), Cantamega (our best selling multivitamin), The Putney Lark and Vitaman. They all did well.

The sales team and other staff after we sold out When we sold out to Nutricia only one of the sales team was offered a job by them and he chose to refuse it. In two of their desk drawers were found piles of visiting cards that gave their names and status of Marketing Director. This was a nonsense – they had made it up as they were just reps. Both of them thought they would be made up to Managing Director and both of them had done everything they could to bring the company down.

WOC went around in the trade complaining he had been sold down the river and that it was thanks to him and his years of tireless work the company had been a success. He was adamant he had received nothing for all his efforts, choosing to forget my half share in Filtro Neto that I had just given him, with a new car and a company pension he had not paid into. RG put the record straight with the alternative health press who were going to make an issue of it.

WOC's girlfriend who managed a health store, helped by WOC, turned out to be one of very few who didn't pay their final bills to Larkhall – several thousand pounds. The debt was never paid.

One of the other salesmen conned the staff he was going to be made MD due to his brilliance. Actually, he was sacked and shown off the premises. This didn't stop him applying for MD type jobs with a glowing CV he had concocted.

One of the laboratory staff went to see RG in her studio and demanded a million pounds for herself and her two colleagues. She said their work had enabled RG to make a fortune out of Trufree and they had been to the tribunal about it. Some of that fortune was owed to them. RG said it was news to her she that she had made a fortune. (What planet were they on?) She told her that a small group of staff had brought the company, including her Trufree brand, to its knees with their criminal behaviour. We had no wish carry on any longer as we were fed up with it and exhausted. It was time for us to retire.

BOOKS and BOOKLETS by Rita Greer

While there was a constant demand for information and knowledge from the public our hands were tied with red tape – the Advertising Standards Authority was ever watchful. The only way to impart the information and knowledge was to have books and booklets published. Here is a list of Rita Greer's contribution.

Allergic to Food – A Self-Help Guide   1985   Dent
Antioxidant Nutrition – Help Fight Cancer (with RJ Woodward)1985
   Souvenir Press
Cooking and Baking with Dried Fruit   1984   Thorsons
Diets to Help Coeliacs and Wheat Sensitivity   1982   Thorsons
Easy Gluten Free Cooking (5 editions, latest title) 1978   HarperCollins
Fruit and Vegetables in Particular   1977   Bunterbird
Gluten-free and Wheat-free Bumper Bake Book   1982   Bunterbird
Healthier Special Diets   1987   Dent
Many Scars and MS Observed   1981   Bunterbird
MS Diet Notebook One -- Information   2006   self-published
MS Diet Notebook Two -- Recipes   2006 self-published
Oat Cuisine   1987   Souvenir Press
Olive Oil the Good Heart Protector (with C. Blau) 1995   Souvenir Press
Rita Greer's Extraordinary Kitchen Notebook   1976   Bunterbird
Rita Greer's Vegetarian Cookbook   1996   Souvenir Press
Simply Gluten Free   2013   Souvenir Press
Soft Options: for adults who have difficulty chewing   2002   Souvenir Press
Superb Soups and Starters   1981   Thorsons
The British Food Fiasco   1984   Bunterbird
The First Clinical Ecology Cookbook 1977   Bunterbird
The Book of Vitamins and Health Food Supplements (with RJ Woodward)
   Souvenir Press 1987   a Retitled version of The Good Nutrients Guide Dent 1985
The Right Way to Cook 1985   Dent
Wheat Free Cooking   1995   Souvenir Press
Wheat, Milk and Egg Free Cooking (several editions)1984   HarperCollins

Some have been translated and published abroad – Italy, Sweden, Holland, Spain etc. Others have been copied in USA.

BOOKLETS
Getting Safely Started -- The Trufree Handbook for Coeliacs
   and Gluten-free/Wheat-free dieters 1981
Healthy Slimming Handbook   1992
Healthier Eating for Schoolchildren   1984
Healthier Eating for Pregnancy   1990

402